THE EMERGENCE OF AN IRON AGE ECONOMY

THE MECKLENBURG GRAVE GROUPS FROM HALLSTATT AND STIČNA

PETER S. WELLS

MECKLENBURG COLLECTION, PART III

BULLETIN 33 · AMERICAN SCHOOL OF PREHISTORIC RESEARCH
PEABODY MUSEUM OF ARCHAEOLOGY AND ETHNOLOGY · HARVARD UNIVERSITY

American School of Prehistoric Research
PEABODY MUSEUM • HARVARD UNIVERSITY
BULLETIN NO. 33

MEMBERS OF
THE AMERICAN SCHOOL OF PREHISTORIC RESEARCH

Kwang-chih Chang
Chairman

C. C. Lamberg-Karlovsky
Director of Prehistoric Research

Noel Morss
Secretary

Robert W. Ehrich   William Howells

Henry Field   Hallam L. Movius, Jr.

Bruce Howe   Peter S. Wells

Stephen Williams

Hugh Hencken
Chairman Emeritus

Goldthwaite H. Dorr
Honorary Chairman

Mrs. George Grant MacCurdy
Honorary Secretary

The Emergence of an Iron Age Economy

The Mecklenburg Grave Groups from Hallstatt and Stična

Peter S. Wells

Mecklenburg Collection, Part III

Illustrations by Symme Burstein

Peabody Museum of Archaeology and Ethnology
Harvard University • Cambridge, Massachusetts

1981

DISTRIBUTED BY HARVARD UNIVERSITY PRESS

Copyright 1981 by the President and Fellows of Harvard College
ISBN 0-87365-536-2
Library of Congress Catalog Card Number 81-81958
Printed in the United States of America
Cover photo by Hillel Burger

This volume is dedicated to
Hugh Hencken
who helped save the Mecklenburg Collection from irrevocable dispersal in the 1930s and assured that this important body of archaeological material would be made available to the scholarly world

Contents

Acknowledgments ix
Introduction 1
    The Mecklenburg Collection 1
    Chronology and Culture History 2
    Notes on the Catalogue Sections 2

PART I: THE MECKLENBURG GRAVE GROUPS FROM HALLSTATT AND STIČNA 5

Hallstatt 7
    Introduction 7
    Catalogue of Graves from Hallstatt 18
    Discussion 27
    Technical Reports 30
        by Erik Trinkaus 30
        by Curt W. Beck and Christopher J. Smart 36
        by J. E. Ericson 37
        by Jill Mefford 39

Stična 45
    Introduction 45
    Catalogue of Graves from Stična 48
    Discussion 87

PART II: SYNTHESIS AND INTERPRETATION 91

The Emergence of an Iron Age Economy in East Alpine Europe 93
    Introduction: The Development of an Iron Age Economy 93
    Early Iron Age Communities in the Eastern Alps 93
    Cemeteries Selected for Comparison 101
    Economic Development beyond Household Needs 101
    Social Organization 116
    A Model for the Changes 122

Afterword 129
Figures 1–193 131–229
References 231
Index 245

Text Figures

Cover. Bronze bovine figure from Hallstatt, Grave 12.
I. Hallstatt   6
II. Salzbergtal at Hallstatt   6
III. Map of Hallstatt   8
IV. Salzbergtal at Hallstatt   9
V. Duchess of Mecklenburg and workmen at Hallstatt   13
VI. Duchess and workmen at Hallstatt   14
VII. Workmen at Hallstatt   15
VIII. Plan of Hallstatt cemetery   16
IX. Hallstatt skulls   33
X. Hallstatt maxillae, mandibles, and dentitions   34
XI. Infrared spectra of amber   37
XII. Graph of energy dispersive X-ray fluorescence of Hallstatt pin   38
XIII. Bimetal sample of pin   39
XIV. X-ray map of iron concentration in pin   39
XV. X-ray map of tin concentration in pin   39
XVI. Halite and textile from Hallstatt   40
XVII. 2-2 twill weave   40
XVIII. 2-2 oblique interlacing   40
XIX. Seam   41
XX. Seam   42
XXI. Diagrams of yarn   43
XXII. Angle of spin   43
XXIII. Plan of Stična   46
XXIV. Map of sites mentioned in text   95
XXV. Schematic representation of relative population sizes   100
XXVI. Graph of amber quantities, Stična, Tumulus IV   112
XXVII. Trade between Eastern Alps and other parts of Europe   116
XXVIII. Trade within Eastern Alps   116
XXIX. Trade between centers and smaller communities   117
XXX. Schematic representations of family units   120
XXXI. Exchange and specialized production   124
XXXII. Growth of specialized community   125
XXXIII. Life-course of bronze objects   127

Tables

1. Grave groups from Hallstatt   26
2. Ceramic vessels in the Hallstatt graves   29
3. Skeletal remains from Hallstatt   31
4. Measurements of Hallstatt skulls   31
5. Dental dimensions and occlusal wear   32
6. Grave groups from Stična, Tumulus IV   88
7. Iron in graves   104
8. Glass in graves   106
9. Bronze in graves   110
10. Amber in graves   111
11. Metal and weapons in graves   118
12. Richer graves in East Alpine Europe   119
13. Weapon graves at Stična   121
14. Late Bronze Age hoards   123

Acknowledgments

In 1976 Dr. Hugh Hencken invited me to assist him in completing the publication of the Mecklenburg Collection. I began my work by helping him to tie up loose ends on his book presenting the grave groups from Magdalenska gora, which was published by the Peabody Museum in 1978. Since that time I have been working on the grave groups from Hallstatt and Stična, which are presented in this volume, while Dr. Hencken has begun work on the La Tène cemetery of Vinica, the other large cemetery site at which the Duchess of Mecklenburg excavated.

Dr. Hencken had already completed much of the essential preliminary work for the Hallstatt and Stična grave groups before I began work on them. He directed the restoration and cleaning of the objects when they reached the Peabody Museum in 1940, and he had most of the drawings done. My task has been to study the surviving written records of the excavations and the objects now in the grave groups, to assemble the catalogues of graves at the two cemeteries presented here, and to write the introductory and synthetic discussions relevant to the two sites and to the broader problems of the Early Iron Age in East Alpine Europe.

I have benefited greatly from the advice and help of many individuals and institutions. Two grants from the National Science Foundation, G18557 in 1961–62 and GS-31 in 1962–63, awarded to Dr. Hencken, helped to provide funding for the drawing of the objects. The National Science Foundation has also generously awarded the Peabody Museum a publication grant, BNS-7913952, to cover the expenses of this volume. I thank Dr. Hugh Hencken for his trust and confidence in permitting me to work with this important archaeological collection. Prof. C. C. Lamberg-Karlovsky, Director of the Peabody Museum, has made all of the facilities of the museum available to me in work on this project, for which I am very grateful.

For various advice and help I wish also to thank the following individuals: Dr. Wilhelm Angeli (Vienna), Prof. H. Arthur Bankoff (Brooklyn), Dr. Fritz Eckart Barth (Vienna), Prof. John Boardman (Oxford), Prof. Joachim Boessneck (Munich), Dr. Peter Bogucki (Cambridge, Mass.), Prof. Larissa Bonfante (New York), Dr. Robert Brill (Corning, N.Y.), Mr. Hillel Burger (Cambridge, Mass.), Ms. Lorna Condon (Cambridge, Mass.), Ms. Donna Dickerson (Cambridge, Mass.), Prof. Franz Fischer (Tübingen), Prof. Otto-Herman Frey (Marburg), Dr. Stane Gabrovec (Ljubljana), Prof. Antonio Gilman (Northridge, Calif.), Mr. Mitja Guštin (Brežice), Dr. Thea Elisabeth Haevernick (Mainz), Prof. George Hanfmann (Cambridge, Mass.), Ms. Ann Hatfield (Cambridge, Mass.), Dr. R. E. Jones (Athens), Dr. Heinz Kimmig (Konstanz), Prof. Wolfgang Kimmig (Tübingen), Prof. Karl Kromer (Innsbruck), Dr. Gustav Mahr (Berlin), Mr. Richard Meadow (Cambridge, Mass.), Prof. David Gordon Mitten (Cambridge, Mass.), Prof. P. R. S. Moorey (Oxford), Dr. Laura Nash (Cambridge, Mass.), Dr. Stefan Nebehay (Vienna), Dr. Ludwig Pauli (Regensburg), Ms. Whitney Powell (Cambridge, Mass.), Ms. Mary Reilly (Somerville, Mass.), Dr. Helmut Schlichtherle (Tübingen), Dr. Eckehart Schubert (Frankfurt), Prof. Emily Vermeule (Cambridge, Mass.), Ms. Barbara Westman (Cambridge, Mass.), and Prof. Wilma Wetterstrom (Cambridge, Mass.).

Introduction

This volume consists of two distinct parts. The first is a catalogue of the grave groups from Hallstatt and Stična excavated by the Duchess of Mecklenburg which are now in the Peabody Museum of Harvard University. For both sites I include introductory sections dealing with their locations, other archaeological research at them, their significance in European prehistory, and the excavations carried out by the Duchess. A brief discussion following the catalogue of graves relates the results of the Duchess's work to other research at these localities. Four technical reports present the results of special studies on some of the materials from Hallstatt.

Hallstatt and Stična are of particular importance to the study of the Early Iron Age in Europe, and both are subjects of extensive ongoing research. It is beyond the scope of this volume to review all of the literature on these sites or to discuss the many issues concerned with each. My review of other research will be brief, and I refer the reader to the principal published studies.

The second part of the volume departs from the presentation of data and attempts to define some of the patterns of change occurring at the beginning of the period of time known as the Iron Age, patterns which are well represented at Hallstatt and Stična. I examine the questions of change particularly in terms of manufacturing and trade systems in East Alpine Europe during this period. My aim in this section is twofold. First, I want to indicate one methodological and theoretical context in which the evidence from Hallstatt and Stična can be profitably examined. Early Iron Age East Alpine Europe provides excellent data pertaining to the kinds of processes of cultural change that are of concern to anthropologically oriented archaeologists today. This material is little known to most archaeologists outside of central Europe, and I hope to bring this important data to the attention of the interested academic community.

Second, by drawing attention to some of the major issues in the prehistory of Europe during this dynamic first half of the last millennium B.C., I hope to define some of the subjects ripe for future research,
both in terms of archaeological excavation and in terms of museum research on existing collections.

Discussion will be organized on three levels. First, relevant archaeological evidence will be presented for an understanding of industry, trade, and social organization in the Early Iron Age of the region. Second, I shall suggest models appropriate to interpreting the archaeological data. Third, I shall outline a model to account for changes in the patterns of evidence between the Late Bronze and Early Iron Ages. In the present state of our knowledge, this third level is of necessity very hypothetical. Yet I believe that it is productive to attempt a coherent picture of change in this context, particularly as a means of posing questions for, and stimulating, further directed research.

Illustrations within the body of the text are designated as text figures and are numbered with Roman numerals. The illustrations of grave groups from Hallstatt and Stična, found at the end of the volume, are designated simply as figures and are numbered with Arabic numerals.

THE MECKLENBURG COLLECTION

The Duchess of Mecklenburg, born Princess Marie of Windischgrätz, excavated extensively in Carniola, in what is now the Yugoslav Republic of Slovenia, and at Hallstatt, Austria, in the years between 1905 and 1914. The principal cemeteries that she investigated were Hallstatt (26 graves), Stična (186 graves), Magdalenska gora (355 graves), and Vinica (353 graves). After a complex series of events, her great collection of Iron Age antiquities was acquired by the Peabody Museum of Harvard University in 1934 and 1940, largely through the efforts of Dr. Hugh Hencken. The history of her work and of the collection has been summarized elsewhere (Mahr 1934; Hencken 1968, 1978, pp. 1–2; Wells 1978a, pp. 215–221). This volume is the third in a series of publications making available to the scholarly world the results of the Duchess's excavations. The first included analyses of the horse bones (Bökönyi 1968) and of the human skeletal material (Angel 1968) in the collection; the second presented the finds from the cemetery at Magdalenska gora (Hencken 1978).

CHRONOLOGY AND CULTURE HISTORY

The literature on the chronology and culture history of the East Alpine region is abundant, and I refer the reader to the principal works on the subject. Those concerned specifically with Hallstatt and Stična will be cited in the introductory sections below. For the regions of Austria under consideration here, Pittioni 1954 is the standard work. See Pauli 1980 for more recent findings and current literature. A series of works by Gabrovec (1966, 1973, 1976, 1980) lays the foundations for study of the Early Iron Age in Slovenia, and his scheme is conveniently summarized in English in Hencken 1978, pp. 3–9. Here I shall not deal with issues of the culture-historical reconstruction, nor with chronological problems, but rather with questions of industry, trade, and cultural change.

A comprehensive study of the chronology of East Alpine Europe is currently in preparation, and the grave groups from Hallstatt and Stična presented here will form a part of that larger study. Thus the chronology of these graves will not be discussed in detail in this volume. Instead, I employ the chronological scheme currently in use in the region, based on the work of Kromer (1959a) for Hallstatt and of Gabrovec (1966, 1973, 1974, 1976; Frey and Gabrovec 1971) for Slovenia.

For making rough estimates of population at some of the sites, I use the years 750 to 400 B.C. as the absolute dates for the Early Iron Age. These years are probably not the correct ones for any single site, but they constitute a very rough average for the various major sites of the region. Adopting these uniform dates is a great oversimplification, but in order to develop any workable comparative data, such a gross scheme is necessary.

The delineation of the concepts "Late Bronze Age" and "Early Iron Age" is still not fully clear (e.g., see Kossack 1959; Müller-Karpe 1959; Gabrovec 1973), and problems of establishing contemporaneity between assemblages at different sites have not been worked out. In the current state of research on the chronology, the absolute dates for the beginning and end of occupation even at the major sites are still uncertain beyond a very rough approximation. For discussion of the absolute chronology of Hallstatt see Pittioni 1954, p. 541, and Kromer 1959a, p. 28. On the neighboring site at the Dürrnberg see Pauli 1978, p. 425, table 23. On the absolute chronology in Slovenia see Gabrovec 1966, 1973; Frey and Gabrovec 1971; Starè 1975a, p. 60; and Guštin 1979, p. 30, fig. 11. Some of the smaller communities mentioned below, such as St. Andrä and Welzelach, are represented by cemeteries covering periods of time considerably shorter than the whole of the Early Iron Age, and absolute dates for them will be cited separately.

For a list of the German names (used in most of the pre–World War I literature and in some later works) of the principal Early Iron Age sites in Slovenia see Gabrovec 1966, pp. 47–48.

NOTES ON THE CATALOGUE SECTIONS

The first paragraph concerning each grave presents all of the information recorded in the notes preserved from the excavations. For Hallstatt, these are sparse, but for some of the tumuli at Stična, particularly Tumulus IV, the records kept by the Duchess's secretary, Gustav Goldberg, are extensive and provide some detailed information about grave structure, burial rite, and placement of grave goods. The most complete accounts come from a notebook kept by Goldberg during the excavations. Other notes are preserved on slips of paper found with the grave groups when the collection was unpacked and studied in Zurich (see references on the history of the Mecklenburg Collection above). Sometimes the notes mention all of the objects now associated with a grave; other times they mention only some of them. The excavators often omitted smaller and less striking objects from their excavation records, though these objects were recovered and kept with the other materials from each grave.

Subsequent paragraphs concerning each grave list and describe the objects now associated with each grave number. In instances in which additional information about the contents of a grave group was noted by the scholars working on the collection in Zurich, I include such information in this section of the catalogue.

Since the notes kept by the excavators are often on separate scraps of paper and do not always agree with one another, it is unclear to what extent the scholars working in Zurich relied on their own judgments in making decisions about associations. This is an uncertainty factor we have to reckon with in those cases in which the excavators' descriptions do not clearly match the objects now with a grave group.

Apparently, some objects included in the packing boxes could not be associated with any distinct grave by those in Zurich, but could be attributed to a specific tumulus. In the interests of maintaining as complete a record as possible, I include such objects in the catalogue as "isolated finds," at the end of the grave groups for each tumulus. I do not cite small, unidentifiable fragments among the isolated finds, though I do record such fragments when they occur in specific graves.

The following abbreviations are used: L.–length; H.–height; W.–width; T.–thickness; D.–diameter; Ext. D.–external diameter; Max. D.–maximum diameter.

The large strings of beads were drawn as they were received by the Peabody Museum. There is no reason to think that the arrangement in the drawings bears any relation to their arrangement when found.

Before the Duchess's collection was exported from Yugoslavia for sale, the museum authorities in Ljubljana were able to select some objects to retain in their collections. These objects have been published by Ložar (1934, pp. 20–22). It should be noted that Ložar's attribution of objects in the Narodni muzej does not always agree with the information preserved in the excavation notes and the objects with the collection in the Peabody Museum.

Part I:
The Mecklenburg Grave Groups from Hallstatt and Stična

Text figure I. View looking west across the Hallstätter See toward the town of Hallstatt and the Salzbergtal above it. From a drawing by F. Simony; photograph courtesy of the Prähistorische Abteilung, Naturhistorisches Museum, Vienna.

Text figure II. View from the Rudolfsturm at the lower end of the Salzbergtal looking westward up the valley toward the heights of the Plassen. The land in the foreground on both sides of the path is the location of the Early Iron Age cemetery. The building in the center of the photograph is the Ökonomiegebäude. Photograph courtesy of the Prähistorische Abteilung, Naturhistorisches Museum, Vienna.

Hallstatt

INTRODUCTION

Location

Hallstatt is situated in the Salzkammergut limestone region of Upper Austria at the northern edge of the Alps, about 50 km southeast of Salzburg (see map, p. 95). It is located on a lake of the same name which occupies a deep glacial valley bounded by the precipitous mountain walls of the Plassen (1,953 m) to the west, the Dachstein (2,996 m) to the south, and the Sarstein (1,975 m) to the east. The Hallstätter See is 8.2 km long and has an average width of 1.05 km. The lake is very deep, particularly in its southern portion on which the town of Hallstatt is situated, attaining a maximum depth of 125.2 m (Morton 1954, p. 106). To the north the narrow valley of the Traun River leads to the resort town of Ischl about 17 km away and eventually joins the waters of the Danube downstream from Linz.

The present town of Hallstatt, with a population of about 1,700 (Morton 1959, p. 5), is situated on the western side of the southern end of the lake. The surface of the lake is 508 m above sea level, that of the town 511 m. The Dachstein massif rises steeply from the lakeshore, leaving only a narrow strip of sloping land along the base on which the town is located.

About 350 m almost directly above the town to the west is the lowest part of the narrow mountain valley extending westward up the part of the Dachstein massif called the Plassen. This valley, the Salzbergtal, is the site of the prehistoric salt mines and of the Early Iron Age cemetery. Below the surface of this valley are deposits of salt, part of the continuous zone of salt-bearing rocks along the northern edge of the limestone Alps in Austria from Hall in the Tirol through Hallein and Hallstatt to Mariazell in northwest Styria. These salt deposits originated when a sea then covering these lands evaporated. During the folding of the earth's crust in the Tertiary Period, when the Alps were formed, the salt deposits were also deformed, resulting in the present configuration of massive salt deposits often high in the mountains between layers of limestone, as at Hallstatt. Those parts of the salt exposed to the elements during this folding process were heavily leached, such that these zones are now bounded by a layer of weathered material of varying thickness (Kromer 1963, p. 26).

The salt deposit at Hallstatt, enclosed by layers of limestone, is some 3,000 m long and 640 m wide; its thickness is known to be greater than 500 m (Lehr 1978, p. 23). Most of the salt is not pure, but is mixed with clay substances and has a purity of about 45 percent salt. This mixture of rock salt and clay minerals is known as *Haselgebirge*. In places this mixture is penetrated by layers or veins of rock salt of up to 80 percent purity, ranging up to about 5 m in thickness (Kromer 1963, p. 26; see Barth 1970a, p. 46 fig. 2; Schauberger 1960). These veins of high purity were the principal goal of the Early Iron Age salt miners. (For further discussion of the topography and geology of Hallstatt see especially Medwenitsch 1954; Morton 1954, 1959.)

Archaeological Research at Hallstatt

Since the reactivation of the salt mines at Hallstatt in A.D. 1311, and perhaps before that as well, people working in the mines or digging in the ground of the Salzbergtal have come across man-made objects from the prehistoric salt mines and cemetery (Simony 1851; Mahr 1925, p. 11; Nebehay 1980, p. 29). On April 1, 1734 miners found the body of a man in a part of the Kilb-Werk that had suffered a cave-in. The body, partly encased in the salt, had been well preserved by the salt, and the records of the time note that the individual's coat and shoes still survived. It was decided that the man probably had not been a Christian, and on April 3, 1734 the body was buried in the modern cemetery, in a part reserved for heathens and criminals (on the find see Simony 1851, p. 4; Mahr 1925, pp. 10–11; Lehr 1978, pp. 34–36).

In more recent times, systematic archaeological research has been conducted on both the extensive cemetery at Hallstatt and in the Early Iron Age salt mines.

The Cemetery. Systematic excavation and recording of finds at the cemetery in the Salzbergtal was begun in 1846 by Johann Georg Ramsauer, Bergmeister at Hallstatt. Ramsauer excavated a total of 980 graves in the years 1846 to 1863, and these graves form the basis of our understanding of the cemetery today (Kromer 1959a; Nebehay 1980). Ramsauer kept generally good records of the objects recovered in the graves, as well as descriptions of the graves themselves. His information is in some instances supplemented by watercolor sketches of the graves and their contents. Ramsauer's excavations were in a roughly oval area measuring about 175 by 100 m south and southwest of the Ökonomiegebäude. He made a plan of the cemetery showing the locations of all of the graves he exca-

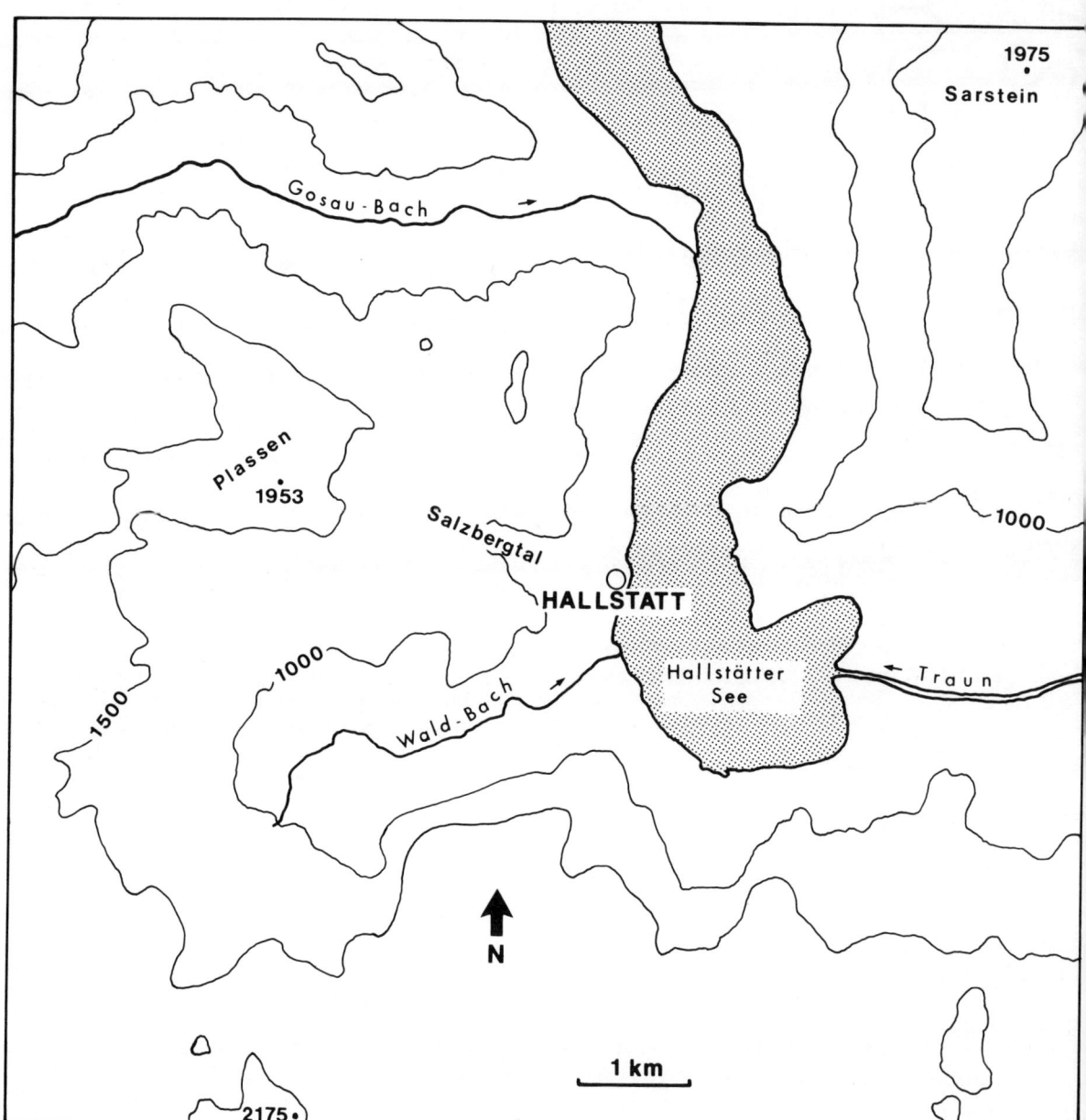

Text figure III. Map showing the topographical situation of Hallstatt, with elevations indicated in meters above sea level. The modern town is located at the edge of the Hallstätter See at an elevation of 508 m. The steeply sloping Salzbergtal, in which the Early Iron Age cemetery and mines are situated, lies several hundred meters above the modern town. The principal streams flowing into the Hallstätter See are also indicated.

vated (Kromer 1959a, map 3). Ramsauer's finds are now in the Prähistorische Abteilung of the Naturhistorisches Museum in Vienna.

The results of Ramsauer's excavations were first comprehensively published by Kromer in his two-volume work of 1959. Since that year a series of important studies of the site have appeared (such as, Kilian-Dirlmeier 1969, 1971; Peroni 1973; Hodson 1977), several of which have dealt with the question of the reliability of Ramsauer's grave associations. The journal kept by Ramsauer during the excavations has been lost, but it may still turn up (Nebehay 1980, p. 36). The principal available information about grave structures and objects found together is contained in the *Protokolle* written by Ramsauer and others at different times after the actual excavation of the graves treated (on these documents see especially Barth and Hodson 1976; Barth 1978–79; Nebehay 1980). These *Protokolle* and other surviving pieces of information about the graves contain various demonstrable inaccuracies and inconsistencies, leading some scholars to reject the possibility of deriving much information of scientific value about grave associations (Pauli 1975a; Schumacher 1978; see also Barth 1976a). It now seems that the *Protokoll* upon which Kromer based his comprehensive publication of Ramsauer's graves is probably not the most accurate one surviving. Information contained in it about individual burials contradicts that in other *Protokolle*, which agree with one another more than they do with that one (Barth and Hodson 1976, p. 161).

A research project initiated by Dr. Fritz Eckart Barth of the Naturhistorisches Museum in Vienna is collecting and collating all available documentation

Text figure IV. View looking eastward down the Salzbergtal toward the southeast end of the Hallstätter See where the Traun River flows into it. The Rudolfsturm, located at the lower end of the Salzbergtal about 350 m above the modern town of Hallstatt, is visible in the center of the photograph, its tower rising above the trees and silhouetted by the lake. The buildings higher up in the Salzbergtal, also visible in text figure II, are part of the modern saltworks. Photograph courtesy of the Prähistorische Abteilung, Naturhistorisches Museum, Vienna.

on Ramsauer's excavations at Hallstatt in order to determine the reliability of the various recorded grave groups. The results so far are very encouraging and suggest that when the project is complete it will be possible to distinguish a substantial number of "good" associations from more questionable ones (Nebehay 1980). A statistical study of the patterning in associations of different kinds of objects from Ramsauer's graves conducted by Hodson suggests that the associations recorded by Ramsauer are probably substantially correct and contributes further to optimism regarding the ultimate scientific validation of at least a good portion of Ramsauer's grave groups (Barth and Hodson 1976, pp. 168–173; Hodson 1977).

No other excavations at Hallstatt were as extensive as those of Ramsauer. In 1864 G. Schubert and E. von Sacken excavated 13 graves, but the location of their excavations is unknown. Between 1868 and 1874 B. Hutter excavated a number of burials; the materials from three of these graves came to the museum in Vienna, but their location in the cemetery is not known. In the years from 1871 to 1876 the Museum Francisco-Carolinum in Linz conducted excavations, first under the direction of G. Schubert and later under J. Stapf. They excavated areas around the margins of the large zone investigated by Ramsauer. In 1877 and 1878 J. Stapf and F. von Hochstetter excavated 27 graves in a small area to the north of the center of Ramsauer's area of excavation. The materials from these graves went to Vienna. In 1886 B. Hutter, F. von Hauer, and J. Szombathy excavated just southwest of the area investigated by Stapf in 1872. Here and at another, unknown, location they found 13 graves, the contents of which also went to Vienna. Between 1884 and 1899 the Museumsverein of Hallstatt excavated 28 graves, the finds from which are in the Hallstatt Museum. In 1907 the Duchess of Mecklenburg excavated 26 graves about which more will be said below. The final systematic excavations in the cemetery at Hallstatt were those of F. Morton in the years 1937 to 1939. He excavated a relatively large area northwest of that explored by Ramsauer and found 61 graves, the contents of which are in the Hallstatt Museum. (For detailed discussion of these various excavations see Kromer 1959a, pp. 6–15.)

The Mines. Unlike the cemetery finds, most of the finds from the mines at Hallstatt have been made accidentally in the course of modern-day mining operations in the mountain. Since A.D. 1311 salt has been mined on a substantial scale at Hallstatt, and this industry is still the economic base of the town (Morton 1954, 1959, pp. 3–4). As new galleries have been cut into the salt deposits of the mountain, a variety of traces of the Early Iron Age mining activity have been found. The extraordinary discovery of the preserved body of a miner has already been mentioned.

As the finds indicate, during the Early Iron Age the miners primarily exploited the purest layers of rock salt, those having a purity of up to 80 percent. Mining was done by tunneling into the rock salt face with picks and other tools, and the chunks of salt were carried to the surface and subsequently traded to other parts of Europe. In medieval and modern times the technique of salt extraction has been different. Rather than extracting the salt as rock salt with picks, the miners excavate cavities in the salt deposits and pump in water to dissolve the salt. When the solution is saturated, the water is pumped out and evaporated (Kromer 1963, p. 26).

Schauberger, a mining engineer at Hallstatt, has conducted an extensive study of the prehistoric remains in the mountain (1960), examining evidence in the galleries currently accessible and collecting information about such discoveries in the available records. He has assembled a table of the find sites and the materials found at them and has drawn maps of these locations within the mountain (1960). He records a total of 57 such sites and, based on his technical knowledge of possible slopes and directions of galleries, constructs a tentative plan of the gallery system of the prehistoric mines. (The galleries themselves are no longer open. Pressure exerted by the mountain closes the open spaces within a relatively short time after the abandonment of a mine. The only traces of the prehistoric mines are the objects left in the galleries by the miners.) Since Schauberger's reconstruction is based on the finds that have been made in modern times and have been recorded, his figures represent a minimum estimate of the extent of the prehistoric system. New discoveries are being made regularly (Schauberger 1976), and systematic research in the areas of the prehistoric mines is currently being carried out by the Prähistorische Abteilung of the Naturhistorisches Museum in Vienna, under the direction of Dr. F. E. Barth, for the purpose of locating more find sites (Barth 1980a and b).

The 57 identified prehistoric find sites within the salt mountain can be divided into three main groups on the basis of location, a north, an east, and a west group. At an early stage in the study of the finds from these groups, Barth noted significant differences in the types of objects recovered in the different groups and in the technique of removal of the rock salt (Barth 1971, 1973, 1976b). These distinctions between the three locational groupings have been confirmed recently by radiocarbon datings on 16 samples of wood from different locations within the three groups, four from the north group, ten from the east group, and two from the west group (Barth, Felber, Schauberger 1975).

These radiocarbon determinations suggest that the sites in the north group belong to the late Urnfield Period (latest Bronze Age), those of the east group to the Hallstatt Period proper (750 to 400 B.C.), the period of the cemetery in the Salzbergtal, and the west group to the Late La Tène Period. Several dendrochronological dates from wood in the Kilb-Werk, part of the east group, confirm the Early Iron Age date of this group of galleries (Hollstein 1974).

For all three groups of sites, Schauberger estimates a total gallery length of 3,750 m and gallery floor area of 156,000 m^2 (1960, p. 12), from which some 2,000,000 m^3 of rock salt and impurities were cut (Pittioni 1976a, p. 256). For the east group alone, which belongs chronologically to the period of the great cemetery, the figures are 1,600 m of galleries, 54,000 m^2 of gallery floor, and 25 of the total recorded 57 find sites (Schauberger 1960, p. 12). In the east group, the deepest recorded point below the surface of the ground is 200 m. This group is situated in a part of the mountain with much purer salt than the other two areas, with much of the salt here of 70 to 84 percent purity (Schauberger 1960, p. 11).

Remains of tools in the mines provide information about the mining procedure, as do a few rare instances of open areas in the prehistoric galleries in which the actual traces of mining techniques are preserved. The cutting of the salt in the mines was done with long pointed bronze winged picks, remains of which have been recovered in the mines (Kromer 1963, pls. 64, 65). These were fastened to wooden handles having right-angle bends, many of which have been recovered, mostly in fragmentary condition (Kromer 1963, pl. 65). In one gallery in the east group evidence of the technique of removal of the salt was found. In order to remove large blocks of rock salt from the relatively pure layers of the mineral, the miners made a deep vertical groove in the face of the salt, then from the top of that groove a curving line to the right and to the left and down to the lower end of the groove, thus forming a heart-shaped pattern (Morton 1949; Barth 1970b, pls. 2, 3). These lines were chipped deeper into the salt face, then the two blocks forming the two halves of the heart were snapped off (Kromer 1963, p. 30). In the Stüger-Werk, also part of the east group, a block of salt so removed was recovered; it was incomplete, but still weighed about 12 kg (Barth 1976b). (On the different techniques of mining employed in Late Bronze and Early Iron Age Hallstatt see Barth 1980a and b.)

Sacks made of the skins of animals and used for carrying salt have been found in the east group galleries. These sacks sometimes contain small chunks of salt, indicating that not only the large blocks were carried to the surface (Barth 1971). Very finely made Late Bronze Age leather sacks with wooden frames have been recovered in the north group of galleries (Kromer 1963, pls. 62, 63).

Both the east and north group have yielded an abundance of fir and spruce splints which provided lighting for the prehistoric miners (Kromer 1963, pl. 66). Those recovered in the north group (Late Bronze Age) are rectangular in section and were burned either singly or in bundles. Those from the east group (Early Iron Age) are wide and flat and have been found only singly. Burned chunks of wood suggest larger fires also as sources of light in these galleries (Barth 1973, pl. I, 1980a, pp. 70–73).

Among other materials of importance for our understanding of the mining operation at prehistoric Hallstatt are wooden shovels and mallets (Kromer 1963, pl. 61; Barth 1971, pl. 5), wooden vessels (Kromer 1963, pls. 67, 68), wooden timbers used to shore up the prehistoric galleries (Kromer 1963, p. 28; Schauberger 1976, p. 156), logs on the floors of galleries which provided secure footing (Schauberger 1976, p. 156, fig. 2), and remains of miners' clothing of fur, leather, wool, and linen (Kromer 1963, pls. 69–72; Hundt 1970). (Important distinctions in the forms of the various tools and equipment recovered in the east and the north galleries are discussed by Barth 1973.)

An altered cow's horn and several bone whistles found in the mines were probably used as signaling devices by the prehistoric miners (Barth 1970c). Food remains found in the mines include the bones of cattle and pig (Barth 1971, p. 38). Study of coprolites from the mines has yielded evidence of vetch, barley, millet, wheat, apple, and cherry (Morton 1953, pl. 20; Aspöck et al. 1973, p. 42, note 4). The coprolites also contain evidence of parasites which afflicted the miners, perhaps causing serious problems in health for the mining population at Hallstatt (Aspöck et al. 1973).

The Question of the Settlement at Hallstatt. Although we have rich archaeological documentation of the cemetery and the mines at Hallstatt, we have very little evidence pertaining to the settlement area or areas of the Early Iron Age community. Traces of cultural layers have been found in various parts of the Salzbergtal over the years (Reitinger 1968, pp. 166–167), and most investigators agree that the settlement should most likely be expected in that mountain valley rather than below at the lakeside on the site of the present town (where no clear evidence of settlement in the Early Iron Age has been found). Besides scattered traces suggestive of settlement remains, several log cabin-type structures have been found at various times during the past two centuries, but it is unclear whether any of these served as actual dwellings (Barth 1976c; Lipp 1976; Pauli 1979). The substantial settlement that must have existed to accommodate the salt-mining population of Hallstatt still has not been found, at least not more than in traces.

Hallstatt in European Prehistory

Hallstatt was the first major Iron Age cemetery in Europe to be extensively and systematically excavated. Ramsauer's work was exceptionally precise for the time, and despite the subsequent disarticulation of some of the grave groups after they had reached Vienna, the graves excavated by him formed the basis of early research on the Early Iron Age in Europe.

Because of its size, the richness of the graves, and the span of time represented by the burials, the Hallstatt cemetery was chosen as the type site for the Early Iron Age of central Europe. At the International Conference of Prehistoric and Protohistoric Sciences in Stockholm in 1874, Hans Hildebrand proposed the designation of the two major stylistically distinct groups of Iron Age material in central Europe by the names of the sites at which each was abundantly represented—in the one case Hallstatt in Upper Austria, in the other La Tène on Lake Neuchâtel in western Switzerland (Hildebrand 1876). Hildebrand's distinction between the two groups was principally stylistic, and he did not emphasize the chronological aspect of the differences. At the end of the last century and beginning of the present one, when the chronological framework for the Early Iron Age was being developed, the graves from Hallstatt played a central role (Reinecke 1900; Hoernes 1905, 1921).

The term "Hallstatt" has been used in three different, sometimes confused, ways. It designates a style of ornament, a culture area, and a period of time. Hildebrand's original use of the term "Hallstatt" was a stylistic one, referring to that decoration represented in the great cemetery and at numerous other sites throughout central Europe.

"Hallstatt" as a culture area refers to that part of Europe in which objects of the Hallstatt style regularly occur. Scholars agree in a general way where this region lies, but as Angeli's map (1970, p. 25, fig. 1) illustrates, there are considerable disagreements on the boundaries of such an area.

Besides a style and a region, "Hallstatt" is also used to designate a period of time. The chronological concept overlaps partly with the stylistic and the geographical, but not completely. Some of the stylistic elements of the Hallstatt material culture are present in the Late Bronze Age Urnfield Period, and some occur in Early La Tène associations. According to the currently accepted chronology, the Hallstatt Period dates roughly 800/750 B.C. to 500/400 B.C. (Pauli 1972, 1978; Dehn and Frey 1979). The beginning and end points are still somewhat unclear, and they vary in different regions of central Europe.

In recent years Hallstatt has remained the focus of chronological studies and has played an important role in research into economic organization in Early Iron Age Europe. The Hallstatt cemetery has been particularly important in recent attempts to correlate chronological sequences in different parts of circum-Alpine Europe (e.g., Kossack 1959; Peroni 1973; Ridgway 1979).

Hallstatt is unique for the wealth of information it embodies concerning industrial activity and trade in Early Iron Age central Europe. The community living there was a specialized one, extracting salt for export trade (see below). The scale of the extractive operation is best documented by the investigations conducted by Schauberger (1960) and Barth (1980a and b) in the galleries of the Early Iron Age mines.

The social organization of this specialized community has been the subject of many studies and much debate. Two principal models have been put forward. One suggests a community made up mainly of able-bodied men, a nontypical, work-camp population (Kromer 1958, 1959a). The other, now with more adherents than the first, views the population represented in the cemetery as a typical community comprising a number of different family units like most other communities (Häusler 1968; Kilian-Dirlmeier 1969, 1971; Angeli 1970; Frey 1971; Maier 1974; Hodson 1977).

Having been a major center of salt extraction and exportation, Hallstatt plays a special role in studies of trade during the Early Iron Age. As Barth has observed (1980a, p. 79), the site of Hallstatt is represented on an extraordinary number of artifact distribution maps, often at the extremity of the distribution of a particular type. Hallstatt displays a wider range of materials from different parts of the continent than any other site. To some extent this fact is due to the large number of graves excavated, but it also reflects the special nature of the community with respect to trade. Among the foreign objects represented in the graves at Hallstatt are fibulae from the northwest Alpine culture area; amber from the Baltic; fibulae, helmets and armor pieces, and ornaments from Slovenia; relief-ornamented situla lids from northeast Italy; and ivory from Africa in the form of sword pommels. The pottery at Hallstatt shows close connections with other parts of Upper Austria, with Lower Austria, and with southern Bavaria (Wells 1978b, pp. 87–88). Thus the community at Hallstatt was connected through commercial relations with many different regions of Europe.

The Excavations at Hallstatt by the Duchess of Mecklenburg

The Duchess excavated at Hallstatt in September and early October of 1907 (de Navarro 1934).* The surviving notes from the excavation indicate an earliest date of September 10 and a latest date of October 9. These dates probably define within a day or two the period during which she excavated there. Langer, who was working at the mines at Hallstatt at the time, gives the dates as September 9 to October 11 (1936, p. 154). By the time the Duchess excavated at Hallstatt in 1907 she had had two summers of experience excavating at large Iron Age cemeteries in Slovenia, at Magdalenska gora, Stična, Vače, and Vinica.

The Duchess received permission from the Austro-Hungarian Emperor Franz Joseph to conduct her excavations at Hallstatt. In a letter written by the Emperor from Vienna on September 16, 1907, now in the Mecklenburg Collection, he acknowledges a letter from her reporting success in the early stages of the work and tells her that he is glad to have been able to help her arrange permission for the digging.

The principal sources of information about the progress of the Duchess's excavations are threefold: (1) the surviving notes from the excavations; (2) several photographs showing the digging; and (3) five pages of a diary kept by the archaeologist Josef Szombathy. Szombathy visited the Duchess's excavations at Hallstatt on September 19, 20, and 21, and recorded some interesting and helpful comments about the work.

Szombathy's diary is now in the Prähistorische Abteilung of the Naturhistorisches Museum in Vienna. I am grateful to Dr. Wilhelm Angeli, Director of the Prähistorische Abteilung, for sending me copies of the pages and for providing me with a transcription of the parts of Szombathy's notes that were written in Gabelsberg shorthand. I further thank Dr. Angeli for his permission to reproduce here the pages of the diary that pertain to the Duchess's work at Hallstatt.

No plan survives indicating where the Duchess excavated, but from the field notes, the photographs, and Szombathy's journal the location can be roughly defined. Szombathy noted that the Duchess began her excavations at Hallstatt in the woods, where she found large stones; underneath them was only salty clay and

---

*A preliminary version of this section, of the catalogue of the Hallstatt graves, and of the discussion following was published in *Germania*, vol. 56, 1978, pp. 66–88.

Text figure V. Photograph of the Duchess of Mecklenburg supervising her excavations at Hallstatt. This view probably shows the initial excavation at the edge of the woods, as recounted by Szombathy.

not the graves which she had hoped to find. The digging here was quickly stopped and the holes were filled in. The photograph in text figure V most likely shows this first excavation attempt. The work is going on at the edge of the forest, probably along the southern edge of the Salzbergtal (see text fig. II), and large stones are visible at the top and bottom of the dirt piles. The second worker from the left has his hand on a large stone block.

Next, according to Szombathy, the Duchess tried excavating *auf der Wiese* (on the meadow), probably somewhere on the cleared area of the Salzbergtal. Again no graves were found.

Finally, she excavated in an area *unterm Ökonomiegebäude* (below the Ökonomiegebäude), and here she discovered graves. The location of this area can be defined quite well on the basis of the notes, the photographs, and Szombathy's records. The photographs in text figures VI and VII show the work in progress in an area enclosed by a fence consisting of three flat boards fastened onto low posts driven into the ground. This fence is probably that enclosing the parcel of land just east of the Ökonomiegebäude bordering on the path running up the Salzbergtal (see text fig. II). The Rudolfsturm is visible in the upper left-hand corner of these photographs, and the small wooden building and the lower end of the Salzbergtal are situated in the center background of the pictures. The slope of the hill up to the right corresponds with the suggested location.

The excavation notes accompanying Graves 4, 6, 14, and 15 indicate that these graves were "near" the Rudolfsturm, a description that would certainly fit the suggested area. Notes for Grave 19 indicate a location "at the fence," referring most likely to that in the photographs here, and that enclosing the parcel of land east of the Ökonomiegebäude.

In his journal Szombathy mentions a location between the Ökonomiegebäude and the path as one in which graves were found by the Duchess. He further

Text figure VI. Photograph showing the Duchess (center, wearing apron) at work at Hallstatt, surrounded by visitors and workmen.

notes that unexcavated graves were known to exist in one of the fields on which turnips were growing. At the time of his visit, September 19 to 21, the turnips had not yet been harvested; Szombathy writes that the Duchess would have to wait until October, when they would be, to excavate in that area. Since in the various photographs of the lower part of the Salzbergtal (text fig. II; Morton 1959, p. 3, fig. 1, pl. I), the enclosed parcel of land east of the Ökonomiegebäude is the only visible land used for growing crops, this evidence further supports the interpretation of that area as the one in which the Duchess excavated the graves.

Langer (1936, p. 154) also mentions these three areas in which the Duchess excavated: in the woods, on the meadow, and in the garden of the Ökonomiegebäude. He adds the information that the place on the meadow where she excavated was between the Rudolfsturm and the Ökonomiegebäude and that the area opened in this location was 106 m², that in the fenced-in garden location, 176 m². He states that one cremation burial was found on the meadow, and all her other finds were made in the garden area.

A notebook kept by the archaeologist, Josef Bayer, describing a visit to Hallstatt in 1928, also in the archives of the Prähistorische Abteilung of the Naturhistorisches Museum in Vienna, contains various information gathered by Bayer about the Duchess's investigations. Many of the details are inaccurately remembered by Bayer's informants after the 21-year interval, but there is agreement on the fact that the majority of the finds were made in the garden of the Ökonomiegebäude.

In his brief account of the Duchess's work at Hallstatt, Langer presents some facts that agree with the surviving notes and some that do not. He writes that excavation went as deep as 2.5 m in places and that the Duchess's excavations uncovered a total of 20 cremation burials and 14 inhumations. He mentions three objects found in the graves which he considered of special interest: the bronze bull and the bronze pin

Text figure VII. Photograph showing workmen at the excavations of the Duchess at Hallstatt. Courtesy of the Prähistorische Abteilung, Naturhistorisches Museum, Vienna.

with iron wire inlay (the latter he records as 35 cm long, whereas it is actually about 25 cm long), which are now part of the Mecklenburg Collection, and a small vessel with a tube-shaped spout of which there is no mention in the collection. Langer also calls attention to a skeleton of an exceptionally large man found in a sitting position facing east, without associated grave goods. According to Langer, the well-preserved skull was sent to the German Kaiser as a gift.

It is difficult to evaluate Langer's information. Some corresponds closely with that provided by the excavation notes and by Szombathy's notebook, but some, particularly concerning the number of graves found, does not. Since Langer's article was written in 1936, it is possible that his recollection of the excavations of 1907 was inaccurate.

For present purposes I rely on the information contained in the excavation notes and objects now in the Mecklenburg Collection, supplemented by the eyewitness account of Szombathy.

In the archives of the Prähistorische Abteilung of the Naturhistorisches Museum in Vienna is a photograph of a plan of the Hallstatt cemetery, a copy of which I include here (text fig. VIII). The plan is undated, but Dr. Stefan Nebehay of the Naturhistorisches Museum advises me that the style of the letters indicates that it was made sometime around the turn of the century. According to the records of the Naturhistorisches Museum, the original photograph had been lent to Adolf Mahr when he was curator of the Prähistorische Abteilung by a man named Krieger from the saltworks at Hallstatt. Dr. Nebehay informs me that it is not known whether the original plan is still in existence.

To the left of the north arrow on the plan are three rectangles colored darker than the surrounding

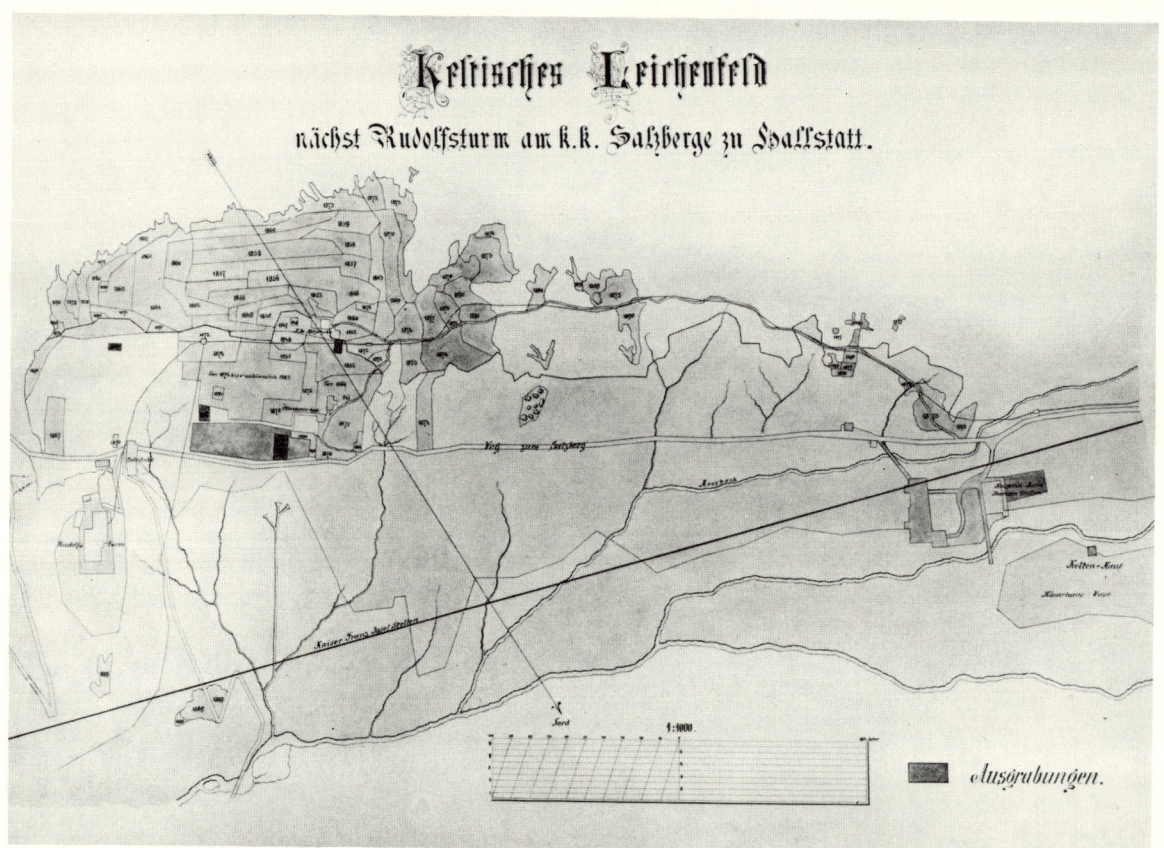

Text figure VIII. Plan of the Hallstatt cemetery indicating areas excavated through 1907. The three dark rectangular areas to the left of the north arrow are labeled 1907, and probably represent the three areas in which the Duchess excavated. Unfortunately, the origin of this plan is unknown, and therefore it is unclear whether or not it is accurate. Note the location of the Rudolfsturm in the lower left and the path running up the valley from left to right through the center of the plan. The Hallstätter See is to the left of the area shown on this plan, about 350 m below.
Photograph courtesy of the Prähistorische Abteilung, Naturhistorisches Museum, Vienna.

areas, each with the year 1907 written in it. These are probably the three areas in which the Duchess excavated, and they correspond with the other evidence regarding the locations of her excavations. It is unfortunate that we do not know who drew this plan of the cemetery, nor the basis for the placement of the three rectangles.

With the kind permission of Dr. Angeli I reproduce here the pages of Szombathy's diary, now in the Prähistorische Abteilung, Naturhistorisches Museum, Vienna, that pertain to his visit to the Duchess's excavations at Hallstatt. Most of the text is in the original German, some has been transcribed into German from Gabelsberg shorthand:

Hallstatt. Grabungen der
Herzogin Marie von Mecklenburg.
19/9 1907. *Gmunden.* Herrn Statthalternrat Gf. Salburg treffe ich nicht an,
da er nach Ischl gefahren ist.
H. Bez.-Komm. Gf. Walderdorf teilt mir
mit, dass infolge der Bitten der Herzogin
Se Majestät dem Gfen Salburg den
Auftrag gab, die Grabg. in Hallstatt zu
ermöglichen.
Das Finanzärar gab nicht nur die
Erlaubnis, sondern bezahlt auch die
Kosten der Grabungen.
Ein Versuch fand vor 14 Tagen
statt, seit 8 Tagen wird gegraben.
Die Herzogin arbeitet selbst mit.
Es dürfte noch nichts Nennenswertes
gefunden worden sein.
20/9 1907. Freitg. Früh Fahrt
nach *Hallstatt.*
Museumsverwalter Roth
Bergrat. v. Kirnbauer Friedrich
Verwalter am Rudolfsturm Langer
Die Herzogin ist um 9h auf den Berg gegangen und wird wohl
    bis abends oben arbeiten.
Der Sohn des Musverwalters Roth ist ja Vorarbeiter, aber
    diesen verfolgt
sie mit ihrem Misstrauen und lässt seine Hände nicht einen
    Augenblick aus dem Auge.
Sie hat bisher verschiedene Kleinigkeiten und eine schöne
    grosse
Urne mit Verzierungen gefunden.
Aber leider noch kein Skelet.
Es ist bekannt, dass auf einem der Felder (wahrscheinlich das
    des früheren Steigers
Engl) noch Gräber zu finden sein würden, aber darauf stehen
    jetzt noch Rüben
und erst gegen Ende Oktober, wenn diese reif sind, kann man
    dort graben.
Das Feld kann man nicht abkaufen, weil die Arbeiter die
    Rüben selbst notwendig haben.
Bergr. v. Kirnbauer teilt mir mit:
die Grabgen gehen auf Kosten des
Salinenärars. Anfangs 22 Arbeiter,
jetzt 11 Arbeiter, deren Abgang im Bergwerk schmerzlich
    empfunden wird.
Die Arbeiter erwarten, dass sie einen höheren Lohn erhalten,
    aber es
ist diesbezüglich noch keine Weisung ergangen.
Die Herzogin ist jeden 2. Tag oben und bleibt dann bis spät
    abends.
Zuerst wurde im Walde gegraben. Es wurde auch telegraph
Schulz aus Laibach berufen, um zu raten.
Auf seinen Rat wurden auch Steinblöcke gesprengt, weil
darunter Gräber sein sollten. Es war aber unter den Steinen
    direkt
der Salzlehm, der gleich wieder bedeckt wurde.
Dann wurde auf der Wiese gegraben. Ohne Erfolg. Dann unter
    dem
Ökonomiegebäude, da wurden Knochen gefunden, aber
kein 1 Skelet. 1 schöner Brarmring,
aber ein wenig gebrochen. Kleinere Fussringe.
1 Kopfschmuck aus 1 Dutz Nadeln, mehrere
Spiralfibeln und 1 Urne, rot mit schwarzen Verzierungen, einige kleinere Gefässe.
Der am Wege gelegene Acker ist im
Gebrauch der Bergverwalter darum wurde er bisher
noch nicht durchgegraben und es ist möglich, dass dort noch
    zahlreiche Gräber
Intakt sind.
Die Herzogin wird jetzt wohl noch 8 Tage hier bleiben, je nach
    dem
Wetter und vielleicht im Okt. wenn die Rüben auf dem Feld
    abgeerntet sind,
wieder kommen. Sie will eine grosse Brurne und ein Schwert
    finden.
Die Herzogin verspricht allen in Hallst. Belohnungen.
Nachmitt. 2½h auf den
Salzberg.
Die Grabg. geht nun die 3. Woche. D. ersten
2 Wochen waren 22, die 3. Woche 11 Arbeiter
und die jungen Leute des Kanzleipersonals
sowie abwechselnd Bergrat od. Bergverwalter bei den Grabungen. Kosten ca 1000 K
Bergrat Kirnbauer stellt mich der Herzogin
vor. Es ist dieselbe Dame, welche vor 1½
Jahren einen Vormittag als "Gräfin X"
in der Sammlung war. Ungnädiger
Empfang, Vorwürfe. Hauptsache
ist die letzte Zuschrift der Z.K. an den
Fürsten Hugo Windischgrätz.
Tratsch des Dr Šmid und des Schulz.
Alles Böse über Petschnik, von Schulz'
gehässiger Darstellung.
Breite Ausmalung der allerhöchsten
Förderungen.
Eigenhändige Ausgrabung d. Herzogin
Skelett 4. zwischen dem Ökonomiegebäude und dem Wege. Es heisst: "Unterkörper verbrannt, Oberkörper beerdigt."
Aber beim Skelett sind Oberschenkel und
Becken vorhanden. Beigaben:
2 Handgelenkringe, 1 Spiralfibel zerbrochen,
1 Dutz Bernsteinperlen. Erhaltungszustand

schlecht in feuchtem Boden.
Ich lehre dem Lakai Goldberg, (der den
Hörnes 7mal genau durchgelesen hat)
wie man die Funde etikettiert.
Abds 7h Abstieg. Gefolge bilden
ich und der Bergrat. Begeisternde
Anekdoten von der Indienreise Ihrer Hoheit
9h–12¾h Privataudienz in Gmunden.
21/9 1907. Morgens mündliche
Anfrage um das Befinden der Hohheit.
Erhalte Pečnik's Brief aus Hl. Kreuz
Mittags Besprechung mit Statthalternrat Gf. Salburg, der den Artikel in d.
N. fr. Pr. nicht geschrieben hat.
2/5 1911. Oberkommissär Langer sagt,
die Herzogin habe mindestens 45 Gräber
geöffnet. Funde: Mehrere schöne Tongefässe,
1 sehr gut erhaltener Bronzestier, schöne Armringe,
mehrere Brfibeln, mehrere Eisenlanzenspitzen, 1
gutes Klappmesser, lange Nadeln mit Knöpfen.
Grabg. 4 Wochen.

CATALOGUE OF GRAVES FROM HALLSTATT

GRAVE 1a

Inhumation burial. The grave was found next to a large stone about 2 m below the surface. The surviving notes mention a small ceramic bowl.

Grave goods:

Two bronze spectacle brooches, one represented by a single surviving spiral; L. of nearly complete one about 10.7 cm (fig. 1a). Bronze fibula bow with ribbing; L. 4.0 cm (fig. 1b). Fragment of sheet bronze with one large boss, a hole at one end, small bosses along the edges, and a circle of small punched indentations around the large boss; L. 2.5 cm (fig. 1c). Iron fragment.

Small grayish-tan bowl. The rim thins out and turns inward. The top half of the exterior is coated with graphite. A small nipple is present near the rim on one side; Ext. D. at mouth 9.9 cm (fig. 1d). Sherd of light brown color coated with a cherry red slip on the exterior. Also on this surface are a small groove and heavy black painted lines (fig. 1e).

GRAVE 1b

The excavation notes call this a *Brand und Skelettgrab*. (On the problem of graves with apparently mixed burial rite see Kromer 1959a, pp. 16–18. The recent excavations at the Dürrnberg have revealed graves containing both unburned skeletal parts and cremated remains [Pauli 1975b, pp. 112–114].) The surviving notes mention two spectacle brooches and 13 small pins, the latter thought to have been jewelry for the head.

Grave goods:

Two bronze spectacle brooches, one represented by only one spiral; L. of complete brooch 9.4 cm (fig. 2a). Thirteen bronze pins. One has dot-and-circle decoration on the head (fig. 2b). Two have roughly spherical heads (one in fig. 2c). Three have mushroom-shaped heads (one in fig. 2d). Seven have lens-shaped heads (one in fig. 2e). L. of complete pins between 7.7 and 8.8 cm.

GRAVE 2

A note says that the ring was found under a tree trunk.

Grave good:

Heavy solid bronze ring with long, thick bosses; Max. Ext. D. 7.5 cm (fig. 3).

GRAVE 3

Cremation burial. A note mentions bronze fragments and buttons.

Grave goods:

At least 50 complete and fragmentary bronze buttons, round, convex, and with eyelets on the backs. D. 1.8 to 1.9 cm (one in fig. 4c). Many are severely misshapen and have fragments of burned bone and charcoal adhering to them. Badly corroded fragments of a bronze ring (fig. 4d). Solid bronze rod, rectangular in section, broken at one end and tapering at the other, probably an awl or chisel; L. 10.6 cm (fig. 4a). Fragmentary bronze object consisting of two rods joined at the top, both of which are broken; L. 7.0 cm (fig. 4b). This object has fragments of charcoal adhering to it. Small fragments of sheet bronze, distorted by heat and in some cases fused together.

GRAVE 4

The notes associated with this grave say "Rudolfsthurm."

Grave goods:

Two small bronze spectacle brooches; L. 5.5 and 4.4 cm (fig. 5a, b). Two spiral rings of thin bronze bands; Ext. D. about 4.0 cm, width of bands about 0.4 cm (fig. 5c).

GRAVE 5

Grave goods:

Bronze Certosa fibula with stop disk and a small

knob on the foot; L. 6.0 cm (fig. 6b). Bronze serpentine fibula with saddle-shaped bend in the bow and a stop disk; L. about 8.4 cm (fig. 6a).

GRAVE 6

Inhumation burial. (De Navarro [1934, p. 71] calls this grave a cremation, but a note preserved from the excavation says *Skelettgrab*.) The notes call this a child's grave. It was found next to a large stone at a depth of 0.75 m. One note says "Rudolfsthurm." The notes mention two broken fibulae, some amber beads, a small arm ring, and a small ceramic vessel.

Grave goods:

Two small bronze spectacle brooches, one represented by a single surviving spiral; L. of complete specimen about 6.0 cm (fig. 7a). Bronze ring with incised line decoration and slightly knobbed ends; Max. Ext. D. 6.2 cm (fig. 7d). Nineteen amber beads including a cylindrical bead 0.9 cm long and a disk-shaped one 1.6 cm in diameter (fig. 7b).

Small pale orange jug with a handle. The vessel is decorated with a row of impressions around the shoulder; these vary in shape from triangular to roughly square. H. 6.1 cm; Max. D. 8.0 cm (fig. 7c).

GRAVE 7

There is some confusion about this grave. One note calls it a cremation burial and mentions as finds a spectacle brooch and a badly preserved arm ring. Another note bearing the same date (September 13, 1907) mentions two urns and says that they belong to a *Skelett- und Brandgrab* found at a depth of 2.05 m; at the bottom of that note and without a clear context a bronze spearhead is mentioned. There is no other evidence of such an object with this grave, and the mention here may refer to the spearhead in Grave 8 (although the notes associated with Grave 8 are dated September 17).

Associated with Grave 7 at present are one ceramic vessel, a spectacle brooch, and an arm ring.

Grave goods:

Bronze spectacle brooch; L. 7.3 cm (fig. 8b). Fragmentary bronze ring with knobbed end; Max. Ext. D. 6.6 cm (fig. 8c).

Wide-mouthed jar or large cup with a handle. The vessel is dark gray and brown. Around the base of the neck is a row of triangular excisions. H. 11.4 cm; Max. D. about 13.0 cm (fig. 8a).

GRAVE 8

A note mentions a bronze spearhead found under a burned layer and suggests that the spearhead probably belonged to a grave containing three urns and some spirals. Another note mentions the spearhead and a garment pin.

Grave goods:

Bronze spearhead with hole through the socket; L. 13.6 cm; D. at socket end 2.3 cm (fig. 9f). Bronze pin with three knobs and guard; L. (slightly bent) 25.7 cm (fig. 9a). Two fragmentary spirals of flattish bronze wire; D. 1.5 and 1.3 cm (fig. 9b, c).

Globular vessel with a short neck and a very small handle between rim and shoulder. The vessel is light brown. On the exterior and the rim interior is a cherry red slip. On the body is a design consisting of concentric chevrons formed by graphite lines. The exterior of the rim is coated with graphite, as is the base. Ext. D. at rim 13.3 cm (fig. 9e). Many sherds of a large light brown vessel. Most of the exterior is coated with a cherry red slip. A pattern, consisting of rhomboids with dots in the centers, crossing lines, and curls beneath the rhomboids is painted in heavy black on the body. The rim is coated with graphite on the exterior and with cherry red slip on the interior. Along the lip on the interior is a heavy black line, and on the interior surface of the rim is what appears to be a zigzag pattern painted in heavy black (fig. 9g). Sherds of a small dark gray bowl of coarse fabric. The exterior is coated with graphite (fig. 9d).

GRAVE 9

Inhumation burial. A skeleton was found at a depth of 0.80 m. Mentioned in the surviving notes are six pins and a button.

Grave goods:

Surviving are three fragmentary pins, two with roughly spherical heads (one in fig. 10c) and one with a lens-shaped head (fig. 10a). Bronze button with a large disk on one side and a smaller one on the other, connected by a thick shaft; D. of front disk 3.0 cm (fig. 10b).

GRAVE 10

Cremation burial. The grave was found next to a large stone at a depth of 1.10 m. A note mentions a small broken fibula, two pins, and a small ring.

Grave goods:

Fragmentary bronze fibula with a twist pattern on the bow. Fragment 4.7 cm long (fig. 11b). Small fragment of what appears to be a similar fibula (fig. 11a). Fragments of two pins with lens-shaped heads (one in fig. 11c). Fragment of a small bronze ring (fig. 11d).

GRAVE 11

Inhumation burial. The grave was found at a depth of 1.80 m. Surviving notes mention an arm ring, a badly preserved spectacle brooch, a skull, and a small fibula found on the left side of the chest of the skeleton.

Grave goods:

Bronze spectacle brooch of which only one spiral survives (fig. 12c). Fragments of a bronze boat-shaped fibula with three bands of incised lines ornamenting the bow; L. of bow about 5 cm (larger fragment in fig. 12a). Open knobbed bronze ring; Max. Ext. D. 7.6 cm (fig. 12b).

GRAVE 12

Cremation burial. The notes mention a bronze bovine or deer figurine and include sketches and measurements which correspond exactly to the figurine now in the collection.

Grave good:

Figurine of a bovine animal of solid bronze with body, legs, tail, long thin neck, small head, very large horns, and bulbous eyes indicated; L. 14.2 cm (fig. 13a, b). (For further discussion and photographs of this figurine see Wells 1978c).

GRAVE 13

Inhumation burial. The grave was found at a depth of 1.90 m. A note mentions a large skull which was photographed. (No such photograph survives in the Mecklenburg Collection. Langer [1936, p. 154, fig. 1] publishes a photograph of an inhumation burial with a well-preserved skull uncovered by the Duchess, but it is unclear whether this is the same one as our Grave 13 or not.)

Grave goods:

Body sherd with a small handle of a thick-walled, fairly coarse-textured brownish-gray vessel (fig. 14). Body sherd of a light brown vessel. The interior has a thin dull black coating, and a cherry red slip coats the exterior.

This grave group also contains a number of animal teeth which were associated with this grave number when the collection was studied in Zurich. One tooth from sheep or goat (*Ovis* or *Capra*), M1 or M2, mandible, left side, individual older than 15 months. One tooth from cow (*Bos taurus*), upper right M1, probably older than 15 months. Two teeth from pig (*Sus*), upper incisors. Two teeth from pig, lower incisors. Four lower canines from male pig, right side. One lower canine from male pig, left side. One lower canine of a young female pig. The minimum number of individuals represented is six pigs, one cow, one sheep or goat. (I am grateful to Richard Meadow of the Department of Anthropology, Harvard University, for identifying the animal remains.)

The scholars studying the collection in Zurich also noted the presence of a human mandible in the grave group. The human skeletal remains from Hallstatt now in the collection cannot be ascribed to specific graves (see pp. 30–36).

GRAVE 14

Cremation burial. This grave was found at a depth of 1.90 m. The notes mention four badly preserved spirals, six pins, and fragments of bones.

Grave goods:

Fragmentary remains of two bronze spectacle brooches (one in fig. 15h). Seven fragmentary bronze pins with heads of roughly spherical (three pins, two in fig. 15d, e), mushroom (one pin, fig. 15c), and lens shape (three pins, two in fig. 15a, b); L. of most complete pin 8.9 cm. Small bronze beads, 162 in all; Ext. D. 0.4 cm, thickness 0.3 cm (fig. 15g). Various bronze fragments severely damaged by fire, including parts of one or more thin rings (fig. 15i–k). Thirty-two blue glass beads with white eyes, D. 0.5 to 0.7 cm; one blue glass bead, D. 0.7 cm; ten very small yellow glass beads, D. 0.3 cm; fourteen very small blue glass beads, D. 0.3 cm; one small greenish-blue bead, D. 0.4 cm (fig. 15f).

Small fragments of burned bone are also preserved.

GRAVE 15

Inhumation burial. This grave was found at a depth of 1.60 m and was *beim Rudolfsturm*. The notes indicate that the grave was surrounded by stones, and coarse yellow sand was scattered about it. The skeleton lay on its back in an extended position. Mentioned as finds are two badly preserved arm rings, a broken spectacle brooch found on the chest, and some small amber beads. A skull was also recovered in the grave.

Grave goods:

Two very similar solid bronze rings with slightly overlapping ends, decorated with groups of three and four incised lines; Max. Ext. D. 6.7 cm (one in fig. 16a). Fragments of a bronze spectacle brooch (fig. 16b). The amber beads are not preserved and were not with the material when it was studied in Zurich. Fragments of the skull were, however, present when the collection was in Zurich, but are no longer associated with this particular grave.

GRAVE 16

Cremation burial. The grave was found at a depth of 0.45 m. Mentioned as finds are an iron knife, a bronze celt, a bronze spearhead badly damaged by fire, three garment pins, and a number of urns (*grosser Urnenkreis*).

Grave goods:

Remains of an iron knife; surviving L. about 14.4 cm (fig. 17b). Two bronze spectacle brooches, one represented by a single spiral; L. of complete one 6.5 cm (fig. 17e). Bronze winged axe with remains of its wooden shaft; L. 17.6 cm, width of blade 6.3 cm (fig. 17i). Bronze spearhead severely damaged by fire; L. 20.2 cm (fig. 17d). Bronze pin with two knobs and mushroom-shaped head, with guard and end attachment. The entire top above the guard is decorated with engraved lines filled with inlay consisting of iron wire (see below, pp. 37–39). L. (bent) 24.8 cm (fig. 17g). Bronze pin with four knobs and flattened mushroom-shaped head and end attachment; L. (bent) 17.2 cm (fig. 17f). Fragmentary bronze pin with four knobs, a guard, and small ridges between the knobs (fig. 17h).

Sherds of a high-necked dark gray vessel. The globular body is decorated with a pattern of double grooves and stamped dots and circles. Around the base of the neck is a row of impressed dots. At four places on the cylindrical neck are perforated lugs. H. of surviving restored portion about 19 cm (fig. 17c). Sherds of a globular vessel of very light brown color with a cherry red slip on much of the exterior and on the interior of the rim. On the neck is a zigzag pattern consisting of three parallel incised lines. On the shoulder is another pattern of three parallel incised lines forming a zigzag, but these are widely spaced and the zones between them are colored by the cherry red slip and graphite. The exteriors of the rim, the neck, and the lower part of the body are also coated with graphite. The lip is flat and coated with graphite (fig. 17j). Sherds of a somewhat similar large vessel of darker brown color. Much of the exterior and the interior of the rim is coated with a cherry red slip. The design on the body is one of alternating bands of cherry red and graphite in a zigzag pattern, but here at least one line is outlined in impressed dots. The exterior of the rim and the flat lip are coated with graphite (fig. 17a).

GRAVE 17

Inhumation burial. A skull was recovered in this grave.

Grave goods:

Two similar solid bronze rings with thickened ends and decorated with sections of ribbing; Max. Ext. D. 6.9 and 7.1 cm (fig. 18a, b). Two bronze spectacle brooches, one very fragmentary. Instead of the figure eight connecting the two spirals characteristic of others in these graves, these specimens have a continuous wire connecting them. L. 8.2 cm (complete one in fig. 18c). Fragment of a perforated whetstone made of a very micaceous black slate; surviving L. 5.7 cm (fig. 18d). (For identification of the rock type I am grateful to Dr. Jutta Binstock of the Department of Geology, Harvard University.)

Fragments of a skull and a few other bone fragments were with this grave when the collection was in Zurich.

GRAVE 18

There is no surviving information about the circumstances of recovery of the material attributed to this grave. The objects were apparently all packed together in a box labeled "Hallstatt" and with the date October 1, 1907. The scholars working on the collection in Zurich attributed these objects to a grave, which they numbered 18, but now it is unclear why they thought that these items all came from one grave.

Objects:

Four similar two-looped bronze fibulae, three with eight knobs on the bow, one with seven knobs, all with ribbing between the knobs; L. of most complete one 4.8 cm (fig. 19a). Two solid bronze rings with Ext. D. of about 7.0 cm, ornamented with sections of ribbing. One (fig. 19c) shows considerable evidence of abrasion against another object, the other (fig. 19b) less so.

GRAVE 19

The notes mention several vessels (*Urnenkreis*) next to a fence (*am Zaun*).

Grave goods:

Sherds of a large light brown globular vessel. Much of the exterior of the body is coated with a cherry red slip. The body is decorated with a dark red zigzag line which defines triangular zones colored cherry red and shiny black (graphite). At the shoulder are three parallel grooves running around the vessel. Just above these grooves the shoulder is coated with graphite. The rim exterior is cherry red, with a dark red zigzag line painted over it. The rim interior is coated with graphite, as is the flattened lip (fig. 20c).

Sherds of another large light brown globular vessel. Much of the exterior is coated with a cherry red slip. The body is decorated with heavy black zigzag lines defining broad zones colored with cherry red and graphite. Of the rim, the exterior, interior, and flattened lip are coated with graphite. Painted on the edge of the lip is a heavy black line (fig. 20b).

Large stepped bowl or dish of light brown color. The interior is coated with graphite. The rim, which flares outward slightly, is decorated on the inside with a zigzag pattern consisting of groups of three parallel lines of small impressed rectangles. These appear to have been made with a tool designed for the purpose, either a stamp or a wheel with teeth on it. The two inner steps are also decorated with lines made with such a tool, as is the base. On each of the two steps is a star pattern consisting of two parallel lines of impressed rectangles and an incised line between them. On the base is a cross made up of three parallel lines of stamped rectangles. Ext. D. at mouth about 44 cm (fig. 20a).

Pale orange bowl with a conical neck and outcurved rim. On the shoulder are six parallel grooves. Below these on the body are four sets of three stamped circles containing crosses. Ext. D. at mouth about 12.5 cm (fig. 20f).

Sherds of a large, high, steep-sided gray bowl. Both surfaces show the presence of a graphite coating. There is a very small handle at the rim on one side; the rim opposite where another handle may have been located is missing. Ext. D. at mouth about 27 cm (fig. 20d).

Many sherds of a large, high pale brown bowl. The body is decorated with pairs of parallel grooves forming vertical and oblique, crossing lines. Between the pairs of grooves are large excised dots. Other dots occur in triangular patterns just below the shoulder. The neck is short and flared and is coated with graphite on both exterior and interior (fig. 20i).

Plain bowl of brownish-gray color. A broad band around the rim on the exterior is coated with graphite. The interior surface also shows the presence of a graphite coating. The rim is turned in and the lip flattened. Ext. D. at mouth about 21.5 cm (fig. 20h).

Brownish-gray bowl with high sides. The rim flares outward slightly. Just below the rim at one point is a small lug; the rim opposite is missing. Ext. D. at mouth about 19 cm (fig. 20g).

Sherds of a pale orange bowl with outcurved rim and an overhang of the rim on the exterior (fig. 20e). Base sherd of a brownish-gray vessel with a flat base decorated on the inside with shallow parallel grooves.

The scholars working on the collection in Zurich noted the presence of bones with this grave group, but they are no longer associated with this material.

GRAVE 20

Cremation burial. An urn is mentioned in a note.

Grave goods:

Bronze ring fragment (fig. 21c). Small irregular lump of bronze, very roughly 2 by 1.5 by 1 cm.

Grayish-brown jar with an outcurved rim. Painted around the outside and inside of the rim is a horizontal heavy black band. From this band, both outside and inside, vertical black bands run down the neck to the top of the shoulder. Around the shoulder are five parallel incised lines. Extending downward from the bottom line are a row of upward-pointing triple chevrons, incised. About 24 cm high and 18 cm in Ext. mouth D. (fig. 21a). Thin-walled light grayish-brown bowl. At the base is an omphalos. Just below the rim are four incised parallel lines running around the vessel. Below these is a row of impressed dots. Most of the body is ornamented with faint shallow grooves forming chevron patterns. Around the omphalos on the exterior is a circle of impressed dots. Both the rim on the exterior and the whole of the interior show traces of graphite coating. H. about 6 cm, Ext. D. at rim about 10.5 cm (fig. 21b). Two small sherds of a coarse-textured pale orange vessel.

Two fragments of burned bone were with this grave when it was studied in Zurich, but they are no longer associated with it.

GRAVE 21

Cremation burial. The grave was found at a depth of 0.45 m between two large stones. Four urns were recovered. One, designated the *Haupturne* by the excavators, was covered with a stone and contained bone remains, which were collected by the excavators. On each side of it was a small ceramic vessel. The fourth was a flat bowl. Also recovered were two small badly preserved rings.

Grave goods:

Light brown globular vessel. The exterior and the rim interior are coated with a cherry red slip. A remnant of a handle survives on the shoulder; the corresponding part of the rim where the handle was attached is missing. The base is coated with graphite, and the body is decorated with zigzag graphite lines. The exterior of the rim is also coated with graphite, as is the lip on the interior. Ext. D. at rim about 11 cm (fig. 22d).

High bowl of dark brownish-gray color with incurved rim and a small handle part way up the body on one side. Ext. D. at rim about 20.5 cm (fig. 22g).

Brownish-gray cup with handle. There are faint traces of graphite on both the neck and the body exterior and on the rim interior. Running down from the shoulder are parallel oblique flutings. Ext. D. at rim about 9 cm (fig. 22c).

Bowl or dish with sharply-defined steps. The exterior is brownish-gray; the interior is coated with graphite. The exterior part of the rim, which flares slightly, is also graphite-coated. Around the inside of the rim is a zigzag pattern consisting of groups of four parallel grooves. On the two steps inside the bowl are star patterns made up of three parallel grooves. The base is ornamented with a pattern of four quadrants, each filled with parallel grooves, such that the grooves in any quadrant run perpendicular to those in the two neighboring quadrants. Ext. D. about 40 cm (fig. 22h).

Sherds of a small dark gray globular vessel. Both exterior and interior surfaces are coated with graphite (fig. 22e). Base sherd of a vessel of thin-walled gray-colored pottery. Both surfaces show some trace of graphite (fig. 22b). Base sherd of another gray vessel with thin wall. On this specimen there are traces of graphite coating on the exterior (fig. 22f). Two creamy tan sherds. The exterior is coated with a cherry red slip. A raised band runs across both sherds; apparently it originally ran around the vessel (one in fig. 22a).

The two small rings mentioned in the excavation notes are not preserved, nor were they present when the material was studied in Zurich.

Remains of the cremated bones were with this grave in Zurich, but are no longer associated with it.

GRAVE 22

Cremation burial. The grave was found at a depth of 0.90 m between two stones.

Grave goods:

Sherds of a small grayish-brown vessel with a bulbous body, a conical neck, and a flaring rim. The whole exterior surface and the rim interior are covered with graphite. Around the neck are two sets of incised lines. The lip is flattened. Max. body D. about 9 cm (fig. 23a).

Small undecorated grayish-brown bowl with graphite coating on both interior and exterior surfaces. H. about 5 cm (fig. 23c).

Rim sherd of a large brown bowl or dish. On the interior is a graphite coating. Incised on the interior are star patterns made up of three parallel lines. Below the bottom line of the middle group is a row of impressed dots. Along the top of the rim is an incised herringbone pattern (fig. 23b).

Remains of the cremated bones with some very badly damaged bronze fragments were with this grave in Zurich, but are no longer associated with it.

GRAVE 23

Cremation burial. At a depth of 1.85 m next to a large stone and on coarse yellow sand were fragments of about five urns in a circle. Found were two badly preserved spectacle brooches, seven small hairpins, and a small iron knife.

Grave goods:

Fragment of an iron knife, 9.6 cm long (fig. 24j). Remains of two small bronze spectacle brooches (fig. 24k, m). Seven bronze pins, all fragmentary, with heads nearly spherical to flattened spherical in shape (four in fig. 24f–i).

Dark gray bowl. There is a small handle at about the middle of the body on one side. Around the top of the vessel exterior is a broad graphite band. On the inside of the bowl are a narrow graphite band along the rim and concentric downward-pointing chevrons formed by graphite lines. The surviving fragments suggest there was a cross of these lines at the base, as on the vessel from Grave 1023 at Hallstatt (Kromer 1959a, pl. 198,6). The rim is thin and slightly outcurved (fig. 24l).

Squat globular vessel light brown in color. The outside and the inside of the rim are coated with a cherry red slip. The lower portion of the body and the exterior of the rim are coated with graphite. The body is decorated with rhomboids painted in graphite. At four places on the rim interior are vertical graphite bands. H. about 12.5 cm, Ext. D. at rim about 18.5 cm (fig. 24e).

Sherds of a bowl of relatively thin dark gray pottery. Both interior and exterior are heavily coated with graphite (fig. 24a). Sherds of a bowl of fairly coarse grayish-brown pottery, the exterior coated with graphite. On the interior are traces of what appear to be linear patterns in graphite, but the remains are too fragmentary to distinguish clearly (fig. 24c). Body sherds of a vessel of rather coarse brown pottery. A cherry red slip covers part of the exterior. Much of the exterior is also coated with graphite. The sherd shown here has part of the shoulder on it (fig. 24d). Base sherd of a thick-walled vessel grayish-brown in color (fig. 24b).

GRAVE 24

Cremation burial. This grave was found at a depth of 2.05 m. It was situated on coarse sand and was surrounded by stones. Mentioned as finds are a palstave, an iron knife, bronze fishhooks, and a bronze pin.

Grave goods:

Fragments of an iron sword (fig. 25b). Small fragmentary iron knife; L. 8.2 cm (fig. 25c). Bronze winged axe (the "palstave"); L. 17.1 cm, width of blade 5.4 cm (fig. 25a). Thin bronze pin with fine ribbing around the head end, bent to nearly a right angle; L. (bent) 14.8 cm (fig. 25m). Three fragmentary bronze fishhooks (fig. 25g, h, o). Numerous fragments of bronze distorted by fire. Among these are a fragment of an undecorated arc fibula (fig. 25e) and a less distinct similar fragment (fig. 25f). Other scraps consist of pieces of thick sheet bronze (one in fig. 25n).

Sherds of a grayish-brown bowl. Decoration consists of a heavy black band painted along the rim, a heavy black zigzag line on the exterior just below the rim, and graphite lines running vertically down the interior from the rim toward the base (fig. 25i).

Sherds of a high thin-walled gray bowl, heavily coated with graphite on both exterior and interior surfaces. The thin rim turns out slightly. Around the lower portion of the body are at least two broad flutings (fig. 25d).

Rim sherd of a flat vessel, a plate or dish, brown in color. The rim flares outward. On its interior is decoration consisting of a row of triangles of incised lines filled by incised hatching. The lip and the interior surface are coated with graphite (fig. 25l).

Sherds of a large stepped bowl or dish brown in color. The rim interior is decorated with a zigzag pattern made up of sets of three parallel incised lines. The interior surface is coated with graphite. Traces of paint of another kind forming chevrons survive on the interior surface (fig. 25j).

Base sherd of a large brown vessel. The interior is coated with graphite (fig. 25k). Sherds of a large light brown vessel with a relatively coarse texture.

Adhering to the sword in this grave was a bone identified as the articular end of a rib, probably of a small cow although possibly of a pig. (I am grateful to Richard Meadow of Harvard University for identifying this specimen.)

GRAVE 25

As in the case of the objects under Grave 18, there is no surviving information about the circumstances of recovery of the following objects, nor any evidence that they constitute a grave group. They were also contained in a box labeled "Hallstatt," and with the date October 1907. It is unclear why the scholars in Zurich attributed these fibulae to a single grave.

Objects:

Nine small fragmentary boat-shaped bronze fibulae, of three varieties. One has only one ridge with incised oblique lines, running across the top of the bow and none on the side (fig. 26a). One has three such ridges, one on top and one on each side, and has relatively thick head and foot ends of the bow without ribbing at these ends (fig. 26b). The other seven have narrow ends of the bow, with both ends decorated with ribbing (one of these in fig. 26c).

STRAY FINDS

The following objects belong to the Duchess's collection of material from Hallstatt, but are not attributable to specific graves. Several are accompanied by notes relating the date and circumstances of recovery.

Flat iron axe with two small side projections (*Ärmchenbeil*) (fig. 27d). L. 17.8 cm in its present condition (the blade is broken), width across the arms 5.7 cm. A note says that the axe was a stray find made on September 10, 1907, the first recorded day of the Duchess's excavations at Hallstatt.

Ring consisting of a strip of sheet bronze with its two edges rolled over to meet (fig. 27b). One end fits inside the other and was held in place by at least two bronze wire rings passing through holes in the large ring. The larger end is broken off, hence it is unclear how great the overlap was originally. Ext. D. of ring originally about 12.5 cm, width about 1 cm, thickness about 0.7 cm. The ring is decorated with groups of parallel incised lines, pairs of holes between these, and dots (actually perforations) in circles on the outside of the holes. Through each hole was apparently a ring of bronze wire 0.7 to 0.8 cm in Ext. D., and still attached to some of the rings are pairs of triangular pendants of sheet bronze. These pendants are decorated with a row of hammered dots down the center and patterns of alternating cutout triangles.

Fragment of a wide curved ring of sheet bronze (fig. 27y). It was originally about 3.6 to 3.9 cm wide and was decorated with broad hammered-out bosses running across the width of the piece, with two thin raised lines between each two bosses, these lines decorated with very fine incised lines running across them. On one boss are remains of at least three and perhaps four perforations. A bronze clip runs through a hole in another boss. A note says that this was an isolated find made on September 10, 1907.

Two fragments of what was probably one or more handles of a bronze vessel (fig. 27a). Both are thicker at the broken end and taper at the other. The broken ends are decorated with incised spiral lines. The unbroken end of the longer fragment is undecorated and is rectangular rather than round in section; the broken end of the smaller has incised lines running part way around and is round in section.

Fragmentary bronze spectacle brooch with the continuous S kind of connection (fig. 27e); L. 9.0 cm. One note says that this object was an isolated find made during clearing on September 16, 1907. Another note indicates that it was found together with the small bronze ring with twist pattern (fig. 27s) on a small burned spot.

Solid open bronze ring with a twist pattern on the outside; Ext. D. 4.5 to 4.6 cm (fig. 27s). A note says that the object was an isolated find made during clearing on September 16, 1907.

Solid bronze ring with overlapping ends and decoration consisting of six groups of ribbing; Ext. D. 4.6 to 5.0 cm (fig. 27r). A note says that this isolated object was found on a burned layer on September 18, 1907.

Bronze ring with open ends that curl around outwards and touch the body of the ring; original Ext. D. about 4 cm (fig. 27x).

Fragmentary iron ring with tang; original Ext. D. about 3 cm (fig. 27t).

Hook of thick bronze wire bent into a T-shape with the bottom end bent upward; H. 4.5 cm, width across top of T 4.8 cm (fig. 27g).

Head of bronze pin (fig. 27f). The pin thickens to accommodate the hole, then constricts again before widening to form the broad head which is flat on top. The zone around the hole is decorated with incised lines in herringbone pattern, and incised lines around the pin border this zone above and below. L. of fragment 5.2 cm. (This object is a characteristic form of the Middle Bronze Age and is especially well represented in southern Bavaria [Holste 1938, pl. 44, 1953, p. 32, fig. 2,1]. A few finds of Bronze Age date are recorded from Hallstatt [Morton 1953, pp. 20–21], and the period is represented by a variety of finds in Upper Austria [Morton 1956, pp. 24–32; Reitinger 1969, pp. 83–144]. Since there is no note accompanying this pin fragment, it is unclear whether it was found in the course of the Duchess's excavations or acquired by her through some other means for her collection. There is no explicit evidence that the fragment even came from Hallstatt, but I include it here since it is now associated with the Hallstatt part of the collection.)

Dark blue glass bead with white wavy line around the outside; D. 1.3 cm (fig. 27w).

Ceramic spindle whorl, light grayish-tan in color (fig. 27v), roughly double conical in shape with diagonal incisions running around the outside; D. 3.2 cm, H. 2.3 cm. A note says that this object was an isolated find made on September 19, 1907.

Textile fragment. This fragment measures about 4 by 2 cm and is of woven material primarily light brown in color but with a dark brown strand running through it. A note indicates that the fragment is from the *Hallstätter Salzberg* (the same term used by the Duchess to refer to the Salzbergtal where she excavated the graves). It was probably found in one of the prehistoric galleries of the salt mines, as were the fragments studied by Hundt (1970, with earlier literature). (See technical study of this fragment, pp. 39–43 below.)

The lump of material on which the textile adheres consists largely, if not almost completely, of halite (sodium chloride). Examination of the piece under the binocular microscope shows the surface to consist of salt crystals. The dirty coloration may be an admixture of clay, or may be dirt accumulated on the surface through handling. (I am grateful to Jutta Binstock of Harvard University for her advice on this object.)

Stray sherds:

A note with the sherds indicates that they are from the Hallstatt cemetery, but there is no explicit indication that they were found in the course of the Duchess's excavations.

Sherds of a thick-walled vessel. The exterior is brown, the interior gray. The rim flares outward slightly. The body is decorated with deep vertical grooves bounding zones containing triangles of deeply incised cross-hatched lines. The exterior of the rim has graphite on it (fig. 27h).

Body sherd of a thick-walled brown vessel. A very small portion of the graphite-coated neck is present. Decoration consists of deep incised vertical lines bounding zones either free or containing vertical rows of deeply stamped dots and circles (fig. 27o).

Rim sherd of a brown bowl. The exterior is coated with a cherry red slip. There is a perforated projection below the rim. On the inside surface is a zigzag line formed by a broad graphite band. The lip is flattened (fig. 27q).

Sherd of a wide-mouthed vessel of brownish-gray pottery. The narrow rim is preserved. Around the shoulder are two parallel incised lines, bordered by two rows of impressed dots. The exterior surface is coated with graphite, as is the interior surface of the rim (fig. 27n).

Rim sherd of a pale orange vessel. On the interior of the neck is a graphite band, and there seem to be traces of one on the neck exterior as well. The lip is an oblique flattened surface. On the shoulder is a small projection extending upward (fig. 27m).

Sherd with perforated projection from a bowl of gray pottery. On the exterior, the upper part of the sherd is coated with graphite. On the interior is a trace of a band of graphite at the top, and bands of graphite running down the interior surface (fig. 27l).

Pale pink sherd. It is ornamented with rows of short vertical impressed grooves (three rows are visible on the sherd), and below them a row of smaller, squarer impressions (fig. 27p).

Handle of a thin-walled cup of brownish-gray pottery. The band-shaped handle rose slightly above the rim of the cup to which it belonged (fig. 27c).

Rim sherd of a steep-sided thin-walled pale orange bowl. The thin rim flares slightly. On the body is a meander pattern formed of two parallel lines made up of small oblique impressions, probably produced by a stamp (fig. 27i).

Sherds of a brownish-gray bowl. The narrow rim is slightly outcurved. At and below the rim on the exterior is a broad band of graphite. On the inside is a

Table 1. The Mecklenburg Hallstatt graves.

Grave No.	Fibulae Spectacle brooch	Fibulae Other	Pins Spherical-headed	Pins Other	Bracelet[1]	Beads	Sword	Spear	Axe	Knife	Large globular vessel[2]	Small globular vessel	Stepped bowl	Bowl	Small bowl/cup[3]	Jar	Other	Other objects	Number of different kinds of objects in grave[5]
1a	2	1													1			Br. pendant Ir. fragment	4
1b	2		13																2
2					1														1
3					1													50+buttons Handle Tool	4
4	2				1														2
5		2																	1
6	2				1	19 amber									1				4
7	1				1										1				3
8				1				1			1	1			1			Small spirals	6
9			3(6)[6]															Button	2
10		2	2															Small ring	3
11	1	1			1														2
12																		Bull	1
13																		Animal teeth	1
14	2		7		1	162 bronze 58 glass													4
15	1				2	(amber beads)													3
16	2			3				1	1	1	2					1			8
17	2				2													Whetstone	3
18		4			2														2
19											2		1	5	1				9
20					1										1	1		Lump of bronze	4
21												1	1	1	2			(2 small rings)	6
22															1	1			2
23	2		7							1				3	1				7
24		2			1		1		1	1				1	1		1	3 fishhooks	9
25		9																	1
No. of graves containing	11	7	5	3	11	2(3)	1	2	2	3	3	2	2	4	10	3	1		
Total no. of specimens	19	21	32 (35)	5	14		1	2	2	3	5	2	2	10	11	3	1		

much narrower band at the rim. There seem to be graphite bands running down the interior of the vessel, but these are not distinct (fig. 27k).

Sherds of a gray bowl with graphite coating on both exterior and interior surfaces (fig. 27j).

DISCUSSION

The graves excavated by the Duchess provide another 26 *reasonably* well-documented groups from the great cemetery of Hallstatt. They are very similar in both grave structure and contents to the majority of the graves from the site published by Kromer (1959a). Of particular interest in these graves is the pottery, since very little ceramic material was preserved from the earlier excavations.

The principal shortcomings of the Mecklenburg graves are the lack of a plan of the area excavated and the sparseness of information preserved in the surviving excavation notes. Especially for cases such as Graves 18 and 25, where it is unclear whether the objects in question represent goods from a grave, more extensive field notes would be very helpful. The materials ascribed to Grave 13 include teeth of at least six pigs, one cow, and one sheep or goat. These animals are often represented in Early Iron Age graves (Koreisl 1934), but the teeth of so many individuals in one grave is very unusual. Here again the lack of full description of the grave contents leaves serious doubts about the integrity of such a group of materials.

I wish to call attention to a few aspects of these graves (see also my earlier report in *Germania*, vol. 56, 1978, pp. 66–88).

Character of the graves

The excavation notes state that seven of the graves were inhumations (Graves 1a, 6, 9, 11, 13, 15, 17), ten were cremations (Graves 3, 10, 12, 14, 16, 20, 21, 22, 23, 24), and three were probably cremations (Graves 1b, 7, 8). For the other six the rite is not recorded.

One or two stones are mentioned in connection with Graves 1a, 6, 10, 21, 22, and 23. Graves 15 and 24 were surrounded by stones. Sand was found in Graves 15, 23, and 24.

In Grave 15 the skeleton was found on its back in an extended position. The spectacle brooch in Grave 15 was on the chest. The fibula in Grave 11 was found on the left side of the chest.

The notes for Grave 21 indicate that the "main" urn was covered with a stone and contained burned bones; on either side of it was a small ceramic vessel.

Depth of grave is recorded for six inhumations, seven cremations, and one probable cremation. Inhumation burials range from 0.75 m to 2.00 m in depth, with a mean of 1.48 m. Cremation burials range from 0.45 m to 2.05 m, with a mean of 1.34 m.

The scanty data which were recorded by the excavators and which have survived correspond well with the findings of other excavators at Hallstatt (Kromer 1959a, pp. 15–16, 20).

Skeletal remains

Human skeletal material from these graves has been preserved, unfortunately unassociated with grave groups (see technical report, pp. 30–36). The notes mention skeletal remains from:

Grave 11—skull
Grave 13—skull
Grave 14—burned bone
Grave 15—skull
Grave 17—skull
Grave 20—burned bone
Grave 21—burned bone

The scholars in Zurich recorded the following skeletal material:

Grave 13—mandible
Grave 14—burned bone
Grave 15—skull fragments ("apparently two skulls")
Grave 17—skull fragments and other bone
Grave 19—bones
Grave 20—burned bone
Grave 21—burned bone
Grave 22—burned bone

---

1. It is not always possible to distinguish bracelets from leg rings when information about location in the grave is lacking. The specimens in these graves are of forms most often found as bracelets, and hence this term is used here. Some of these rings may, however, have been worn on the leg.

2. Large globular vessels have mouth diameters of more than 18 cm; small ones have mouth diameters less than 14 cm.

3. A "small bowl" (or "cup") is distinguished from a "bowl" when the sum of its mouth diameter and its height is less than 25 cm.

4. Individual sherds are omitted from this table (see p. 28).

5. All fibulae are counted as one kind of object; all were worn on the chest or shoulder to fasten clothing. Spherical-headed pins and "other" pins are counted as two kinds of objects. The former were usually worn on women's heads to hold a covering in place; many-knobbed pins and pins with profiled heads were usually worn by men on the chest. Each ceramic vessel is counted separately, since no two are identical, and little is known about the use to which the different forms were put.

6. Objects mentioned in the excavation notes but no longer present in the collection are included here in parentheses.

Grave goods

Since very little written information is preserved concerning the structure and contents of the graves, we have almost no data against which to check the groups as they are now constituted. Given the general care with which the Duchess and her assistants worked and their concern with keeping grave groups intact, it is likely that the groups as defined by the scholars in Zurich and as presented here are for the most part correct.

The character of the grave groups is similar to that of the majority of graves excavated at Hallstatt. Cremation burials are generally more richly equipped with goods than inhumations. Only cremation graves contain weapons (Graves 8, 16, 24), and graves richest in pottery are cremations (Graves 16, 19, 21, 23, 24). None of the graves excavated by the Duchess is as richly outfitted as are many of the sword graves from the cemetery (see Kromer 1958, p. 50), and no gold jewelry or bronze vessels are represented. Graves 16, 19, and 24 are well equipped relative to other Early Iron Age graves in central Europe, but they are not among the richest at Hallstatt.

I wish to call attention briefly to some of the patterns apparent in these graves, without dealing with the entire cemetery of Hallstatt here. The 26 graves can be divided into two groups on the basis of the number of different kinds of objects in each grave (counting, for example, 13 pins of similar form as one kind of object). Graves 8, 16, 19, 21, 23, and 24 all contain six or more different kinds of objects, while all the other graves contain four or fewer kinds. This numerical distinction is reinforced by other, qualitative distinctions in the objects occurring in the graves. Weapons occur only in the graves with six or more forms, as do large ceramic vessels with cherry red slip and graphite decoration and stepped bowls and dishes (I discount the single sherds that may be from such vessels in Graves 1a and 22, since individual sherds may have been mixed in with the material from a grave at any stage from the original digging of the grave on.)

Turning first to the larger group of graves with four or fewer kinds of objects, the great majority (17 out of 20) contain principally bronze items of personal adornment. Bracelets (or possibly leg rings) occur in 11 graves, in seven singly, in three as two rings, in Grave 14 in very fragmentary condition. Spectacle brooches occur in nine graves, six times in pairs and three times singly. Fibulae are present in six graves, if Graves 18 and 25 really are grave groups. Bulbous-headed pins occur in four graves, with two, three, seven, and 13 pins in the graves, respectively. Four of these graves also contain ceramic vessels; in three cases a single small vessel, in the case of Grave 20 a large and a small one.

Other items of personal adornment are present in isolated instances among these graves, including amber beads, glass beads, bronze beads, and bronze buttons. It is interesting to note, although the meaning is unclear at this stage, that all of these objects belong to one of the two groups of grave materials at Hallstatt that Hodson was able to distinguish through single-link cluster analysis (1977, p. 402, fig. 3). Hodson suggests (1977, pp. 399–401) that this group may represent the burial inventories of women, though, as in his sample, the number of graves of this character among the Mecklenburg groups would seem to be excessively large.

Three of the 20 graves with four or fewer kinds of objects do not contain such items of personal adornment. Grave 13 contained two sherds of different vessels and a number of animal teeth. Grave 22 contained one complete and one nearly complete ceramic vessel, both small, and a single sherd of a stepped bowl. Grave 12 contained only the bronze bull.

The six graves with six or more kinds of objects in them are quite different in character. The feature all have in common, besides the range of grave goods, is the presence of a rich set of pottery vessels. All contain large and ornate vessels, including the large stepped bowls and dishes with incised or impressed linear ornament and graphite coating, and large globular vessels with a cherry red slip and linear decoration in graphite or black paint. These differ greatly from the small vessels in the other group of graves. Graves 19 and 21, with nine and eight ceramic vessels respectively, each contains a wide range of vessel forms which can be interpreted as constituents of a set (see Kossack 1970; Pauli 1978, pp. 71–73).

The other distinctive feature of these six graves is the presence of weapons in half of them. Grave 24 contained an iron sword and a bronze axe, Grave 16 had a spearhead and an axe, both of bronze, and Grave 8 contained a bronze spearhead. Iron knives are present in three of these graves, twice in association with weapons (Graves 16 and 24) and once without (Grave 23). Many-knobbed pins occur only with weapons (Graves 8 and 16), and the other weapon grave (Grave 24) had in it a pin with profiled head.

I shall discuss briefly the pottery in these graves. The various jewelry forms, which are the most abundantly represented kind of object in these graves, are well treated in the published literature. Relatively little pottery from the Hallstatt cemetery has been published, since little was preserved from the earlier excavations (Barth 1980a, p. 76), hence this group of objects deserves some special attention. In the earlier article on these graves (Wells 1978b, pp. 86–88), I discussed the main forms represented and cited vessels from other sites that share features with those in the Mecklenburg graves. Here I wish to consider some of the patterns of vessels in the graves. I eliminate from consideration any single sherds in a grave group as well as small fragments (less than 10 percent) of originally large vessels. We know that many graves overlapped at Hallstatt, and a certain amount of mixing of materials no doubt occurred when a later grave was dug into part of an earlier one. During the complex history of the Mecklenburg Collection single sherds may have found their way into incorrect grave groups.

Eleven graves contain pottery (excluding Grave 13, which contains only two sherds, each from a different vessel). After eliminating vessels represented by only a few small fragments, we find the following:

Three graves contain one vessel (Graves 1a, 6, 7).
Two graves contain two vessels (Graves 20, 22).
Three graves contain three vessels (Graves 8, 16, 24).
One grave contains four vessels (Grave 23), one contains five (Grave 21), and one contains nine (Grave 19).

The most common ceramic form is the small bowl or cup, with or without a handle. Each grave with pottery except Grave 16 contains one, and this is the only vessel form in the three graves that have just one vessel. These bowls or cups bear neither painted decoration nor cherry red slip, but some are ornamented with patterns of incised or impressed lines, grooves, and dots, as well as with graphite coating. These vessels are likely to have been used as drinking cups, as shown in the banquet scenes on the Vače and Kuffarn situlae (Lucke and Frey 1962, pls. 73, 75).

Large globular vessels occur in three graves, Grave 8 (one specimen), Grave 16 (two), and Grave 19 (two). Visually these are the most striking of the vessels in these 26 graves, principally because of their size and their decoration. All five are coated with cherry red slip and have portions coated with graphite. Ornamentation on the body of the vessels consists of linear patterns, in four of the five cases zigzag bands of alternating colors.

Smaller versions of the globular vessels with similar coloration and ornamental patterns occur in Graves 8 and 21.

Large stepped bowls or dishes occur in Graves 19 and 21. (Others are represented by individual sherds in Graves 22 and 24.) These vessels are decorated with elaborate incised and impressed linear patterns and with graphite coating on the interior.

All but three of the remaining vessels can be classified generally as bowls; all are relatively low and flat and have wide mouths. Size, shape, and color vary. The three vessels that do not fit into any of the categories might be called jars. Each has a constricted mouth and is high relative to its maximum diameter.

Besides these surviving ceramic vessels, wooden vessels may also have been placed in these graves (see Pauli 1978, pp. 350–353).

The specific purpose of the different forms of vessels is difficult to determine on the basis of present evidence. Pauli (1978, pp. 71–73) suggests that at the Dürrnberg Early Iron Age cemetery large vessels were used to hold liquids, bowls to hold dry foods, and cups for drinking. Until we have the results of more analyses of the contents of vessels, it will be impossible to make any more precise statements about the use to which the different vessel forms were put.

Table 2. Ceramic vessels in the Mecklenburg Hallstatt graves.*

Grave	Globular vessel Large (Mouth D. > 18 cm)	Globular vessel Small (Mouth D. < 14 cm)	Stepped dish	Large bowl (Mouth D. + H. > 25 cm)	Jar	Small bowl or cup (Mouth D. + H. < 25 cm)	Other
19	2		1	5		1	
16	2				1		
8	1	1				1	
21		1	1	1		2	
23				3		1	
24				1		1	1
20					1	1	
22					1	1	
1a						1	
6						1	
7						1	

* Excluding small sherds, see page 28.

Chronology

Since a larger work concerned with the chronology of the Early Iron Age in the East Alpine area is in preparation, I wish to make only a few general remarks on the subject here. Among the grave materials recovered by the Duchess at Hallstatt, both the earlier and later phases of the cemetery, as defined by Kromer (1959a, pp. 23–28), are represented. Characteristic of the earlier are the knobbed two-looped fibulae in Grave 18, the two bronze spearheads, the sword in Grave 24, and the ceramic vessels with polychrome zonal decoration. The later period is represented by the Certosa fibula in Grave 5 and by the ring with large bosses in Grave 2. Many of the jewelry items in these graves are abundantly represented in both phases.

The absolute dates for the Hallstatt cemetery are generally given as roughly 800 or 750 to 500 or 400 B.C. (Kromer 1959a, p. 28). I agree with Pauli (1978, p. 425, table 23) in seeing the Hallstatt material culture continuing well into the fifth century B.C. in some regions of central Europe, while the Early La Tène style was developing in other areas. The cemetery of Hallstatt, like most of the East Alpine area, was not a locus of early adoption of La Tène motifs, and I would date the main part of the Hallstatt cemetery down to at least 400 B.C. Further discussion of this point will be developed in another context.

TECHNICAL REPORTS

The Human Skeletal Remains*
by ERIK TRINKAUS

The Mecklenburg Collection includes the partial skeletons of at least nine individuals from Hallstatt. The skeletal remains are primarily cranial and dental, but some fragmentary postcranial bones are included. Since only a few of the human remains from Hallstatt have been preserved and described (Ehgartner and Kloiber 1959), a brief description of the skeletal material in the Peabody Museum is presented here.

Between the time of excavation and the cataloguing of the bones in the Peabody Museum, the bones became partially mixed. Some of the bones cannot be associated by individual except by morphology, and it is not possible to associate accurately specific individuals with specific graves. The four graves that yielded burnt bones, Graves 14, 20, 21, and 22, undoubtedly correspond to the four collections of burnt bones, Peabody Museum numbers N/3737, N/3740, N/3741, and N/3742. As catalogued in the Peabody Museum (apparently following the sorting of the material in Zurich), there are several individuals with one number and portions of an individual with different numbers. For this reason these specimens have been partially renumbered (table 3).

If the sorting in Zurich was correct, it may be possible to associate individuals with graves as follows: N/3736a with Grave 13, N/3738a plus N/3738b or N/3738c with Grave 15, N/3739a with Grave 17, and N/3738b or N/3738c with Grave 19. Given the state of the material, however, any sorting must remain conjecture.

All of the measurements are in millimeters; M-## refers to the number of the equivalent measurement in Martin (1928).

N/3736a (tables 4 and 5; text figs. IX and X). The remains consist of a largely complete cranium, most of the mandible and dentition, and portions of the atlas and axis. The cranium, dentition, and vertebrae were originally catalogued as N/3738, but they are clearly associated with the N/3736 mandible.

The cranium is undistorted and is lacking only the glabellar and superior nasal region, the left zygomatic bone, left and right portions of the occipital bone, and the left greater wing of the sphenoid bone. The mandibular corpus is complete; but the right ramus lacks its condyle, and the posterior two-thirds of the left ramus is absent. The dentition is exceptionally intact, since only the right I^1, left I^2, and left I_1 are missing. However, the right M^1 and left M_1 suffered severe abscesses which removed all of the crowns and most of the roots and extended onto the mandible and maxilla well beyond the alveoli.

On the basis of the general rugosity of the bones and the large size of the mastoid processes, this individual is assumed to be male. The minimal dental wear and openness of the cranial vault sutures suggest a young age; however the full eruption of the third molars and the fusion of the spheno-occipital synchondrosis confirm his adult status. An age between 20 and 30 years is therefore suggested.

N/3736b. This piece consists of a right scapula which preserves most of the glenoid fossa, acromion, coracoid process, and axillary border. It may be from the same arm as the N/3739b right humerus, and its association with the N/3736a skull and vertebrae is uncertain. Morphologically it presents a relatively large glenoid fossa (length [M-12] = 41.0) and a ventral sulcus on the axillary border.

N/3737. Six pieces of burnt bone are preserved

---

*This study originally appeared in *Germania*, vol. 56, 1978, pp. 88–93, and is reprinted here with permission of the Römisch-Germanische Kommission des Deutschen Archäologischen Instituts, Frankfurt.

Table 3. Renumbering of the Hallstatt partial skeletons.

Peabody Museum number	Skeletal remains	New number
N/3736	Mandible	N/3736a
	Scapula	N/3736b
N/3738	Cranium and dentition (same individual as N/3736 mandible)	N/3736a
	Cranium, mandible, and dentition	N/3738a
	Maxilla, cranial fragments, mandible, and dentition	N/3738b
	Maxilla and frontal	N/3738c
N/3739	Cranium, mandible, dentition, and postcranial pieces	N/3739a
	Humerus	N/3739b

Table 4. Cranial and mandibular measurements of the Hallstatt skulls.*

		N/3736a	N/3738a	N/3738b	N/3739a
Glabello-occipital length		—	181.5	—	—
Nasio-occipital length		—	177.0	—	—
Basion-bregma height		145.5	—	—	—
Maximum cranial breadth		154.5	144.5	—	—
Maximum frontal breadth		126.0	(139.0)**	—	—
Bistephanic breadth		119.5	—	—	(112.0)**
Biasterionic breadth		111.0	—	—	(108.0)**
Basion-prosthion length		104.7	—	—	—
External palate breadth		64.0	—	(63.5)	—
Mastoid height		30.3(rt)	25.0(lt)	—	—
Bifrontal breadth		97.0	—	—	(94.0)**
Foramen magnum length		43.7	—	—	—
Nasion-bregma chord		—	114.4	—	111.0
Nasion-bregma arc		—	136.0	—	131.0
Bregma-lambda chord		124.0	125.0	—	113.8
Bregma-lambda arc		136.0	147.0	—	122.0
Lambda-opisthion chord		100.0	—	—	—
Lambda-opisthion arc		117.0	—	—	—
Bicond. max. breadth (M-65)		—	116.2	(124.0)**	—
Bigonial breadth (M-66)		(102.0)	88.0	(90.0)**	—
M_1 external breadth		63.0	57.7	59.0	—
Symphyseal height (M-69)		34.9	31.4	27.5	34.7
Symphyseal thickness		14.3	12.3	17.4	14.7
Corpus height (M-69-2)	Rt	31.4	(26.4)	26.4	—
	Lt	31.4	28.0	27.0	(29.5)
Corpus thickness	Rt	14.1	11.8	15.4	—
	Lt	14.5	11.9	—	(14.0)
Ramus height (M-70)	Rt	—	54.0	—	—
	Lt	—	55.0	57.0	—
Ramus breadth (M-71)	Rt	35.0	35.7	—	—
	Lt	—	33.9	33.1	—

*The cranial measurements are from Howells (1973); the mandibular measurements are adapted from Martin (1928).
**Indicate a measurement that is twice the distance from the midline to the preserved side.

Table 5. Dental dimensions and occlusal wear.*

		N/3736a Length M-D	N/3736a Breadth B-L	Wear Category	N/3738a Length M-D	N/3738a Breadth B-L	Wear Category	N/3738b Length M-D	N/3738b Breadth B-L	Wear Category	N/3739a Length M-D	N/3739a Breadth B-L	Wear Category
MAXILLA													
I-1	Rt	postmortem loss			postmortem loss			8.2	7.8	3	8.4	7.4	3
	Lt	8.3	7.7	3	postmortem loss			8.4	7.8	3	8.7	7.0	3
I-2	Rt	6.0	7.0	2	5.7	5.8	5	6.9	7.0	1	6.5	6.9	3
	Lt	postmortem loss			5.6	5.5	5	7.2	6.8	1	6.8	6.8	3
C	Rt	7.4	8.7	2	7.1	7.6	5	7.7	8.3	2	8.2	8.5	3
	Lt	7.5	8.5	1	7.0	7.6	5	7.5	8.4	1	8.0	8.3	3
P-3	Rt	6.8	8.8	2	6.1	8.0	4	7.3	9.1	1	6.9	9.0	3
	Lt	6.6	9.1	1	postmortem loss			7.1	9.1	1	6.9	8.9	3
P-4	Rt	6.6	9.5	2	6.0	8.6	3	7.1	9.6	1	6.8	8.8	3
	Lt	6.4	9.4	1	postmortem loss			7.0	9.4	1	6.7	8.7	3
M-1	Rt	antemortem loss			9.7	11.0	4	10.4	11.0	3	postmortem loss		
	Lt	11.2	12.1	3	9.4	10.9	5	10.7	11.1	3	—	—	—
M-2	Rt	8.3	12.3	2	9.4	10.8	2	9.2	11.4	1	—	—	—
	Lt	10.1	12.2	2	9.4	10.7	2	9.1	11.2	1	—	—	—
M-3	Rt	8.0	11.8	1	7.2	8.0	1	8.0	10.2	1	9.3	11.3	2
	Lt	7.5	11.6	1	agenesis			8.9	10.8	1	—	—	—
MANDIBLE													
I-1	Rt	5.3	6.3	3	4.8	5.5	4	5.2	6.1	3	postmortem loss		
	Lt	postmortem loss			postmortem loss			postmortem loss			5.3	5.8	3
I-2	Rt	5.7	6.4	2	5.1	6.0	4	6.0	6.5	2	postmortem loss		
	Lt	6.0	6.6	2	postmortem loss			6.9	6.5	2	5.9	6.3	3
C	Rt	6.7	8.4	2	6.3	7.1	3	6.8	7.6	2	postmortem loss		
	Lt	6.9	8.5	1	postmortem loss			6.6	7.6	1	—	7.4	—
P-3	Rt	6.7	7.8	1	6.2	7.5	3	7.0	8.1	1	6.9	7.6	2
	Lt	6.6	7.7	1	6.0	7.1	3	7.4	8.1	1	6.7	7.7	2
P-4	Rt	7.0	8.1	1	6.7	8.0	3	7.5	8.7	1	6.7	8.4	3
	Lt	7.1	8.2	1	6.3	8.6	3	postmortem loss			6.9	8.2	3
M-1	Rt	11.3	11.0	3	antemortem loss			11.1	10.6	3	postmortem loss		
	Lt	antemortem loss			10.7	10.3	5	postmortem loss			10.7	11.0	4
M-2	Rt	10.7	10.6	2	postmortem loss			11.0	10.0	1	antemortem loss		
	Lt	10.9	10.5	2	10.5	9.6	3	11.1	10.0	1	—	—	—
M-3	Rt	11.4	10.4	2	agenesis			11.0	9.9	1	postmortem loss		
	Lt	11.1	10.4	1	agenesis			10.9	9.8	1	antemortem loss		

* The dimensions are in millimeters; the wear categories follow those of Molnar (1971) in which "1" indicates an unworn tooth and "8"

here, some of which may be human. None is sufficiently intact for precise identification. Three exhibit copper staining.

N/3738a (tables 4 and 5; text figs. IX and X). This individual retains much of the cranium, an intact mandible, and most of the dentition. The cranium, as reconstructed, consists of most of the parietals, the frontal bone, the squamous occipital, and the right temporal bone, zygomatic bone, and greater wing of the sphenoid bone. The left temporal bone and greater wing of the sphenoid bone, the basioccipital, and the anterior half of the maxilla are preserved separately. There has been some postmortem distortion of the cra-

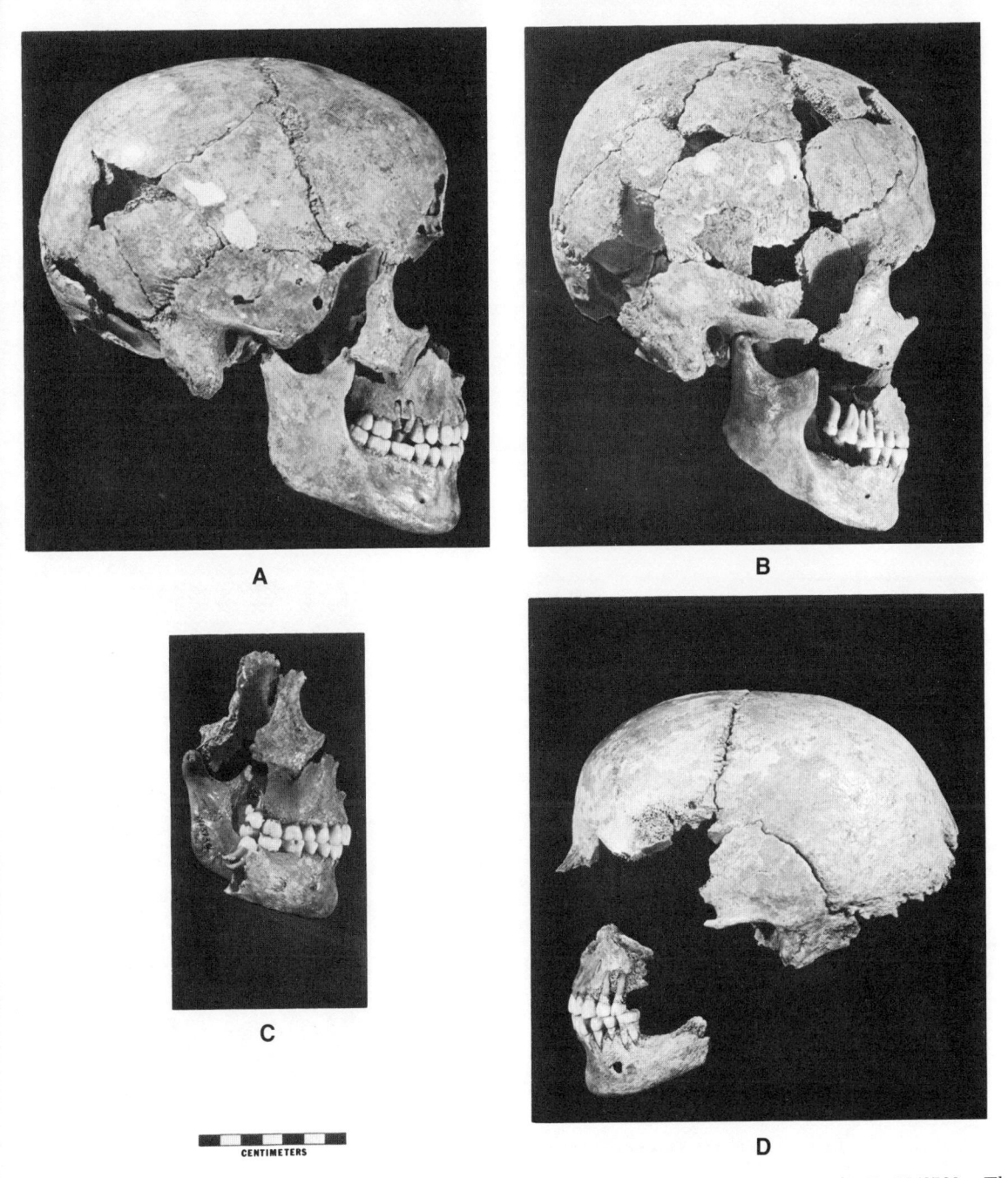

Text figure IX. The Hallstatt skulls in *norma lateralis*. A. N/3736a; B. N/3738a; C. N/3738b; D. N/3739a. The positions of the N/3738a and N/3739a maxillae are approximate.

nial vault. The maxillary dentition is complete on the right from I² to M³ and retains the left I², C, M¹, and M², whereas the mandibular dentition is complete from I₁ to P₄ on the right and from P₃ to M₂ on the left.

Pathology is limited to the antemortem loss of the right M_1. However, the individual had agenesis of the left M^3, the right M_3, and the left M_3, while the right M^3 is highly reduced. There is slight copper staining

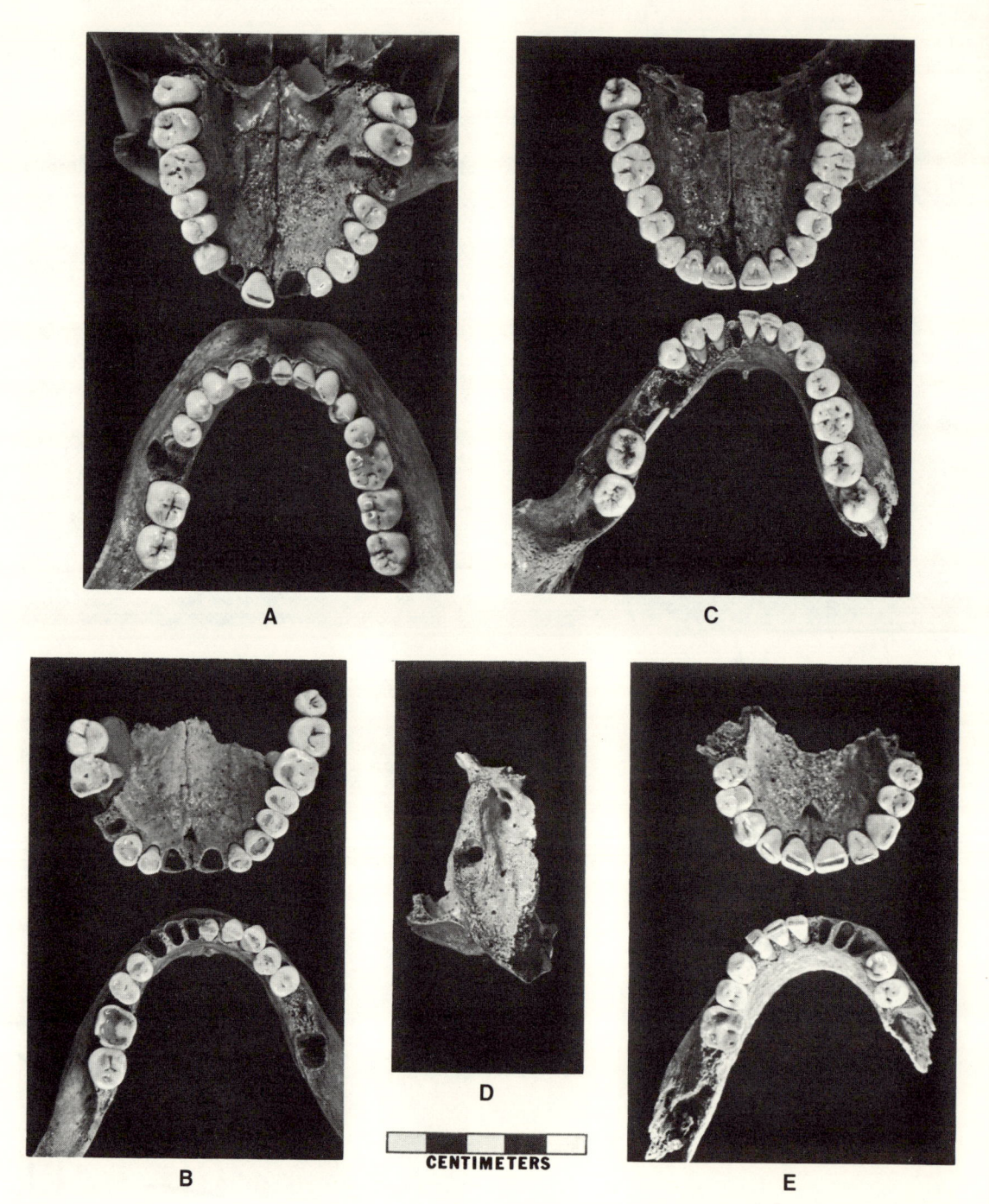

Text figure X. Occlusal views of the Hallstatt maxillae, mandibles, and dentitions. A. N/3736a; B. N/3738a; C. N/3738b; D. N/3738c; E. N/3739a. Note the minimal to moderate occlusal wear and the abscesses on the N/3736a right M^1 and left M_1.

on the right mandibular ramus, M³, and temporal squamous.

The robustness of the cranial vault suggests that this was a male, and the moderate to heavy dental wear and the thickening of the cranial vault bones, in particular of the diploe, suggests an advanced age, probably 40 to 60 years.

N/3738b (tables 4 and 5; text figs. IX and X). Nothing remains of the cranial vault for this individual, but the maxilla and mandible are largely complete and have associated with them the right zygomatic bone, the right halves of the sphenoid bone and basioccipital, and a virtually complete dentition. Only the left I_1, P_4, and M_1 are missing from the dentition. The sex of these remains is indeterminate, but the age can be accurately assessed since the third molars are fully formed, and three of them had just reached full occlusion. This suggests an age between 17 and 20 years.

N/3738c (text fig. X). Three pieces of an old adult cranium are preserved which are probably associated. They consist of a large portion of a left frontal squamous, the lateral half of the left orbital portion of a frontal bone, and most of the left maxilla. The alveolus shows antemortem loss of all of the teeth except the M^1 and complete resorption of the sockets. Even the M^1 may have been lost antemortem, since the socket shows evidence of bony resorption.

N/3739a (tables 4 and 5; text figs. IX and X). The associated bones for this individual include portions of the cranium, mandible and dentition, and several postcranial pieces. The reconstructed portion of the cranial vault consists of the left parietal and temporal bones, the frontal bone damaged on the right side, and the nasal bones. The frontal bone is bisected by a persistent metopic suture. In addition there are portions of the right parietal bone, the occipital squamous, the left temporal bone, and the anterior maxilla. Both of the parietals, especially the right one, are warped, and all of the vault bones show some postmortem erosion. The mandible preserves the corpus to M_1 on the right and to M_3 on the left with a fragmentary anterior margin of the right ramus. The maxillary dentition is complete from I^1 to P^4 on both sides and retains the right M^3 as well; the mandibular dentition is complete from I_1 to M_1 on the left and preserves the left P_3 and P_4. From the region of the left I-1 to the right P-4 there is strong copper staining on both the maxilla and the mandible.

The postcranial remains consist of a right rib fragment, a metacarpal diaphysis and head, the left pisiform bone (length [M-1] = 13.3), a middle phalanx of the hand (length = 21.4), and a pedal proximal phalanx II (length = 25.6).

The only pathology present is the antemortem loss of the left M_2 and M_3. On the basis of the cranial gracility and the moderate dental wear, the remains are probably those of a young adult female.

N/3739b. Questionably associated with the N/3739a remains is a right humerus with minor damage to the proximal and distal ends. It was stained by copper postmortem along its proximal 70 to 75 mm; since the face of N/3739a was stained by copper on the right side, this supports their association. The humerus agrees in size with the N/3736b scapula, which suggests that the scapula and humerus may both be associated with N/3739a or may represent another individual. The measurements of the humerus are: maximum length (M-1) = 293.0; maximum diameter (M-5) = 22.0; minimum diameter (M-6) = 17.4; sagittal head diameter (M-9) = (39.0); distal articular breadth (M-12a) = 36.7.

N/3740. These fragmentary remains consist of a burnt human femoral diaphyseal fragment, two possibly human rib fragments, a piece of an iliac blade, and seven pieces of bone of questionable identity.

N/3741. This collection includes 15 burnt human bones of varying completeness. There are seven cranial vault fragments, including a major portion of the right parietal bone and part of the left orbital portion of the frontal bone, two thoracic vertebral bodies, three femoral diaphyseal fragments, a complete right patella, a proximal diaphyseal section of the right fibula, and the trochlea of the right talus. The measurements of the complete patella are: height (M-1) = 38.7; breadth (M-2) = 36.4; thickness (M-3) = 18.0; articular height (M-4) = 27.5. The talus has a trochlear breadth (M-5) of 28.7.

N/3742. These remains consist of 22 bone fragments, some of which are nonhominid and some of which may be hominid, and three of which exhibit copper staining. In addition, there is a portion of a right talar trochlea (trochlear breadth [M-5] = 24.5).

Discussion. These few fragmentary human remains from Hallstatt do not provide sufficient data to permit statistical comparisons with contemporaneous human skeletal material. However, they indicate several patterns. Pathology, except for antemortem tooth loss and subsequent resorption of the sockets, is minimal. Nondental pathology, caries, and generalized periodontal inflammation are virtually absent. The only inflammation is on the N/3736a first molars, which may have been periodontal or cariogenic in origin. In addition, occlusal dental wear and interstitial wear are minimal; only the oldest individuals show more than the slightest exposure of dentin, and the adolescent N/3738b has a practically unworn dentition. These patterns suggest a diet of highly processed foods with a minimum of grit.

Dr. Erik Trinkaus, Department of Anthropology, Harvard University, Cambridge, Massachusetts.

The Provenience of Amber in Grave 6
by CURT W. BECK and CHRISTOPHER J. SMART

The excavation of the grave field at Hallstatt has yielded large amounts of amber. In the first comprehensive report on the site, E. von Sacken recorded 240 amber finds (1868, pp. 60–63, 75–87). He noted the "fiery and red" color of some amber beads, and it seems to have been this unusual color that led him to suggest that these beads might be of a "resin composition" other than that of the usually golden-yellow amber of the Baltic. (The familiar amber of northern Europe, which mineralogists call succinite, is often called "Baltic amber." Although the shores of the Baltic Sea, from Denmark to the former Baltic States, yield the greatest quantity of this resin, it is also found on the British, Dutch, and German shores of the North Sea and inland throughout Poland and deep into European Russia.)

In 1885 A. B. Meyer (1885, pp. 14–17) sent fragments of an amber bead from Hallstatt to O. Helm, who had some years earlier developed a chemical test for Baltic amber. The test (Helm 1877) used the presence of 3 to 8 percent of succinic acid (first discovered in amber by Agricola in 1546) as an indication that an amber find was of Baltic amber or succinite, but Helm himself soon discovered that this was not a reliable criterion as similar amounts of acid occur in amber from Rumania, Italy, France, and Portugal (Beck 1970). Helm found 4.2 percent of succinic acid in the Hallstatt amber, and although he explicitly conceded that this did not rule out a Rumanian source, he concluded from the appearance and from the odor on burning that the sample was of Baltic amber. Meyer quite rightly did not consider this reliable evidence; he appended a list of Austrian sources of amber and entertained the possibility that, like so many other imports to Hallstatt, the amber may have been of Italian origin.

In spite of the uncertainties of the succinic acid test, it remained in use as a means of determining the provenience of amber for almost a century. In one of these studies, Hedinger (1903, pp. 26, 29) had 16 archaeological amber artifacts analyzed in the commercial laboratory of Hundeshagen and Philipp, including fragments of several beads from Grave 42 at Hallstatt. The chemists found 3.4 percent of succinic acid.

The succinic acid test was also used in the first laboratory established solely for research in archaeological chemistry in Berlin by Rathgen. He and Olshausen analyzed almost a hundred amber artifacts; the results were later published by La Baume (1935). They include two samples from Hallstatt: Fragments of several small beads (Vienna Hofmuseum Inventory No. 26 848) yielded 5.83 percent of succinic acid, and a single ring bead (Vienna Hofmuseum Inventory No. 26 843) gave 9.04 percent of the acid.

The inconclusive succinic acid test has since been superseded by a spectroscopic method (Beck, Wilbur, and Meret 1964) that identifies Baltic amber with a statistical certainty of 97.5 percent (the exceptions are samples that have deteriorated so extensively that no diagnostically useful spectrum can be obtained). No known European fossil resin gives an infrared spectrum that can be mistaken for one of Baltic amber, and the spectra can be classified on a purely empirical basis by a computer (Beck et al. 1971).

Infrared spectra of freshly dug Baltic amber are distinguished by an almost perfectly horizontal "shoulder" between 8.0 and 8.5 μ (microns), followed by an absorption maximum at 8.7 μ. Baltic amber also has an absorption at 11.3 μ. This is not of diagnostic value (it is shared by most samples of Sicilian amber and by many recent resins, especially copals), but it is a measure of the state of preservation of the sample; progressive oxidation (weathering) reduces this absorption feature and at the same time changes the slope of the "shoulder" to increasingly negative values. The chemistry of these changes is relevant to an understanding of the structure of amber (Beck et al. 1965); for the provenience of amber artifacts it is sufficient to say that even after moderate weathering, the spectra remain identifiable as Baltic amber.

The spectrum of a sample of well-preserved Baltic amber is shown in text figure XI (Spectrum 4247).

The amber from Grave 6 at Hallstatt in the Mecklenburg Collection is the first to have been analyzed by infrared spectroscopy. The sample was taken from the largest of the 19 beads found in this grave (the lentoid bead of 1.6 cm diameter), because it is the only bead with a break that exposes the transparent interior beneath the brown weathering crust. The color of the interior is a dark reddish brown (Munsell Soil Color Chart No. 2.5 YR 2.5/4).

The spectrum of this bead is quite clearly that of Baltic amber (Spectrum 2040 in text fig. XI). There is a degree of weathering that is common to nearly all archaeological amber finds, and it is the cause of the dark reddish color. The absorption band at 11.3 μ is almost completely lost, and the "shoulder" between 8.0 and 8.5 μ has a moderately negative slope. But the spectrum retains the characteristic features of Baltic amber and cannot be confused with any of the numerous deposits of amber and amberlike fossil resins that are native to Europe outside the natural distribution of Baltic amber or succinite.

Since the completion of this analysis we have had occasion to analyze other amber artifacts from Hallstatt. They include a necklace of 18 beads and one spacer with two perforations (National Museum, Budapest, Inventory No. 199.1871.22) and a series of finds excavated by Sir John Lubbock (later Lord Avebury) in 1869 and presented to the British Museum in 1916 (Read and Smith 1916). Nine samples of the Budapest necklace and eight of the British Museum finds all gave infrared spectra readily identifiable as Baltic amber (Beck and Sprincz, in press). None of these amber objects can be assigned to graves and hence none can be dated.

While it will be desirable to test further amber finds from the Hallstatt cemetery, it is now certain that all of 18 finds that have been analyzed by an unambiguous method are definitely of Baltic amber.

The authors thank the National Science Foundation for the support of this work under Grant No. BNS79-07250 (Anthropology).

Dr. Curt W. Beck and Dr. Christopher J. Smart, Amber Research Laboratory, Department of Chemistry, Vassar College, Poughkeepsie, New York.

Some Technical Notes on a Bronze Pin
by J. E. ERICSON

The bronze pin from Grave 16 of the Hallstatt site (fig. 17g) was analyzed in the facilities of the Center for Archaeological Research and Development, Peabody Museum of Archaeology and Ethnology and the Gordon McKay Laboratories, Harvard University.

The pin is 26.73 cm long and 0.33 cm in diameter along its central shaft. It weighs 27.1 gm. The surface corrosion is mottled light and dark green, characteristic of the corrosion products of a bronze. At the upper end of the pin are the head, two knobs, and three zones of black and ochre-colored corrosion, characteristic of iron corrosion, suggesting goethite and limonite. This corrosion suggests that iron wire had been inlaid into the original bronze pin. This would have appeared originally as "a golden pin with 'silver' inlay" in its uncorroded state.

The parent bronze metal and winding areas were sampled for energy dispersive X-ray fluorescence analysis in a scanning electron microscope, a JEOL, model JSM35, located in the Gordon McKay Laboratories. A very small bimetal sample was carefully removed from the top portion of the pin containing both corrosion types. This was encapsulated in thermal plastic forming a cylindrical container and coated with carbon in a vacuum chamber.

A qualitative EDX analysis was performed on both areas, using a 200-second count, three condensers,

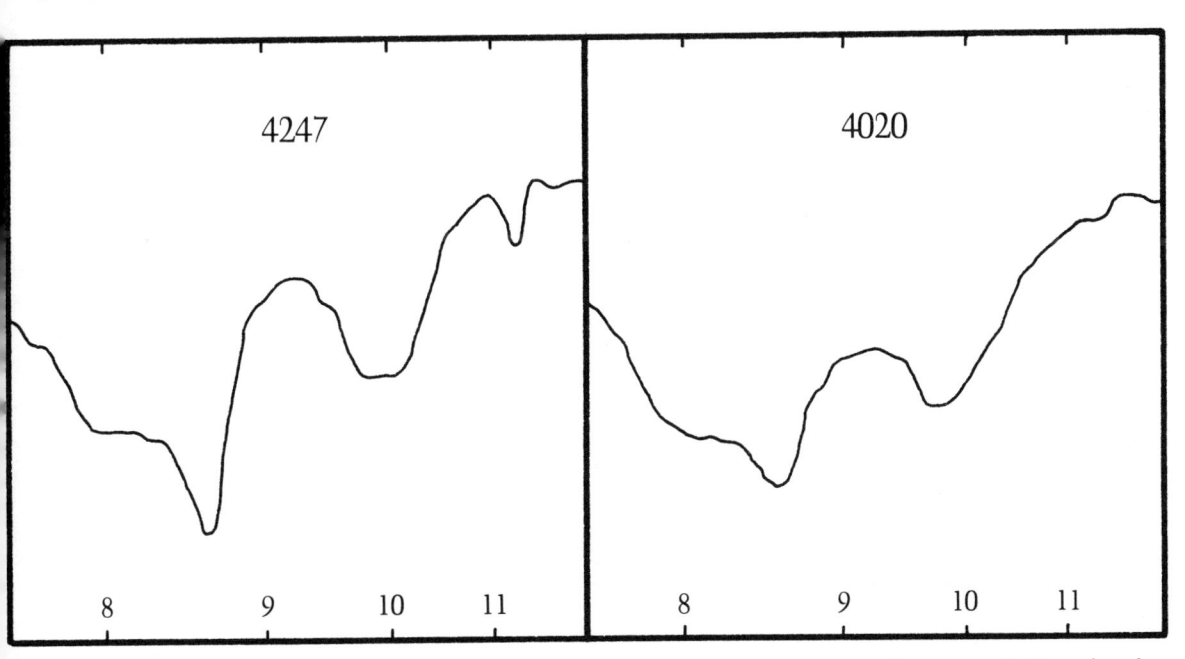

Text figure XI. Partial infrared spectra over the range of 7.5 to 12.0 μ of Baltic amber (Spectrum 4247) and amber from Grave 6 at Hallstatt (Spectrum 4020).

200 microamps, and 20 kilovolts. The scan of the bronze area revealed the presence of copper, iron, tin, and slight traces of calcium, phosphorus, aluminum, silicon, and sulfur (shown in text fig. XII). There was no sign of gold or silver. The trace element constituents may have been the result of burial conditions in a cemetery environment. The analysis of the winding area indicates the presence of predominantly iron with some copper and tin (text fig. XII). The copper and tin may have been the result of the migration of secondary copper corrosion products during burial.

A secondary image of the boundary of the two layers reveals a straight line and tight fit of the two original metals shown in text figure XIII. Scans of the two areas produced X-ray maps which show the iron-rich and tin-rich areas, respectively text figures XIV and XV.

In conclusion, the Hallstatt pin appears to be a bronze with iron winding on its top and bottom portions. The iron wire was tightly inlaid into the bronze as indicated by the sharp line of demarcation between the two metals. The pin would have been a handsome

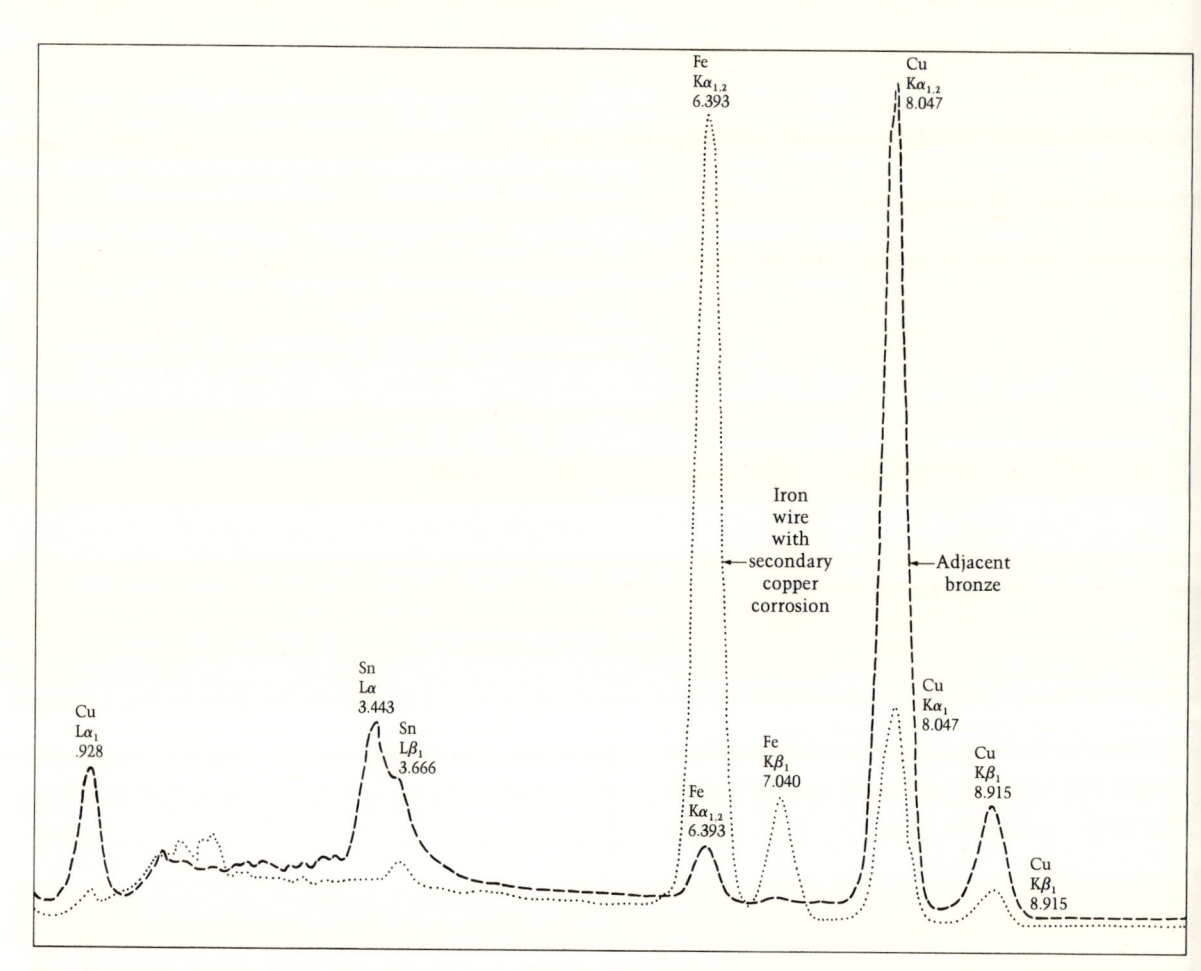

Text figure XII. Energy dispersive X-ray fluorescence analysis of the Hallstatt bronze pin (dashed) with wire inlay (dotted). The spectra were redrawn from the original graphic output. The dotted spectrum represents the major constituent of the wire—iron with some copper. (A brassy area was observed along the wire which may be chalcopyrite, a compound of copper, iron, and sulphur. This was not verified by X-ray diffraction analysis. It is not certain whether chalcopyrite is capable of being formed in burial or museum environments.) The dashed spectrum represents the major constituents of the bronze pin—copper and tin. Slight traces of calcium, phosphorus, aluminum, silicon, and sulphur were observed. No gold or silver were observed.

The analyses were performed on the screening electron microscope at the Gordon McKay Laboratories using a 200-second count, three condensers, 200 μA aperture, set at 20 kilovolts.

piece having the appearance of gold and silver. Originally, the piece would have tarnished easily in a humid environment or if handled very much.

The author acknowledges the assistance of Kim Jones, Gordon McKay Laboratories, CARD publication 11.

Dr. J. E. Ericson, Department of Anthropology, Harvard University, Cambridge, Massachusetts.

Text figure XIII. Secondary image of the bimetal sample. The bronze area is larger. The smaller area is the iron wire. A ridge separates the two metals. A scale is provided as a white line which is 1,000 microns (same for text fig. XIV).

Text figure XIV. X-ray map of the bimetal sample of iron concentration. Bright field dots represent sites of iron. The lower iron area is well differentiated from the bronze above. A portion of the iron in the bronze area originated from the soil.

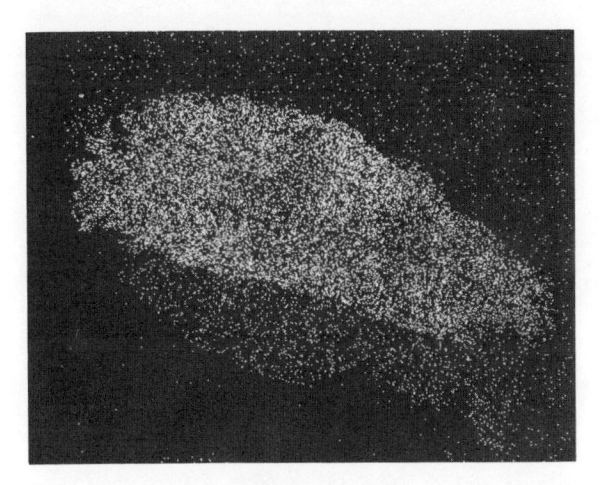

Text figure XV. X-ray map of the bimetal sample of tin concentration. Bright field dots represent sites of tin. The upper area is likewise well differentiated from the iron wire, the lower portion of the sample. The tin in the iron area may be a combination of corrosion product and background. Scale is the same as in text figure XIII.

The Textile Fragment
by JILL MEFFORD

No textile remains survive among the grave goods recovered by the Duchess at Hallstatt, nor is mention made in the field notes of textile remains or impressions. Yet the Duchess's collection contains a fragment of cloth labeled only *Gewandreste aus dem Hallstätter Salzberg* (text fig. XVI). Its exact provenience is unknown. The scrap of wool cloth measures 4 by 1.8 cm and adheres to a piece of salt 6 by 4.5 by 2.5 cm (see p. 25). It is undoubtedly to this contact with salt that the fabric owes its exceptional preservation. Association of salt with the textile confirms to some extent the information that the find came from the mines rather than from a burial, and so belongs to the considerable body of textile fragments preserved in the galleries of the Hallstatt salt mountain and reported in Hundt's studies entitled "Vorgeschichtliche Gewebe aus dem Hallstätter Salzberg" (1959, 1960, 1967). This report is intended to add a small scrap (literally) to the existing information on the art and technology of textiles during the Hallstatt Iron Age (see also Brandford 1978; Hundt 1961, 1970).

Construction of the Fragment. The fabric is a 2-2 twill weave (text fig. XVII), constructed generally as follows: The warp yarns are held parallel and taut while the weft yarn—the active element—passes back and forth across the cloth perpendicular to the warps, moving over two, then under two warp yarns. Each time the weft reaches the edge of the cloth and turns to recross the cloth, the over-under sequence shifts one yarn to the right or left. This offsetting of the sequence sets up the diagonal pattern in the weave which is so characteristic of twill. In this fragment the diagonal is continuous, though it can also be reversed at intervals to form "herringbone" twill. By means of a simple loom with four lifting devices, the yarns can be raised mechanically in this offset sequence: 1-2, 2-3, 3-4, 4-1, and large cloths manufactured fairly quickly.

If woven on a loom as just described, the angle of warp-weft intersection is 90°. In this fragment, however, the angle of intersection is sometimes as low as 60° suggesting that instead of being loom woven, the piece was constructed by the older method of "oblique interlacing," known generally as plaiting or braiding (text fig. XVIII). In this technique, classed as "finger weaving" because it is produced entirely by hand manipulations, all the yarns are "active," crossing over and under each other in the manner of the simple three-strand braid. Each yarn meets the edge of the cloth at an oblique angle and turns to recross the cloth at the same angle.

However, despite appearances, two things argue that the piece was loom woven. First, the fragment conforms to the contours of the salt as though the two were fused together under some pressure. If in this situation the cloth were under diagonal tension, the normal alignment of yarns could easily be distorted. Second, all previously published textiles from Hallstatt are woven: Of the 75 fragments reported, 47 are woven twills, 26 are plain weaves (Hundt 1959, 1960, 1967). The less efficient technique of oblique interlacing became obsolete during the Neolithic, as the loom came into general use (Hundt 1970, p. 55). Given existing knowledge of textiles of the time, it is easier to postulate a woven construction for this piece, though without the evidence which the edges (selvages) of the cloth provide, it is not possible to be absolutely certain.

A row of dark brown overcasting stitches crosses the fragment (a–b in text fig. XIX). Stitches are 2 mm long and spaced 4 to 6 mm apart. A single stitch (c) at the inner edge belongs to a second row (c–d) only faintly visible. Between these two rows of stitches the cloth layer is double, while beyond row a–b the cloth is a single layer. This then is a seam, with two pieces of

Text figure XVI. Lump of halite from Hallstatt, measuring 6.2 cm in length, with the textile fragment adhering to it.

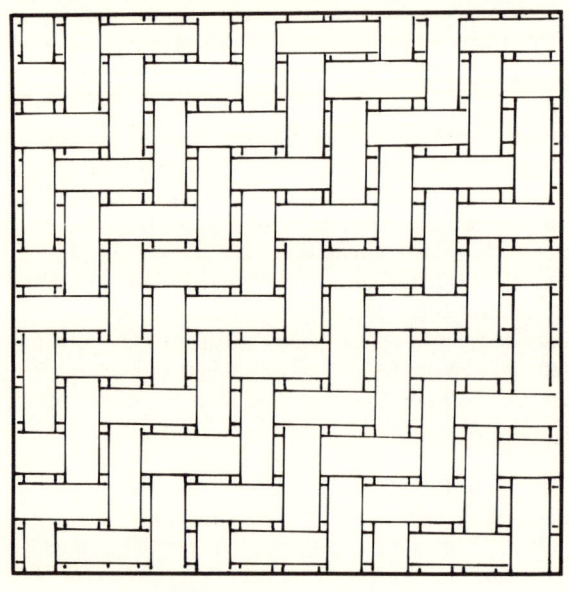

Text figure XVII. 2-2 twill weave.

Text figure XVIII. 2-2 oblique interlacing.

Text figure XIX. The seam. Two fabrics are turned under and stitched together along lines a–b and c–d.

cloth overlapped slightly, the cut edges turned under, then sewed together with a double row of stitches (text fig. XX). Three examples of this type of seam *(Kappnaht)* are reported from Hallstatt, though the more common type is the simple rolled seam (Hundt 1959, pp. 84–85, 1960, p. 138, 1967, p. 46).

Fibers and Yarns. Both yarns used in the cloth are sheep's wool and both are probably naturally occurring shades, perhaps somewhat darkened with time. No chemical analysis is possible at present, and the use of dyes cannot definitely be ruled out.

The brown yarn of the twill weave is Z-spun (text fig. XXI, b) used singly. The angle of spin always varies within a single yarn and certainly within a fabric; the range here is between 25° and 60°—decidedly "tight" (text fig. XXII). The diameter of the brown yarn is 0.4 to 0.6 mm, and the yarns are spaced 14 per centimeter in both directions. Since no selvages are present it is not possible to determine warp and weft directions.

The dark brown yarn of the seam is also Z-spun, but with two yarns twisted, or plied, together with the S direction (text fig. XXI, c). It measures 0.8 to 1 mm in diameter.

Conclusions. No conclusions are possible as to the original function of this tiny fragment, but in both materials and techniques it matches closely the textiles recovered from the Hallstatt salt mountain. In particular it resembles specimens collected from the Kaiser Joseph Stollen in the course of the nineteenth century. This shaft in the eastern section of the mountain is no longer accessible, as movement of the semifluid salt masses has since sealed the opening. Of the 18 different textiles represented in the Kaiser Joseph Stollen Collection, now in the Naturhistorisches Museum, Vienna, ten are fully comparable to this fragment. They are all 2-2 twills of undyed brown wool; yarn is Z-spun (for the most part tightly spun), 0.4 to 0.8 mm in diameter and spaced 10 to 14 per centimeter. Of the remaining eight, four are plain weaves, four differ in spin direction and/or use of dyes. The uniformity of the sample is surprising. One might suspect that perhaps all these scraps were once a single textile, but wool shades, densities, and so forth vary enough that it appears we are dealing with 18 distinct cloths. This degree of standardization might suggest a single source—a workshop turning out a uniform product, rather than manufacture in individual households. Perhaps it is not unreasonable to speculate that such a mining operation was supported by comparable division of labor in other trades. Or perhaps there was a company store.

The Kaiser Joseph Stollen was recently dated by a carbon 14 count made on remains of a tool and other unidentified material from the Querschlag, an exploratory shaft which intersects the prehistoric one (Barth, Felber, and Schauberger 1975). Two counts, 860± 90 B.C. and 645± 50 B.C., suggest continued use of the shaft over a fairly long period. The only other sizable group of Hallstatt textiles available for comparison comes from the Kilb-Werk, further down the Kaiser Joseph Stollen. These 43 fragments collected in the 1960s show greater diversity of weave, of patterning based on contrasting spin direction, and patterning involving color contrast. They include five basket weaves, four herringbone twills, one broken twill; thirteen use alternation of spin direction to create pattern, and seven are plaids. This increased elaboration might suggest a later date for these textiles—a supposition in line with the radiocarbon date for the Kilb-Werk: 515± 35 B.C. (Barth, Felber, and Schauberger 1975).

An additional small group of textiles comes from the north side of the mountain, believed to be the oldest of the three Iron Age mining areas (north, east, west). Two carbon 14 counts from the Grüner-Werk yielded 1000± 35 B.C. and 860± 90 B.C. (Barth, Felber, and Schauberger 1975). Of the nine textiles from the Grüner-Werk, seven are wool plain weaves, and two twill cloths are linen. The sample is much too small to be a reliable indication, but the frequent occurrence of plain weaves agrees with Hundt's state-

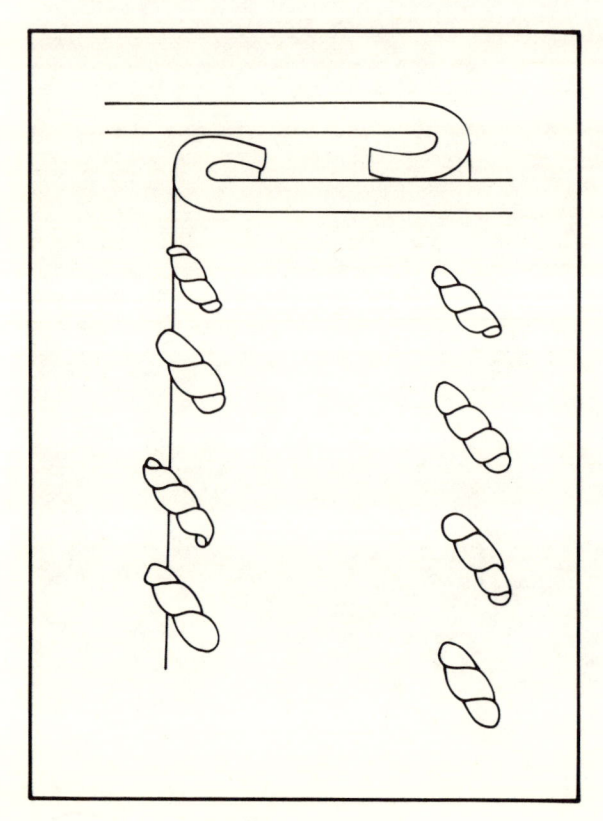

Text figure XX. Seam.

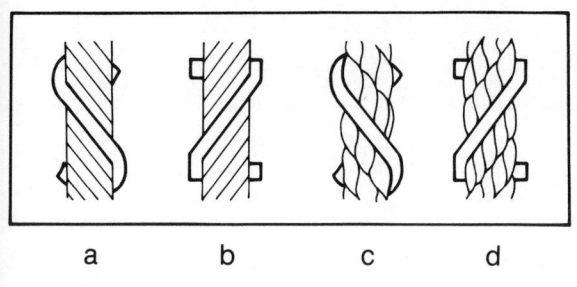

Text figure XXI. Schematic diagrams of: a. S-spun yarn; b. Z-spun yarn; c. S-plied yarn; d. Z-plied yarn.

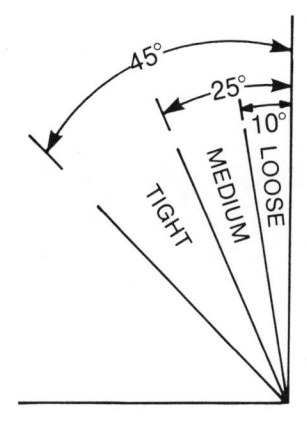

Text figure XXII. Measurement of angle of spin.

ment (1970, p. 57) that for the Bronze Age plain weave was the predominant weave. It was only in the Hallstatt period that twill came into general use. Greater use of plain weave in the Grüner-Werk is in line—as far as it goes—with the early date. The occurrence of linen is less easy to explain. These are the only two examples of linen textiles found to date in the Hallstatt salt mines.

These comparisons are intended only to indicate that the conventions—or fashions—of textile construction changed considerably in the course of mining operations at Hallstatt, a period of perhaps 1,000 years. Where the samples are adequate these changes offer possibilities for relative dating, but in this case we have only a single fragment in the Mecklenburg Collection. On the basis of comparison we can conclude with probability that it came from the Hallstatt salt mountain, as claimed. Possibly it came from the Kaiser Joseph Stollen, reopened in the later half of the nineteenth century. The type of cloth represented by the fragment was most common in the Kaiser Joseph sample in contrast with samples from the Kilb-Werk and Grüner-Werk. However, we cannot rule out that it could have come from any of these three locations or from one of the many galleries not well represented by textile remains.

Ms. Jill Mefford, Peabody Museum, Harvard University, Cambridge, Massachusetts.

Stična

INTRODUCTION

Location

Slovenia, the northernmost and westernmost republic of Yugoslavia, is made up structurally largely of high mountains and deep valleys; it belongs to the eastern part of the Alpine network. In the northwest and northern parts of Slovenia are the high Alps; in the southwest and south, the Dinaric range. In the angle between these are the foothill regions of Slovenia, opening onto the Pannonian Plain to the east. The river valleys, of which the Sava and the Drava are the most important, provide both fertile agricultural lands and important routes of communication. The climate and vegetation of Slovenia are typically Alpine. The country is heavily forested, and rich pasture lands and fertile valleys occupy the river basins.

Stična (German Sittig or Sittich) lies in that part of Slovenia known as Lower Carniola, Dolenjsko in Slovene, in the foothills of the mountains. The site is located about 30 km east-southeast of Ljubljana, the capital city of Slovenia, and close to the modern highway between Ljubljana and Zagreb (see map, p. 95).

Both the settlement of Early Iron Age Stična and its cemetery are clearly visible today. The settlement is situated on a low flat-topped hill overlooking the plain around it and is bounded by man-made ramparts, now in the form of earthen walls. The enclosed settlement area measures roughly 800 by 400 m and is the largest of the enclosed hilltop settlement sites of the area (Frey 1974a, p. 152). South and southeast of the settlement are the tumuli, about 140 of which are still identifiable despite intensive modern agricultural activity in the area.

Archaeological Research at Stična

Since only very small-scale diggings were done at Stična during the second half of the nineteenth century, in contrast to many of the Early Iron Age sites of the region, Stična is one of the best-preserved sites in Slovenia (on the history of excavations at Stična see Gabrovec, Frey, Foltiny 1970, pp. 16–18; Gabrovec 1974, pp. 170–172). The first major excavations at the site were those conducted by the Duchess of Mecklenburg between 1905 and 1914, when she excavated 10 complete tumuli and part of another.

Between the world wars a farmer named Hrast unsystematically excavated a large number of tumuli. Fortunately, some of the important material from the graves he opened was able to be rescued for the Narodni muzej in Ljubljana, but he did considerable damage to then intact burial mounds (Gabrovec 1974, pp. 170–172).

In 1946 the Narodni muzej began excavation of a large tumulus at the site and carried out excavation in the years 1952 to 1953 and 1960 to 1964 (Gabrovec 1971, 1974). At the start of the excavations the mound had a diameter of 60 m and a height of 6 m. The excavators found evidence of a grave robber's tunnel and of plundered burials, but the tumulus as a whole was not badly damaged (Gabrovec 1974, p. 172). A total of 183 graves were found in the mound, arranged concentrically around the center which was empty (plan in Gabrovec 1974, pp. 168–169, plan 1). Four were cremation burials, the other 179 inhumation. Wooden coffins could be detected in most of the graves; in a few cases the coffins were covered with stones or with a stone slab. Around the outside of the tumulus was a stone wall about 1 m high made of unworked but carefully selected and packed stones (Gabrovec 1974, pls. 2, 3).

Stratigraphic observations in the course of excavation revealed that the tumulus was built up of three distinct tumuli arranged concentrically on top of one another (Gabrovec 1974, pp. 174–175, plan 2). The grave goods recovered indicate that the tumulus served as a cemetery from the eighth century to the fifth or fourth B.C. Gabrovec suggests that the tumulus was used as the cemetery of one family group throughout this time period (1971, p. 230, 1974, pp. 180–182).

In 1967 the Narodni muzej in Ljubljana, in collaboration with the Institute of Advanced Study in

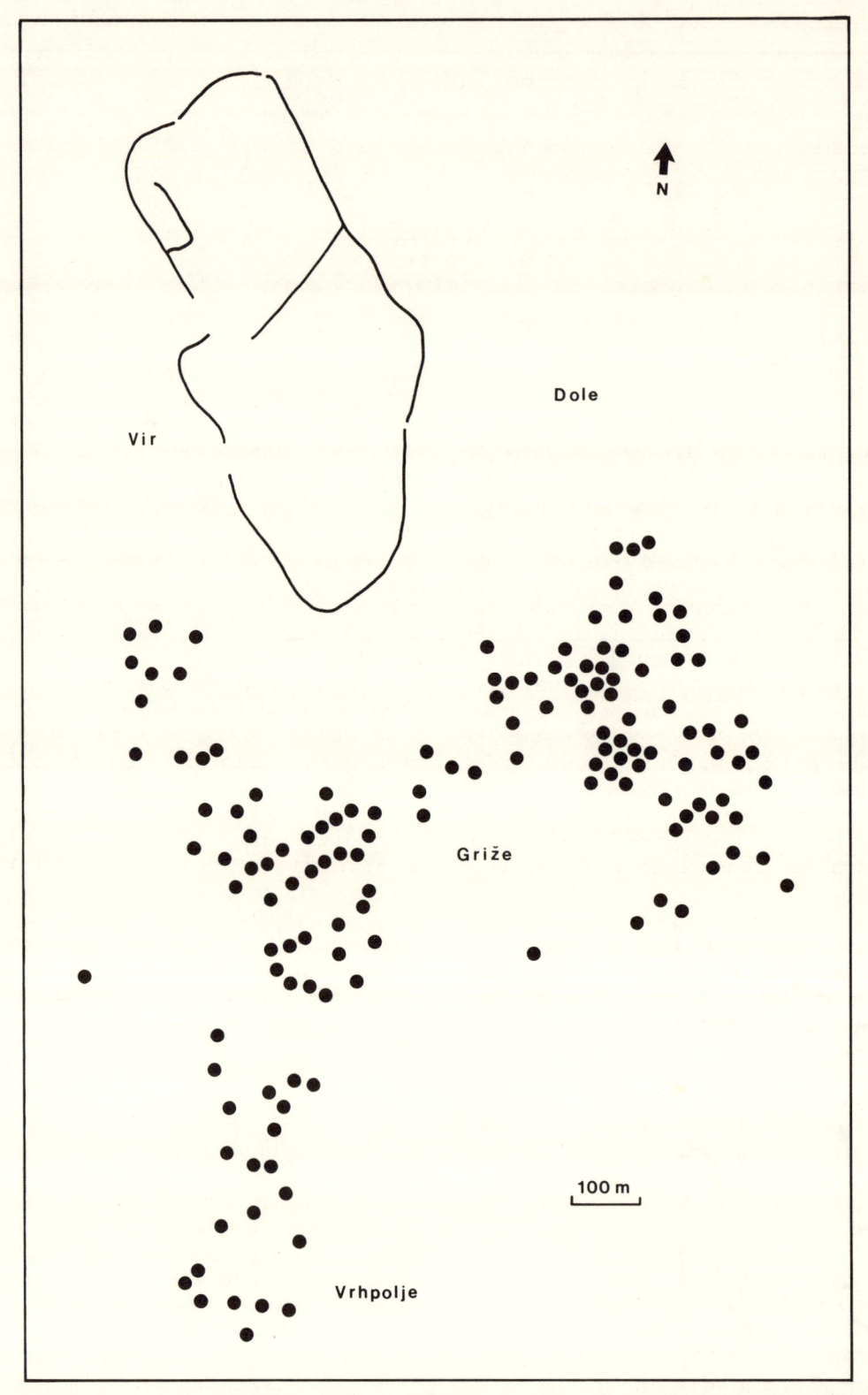

Text figure XXIII. Plan showing the wall system of the hillfort at Stična and the accompanying tumuli that are now visible. The names are those of four of the neighboring hamlets. Based on a plan by O.-H. Frey.

Princeton and the Seminar für Vor- und Frühgeschichte of Marburg University, began excavation on the settlement at Stična. The work centered on investigation of the defenses surrounding the settlement area (Gabrovec, Frey, Foltiny 1970; Frey 1974a). Found were walls of stone and earth, datable by associated artifactual material from the beginning of Hallstatt C through to Hallstatt D3 (Gabrovec, Frey, Foltiny 1970, p. 18), thus spanning the period represented by the graves in the excavated tumuli. Very little of the settlement itself has been revealed as yet (see p. 96).

Stična in European Prehistory

Since systematic research at Stična, aside from that by the Duchess of Mecklenburg, began in 1946 with the Narodni muzej's excavations of the tumulus, Stična has only recently become generally known among European prehistorians. Two important richly equipped graves from the site were published by Ložar (1937a and b) and discussed by Jacobsthal (1956, pp. 178–179, figs. 582–584, 588–592), and some other early finds have been cited in the literature (see Kastelic 1960, pp. 3–4, 18). In some of the past studies dealing with material from Stična there has been confusion about place-names. Many of the finds are known by the names of the hamlets in which the individual tumuli are located (Vir, Griže, Vrhpolje, Pece). Since the tumuli all form a single large, cohesive necropolis, modern researchers advocate using the designation Stična to cover all of these finds (Kastelic 1960, p. 18; Gabrovec 1974, p. 170).

The recent work at the great tumulus at Stična conducted by the Narodni muzej has been of major importance for modern studies of chronology and burial practices of the southeast Alpine area during the Early Iron Age. It was the first exceptionally large tumulus in Lower Carniola to be excavated using modern techniques, and thus provides much important information unavailable from earlier excavations such as those by the Duchess of Mecklenburg. Gabrovec has based much of his recent chronological work on the southeast Alpine region on the results of that excavation (1966, 1974; Frey and Gabrovec 1971).

Since the publication of the results of the first seasons of excavation at the settlement of Stična (Gabrovec, Frey, Foltiny 1970; Frey 1974a), the site complex (settlement and cemetery) has been viewed as a model of an Early Iron Age center in Lower Carniola. Modern archaeological research has not yet been carried out at the nearby contemporaneous sites such as Magdalenska gora and Vače, and at the present the grave finds from these sites are often viewed in a context based on the model of the settlement complex of Stična (Frey 1974a).

Excavations by the Duchess of Mecklenburg

Between 1905 and 1914 the Duchess excavated 11 tumuli at Stična (de Tompa 1934; Wells 1978a). Eight tumuli were in the part of the cemetery designated by her as St. Veit (Šentvid), one was at Vas Vir, one at Vas Pece, and one at Vas Glogovica. The eight tumuli in St. Veit/Šentvid were excavated in 1905 (Tumulus I), 1910 (II), 1912 (III), 1913 (IV, V, VI, VII), and 1914 (VIII). The Duchess had excavated only two graves in the eighth tumulus in 1914 when World War I broke out. She excavated the mound at Vas Glogovica in 1910, and the tumuli at Vas Pece and Vas Vir in 1912. She found a total of 186 graves. From the surviving records of the Duchess's excavations it is not at present possible to identify the mounds which she investigated on the main plan of the cemetery.

The records kept by the Duchess's secretary, Gustav Goldberg, often include information about the depth and structure of graves and whether they contained inhumation or cremation burials. In general the excavation notes from Stična are considerably more detailed than those from Hallstatt, since Goldberg kept more complete records of the excavation work as he became more experienced. In 1913 many more photographs were taken of the excavations than in earlier years, or at least more have survived in the collection, hence the photographic record of the Stična work is much more complete than is that of the excavations at Hallstatt. Photographs provide useful information about the size and form of the tumuli (e.g., figs. 111, 162a, b), about the excavation work (figs. 112, 113), and about some individual graves and their contents (figs. 85a, b, 129).

For many well-documented graves excavated by the Duchess at Stična, different sources of information confirm the composition of a grave group. Goldberg's field notes often record the grave goods recovered in a burial and include details making identification with objects in the Mecklenburg Collection certain. Slips of paper once attached to the boxes in which grave groups were packed often provide information about associations. In some instances objects that are not mentioned in any of the surviving notes were found packed with grave groups when the collection was studied in Zurich. In such cases, I rely on the judgment of the scholars working in Zurich regarding associations. Several small objects not noticed by the excavators or by the scholars in Zurich have been found as a result of the cleaning of larger items at the Peabody Museum.

The principal shortcoming of the Duchess's material from Stična is the lack of plans showing locations of graves in the tumuli. Only one such plan survives—of the Vas Vir tumulus, which shows just 19 of the 27 graves (fig. 170). The plan shows horizontal relationships between graves, but not vertical positions. The lack of plans and section drawings for the other tumuli is puzzling when we consider the care and detail with which Goldberg recorded information about the individual graves and the number of good documentary photographs taken in the later years of the excavations. A letter written by Oscar Montelius to the Duchess on December 16, 1913 describing his visit to her cousin Kaiser Wilhelm II of Germany includes the following sentence, "Besonders betonte ich, dass Sie einen Künstler haben kommen lassen, um Pläne für die Hügel und die verschiedenen Gräber zu machen, und durch Profile die Lage der Gräber im Verhältnis zu einander klar zu machen" [I emphasized especially that you engaged an artist to make plans of the tumuli and of the different graves, and through the use of profiles to make the position of graves with respect to one another clear]. Apparently the Duchess was aware of the importance of recording horizontal and vertical relationships of graves. It is possible that other plans were made but were lost at some stage in the complex history of the collection.

CATALOGUE OF GRAVES FROM STIČNA

Tumulus I

This tumulus was excavated between August 4 and September 7, 1905. Seven graves were found.

GRAVE 1

A cremation burial was found at a depth of 1.4 m in the tumulus. In the grave were a fibula, a spindle whorl, and an amber bead.

Grave goods:

Bronze Certosa fibula of the Slovenian variety with a stop disk and a knob on the foot; L. about 7.0 cm (fig. 28b). Amber bead; D. 1.45 cm (fig. 28c). Spindle whorl; H. 2.2 cm, D. 2.8 cm (fig. 28a).

GRAVE 2

Associated with a burned area found at a depth of 6.25 m were a helmet or some kind of head covering of thin sheet bronze, a bronze figurine, a fragmentary long bronze platform on which the figurine had stood, a ribbed bucket with two movable handles resembling twisted wire, a white, a yellow, and two blue glass beads, and a small ceramic vessel. One note states that the ceramic vessel was found 1.1 m from the bronze vessel and the helmet.

Grave goods:

Solid bronze figurine of a human, probably a woman (see Wells 1978d), 9.4 cm high. The excavation notes mention that a piece of one of the arms was broken off when the object was removed from the ground, hence the arms were once longer than they are now (fig. 29g, h). Ribbed bucket of sheet bronze, missing and not represented by any surviving drawing or photograph. From the notes it is clear that it had two movable top handles with a twisted pattern on them, such as those in Stjernquist 1967, vol. II, pl. 2,1.2. Disk of sheet bronze with a raised center culminating in a cast bronze top, a phalerae. D. about 23 cm (fig. 29c). This is the object that the excavators thought was a helmet.

Four glass beads: One dark blue with blue-and-yellow eyes; D. 1.7 cm (fig. 29a). One dark blue barrel-shaped bead with blue-and-white eyes; L. 2.0 cm (fig. 29b). One four-sided bead of clear glass with yellow spirals at the four corners; W. across diagonal 2.1 cm (fig. 29d). One clear glass melon-shaped bead; L. 1.7 cm (fig. 29e).

Small low cylindrical ceramic vessel of grayish-brown color; H. about 4.3 cm (fig. 29f).

The object thought to have been a platform for the figurine was missing when the collection was studied in Zurich, and no description or drawing of it survives.

GRAVE 3

In this grave were remains of wood which the excavators interpreted to be part of a burial chamber. Round wooden posts are mentioned. On the bottom of the grave were the rotting remains of one or more boards, in which a bronze nail was stuck. The excavators interpreted the position of the wooden fragments as an indication that the grave had been robbed.

Grave good:

Bronze rod with mushroom-shaped head. The upper part of the shaft is eight-sided, the lower part round in section. The upper part is decorated with patterns of incised lines. The lower end is broken off; surviving L. 18.9 cm (fig. 30).

GRAVE 4

Eight centimeters from a stone and associated with bone remains were two bronze fastenings and many small longish bronze rings attached to leather which disintegrated as the objects were being removed.

Grave goods:

Remains of two sheet bronze belt attachments

with rivets (one in fig. 31b). Solid bronze ring with evidence of wear at one edge; Ext. D. 2.2 cm (fig. 31a). When the material was studied in Zurich, the ring was attached to the fragmentary loop of the belt attachment illustrated here. About 100 small bronze rings or loops of roughly rectangular shape with three knobs on one side, most of them fragmentary; L. about 1.2 cm (fig. 31d). Cross-shaped bronze knob, originally with a loop on the back (fig. 31c). Similar knob, badly corroded.

Fragments of burned bone. On the basis of these fragments, the scholars in Zurich suggested that the burial was a cremation.

GRAVE 5

At a depth of 1.24 m, 9 cm below a carbonized tree trunk, were found a bronze fastening, a red urn, bronze fragments and rivets, and two collared amber beads. One note indicates that the bronze fastening was recovered 0.85 m from the red urn, another that the two amber beads were 10 cm from the fastening.

Grave goods:

Fragments of a bronze belt plate with a row of three rivets at each end, decorated with incised horizontal grooves (fig. 32a). Fragments of several bronze strap attachments with rivets. One, of metal 0.2 cm thick, is complete and has a loop at one end; L. 9.9 cm (fig. 32b). Other attachments are of thin sheet bronze (fig. 32d, e). Fragments of sheet bronze ornamented with rows of hammered dots, with rivets fastening two layers of metal tightly together (fig. 32f–h). Solid bronze ring with diamond-shaped section and Ext. D. of 2.8 cm (fig. 32c). Fragments of a small segmented bronze ring; original Ext. D. around 2.4 cm (fig. 32i).

The amber beads and urn are missing as they were when the collection was studied in Zurich.

GRAVE 6

Found in this grave were a small iron fastening with a bronze pin, a palstave or celt, and three small bronze rings and fragments of others. One note states that the palstave or celt was found 12 cm from the fastening.

Grave goods:

Two badly rusted iron rings, both with fragmentary iron rods projecting from the rings at 90° angles, and one connected to a thick iron shaft which is broken; Ext. D. of rings now about 4 cm (fig. 33a, c). Fragments of wood adhere to them. Fragmentary small conical iron object; surviving L. 3.2 cm (fig. 33b).

Fragments of three very small bronze rings. The smallest (fig. 33e) has a round section and an Ext. D. of 0.8 cm. The other two have diamond-shaped sections and Ext. D. of 1.2 cm (one fragment in fig. 33d).

The iron axe (palstave, celt) is missing.

GRAVE 7

Found were long Egyptian-looking glass beads ornamented with wavy lines and with yellow-and-blue ends.

Grave goods:

Sixty-nine glass beads (fig. 34): Seven long barrel-shaped beads with a dark blue-and-white wavy line pattern; L. 2.2 to 2.4 cm; four of them with yellow ends and three with light greenish-blue ends. Twelve light greenish-blue beads with dark blue-and-white double eyes; D. 0.7 cm. Two clear barrel-shaped beads with knobs projecting around the middle and with collars at the ends; L. 0.8 and 0.9 cm. Thirty plain dark blue beads; D. 0.6 to 0.9 cm. Eleven plain clear dark yellow beads; D. 0.6 to 0.8 cm. Seven plain clear colorless beads; D. 0.6 to 0.7 cm.

(Only one note made at the time of the excavation survives; it says Tumulus I, St. Veit and describes the beads but gives neither grave number nor information about depth or association. Mahr and his colleagues in Zurich considered the beads to have come from a distinct grave but do not say why.)

ISOLATED FINDS, TUMULUS I

Two segmented bronze rings with Ext. D. of 4.1 to 4.4 cm and 4.7 to 4.8 cm (fig. 35b, d). Badly corroded bronze ring; Ext. D. 5.7 to 6.0 cm (fig. 35a). Fragmentary bronze serpentine fibula with saddle-shaped bend in bow and stop disk; L. of surviving fragment 5.8 cm (fig. 35c). Fragmentary small bronze ring with a groove running around the middle; Ext. D. of fragment 2.4 cm (fig. 35e).

Tumulus II

Tumulus II was excavated between August 9 and 23, 1910. Sixteen graves were found. One note refers to the tumulus as Vas Griže, the village in which it was located.

GRAVE 1

Found were fragments from the bottom of a bronze vessel.

Grave goods:

All that survive from this grave are some small

fragments of sheet bronze, very likely the remains of a vessel.

GRAVE 2

At a depth of 0.25 m under the sod were found many small glass beads spread over an area some 2.5 m across. Among them were a few amber beads and two large blue-and-yellow eye beads. The excavators thought that the grave had been damaged by plowing. One note mentions a bronze vessel.

Grave goods:

Now associated with this grave number are remains of at least two bronze vessels. Substantial fragments of two handles survive as well as numerous small body fragments. The more completely preserved handle (fig. 36a) was fastened at its bottom end onto the outside of the vessel and extended upward forming a long curved opening for the hand. The upper end was attached to the inside of the rim.

The general form of the other handle (fig. 36b) is similar, but it does not rise as high above the vessel rim as does the first. The rim of the second vessel is ornamented with incised parallel lines, with very fine vertical lines forming triangles between them.

About 2,555 glass beads, 717 amber beads, and one bronze bead, shown here (fig. 36c) strung on three strings as they were when the Mecklenburg Collection arrived at the Peabody Museum. There is no reason to believe that the beads were found in any arrangement that might have suggested the patterns of these strings.

Glass beads: 991 very small blue beads, most of them dark blue, some lighter, D. 0.3 to 0.7 cm, most 0.3 to 0.4 cm; 1,503 very small white beads, D. 0.4 to 0.5 cm; 29 very small dark yellow beads, D. 0.4 cm; 30 very small yellow opaque beads, D. 0.4 to 0.6 cm; 5 very small broad beads of a dark gold color, D. 0.45 to 0.5 cm; 7 very small light green beads, D. 0.4 cm.

Amber beads: 15 spacer beads, rectangular in form. Longest complete bead 2.9 cm long, width of all about 0.5 cm, thickness of all about 0.3 cm. Each spacer bead has between six and nine perforations. All 15 are plain on one side and decorated on the other. Nine are decorated with horizontal grooves and ridges; the other six have grooves and in addition very fine incised lines in zigzag patterns. 635 very small, round beads, D. 0.3 cm. Twenty-nine amber beads, D. 0.6 to 1.0 cm. Thirty-six amber beads, D. 1.1 to 2.0 cm. One barrel-shaped bead, L. 0.7 cm, thickness 0.5 cm. Amber pendant, L. 2.5 cm, width 1.8 cm, thickness 0.6 cm.

Very small bronze bead, disk-shaped, D. 0.45 cm.

GRAVE 2a

An urn was found on a burned layer near the middle of the tumulus at a depth of 2.1 m. Next to the urn were two iron spearheads. A note written by the scholars working in Zurich indicates that the two spearheads, both in bad condition, were thrown away. The pot was not with the collection when it was in Zurich.

GRAVE 3

Associated with a burned area at a depth of 2.1 m was a poorly preserved bronze cauldron. Also found were a fragmentary hollow bronze ring, small bronze rings, three small amber beads, an urn, and a ceramic bowl.

Grave goods:

Bronze cauldron with cross-shaped handle attachments and a pair of smooth handles ending in stylized animal heads (fig. 37a). On the exterior just below the rim are bands of incised linear ornament. The bottom of the vessel is missing; the Ext. D. of rim ranges from 24 to 26.5 cm. Hollow bronze ring with one end fitted into the other and held in place by a bronze rivet. The ring is decorated with sections of ribbing. Original Ext D. about 8.0 to 8.5 cm, W. about 1.5 cm (fig. 37b). Three small closed solid bronze rings; one with a diamond-shaped section is 4.4 cm in Ext. D. (fig. 37d); another with diamond-shaped section is 4.8 cm in Ext. D. (fig. 37c); one with an oval section is 3.9 cm in Ext. D. (fig. 37e).

Two amber beads, one flat around the outside. This one has a D. of 1.0 cm (fig. 37g); the other has a D. of 1.1 cm (fig. 37f).

Sherds of several vessels are now associated with this grave. Pinkish-brown bowl. There is a groove just below the rim on the exterior of the vessel and a small nipple on one side; H. 5.5 to 6.0 cm (fig. 37h). Sherds of a large gray vessel with profiled foot (fig. 37l). The upper part of the vessel has profiled bands, some coated with graphite. Sherds of a lid, including the handle, perhaps belonging with the large footed vessel (fig. 37k). Sherds of a thick-walled bowl of gray pottery with a slightly indented base (fig. 37m). Low foot with slight profiling from a fairly thick-walled gray vessel (fig. 37j). The rim fragment (fig. 37i) is probably part of the large gray vessel shown in figure 37.

GRAVE 4

At a depth of 3.2 m and associated with a burned area were a hollow bronze ring and many small glass beads. Also found were fragments of a small bronze situla and a bronze "Cista Certosa," wood remains with bronze fragments, and fragments of ceramic vessels including a footed one, a brown one, and a red one.

Grave goods:

Fragments of a ribbed bucket of sheet bronze (fig. 38c). Fragments of a bronze vessel with a plain movable handle, the ends of which are stylized animal heads, two loop attachments riveted to the sides just below the rim, and a rim constructed over a heavy metal core (fig. 38f). Fragment of the side of a bronze cauldron with incised horizontal lines (fig. 38a). This fragment is similar to the remains of cauldrons from Tumulus V, Graves 14 (fig. 124b) and 18 (fig. 128b), but on this piece there is no trace of fine vertical lines between the horizontal ones. Probably from the same vessel are three small fragments of cross-shaped handle attachments. Fragments of a flat round object of thin sheet bronze (fig. 38b). Around the edge are two ridges, a higher inside one and a lower outside, with a row of closely spaced dots hammered out along the top of each; original D. of object about 30 to 35 cm. Long fragment of thin sheet bronze, probably from another vessel (fig. 38g).

Fragmentary hollow bronze ring with an original Ext. D. of about 16 to 18 cm, decorated with patterns of incised lines (fig. 38j). Fragments of two or more bronze belt attachments with rivets (one in fig. 38e). Solid bronze ring with diamond-shaped section, Ext. D. 2.8 cm (fig. 38h). Fragmentary long thin flat object of bronze with at least three large holes, 2.5 cm wide and 0.2 cm thick (fig. 38d).

Glass beads (fig. 38i): Dark blue bead, D. 1.0 cm. Pale greenish-blue bead with dark blue-and-white double eyes, D. 0.7 cm. Very small glass beads, D. 0.4 cm: 91 dark blue, 150 white, 16 brown transparent.

Dark gray ceramic vessel once on a foot (fig. 38n). The upper part of the exterior has a shiny black coating of graphite. Light orange footed vessel (fig. 38l). The pottery is heavily weathered, but traces of graphite are visible on the interior of the neck. Sherds of two other large light orange vessels (fig. 38k, o). In each case the profiled neck has a dull cherry red slip and black graphite bands; the graphite appears to have been applied over the red slip. One has a low foot, the other a high one. Both feet are decorated with profiling and red and black bands. Other sherds are associated with this grave group, including a reddish-orange foot bearing traces of cherry red slip (fig. 38m).

GRAVE 5

The grave was found at a depth of 2.4 m and contained a burned area. Strewn about on it were seven glass beads and several fragments of gold foil. Also found were a small broken ring and at least one urn.

Grave goods:

Several small fragments of very thin gold foil, about 4 cm^2 all together. The original form of the pieces is unclear. Very small glass beads, Ext. D. 0.3 to 0.45 cm: 63 dark blue, 75 white, 6 brown transparent (fig. 39e).

Sherds of a large thick-walled footed vessel of dark grayish-brown color (fig. 39b). The upper part has large bulges on it and is coated with graphite on the exterior. This is the only vessel mentioned in the inventory of this grave made by the scholars in Zurich. Now remains of three other vessels are associated with the grave.

Sherds of dark reddish-brown pottery with a lip curving sharply outward and with a groove high up on the shoulder (fig. 39d). Sherds of two lids including their handles; one is dark grayish-brown (fig. 39c), the other pale tan (fig. 39a). The latter has a reddish slip or paint covering much of the exterior.

GRAVE 6

A bronze vessel, an urn, and the remains of a skull were found.

Grave goods:

Fragments of a bronze cauldron with cross-shaped handle attachments and two handles with twist patterns and stylized animal-head ends (fig. 40a). This cauldron has no incised ornament around the rim exterior.

Sherds of a low light grayish-brown bowl (fig. 40b). Just below the rim on the exterior is a deep groove setting off the rim from the body of the vessel. On the shoulder is a nipple (other nipples may have existed, but are not preserved). Sherds of a light brown vessel, much of the exterior coated with graphite (fig. 40c). The neck is decorated with horizontal grooves and on the body are broad vertical bulges. Other sherds of the same character and color may be from the same vessel, or they may be from a different one. They are coated with graphite on the exterior, and have a horizontal raised ridge on the exterior (fig. 40d).

GRAVE 7

At a depth of 2.9 m a grave was found which had been dug 0.2 m into the natural ground beneath the tumulus. It was 3.1 m long and 2.1 m wide. On a thin burned layer were 24 glass beads, a small iron rod, and a small ceramic bowl. One note mentions fragments of a small bronze vessel.

Grave goods:

Only the ceramic vessel survives. It is a kylix or handled drinking cup on a foot of a form common in the Greek world (fig. 41). The pottery is brick orange in color, and much of the surface on both interior and exterior is covered with a black coating. Since much of the coating has worn off, the painted pattern is difficult to discern. Outer rim D. about 13.5 cm, H. about 6.5 cm.

(This kylix has been published by Jacobsthal [1956, pp. 177–178, figs. 579–581], who suggests that the clay and firing are not Attic or Ionic, though the throwing looks Greek. He considers it a good copy of an Attic model, proposing a date of manufacture in the first quarter of the fifth century B.C., in a workshop on the east coast of the Adriatic.

Prof. G. M. A. Hanfmann advises me that a date in the first half of the fifth century B.C. is perhaps safer than Jacobsthal's narrower dating and suggests that "east coast of the Adriatic" may also be too specific a designation considering the present state of knowledge.

Dr. R. E. Jones of the Fitch Laboratory, British School at Athens, generously analyzed a sample of clay from this vessel by optical emission spectroscopy, using the method described by Schweizer in Prag et al. 1974. The results, kindly provided by Dr. Jones, show the composition of the sample in nine elements to be the following: Al 21.2 percent, Mg 3.3 percent, Fe 8.6 percent, Ti 1.06 percent, Mn 0.150 percent, Cr 0.022 percent, Ca 8.2 percent, Na 0.75 percent, Ni 0.007 percent. Dr. Jones calls attention to the comparison between these figures and those for Attic pottery [Boardman and Schweizer 1973; Prag et al. 1974], noting particularly that the Attic pottery has significantly higher Cr and Ni contents. On this basis, Dr. Jones advises me that this kylix is probably not Attic. Dr. John Boardman further advises me that the pottery may have its origin in a region on the fringes of the Greek area, perhaps in the north, though he emphasizes the current lack of sufficient comparative materials to allow more specific delineation of possible sources.)

GRAVE 8

No notes about the grave survive, and the finds are missing.

GRAVE 9

The grave was found at a depth of 2.1 m and contained an arm ring, a large amber bead, and remains of wood.

Grave goods:

Hollow bronze ring with overlapping ends, decorated with groups of incised lines; Ext. D. about 8.5 cm (fig. 42a). Large amber bead; D. 2.5 cm; H. 1.9 cm (fig. 42c). Three bronze nails 2.7, 2.7, and 2.2 cm in length. Two are still attached to fragments of iron and wood (one in fig. 42b). On the underside of the iron fragment shown here are remains of wood, apparently from an object to which the iron was attached by means of the bronze nail. Two fragments of wood, the larger about 34 cm long and 4.5 cm wide at the widest part, with a roughly triangular section (fig. 42d).

GRAVES 10 to 13

Neither excavation notes nor finds survive.

GRAVE 14

Bronze chains and two bronze disks were found.

Grave goods:

Fragments of spirals made of heavy bronze wire. Some of the segments are of wire of triangular section, others of round section; D. of the spirals about 0.8 cm. The total surviving length of these spirals is about 36 cm (fig. 43a). Three bronze disks originally about 5.5 cm in D. (one in fig. 43b). On the back of each are two bronze loops. Abundant traces of iron survive on the back of one disk. A badly corroded iron fragment about 5 cm long is now associated with this grave.

GRAVE 15

In a cremation grave a hairpin and a small button were found.

Grave goods:

Fragmentary many-knobbed bronze pin with head, two surviving knobs, and a guard (fig. 44a). Additional knobs may have been present above the break. (The head is probably the button mentioned in the excavation notes.) Small bronze ring with Ext. D. of 2.7 cm and a triangular section (fig. 44b). Attached are seven small wire rings onto each of which is attached a very small bronze chain.

ISOLATED FINDS, TUMULUS II

Nine small solid rings of bronze: One with diamond-shaped section and Ext. D. of 5.2 to 5.3 cm (fig. 45o). One with drop-shaped section and Ext. D. of 4.6 cm (fig. 45p). One with diamond-shaped section and Ext. D. of 4.2 cm (fig. 45q). One with oval section and Ext. D. of 3.7 cm (fig. 45r). One with diamond-shaped section and Ext. D. of 3.45 cm (fig. 45v). One with diamond-shaped section and Ext. D. of 3.3 cm (fig. 45u). One with round section and Ext. D. of 2.6 cm (fig. 45t). One with diamond-shaped section and Ext. D. of 2.3 cm (fig. 45s). Ring flat on one side and rounded on the other, with a fragmentary tang and Ext. D. of 2.1 cm (fig. 45ii).

Solid bronze ring with overlapping ends and incised line decoration; Ext. D. about 7.5 cm (fig. 45m). Fragments of one or more rings of thin bronze wire;

Ext. D. about 5 cm (fig. 45n). Small spiral ring of bronze wire, Ext. D. about 2.2 cm (fig. 45g). Flat ring, Ext. D. 7 cm, with holes around two-thirds of the circumference and with linear ornamentation of incised lines. Attached to the ring were chains of small bronze pendants (fig. 45jj). Fragmentary La Tène fibula missing its foot, with a long spiral spring and external wire; L. of spring 3.8 cm (fig. 45c). Fragmentary Middle La Tène fibula with the foot clasping the back of the bow (fig. 45b). Fragmentary very small Certosa fibula with incised lines on the top of the bow; L. 3.6 cm (fig. 45a). Two bronze pendants 3.2 cm long with a globular end, thin shaft, and loop at end containing iron remains (one in fig. 45d). Three small vase-shaped knobs of bronze, each perforated with a large hole. One 1.85 cm in D. with a square perforation (fig. 45h); one 1.4 cm in D. with a round perforation (fig. 45i); one 1.6 cm in D. with a round perforation, its upper part broken off (fig. 45j).

Hollow bronze button 1.6 cm in D. with a loop on the back (fig. 45k). Fragmentary flat bronze pendant with large loop, and triangular base with a row of small holes at the bottom for the attachment of other objects (fig. 45e). Fragment of a sheet bronze pendant with boss and hammered dots (fig. 45ll). About 350 small round bronze bosses with loops on the backs; D. about 1.0 cm (one in fig. 45mm). Remains of about ten sheet bronze attachments, long and thin with each end bent over and connected with the front by a rivet. Some are decorated with two parallel grooves running the length of the band and small oblique incised lines along each edge; L. of complete specimen 6.9 cm, W. 0.5 cm (one in fig. 45f). Fragments of two bronze vessel handles, both with twist pattern (fig. 45gg, hh). Two fragments of a sheet bronze band 2.0 cm wide ornamented with small hammered bosses along the edges; along the edges are also nail holes (one in fig. 45l).

Bone handle for an iron object, probably a knife (fig. 45w). Both sides of the bone are decorated with incised dot-and-circle patterns connected by two parallel lines. Between the two layers of bone is preserved part of the iron object. At one end is a fragmentary sheet bronze clamp riveted through the object.

Fragmentary remains of 12 to 14 long cylindrical beads consisting of hollow bronze core with ribbing, with a band of sheet gold rolled around it and pressed into the grooves of the core. Surviving L. up to 2.5 cm. Figure 45x shows remains of a bronze core; figure 45y shows the complete gold-covered beads.

Glass beads (fig. 45ff): Two dark blue beads with a white wavy line, D. 1.2 and 1.3 cm. One pale green bead, D. 1.6 cm. One pale green bead with a yellow wavy line, D. 1.4 cm. One pale green bead with yellow and black spirals on four knobs, each at one corner; 1.6 cm across diagonal.

Glass beads (fig. 45y): One dark blue bead with white wavy line, D. 1.4 cm. One greenish-blue bead with blue-and-white double eyes, D. 1.7 cm.

Amber beads (fig. 45y): Two cylindrical beads with ribbing resembling the gold-covered bronze ones, L. 1.4 and 1.0 cm. Pendant. Nine wafer-shaped beads with one flat side and one low rounded side, D. 1.5 to 2.5 cm. Seven beads of varying form and size.

Amber beads (some in fig. 45kk): Thirteen small beads, D. 0.6 to 1.1 cm.

Eight spindle whorls: One bell-shaped with a Max. D. of 3.7 cm (fig. 45z). One conical with a Max. D. of 3.2 cm (fig. 45aa). Three conical with Max. D. of 2.8, 2.6, 2.6 cm (one in fig. 45bb). One double-conical with Max. D. of 3.2 cm (fig. 45ee). One rounded-conical with Max. D. of 3.0 to 3.1 cm (fig. 45cc). Low one with D. of 2.6 cm (fig. 45dd).

Sherds of orange-brown pottery including fragments of a footed vessel and of a handled lid.

Tumulus III

This tumulus was called the *Waldtumulus* and was located on the imperial road (*Reichsstrasse*) through Carniola. Work here was carried out from June 4 or 8 through July 13, 1912. The tumulus had a diameter of 18 m east-west and 15 m north-south and was 2.8 m high and consisted of yellow earth.

The information about the graves and the associations of objects in this tumulus is exceptionally poor. No detailed excavation notes survive, such as those for Tumulus IV, and in the brief notes that do survive are confusing and sometimes contradictory data. For the attribution of objects to individual graves in this tumulus, I have relied very heavily on the judgment of the scholars working in Zurich who unpacked the materials and the surviving notes. I do not have confidence in these associations.

GRAVE 1a

At a depth of 1.1 m on the natural ground surface were a small arm ring and a small iron fragment with bronze rivets.

Grave goods:

Fragments of a bronze ring decorated with segmentations on part of its surface; Ext. D. of surviving fragment 6.5 cm (fig. 46a). Four small bronze rivets 1.4 to 1.7 cm long (fig. 46c). Two have mushroom-shaped heads and taper at one end. One of these has remains of sheet bronze attached just below the head. Two are cylindrical with slightly broadened heads. Associated with this grave when the collection was studied in Zurich and still present are 16 amber beads of lozenge shape. These beads range in length from 0.8 to 2.2 cm (fig. 46b).

GRAVE 1b

Two meters away from Grave 1a was a stone slab about 0.8 m in diameter. Beneath it were remains of a human skeleton; only the foot bones survived. Next to the slab was a reddish urn. One note indicates that the grave was 1.6 m deep in the tumulus, 3.1 m long, 1.05 m wide, and had been dug 0.25 m into the ground.

No objects are preserved from this grave.

GRAVE 2a

Two sets of notes give depths of 1.6 and 1.9 m respectively. Various notes indicate that the grave was 3.2 m long, 1.1 m wide, and had been dug 0.6 m into the ground. Finds mentioned are two arm rings, two leg rings, two serpentine fibulae, a spectacle pendant, and several amber and glass beads. Because the arm rings were small, Goldberg called this a child's grave.

Grave goods:

Two very similar small solid bronze rings with overlapping ends, decorated with zones of ribbing; Ext. D. about 4 cm (one in fig. 47c). Solid bronze ring ornamented with groups of incised lines; Ext. D. about 6.0 to 6.5 cm (fig. 47b). Fragmentary small bronze spectacle pendant; L. about 3.3 cm (fig. 47a). Two dark blue glass beads with white zigzag lines; D. 1.2 cm (fig. 47d, e). The one with the smaller hole has thinner white lines than the other. (The serpentine fibulae and amber beads are missing.)

GRAVE 2b

The grave was covered with three stone slabs and was 1.9 m deep in the tumulus, 2.4 m long, and 0.6 m wide. The skull and other skeletal remains were preserved; the skeleton was stretched out, and at the head and foot were brown urns. Along one side was a layer of burned wood. Recovered were a bronze garment pin with a thick smooth head, several fragmentary iron rings, perhaps bracelets, found together at the chest of the skeleton, three or four bronze buttons or knobs near the rings, a bronze attachment with rivets and with remains of wood and leather, thought to be a belt hook, and a fragment of a small iron knife.

All of the finds were missing when the collection was studied in Zurich.

GRAVE 2c

Near the center of the tumulus at a depth of 1.6 m was found a packing of three stone slabs 0.9 to 1.1 m in diameter. Under the slabs was a burned area.

On or in the burned area were remains of a brownish urn, burned bones, and many small bronze nails and rivets. The burned area was found to extend deep into the ground, and many more bronze nails were recovered as the burned area was investigated. Leather remains are mentioned in connection with the nails.

Grave goods:

Fragments of four bronze nails survive; L. of most complete one 1.4 cm; D. of head 0.6 cm (fig. 48). They have thin heads of sheet bronze and shafts of thin bronze wire rectangular in section.

Near Grave 2c were two small stone slabs at the same depth as those covering Grave 2c, apparently close together. Underneath them were animal bones and several teeth of what was probably a horse. (It is not clear whether Goldberg thought these finds were part of Grave 2c or a separate grave. Mahr and his associates in Zurich interpreted the notes to indicate that they were part of Grave 2c.)

GRAVE 3

This grave was 4 m long, 1.25 m wide, and had been dug 0.5 m into the ground. It was 1.7 m deep in the tumulus. In the grave were an urn, a spindle whorl, 70 small amber beads, 22 glass beads, and a badly damaged ear pendant.

All of the finds are missing.

GRAVE 4

Found in this grave were many glass beads and an "ambrosa" (*Armbrust?*) fibula in fragments.

The objects are missing.

GRAVE 5

In this grave were a bronze knife, a spearhead, and an iron celt, all of them very badly preserved. Also recovered were two belt rings.

All of the finds are missing.

GRAVE 6

The grave was found at a depth of 1.85 m. It was 3.7 m long, 1.3 m wide, and had been dug 0.3 m into the ground.

Grave goods:

Associated with a slip of paper bearing this grave description when the collection was studied in Zurich were the following objects: Globular footed dark gray vessel; the body is decorated with six rows of three nipples arranged vertically (fig. 49b). Sherds of a similar vessel with less pointed nipples and a lower and broader foot. Remains of two lids of the same dark gray pottery (one, with a D. of 18 to 19 cm, in fig. 49a).

GRAVE 7

Goldberg called this a child's grave. The only recorded find is a reddish urn.

Grave goods:

Associated with this grave now are sherds of at least two vessels. One is a small globular vessel with three small nipples just above the middle of the body; Max. D. 11.0 to 11.5 cm; H. 8.0 to 8.5 cm (fig. 50). The vessel is dull orange and of rather coarse texture. The other sherds are of similar color, but the character of the other vessel is unclear.

GRAVE 8

This was also called a child's grave and contained a reddish vessel found at a depth of 25 to 30 cm and a small urn found at a depth of 25 cm. One note says that the latter vessel belongs with a small finger ring, two arm rings, a foot ring, and three beads.

Grave goods:

Sherds of a footed vessel of dull reddish-orange color, with sets of three vertical ridges on the body (fig. 51a). Small conical vessel of coarse black pottery; H. 6.0 to 6.5 cm (fig. 51b). Small round-bodied vessel of pale reddish color with two surviving nipples (there was probably a third originally); H. 7.5 cm (fig. 51c).

GRAVE 9

A note mentions a bronze belt plate found at a depth of 20 cm next to a stone.

Grave good:

Fragmentary belt plate of sheet bronze (fig. 52). It consists of two pieces of bronze riveted together by three bronze rivets. A flat iron bar with projecting fragmentary hook is riveted to the end of the bronze plate with three bronze rivets (two survive). Surviving L. 11.3 cm; W. 5.3 cm.

GRAVE 10

Notes mention an arm ring, fragments of arm rings, and amber beads.

Grave goods:

Bronze ring with overlapping ends, solid and decorated with groups of incised lines. The ends are ornamented with ribbing. Ext. D. about 7 cm (fig. 53a). Seventy-nine very small amber beads, D. 0.2 to 0.5 cm (some in fig. 53b).

ISOLATED FINDS, TUMULUS III

Narrow segmented bronze ring with overlapping ends; Ext. D. about 6.5 cm (fig. 54b). Fragmentary bronze serpentine fibula with stop disk, saddle-shaped bend in the bow, a pair of horns ending in lens-shaped knobs, and a rivet passing through the bow with a disk on either end (fig. 54a).

Glass beads (fig. 54c): Dark blue bead with white zigzag line; D. 1.4 cm. Plain dark blue bead; D. 1.4 cm. Light greenish-blue bead with dark blue-and-white double eyes; D. 0.75 cm. Eight yellow to yellow-brown beads; D. 0.7 to 0.8 cm. Fifty-one small dark blue beads; D. 0.5 to 0.8 cm. About 160 very small dark blue beads; D. 0.3 to 0.4 cm. Twenty-eight very small white beads; D. 0.3 to 0.4 cm.

Amber beads: 263 of various shapes, ranging in D. from 0.3 to 1.7 cm (some in fig. 54d, e).

A five-minute walk away from Tumulus III was another tumulus which Goldberg and the workmen excavated. It was located on the farmland of an Anton Liscak. Goldberg wrote of the mound's peculiar formation: At the center of the tumulus the natural ground surface rose up so that the earth was only some 1.1 m deep above it. At the other parts of the mound, however, the tumulus was 1.6 to 2.0 m deep. At first Goldberg thought the mound might have been a natural feature, but some charcoal was found, as well as sherds of pottery, and two stones which he interpreted as having been set in place. The mound was apparently abandoned by the excavators without full excavation.

Tumulus IV

This tumulus was generally called Tumulus Trondel, after the landowner Jacob Trondel, and was also referred to as the Great Tumulus (*Grosse Gomila*). It was excavated from March 28 through April 29, 1913. Fifty-seven graves were found.

The documentation for this tumulus is exceptionally good. The original excavation notes are preserved for each grave. These notes include information about the character and structure of each grave, about the objects found in it, and often about the locations of the objects. The materials now associated with each grave correspond very well to the descriptions in the excavation notes. Thus I judge the associations in this tumulus to be thoroughly trustworthy.

GRAVE 1

This grave was oriented east-west and was 2.7 m long and 1.05 m wide. It was situated at a depth of 1.6 m and had been dug 0.9 m into the ground. At the foot end were a brownish urn, 35 blue-and-white glass beads, and a spindle whorl.

Grave goods:

Thirty-five glass beads: Two four-sided dark blue

beads with white spirals at the corners; W. 1.6 cm (fig. 55f). Seven dark blue beads of nearly spherical shape, each with three white spirals; D. 1.6 to 1.7 cm (four in fig. 55e). Dark blue bead with two white eyes and one white spiral; D. 1.75 cm (fig. 55b). Dark blue bead with four white eyes; D. 1.5 cm (fig. 55d). Two dark blue beads with three white eyes; D. 1.3 and 1.35 cm (one in fig. 55c). Ten dark blue beads with white zigzag lines; D. 1.0 to 1.7 cm (five in fig. 55a). Eleven dark blue beads with white wavy lines; D. 1.35 to 1.7 cm (four in fig. 55g). Dark blue bead with a yellow zigzag line; D. 1.2 cm (fig. 55h).

Dark grayish-brown vessel with broad horizontal flutings on high conical neck and narrow oblique flutings on shoulder (fig. 55i). Dull orange spindle whorl; D. 3.4 cm (fig. 55j).

GRAVE 2

This grave is described as an extension of Grave 1. Covering the grave was a stone slab with a diameter of 0.85 m. The grave was situated at a depth of 1.65 m and contained a skeleton oriented east-west; it was 2.8 m long, 0.85 m wide, and had been dug 0.6 m into the ground. At the head end were two glass beads and a serpentine fibula. At the foot end were two leg rings around the surviving leg bones. Also at the foot end were an urn and a spindle whorl.

Grave goods:

Two similar thin segmented bronze rings; Ext. D. about 10 to 11 cm (one in fig. 56a). Fragmentary bronze serpentine fibula with saddle-shaped bend in the bow and round knob on foot; L. about 9 cm (fig. 56e). Two transparent pale blue glass beads; D. 1.1 cm (fig. 56c). Small nearly spherical vessel of light brown color and coarse texture; H. about 5.5 cm (fig. 56b). Tan spindle whorl; D. 3.4 cm (fig. 56d).

GRAVE 3

This grave, found 3.8 m from Graves 1 and 2, was situated at a depth of 1.65 m. It was 3.5 m long, 1.05 m wide, and had been dug 0.6 m into the ground. Above the grave were remains of a reddish urn and an iron celt, which the excavators believed to have belonged to the grave. No other objects were found in the grave.

Grave goods:

Fragmentary socketed iron axe (fig. 57b). Sherds of an orange footed vessel with a slip of darker orange-red color on the exterior. At least three bands of graphite encircle the vessel (fig. 57a).

GRAVE 4

This grave was 4.8 m from Grave 3 and 2.15 m deep in the tumulus. It was 3.6 m long, 1.25 m wide, and had been dug 0.7 m into the ground. In the middle of the grave on each side a stone had been placed. On the bottom of the grave was a small burned layer. Found were two hollow arm rings, broken by a workman, 15 small amber beads, and sherds of a reddish urn. Goldberg suggested that the grave had been disturbed but did not say why.

Grave goods:

Fragmentary remains of one or more hollow bronze rings decorated with ribbing (fig. 58a). Fifteen amber beads, D. 1.2 to 2.3 cm (some in fig. 58b). Sherds of a thin-walled light tan vessel.

GRAVE 5

Cremation. This grave was west of Grave 1 and was 3.2 m long, 1.15 m wide, and had been dug 1.05 m into the ground. The total depth to the bottom of the grave was 1.7 m. In the grave were a large red urn and a small black one, a very badly rusted iron celt, a spindle whorl, and a badly preserved iron spearhead.

Grave goods:

Very fragmentary remains of an iron axe and an iron spearhead. Sherds of a thin-walled gray and tan vessel with a conical neck and two lugs on opposite sides of the shoulder, each perforated vertically (fig. 59a). Sherds of a reddish-brown and gray vessel with oblique flutings on the shoulder and broad horizontal flutings on the conical neck (fig. 59b). Pinkish-tan spindle whorl with many small holes in the surface of the sides and bottom; D. 3.6 cm (fig. 59c).

GRAVE 6

This grave was near Grave 5. It was 3.4 m long, 0.9 m wide, and had been dug 0.6 m into the ground. Its total depth was 1.55 m. Above the grave at the foot end were two stones. Near them was a burned area in which were strewn 15 blue-and-white glass beads. Somewhat deeper were sherds of a brownish urn.

Grave goods:

Fifteen small glass beads (five in fig. 60). All are pale greenish-blue and have dark blue eyes surrounded by white. Ten have four double eyes; D. of these 0.6 to 0.7 cm. Three have three double eyes and one single eye; D. 0.6, 0.7, 0.8 cm. One has two double eyes and two single eyes; D. 0.8 cm. One has three single eyes; D. 0.8 cm.

Sherds of a reddish-brown and gray vessel, of fairly coarse texture and without decoration.

GRAVE 7

This grave was near Grave 2 and was 2.6 m long, 0.7 m wide, and had been dug 0.4 m into the ground. The bottom of the grave was at a depth of 1.1 m. Found were an arm ring, a broken fibula, and many small glass beads. At the foot end were sherds of a brownish urn. The notes mention a streak of gray earthy material and add that the Duchess believed this to be composed of decayed glass beads, while Goldberg held it to be from disintegrated lead.

Grave goods:

Fragmentary boat-shaped fibula with two knobs sticking out from the sides of the bow, a long catch decorated on the top with incised lines, and a knob on the foot; L. of bow and catch fragment 8.7 cm (fig. 61a). At the head end of the bow is a hole containing remains of an iron rivet. Ring with overlapping ends consisting of a bronze band with a constriction and decorated with incised lines; greatest Ext. D. about 5.8 cm, width of band 0.8 cm (fig. 61b).

Glass beads, 176 in all, of very small size (fig. 61c): 30 dark blue beads, D. 0.3 to 0.6 cm; 7 yellow beads, D. 0.4 cm; 11 yellow beads with dull surface, D. 0.4 cm; 30 white beads, D. 0.3 to 0.45 cm; 2 white beads with dull surface, D. 0.35 and 0.4 cm; 96 pale greenish-blue beads, D. 0.4 to 0.5 cm.

Five flat beads of bronze, D. 0.3 to 0.6 cm.

Sherds of a brownish-gray vessel, probably a bowl, with indented circle at base and a raised bulge in the interior (fig. 61d).

GRAVE 8

This grave was west of Grave 6. A circle of 11 arranged stones was 1.1 m above it. The grave was 3.3 m long, 2.15 m wide, and had been dug 0.4 m into the ground. The total depth to the bottom of the grave was 1.55 m. On the bottom of the grave was a burned area in which were pottery sherds and badly preserved glass beads. The scattered nature of the objects suggested to Goldberg that the grave had been disturbed. Found were 12 whole beads, 8 broken ones, and several small ones, and a spindle whorl.

Grave goods:

Eight large dark blue glass beads; D. 1.6 to 1.95 cm (three in fig. 62a). Three dark blue beads with white zigzag lines; D. 1.2 cm (fig. 62a). Three large pale greenish-blue transparent beads; D. 1.6, 1.6, 1.8 cm (two in fig. 62b). Very pale green transparent bead; D. 1.2 cm (fig. 62b). Ninety-two very small dark blue beads; D. 0.5 to 0.7 cm (some in fig. 62a).

Sherds of a lid light red in color with a cherry red slip on the exterior. On the rim exterior is a graphite band, and others run from this band up toward the top (fig. 62e). Sherds of a cylindrical light tan vessel with a raised band encircling the vessel just below the rim, decorated with finger impressions; H. about 15.3 cm (fig. 62d). Grayish-tan spindle whorl; D. 2.65 cm (fig. 62c).

GRAVE 9

This grave was southeast of Grave 8 and at a depth of 1.6 m. It was 3.6 m long, 0.9 m wide, and had been dug 0.4 m into the ground. Three stones had been placed in the grave. At the foot end was an urn. Also found were three large glass beads, a spindle whorl, and a fragment of an earring.

Grave goods:

Fragmentary bronze ring about 3 cm in Ext. D. (fig. 63c). Three large pale green transparent glass beads; D. 1.9, 1.9, 2.0 cm (fig. 63b). Rim sherd of a thin-walled brownish-gray bowl with an outcurved rim (fig. 63d). Sherds of a large footed vessel of reddish color (fig. 63e). On the exterior are traces of bands of graphite as well as of a reddish slip. On the interior is a dull black coating. The neck has broad horizontal flutings on it. Grayish-brown spindle whorl; D. 2.9 cm (fig. 63a).

GRAVE 10

This grave was found higher up than the preceding ones, at a depth of 0.45 m, and near the center of the tumulus. Some burned bones were found, along with sherds, fragments of a badly preserved bronze belt plate, and the bow of a fibula with an animal head on it, representing a hare or a roe deer.

Grave goods:

Fragmentary bronze animal-head fibula of crossbow construction. The bow with catch and animal head is complete; also surviving are the axle and part of the spring. L. of the bow 7.2 cm (fig. 64j). Fragmentary remains of one or more bronze belt plates with rivets (fig. 64b, c, d). On the underside of the fragment in figure 64c, the third rivet from the top holds remains of iron, probably from the iron hook which was attached to that plate (fig. 64h, i). The arrangements of the other fragments is unclear, as is the form of the original plate(s). Fragments of burned bone adhere to several pieces of sheet bronze. Fragmentary bronze belt attachment (fig. 64f) with fragmentary solid bronze ring (fig. 64e). Two fragmentary bronze attachments of thin bands of rectangular section (larger fragment in fig. 64g).

Fragmentary iron knife with pieces of bone and remains of textile adhering to it (fig. 64a).

Sherds of grayish-tan pottery.

GRAVE 10a

This was called a child's grave. Below a circle of stones were a glass pendant in the shape of two breasts, a small fibula, and some small glass and amber beads.

Grave goods:

The objects mentioned in the notes were missing when the collection was studied in Zurich. Associated with this grave number in Zurich and still present is a small fragmentary ring of sheet bronze (fig. 65).

GRAVE 11

Found in this grave were two arm rings, six glass beads, an amber bead, a spindle whorl, and a small bronze ring.

Grave goods:

Two solid bronze rings with overlapping ends. One is decorated with groups of ribbing; Max. Ext. D. 7.2 cm (fig. 66b). The other is decorated with incised lines and with groups of four deep and broad grooves; Max. Ext. D. 6.9 cm (fig. 66a). Small solid bronze ring with six knobs on the outside; D. across knobs 2.7 cm (fig. 66d). Six glass beads (fig. 66c): one transparent pale green (very fragmentary); one transparent pale bluish-green, D. 1.5 cm; one dark blue, D. 1.3 cm; one brown with three white-and-brown eyes, D. 1.0 cm; one amber-colored (the "amber bead"), D. 0.8 cm; one greenish-blue with blue-and-white eyes and yellow projections, D. across eyes 1.2 cm. The spindle whorl is missing.

GRAVE 12

In this grave were found two badly preserved arm rings, fragments of an earring, two glass beads, a serpentine fibula, and the bow of a poorly preserved boat-shaped fibula.

Grave goods:

Two similar segmented bronze rings with overlapping ends; Max. Ext. D. 10.2 cm (one in fig. 67a). Serpentine fibula with saddle-shaped bend in bow and disk; surviving L. 7.6 cm (fig. 67d). Fragmentary solid bow of leech-shaped fibula (fig. 67b). Two glass beads of transparent pale green color, D. 1.2 and 1.8 cm (fig. 67c). The fragments of an earring are missing.

GRAVE 13

No objects were found in this grave.

GRAVE 14

Associated with nine stones which had been arranged were 52 amber beads, a spindle whorl, and remains of an urn.

Grave goods:

Fifty-two amber beads of different shapes and sizes, the largest 3.0 cm in D. (some in fig. 68a). Sherds of two undecorated tan-and-gray vessels (fig. 68b, d). Grayish-tan spindle whorl, D. 4.2 cm (fig. 68c).

GRAVE 15

Associated with a large burned area were fragments of sheet bronze, thought by the excavators to be fragments of a sieve, 72 small amber beads, and interwoven wood and straw remains.

Grave goods:

Seventy-two amber beads of various sizes (some in fig. 69c). Fragments of a bronze sieve with a handle. Surviving are the attachments of the loop handle and part of the side of the vessel (fig. 69a), as well as two small fragments of sheet bronze with many perforations, probably the bottom of the sieve (fig. 69b).

GRAVE 16

This grave was oriented east-west and was 3.5 m long, 1.3 m wide, and 0.7 m from top to bottom. The bottom of the grave was 1.8 m below the surface of the tumulus. Around the four sides of the grave had been placed 21 stones. At the foot end were two spearheads and an iron celt. At the head end were horse bones, including bones of the feet, hooves, and teeth. A fragmentary brown urn, together with many iron fragments (the excavation notes suggest *von Platte oder Schild*), and a bronze belt plate, which was broken by the workmen, were on one side of the grave. Also found were a large red urn and two lids.

Grave goods:

Two iron spearheads, both fragmentary. The nearly whole one is 30.1 cm long in its present state; the base of the socket is decorated with linear patterns (fig. 70a). The other, which was larger, is more fragmentary; its socket is also decorated with linear ornament (fig. 70b). Fragmentary iron axe (fig. 70e). Fragments of a sheet bronze belt plate decorated with very fine incised lines (fig. 70c). Fragments of an iron knife (fig. 70d). Many other iron fragments, most of them flattish.

Sherds of a gray vessel on a foot, ornamented with three sets of three vertical ridges on the shoulder; restored H. about 23.5 cm (fig. 70h). The exterior has a shiny black surface. Sherds of a large globular footed vessel of light reddish color. On the exterior are traces of zones of a bright red slip and of graphite bands. Rim sherds of two similar large globular vessels of reddish pottery, both with profiled necks and bands of graphite and red slip on rim, neck, and shoulder. One of the sets of rim sherds probably belongs to the vessel with the foot, above. A composite reconstruction from parts of both vessels, which were very similar, is in figure 70g. Two lids represented by two handles and other sherds; both graphite and red slip are present on them (one in fig. 70f). Sherds of a vessel of brown color and coarse texture, apparently undecorated (fig. 70i).

Teeth and bone fragments from a horse. Bökönyi (1968, pp. 15–16) has identified these as remains of an adult horse.

GRAVE 17

On a burned layer 0.3 m from the ground level at a depth of 2.1 m below the surface of the tumulus were found about 80 amber beads, almost all of them broken. With them were two fibulae, also broken, and other bronze objects including earrings. Fine bronze wire was observed inside the amber beads by the excavators, leading them to suggest that the beads had been strung on a bracelet.

Grave goods:

Fragment of a bronze serpentine fibula with a saddle-shaped bend in the bow and a disk (fig. 71c). Bow of a bronze fibula with a knob on top (fig. 71b). Fragmentary springs from fibulae (fig. 71e–g). Fragments of a thin bronze ring, perhaps the earrings mentioned in the excavation notes (fig. 71d). Fragments of about 20 amber beads survive (four in fig. 71a).

GRAVE 18

This grave was about 2 m from Grave 17. On a burned area were a bronze belt plate, a badly corroded iron celt, two small broken rings for a belt or for a weapon, and remains of a brown vessel. The belt plate could only be removed from the grave in fragments.

Grave goods:

Fragmentary belt attachments of sheet bronze with bronze rivets (fig. 72b–e, g). Sheet bronze attachment with a central hole, held together by two iron rivets (fig. 72f). Two small segmented bronze rings, Ext. D. about 2.4 cm. One has remains of what is probably leather adhering to it (fig. 72h). Fragments of two pairs of bronze tweezers (fig. 72i, j).

Fragmentary iron socketed axe (fig. 72a). Many flattish fragments of iron are now associated with this grave.

The pottery was already missing when the collection was organized in Zurich.

GRAVE 19

Cremation grave. Near the center of the tumulus at a depth of 4.8 m the excavators came upon intensely burned earth and a stone slab laid over a burned area. Beneath the slab was the grave, designated the *Mittelgrab* of this tumulus by the excavators. It was oriented north-south. The slab was great trouble to lift, being 1.6 m wide, 3.4 m long, and 12 to 15 cm thick. The length of the grave was 3.5 m, its width 1.4 m, and it had been dug 0.45 m deep into the ground. Along the side of the grave at the head and foot ends were burned streaks. At the foot end were remains of three blackish-brown footed urns and a bronze *Patellenhut* (dish-shaped hat?). Also found were two broken hair or garment pins at the head end, a bronze knob from a dagger or knife, and at the foot end along with the urns and *Patellenhut* two iron points.

Grave goods:

Fragmentary sheet bronze socket with two iron rivets perpendicular to each other (fig. 73f). Fragmentary remains of iron spearheads, probably of two (fig. 73d, e, g). Two fragmentary bronze shepherd's crook pins (fig. 73a, b). The bronze *Patellenhut* is missing, as it was when the collection was in Zurich.

Sherds of one or more large vessels of reddish-brown and dark gray color with thick walls. Below the rim were nipples (fig. 73i). Sherds of a reddish-brown vessel with thin, straight walls and a flat narrow rim (fig. 73c). Sherds of a vessel of dark gray color and fine fabric; above the shoulder are three vertical ridges (fig. 73j). Sherds of a large dark gray lid; it is decorated with grooves in zigzag or chevron patterns. The handle is shaped like a vessel and has oblique flutings around the body (fig. 73h).

GRAVE 19a

In the remains of what the excavators interpreted as a badly disturbed grave just east of the main grave (Grave 19) were found decorated fragments of sheet gold.

Grave goods:

Numerous fragments of sheet gold decorated with raised circles and tiny impressed dots around them. Among the fragments is one of triangular shape (fig. 74).

Associated with this grave when it was studied in Zurich was a string of glass and amber beads (fig. 74a, b), but these are not mentioned in the excavation notes. Dark blue four-cornered bead with white spirals at the corners, D. across the corners 1.8 cm. Dark blue bead intermediate in shape between four-cornered and round, with four white spirals, D. 1.35 cm. Three dark blue beads with white zigzag lines, D. 1.3, 1.3, 1.2 cm. Dark blue bead, D. 1.0 cm. Small dark blue beads, 157 in all, D. 0.3 to 0.4 cm. Yellow bead, D. 0.4 cm. Nine amber beads, D. about 0.4 cm.

GRAVE 20

Beneath two stones and in a burned layer were the remains of a brown vessel, two arm rings, and at least 15 amber beads.

Grave goods:

Two thin bronze rings with overlapping ends. The better preserved one has zones of segmentation (fig. 75a). The other may have had similar ornament but is badly corroded (fig. 75b). Fifteen amber beads, ranging in D. from 1.6 to 2.4 cm (fig. 75c). Weathered sherds of brownish-gray pottery, some with graphite coating on the exterior.

GRAVE 21

The excavation notes call this a child's grave. Its base was situated at a depth of 1.8 m below the surface of the tumulus. The grave was 1.4 m long, 0.7 m wide, and 0.4 m deep. Found at the foot end of the grave were a ceramic vessel and eight small arm rings, as well as 20 small beads of amber and glass. A lid is also mentioned.

Grave goods:

Fragments of eight or nine solid-bronze rings, all of them segmented (four in fig. 76a–d). The Ext. D. range from 4.7 to 6.2 cm. Nineteen beads survive of the 20 recorded by the excavators (fig. 76e). One is bronze, D. 0.7 cm; four are amber, D. 0.9 to 1.1 cm; one is white glass, D. 0.8 cm; one colorless transparent glass, D. 0.9 cm; seven dark blue glass, D. 0.7 to 0.9 cm; one dark blue glass with three solid white eyes, D. 0.9 cm; two dark blue glass with three blue-and-white eyes, D. 0.8 and 0.9 cm; and two dark blue glass with yellow zigzag lines, D. 0.9 and 1.1 cm.

Sherds of a red lid. A red slip covers the exterior; a graphite band covers the rim exterior, and more graphite coating covers the central portion (fig. 76f). Sherds of another vessel of similar pottery and probably of similar form, also with red slip and graphite coating.

GRAVE 22

At the level of the natural ground surface were found some 90 amber beads and eight badly preserved earrings. The length of the grave was 3.5 m, its width 0.9 m, and it had been dug 0.05 m into the natural ground. The bottom of the grave was 1.1 m below the surface of the tumulus.

Grave goods:

Fragments of at least three bronze band earrings decorated with repoussé lines and dots (fig. 77a, f, g). Fragments of a broad band ring of bronze, wider than the earrings, with holes at the ends, flat parallel grooves in the surface, and very fine oblique incised lines along some of the ridges (one fragment in fig. 77b). Fragment of a similar ring without the very fine oblique incised lines (fig. 77c). Other fragments of sheet bronze with repoussé ornament (two in fig. 77d, e). Seventy-two amber beads, D. 0.9 to 1.4 cm (fig. 77h).

GRAVE 23

The grave was oriented south-north and was 2.1 m long, 0.9 m wide, and had been dug 0.15 m into the natural ground beneath the tumulus. The bottom of the grave was 1.6 m below the surface of the tumulus. At the head end was a high packing of five stones. In the grave were 94 amber beads, a broken glass bead, and two small arm rings, one of them broken. One note further mentions a spindle whorl.

Grave goods:

Two solid bronze rings with overlapping ends, decorated with groups of incised lines; Ext. D. of complete one 5.4 cm (fig. 78b). Eighty-nine amber beads, D. 0.9 to 2.7 cm; the long bead in the drawing is 2.7 cm long, 1.8 cm wide, and 1.1 cm thick (fig. 78a). Large glass bead of transparent pale green color, D. 2.1 cm (fig. 78c). Brown spindle whorl with two grooves around the lower portion, D. 3.1 cm (fig. 78d).

GRAVE 24

This grave was 2.1 m long and 0.6 m wide, and it had been dug 0.15 m into the natural ground beneath the tumulus. The bottom of the grave was 1.4 m below the surface of the mound. At the foot end were an urn and a fragment of a knife.

Grave goods:

Fragment of an iron knife; near one end is a rectangular hole; surviving L. 8.5 cm (fig. 79b). Sherds of a footed vessel dark gray in color with rows of three pointed nipples on the upper part of the body (fig. 79a). The exterior surface is shiny dark gray.

GRAVE 25

This grave was 2.4 m long, 1.2 m wide, and had been dug 0.2 m into the natural ground beneath the tumulus. The depth from the tumulus surface to the bottom of the grave was 1.8 m. Two high-standing stones were found in the grave, as well as a blue glass bead, sherds of pottery, and a small arm ring. Goldberg interpreted the small number of sherds recovered to indicate that the grave had been robbed.

Grave goods:

Segmented bronze ring; Ext. D. 5.9 cm (fig. 80a). Dark blue glass bead, D. 1.9 cm (fig. 80b). Sherds of a reddish-brown vessel.

GRAVE 26

Associated with a small burned area and a stone were sherds of an urn and two broken leg rings. Goldberg suggested that this grave may have been disturbed, apparently because of the small number of sherds from the urn recovered.

Grave goods:

Fragments of two thin segmented bronze rings, Ext. D. around 10 cm (one in fig. 81). Sherds of a large reddish-brown vessel.

GRAVE 27

Cremation grave. Beneath the stone packing at the head end of Grave 23 were burned bones, an iron knife, a small bronze weapon ring, and a knob and loop fitting for the knife. One note mentions a second weapon ring.

Grave goods:

Fragment of an iron knife; L. now 11.5 cm (fig. 82b). Another iron fragment, probably part of a smaller knife; surviving L. 7.1 cm (fig. 82a). Sheet bronze attachment with six bronze rivets holding front and back together; L. 5.8 cm, W. 3.1 cm (fig. 82c). Small bronze profiled three-sided ornament on a fragmentary belt attachment of sheet bronze, L. of ornament 3.2 cm (fig. 82d). Small plain solid bronze ring; Ext. D. 2.4 cm (fig. 82f). Fragments of a thin flattish bronze ring with a groove in the middle surrounded by two ridges; the tapering end is decorated with incised lines in herringbone pattern (fig. 82g). Solid lump of bronze, roughly 2.1 by 1.4 by 1.4 cm (fig. 82e).

Many fragments of burned bone, too small to be identified as human or animal.

Among the burned bone fragments were several small bronze objects encrusted with charcoal and ash, apparently not noticed by the excavators or by the scholars organizing the collection in Zurich. Cleaning of the fragments revealed feet of three fibulae and three other fibula parts. Foot of a long Certosa fibula, too badly corroded to tell whether or not the top was originally decorated (fig. 82l). Feet of two smaller Certosa fibulae, one with a flattish knob surviving on the end (fig. 82h, j). Bow of a fibula, probably belonging with the foot with the surviving knob (fig. 82i). Small fragment of a fibula bow (fig. 82m). Fragmentary spring of a fibula (fig. 82k).

GRAVE 28

Cremation grave. In this grave were two broken upper arm rings and another arm ring. Mentioned in other notes are two red and two black urns, a small pot, and a spindle whorl.

Grave goods:

Fragments of two large segmented bronze rings (one in fig. 83a). Smaller segmented bronze ring, closed; Ext. D. 7.7 cm (fig. 83b).

Associated with this grave group in Zurich and still present (but not mentioned in the excavation notes) is a fragmentary object of sheet bronze. In the center is a raised circular boss, riveted onto another piece of sheet bronze with a circular cutout in it (fig. 83h). (The object bears some morphological resemblance to an iron shield boss from Vinji Vrh [Stare 1973a, pl. 51,6].)

Sherds of a large black footed bowl with broad vertical flutings on the shoulder; restored mouth D. about 21 cm (fig. 83i). The exterior had a shiny black surface. Sherds of a small globular vessel of light to dark gray pottery; around the base of the neck is a row of impressions. Restored H. about 14 cm (fig. 83j). The neck and at least part of the body have a shiny black coating on the exterior. Sherds of a grayish-brown cylindrical vessel with lugs shaped like upside-down U's just below the rim (fig. 83k). Rim sherds of a lid of reddish color with a brick red slip and graphite band on the exterior (fig. 83d). Sherds of a pinkish-cream vessel; some have a raised band on them similar to those of vessels from Este. Traces of red slip remain on some (fig. 83e, f). Sherd of a reddish vessel with remains of roughly rectangular lug (fig. 83g). Dark gray spindle whorl, D. 3.4 cm (fig. 83c).

(The lack of correspondence between the scanty notes on this grave and the relative abundance of material now associated with this grave number makes the integrity of this group open to question.)

GRAVE 29

At a depth of 1.2 m next to a stone were two arm rings, 64 amber beads, and two blue glass beads.

Grave goods:

Two segmented bronze rings with overlapping ends and Ext. D. of 7.5 cm (one in fig. 84b). Sixty-four amber beads, D. 1.0 to 3.4 cm, and two dark blue glass beads with white zigzag lines, D. 1.1 and 1.2 cm (fig. 84a).

GRAVE 30

A large packing of stone slabs covered this grave (fig. 85a). Beneath a layer of earth containing much iron at a depth of 4.9 m in the tumulus was a burned layer in a pit which had been dug 30 cm into the natural ground beneath the tumulus. The grave was 3.1 m long and 1.1 m wide, and the depth from the surface of the tumulus to the bottom of the grave was 5.2 m. Directly beneath the stone slabs in the grave were a bronze cuirasse (fig. 85b), well preserved though somewhat crushed, and in a circle three ceramic vessels, two of them of unusual shape. One had four little vessels at the rim (to the right of the cuirasse in fig. 85b). Also recovered in the grave were two iron spearheads and some round buttons.

Grave goods:

The Duchess gave the sheet bronze cuirasse, along with other special objects from her excavations, to Kaiser Wilhelm II, who presented it on loan to the Prehistoric Museum (now the Staatliches Museum für Vor- und Frühgeschichte) in Berlin. It has been missing since World War II. Several photographs of the cuirasse taken during and after its removal from the grave survive in the Mecklenburg Collection (fig. 85 c–e). (See also the published photograph of the object in Schmid 1933, p. 275, fig. 48, and Schuchhardt 1935, p. 185, fig. 158 [the helmet shown in the photograph was not found with the cuirasse].)

Sixty-seven bronze buttons, most with a small boss in the middle; on the backs are loops. D. of majority 1.6 to 1.7 cm (some in fig. 85l, m). Two iron spearheads, both badly preserved; surviving L. 28.0 and 22.6 cm (fig. 85f, g).

Sherds of a large reddish-brown vessel with broad vertical ribs outlined at the top by shallow grooves. The high cylindrical neck had two raised bands at its base. Much of the body exterior is coated with a reddish slip (fig. 85h). Small undecorated light brown vessel of coarse texture (fig. 85j). Sherds of a brownish footed vessel. The join between foot and body is decorated with broad flat flutings and coated with graphite. Much of the body is also graphite-coated (fig. 85i). Sherds of two lids of reddish color with traces of graphite coating (one in fig. 85k).

The ceramic vessel with four small vessels on its shoulder is now at the Staatliches Museum für Vor- und Frühgeschichte in Berlin (fig. 85n–p). (This vessel has been published; see Schuchhardt 1935, p. 184, fig. 157c.)

GRAVE 31

The excavation notes call this a child's grave. It was 2.5 m long, 0.6 m wide, and had been dug down 0.2 m into the ground. The bottom of the grave was 2.45 m below the surface of the tumulus. Two stones were found, and next to them two bowls, two glass beads, and remains of an earring.

Grave goods:

Dark blue glass bead with white wavy line, D. 1.4 cm (fig. 86e). Lighter blue glass bead with five large rounded knobs, D. 1.4 cm (fig. 86d). Fragment of a small bronze band ring with two longitudinal grooves and incised lines along the edges of the surviving end; Ext. D. about 2.0 cm (fig. 86f).

When the collection arrived at the Peabody Museum three ceramic vessels were associated with this grave. Small undecorated grayish-brown vessel, H. about 9.75 cm (fig. 86a). Small undecorated vessel of double conical form and grayish-tan color, H. about 12 cm (fig. 86b). Small undecorated pinkish-cream vessel with a globular body and with remains of a shiny black coating (not graphite) on the exterior (fig. 86c).

The first two are represented in the photographs of the contents of this grave taken in Zurich. Under Grave 33 the Zurich group recorded a "small urn, in sherds," which would fit figure 86c here. Hence the vessel in figure 86c probably belongs with Grave 33. I include it in the figure with this grave because its correct association cannot be determined with certainty, and because it arrived associated with Grave 31.

GRAVE 32

This grave was covered by a stone slab, and other slabs had been placed along the sides. The length of the grave was 4.05 m, its width 0.9 m (in another note 1.35 m), and it had been dug 1.05 m into the ground. The bottom was 2.45 m or 1.9 m below the surface of the mound. It was the deepest grave found so far in Tumulus IV. At the bottom of the grave was a gray clayey layer on which were 190 (or 160) amber beads. The grave was divided in the middle by a stone slab, and Goldberg suggested that the grave was probably a double one. On one side were two large ear pendants and two large earrings of bronze wire. Mentioned in other notes are parts of a fibula with birds on it, a flower (*Blumen*) fibula, and a belt fastening.

Grave goods:

Fragmentary bronze serpentine fibula with two pairs of horns ornamented with large balls bearing smaller ones on top. On the bow is riveted a small bird figurine (fig. 87a). Sheet bronze attachment for a belt with ribbed bronze ring attached; one side of the attachment is decorated with rows of small bosses on the edges and a wave pattern of tiny hammered dots between them (fig. 87b). Solid bronze ring of diamond-shaped section, Ext. D. 3.6 cm (fig. 87c). Many fragments of rings of thick bronze wire with a twist pattern (fig. 87d, f). Fragments of thin bronze bands from a ring (fig. 87e). Small fragment of bronze spiral with a straight piece extending from it, perhaps part of a fibula (fig. 87g). Several fragments of spirals consisting of flat bronze wire, D. of spiral 0.9 cm (one in fig. 87i). Amber beads, 159 in all, D. 0.7 to 0.9 cm (fig. 87h).

GRAVE 33

This grave was 4.7 (or 2.7) m long and 1.65 m wide. It had been dug down 0.35 m into the ground. From the grass on top of the tumulus to the bottom of the grave was 2.1 m. Mentioned as finds were small fragments of sheet gold, some small amber beads, two earrings, a small urn, and a spindle whorl. The excavators suggested that the grave had been robbed, apparently because of the poor quality of the objects recovered relative to the large size of the grave.

Grave goods:

Small folded bits of gold foil. Ten amber beads, D. 0.7 to 1.0 cm (some in fig. 88c). Small hollow ring of sheet bronze, Ext. D. about 2 cm (fig. 88b). Pale orange and gray spindle whorl, D. 3.8 cm (fig. 88a). The inventory made in Zurich mentions sherds of a small urn. The vessel from this grave may be that in figure 86c (see Grave 31, above).

GRAVE 34

Neither information about the grave nor grave goods survive.

GRAVE 35

This grave was 2.75 m long, 0.9 m wide, and had been dug 0.5 m into the ground. The depth from the tumulus surface to the top of the grave was 1.6 m, to the bottom it was 2.1 m. Three small stones had been placed at the head end of the grave. A brown ceramic urn was found at the foot end. Fifty-seven small amber beads were found as well as a small broken earring and two badly preserved arm rings.

Grave goods:

Fragments of two bronze rings consisting of bands with three ridges and two grooves and with incised chevrons at the ends; W. 0.7 cm (one in fig. 89b). Small fragmentary ring of sheet bronze with three ridges (fig. 89d). Fifty amber beads and fragments of several others, D. 0.7 to 1.0 cm (some in fig. 89c).

Sherds of a gray bowl on a low foot (fig. 89a).

GRAVE 36

This grave was next to Grave 35. Two small stones had been placed at the head end of the grave, and at the foot end was an urn. Near the urn were approximately 30 very small blue glass beads. Also found were a small bronze ring from a belt fastener and a bronze belt hook. These last two were recovered in the process of clearing and were thought to belong to Grave 36.

Grave goods:

Fragments of a sheet bronze belt plate with bronze hook riveted to it with bronze rivets (fig. 90c). Fragmentary loop of sheet bronze from a belt attachment, with a bronze rivet (fig. 90d). Solid bronze ring much worn on the interior on one side; Ext. D. 2.6 cm (fig. 90b). Fragment of sheet bronze, apparently damaged by heat. Thirty-eight very small dark blue glass beads, D. 0.3 to 0.4 cm (some in fig. 90e).

Sherds of a dark brownish-gray vessel of double conical form, with three nipples on the upper part, and around and below these a semicircular area of excised or impressed dots (fig. 90a). On the shoulder are short, oblique flutings.

GRAVE 37

This grave was close to Grave 36. At the foot end were a brown bowl, an iron knife, and an iron hook.

Grave goods:

Fragment of an iron spearhead (the "knife" of the excavation notes) (fig. 91a). Sherds of a bowl of brownish-gray color with a perforated lug on one side (the rim opposite is missing); Ext. mouth D. about 19.5 cm (fig. 91b). The iron hook is missing, as it was when the collection was organized in Zurich.

GRAVE 38

Underneath a stone was found a high urn, a large arm ring as well as a small child's, and 27 amber beads. Above these objects were three teeth, the only remains of the body. The bottom of the grave lay at a depth of 2.05 m from the surface of the tumulus. A small burned area is mentioned. Other notes mention a celt and an iron spearhead found above the other objects.

(It is unclear from the notes whether the celt and spearhead were part of the same grave as the other objects. The notes do not indicate how far above the other items these weapons were found. Although all of these objects may have belonged to the same grave as the scholars in Zurich thought, I am not fully confident of the integrity of this group.)

Grave goods:

Segmented bronze ring with ends that meet; Ext. D. 7.4 cm (fig. 92f). Segmented bronze ring with overlapping ends; Ext. D. 5.0 cm (fig. 92g). Fragments of two iron spearheads: two fragments of the middle parts, with the upper portion of the socket and the beginning of the midrib preserved in each case (fig. 92a, b). Fragmentary base of one of the spearheads, with a small hole in it 3.2 cm from the bottom (fig. 92c). Very small fragments of an iron axe. Twenty-seven amber beads, D. 0.7 to 1.2 cm (some in fig. 92e).

Sherds of a light grayish-brown vessel of situla form, with small nipples just below the shoulder, probably originally four of them (fig. 92d).

GRAVE 39

This grave was 2.35 m long, 1.05 m wide, and it had been dug down 0.8 m into the ground. The top of the grave was 1.6 m below the surface of the tumulus, the bottom was 2.4 m below it. The grave was oriented west-east. At the foot end were found scattered sherds of a brown bowl. Goldberg thought that the grave had been robbed.

Grave good:

Sherds of a dark grayish-brown bowl with a perforated lug just below the rim on one side; Ext. mouth D. about 17 cm (fig. 93).

GRAVE 40

Cremation grave. The grave was 2.85 m long, 0.95 m wide, and had been dug down 15 cm into the ground. The top of the grave was 2.1 m below the surface of the tumulus, its bottom 2.25 m below it. The grave was oriented southeast-northwest. At the northwest end were a brown urn with a lid, together with a ceramic bowl. In the bowl were two broken arm rings. At the southwest side of the grave were a broken bronze belt plate, an iron point, and a small decorative or weapon ring. In the middle of the grave was an area of burned bones among which were remains of an arm ring. One note further mentions a spindle whorl.

Grave goods:

Fragments of two hollow bronze rings. One has a width of 1.1 cm and is decorated with regular ribbing (fig. 94g). This ring appears to have been damaged by fire. The other is 0.7 cm wide and decorated with groups of three raised ridges separated by broader bulges (fig. 94e). Fragments of a small sheet bronze belt plate with bronze hook and rivets (fig. 94k). Fragment of another sheet bronze belt plate with remains of an iron hook and of an iron band riveted to the back of the plate (fig. 94j). Fragmentary belt attachment of sheet bronze with three bronze rivets and oblique incised lines along the edges (fig. 94l). Fragmentary sheet bronze belt attachment with a loop (fig. 94m). Small segmented bronze ring, Ext. D. 2.4 cm (fig. 94h). Other fragments of sheet bronze, one with two bronze rivets (fig. 94n).

Fragment of an iron spearhead (fig. 94i).

Sherds of a footed vessel of pinkish-cream color with a dark red slip on the exterior and graphite bands on the neck and lower part of the body (fig. 94b). The interiors of the rim and the foot have a shiny black coating (not graphite) on them. Handle and other sherds of a pale orange lid with traces of graphite bands (fig. 94a). Handle of a lid, tan in color (fig. 94d). Sherds of a cylindrical vessel of coarse brown pottery (fig. 94c). Spindle whorl of spherical shape and dark reddish-gray color, D. 3.8 cm (fig. 94f).

GRAVE 41a

The excavation records assembled in Zurich with Grave 41 form two groups, each describing a particular grave location and inventory of objects which do not overlap with the other. Probably two distinct graves were assigned the same number by the excavators through an oversight. I call one Grave 41a and the other Grave 41b.

Between two arranged stones at a depth of 1.2 m in the tumulus was a small burned area about 0.4 by 0.7 m. In this burned area were an iron celt, a fragment of an iron knife, a fire-damaged horse bit, four bronze knobs from a harness, nine (or ten) iron arrowheads, and three small bronze decorative or weapon rings.

Grave goods:

Four bronze knobs, two with remains of bands of leather still inside the loops. Each is round with a projecting nipple and has a four-way loop on the back; D. 2.9 cm (one in fig. 95e). Three small six-sided bronze rings. Two have round projecting knobs at the six corners; Max. diagonal across knobs 3.1 cm (one in fig. 95f). The other has a Max. diagonal of 2.7 cm (fig. 95d). Socketed iron axe with remains of wood inside socket; surviving L. 17.3 cm (fig. 95a). Badly corroded iron horse bit of twisted heavy wire (fig. 95c). Fragment of an iron knife (fig. 95b). Numerous other iron fragments.

GRAVE 41b

Just 35 cm beneath the sod were some glass beads and a broken arm ring. Also found were some amber beads.

Grave goods:

Fragment of a bronze ring decorated with zones defined by ridges, containing oblique incised lines; at the surviving end is ribbing (fig. 96c). Glass beads (some in fig. 96b): 56 small blue beads with many projecting knobs, D. 0.6 cm; 64 small white beads with projecting knobs, D. 0.6 cm; 26 small light green beads, D. 0.6 cm; 31 small beads with sheen like mother-of-pearl, D. 0.5 cm; 2 small white beads in the shape of a spool, D. 0.5 cm; 3 small blue beads in the shape of a spool, D. 0.5 cm; dark blue bead with dark blue-and-white eyes arranged obliquely, D. 1.1 cm; dark blue bead with four irregular dark blue-and-white eyes, D. 0.8 cm; dark blue bead with three dark blue-and-white eyes, one of them with an outer circle of yellow instead of white, D. 0.9 cm; dark blue bead with two dark blue-and-white eyes, one of them with an outer circle of yellow, D. 0.8 cm; 1 light blue bead with white-and-dark blue eyes, D. 1.0 cm.

Forty-seven amber beads, D. 1.3 to 3.3 cm (some in fig. 96a).

GRAVE 42

This grave was found above Grave 40, at a depth of 1.7 m below the sod. In the grave were a large string of blue glass beads, a small string of glass beads, a string with very small blue glass beads, and five other glass beads (three blue, one green, one small yellow). Also found was a cross of beads. Notes also mention an arm ring and a very small pendant, perhaps of bronze and amber.

Grave goods:

Glass beads: 54 light greenish-blue beads with white-and-dark blue eyes, some with single eyes, some with double, and some mixed, D. 0.6 to 1.3 cm (some in fig. 97a); 30 beads of light greenish-blue color with dark blue-and-white eyes and many small projecting knobs of yellow paste, D. 1.2 to 1.3 cm (some in fig. 97a); 5 small barrel-shaped beads of dark blue color with knobs projecting from all four sides, L. 0.8 to 1.2 cm (three in fig. 97b); 205 beads ranging in color from lightish to dark blue and in size from D. 0.5 to 1.3 cm (some in fig. 97b); dark blue bead with three white eyes, D. 0.8 cm (fig. 97b).

Small cross-shaped perforated pendant of amber, surviving H. 1.5 cm (fig. 97c).

The arm ring mentioned in the excavation notes is missing.

GRAVE 43

This grave was oriented south-north and was 2.8 m long, 0.95 m wide, and had been dug 0.45 m into the ground (fig. 98a). The top of the grave was 1.80 m below the surface of the tumulus, the bottom 2.25 m below it. In the grave were two large foot rings. At the head end toward the north were 50 amber beads and six glass beads, a small corroded fibula, and in the area of the chest a rod with clappers (*Klapperstäbchen*) and corroded fragments of pendants. At the head end were also an urn and a lid. At the foot end toward the south, just 20 cm from the two large foot rings, were a black bowl and a red vessel.

Grave goods:

Two hollow closed segmented bronze rings, Ext. D. 11.2 cm (one in fig. 98e). Forty-six amber beads, D. 1.0 to 1.7 cm (some in fig. 98g). The cylindrical bead in the illustration is 0.8 cm long. Six glass beads: one pale green bead, D. 1.6 cm; one brown bead with white zig-zag line, D. 1.3 cm; one small brown bead, D. 0.7 cm; and three small dark blue beads, D. 0.6, 0.6, 0.7 cm (fig. 98f).

Sherds of a dark grayish-brown footed vessel with profiled neck (fig. 98c). Handle and other sherds of a light gray lid (fig. 98b). Sherds of a thin-walled light reddish-brown vessel with profiled neck and broad vertical ribs on the shoulder (fig. 98d). Sherds of a second lid of light gray color, this one much thinner than the other (fig. 98h).

The fibula and the *Klapperstäbchen* mentioned in the excavation notes were already missing when the collection was organized in Zurich. The latter was almost certainly one of the group studied by Stare (1973b).

GRAVE 44

This grave was 3.5 m long, 1.1 m wide, and had been dug 0.5 m into the ground. The top of the grave was 1.8 m below the surface of the tumulus, the bottom 2.3 m below it. As the grave was uncovered scattered sherds and burned bones were found. On one side of the grave two stones had been placed. At the west end was an area of broken pottery.

The objects are missing, as they were when the collection was in Zurich.

GRAVE 45

This was called a child's grave. It was oriented east-west and was 2.1 m long, 0.5 m wide, and had been dug 0.35 m into the ground. The top of the grave was 1.3 m below the surface of the tumulus, the bottom 1.65 m below it. In the grave were a small arm ring, a brown bowl, and 12 blue beads.

Grave goods:

Bronze ring with overlapping ends; the outside is profiled and both ends are segmented; Ext. D. 4.5 cm (fig. 99b). Twelve dark blue glass beads, D. 1.2 to 1.3 cm (some in fig. 99c). Dark grayish-brown bowl (fig. 99a).

GRAVE 46

This grave was oriented east-west and was 2.9 m long, 0.9 m wide, and had been dug 0.3 m into the ground. The top of the grave was 1.8 m below the surface of the tumulus, the bottom 2.1 m below it. At the foot end was a red urn; no other grave goods were present.

Grave goods:

Light red footed vessel of situla form. The body is coated with a red slip and has at least three graphite bands on it (fig. 100).

GRAVE 47

This grave was oriented southeast-northwest. At the northwest end under a stone packing were remains of animal bones, thought to be horse bones. The whole grave was laid out with stones, found lying on top of one another. Scattered sherds were recovered in the grave, as were 16 small amber beads, a glass bead, and a spindle whorl. At the southeast end of the grave were more stones and under them burned bones. Among the bones were fragments of a foot ring and of a horse mandible. The length of the grave was 2.8 m, its width 1.25 m, and it had been dug 0.8 m into the ground. The top of the grave was 1.5 m below the surface of the tumulus, the bottom 2.3 m below it. On the basis of the scattered nature of the beads and fragments of a foot ring, the excavators suggested that the grave had been robbed.

Grave goods:

Fragments of a large solid segmented bronze ring (fig. 101c). Sixteen amber beads, D. 0.9 to 1.1 cm (some in fig. 101e). Dark blue glass bead, D. 1.8 cm (fig. 101d).

Sherds of a ram's head rhyton (fig. 101a). (The piece is described by Hoffmann [1966, pp. 96–97]. The pottery is of light tan or buff color. Traces of a black coating survive on parts of the surface. For this object Hoffmann suggests an eastern Adriatic origin, as does Jacobsthal [in a letter of Jan. 5, 1955], and a fourth or third century B.C. date.)

Spindle whorl of dark gray color, D. 3.3 cm (fig. 101b).

Teeth and bone fragments from an adult horse (Bökönyi 1968, p. 16).

GRAVE 48

This grave was very close to Grave 47. It was 3 m long, 1.2 m wide, and had been dug 0.7 m into the ground. The top of the grave lay 1.6 m below the surface of the tumulus, the bottom 2.3 m below it. The excavators found scattered sherds and a fragment of a small iron knife. Because of the scattered sherds, the excavators suggested that the grave had been robbed.

Grave goods:

Fragments of an iron knife (fig. 102b). Sherds of a large footed vessel of reddish color and situla form. The exterior is covered with a red slip and the neck coated with graphite (fig. 102a). Sherds of a vessel of relatively coarse brown pottery (fig. 102c).

GRAVE 49

At its southwest end this grave was connected to Grave 48. It was 3.7 m long, 1.05 m wide, and had been dug 0.6 m into the ground. The top of the grave was 1.45 m below the surface of the tumulus, the bottom 2.05 m below it. On the bottom of the grave toward the northwest was a small broken urn. Above the grave were two spindle whorls.

Grave goods:

Sherds of a low bowl of brown color. Much of the exterior is coated with graphite (fig. 103a). Sherds of a tan vessel; not enough remains to distinguish its form. Two light tan spindle whorls, D. 3.1 and 3.2 cm (fig. 103b, c).

GRAVE 50

Next to two placed stones at a depth of 0.6 m was an area containing intensely burned bones and sherds of a vessel. Two arm rings showing signs of fire were found associated with these items. An oval 4.5 by 3 m formed by placed stones was uncovered, many of the stones of odd shape. This arrangement was situated on an intensely burned area 1.4 m deep in the tumulus. In the middle of the oval was a group of urns. One was a black bowl in relatively good condition. There were sherds of some three other vessels. One meter away was another group of urns. One of these was nearly intact while the others were very fragmentary.

(To judge by the description, two or possibly three graves may be represented by these finds. The burned bones, sherds, and two rings associated with the two stones at a depth of 0.6 m may have been one, and the two groups of urns a meter apart at a depth of 1.4 m may represent a single grave or may be the grave goods from two burials. Since only one vessel is described, the black bowl, it is impossible now to separate the objects into two or three units.)

Grave goods:

Two segmented bronze rings with overlapping ends; Ext. D. 7.4 cm (one in fig. 104m). Sherds of a large black footed vessel decorated with five vertical rows of nipples and pairs of parallel grooves on each side of the rows of nipples (fig. 104g). Sherds of a thin-walled light brown vessel with remains of an upward-pointing nipple on the shoulder (others may also have been present originally) (fig. 104h). Sherds of a brownish-gray bowl with a neck (fig. 104d). Sherds of a brownish-gray bowl with rounded profile (fig. 104c). Sherd of fairly thick brownish-gray pottery with a perforated lug (fig. 104n). Rim sherd of a grayish-tan vessel with a ridge just below the rim (fig. 104b). Sherds of a base of a light tan vessel (fig. 104f). Base sherds of a pinkish-tan vessel (fig. 104e). Sherds of a light pinkish-tan vessel with a red slip and a shiny black coating (not graphite) on parts of the exterior (fig. 104o). Sherds of a thin-walled bowl of tan color with four horizontal grooves just below the rim and broad vertical ribs on the shoulder (fig. 104k). Both interior and exterior are coated with graphite. Dull black sherd with a high pointed nipple (fig. 104j). Sherd of black pottery with a shiny black surface, not graphite (fig. 104o).

GRAVE 51

Cremation grave. One meter from the stone oval of Grave 50 between two placed stones at a depth of 0.5 m was an area of burned bones and burned earth. Associated with this area were a spindle whorl and two large upper arm rings or foot rings.

Grave goods:

Two similar large, closed, segmented, solid bronze rings. One segment on each is flat and is decorated with cross-hatched incised lines; Ext. D. 12.8 cm (one in fig. 105a). Brownish-gray spindle whorl, D. 3.3 cm (fig. 105b).

GRAVE 52

The notes call this a child's grave. It was oriented east-west and was 2.05 m long, 0.45 m wide, and had been dug 0.15 m into the ground. The top of the grave was 0.90 m below the surface of the tumulus, the bottom 1.05 m below it. At the west end was a ceramic bowl, at the east end a spindle whorl.

Grave goods:

Sherds of a dark grayish-brown vessel on a low foot with a high profiled neck (fig. 106b). Thin shallow grooves run around the upper part of the body. Spindle whorl of very light tan color, D. 3.3 cm (fig. 106a).

GRAVE 53

This grave was on the natural ground surface at a depth of 1.9 m below the surface of the tumulus. A small red bowl was found, along with two small arm rings, two exceptionally fine blue beads with yellow dots, three ordinary glass beads, and a serpentine fibula.

Grave goods:

Fragment of a bronze serpentine fibula with a saddle-shaped bend in the bow and a stop disk (fig. 107c). Remains of two similar small segmented bronze rings with overlapping ends, Ext. D. 5.2 cm (one in fig. 107b). Five glass beads: three are dark blue, D. 1.6, 1.7, 1.8 cm; two light blue with four white-and-dark blue eyes and with many small yellow projections, D. across diagonal 1.2 and 1.3 cm (fig. 107d).

Sherds of a wide low footed bowl of orange color. The body is decorated with three horizontal raised bands. The exterior is coated with a reddish-orange slip, and along the rim on the interior is a band of graphite (fig. 107a).

GRAVE 54

Cremation grave. Beneath a stone at a depth of 0.5 m were a broken bowl together with burned bones and two arm rings. From the scattered situation of the sherds the excavators concluded that the grave had been disturbed by a plow or other agency.

Grave goods:

Two similar segmented bronze rings with ends that meet, Ext. D. 7.6 cm (fig. 108d, e). Sherds of a vessel of cylindrical shape. The pottery is orange, and the exterior is coated with an orange-red slip. Around the body are several horizontal grooves and traces of graphite on the exterior. Along the top of the rim is a groove (fig. 108a). Sherds of a large tan foot with profiling and graphite coating on the exterior (fig. 108b). Rim of a bowl of pale orange color coated on the exterior with a reddish-orange slip. Just below the rim on the exterior is a groove (fig. 108c).

GRAVE 55

This grave was covered with large stone slabs; the covering measured 3.65 by 1.80 m. Under the slabs was an intensely burned area. Beneath one of the slabs were scattered fragments of fruit shells or husks (*Fruchtschalen*). The grave had been dug 0.3 m into the ground and was 3.4 m long and 1.3 m wide. The top of the grave was 5.40 m below the surface of the tumulus, the bottom 5.70 m below it. The grave was oriented southeast-northwest. At the southeast end were two bronze wire rings and five amber beads. At the northwest end were two black ceramic vessels. Another note concerning this grave mentions 92 small amber beads, eight spindle whorls, and a small arm ring.

(There is no clear connection in the notes between these two groups of grave goods. The 92 amber beads, eight spindle whorls, and small arm ring are not mentioned in connection with any specific grave features, and these may be from another grave, the description of which is missing.)

Grave goods:

Small closed undecorated bronze ring of oval section, Ext. D. 5.7 cm (fig. 109a). Ninety-two amber beads, most of them barrel-shaped, L. 0.5 to 1.5 cm (some in fig. 109b). Eight spindle whorls of brown, tan, and gray color, D. 2.7 to 3.5 cm (fig. 109c–j). The pottery is missing.

ISOLATED FINDS, TUMULUS IV

Two very similar solid bronze rings with groups of incised lines (one in fig. 110a). Bronze band ring with four grooves around it and a narrow section in the middle (fig. 110c). Fragmentary bronze serpentine fibula with saddle-shaped bend in the bow and two holes at head end (fig. 110f). Two fragmentary small belt attachments of sheet bronze with bronze rivets and solid bronze rings attached. One ring is segmented, Ext. D. 2.4 cm (fig. 110g). The other is not, Ext. D. 2.5 cm (fig. 110b). Foot of a Certosa-type bronze fibula with dot-and-circle ornament (fig. 110h). Two blue glass beads of barrel shape with projections, L. of more complete one 1.2 cm (fig. 110e). Amber bead, D. 1.7 cm (fig. 110d). Two flattish lumps of bronze, one roughly 3 by 3.5 by 1 cm, the other roughly 3 by 2.5 by 0.8 cm.

Tumulus V

Tumulus V was excavated from the beginning of October through October 28, 1913. Twenty graves were found. Figures 111 to 113 show the tumulus and the excavations in progress.

GRAVE 1

Neither information about the grave nor finds are preserved.

GRAVE 2

This grave was found at a depth of 3.65 m in the northeast part of the tumulus (the part nearest the woods). It is described as a child's grave. In the grave were a fine black urn, a wide range of glass and amber beads, a small child's arm ring, four chains, and fragments of spectacle pendants.

Grave goods:

Small bronze ring with overlapping ends, decorated with groups of lines; Ext. D. 4.4 cm (fig. 114g). Parts of at least eight bronze spectacle pendants of various sizes (fig. 114b–h).

Two very large glass beads of opaque greenish-blue color (fig. 114m, o). They are 2.7 and 2.8 cm long, respectively. The smaller is decorated with five dark blue projecting eyes on a white background, with two circles of brown color around each dark blue end. Above and below the projecting eyes is a row of small white opaque glass projections. Around one end is a row of opaque yellow projections. The larger bead has seven dark blue-and-white projecting eyes around its middle. These do not project as far as those on the middle of the other bead, and they consist of a central circle of dark blue color surrounded by two bands of dark blue. Above and below these eyes are two rows of projections of opaque yellow glass.

Twenty dark blue barrel-shaped beads, each with three projections from the middle, L. 0.6 to 1.6 cm (some in fig. 114k). One bead has three yellow projections, one has white ends and white projections.

Twenty-eight opaque greenish-blue beads with dark blue-and-white eyes and projections of opaque yellow glass, D. 1.1 to 1.3 (some in fig. 114l). Twenty-one dark blue beads, D. 0.6 to 0.9 cm (some in fig. 114l). Thirty-five dark blue beads, with white zigzag lines around middles, D. 1.2 to 1.5 cm (some in fig. 114l). Thirty-eight small beads of various colors, some with eyes, some with other decoration, and others plain, D. 0.6 to 0.7 cm (some in fig. 114l). Melon-shaped bead of gray color, D. 1.5 cm (fig. 114l). Opaque yellow bead consisting of a medium-sized bead and a small bead joined together, D. 1.0 cm (fig. 114l).

Two beads with double animal heads facing opposite directions (one in fig. 114n). They are of very light transparent greenish glass with trim of opaque yellow glass. Bands of this yellow glass occur at the top and bottom of the perforated shaft, as well as forming the ears and nose of the animals, and a further projection of this yellow glass occurs on each side of the perforated shaft. The kind of animal represented is unclear. L. 2.4 and 2.5 cm (the latter specimen is missing the nose from one of the heads).

Cross-shaped bead of opaque white glass consisting of two perforated cylinders with a twist pattern on them, joined together at their middles, L. across the arms 5.0 and 4.7 cm (fig. 114n).

Twisted fragment of bronze wire (fig. 114j).

Sixty-nine amber beads (some in fig. 114i). One 2.3 cm long and 1.8 cm in D., one 1.9 cm in D., the rest 0.4 to 1.4 cm in D.

Sherds of a large vessel with a dull black coating over an orange-brown fabric (fig. 114a). The vessel has a broad cylindrical neck, and around the shoulder is a row of roughly rectangular bosses pushed out from the inside.

GRAVE 3

This grave was found at a depth of 4.8 m and contained a red urn.

Grave goods:

Sherds of a footed vessel of situla form of pale pinkish-orange color with a dull red slip on the body exterior. On the neck, the base of the foot, and elsewhere on the body exterior are bands of graphite (fig. 115a). Sherds of a lid of the same kind of pottery, also with a dull red slip and graphite bands. The handle is hollow and shaped like a pot with a rounded body (fig. 115b).

GRAVE 4

Neither information about the grave nor grave goods are preserved.

GRAVE 5

Next to an urn in what the excavators called a double grave were two spindle whorls.

Grave goods:

Two brownish-gray spindle whorls, D. 1.9 and 3.1 cm (fig. 116a, b). The vessel is not preserved.

GRAVE 6

Two small pendants were found in a grave that contained some gold.

Grave goods:

Remains of gold foil. On the largest fragment, now about 3.2 cm long, are decorative bands of pressed lines (fig. 117c). Cylindrical bronze rod with an iron core. The end, which has been damaged, perhaps through exposure to fire, has a collar and a bulb on it; D. of the rod about 0.85 cm, surviving L. 8.1 cm (fig. 117a). Fragmentary object consisting of a thin piece of iron sandwiched between two pieces of bone, perhaps the remains of an iron knife with a bone handle (fig. 117b).

GRAVE 7

In this grave were found small beads, a large fibula, an arm ring, and a large clay pendant.

Grave goods:

Fragmentary segmented bronze ring, Ext. D. 7.9 cm (fig. 118b). Remains of a large bronze fibula, probably of the two-looped variety. The hollow bow is decorated on one side only with groups of incised lines. Adhering to the head end is a solid bronze ring of diamond-shaped section with an Ext. D. of about 4.0 cm and a mass of burned material including bronze, charcoal, bone, and textile (fig. 118d).

Pendant of weathered amber (the excavators thought this was clay) perforated by two holes, L. 4.4 cm, W. 3.2 cm, T. 1.0 cm (fig. 118a). Small amber beads, 227 in all, D. 0.4 to 1.1 cm (some in fig. 118c).

GRAVE 8

In this grave were found a glass ram's head, light blue glass beads, long divided beads, a small glass sun ring, and a long oval enamel bead with wave-shaped line design on top and on bottom blue or yellow borders.

Grave goods:

Greenish-blue glass ring with three small animal heads on the outside. The excavators called them ram's heads, but they are so stylized that any such specific identification is impossible, Ext. D. of ring (not including animal heads) 2.4 cm (fig. 119e). Long thin blue bead, thicker in the middle and thinner at the ends. At the one surviving end is a double collar. The body is decorated with four sets of white zigzag lines, surviving L. 4.45 cm (fig. 119d). Fragmentary small animal head of opaque light blue glass. The eyes are represented by two dark blue-and-white knobs. At the end of the snout is a white spot with two dark blue spirals. A hole up into the head from the shoulder/neck area does not come out the top of the head. The object was apparently placed at the end of a thin projection, surviving L. 1.2 cm (fig. 119c). Four dark blue glass beads, each with four corners ornamented with white spirals; D. across diagonal 1.3 to 1.6 cm (two in fig. 119b). Four dark blue barrel-shaped beads with single white zigzag lines around middles and opaque yellow bands around ends, L. 1.1 to 1.6 cm (two in fig. 119b). Thirty-three small dark blue beads, D. 0.7 cm (some in fig. 119b).

Two long thin amber beads, thickest in the middle and tapering toward the ends, which are profiled, L. 2.9 and 1.8 cm (fig. 119a). Amber bead with three rounded segments, perforated longitudinally, and with a hole through each end segment, L. 2.5 cm (fig. 119a). Two small amber beads, D. 0.7 and 0.8 cm (one in fig. 119a).

GRAVE 9

Cremation grave. A note says that the grave was found at a depth of 0.8 m and contained an urn with some burned bones in it, but no other grave goods.

Grave goods:

Sherds of a dark gray footed vessel. On the shoulder are four sharp nipples pointing upward. Around the body are sets of two parallel grooves placed obliquely, forming a zigzag pattern. In the triangular areas above and below these grooves are large impressed dots surrounded by slightly impressed circles and by outer circles of smaller impressed dots. Original H. about 23 cm (fig. 120).

GRAVE 10

In the grave were found large earrings and two boat-shaped fibulae, one with a pendant hanging from it.

Grave goods:

Fragments of two rings consisting of flat bronze bands. The better preserved one has a Max. Ext. D. of about 6.5 cm (fig. 121b). Fragment of a bow and spring from a bronze arc fibula. The bow is solid, D-shaped in section, and decorated only with two groups of incised lines near the spring (fig. 121c). Fragment of a bronze fibula with three projecting knobs, all apparently broken off. The top of the bow is decorated with many small dots and circles. Both ends are ornamented with heavy profiling (fig. 121a). Acorn- or basket-shaped bronze pendant decorated with two incised lines around the body and a band of cross-hatched incised lines, H. 4.5 cm. The middle of the body is perforated by a small hole (fig. 121e). Bronze pendant consisting of a sphere at one end, a shaft, and an eyelet containing traces of iron, H. 3.2 cm (fig. 121d).

GRAVE 11

At a depth of 2.9 m was a grave which had been dug 0.15 m into the ground. It contained 24 identical glass beads, a small broken bronze ring, and a small bronze plaque.

Grave goods:

Fragment of a solid bronze ring decorated with incised lines (fig. 122c). Fragments of a pair of bronze tweezers (fig. 122a). Fragmentary pendant of sheet bronze with a large boss and a hole in it (fig. 122d). Fragment of another object of sheet bronze, probably a pendant, with a large boss surrounded by impressed dots (fig. 122f). Fragmentary bronze pendant of triangular shape (fig. 122g). Fragmentary narrow band of sheet bronze with fine incised lines along both edges on one face (fig. 122e). Other small fragments of sheet bronze.

Twenty-five vase-shaped beads of colorless transparent glass, L. 1.6 to 2.1 cm (some in fig. 122b).

GRAVE 12

Neither information about the grave nor finds are preserved.

GRAVE 13

This grave was found at a depth of 3.65 m and was called a child's grave by the excavators. In it were two small urns, a small arm ring, and several small blue glass beads.

Grave goods:

Small solid bronze ring with diamond-shaped section, decorated with incised lines, some lateral and others forming chevrons, Ext. D. 4.1 cm (fig. 123d).

Twenty-four blue glass beads, ranging in color from light blue to dark blue, D. 0.35 to 0.7 cm (some in fig. 123a).

Small grayish-brown vessel of coarse texture, H. about 9 cm (fig. 123c). Small brownish-orange vessel with rounded sides, with three small nipples, H. about 5 cm (fig. 123b).

GRAVE 14

At a depth of about 4 m was a layer of wood, and on it was a largely disintegrated bronze cauldron (fig. 124a).

Grave good:

Remains of a bronze cauldron with double cross handle attachments. Just below the rim on the exterior is a series of parallel incised lines with incised linear patterns between some of them. The handles are thin and undecorated (fig. 124b).

(The photograph of this cauldron in the grave [fig. 124a] shows a vessel with handles ornamented with a twist pattern. Either the photograph or the cauldron now associated with this grave must be incorrectly attributed. The photograph and the cauldron fragments now with this grave number were attributed to the same grave by the scholars working in Zurich, probably through an oversight.)

GRAVE 15

At a depth of 5.2 m was a long burned area and on it were two spearheads, a badly preserved double-crested helmet, an iron celt, and iron remains thought by the excavators to be parts of a horse bit.

Grave goods:

Sheet bronze fragments of a helmet, probably of the type consisting of separate pieces riveted together (*mit zusammengesetzter Kalotte*). Most of the surviving fragments are parts of the brim and are decorated with two rows of bosses (largest fragment in fig. 125f). (Very similar fragments were found in Tumulus I, Grave 37 at Brezje [Kromer 1959b, pl. 7; see discussion of the type with illustrations in Gabrovec 1960, pp. 39, 55–56, 59–61, 72–79, figs. 2, 8–15].) Small pin made of sheet bronze folded together, with hole at one end, perhaps part of the helmet; surviving L. 2.7 cm (fig. 125e). Socketed iron axe, now 19.5 cm long, containing remains of wood (fig. 125b). Fragmentary iron spearhead with long socket and small head, without a distinct midrib; surviving L. 17 cm (fig. 125c). Large iron spearhead with distinct midrib; surviving L. 32.5 cm (fig. 125a). Fragments of an iron horse bit (fig. 125d).

GRAVE 16

On a burned layer were found many beads of various kinds, including some especially fine glass beads.

Grave goods:

Glass beads (fig. 126a): Fifteen beads of pale green color, transparent, with a yellow zigzag line around middle, D. 1.2 to 1.7 cm. Two light brown transparent beads with white zigzag line around middle; D. 1.2 and 1.3 cm. Two dark yellow transparent beads with white zigzag line around middle; D. 1.3 cm. Five dark blue beads, D. 1.0 to 1.3 cm. Nine dark blue beads with white zigzag line around middle, D. 1.2 to 1.4 cm. About 135 very small dark blue glass beads, D. 0.3 to 0.5 cm. About 355 very small white glass beads, D. 0.3 to 0.5 cm. About 92 very small yellow glass beads, D. 0.4 to 0.5 cm.

Three disk-shaped bronze beads, D. 0.4 to 0.5 cm (two in fig. 126d).

Small iron object, perforated as a bead or pendant, with broken shaft (fig. 126c).

Amber beads, 202 in all, D. 0.3 to 1.1 cm (some in fig. 126b).

GRAVE 17

This grave, called a child's grave by the excavators, was situated 0.9 m below the humus. Found were two small arm rings, some small glass beads, some amber beads, and a neck ring.

Grave goods:

Remains of a large bronze ring decorated with at least three groups of grooves (fig. 127b). Iron remains adhere to one end. Two small segmented bronze rings with overlapping ends, Ext. D. 4.9 and 4.2 cm (fig. 127c, d). Many fragments of a socketed iron axe (fig. 127a).

Glass beads (fig. 127e): Fourteen very small dark blue beads, D. 0.4 to 0.5 cm. Four very small light blue beads, D. 0.5 cm. Eighteen very small white beads, D. 0.4 cm. One very small yellow bead, D. 0.4 cm.

Three very small amber beads, D. 0.4, 0.5, 0.6 cm (fig. 127f).

GRAVE 18

At a depth of 1.6 m on the west side of the tumulus were found a badly preserved double-crested helmet and an iron celt. A badly damaged bronze cauldron was found 1.8 m west of the helmet and celt.

Grave goods:

Fragments of a bronze cauldron with cross-shaped handle attachments. The handles are decorated with a twist pattern. Below the rim on the exterior are parallel incised lines, and some of the zones between them are decorated with groups of fine incised lines (fig. 128b). Fragments of a double-crested helmet of sheet bronze: including one comprising some of the lower part of the front or back with a riveted perforated attachment and part of the brim (fig. 128d); and a fragment from part way up the helmet with remains of three bronze rivets which held the parts of the helmet together (fig. 128c). (For discussion and illustrations of this type of helmet see Gabrovec 1962–1963.) Iron double-winged axe, now 18.7 cm long (fig. 128a).

GRAVE 19

This grave was designated the "central grave" by the excavators. The stone packing over it was situated at a depth of 4.2 m and was 4.05 m long and 1.6 m wide (fig. 129). No grave goods were found. The excavators state that the grave was investigated very carefully, and they interpret the lack of finds to indicate that the grave had been robbed.

GRAVE 20

The notes mention six round amber beads.

Grave goods:

Associated with this grave are six disk-shaped

amber beads, each with a perforation through the center and through one edge and with three dots and circles on one side; D. 2.4 to 2.8 cm, T. 0.6 to 1.0 cm (three in fig. 130).

(It is unclear from the notes whether these beads constitute the goods from a distinct grave.)

Tumulus VI

This tumulus was excavated between November 10 and December 15, 1913 (fig. 131). The mound was on the property of Jacob Trondel. It was oval in shape, measuring 48 m in one direction and 30 m in the other. Work began on the northeast side, which bordered on the north side of Tumulus V. Thirty-two graves were excavated by the Duchess.

GRAVE 1

This was called a child's grave by the excavators. The top of the grave was 1.6 m deep in the tumulus. The grave had been dug 0.28 m into the ground, hence its bottom was 1.88 m below the surface of the tumulus. The grave was 1.6 m long, 0.67 m wide, and it was oriented north-south. On the bottom of the grave was a thin burned layer. On it were a fibula, two small arm rings, some small amber beads, and a small broken boat-shaped fibula.

Grave goods:

Two small segmented bronze rings with overlapping ends, Ext. D. between 5.0 and 5.5 cm (fig. 132a, b). Thirty-three amber beads, D. 1.0 to 1.3 cm (some in fig. 132c).

The two fibulae are missing, and apparently they were missing when the collection was in Zurich.

(Now associated with this grave are two enormous amber beads, each with two large amber beads attached by a bronze and an iron pin, respectively. These beads are not mentioned in the excavation notes, and it is unlikely that such exceptionally large specimens would have escaped mention. A note written by one of the scholars in Zurich on one of the index cards suggests that these beads may belong to the material excavated by the Duchess at Vinica.)

GRAVE 2

This grave was found 1.6 m north of Grave 1. It was situated at a depth of 2.05 m, and it had been dug 8 cm into the natural ground below the tumulus. It was oriented north-south and was 2.05 m long and 0.86 m wide. At one end was a crushed reddish-brown urn. No other objects were found.

Grave goods:

Sherds from several vessels are now associated with this grave number. One is an orange situla on a low foot with a broad graphite band around the neck and traces of another on the foot; H. about 21 cm (fig. 133b). Sherds of a dark reddish-brown vessel of globular form with disk-shaped nipples applied as separate pieces to the shoulder (three survive on the extant sherds) (fig. 133a). Sherds of a light reddish-brown foot with graphite coating on the exterior (fig. 133c).

(Since the excavation notes mention only one urn, there is some confusion here. Some of the sherds belonging to these vessels are labeled Grave 3, hence some mixing probably occurred.)

GRAVE 3

This grave was found at a depth of 1.85 m. It was covered with stone slabs placed obliquely and was oriented southeast-northwest. The stone packing was 3.9 m long and 1.05 (or 0.95) m wide. The grave itself was 3.2 m long, 1.05 m wide, and had been dug 20 cm into the ground. Thus the bottom of the grave was 2.05 m below the surface of the tumulus. During the excavation the investigators recognized what they interpreted as evidence for disturbance of the grave. The stone packing was disturbed, and pottery and bones were scattered about. On the stone packing were found a fragment of a skull and leg and arm bones. Goldberg wrote that although the grave was excavated with great care, only three black urns, a red footed urn, and an amber bead were found.

Grave goods:

Many sherds of a large pale orange vessel. The body exterior and the interior of the rim are coated with a dull red slip, and around the middle is a graphite band. On the neck are three bands bordered by ridges, the top band coated with graphite. The foot is now missing (fig. 134a). Sherds of a small polished black vessel, probably once with a foot. The color and general character suggest Etruscan bucchero. On the shoulder are four groups of three parallel vertical ridges (fig. 134b). Sherd from the join of the foot and body of a large reddish-brown vessel (fig. 134c). This may be part of the same vessel as the fragmentary foot now associated with Grave 2 (fig. 133c). Sherds of thick, dark brownish-gray pottery.

Amber bead, D. 1.8 cm (fig. 134d).

GRAVE 4

This grave was found 3.2 m southeast of Grave 3. It was 1.9 m deep in the tumulus and had been dug 8 cm into the natural ground. It was oriented southeast-northwest and was 2.3 m long and 0.8 m wide. At the southeast end was a ceramic vessel; one set of notes says it was a crushed red urn, the other that it was a crushed black footed urn. No other objects were found.

Grave good:

Brownish-gray vessel with four large perforated lugs on the shoulder, restored H. about 20 cm (fig. 135).

(This vessel does not fit the description of the urn in either set of excavation notes.)

GRAVE 5

This grave was found at a depth of 1.3 m. It was 2.4 m long, 0.85 m wide, and had been dug 20 cm into the ground. The bottom of the grave was thus 1.5 m below the surface of the tumulus. The grave was oriented northeast-southwest. Figure 136 shows Graves 5, 6, and 7, all of which were thought to have been dug into the natural ground beneath the tumulus.

No objects were found in Grave 5.

GRAVE 6

This grave was oriented east-west and was at a depth of 1.95 m. It was situated on the level of the natural ground surface. On the bottom of the grave four stones had been placed obliquely, and in the middle was a reddish-white sandstone slab 2.85 m long and 1.1 m wide. Underneath it was a black burned area.

No objects were found in this grave.

GRAVE 7

This grave was found at a depth of 1.8 m. Above the grave in an area some 2 m in D. were many small red and black sherds, many small blue and white glass beads, small amber beads, and a fragment of an amber fibula bearing a carved bird figure. Also found was a small piece of gold sheet or foil. Since no other objects were recovered, Goldberg concluded that the grave had been robbed.

Grave goods:

Perforated carved piece of amber, probably originally attached to the bow of a fibula. It is made of three pieces of amber fastened together. On the top of the largest piece is a small figure of a sitting bird, perhaps a duck. At the outer end of this piece are nine very small holes surrounding the central perforation. Remains of metal, probably bronze, are visible inside the perforation. L. 2.0 cm (fig. 137m).

Twelve small amber beads, D. 0.5 to 1.2 cm (nine in fig. 137j).

Glass beads (fig. 137l): 27 small dark blue beads, D. 0.7 to 0.8 cm; 202 very small dark blue beads, D. 0.3 to 0.5 cm; 38 very small white beads, D. 0.3 to 0.5 cm; 175 very small pale blue beads, D. 0.3 to 0.5 cm; 9 very small yellow beads, D. 0.3 to 0.4 cm.

Three very small bronze beads, D. 0.3 to 0.4 cm (two in fig. 137k).

Two small fragments of gold foil.

Sherds of a footed vessel of orange color, the exterior coated with a dull red slip. Around the neck is a graphite band (fig. 137b). Sherds of a reddish-orange bowl, coated on the exterior with a dull red slip and with a graphite band just below the rim (fig. 137e). Sherds of a vessel of shiny black pottery resembling Etruscan bucchero (fig. 137h).

Several other objects now associated with this grave were thought by the scholars in Zurich to belong with it. It is unclear why they thought so; perhaps they were packed in boxes labeled with this grave number. Since Goldberg's notes state explicitly that no further finds other than those mentioned were made, it seems unlikely that these belong to Grave 7. The slips of paper associated with these objects indicate that they come from Tumulus VI. The items in question are the following:

Fragmentary bronze pendant with human head. The facial features are distinctly indicated. On top of the head is an eyelet for suspension. On the throat is a dot and circle, similar to the eyes, and below this double parallel lines (fig. 137a). Fragments of three bronze pendants in the form of roosters. The head has a comb and dot-and-circle eyes; the tail is decorated with incised lines. Dots and circles ornament the body. Rising from the middle is a shaft with an eyelet (fig. 137d, g, i). Fragment of a fourth rooster pendant. Hollow triangular ornament of sheet bronze with relief decoration of concentric circles and with an outside circle of small hammered dots (fig. 137c). Small knobbed bronze fragment, perhaps part of another pendant (fig. 137f).

GRAVE 8

Near the southeast edge of the mound at a depth of 1.6 m was a bronze kettle in a burned area. In the kettle were knobs with loops, thought to be ornaments for a horse.

Grave goods:

Remains of a cauldron of sheet bronze with joined cross-shaped handle attachments and smooth handles round in section. There is no trace of incised ornament on the exterior. Ext. D. at rim about 25.5 cm (fig. 138a). Four bronze knobs, round with a projecting central point. On the back of each knob is a four-part loop. The loop on one knob contains remains of leather crossing straps (fig. 138g); D. 2.9 cm. Four sheet bronze belt attachments with loops and rings and with four bronze rivets each. One has both edges folded under; surviving L. 9.3 cm (fig. 138f). The other three do not have folded-under edges. One has an additional attachment, perpendicular to the main part; L. 8.2 cm (fig. 138e). Three small solid bronze rings, Ext. D. 2.9, 3.4, 3.7 cm (fig. 138b–d). Fragment of a sheet bronze attachment with remains of two rivets (fig. 138h). Small iron fragment with a hole filled by a bronze rivet (fig. 138i).

GRAVE 9

This grave was found at a depth of 2.1 m. Above a setting of blue stone slabs were two reddish-white sandstone slabs. The grave was oriented southeast-northwest and was on the natural ground surface. At the base of the grave was a thin burned layer. On it at the southeast end were two broken black urns. Also on the burned layer were some small bronze beads and amber beads, as well as a dress pin.

Grave goods:

Seventeen small bronze beads, D. 0.6 to 0.9 cm (six in fig. 139b). Fragments of a many-knobbed bronze pin (fig. 139a). Eleven amber beads, D. 1.0 to 1.6 cm (five in fig. 139c).

The pottery is missing, as it was when the collection was in Zurich.

GRAVE 10

At a depth of 2.1 (or 2.2) m and 3.4 m away from Grave 9 was a setting of obliquely placed blue stone slabs, oriented southwest-northeast. Beneath it was a grave 3.05 m long and 1.05 m wide which had been dug 25 cm into the natural ground. On the bottom of the grave was a thin burned layer in which were found remains of a skull, vertebrae, ribs, and leg bones. At the northeast end of the grave were two crushed black urns, and next to them were two badly preserved iron spearheads with points toward the northeast and a small iron ring.

Grave goods:

Two similar iron spearheads with large midribs, both badly preserved (one in fig. 140a). Remains of two iron rings (one in fig. 140d). Small dark gray vessel with some orange coloration, restored H. about 11 cm (fig. 140c). Cylindrical vessel of very coarse texture and reddish-brown color, restored H. about 14 cm (fig. 140b).

GRAVE 11

This grave was found at a depth of 1.5 (or 1.8) m and was oriented north-south. It was 2.1 m long, 0.65 m wide, and had been dug 25 (or 12) cm into the natural ground beneath the tumulus. At the south end of the grave was a bulgy red urn, and near the north end were scattered many small blue-and-white glass beads and a small arm ring.

Grave goods:

Small segmented bronze ring, Ext. D. 6.1 to 6.5 cm (fig. 141e). About 750 very small beads: glass, of dark blue, pale blue, yellow, and white color, and bronze; D. 0.3 to 0.7 cm (fig. 141b, c). Nine very small amber beads, D. 0.4 to 0.6 cm (four in fig. 141d). One longer amber bead with a collar, L. 0.8 cm (fig. 141d). Sherds of a reddish vessel with a dull red slip on the exterior. It probably had a foot originally (fig. 141a).

GRAVE 12

This grave was found at a depth of 2.4 m. It was oriented north-south. Large blue stone slabs were found laid on the natural ground surface, beneath them was a grave which had been dug into the natural ground. The stone slab setting was 3.55 m long, 1.60 m wide. The grave was 3.1 m long, 1.05 m wide, and had been dug 15 cm into the ground. In the grave were four black footed urns at the south end, a knob from a fibula, and two spindle whorls.

Above the urn group under a small stone slab was a "nest" of small blue glass beads, two small arc fibulae, a small earring, and a small arm ring. The excavators thought that this "nest" represented a child's grave placed at the feet of the other burial.

Goldberg suggested that the main grave must have been robbed, since so few grave goods were found associated with the elaborate grave structure. He wrote that perhaps when the large grave was robbed, the small "nest" of objects was overlooked. He suggested that another possibility was that the small "nest" may have been a later burial than the main one and that when it was placed in the tumulus the main grave was discovered and looted.

Grave goods:

Main grave (12a): Spherical knob on the foot end of a bronze fibula (fig. 142d). Sherds of a large pale orange ceramic bowl with a dark gray coating, ornamented with large bulging ribs pushed out from inside. On the neck are two broad grooves. On much of the vessel, particularly on the neck, are traces of what was probably a graphite coating, too faint to indicate in the drawing (fig. 142b). Two spindle whorls, one of pinkish-orange color, D. 3.5 cm (fig. 142c), the other of grayish-orange color and with linear decoration, D. 4.9 cm (fig. 142a).

The other vessels are missing, as they were when the collection was in Zurich.

Other grave (12b): Remains of a solid bronze ring with overlapping ends, decorated with linear patterns (fig. 143b). Fragmentary small bronze ring, Ext. D. about 5 cm (fig. 143c). Fragmentary small thin bronze ring, Ext. D. 2.2 cm (fig. 143j). Two fragmentary very small bronze fibulae of a form related to the Certosa fibula, one ornamented with lines on the bow (fig. 143h, i).

Ten fragmentary very small glass animal-head beads: The head is of dark blue glass, the eyes and end of the nose of light greenish-blue. From the bottom of the head is a hole which does not come out the top, surviving L. about 1 cm (two in fig. 143d). Two very small animal-head beads complete with horns and facial features. The more distinct of the two is light greenish-blue with eyes and nose of dark blue-and-white and horns of white-and-brown. The head is attached to a blue bead, L. 1.1 cm (fig. 143d). Seventeen very small glass beads of dark blue color with white-and-blue eyes and small yellow projections, D. 0.3 to 0.4 cm (three in fig. 143e). Two very small transparent light brown beads, D. 0.5 cm. Very small yellow bead, D. 0.4 cm (fig. 143d). Very small transparent pale blue bead, D. 0.4 cm (fig. 143d). Very small opaque pale blue bead, D. 0.5 cm (fig. 143d). Six dark blue-and-yellow beads with four yellow projections, D. across diagonal 1.3 cm (two in fig. 143e). Sixteen small cylindrical beads of white glass, D. 0.5 to 0.6 cm (four in fig. 143e).

Sixty-six flat disk-shaped bone beads, D. 0.7 to 1.3 cm (some in fig. 143g).

One bronze bead, D. 0.5 cm.

Fragmentary long amber bead with collar (fig. 143f).

GRAVE 13

Another grave covered with stone slabs was found 4.5 m south of Grave 12 at a depth of 3.5 m on the natural ground surface. The stone packing was 3.55 m long and 1.1 m wide, and it was oriented south-north. Apparently some slabs had been set vertically, and others laid across them. Beneath the slabs was a grave 3.2 m long and 1.1 m wide which had been dug 35 cm into the natural ground. On the bottom of the grave, which lay 3.85 m below the surface of the tumulus, was a thin burned layer. In the middle of the grave on a wood layer in the chest area of the skeletal remains was a disk-helmet (*Schüsselhelm*). At the lower left arm was an iron celt, at the left temple a badly preserved iron spearhead, and at the feet (at the south end) was a group of urns, three bulgy black footed vessels and a red one.

Grave goods:

Parts of a disk-helmet (*Schüsselhelm*). There are five concave disks of sheet bronze, ranging from about 13 to about 14.5 cm in D. In the center of each is a hole through which passes a fastener consisting of a thin rod of bronze with rectangular cross section. At the outer end of this rod is a conical head. There are also six small disks, about 2.5 to 3 cm in D., also concave in shape and each with a small nipple at the center of the exterior. At the center of the interior of each is a small loop. Some wickerwork is preserved from the crown. This apparently formed part of the original padded interior of the helmet (fig. 144c).

Six-pointed bronze star, probably part of the helmet; Max. L. between points is 5.0 cm (fig. 144a).

Fragments of a socketed iron axe (fig. 144h). Fragments of an iron spearhead with a small bronze band around the base of the socket (fig. 144g).

Sherds of a cylindrical vessel of reddish-orange color. On the exterior are two horizontal ridges forming lugs, decorated with indentations. A probable original third lug is missing. Restored H. about 18.5 cm (fig. 144i).

The other vessels are missing, as they were when the collection was in Zurich.

Profiled amber rod on a bronze pin. Three zones are engraved with zigzag lines, perhaps once containing inlay. Present L. 3.7 cm. The amber part of the object may be its original length; the bottom is not broken, and part of the top border appears to be intact (fig. 144e). Another profiled amber rod on a bronze pin, decorated with ridges, present L. 4.7 cm. The amber part may be its original length (fig. 144f). Two amber beads on a thin bronze pin or wire and three on a thin pin (one set in fig. 144d), D. of largest bead 1.3 cm. Both groups look as though they may have been attached to the profiled amber rods.

Also with this material now, though not mentioned in the excavation notes, are five very small convex bronze disks, about 0.6 cm in D., each with a small pin on the underside (fig. 144b).

GRAVE 14

Southeast of Grave 13 and at the same depth was another grave covered with stone slabs (fig. 145a). The length of the stone packing was 3.6 m and its width 1.2 m. The packing consisted of blue slabs with Ds. of 0.8 to 1.6 m, and thicknesses of 12 to 15 cm. Beneath the slabs was a grave 3.4 m long and 1.1 m wide which had been dug 35 cm into the natural ground beneath the tumulus. It was oriented north-south with the head to the south. On the bottom of the grave was a burned layer, and in places were remains of a wood layer. Among the remains were many small bronze buttons and amber beads. Remains of what was thought to be textile were also found and removed with great care. In the area of the chest among the bronze buttons were at least four fibulae (one set of notes mentions one serpentine fibula and three other fibulae; another set mentions four serpentine fibulae and three others) and a twisted wire earring. At the north end of the grave was a group of three black footed urns.

Grave goods:

About 600 very small hemispherical bronze buttons 0.5 cm in D. Across the back of each is a loop (some in fig. 145b). Eleven larger disk-shaped bronze buttons, 1.1 cm in D. (three in fig. 145g). Fragment of a small ring of bronze wire, perhaps the earring of the excavation notes (fig. 145d). Sixteen very small amber beads, D. 0.3 to 0.5 cm (six in fig. 145i).

Sherds of a shiny black jug with squat body and high thin neck. On the body are large vertical swellings, and on the neck are parallel grooves (fig. 145e). Sherds of a small bowl of shiny black color with sets of broad parallel vertical grooves on the body (fig. 145h). Sherds of a vessel of grayish-brown color with flattened globular body and neck decorated with grooves and ridges (fig. 145f). Restored H. about 17.5 cm. Low bowl of light grayish-tan color with a perforated lug on one side. On the exterior the rim is set off from the body by a slight groove. Ext. rim D. about 18 cm (fig. 145c).

None of the fibulae mentioned in the excavation notes is preserved; they were already missing when the collection was in Zurich.

GRAVE 14a

Near Grave 14 the excavators found what they interpreted to be a large grave, oriented north-south. It was 6 m [sic] long, 1.8 m wide, and had been dug 45 cm into the natural ground. There was no slab covering, and the excavators took the remains to be those of a looted and destroyed grave chamber. A burned layer in the grave had been disturbed, and many urn fragments were strewn about. No other objects were found.

No objects are preserved from the grave.

GRAVE 15

The bottom of this grave was situated at a depth of 3.2 m. The grave was 2.3 m long, 0.9 m wide, and had been dug 15 cm into the natural ground. Beneath a packing of stone slabs was the grave. On the bottom of the grave at the north end were two urns and a spindle whorl. In the middle of the grave were two arc fibulae, a small boat-shaped fibula, and two large earrings.

Grave goods:

Several hundred very small bronze rivets or nails with heads, now about 0.8 cm long with heads about 0.4 cm in D. (one in fig. 146c). Bow of a boat-shaped bronze fibula decorated with raised bands bearing oblique incised lines, surviving L. 4.5 cm (fig. 146f). Three-knobbed bronze fibula. Each knob has an indentation at the end. At the end of the long foot is a sunburst with an indentation in the center, L. 7.5 cm (fig. 146g). (The other fibula mentioned in the excavation notes is missing.) Two small rings consisting of thin bronze bands, both with overlapping ends. Ext. D. 1.9 and 2.0 cm (fig. 146a, b).

Large black footed bowl decorated with broad and narrow vertical ribs on the shoulder. The neck is divided into two zones by grooves, each of which contains zigzag lines formed by grooves. Traces of a shiny black coating survive (fig. 146e). Brownish-gray spindle whorl, D. 4.4 cm (fig. 146d).

GRAVE 16

This grave was found at a depth of 2.8 m. The excavators thought from the start that it had been disturbed because the stone setting was irregular and beads were scattered at the ends and sides of the grave. A large number of glass and amber beads were found.

Grave goods:

Glass beads (fig. 147e, f): About 345 very small pale blue beads, D. 0.4 to 0.5 cm; 277 very small and small blue beads, from light blue to dark blue, D. 0.3 to 0.7 cm; 140 very small white beads, D. 0.3 to 0.5 cm; 90 very small yellow beads, D. 0.4 to 0.5 cm; 17 very small greenish-blue beads, D. 0.3 to 0.4 cm; 4 very small yellow beads with three dark blue-and-white eyes, D. 0.4 to 0.45 cm; 20 small brown translucent beads, D. 0.6 cm; 3 small white beads, D. 0.5 to 0.6 cm; 12 small green transparent beads, D. 0.8 to 0.9 cm; 4 dark blue beads, D. 0.8, 0.9, 1.0, 1.4 cm; 1 dark blue bead with white zigzag line, D. 1.2 cm; 1 dark blue bead with three yellow dots, D. 1.1 cm; 1 dark blue bead with three yellow circles forming eyes, D. 1.0 cm; 2 yellow beads with three dark blue-and-white eyes, with six light greenish-blue projections at each end, D. 1.3 and 1.5 cm; 3 light greenish-blue beads, each with three dark blue-and-white eyes and with six yellow projections at each end, D. 1.3, 1.3, 1.4 cm. Barrel-shaped bead with collared end; dark blue with yellow zigzag lines, collars yellow; surviving L. 1.8 cm. Transparent colorless bead, D. 1.7 cm. Brown vase-shaped pendant, H. 2.1 cm.

Bronze beads: Seventy-four small beads, D. 0.25 to 0.5 cm (some in fig. 147b).

Bone beads: Nine thin beads, D. 1.1 to 1.2 cm (three in fig. 147a).

Amber beads (fig. 147c): Four fragmentary wafer-shaped pendants, W. of three best-preserved 2.6, 3.2,

3.9 cm. Five fragmentary large disk-shaped beads, D. 2.8, 3.1, 3.6, 4.0, 4.7 cm. Ten round beads with central perforations and with a hole through an arc of the circle, D. 1.4 to 1.6 cm. All are concave on both sides. Two round beads with central perforation and with a hole through an arc of the circle, but not concave on either side, D. 2.1 and 2.5 cm. Four plain beads, D. 1.0 to 1.2 cm. Twelve small and very small beads, D. 0.4 to 0.8 cm. Ten barrel-shaped beads, L. 0.7 to 1.4 cm.

Two small fragments of one or more bronze objects consisting of a rod and large connected loops. Both rods and loops have a diamond-shaped section (larger fragment in fig. 147d).

GRAVE 17

This grave was oriented south-north and was 2.8 m deep in the tumulus. It was 3.5 m long, 0.85 m wide, and had been dug 45 cm into the ground. The excavators interpreted their findings to indicate that the grave had been disturbed. The burned area in the grave had been dug through, and strewn about the grave were sherds of red and black urns. Eighty cm above the grave toward the north was a burned layer with remains of wood on it. Here also was evidence of disturbance. On the burned area in the grave itself were traces of corroded bronze and some unrecognizable iron fragments. Also recovered were fragments of a bronze belt plate and some belt rings.

Grave goods:

Fragmentary bronze belt hook. The back portion is decorated with tremolo lines in patterns of rectangles and diagonals (fig. 148b). Remains of two or three sheet bronze belt attachments with bronze rivets, forming loops holding solid bronze rings (fig. 148c, d). The better preserved ring has a diamond-shaped section.

Sherds of a dark reddish vessel, the neck coated with graphite (fig. 148a).

GRAVE 18

Another burned layer was 2.1 m south of Grave 17 at the same depth and in the same orientation. On it were iron fragments, thought to be the remains of an iron bit, and a belt loop with a ring, two additional fragments, and two iron objects some 90 cm long, designated as roasting spits.

Grave goods:

Loop and attachments held together by rivets, with a solid bronze ring about 2.8 cm in Ext. D. in the loop. The ring is decorated with lines in a herringbone pattern and is of diamond-shaped section (fig. 149h). Solid bronze ring 5.0 to 5.5 cm in Ext. D. of roughly round section (slightly flattened on the interior) with linear decoration. Some lines run around the ring, others form chevrons (fig. 149i). Iron fragments of a horse bit (one in fig. 149e). Two fragmentary iron "roasting spits," both square in section, with a twist pattern near the end and with a twisted loop at the end (fig. 149a, b). On one the loop is intact, and a small iron ring is attached to it. Surviving L. 59.5 and 43 cm. Another fragment, perhaps from the one with the broken loop, is 49 cm long (fig. 149a).

Now associated with the grave though not mentioned in the excavation notes are beads and pottery.

Glass beads (fig. 149f): Sixteen small white beads, D. 0.6 to 0.8 cm. Eighteen small dark blue beads, D. 0.6 to 1.1 cm. Seven small dark blue beads with white dots, D. 0.7 to 0.8 cm. Dark blue bead with white spirals, D. 1.5 cm. Broad yellowish-green transparent bead, L. 1.0 cm.

Two barrel-shaped amber beads, L. 1.4 cm (fig. 149g).

Sherds of a dull reddish-brown vessel with gray exterior. The shoulder is decorated with upward-pointing nipples, of which three survive (a fourth is missing). The vessel stood on a short foot (fig. 149c). Sherds of a grayish-brown bowl with a perforated lug on one side (fig. 149d).

GRAVE 19

Near Grave 17 at a depth of 2.2 m were two blue slabs with D. of 60 cm (fig. 150a). Beneath them in a grave 1.2 m long and 0.85 m wide were a black ceramic bowl and a small red footed vessel. Also in the grave were two fibulae, one of them of unusual form, and a small torque.

Grave goods:

Broken and partly melted remains of at least two hollow bronze rings made of thick sheet bronze decorated with groups of lines (one in fig. 150b). Two small bronze rings, 2.1 and 1.9 cm in Ext. D. (fig. 150c, i). Fragment of a bronze fibula. Surviving are part of the thin ribbed bow, a large solid lump at the head forming a stop guard, and part of the pin (fig. 150h). Small dark blue glass bead, D. 1.0 cm, and 21 amber beads, D. 0.7 to 1.5 cm (fig. 150g).

Sherds of a light brown bowl with three small nipples on the shoulder and an omphalos in the center of the flat base, restored H. about 7.5 cm (fig. 150e). Sherds of a gray vessel of roughly double conical form, originally with a foot (fig. 150d). Very small brownish-gray bowl, H. about 3 cm (fig. 150f).

(The objects now associated with this grave do not correspond very closely with the description in the excavation notes. It is possible that the notes were written somewhat carelessly, but more likely that some of the wrong objects were placed with this grave number.)

GRAVE 20

This grave was found at a depth of 2.8 m and was 4.2 m from Grave 19. It was oriented north-south and had been dug 20 cm into the natural ground. At the north end of the grave was a black urn. No other objects were found. The excavators thought that the grave had been disturbed and suggested that it may have been robbed.

Grave good:

Sherds of a vessel with a shiny black exterior, with broad shallow grooves running obliquely up the shoulder from right to left. On the shoulder are three nipples pointing upward. Restored H. about 16.5 cm, Ext. mouth D. about 13 cm (fig. 151).

GRAVE 21

This grave was below the burned layer on which the two roasting spits were found (Grave 18). The grave was found at a depth of 3.4 m. It was oriented north-south. It was 3.4 m long, 1.4 m wide, and had been dug 25 cm into the natural ground. The bottom of the grave lay 3.65 m below the surface of the tumulus. On the bottom of the grave was a thin burned layer, and the two sides also showed burned traces. Also on the bottom (it is unclear whether above or below the burned layer) was a layer of stamped gray-green clay, and on this were many sherds of black and red urns as well as a small unidentifiable iron fragment. At each end of the grave was a hollow. The excavators interpreted these hollows as locations of balks of the grave structure. No other objects were recovered. Goldberg suggests that this grave had been robbed, apparently on the basis of the poor finds.

Grave good:

Sherds of a shiny black bowl or large cup with a high handle. A three-part animal head survives on top of the handle on one side. Around the shoulder are groups of vertical grooves, and above these are three grooves running around the vessel. In the center of the base is an omphalos (fig. 152).

GRAVE 21a

This grave was found near Grave 21 at a depth of 3.25 m, just 20 cm above the natural ground surface. It was oriented southeast-northwest. The excavators thought this too was a disturbed burial chamber, since wood remains and sherds from black and red urns were found scattered about. Also found were a fairly well preserved bowl, an unidentifiable iron fragment, and a badly rusted iron celt. In this grave too were remains of a burned layer.

Grave good:

Only the iron axe survives. It is of the socketed type and measures 16.4 cm in length (fig. 153).

All of the other objects mentioned in the excavation notes were already missing when the collection was in Zurich.

GRAVE 22

This grave was found on the west side of the mound (fig. 154), at a depth of 2.4 m to the stone packing which was 0.9 m above the natural ground surface. The stone packing was oriented east-west and was 2.1 m long and 1.5 m wide. It consisted of blue slabs which had sunk over the middle of the grave. Underneath on the natural ground level was a burned layer. At the east end of the grave were two small black ceramic urns and a small bowl. Six teeth were found on the burned layer. No other objects were recovered.

All of the objects mentioned were already missing when the collection was in Zurich.

GRAVE 23

This grave was found 3.1 m from Grave 22 and was also oriented east-west (fig. 154). It was 2.4 m deep and 1.25 m above the natural ground surface. The grave was covered with a stone packing 1.2 m wide and 1.25 m long consisting of four slabs. Under them were three black footed urns. Also under the slabs was a burned layer on which were found a small iron fragment and small child's arm ring.

Grave goods:

Solid bronze ring with D-shaped section and overlapping ends, decorated with groups of lines. The outside appears to be worn smooth; Ext. D. 6.9 cm (fig. 155d). Sherds of a dark brownish-gray vessel on a relatively high foot. The shoulder is ornamented with long vertical ridges. The vessel originally had a shiny black coating which survives only in places; restored H. about 20 cm (fig. 155a). Sherds of a vessel of shiny black color similar in form to the preceding. On the shoulder are six groups of broad vertical grooves—five groups of five grooves and one of six; restored Ext. mouth D. about 15.5 cm (fig. 155b). The vessel is likely to have had a foot, but no sherds of it survive. Rim sherd of a vessel of dark gray pottery, coated on both surfaces with graphite. The top part of a broad vertical groove survives (fig. 155e).

Now among the material from this grave at the Peabody Museum are sherds of a brown and gray globular vessel decorated with six vertical ridges bordering zones containing three parallel vertical grooves and other zones containing patterns of concentric rhomoids, triangles, and spirals all formed by shallow grooves. On the shoulder are remains of three large nipples (fig. 155c). (The sherds were partly with the materials from Grave 23, partly with those from Grave 24, hence the provenience of the vessel is uncertain.)

GRAVE 24

This grave was found at a depth of 2.5 m, still 1.5 (or 1.25) m above the natural ground level. It was oriented east-west (or southeast-northwest) and was 1.8 m long and 0.8 m wide (fig. 154). Beneath gray stone slabs were a small black urn and a small low drinking vessel which was recovered intact. No other objects were found.

Grave goods:

Sherds from at least six vessels are now associated with this grave. Since the excavation notes state that only two vessels were found and the accompanying photograph shows the two, most of these must be strays from elsewhere.

Certainly belonging to this grave is the handled cup or bowl. It is intact, of dark brownish-gray color. Around the shoulder are short, broad, shallow vertical grooves. It has a high and wide band-shaped handle. H. of vessel 5.5 cm, Ext. mouth D. about 11 cm (fig. 156b). On the bottom is an omphalos.

The other sherds now associated with the grave come from dark gray vessels: low foot (fig. 156f); bowl with a perforated lug at the rim (fig. 156a); small steep-sided bowl (fig. 156c); wide base with bottom part of vessel wall (fig. 156e); low conical foot (fig. 156d).

GRAVE 25

This grave was found at a depth of 3.1 m on the east side of the tumulus and was situated on the natural ground surface. On the bottom of the grave was a thin gray clay layer, and on it was a thin burned layer oriented southwest-northeast. On the burned layer were some large amber beads, including large flat ones, a broken earring, and a fragment of a fibula.

Grave goods:

Fragmentary serpentine fibula. On the bow one horn with a ball on the end survives. It is attached to the bow by a small bronze rivet. Toward the foot are two stumps which are probably remains of two further horns, cast as part of the bow (fig. 157a). Fragments of one or two bronze wire rings, round in section; Max. Ext. D. about 5 cm (fig. 157d, showing the fragments reconstructed as one ring). Fifteen large amber beads, most flattish in shape. Ten have holes through one edge as well as through the center; D. of these 2.3 to 3.5 cm (five of these in fig. 157c); D. of the other five 2.3 to 2.7 cm (three in fig. 157b).

GRAVE 26

A stone slab-covered grave oriented northeast-southwest south of the middle of the mound was found at a depth of 3.1 m (fig. 158a). The stone setting was 3.7 m long and 1.05 m wide. Beneath it was a grave 3.1 m long and 0.95 m wide, which had been dug 25 cm into the natural ground. Beneath the slabs the excavators came upon a thick burned layer. A wood structure was found, largely carbonized. At the northeast end was a bronze plaque, at first thought to be a belt plate. It was 15 to 18 cm wide and 25 cm long. Attached to it were unidentifiable iron fragments. At the southwest end of the grave was a group of crushed urns consisting probably of three black urns and a flat bowl. No other objects were found.

Grave goods:

Plaque of sheet bronze 29.3 to 29.5 cm long, about 15.4 cm wide. All four edges are rolled over pieces of thick bronze wire. Ten rivet holes occur around the outer edge, some with remains of iron rivets in them. In a band about 5 cm wide running along one end of the back of the object are additional traces of iron from an object either fastened or positioned close to the plaque in the grave. Also adhering to the back are fragments of textile; fragments of wood adhere to the front (fig. 158b).

The pottery is missing, as it was when the collection was in Zurich.

GRAVE 27

This grave was found at a depth of 3.1 m on the west side of the tumulus. It was oriented southeast-northwest. It was 3.1 m long, 1.05 m wide, and had been dug 40 cm into the ground. In the grave were scattered sherds. The excavators interpreted the evidence to indicate that the grave had been robbed. No finds are preserved.

GRAVE 28

This grave was found at a depth of 1.8 m in the west part of the tumulus. Four arranged stones were found. Beneath one were a crushed black urn and burned bones and three small amber beads.

The finds are missing, as they were when the collection was in Zurich.

GRAVE 29

At a depth of 2.9 m at the level of the ground a

grave was found which had been dug down into the natural soil. The nature of the remains suggested to the excavators that this grave had been looted. A fragment of an unusual fibula, an unidentifiable iron fragment with small bronze rivets, and two broken crossbow fibulae were found.

Grave goods:

Mahr and his associates in Zurich attributed two similar Middle La Tène fibulae with long springs to this grave (more complete one in fig. 159b). Fragment of an iron horse bit with rings and with small bronze clamps now corroded onto the rusted iron; L. of bit now 10.0 to 10.5 cm (fig. 159a).

Mahr also attributed a large number of other bronze objects to this grave, although none is mentioned in the excavation notes. Because of this confusion it is best to consider these objects among the isolated finds from this tumulus (see below).

GRAVE 30

This grave was oriented south-north and was found at a depth of 3.05 m. It was 3.1 m long, 1.05 m wide, and had been dug 15 to 20 cm into the natural ground. A thick burned layer was found, with remains of a wood layer still present, and among the remains a fragmentary double-crested helmet. In and around the helmet were fragments of iron, thought to have been the remains of a shield or harness. Associated with these was a badly preserved belt plate. Also recovered was a fragment of a spearhead.

All of the objects mentioned were already missing when the collection was in Zurich, but the helmet and harness disk are visible in a photograph which survives (fig. 160).

ISOLATED FINDS, TUMULUS VI

Sherds of a brown barrel-shaped vessel with a ridge on the shoulder (fig. 161d). Double glass bead of dark blue color. One part of the bead consists of a flattish bead with seven projecting light blue-and-white eyes; the center is pale blue, around it are darker blue circles, D. 1.5 cm. The other part of the bead consists of a smaller disk with two white bands around it and a row of eight small white projections (fig. 161j). Bead similar to the lower part of the preceding one, but with eight eyes instead of seven, D. 1.6 cm (fig. 161h). Dark blue vase-shaped bead, L. 1.7 cm (fig. 161m). Fragment of a dark blue-and-white double animal-head bead (fig. 161k). Ram's head bead of brown color, L. 1.8 cm (fig. 161i). Fragments of at least ten light blue beads with side projections, white and blue. One has a white collar at one end (fig. 161n). Some or all of the others may have had similar collars. Remains of small hollow iron cylinders survive in three of these beads.

Fragment of an animal-head bead of dark blue color with white projections (fig. 161l).

Three bronze cruciform knobs with loops on the back, Max. L. 2.4, 2.5, 2.5 cm (fig. 161e). Many small bronze buttons of various sizes with loops (fig. 161a). Six fragmentary bronze rivets (four in fig. 161g). Six rectangular bronze loops, each with knobs on one side, L. 1.2 to 1.5 cm (two in fig. 161b). Disk-shaped button with four-part loop on the back, D. 1.6 cm (fig. 161f). Pieces of at least eight thin bronze fastenings of rectangular section, bent into rectangular shape (three in fig. 161q). Bronze rivet with large flattish head, D. 1.6 cm (fig. 161p). Bronze pin, L. 2.7 cm, with an eye and with a sheet bronze disk near the eye (fig. 161o). Fragments of bands of sheet bronze, some with surviving wood fragments, fastened together with thin band-shaped pieces of bronze wire (fig. 161c).

Tumulus VII

This tumulus was also called Gomila Spandal. It was excavated from December 15 through 20, 1913, and it contained seven graves. Two photographs show the tumulus under excavation (fig. 162a, b).

GRAVE 1

Glass and amber beads were found.

Grave goods:

Various beads (fig. 163a): Dark blue glass bead, D. 1.3 cm. Dark blue barrel-shaped bead with three projections, L. 1.4 cm. Seven small dark blue beads, D. 0.6 to 0.7 cm. Six small yellow beads, D. 0.5 to 0.6 cm. Two transparent colorless beads, D. 0.6 and 0.7 cm. Two white beads, D. 0.5 and 0.6 cm. Two small amber-colored beads, D. 0.55 cm. Small bronze ring bead, D. 0.9 cm, and small bronze spiral of four turns, D. 0.4 cm. Fragment of a dark blue animal-head bead with light greenish-blue projections for eyes and nostrils. Semicircular amber spacer bead with five perforations and dot-and-circle ornament on one side, D. 2.4 cm.

Twenty-one amber beads, most of them flattish, D. 0.6 to 2.3 cm (19 shown in fig. 163b).

GRAVE 2

In this grave were four fibulae, two of them small, and a spindle whorl.

Grave goods:

Fragments of two small boat-shaped bronze fibulae, their bows decorated with transverse lines at both ends (fig. 164a, c). Fragment of a bronze fibula of Middle La Tène character (fig. 164b). Two small dark blue barrel-shaped glass beads with side projections, L.

0.7 and 0.9 cm (fig. 164e). Small brownish-gray spindle whorl, D. 2.6 cm (fig. 164f).

GRAVE 3

A leg ring, an arm ring, and a broken fibula were found in this grave.

Grave goods:

Solid bronze ring with a twist pattern. The original form of the corroded ends is unclear. Max Ext. D. about 12 cm (fig. 165a). Fragmentary solid bronze ring with overlapping ends, decorated with transverse linear patterns; Ext. D. about 7.5 cm (fig. 165b).

The fibula is missing, as it was when the collection was in Zurich.

GRAVE 4

In this grave were found two wide-ribbed earrings, two fibulae, some beads, and an amber cross-shaped object.

The objects were already missing when the collection was in Zurich.

GRAVE 5

Neither information about the grave nor finds survive.

GRAVE 6

Neither information about the grave nor finds survive.

GRAVE 7

An arm ring was found in this grave.

Grave good:

Solid bronze ring with overlapping ends and ornamental lines running longitudinally; Ext. D. about 8.5 cm (fig. 166).

ISOLATED FINDS, TUMULUS VII

Thin solid bronze ring with overlapping ends, Ext. D. about 7 cm. Four dark blue glass beads: one with yellow zigzag line around the middle, D. 1.4 cm; one with white wavy line, D. 1.3 cm; two with yellow eyes, D. 1.2 and 1.4 cm. Small disk-shaped amber bead, D. 1.6 cm (fig. 167).

Tumulus VIII

This tumulus was located in the community of Studenz bei Vir. The Duchess had excavated two graves between July 29 and August 2, 1914, when the outbreak of World War I put an end to her work.

GRAVE 1

The excavators called this a child's grave. Found were beads and an amber cross.

Grave goods:

Fragment of a bronze fibula with the bow in the form of an animal, perhaps a dog. On the end of the foot is the head of another animal, too damaged to identify. Surviving L. 4.5 cm (fig. 168b). Three very small glass beads: one very dark blue or black, D. 0.6 cm; one dark blue, D. 0.6 cm; one white, D. 0.6 cm (fig. 168c). Cross-shaped amber bead with perforations through both arms, Max. L. between ends of arms 2.6 cm (fig. 168a).

GRAVE 2

A bronze cauldron was found in this grave. One note mentions a horse mandible associated with it; another mentions straw and wood wickerwork.

Grave goods:

Fragmentary bronze cauldron with joined cross-shaped handle attachments. Below the rim on the exterior are two pairs of incised lines around the vessel. Several fragments of the bottom show ancient repairs—sheet bronze patches attached by bronze rivets. Both handles are round in section and have a twist pattern on them (fig. 169a). Bronze pendant 4.2 cm long with a large loop and two "legs" spreading out from a shaft. Attached are two small solid bronze rings (fig. 169b).

Vas Vir

The Duchess excavated one tumulus, referred to as the *Vogel* (bird) tumulus, in the village of Vir just southwest of the hillfort. It was investigated between July 14 and August 3, 1912. Twenty-seven graves were found. A plan indicating the relative locations horizontally of 19 of the graves survives. It shows one grave in the center of the mound and the other 18 arranged concentrically around it (fig. 170).

GRAVE 1

Cremation grave. In this grave were five weapon rings, a small bronze knob, several spirals, and small bronze beads.

Grave goods:

Five bronze rings, closed. Three are about 4.7 cm

in Ext. D. and have diamond-shaped sections (one in fig. 171a). One is about 3.5 cm in Ext. D. and has a round section (fig. 171b). The fifth is about 2 cm in Ext. D. and has a diamond-shaped section (fig. 171c). Vase-shaped bronze bead, H. 1.6 cm, D. 2.0 cm (fig. 171d). Nine small bronze beads, D. 0.7 to 0.9 cm (four in fig. 171e). Many fragments of bronze wire spirals; a total length of about 20 cm survives; D. 0.7 to 0.8 cm (fig. 171f–h).

GRAVE 2

Cremation grave. The grave was found at a depth of 1.4 m and was covered by stone slabs. In the grave were two iron spearheads, a ring, and fragments of spirals.

Grave goods:

Remains of two iron spearheads, both with distinct midribs. Surviving L. of better preserved one about 20.5 cm (fig. 172a, f). Closed bronze ring with lentoid section, somewhat sharper on the outside and more rounded on the inside, Ext. D. 5.1 to 5.3 cm (fig. 172c). Three small bronze beads, D. 0.8 cm (fig. 172e). Small bronze rivet with a wide conical sheet bronze head, L. 1.0 cm, D. of head 1.0 cm (fig. 172d).

Now with the grave material (and with it in Zurich) is a low light pinkish-brown bowl with traces of a foot which does not survive. The shoulder is decorated with broad vertical ribs and wider bulges, pushed out from the inside. Restored Ext. mouth D. about 21 cm (fig. 172b). On the neck are traces of graphite.

GRAVE 3

This grave is described as a cremation grave with stone covering slabs. Listed as finds are an arm ring, some amber beads, a blue glass bead, an iron celt, a small spearhead, an urn, and a fibula of the Glasinac type.

Grave goods:

Fragmentary bronze ring, part of it decorated with segmenting. The original form of the two corroded ends is unclear. Max. Ext. D. about 6.5 cm (fig. 173b). Small closed bronze ring with distinct profiling, Ext. D. 3.5 cm (fig. 173f). Two-looped bronze fibula with large decorated catch plate and incised lines around both ends of the bow, L. 8.3 cm (fig. 173e). Two iron fragments, probably from a spearhead (fig. 173d). Large blue glass bead, D. 1.9 cm (fig. 173g). Twenty-eight amber beads, D. 0.9 to 1.4 cm (some in fig. 173h).

Sherds of a large footed vessel with a dark gray exterior. Along the shoulder are six rounded bulges pushed out from the inside, with another row of them below the shoulder. At the base of the neck are two broad shallow grooves. On the neck are remains of a graphite coating, and other remains of graphite on the body indicate patterns of crisscross bands (fig. 173a). Sherds of a low grayish-brown bowl with remains of a lug on one side (fig. 173c).

The iron celt or axe is missing.

GRAVE 4

This grave was found at a depth of 1.8 m and had a stone packing covering it. In the grave were an arm ring, a small earring, and some amber beads.

Another note with this grave number mentions three iron rings, two spearheads, and an iron knife. Since none of the objects cited in this second note was with the collection when it was studied in Zurich, although all of the objects mentioned in the first set of notes were present, the six iron objects may have been incorrectly attributed to this grave.

Grave goods:

Bronze ring with overlapping ends, decorated with groups of lines running laterally and with segmenting at the ends (fig. 174b). Closed bronze ring with a large ridge running around the center on the exterior, Ext. D. 3.6 cm (fig. 174a). Fragment of one or two small rings consisting of a bronze band with two longitudinal grooves and ends narrowing to a point. At each end are short oblique incised lines meeting to form chevrons (fig. 174c). Eighty-eight amber beads, cylindrical, round, barrel-shaped, and disk-shaped; D. up to 1.5 cm, L. up to 1.9 cm (some in fig. 174d).

(The two spearheads, iron knife, and three iron rings which may or may not belong with this grave are missing.)

GRAVE 5

In a grave under a stone slab at a depth of 1.6 m were a small low urn with lid found in a black urn, a fibula, and two fragmentary earrings.

Grave goods:

Three fragments of bronze wire rings, Ext. D. about 5 cm. One has incised lines around it suggesting a twist pattern (fig. 175a, c). Twenty amber beads ranging in D. from 0.8 to 2.6 cm (some in fig. 175d).

Small handled cup of dark gray color and very fine texture, H. to rim about 4.5 cm (fig. 175b). Small pinkish-cream vessel of coarse texture with two small lugs at the rim perforated vertically with very small holes. A small lid is perforated in two places matching those on the vessel rim; H. to rim about 5.25 cm (fig. 175e). Very small plain globular vessel of reddish-amber color, H. about 4 cm (fig. 175f). Sherds of a grayish-brown vessel on a low foot, restored H. about 21 cm (fig. 175g).

The fibula is missing, as it was when the collection was in Zurich.

The inventory made in Zurich also mentions remains of a child's skull among the grave's objects; this skull is now missing.

GRAVE 6

Found in this grave were amber beads, a small low urn in another urn, a fragmentary wire bracelet, spectacle spirals, fragments of a fibula, some pendants, and a hollow neck ring.

Grave goods:

Hollow bronze ring made of thick sheet metal, decorated with groups of ribbing, W. 1.2 cm, Ext. D. about 8 cm (fig. 176c). Many fragments of one or more thin wire rings, most of them with a twist pattern (fig. 176g, i). Fragments of thin sheet bronze decorated with rows of large and small hammered bosses and circles (fig. 176m). One complete small triangular pendant set and fragments of at least two others. Each consists of two similar pendants attached to a tiny bronze ring. These pendants are decorated around the edges with rows of tiny hammered bosses, with a row of larger bosses in the middle (complete pair in fig. 176k). Small fragments of a bronze band decorated longitudinally with incised lines; some of the zones so defined are ornamented with oblique incisions (fig. 176l). Sheet bronze attachment shaped like a figure eight with a rivet near the middle, W. about 1.2 to 1.3 cm. On the edges are tiny hammered bosses (fig. 176f). Fragments of three bronze fibulae. Two are three-knobbed, each knob with an indentation at the end, both having a long foot and flat star pattern at the end with a small indentation in the center (one in fig. 176a). Catch plate and lower fragment of the bow of a boat-shaped fibula with a long foot. On the bow fragment is a band of oblique incised lines (fig. 176n). Fifty-nine amber beads of round, barrel-shaped, and cylindrical form, D. up to 1.2 cm, L. up to 1.5 cm; five tiny amber beads, D. 0.3 cm (some in fig. 176j).

Sherds of a yellowish-brown vessel of coarse texture, roughly globular in form and with a short flaring neck (fig. 176b). Base sherd of a brownish globular vessel (fig. 176h). Sherds of a dull orange-red thick-walled vessel (fig. 176e).

GRAVE 7

The excavators called this a child's grave. Found in it were four child's arm rings, amber beads, one or two small vessels, one of them decorated, a badly preserved iron spearhead, a greenish glass ball, two large neck rings, and fragmentary pendants.

Grave goods:

Fragments of one or more small bronze wire rings, Ext. D. about 4 cm (fig. 177f). Fragments of at least five pairs of small triangular bronze pendants like those in Grave 6 (one in fig. 177d). Two similar fragmentary solid bronze rings with knobs and ridges between the knobs. The ends are curled (one in fig. 177b). Large round transparent glass bead of very pale greenish color, D. 2.2 cm (fig. 177c).

Small handled cup of dull orange color with a dull cherry red slip covering both exterior and interior. The exterior is decorated with large painted graphite chevrons pointing upward. On the top of the handle are two small projections. H. to rim about 5 cm, to top of handle about 7.5 cm (fig. 177e). Fragmentary remains of a very small light blue vessel of porous lightweight glasslike material. Some fragments show the presence of white "eyes" in the light pale blue base (reconstruction in fig. 177a).

The spearhead is missing, as it was when the collection was in Zurich. Since it is described as "very badly preserved," it may well have been thrown away by the excavators. The amber beads were also missing when the collection was in Zurich.

GRAVE 8

The excavators called this a child's grave. In it were four child's arm rings, a small bronze ring, a triangular ring, and some amber beads.

Grave goods:

Fragments of spiral rings of bronze wire, some of them with a twist pattern; Ext. D. about 5 cm. At least two and perhaps three separate objects are represented (one in fig. 178b). Solid bronze ring with diamond-shaped section, Ext. D. 3.3 cm (fig. 178a).

The "triangular ring" and the amber beads are missing.

GRAVE 8a

Above Grave 8, and attributed by the excavators to a separate grave, were an iron celt, an iron knife, and a small ring.

Grave good:

Socketed iron axe, surviving L. about 17 cm (fig. 179).

The other objects are missing.

GRAVE 9

The notes mention an urn as a grave good.

Grave goods:

Sherds of a large dark gray vessel on a foot, decorated with groups of three nipples arranged in vertical rows on the shoulder (fig. 180b). Some of the sherds have small holes drilled in them, suggesting repair of the vessel during its use life. Sherds of a lid of similar color and fabric (fig. 180a).

GRAVE 10

Found were a small very badly preserved spearhead, two small child's wire arm rings, a small fibula, and a spindle whorl.

All of the objects are missing, as they were when the collection was in Zurich.

GRAVE 11

This grave was called the middle grave by the excavators, and it is shown in this location on the plan (fig. 170). It was covered by a large stone packing. Found in the grave were a ceramic vessel with two animal heads on it, a ceramic bowl, some small bronze buttons or knobs, two very badly preserved iron spearheads, an iron celt, and two arm rings.

Grave goods:

Two bronze rings with overlapping ends, decorated with groups of lateral lines, Ext. D. 7.25 cm (one in fig. 181c). Fragmentary remains of two iron spearheads (fig. 181a, f). Many broken fragments of iron, perhaps of the axe mentioned in the excavation notes ("celt"). Fragments of leather with many tiny bronze studs inserted into regularly spaced holes. The heads of the studs are about 0.2 cm in D. (fig. 181d). Other fragments of leather.

Sherds of a gray cylindrical vessel with a raised zigzag ridge around the middle and a horizontal ridge near the bottom. Through one side of the vessel just below the rim is a perforation (the part of the vessel opposite is missing). On the lid, which is of the same material, are the heads and necks of two opposite-facing animals. One has a mane and may be a horse. The other looks like a ram or a bull. Between the heads is a perforation through the lid. H. of vessel without lid about 11 cm, Ext. mouth D. about 8 cm (fig. 181e). Low brown bowl; a groove just below the rim sets off the rim from the body. At the middle of the body on one side is a nipple, and there is a slight omphalos at the center of the base. Restored H. about 6 cm (fig. 181b).

The notes made in Zurich mention parts of a disk-helmet that may belong to this grave. The object is shown in a photograph taken by the excavators after the object had been removed from the ground. In the photograph groups of tiny bronze studs can be seen between the disks. These studs are similar to those associated with the leather remains in this grave. The scholars in Zurich were confused as to the provenience of this helmet. It was not present when they studied the collection. If it was found in this grave, it is odd that the excavators would not have mentioned it in the notes. Since its origin is unclear, it seems best not to consider the helmet as part of this grave group.

GRAVE 12

This grave was found at a depth of 20 cm. The excavators thought it had been disturbed by farming activity. In it were two heavy arm rings with overlapping ends, 17 large amber beads, some long amber beads, sherds of a reddish urn, a boat-shaped fibula, earrings, and four loom weights.

Grave goods:

Two hollow rings of thick sheet bronze, decorated with groups of transverse lines; Ext. D. about 8.4 cm (one in fig. 182g). Fragments of a thin bronze band with longitudinal incised lines defining narrow zones, some of them containing short oblique incised lines (fig. 182f). Fragmentary ring consisting of a thin bronze band with three longitudinal ridges, the two outer ones decorated with short oblique incised lines. The surviving end is pointed and has incised lines running across the point. Original Ext. D. about 4.5 cm (fig. 182h). Fifteen amber beads, roughly barrel-shaped; L. 0.8 to 1.7 cm (some in fig. 182l).

Three pyramidal ceramic loom weights, H. of the two best preserved ones 12.0 and 9.0 cm (fig. 182i–k). Four spindle whorls, two of them ornamented with impressed dots; D. 3.5 to 4.0 cm (fig. 182a, b, d, e). Dull orange vessel with four vertical perforated lugs around the neck (fig. 182c).

Now associated with this grave but not mentioned in the excavation notes are a fragment of a Middle La Tène bronze fibula with the foot grasping the bow (fig. 182m) and fragments of a ribbed bronze ring with a flattish area containing remains of two iron rivets (fig. 182n).

GRAVE 13

Neither information about the grave nor finds survive.

GRAVE 14

The notes mention two arm rings and a small ring. The objects were already missing when the collection was in Zurich.

GRAVE 15

Neither information about the grave nor finds survive.

GRAVE 16

One note calls this a double grave. Found were some small bronze studs, small amber beads, and some teeth.

Grave goods:

About 4,370 tiny bronze studs, each consisting of a dome of sheet bronze with a tiny loop of thin bronze wire on the inside; D. of the dome about .6 cm (fig. 183a). Small bronze ring with lens-shaped section, Ext. D. 1.9 cm (fig. 183g). Fragment of the catch plate and end knob of a bronze fibula (fig. 183f). Five small bronze beads, D. 0.5 to 0.6 cm (two in fig. 183d). Fragmentary cylinder of sheet bronze (fig. 183c). Seventy-four very small round amber beads, D. 0.3 to .6 cm (fig. 183b). Small fragmentary conical bone object with a central perforation and with three ridges surrounding it (fig. 183e).

Twenty-two teeth accompanied the grave goods. L. Angel examined them and concluded that they were teeth of a child approximately ten years old.

The notes made in Zurich indicate that fragments of a skull were also among the materials with this grave.

GRAVE 17

According to the plan (fig. 170) this was a child's grave. It was 1.9 m long, 0.8 m wide, and 25 cm deep. The bottom of the grave was 1.6 m below the surface of the tumulus. There are no surviving notes recording finds, nor are there any objects preserved.

GRAVE 18

This grave had a stone packing over it. In the grave were a boat-shaped fibula, a serpentine fibula, an iron dagger point with a bronze knob, and two arm rings.

Grave goods:

Bronze ring with overlapping ends, decorated with narrow and wide ribbing; Ext. D. 7.0 to 7.5 cm (fig. 184d). Bronze serpentine fibula with a stop disk, a round knob and projection at the end of the foot, and a saddle-shaped bend in the bow covered by a rectangular plate decorated with six dots and circles; L. 3 cm (fig. 184b). Fragmentary bronze arc fibula with solid bow. Corrosion may obscure a decoration once present on the bow. The catch plate is long and has a small spherical knob at the end. Original L. about 7.5 cm (fig. 184c). Iron shaft fragment with square section. Another fragment of what appears to be the same shaft has a bronze knob at the end. This knob appears to have been damaged by heat (fig. 184a).

The other arm ring was already missing when the collection was in Zurich.

GRAVE 19

A boat-shaped fibula and a serpentine fibula were found.

Grave goods:

A bronze bow fragment of a three-knobbed fibula is all that survives. Both ends are decorated with deeply incised lines (fig. 185).

The serpentine fibula was already missing when the collection was in Zurich.

GRAVE 20

Neither information about the grave nor finds survive.

GRAVE 21

Neither information about the grave nor finds survive.

GRAVE 22

No information survives.

Grave good:

Sherds of a large footed vessel of very pale orange color with traces of a dull cherry red slip and with graphite coating on the neck; restored H. about 30 cm, Ext. rim D. about 20.5 cm (fig. 186).

GRAVE 23

Neither information about the grave nor finds survive.

GRAVE 24

A bronze cauldron containing remains of *Feldfrüchten* was found.

Both the vessel and the remains were already missing when the collection was in Zurich.

GRAVE 25

This grave was 1.7 m long, 0.45 m wide, and 0.8 m deep. There is no record of finds, and none survives.

GRAVE 26

This grave was found near the edge of the tumulus and was 1.7 m long, 0.55 m wide, and 0.5 m deep.

Grave good:

Sherds of a small gray footed vessel decorated with broad vertical ribs. Traces of graphite coating appear on both interior and exterior surfaces. Restored H. about 7.5 cm, Ext. mouth D. about 10.5 cm (fig. 187).

ISOLATED FINDS, VAS VIR TUMULUS

Six fragmentary bronze fibulae with birds on the bows (four in fig. 188a–d).

Vas Pece

In the village of Pece on July 5 and 6, 1912, the Duchess excavated two graves in a tumulus referred to as the *Waldtumulus*.

GRAVE 1

An urn and a hollow arm ring were found.

Grave goods:

Fragmentary hollow bronze ring with fine ribbing. One end fits inside the other. Ext. D. about 8.6 cm (fig. 189b). Large thick bronze belt plate 9.3 cm wide and about 31.5 cm long. At each end are five bronze rivets with large round heads, all but two ornamented with incised concentric circles. The bronze hook is in the shape of a human hand with four fingers bent to form the hook and the thumb held straight (fig. 189f). Glass beads: Two dark blue with white wavy lines, D. 1.6 cm (fig. 189c). Forty-one dark blue, D. 0.7 to 1.4 cm (some in fig. 189d). Pale transparent green bead with traces of a zigzag line, D. 1.6 cm. Brown bead, D. 0.7 cm (fig. 189a). Seventeen amber beads, D. 0.6 to 1.8 cm (some in fig. 189e).

Sherds of a large dull orange-brown vessel.

GRAVE 2

A bowl, a spindle whorl, and a glass bead were found.

Grave goods:

Fragmentary one-edged iron dagger in a bronze sheath with a bronze covering over the T-shaped hilt. Both hilt and sheath are held together by bronze rivets (fig. 190a). Dark blue glass bead with white circles forming eyes, D. 1.3 cm (fig. 190c).

Small dull orange and gray vessel with three small nipples on the shoulder and traces of two others; H. about 8.5 cm (fig. 190e). Sherds of a low grayish-tan bowl. Just below the rim on the exterior is a groove setting off the rim from the body (fig. 190h). Sherds of a low brownish-gray bowl with a broad flat base with a small circular indentation at the center surrounded by a larger impressed circle (fig. 190i). Sherds of a grayish-brown vessel. The vertical neck has grooves and ridge on it (fig. 190f). Sherds of a base with a small omphalos (fig. 190g). The appearance of the pottery suggests this base may be part of the same vessel as the preceding neck sherds. Two spindle whorls, one cylindrical and grayish-brick color, D. 4.0 cm (fig. 190b) the other conical and grayish-tan color, D. 3.2 cm (fig 190d).

Vas Glogovica

The Duchess excavated a small tumulus in the village of Glogovica from November 15 through 23 1910. Only three graves were found. Goldberg wrote that the entire mound had been explored, hence no other graves were present.

GRAVE 1

Neither information about the grave nor finds survive.

GRAVE 2

This grave was 3.7 m long, 1.2 m wide, and 0.8 m deep. It was found 1.4 m east of Grave 1. In the grave were two small spearheads, a small iron celt, a glass bead, and a fragmentary urn.

Grave goods:

Remains of two iron spearheads. The better preserved one has a broad blade. At the base of the socket is a hole with a bronze pin in it (fig. 191a). Glass beads (fig. 191b): Four large blue beads, all showing fire damage, D. 1.5 to 1.8 cm. Dark blue bead with three white eyes, D. 1.3 cm. Eight beads, probably originally blue, each with four white eyes, much damaged by fire, D. 1.1 to 1.2 cm. Fragmentary blue bead with three projections of blue-and-white circles. Barrel-shaped yellowish-brown bead, L. 0.9 cm. Fragmentary light greenish-blue bead with broad longitudinal ribs and collars at the ends.

GRAVE 3

Two small earrings, a small brown vessel, and a spindle whorl were found.

Grave goods:

Small vessel consisting of a hemisphere with

three fragmentary perforated projections. The projections may have been legs on which the vessel stood as a bowl. The rim does not survive, hence the form of the object is unclear (fig. 192a). Gray spindle whorl, D. 3.0 cm (fig. 192b).

St. Vid

In the Mecklenburg Collection is a fragmentary bronze vessel labeled "St. Vid bei Stična, Hügelgrab." It is unclear where either this grave or the tumulus was located, and whether it was excavated by the Duchess. Surviving are two bronze handles, solid and smooth with a round section and with three of the four attachments, and fragments of the vessel rim with its iron core (fig. 193).

DISCUSSION

The graves excavated by the Duchess at Stična are similar in the described structures, burial rites, and assemblages of grave goods to those in the recently excavated tumulus at the site (Gabrovec 1974). Since the notes accompanying the grave groups excavated by the Duchess, even though relatively complete for the time, do not provide all the data required for modern analysis of the findings, full assessment of the results of her excavations must await publication of that other tumulus. For the present, I wish to call attention to some of the aspects of the graves in the tumulus for which the best records survive, Tumulus IV (see p. 55).

For the graves in this tumulus, the excavation notes record both inhumation and cremation burials. The association of stones with the graves is noted in many instances, including large stone covering slabs (as in Grave 19) and encircling arrangements of stones (as in Grave 16). The sparse information preserved about locations of objects in the graves indicates patterns similar to those in other tumuli at Stična and at other sites in Slovenia (see e.g., Teržan 1978).

In table 6 (pp. 88–89) I present an overview of the contents of the 50 graves in Tumulus IV that I judge to be reliably documented; for the other graves there is some doubt as to contents, and I omit them from this table. The numbers in the table indicate quantities of the various categories of objects. In the case of glass and amber beads I include the total weights of the beads beneath the numbers of beads, since beads vary greatly in size. The different categories of pottery are defined strictly on the basis of morphology. The combinations of grave goods are similar to those in the other tumuli excavated by the Duchess at Stična.

In an effort to provide some quantitative information about the grave goods, I have weighed all of the glass and amber beads in these graves and all of the bronze objects. In the case of the bronze objects, I have estimated the weight of missing portions of fragmentary items. The total weight of glass beads in these 50 graves is 472.4 gm (1.04 lb). The weight of amber beads is 738.0 gm (1.63 lb). The weight of bronze I estimate at about 2,700 gm (about 6 lb). Until more quantitative data from other sites become available, isolated weights such as these are difficult to assess, but we can gain some impression of the total quantities of these materials in the cemetery at Stična by calculating the probable quantities for the estimated 5,610 graves at the site (see p. 99) on the basis of these figures for Tumulus IV. The total weights would be 53 kg of glass (about 117 lb), 82.8 kg of amber (about 183 lb), and 303 kg of bronze (about 666 lb). These are only very rough estimates based upon scanty data, but they do provide an impression of the quantities involved.

Table 6. Stična Tumulus IV, the reliable graves.*

Grave No.	Fibula	Bracelet/leg ring	Earring	Beads Glass	Beads Amber	Beads Bronze	Belt plate	Belt attachments	Axe	Spear	Knife	Footed vessel	Lid	Bowl	Cup	Jar	Unclear pottery fragments	Spindle whorl	Other
1				35 / 109.6g												1		1	
2	1	2		2 / 2.5g											1			1	
3									1			1							
4		2			15 / 41.0g												1		
5							1	1								2		1	
6				15 / 5.3g													1		
7	1	1		176 / 7.3g		5											1		
8				107 / 67.5g									1			1		1	
9				3 / 19.5g								1						1	Small bronze ring
10	1						1	1			1						1		
11		2		6 / 9.0g													(1)		6-sided ring
12	2	2	(1)	2 / 6.4g															
13																			
14					52 / 33.6g								1				1	1	
15					72 / 46.4g														Bronze vessel (sieve)
16							1		1	2	1	3	2				1		Horse bones, Iron object
17	2			20 / 33.7g															Bronze wire
18							1	1	1								(1)		Bronze tweezers
19										2			1			1	2		(Patellenhut) 2 pins, Bronze socket
20		2			15 / 52.0g												1		
21		8		14 / 6.8g	4 / 1.2g	1							1				(1)		
22		2	3		72 / 42.6g														Sheet bronze fragments
23		2		1 / 9.2g	89 / 117.0g													1	
24											1	1							
25		1		1 / 6.6g													1		

*See table 1 (p. 26) for explanation of table.

Table 6. (Continued)

Grave No.	Fibula	Bracelet/leg ring	Earring	Beads Glass	Beads Amber	Beads Bronze	Belt plate	Belt attachments	Axe	Spear	Knife	Footed vessel	Lid	Bowl	Cup	Jar	Unclear pottery fragments	Spindle whorl	Other
26		2															1		
27	3	1						1			2								Lump of bronze
29		2		2 3.2g	64 110.9g														
30										2		1	2		1	2			Cuirasse, Buttons
31			?	2 3.9g											2				Ear or finger ring
32	2	2+			159 38.7g			1											Small ring
33					10 3.4g										1			1	Gold foil 1 + (1) small bronze rings
35		2			50+ 16.8g									1					Finger ring (?)
37											1			1					(Iron hook)
39														1					
40		2					1	1		1		1	2			1		1	
41a									1	1									Horse bit, 4 harness knobs, 9/10 arrowheads, 3 6-sided rings
41b		1		187 35.5g	47 159.4g														
42		(1)		295 145.2g	1 0.5g														
43	(1)	2		6 6.9g	46 34.6g							1	1	1			1		(Klapperstäbchen)
44																(+)			
45		1		12 8.3g										1					
46												1							
47		1		1 4.9g	16 6.2g													1	Horse bones, Ceramic rhyton
48											1	1				1			
49														1				2	
51		2																1	
52																1		1	
53	1	2		5 14.8g								1							
54		2										1		2					

STIČNA 89

Part II:
Synthesis and Interpretation

The Emergence of an Iron Age Economy in East Alpine Europe

INTRODUCTION: THE DEVELOPMENT OF AN IRON AGE ECONOMY

Societies of the last millennium before Christ in central Europe differed substantially from their predecessors. The most apparent change that occurred between 1000 B.C. and the birth of Christ was the emergence of centers of industrial and commercial activity. Such centers appeared first in the East Alpine region—at Hallstatt and in Lower Carniola in Slovenia. After about 600 B.C. a similar development of economic centers took place in west-central Europe, where the Heuneburg, the Hohenasperg, and Mont Lassois are already well known (Kimmig 1969; Wells 1980a), and other apparently similar sites are now being investigated. In the final centuries before the birth of Christ the oppida came to dominate the cultural landscape of central Europe (Collis 1975).

The Iron Age centers, from the earliest at such sites as Hallstatt and Stična to the major oppida of Bibracte, Manching, and Stradonice, had in common a level of manufacturing and commercial activity unknown in central Europe before 1000 B.C. A range of specialized industries is represented at these centers, including working of iron, bronze, gold, and glass.

Accompanying the centralization of manufacturing and trade were changes in society. The economic centers had considerably greater populations than settlements of preceding periods, ranging from several hundred at the early centers of the Eastern Alps to several thousand at the Late La Tène oppida. The larger communities required more complex organizational structures than those needed by smaller communities (Gall and Saxe 1977), and these more complex structures are evident in new, more differentiated burial patterns.

These economic and social aspects of societies of the last millennium B.C. set them apart from those of the preceding periods and permit us to speak of an "Iron Age economy" distinct from that of the Neolithic and Bronze Age in central Europe.

In this section I shall suggest one set of mechanisms that can account for the first stages of this major change in central European cultural life, represented at the earliest such centers to emerge, those of the East Alpine region.

EARLY IRON AGE COMMUNITIES IN THE EASTERN ALPS

The purpose of this section is to address several issues important to the subsequent discussion. Here I wish to indicate the kinds of evidence we have to work with and the very rough picture that can be put together of subsistence patterns, population sizes, and patterns of daily life.

Life in Preindustrial Societies

In examining problems of the past, it is important for the archaeologist or historian to consider some of the principal differences between life in the context he is studying and life in his own world. In doing so he is more likely to be able to separate his interpretation of the past from his own experiences in the modern world. The Industrial Revolution brought to the West vast changes not only in the way man produced his goods but also in most other aspects of life, such as social organization, medicine, techniques of food production, population size, and settlement patterns (Polanyi 1944; Laslett 1973). As members of industrial societies having very little direct familiarity with any nonindustrial cultures, we should be aware of some of the essential features of preindustrial life in Europe. I shall cite just three aspects of particular concern to this study.

Perhaps most important is the difference in scale between preindustrial and modern Western societies (Redfield 1953, pp. 1–25). A glance at any graphs showing population trends through history for any part of the world will indicate immediately the enormous changes that came about through improved medical care and nutrition accompanying the arrival of full-scale industrialization (McEvedy and Jones 1978). Before those changes, both regional population sizes and individual communities in which people lived were much smaller than their modern counterparts (Laslett 1973, pp. 55–60).

The societies of the preindustrial world were organized principally upon the basis of families. Whereas in the modern world relations between persons are frequently based upon sharing the same work place or leisure interests, in the preindustrial context personal relations were principally based upon family relations (Redfield 1953, p. 6). The family was the essential unit of economic relations as well as of social ones (Laslett 1973).

These small-scale, family-based societies of the preindustrial world were thoroughly agrarian in their economic foundations. Even those societies that engaged in active manufacturing and trade were basically agrarian, with only a very small percentage of the population, perhaps 5 to 10 percent at most, engaged primarily in pursuits other than food production. All other activities, such as manufacturing, trade, feasting, and religious celebration, revolved around the schedule of agriculture (Cipolla 1970, p. 65; Laslett 1973, pp. 13–14). Homans (1942) and Fél and Hofer (1972) provide studies of medieval and modern European contexts that illustrate this point well.

These three features—small scale, family-based organization, and heavily agrarian economic system—are critical for understanding the evidence from prehistoric East Alpine Europe. The small scale of the Late Bronze and Early Iron Age societies is apparent in the character of the settlements and in the size of the cemeteries. The strongly familial aspect of social organization is difficult to demonstrate archaeologically with evidence available at present, but as Filip (1961), Gabrovec (1974, pp. 180–182), and Urleb (1974, pp. 83–88) have shown, such an organizational basis would correspond well with patterns in the cemetery evidence. In the present state of our knowledge, it is very difficult to compare relative amounts of time or energy devoted by the members of any community to agricultural production with that devoted to manufacturing and trade, though such comparisons may be possible in the future.

The Character of the Archaeological Evidence

By the beginning of the Late Bronze Age, around 1200 B.C., most parts of the East Alpine region were settled, except the least hospitable mountainous terrain. (On the archaeological remains of Palaeolithic, Neolithic, and Bronze Age communities in these regions see especially Pittioni 1954 for the Austrian areas and *Arheološka Najdišča Slovenije* 1975 for Slovenia.) The Late Bronze Age habitation of the region is best documented from the graves of the period. Hoards are also an important source of information about cultural life of the time. Settlements are known, though very few have been investigated in systematic fashion (see references in the works cited above).

The evidence of occupation of the region during the Early Iron Age (750 to 400 B.C.) is considerably more abundant than that of the preceding period and suggests an increase in the number of communities and in the number of people (Čović and Gabrovec 1971, p. 327; *Arheološka Najdišča Slovenije* 1975). In the Early Iron Age too the principal source of information comes from the burials. In most parts of the East Alpine area, as in other parts of central Europe, graves were placed beneath or within tumuli of earth and stone during the Early Iron Age. Some of these tumuli survive today and constitute the main apparent remains of the Early Iron Age occupation. In the latter half of the nineteenth century, when interest in the archaeological remains of the various countries of central Europe flourished, thousands of burial mounds were opened and their graves emptied of grave goods. Some of these mounds were excavated under relatively controlled conditions, but most were not (Gabrovec 1966, pp. 1–5). Also at some sites where the burial practice did not involve tumuli but rather flat graves, as at Hallstatt, Vače, and Most na Soči, large-scale excavation was carried out in the last century. The result of this great amount of digging is that many museums of East Alpine Europe, particularly those in Vienna and Ljubljana, have large collections of grave goods from these Early Iron Age cemeteries. Much of this material was studied and partly published by the early authorities such as Hoernes and Szombathy, but most of the large collections have only recently become available to the scholarly world through systematic publication. Examples include the grave groups from Hallstatt (Kromer 1959a), Vače (Starè 1955), Brezje (Kromer 1959b), Šmarjeta (Stare 1973a), Podzemelj (Barth 1969; Dular 1978), Libna (Guštin 1976), and Magdalenska gora (Hencken 1978).

In the case of some of these early excavations, as at Hallstatt, the evidence of the grave groups is relatively good and the associations can be used for various kinds of analyses. But in many cases—Vače, Brezje, and Šmarjeta, for example—the grave groups were not kept intact. In these instances, the objects themselves provide information about the material culture and wealth of the communities and about import trade with the outside world, but information concerning grave groups has been lost.

Since settlements are much more poorly known

than graves, the cemeteries provide the best evidence of the distribution of human habitation. The great tumulus cemeteries around the hillforts of Lower Carniola, with up to 140 tumuli at Stična containing as many as 200 graves each, suggest a concentration of population and material wealth at these sites. Large cemeteries are also found elsewhere in Slovenia, as at Most na Soči in northwestern Slovenia (Guštin 1979; see distribution maps of Early Iron Age cemeteries in Gabrovec 1966 and *Arheološka Najdišča Slovenije*

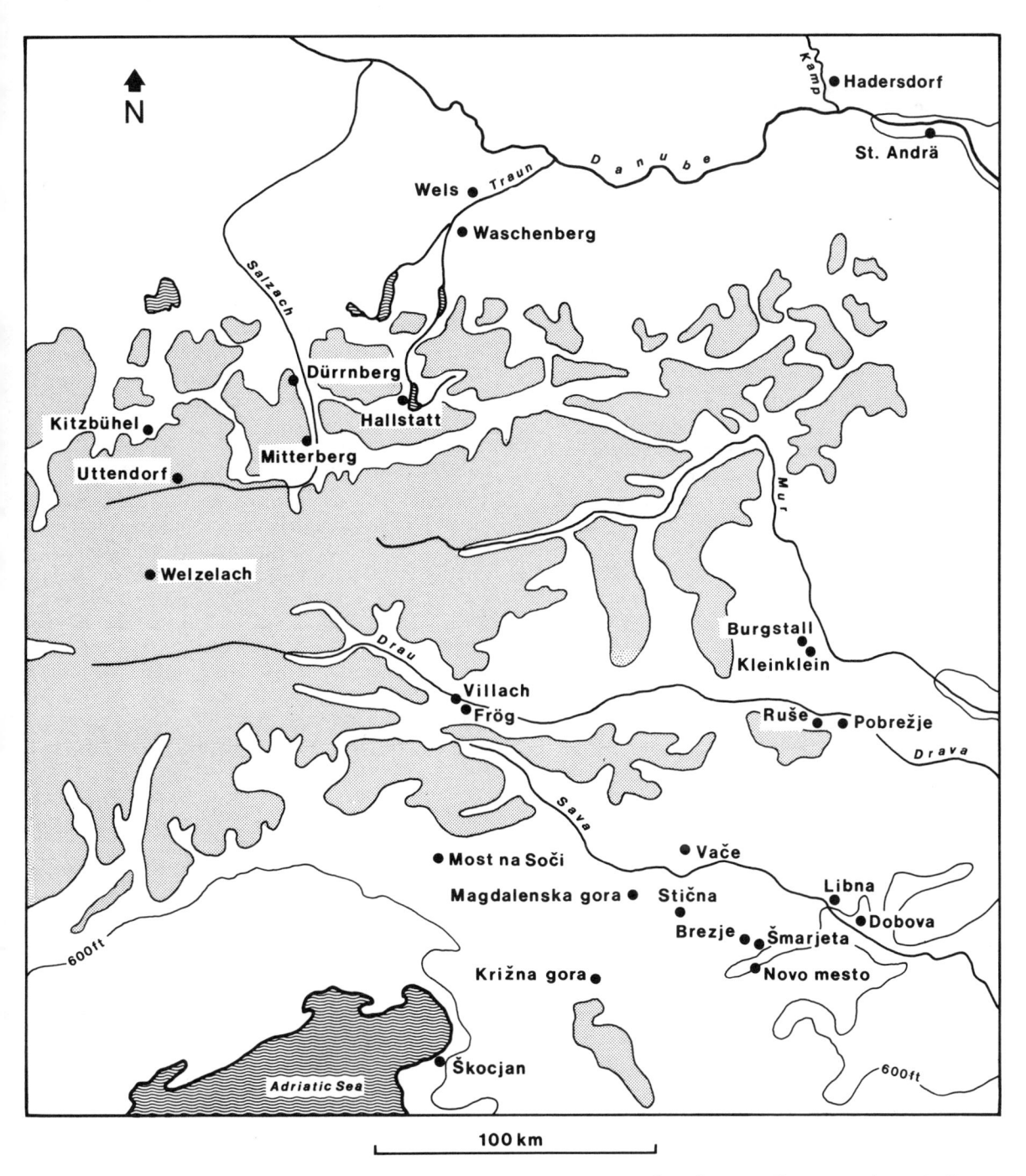

Text figure XXIV. Map showing locations of the principal sites mentioned in the text. The screened area indicates lands over 3,000 ft (914 m) above sea level.

1975). In the Alpine regions of Upper Austria, Carinthia, and Styria, such large numbers of graves are less frequent, though at Hallstatt some 2,000 graves have been excavated, and around 700 were identified at the Burgstall near Wies in Styria (Szombathy 1890). More common in the Alpine regions are small cemeteries, as at Leoben (Modrijan 1963) and in the Drava River valley of northern Slovenia (Pahič 1973). The catalogue of archaeological materials from Upper Austria compiled by Reitinger (1968), with maps showing locations of sites, provides a good picture of the distribution of occupation remains in the Alpine areas.

Our knowledge of the settlements is sparse because of relatively little research attention directed to them. In Slovenia there has been considerable surface study of Early Iron Age hillforts (Guštin 1978), and some of the sites around which tumuli are grouped have been partially excavated. Recent fieldwork at Stična (Gabrovec, Frey, Foltiny 1970; Frey 1974a), Libna (Guštin 1976), and Most na Soči (Svoljšak 1974) is providing good data on these sites. The amount of surface excavation has not been sufficient to provide settlement plans, but remains of buildings at two sites indicate structures similar to contemporary ones on settlements north of the Alps.

At Stična the excavators uncovered the remains of a house dating to the latter part of the Early Iron Age. It was a log cabin-type structure, with its walls resting on a foundation of stones (Gabrovec, Frey, Foltiny 1970, p. 29, pl. 6,2). Also of the latter part of the Early Iron Age is a complete building uncovered in recent excavations at Most na Soči in the mountainous region of western Slovenia. Here the excavators found the building constructed in log cabin fashion, as at Stična, the walls again resting on a foundation of stones. This was a two-room structure (Švoljsak 1974, pp. 16–18, 32, figs. 2, 4, and pl. 7).

As the synthetic study by Guštin (1978) indicates, there is considerable variation in locational type, wall system, and construction of the hillforts. Thus the concept "hillfort" here encompasses a range of different habitation sites, perhaps some densely occupied, townlike settlements with substantial populations evident in the thousands of graves (as at Stična), others with much smaller numbers of inhabitants. We know very little about habitation sites other than the hillforts (Guštin, pers. comm.). The population and material wealth in the graves at the major settlements, including fine crafts products and imports from distant areas, suggest that some of these sites were centers of regional importance; but until other settlements have been explored (even in their cemetery aspects), little can be said about the centrality of these sites. Future research may show that the organization of Early Iron Age society was along similar lines to that in southwest Germany, where there is good evidence for the existence of manufacturing, commercial, and demographic centers; for smaller communities in the same regions; and for economic and sociopolitical interaction between major centers and smaller communities (Kimmig 1969; Frankenstein and Rowlands 1978; Wells 1980a).

In the Austrian regions, a number of settlements have been identified, but very few systematically excavated (see e. g., Hell 1948). At Hallstatt the settlement contemporaneous with the great cemetery has not yet been found (pp. 11–12). The recent excavations by Pertlwieser at the Waschenberg near Wels in Upper Austria are especially important in providing a fairly complete picture of an Early Iron Age settlement. The investigations have yielded a plan of the site, with a number of buildings, apparently dwellings, and features connected with iron smelting and forging (Pertlwieser 1969, 1970). The findings at the Waschenberg indicate what we might expect to find in other parts of the East Alpine region as more settlements are investigated.

Subsistence

The ability of a community (and, on a larger scale, a society) to produce food determines the extent to which specialists can be maintained whose principal energies are devoted to activities other than the production of food (Sherratt 1972). If a community's subsistence base is poor, it is less likely that the community will be able to support specialists than if it has a rich and varied subsistence base, in which case it can generate surpluses to sustain such persons as miners, metalworkers, and merchants.

Most of the communities living in the East Alpine region were probably self-sufficient for their food. Slovenia and the Alpine valleys of Carinthia, Styria, and Upper Austria possess rich soils capable of supporting the relatively small communities of the Early Iron Age. The community at Hallstatt, living in the narrow, infertile, and shaded Salzbergtal, is likely to have imported most of its food, if only from the valley area at the level of the lake below. Other specialized communities, such as that of copper miners at Welzelach, were probably small enough to have produced most, if not all, of their food.

To date there has been little systematic publication of data relating to subsistence of the communities of prehistoric East Alpine Europe, and as a result not much can be said about the nature of the subsistence economy. Data are available on the plants and animals raised, but very little on relative quantities of different species in use. Werneck (1961, 1969, pp. 9–14) reports the following plants recovered in East Alpine contexts of the Early Iron Age or earlier. Grains represented are einkorn wheat (*Triticum monococcum* L.), club wheat (*Triticum aestivum* L. subsp. *compactum* Host), emmer wheat (*Triticum dicoccum* Schr.), spelt wheat (*Triticum spelta* L.), rye (*Secale cereale* L.), broomcorn millet (*Panicum miliaceum* L.), Italian millet (*Setaria italica* L.), barnyard millet (*Echinochloa crusgalli* L.), oats (*Avena sativa*), four-row barley (*Hordeum vulgare* L. subsp. *vulgare* L.), and naked six-row barley (*Hordeum vulgare* var. *coeleste* L.). Among legumes represented are horse bean (*Vicia faba* L. var. *minor* Peterm. subv. *celtica nana* Heer), pea (*Pisum sativum* L.), lentil (*Lens esculenta*), and bitter vetch (*Vicia ervilia*). Wild foods present in archaeological contexts include grape, plum, cherry, apple, and hazel nuts (see also Morton 1953, pl. 20; Lippert 1972, p. 9; Aspöck et al. 1973, p. 42, note 4). These plants identified in the East Alpine area correspond closely with those known on archaeological sites from Neolithic, Bronze, and Early Iron Age settlements north of the Alps (Jankuhn 1969, p. 71; Wyss 1969, pp. 117–124; Kimmig 1979, p. 51; Quillian 1980).

Further evidence for cultivation of plants is provided by scenes in the situla art. The situlae from Certosa, Sanzeno, and Montebelluna (Lucke and Frey 1962, pls. 64, 67; Frey 1966, p. 68, fig. 1) bear scenes of plowing with a draft animal. The plows represented closely resemble wood plows found intact in boggy regions of northern Europe (Jankuhn 1969, p. 75, pl. 6). Many Late Bronze Age hoards from the East Alpine region contain bronze sickles, another principal component of grain cultivation technology (see p. 123).

Among domestic animals, cattle, pigs, sheep, goats, horses, and dogs are represented both on settlement sites and in graves (Koreisl 1934, pp. 239–240; Amschler 1949; Guštin 1976, p. 17; see also Bökönyi 1974). Bones of pig and cattle have been recovered in the salt mines at Hallstatt (Barth 1971, p. 38). Wild animals present in archaeological contexts include red deer, roe deer, wild boar, and beaver (Koreisl 1934, pp. 239–240; Guštin 1976, p. 17). This spectrum of domestic and wild animals corresponds to that at contemporaneous sites north of the Alps (Jankuhn 1969, pp. 75–77, 80) and Late Neolithic faunal assemblages from Ljubljana (Drobne 1973). Hunting of wild animals is also attested by scenes in the situla art that show the hunting of rabbits and deer (Lucke and Frey 1962, pls. 64, 67).

Thus the evidence of the various species of food plants and animals represented indicates that a wide range of foods was available to the Early Iron Age inhabitants of the East Alpine part of Europe. Until large-scale systematic studies of plant and animal remains are undertaken at settlements of the period, it will be impossible to document the nature of the subsistence economy of communities in specific terms or to show which plants and animals were the principal food sources of the different regions and settlements.

The present evidence suggests a rich and varied subsistence base, offering alternate possibilities should one or two species of plants or animals fail through disease or drought. Such a broad and reliable subsistence base can open to a society the possibility of a substantial amount of activities other than the production of food. For a full understanding of the changes that came about in East Alpine Europe during the Early Iron Age it would be important to document changes in subsistence patterns. Future research directed toward the plant and animal remains on the settlements may provide the evidence necessary for such documentation.

Population

As noted above, one of the essential differences between Early Iron Age and modern Europe is that of the scale of human populations and institutions. In order to suggest reasonable models for the patterns of change, it is necessary to develop some information, however hypothetical, regarding the sizes of the populations of the various communities under consideration.

The problems of dealing with the issue of past population sizes are numerous. For prehistoric contexts, where no written documents exist to aid in estimating populations, the difficulties are that much greater (see Cowgill 1975; Petersen 1975; Cunliffe 1978). Nonetheless, from the available archaeological data very rough estimates can be made. These estimates are working hypotheses, to be used until new data become available.

Among the potentially useful sources of information on prehistoric population sizes are the sizes of settlements, sizes and numbers of houses within settlements, quantities of animal bones on sites, and numbers of graves associated with communities (Phillips 1972). For Early Iron Age Europe, the best source of information is the cemeteries.

Several assumptions must be made in estimating population sizes from graves. First, we must assume that the cemetery was used by one community and by one only and that that community did not use any other cemeteries at the same time. The evidence from many sites of different periods in central Europe suggests that this association of one community with one cemetery is generally correct (Donat and Ullrich 1976, p. 349).

Second, we must assume that all individuals were buried in the cemetery. In many contexts, including most of the Early Iron Age sites of East Alpine

Europe, infants were buried in areas different from the main community cemetery (Donat and Ullrich 1976, p. 349; Pauli 1980, p. 134). In such cases, a population estimate made from the main cemetery will give the number of noninfant individuals in the community. If some deceased persons were disposed of in ways other than burial (examples in Ucko 1969), estimates of community size based on the cemeteries would be incorrectly low, but for Early Iron Age East Alpine Europe there is no evidence to suggest that other means of disposal were used.

Other sources of potential inaccuracy come from the nature of the archaeological data itself. Even if all individuals were buried in the same cemetery, the archaeologist excavating can miss some graves. Since a large proportion of Early Iron Age cemeteries was excavated during the last century or the beginning of this one under less than ideal conditions, it is likely that some graves were overlooked.

For our purposes of making rough estimates of populations of various Late Bronze and Early Iron Age communities, I adopt the formula developed by Acsádi and Nemeskéri (1970, pp. 65–66; see also Donat and Ullrich 1976, p. 349):

$$P = \frac{De_o^o}{t} + k.$$

P is the average population size of the living community; D is the total number of dead in the cemetery; e_o^o is the average life expectancy at birth; t is the number of years during which the cemetery was in use; k is a correction factor of 20 percent of the fraction. (Acsádi and Nemeskéri and Donat and Ullrich suggest a correction factor of 10 percent, but since the majority of the East Alpine cemeteries were excavated under less than ideal conditions, I feel that a larger correction factor is in order.)

The number of dead (D) is the number of individuals represented in the cemetery. Since few cemeteries in the Eastern Alps have been completely excavated, this number must often be estimated on the basis of the number of graves found and the predicted extent of the cemetery. The correction factor helps to compensate for destroyed graves and graves missed by the excavators.

Life expectancy (e_o^o) is very difficult to determine in prehistoric contexts, even in those rare instances in which we have a substantial number of well-preserved skeletons (Acsádi and Nemeskéri 1970, pp. 60–72, 182–214). For the life expectancy at birth in the Late Bronze and Early Iron Ages, I arbitrarily adopt a figure of 30 years. This figure is based on a rough average of life expectancies derived through skeletal study of different Metal Age populations of central Europe (Acsádi and Nemeskéri 1970, p. 211; Pauli 1980, pp. 135, 314, note 19; see also Cipolla 1970, p. 83). In reality the life expectancies for different communities in a region (and for different individuals) varied, depending upon local environmental and cultural circumstances, including nutrition, and the average life expectancy for any given community was changing over time. For the present we must overlook such fine distinctions, since so few skeletal populations have been subjects of physical anthropological analysis in East Alpine Europe. The figure of 30 years for average life expectancy at birth represents a reasonable one for the period under consideration.

The number of years during which each cemetery was in use can be roughly estimated on the basis of the chronological system for the area (see p. 2).

Each of the variables in the formula can only be approximated. Nonetheless from reasonable estimates it is possible to arrive at workable population sizes for the communities. I emphasize that these figures are very tentative, since the evidence upon which they are based is scanty. Another variable involved is change in population sizes of communities over time. For present purposes, I am calculating a single population estimate for the duration of each cemetery, but at many sites, Magdalenska gora, for example (Hencken 1978), the number of later graves substantially outnumbers the earlier ones, suggesting a gradual growth in population over time.

Using the formula

$$P = \frac{De_o^o}{t} + k,$$

I make the following calculations from excavated cemeteries, with e_o^o always equal to 30.

Hallstatt. Kromer's publication of the cemetery (1959a) deals with 1,111 grave groups which are well documented; another 26 graves from the cemetery have been presented here. A large number of other graves have been excavated at Hallstatt, most under unsystematic conditions (see Kromer 1959a, pp. 6–15). Records and finds from many such excavations do not survive. It has been estimated that some 2,000 graves have been uncovered at the site (Angeli 1970, p. 15), a figure that I shall work with here: 2,000 graves over 350 years equals

$$\frac{2,000 \times 30}{350} + \left(\frac{2,000 \times 30}{350}\right)(.20) = 206,$$

a rough approximation of the average population at Hallstatt.

Stična. About 140 tumuli are now visible at Stična (Gabrovec 1974, p. 170). Since the land on which the tumuli are located is largely agricultural, other mounds may have once existed which have been eroded through farming activities. In order to compensate roughly for such a likely loss, I shall add another third as many tumuli, thus working with the number 187. The average number of graves in the ten tumuli excavated by the Duchess (excluding Tumulus VIII which she had only begun to explore when World War I broke out in 1914) was 18.4. The Great Tumulus excavated by the Narodni muzej contained 183 graves (see p. 45); this one was exceptionally large among those surviving. If we work with an average of 30 graves per tumulus (probably on the high side), we arrive at a total of 5,610 graves. Over 350 years these would represent an average population of 577.

Magdalenska gora. Forty tumuli are now visible (Hencken 1978, p. 94, fig. 2). Adding another third as many to compensate for tumuli that no longer survive yields a hypothetical total of 53. The average number of graves in the tumuli excavated by the Duchess was 35.5, thus the total number of graves may have been around 1,882. Over 350 years these would represent an average population of 194.

Brezje. Of the 19 tumuli reported in the vicinity of Brezje, Kromer (1959b) publishes the grave groups from the six that are in Vienna. The number of graves per tumulus varies greatly, averaging 32.67. Working with a guessed total original number of tumuli of 25, I arrive at a figure of 817 graves. Over 350 years this would provide a figure of 84 persons on the average.

Vače. The number of graves excavated and those remaining at Vače is unknown, but Staré judges that at least 2,000 were excavated (1955, p. 69). Allowing another third again as many, I reckon with some 2,667 graves. Over 350 years the average population would have been around 274.

Libna. Guštin reckons with a maximum of 300 graves in the roughly 70 tumuli surviving at the site (pers. comm.). Allowing for another third as many graves in destroyed tumuli, 400, the average population over 350 years would have been around 41.

Welzelach. It is unlikely that many, if any, graves were missed by the excavators at Welzelach. The cemetery was compact, and the graves were marked by stone cists. The 56 graves over a period of 150 years (Lippert 1972) would have represented a population averaging about 13. If the cemetery was used for only 100 years, the average population would have been about 20. (These figures agree with those suggested by Lippert 1972, p. 43 and Kilian-Dirlmeier 1973, p. 218.)

Frög. In the second half of the last century a cemetery comprising about 300 tumuli, most containing a single burial, was excavated at Frög (Modrijan 1957, p. 5). Allowing another third as many graves for the few cases of multiple burials in single tumuli and tumuli that were no longer visible, I reckon with roughly 400 graves. Over 350 years the average population would have been around 41.

Burgstall at Wies. As at Frög, in the latter half of the nineteenth century several large cemeteries of tumulus graves, most of them containing a single burial, were explored and partly excavated at Wies. Szombathy (1890, p. 171) records a total of 654 tumuli. Allowing another third for multiple burials in tumuli and for unidentified tumuli, the total number of graves may have been around 872. Over 350 years the average population using the cemetery would have been about 90.

St. Andrä. Thirty-six graves were excavated, and others may lie in the unexcavated areas adjacent to them (Eibner 1974, p. 13, fig. 3). Adding another third to allow for such undiscovered graves, the tentative total would have been 48 graves. Over about 180 years (Eibner 1974, p. 106) these may represent an average population of about ten.

I emphasize that these calculations are all done with very uncertain quantities. My aim here is to develop a relatively consistent means of arriving at very rough estimates of possible average populations for the different sites. The method is full of inadequacies, but I know of none better in the present state of the art.

These estimates agree well in principle with those made by Kossack (1959, pp. 86, 124–125, 1972, p. 92) when he suggests that the settlements of Early Iron Age southern Bavaria were inhabited only by very small communities, usually fewer than 30 individuals. These settlements he designates as farmsteads and hamlets. Killian-Dirlmeier (1974) suggests a similar scale of settlement at Mühlacker in northern Württemberg. (My estimates for the various Early Iron Age communities of the East Alpine region would agree in principle with those made for early medieval sites in central Europe [Donat and Ullrich 1976, p. 351, fig. 74], allowing for the gradual increase in population throughout Europe between the Iron Age and the early medieval period [McEvedy and Jones 1978, pp. 18, 89]).

If these estimates for Early Iron Age sites are on the right order of magnitude, then many of the published calculations for population sizes in prehistoric Europe may be much too high. For example, Phillips (1972) sugests that many Neolithic communities had populations over 200, and sizes up to 400 and 500 have been proposed for Late Bronze Age settlements such as

Wasserburg Buchau (Härke 1979, p. 235) and Zurich-Alpenquai (Wyss 1971, p. 104). These high figures have generally been proposed on the basis of settlement evidence rather than graves. An instructive warning on the use of settlement data for calculating population sizes is provided by the Late Bronze Age (in this case roughly 1280 to 805 B.C.) site of Elp in Drenthe in the Netherlands (Waterbolk 1964), which would appear from plans to have been occupied by a community utilizing some 30 buildings. Careful excavation and obser-

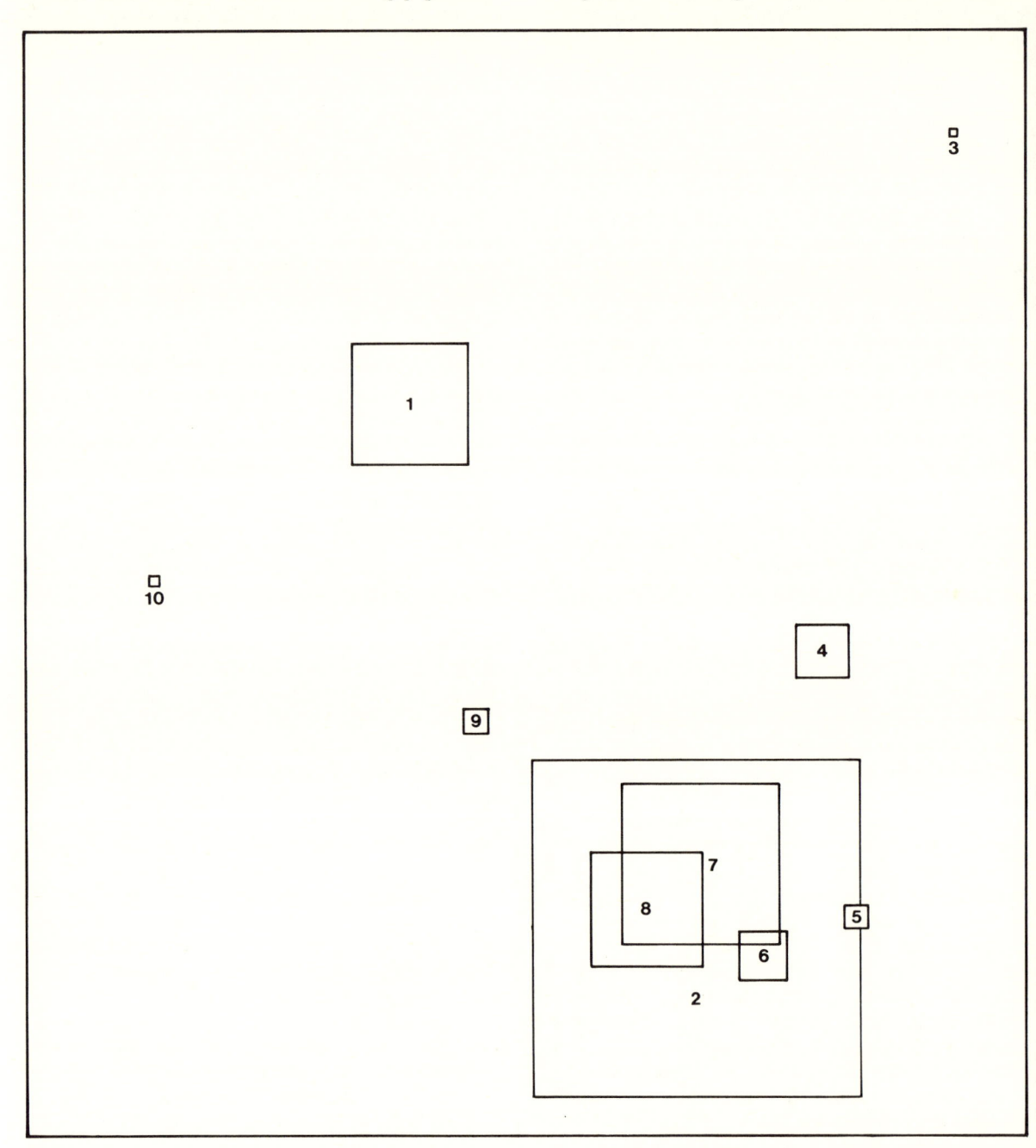

Text figure XXV. Schematic representation of relative population sizes hypothesized for ten sites in the East Alpine area. The length of each square varies directly with the estimated population. The sites indicated by numbers are as follows: 1. Hallstatt, 2. Stična (the largest square), 3. St. Andrä, 4. Kleinklein, 5. Libna, 6. Šmarjeta, 7. Vače, 8. Magdalenska gora, 9. Frög, 10. Welzelach.

vation, and application of several radiocarbon determinations, led to the conclusion that the site consisted of a single farmstead, its main building having been relocated within a single limited area throughout this roughly 500-year period. I suspect that many other settlements were much smaller than they appear, because the structural remains recovered by the archaeologists date from an extended period of time, during which the occupants rebuilt their houses and barns a short distance from their previous locations.

On the basis of the population sizes for Early Iron Age sites proposed here, there is a considerable range in size from the small farmstead of St. Andrä to large villages of the size of Stična. For the larger sites it is necessary to reckon with the possibility that the cemeteries served not only the local inhabitants but also those of surrounding smaller communities, as Szombathy has suggested for the cemetery at the Burgstall (1890, p. 171). In any cultural landscape, settlements vary substantially in population size. In the population estimates made here I see no distinct breaks between different types of community (farmstead, hamlet, village), but rather a continuum with farmsteads on one end of the spectrum and substantial villages on the other.

CEMETERIES SELECTED FOR COMPARISON

In the discussion of changes in the patterns of the archaeological evidence from the Late Bronze to the Early Iron Age, I shall make use wherever possible of quantitative data from the principal source of evidence on these periods—the cemeteries. I believe that the use of numerical data enables us to discuss patterns and changes much more precisely than is possible from more qualitative kinds of information. As sources for this numerical data, I have selected 12 cemeteries from different parts of the East Alpine region which are at least reasonably well documented. Seven of these date to the Late Bronze Age, five to the Early Iron Age. Many other cemeteries could have been chosen, and I have used no special criteria in selecting these aside from their above-average state of documentation. Since my purpose is to draw attention to patterns of change between the Late Bronze and Early Iron Ages, I have chosen only cemeteries that, according to the conventional chronological sequences, belong to one period or the other, but not both. Thus I do not make use of the very well-documented cemetery at Ljubljana SAZU, because it was used continuously through both periods (Starè 1954; Puš 1971; Gabrovec 1973, 1976).

I list here the cemeteries that are represented in the tables below, with the principal literature dealing with each. Their locations are shown on the map on page 95.

Late Bronze Age cemeteries

Dobova (Starè 1975b)
Hadersdorf (Scheibenreiter 1954)
Novo mesto, Mestne njijve (Knez 1966)
Pobrežje (Pahič 1972)
Ruše (Wurmbrand 1879; Pahič 1957)
St. Andrä (Eibner 1974)
Wels (Willvonseder 1950)

Early Iron Age cemeteries

Hallstatt, Mecklenburg excavations
Križna gora (Urleb 1974)
Magdalenska gora, Tumuli IV, VII, X (the tumuli containing the largest numbers of reliable grave groups) (Hencken 1978)
Stična, Mecklenburg excavations
Welzelach (Lippert 1972)

In each case, I use only those graves that appear from the published reports to have been intact when excavated. In the tables, the column labeled "No. reliable graves" reflects this selection on my part of those grave groups that were intact, as far as I can judge from the published reports.

ECONOMIC DEVELOPMENT BEYOND HOUSEHOLD NEEDS

The amount of time and energy devoted by communities of the Late Bronze and Early Iron Ages to manufacturing beyond immediate household needs and to trade with the outside world was probably very small compared with that applied to primary agricultural production and to everyday household needs. Yet in the industrial and commercial aspects of any agrarian economy lies potential for great change and growth (Cipolla 1970, p. 66), and it was in these aspects that the principal changes took place that led to the development of Early Iron Age economic and social patterns.

In this section I shall review some of the evidence for manufacturing and trade and suggest models to aid in the understanding of the organization behind these processes.

Manufacturing

Iron Production. The problem of the origins of iron technology in the East Alpine region is a complex one. Iron was in use for a long period in the Near East, Anatolia, and Egypt before it began to appear regularly in Europe (Tylecote 1976, pp. 40–52; Coghlan 1977), and it is most likely that knowledge of recognition and processing of iron ores was introduced by specialists from outside central Europe (Pleiner 1980, p. 375). The East Alpine area was probably among the first parts of Europe north of the Mediterranean to develop active iron production (Rieth 1942).

Investigators working on questions of early iron metallurgy in Europe have argued for sources of the new technical knowledge from Asia Minor via Greece and the Danube River valley (Rieth 1942, pp. 77, 121, 137; Tylecote 1976, p. 46) and from Italy, and from both sources (Gabrovec 1980, p. 42; Drescher 1980, p. 56; Pleiner 1980, p. 381). The possibility of more or less independent development of iron metallurgy in East Alpine Europe has been raised (Rieth 1942, p. 137; see also Tylecote 1976, p. 40), but the abundant evidence of contact between this part of Europe and Mediterranean regions makes such an independent development less likely than the introduction of the technology from outside. Information about iron metallurgy may have been introduced by a number of different possible mechanisms (ironworkers coming in from outside and setting themselves up in local production or East Alpine persons learning the techniques in Mediterranean lands and bringing the knowledge back with them), and we may never be able to arrive at a satisfactory account of its introduction. The important aspect of the issue is not how, when, and where the knowledge of iron metallurgy was first introduced to the region, but rather why and how it became so very important after about 800 B.C., when the knowledge of the metal and of techniques for working it had been present in the area for at least a couple of hundred years.

Iron objects have been recovered from several contexts dating before 1000 B.C. in Europe north of the Mediterranean (Rieth 1942, p. 7; Pleiner 1980, pp. 376–378). In the period 1000 to 800 B.C. iron is not uncommon (list of finds in Kimmig 1964, pp. 274–281). During this period iron occurs frequently as inlay in bronze objects such as swords, rings, and pins, and also in composite tools made of bronze handles and iron blades, especially swords and knives. Implements with iron inlay and with iron blades are particularly well represented in the Late Bronze Age Swiss lakeshore settlements (Rieth 1942, pp. 10–12; Vogt 1949–1950). In the East Alpine area, small objects of iron occur in a number of Late Bronze Age cemeteries, for example a knife handle and neck ring from Ruše (Wurmbrand 1879, p. 418), a knife from Hadersdorf (Scheibenreiter 1954, p. 13, pl. 11, 5), and fragments from Kitzbühel (Eibner, Plank, Pittioni 1966, pp. 242–243) and St. Andrä (Eibner 1974, pp. 33–34). An iron sword of the *Griffzungen* type was found in the Mušja jama (Fliegenhöhle) at Škocjan (Szombathy 1937, p. 148, fig. 92; Rieth 1942, p. 15, fig. 9).

This relatively frequent occurrence of small amounts of iron in contexts well before the start of what is considered the "Iron Age" (see Pleiner 1980, p. 383, fig. 11.3) is significant. Apparently, iron was being produced and worked in parts of central Europe for a couple of centuries before it began to replace bronze as the principal metal used in making tools and weapons.

The Eastern Alps are richly endowed with iron ore, more so than the west Hallstatt culture area (Rieth 1942, p. 80). Hematite and limonite occur abundantly in fissures and gullies in deposits of mountain detritus, gravels, and clays (Müllner 1908, pp. 38–39). Many such deposits are surface outcrops, hence the ore could be collected in substantial quantities without underground mining (Davies 1935, pp. 182–184). Small deposits of iron ore occur throughout these Alpine regions. For example, even the inhabitants of Hallstatt had close access to small pockets of iron ore (Morton 1951). Müllner's map (1908, p. 53) shows the distribution of iron ore sources throughout Carniola. Many of the ore deposits are rich in metal, with an iron content up to 50 percent (Rieth 1942, p. 80). The large scale of Roman period and later iron production in Carinthia, Styria, and Slovenia attests to the abundance and quality of the ores (Müllner 1908; Davies 1935, pp. 173, 182–183; Egger 1961; Alföldy 1974, pp. 113–114). These same regions have remained major producers of iron into modern times (Mutton 1961, pp. 145–146; Pounds 1969, pp. 706, 710).

Most traces of Early Iron Age exploitation of ore sources have been obliterated by subsequent workings on the same locations. In Slovenia good evidence of prehistoric iron production exists in the vast quantities of slag on Early Iron Age settlements (Müllner 1908, pp. 39–88). In general these slag deposits are not datable, and since many of the Early Iron Age sites were occupied during La Tène, Roman, and medieval times some or much of the slag may belong to these later occupations. Fragments of iron ore and slag found in Early Iron Age graves at sites such as Vače (Müllner 1908, p. 63), Toplice (Müllner 1908, p. 64), and Magdalenska gora (Rieth 1942, pp. 81–82) provide a direct connection between ironworking and the Early Iron Age occupation.

Although a number of iron smelting and forging sites have been found in the East Alpine area (Müllner 1908, pp. 68–70; Tylecote 1976, pp. 46–47; Coghlan 1977, pp. 21–38), only that on the Waschenberg near Wels in Upper Austria (Pertlwieser 1970; Pleiner 1980, pp. 386–387) can be confidently dated to the Early Iron Age. The context of the Waschenberg settlement suggests small-scale iron production in a small hamlet community (Pertlwieser 1969). Some evidence of the tools used by blacksmiths of the period is provided by the remarkable find in the Býcî Skála cave in Moravia, dating to the sixth century B.C. The remains of a blacksmith's shop were found, including ash and charcoal from the furnace, lumps of smelted but not forged iron, and iron tools including hammers, anvils, and tongs (Wankel 1882, p. 379–416; Pleiner 1962, p. 62, fig. 10, 1980, pp. 387, 392, fig. 11, 6).

The results of chemical and metallographic analyses of iron objects from Early Iron Age East Alpine Europe (Rieth 1942, pp. 148, 155–156; Coghlan 1977, pp. 118–119) show that metalworking knowledge and techniques there were similar to those in the regions of Europe for which more detailed analysis of iron objects has been carried out (Pleiner 1962, 1968; Piaskowski 1970). Many of the iron objects of the period are made of plain wrought iron, others of iron that had been heat-treated in order to improve the hardness of the object (Plöckinger 1976; Drescher 1980; Pleiner 1980, pp. 388–390). Examples of packet welding of iron and harder, more brittle steel in order to produce cutting tools combining the advantages of both materials have been identified (Pleiner 1962, pp. 259–261, 1968, p. 39). Techniques required to harden iron can be identified already in iron objects dating from the Late Bronze Age (Pleiner 1968, p. 41), hence any kind of developmental sequence of ironworking techniques over time is difficult to recognize at the present state of research. Apparently, sophisticated and advanced techniques were available to some Early Iron Age smiths, though such techniques were not always applied. It is possible that only a few of the smiths working at the time knew the more sophisticated techniques or that such techniques were used only for the production of iron implements for certain customers (Pleiner 1980, p. 390).

Without the archaeological evidence of ironworking sites, it is difficult to discuss the organization of iron production. The evidence from the Waschenberg suggests small-scale production at that site, but the lack of comparable finds makes evaluation difficult. Most needed is archaeological exploration and investigation of smelting and forging sites in order to provide the evidence for scale and organization of the industry.

Table 7 shows the quantities of iron in the Late Bronze and Early Iron Age cemeteries being considered here. The table records only the numbers of objects and does not take account of their sizes. Iron objects in Late Bronze Age contexts are generally small, such as jewelry objects and knives. If sizes of objects could be included in this table (by weight; see Pleiner 1980, p. 408, note 13, for typical weights of different iron objects), the differences between the Late Bronze and Early Iron Age cemeteries would be even greater.

In the Late Bronze Age cemeteries represented in the table, the percentage of all metal objects that are of iron never exceeds 4 percent, whereas in the Early Iron Age cemeteries it is consistently more than 20 percent, with the exception of the Mecklenburg graves from Hallstatt. The average numbers of bronze objects per grave are also important (see table 9), because they show that the increase in iron in the Early Iron Age was not accompanied by a decrease in bronze, but rather by an increase in that metal as well.

The most common iron objects in Early Iron Age graves are knives, spearheads, axes, fibulae, rings, and swords, all of which are represented among the grave goods in the Mecklenburg graves from Hallstatt and Stična.

Bronzeworking. Two aspects of bronzeworking in East Alpine Europe must be considered: (1) the acquisition of the copper and tin; and (2) the manufacture of finished products from bronze metal. Bronzeworking is a different matter from iron production, because copper does not occur in all parts of the region and, where it does occur, it must be mined in underground galleries; tin must be imported from other parts of Europe.

COPPER MINING. Since the 1930s Austrian prehistorians and mining engineers have been studying ancient copper mining sites in the Austrian Alps (summaries in Pittioni 1951; 1976b). The principal regions of prehistoric copper mining in Austria are in Land Salzburg and in the Tirol (map in Pittioni 1951, p. 17, fig. 1), where numerous mines have been identified and investigated (map 1 in Neuninger, Pittioni, Preuschen 1969). Other prehistoric mines have been studied in Lower Austria (Hampl 1976; Kerchler 1976) and Styria (Presslinger et al. 1980). The copper ores in the main mining regions are copper pyrites, that is sulphide ores (Pittioni 1951, p. 19). The ore deposits occur as thin veins of these pyrites in the graywacke zone of the slate Alps (*Schieferalpen*) (Pittioni 1951, pp. 17, 19). The gangue is principally quartz. Since the lode material is of a harder composition than the surrounding rock, the lode is often found protruding from the weathered surfaces of the mountains, and it was probably this feature that made the ore outcrops readily identifiable to experienced prehistoric prospectors (Pittioni 1951, p. 20).

Three different kinds of sites involved in copper mining have been studied at a number of different locations: (1) mine shafts cut into the copper lodes; (2) sites at which lode material was broken up to separate copper ore from surrounding rock; and (3) smelting sites (Pittioni 1951, pp. 20–21). Technical details of the processing of the ore can be found in literature cited in Pittioni 1976b.

Of particular interest to this study are estimates made of the total amounts of copper produced and of the numbers of miners involved. It is important to note that these studies have been carried out by archaeologists and mining specialists working together. Based on the technology available, the techniques of mining employed, and the quantities of ore removed from the galleries, investigators estimate that for the Salzburg area mines some 500 to 600 workers were employed in producing copper metal, cutting the mine shafts, collecting and preparing timber for gallery supports, separating ore from stone, transporting ore, and supervising the operations (Pittioni 1951, pp. 30–31). For the area around Kitzbühel in the Tirol, another 300 to 400 workers are estimated. Thus a total of some 800 to 1,000 individuals are thought to have taken active part in the production of the metal, probably on a year-round basis.

For the Mitterberg mines, among the most extensively investigated, and others in the vicinity of Bischofshofen in Land Salzburg, the total mass of ore removed by prehistoric miners is estimated at 1,300,000 tons, yielding some 20,000 tons of copper metal (Pittioni 1951, pp. 31–32). For all of the Austrian Alpine copper mines Pittioni estimates a copper output of some 50,000 tons (p. 32). These figures apply to total copper production from Early Bronze Age times through the Early Iron Age, and on present evidence it is not possible to separate phases of metal extraction into chronological periods. Pittioni and others have noted evidence for a marked increase in copper mining during the Late Bronze Age, but it is difficult to

Table 7. Iron in graves.

Cemetery	No. reliable graves	No. iron objects	Iron objects as % of all metal objects
Dobova	310	0	0
Hadersdorf	125	1	3.1
Novo mesto	44	2	33.3
Pobrežje	134	0	0
Ruše	206	4	3.08
St. Andrä	36	1	2.3
Wels	56	0	0
Hallstatt, M.*	24	5	5.0
Križna gora	153	82	34.0
Magdalenska gora, M. IV, VII, X	174	177	25.7
Stična, M. IV	50	24	17.3
Stična, other M.	98	49	15.3
Welzelach	56	58	38.2

*M. = Mecklenburg graves.

Explanation of tables 7 to 11. Tables 7 to 11 present numerical data from the seven Late Bronze Age and five Early Iron Age cemeteries selected for comparison (p. 101). Only those graves that seem to have been intact when excavated, as well as can be determined from the literature, are used. The column in each table labeled "number of reliable graves" indicates the number of well-documented grave groups. When only fragments of objects survive, I estimate the original number on the basis of the information contained in the publications.

These tables constitute a first, very rough, attempt to make use of such numerical data for comparison of cemeteries in this context. Except in the case of the Mecklenburg grave groups from Hallstatt, Stična, and Magdalenska gora, I have been unable to examine the objects themselves and hence have worked from the published literature. Ideally, a study of this kind would make use of the mass of the substances in question in each grave group. Surviving objects could be weighed, and the weights of fragmentary and missing objects could be estimated on the basis of surviving materials. In the absence of information about the mass of each object in all the graves, I feel that the numerical data contained in these tables illustrate significant patterns of change between the Late Bronze and Early Iron Ages.

In the category of weapons I include swords, spearheads, axes, helmets, and cuirasses, but not knives (which I consider as tools) or arrowheads (for hunting?).

find good data for comparing Late Bronze and Early Iron Age production (on Early Iron Age mining in these areas see Neuninger, Pittioni, Preuschen 1969, p. 68; Lippert 1972, p. 43; Moosleitner 1977; Pauli 1978, p. 403).

A number of cemeteries have been excavated in the vicinity of copper-mining and ore-processing sites in the Austrian Alps, providing information on the dating of the mining activity and on material culture, trade relations, and social structure of the communities producing copper. At Lebenberg (Kitzbühel, Tirol), for example, a small cemetery of 16 graves of Late Bronze Age date included one exceptional grave containing a bronze sword and spearhead, while the others contained typical modest inventories of the period (Pittioni 1952; Eibner, Plank, Pittioni 1966). Early Iron Age cemeteries associated with copper deposits have been studied at Zedlach (Lippert 1970), Welzelach (Lippert 1972), and Uttendorf (Moosleitner 1977), all in the Tirol. Each cemetery is characterized by graves more richly equipped with metal grave goods than most of the period. At Uttendorf, the presence of two-looped fibulae in the graves suggests interactions with communities in Slovenia, probably part of a trade in copper (Moosleitner 1977, p. 117).

TIN. Substantial deposits of tin that might have been worked in Early Iron Age times are lacking in the East Alpine region, hence the tin for bronze had to be imported from outside. See below (pp. 110–111) for discussion of the problems.

BRONZE INDUSTRY. The distributions of the various types of bronze fibulae, bracelets, belt attachments, weapons, and vessels (e.g., Gabrovec 1962-63, pp. 294, 321, maps 1, 2, 1970, pp. 25, 29, maps 4, 8) suggest that a large number of local bronzeworking centers were producing objects for local clientele in different parts of the East Alpine region. The frequency of nonlocal types in most cemeteries indicates that regular circulation of materials went on between different communities, but most of the bronze objects found in graves were produced within the region in which they were found. The Hallstatt cemetery is a major exception in the quantity of objects recovered in the graves that were probably produced elsewhere and brought to the site.

Because of the dearth of excavated settlements, we have very little good evidence bearing on the question of the distribution and organization of bronze workshops in the East Alpine region. In another part of central Europe, at the Heuneburg in southern Württemberg, a site comparable to Stična in some respects, evidence for bronzeworking has been recovered in the form of casting molds (Bittel and Rieth 1951, pl. 11,5; Schiek 1959, p. 121, fig. 2; Kimmig and von Vacano 1973) and bronze droplets from the casting process (Gersbach 1971, p. 74). These kinds of evidence of metalworking can be expected from the major settlements of the East Alpine region. A well-documented bronzeworking center of Late Bronze and Early Iron Age date was at Velem Szentvid in western Hungary, just east of the region under consideration. Unworked copper metal, tools used in the casting process, and a variety of stone molds have been recovered at that settlement (von Miske 1929; Foltiny 1958), providing a good impression of the probable character of contemporaneous bronze workshops of Austria and Slovenia.

From the bronze objects themselves we can note a major change in technique beginning during the Late Bronze Age and continuing in the Early Iron Age. This is the development of methods for producing large objects of sheet bronze (Drescher 1980) which either had not been made previously or only in very isolated instances. These objects include particularly vessels (e.g., fig. 37a), helmets (e.g., fig. 160), and cuirasses (e.g., fig. 85c–e), but also smaller and more common objects such as belt plates (e.g., fig. 70c), earrings (e.g., fig. 77a, f, g), and hollow arm and leg rings (e.g., fig. 189b). The production of the new, larger objects probably reflects the availability of greater quantities of bronze and the new ability of communities to support more specialized craftsmen who could learn and carry out the techniques necessary to produce such luxury objects. Also new in the Early Iron Age is the use of the lathe, apparent in the production of the phalerae at Hallstatt and Stična (fig. 29c; Pauli 1978, pp. 402–403; Drescher 1980, pp. 58–60).

Glassworking. Glass appears as early as the Middle Bronze Age in grave contexts in the East Alpine region, and during the Urnfield Period small glass beads, particularly of blue color, are found with some frequency in graves there and elsewhere in central Europe (Neuninger and Pittioni 1959; 1961; Haevernick 1978). In the Early Iron Age the quantities of glass occurring in graves increases greatly, particularly in Slovenia. Of the Late Bronze Age cemeteries listed in table 8, only two contained a single glass bead each, whereas all of the Early Iron Age cemeteries contained some glass, and in the tumuli at Stična about one-third of all graves contained some glass beads.

The quantities of glass beads are often large. In Tumulus II, Grave 2 of the Mecklenburg Collection from Stična were some 2,500 glass beads (p. 50 and fig. 36); given the excavation techniques, it is likely that there were other beads in the grave that were not recovered. In the tumulus at Stična excavated in the 1950s by the Narodni muzej of Ljubljana, six graves contained a total of some 20,500 glass beads (Haevernick 1974a, p. 62). Slovenia stands out not only as the

Table 8. Glass in graves.

Cemetery	No. reliable graves	No. graves with glass	% graves with glass
Dobova	310	1	0.32
Hadersdorf	125	0	0
Novo mesto	44	0**	0
Pobrežje	134	0	0
Ruše	206	0	0
St. Andrä	36	1	2.78
Wels	56	0	0
Hallstatt, M.*	24	1	4.17
Hallstatt, Ramsauer Excs.	980	70	7.14
Križna gora	153	9	5.88
Magdalenska gora, M. IV, VII, X	174	24	13.79
Stična, M. IV	50	19	38.00
Stična, other M.	98	26	26.53
Welzelach	56	1	1.79

*M. = Mecklenburg graves.
**Several glass beads were found as strays in the Novo mesto cemetery.

richest region of central Europe in numbers of glass beads, but also in the range of different kinds and colors of beads (Haevernick 1974a). The glass workshops in Slovenia produced beads for export as well as for local use (Haevernick 1974b, p. 152). No workshop sites have been identified as yet in the region, a situation that will probably change as more settlement research is carried out. The extraordinarily large numbers of glass beads in the graves at Stična (table 8), even relative to those at other sites in the vicinity such as Magdalenska gora, suggest that Stična may have been the principal center for the production of beads. The sizes of regions served by different glass workshops could be studied by numerical comparison of different kinds of glass beads at different cemeteries, but such an investigation has not yet been undertaken (on the problem of organization of glass bead production see Haevernick 1979, pp. 116, 118–119).

Goldworking. To judge by the small number of finds in the East Alpine region, goldworking was not a major industry. Yet the metal is of interest to this study because it occurs much more frequently in Early Iron Age contexts than in Late Bronze Age ones. Gold occurs in 23 of the 980 graves excavated by Ramsauer at Hallstatt, most often in very small quantities as spiral wire rings and thin gold-leaf covering on bronze ornaments. Exceptional is Grave 505 with a belt plate covering, two earrings, and an armband, all of sheet gold.

At the centers of Early Iron Age Slovenia, the principal occurrence of gold is in the form of "diadems" or fragments thereof, sheet gold cut into a variety of geometrical forms with impressed circular and linear patterns. The accompanying grave goods suggest that most of these "diadems" occur in the graves of women (Knez 1974, p. 118). The greatest quantity of gold in such a form, comprising a total of 2.94 gm, was recovered in Grave 27 of the Great Tumulus at Stična excavated by the Narodni muzej (Kastelic 1960; Gabrovec 1966, pp. 20–21, figs. 10, 11). Two similar fragments were found in Grave 40 of the same tumulus (Kastelic 1960, p. 21, pl. 5, 4–5). Fragments of sheet gold of more or less similar form and decoration to these occur in a number of other burial contexts in Slovenia, at Šmarjeta, Malence, Podzemelj, Loka pri Črnomlju, Libna, and Novo mesto (Kastelic 1960, pp. 21–24, 26, fig. 3; Knez 1974). Fragments very much like those from Grave 27 of the Great Tumulus were found by the Duchess in Grave IV/19a (fig. 74). (Other gold finds recovered by the Duchess at Stična include fragments of foil [Graves IV/33, VI/7], a band of sheet gold with impressed linear ornamentation [fig. 117c], and gold-leaf covering on bronze beads [fig. 45x, y].)

The gold at Hallstatt, Stična, and other East Alpine sites was most likely panned from streams in the different local regions (Pauli 1980, pp. 277–278). Many of the Alpine streams are relatively rich in the metal, and gold has been panned from them throughout historical times (Davies 1935, p. 175; Friedrich 1958).

Models of Scale and Organization. For the extractive industries in salt and copper in the Eastern Alps we have some evidence of the scale of operations in the cemeteries of the miners. For Hallstatt I have suggested an average population of some 206 people (p. 98), an estimate that agrees with that of Kromer (1958). If, as Häusler (1968) and later authors argue, the community at Hallstatt consisted of family units rather than of a special male-dominated work camp, then of these 206, the number of adult men in their prime may have been between 40 and 60. At Hallstatt it is likely that all family members played some active role in the production of salt, as was the case in the nineteenth century (Morton 1954, p. 68). Not all of the individuals working would have been in the mines cutting at the salt face, since many other tasks were necessary for the complete operation (see below).

Pittioni and his colleagues have estimated that some 800 to 1,000 individuals were involved at one time in the extraction of copper in the Austrian mining regions. Since a large number of prehistoric mines have been identified, none of the operations would have had to have been very large. The population of the copper-mining community represented in the cemetery at Welzelach was probably in the range of 10 to 20 (p. 99).

The scale of the manufacturing of finished products was similar. An examination of the quantities of iron objects in the graves at Stična will provide an example. Among the graves excavated there by the Duchess the most common iron objects are spearheads (26 specimens), axes (15 specimens), and knives (10). Other kinds of iron objects are much less frequently represented, such as roasting spits (fig. 149a, b), bits (fig. 159a), and rings of various types (figs. 33a, c, 140d). The kinds and quantities of iron objects in the 186 graves excavated by the Duchess are very similar to those recovered by other excavators at Stična (Gabrovec 1966; 1974).

The 186 graves excavated by the Duchess contained 26 spears, or 1 per 7.15 graves, 15 axes, or 1 per 12.4 graves, and 10 knives, or 1 per 18.6 graves. Working with the estimate of 5,610 Early Iron Age graves at Stična (p. 99), if the average number of spears, axes, and knives was the same throughout the cemetery, we could expect totals of 785 spears, 452 axes, and 302 knives in the cemetery. Taken over the estimated 350-year period of use of the cemetery, these figures represent just 2.2 spears, 1.3 axes, and 0.9 knives per year, on the average. Since the numbers of weapons in graves increase after about 600 B.C. (see e.g., Hencken 1978), we could calculate the numbers on the basis of the 200-year period 600 to 400 B.C., in which case we would get 3.9 spears and 2.3 axes per year, still very small numbers.

These numbers of iron objects do not necessarily represent the quantities produced, but only the quantities placed in graves. Yet the numbers are significant, because they represent the number of objects being removed from circulation and thus necessitating replacement for the living. If the number of individuals at Stična requiring spears, axes, and knives remained more or less constant during the period 600 to 400 B.C., then the number in the cemeteries would be the same as the number manufactured per year to keep the living communities equipped (leaving the issue of export trade aside for the moment). The striking aspect of these numbers is that they are so low. Even if we reckon with the other less frequently represented iron objects, and with other possible categories of iron objects not represented in the graves, such as plowshares and sickles, the scale of production of iron tools and weapons for local use was very small indeed and certainly would not have required the services of a full-time blacksmith at Stična.

The same kind of calculations can be made for the bronze objects in the graves, and again one is struck by the small level of production. The reason why the scale of manufacture appears to have been so large is because we tend to overlook the length of time involved. When the great quantities of fibulae, arm rings, glass beads, and other materials are reckoned over 200 or 350 years, the annual rate of production is seen to have been small.

The issue of the organization of industrial activity can be conveniently considered in two aspects, that of the extractive industries on the one hand and that of manufacturing on the other. The extraction of salt and copper by miners was limited geographically by nature; both minerals occur only in certain areas, in which miners must work in order to obtain them. In the case of each mineral, the actual mining operation had to be accompanied by a range of supporting activities such as felling, preparing, and transporting timber to build gallery supports, and carrying the mined salt and copper ore from the mine face to the surface for further processing. The persons doing these different tasks had to be working in close concert, since each effort had to coordinate smoothly with the others for efficient production. A managerial function had to be exercised by an individual or individuals in order to assure coordination of the various tasks. Such a managing role may well have been played by someone actively involved in the physical labors, since the size of these mining operations was small.

The only evidence available at present on the organization of the mining operations is that of the burials in the associated cemeteries. At Hallstatt and at the cemeteries associated with copper mining (such as Welzelach, Zedlach, Uttendorf), the graves are considerably more richly equipped with grave goods than most other graves of the period. This exceptional wealth is in the form of bronze vessels, bronze and iron weapons, and other metal objects, and, at Hallstatt in particular, substantial quantities of amber beads. The general high level of material wealth suggests that entire communities benefited from the profits of mineral extraction and export trade (Pittioni 1951, p. 39). It is particularly significant that these cemeteries associated with mining sites do not contain any extraordinarily rich burials. Even at Hallstatt, where some graves containing ornate swords, bronze vessels, gold, and imports appear considerably wealthier than many of the graves, still these richer graves are not topographically distinguished from their fellows, nor do they contain objects that occur exclusively in rich graves. Among the Hallstatt graves there is a continuum of wealth rather than any distinct breaks between plain and rich graves (Hodson 1977).

It is likely that the sword graves are those of individuals who were of above-average status and authority in the community, as swords are generally believed to mark the burials of community leaders in the early part of the Early Iron Age (Kossack 1972, p. 92). The 1,111 graves from Hallstatt studied by Kromer (1959a) include 19 graves with swords. Adding Mecklenburg Grave 24, we have a total of 20 sword graves out of 1,137. According to the current chronology, these graves date to the earlier period at Hallstatt, roughly 750 to 600 B.C. Projecting the rate of 20 sword graves per 1,137 over the rest of the rough total of 2,000 graves believed to have been excavated at Hallstatt, we can estimate a total of 35 sword graves. If we assume for the moment that each individual who possessed a sword had it for an average of 20 years (age 20 to 40), then using the formula

$$P = \frac{De_o^o}{t} + k,$$

where D is the number of sword graves and e is 20, we get a result of six individuals possessing a sword at any one time, on the average. In a community with a total population of some 206, six individuals with swords would represent one out of every 34 persons, a ratio similar to that of sword graves to other graves in the small communities throughout central Europe (Kossack 1959, p. 86, 1972, p. 90). If the model of the Hallstatt salt mines as operations carried on by several cooperating extended family units is correct (as Kilian-Dirlmeier 1969, 1971 and Maier 1974 argue; see also Pauli 1978, pp. 509–510 on the Dürrnberg), then these sword bearers can be viewed as leaders of extended family units (see below).

Among the sword graves at Hallstatt, there is little indication of differences in wealth to suggest any kind of ranking of these sword-bearing individuals. Instead, they share more or less similar burial inventories (Kromer 1958, p. 50). There are no graves at Hallstatt, nor at any of the copper-mining cemeteries, that differ markedly from other graves of their communities and that are distinguished topographically from the rest, as are the *Fürstengräber* of the Late Hallstatt Period in west-central Europe, such as Vix (Joffroy 1954), Hochdorf (Biel 1978), and Grafenbühl (Zürn 1970). Thus in the burial evidence at these mineral extraction sites we have no indication of one or more individuals having had much greater wealth and power than his fellows.

The essential aspect of these salt- and copper-mining industries is their organization on the basis of family units, and it is in this respect that they differ most from mines of the classical world and of more modern times. All of the evidence from Hallstatt, the Dürrnberg, Welzelach, and the others suggests that the individuals represented in the graves took part in the labors of the extractive process and also shared in the profits of the export trade. There is no evidence to suggest the existence of slavery at the mines (Pittioni 1951, p. 39; Pauli 1978, p. 510), and analysis of the skeletal remains in the graves at the Dürrnberg provides evidence that those individuals worked in the strenuous physical tasks of mining (Pauli 1978, p. 510; Schultz 1978).

Since such mining operations demanded not only hard work and good organization but also considerable technical knowledge and skill, it is likely that the family groups that worked the mines were highly specialized in this task and that members of such groups continued the family occupational tradition through the passing of generations. It will be interesting to see whether future physical anthropological studies may be able to identify specific family traits in the skeletal remains of mining populations as excavation on such sites continues.

For the production of iron from its ore the questions are different. In the East Alpine region iron is not restricted in its natural occurrence to certain ore bodies, like copper, but occurs in deposits of varying richness in metal and accessibility throughout the region (see p. 102). Thus the collection procedure does not require the degree of specialization as does the mining of copper and salt, nor did groups of miners need to travel far into otherwise sparsely inhabited mountainous regions in order to locate and extract the metal. The smelting of the iron ores required highly specialized technical knowledge, but the possessors of such knowledge did not have to form communities geographically separated from the main centers of population. Because of this geographical difference between the occurrences of copper and salt and iron, it is likely that the technical knowledge of identifying suitable iron ore and of iron smelting was transmitted fairly rapidly from one individual to another, whereas the knowledge of the techniques for extracting salt and copper from the mountains could have remained restricted for a long time.

Beyond production of the raw materials, the two principal issues of concern here are the extent to which full-time specialized craftsmen manufactured the finished products and the extent to which manufacturing was centered at a limited number of sites. As the discussion on page 107 indicates, the number of manufactured objects in East Alpine Europe was not as large as an initial impression suggests. The regular burial of a wide range of local bronze, iron, and glass products (and probably organic ones which have not survived) meant that manufacture of such goods had to be maintained in order to keep up the supply for the living, but the numbers of objects represented in the graves do not suggest the necessity of full-time craftsmen resident at the sites for production of goods for local consumption alone.

The manufacture of objects in metals and glass required considerable training and skill, and it is unlikely that more than just a few specialists were able to work in these materials. Bronze vessels, fibulae, helmets, and bracelets, not to mention the elegant products of the situla art, all required high levels of technical knowledge and experience to produce them (Drescher 1958, 1980). The same applies to iron spearheads, axes, knives, bits, and other objects, and to glass beads.

It is likely that the larger communities of East Alpine Europe, such as Stična, had resident in them full-time crafts specialists producing for that community and for other smaller communities in the greater vicinity and for export trade to more distant communities. The strong similarity of bronze and iron objects from many different sites in Lower Carniola would suggest such standardized and centralized production, perhaps by metalworkers at Stična. A community the size of Stična, with an average population of some 400 to 500, could probably have supported several such specialists, whereas smaller communities, such as Libna and Brezje, probably could not have. The same point applies to glass beads. For gold also, the great similarity of the fragments of "diadems" from the different sites suggests a common origin in a goldsmith's shop.

Trade

My concern here is with trade from the point of view of its importance in the changes that brought about the conditions that I call the Early Iron Age economy.

A convenient definition of trade is that offered by Polanyi: "the mutual appropriative movement of goods between hands" (1957, p. 266). Two aspects are of importance: (1) that the interaction is mutual (distinguishing trade from forceful seizures of goods); and (2) that the goods move.

Trade is unlikely to have contributed in any major way to the basic survival of communities of the East Alpine region. Since the lands are generally fertile and well watered, and the subsistence base was broad by the Late Bronze Age (see pp. 96–97), communities there, as in other parts of central Europe, could produce all of their foodstuffs locally. Other materials required for a comfortable existence, such as wood, leather, hides, and clay were readily available throughout the region.

Communities in East Alpine Europe were dependent upon trade for bronze, but this material I would not classify as a necessity. Surely bronze sickles, saws, axes, and knives improved the efficiency of agricultural production, building, and forest clearing, but they were not essential to human life. Salt in this context also cannot be considered a necessity. With the mixed animal and vegetable diet of the region, it is unlikely that the inhabitants required additional salt in order to stay alive; salt was a condiment and was used as a preservative for meat and fish (p. 113).

Although trade in the East Alpine region did not provide necessities for most of the inhabitants, the communities that were directly involved in the extractive industries came to depend upon the trade systems for their material wealth and probably to some extent for necessities. Copper miners, such as those at Lebenberg (Eibner, Plank, Pittioni 1966), Welzelach (Lippert 1972), and Uttendorf (Moosleitner 1977), gained the wealth so apparent in their graves, and probably other items such as foods and textiles, from export trade in the metal they mined. The large community of salt miners at Hallstatt probably depended largely upon imports of food and other necessities to maintain themselves, since the Salzbergtal and environs could not have provided many of the necessities of life. These specialized mining communities of the Alpine regions were very different from the large communities that developed in the fertile lands of Carniola.

Three aspects of trade are of particular interest here. First, trade is a means of acquiring goods not available to a community locally, including both raw materials such as copper and tin and luxury products manufactured elsewhere. A community can overcome the shortcomings of its natural environment by importing raw materials and can acquire finished products from other cultural traditions. Second, trade serves to initiate and maintain contact between communities and between societies. Such contact can play an important part in effecting cultural change (Wells 1980a). Third, trade can function as an outlet and stimulus for a growing economy. A community that is able to produce a surplus beyond its own needs of a material that is in demand by another community is able to grow in wealth through increased production and trade of that material.

Here I shall discuss briefly the principal traded materials in the Eastern Alps.

Copper. As the principal component of bronze, copper was essential in the metal production of the Late Bronze and Early Iron Ages. The sources of the copper for the East Alpine region were probably the various mines in the Austrian Alps, particularly those in the Tirol and Salzburg (Pittioni 1952; Lippert 1972, pp. 54–55; Moosleitner 1977, p. 117). The archaeological remains of the mining and smelting operations indicate many different mines operating simultaneously and generating substantial quantities of metal (see above).

In the graves of the Late Bronze Age copper metal is present in the form of bronze jewelry and occasionally larger objects. As table 9 indicates, usually less than half of the graves in cemeteries of this period have any bronze in them. The most frequent kind of bronze object in the graves is a small garment pin or an arm ring. Fibulae, neck rings, and other such ornaments also occur with some frequency (Müller-Karpe 1959). Bronze knives occur infrequently. Larger bronze objects are rare. The quantities of bronze in the graves in this period are small relative to those of the following Early Iron Age. Hoards contain considerable quantities of the metal, usually in the form of broken objects intended for remelting and recasting (see pp. 122–123).

Bronze is much more abundant in graves of the Early Iron Age than in those of the Late Bronze Age. Table 9 shows the percentages of graves at the several cemeteries containing bronze objects and also the average number of bronze objects per grave. In every case well over half of the graves contain bronze. In addition, the quantities of the metal are much greater than in the Late Bronze Age. The average number of bronze objects per grave gives an impression of this difference between the two periods, but does not indicate that Early Iron Age graves often contain much larger bronze objects, such as swords, vessels, helmets, cuirasses, and large rings, all of which are rare in Late Bronze Age graves. This change occurs throughout the East Alpine area—at Hallstatt, in the inner Alpine regions, and in Slovenia. A glance at any of the published catalogues of the Early Iron Age cemeteries will make this aspect immediately apparent.

This evidence indicates that great quantities of copper were being traded from the mining and processing sites to settlements throughout East Alpine Europe during the Early Iron Age, quantities much greater than those of the Late Bronze Age.

Tin. There is no evidence for mining and processing of tin in the East Alpine region, nor in any immediately adjacent region; therefore, unlike copper the tin was probably being imported from some dis-

Table 9. Bronze in graves.

Cemetery	No. reliable graves	% graves with bronze	Average no. bronze objects per grave
Dobova	310	31.6	0.68
Hadersdorf	125	16.0	0.25
Novo mesto	44	9.1	0.09
Pobrežje	134	42.5	0.95
Ruše	206	28.6	0.61
St. Andrä	36	55.6	1.17
Wels	56	44.6	0.98
Hallstatt, M.*	24	87.5	3.96**
Križna gora	153	44.4	1.04
Magdalenska gora, M. IV, VII, X	174	64.4	2.94
Stična, M. IV	50	68.0	2.30***
Stična, other M.	98	72.4	2.77
Welzelach	56	62.5	1.68

*M. = Mecklenburg graves.
**For this calculation, the buttons in Grave 3 are counted as three objects; the beads in Grave 14 as two objects.
***For this calculation, the beads in Grave 7 are counted as one object; the buttons in Grave 30 as five objects.

Table 10. Amber in graves.

Cemetery	No. reliable graves	No. graves with amber	% graves with amber
Dobova	310	0	0
Hadersdorf	125	0	0
Novo mesto	44	0	0
Pobrežje	134	0	0
Ruše	206	0	0
St. Andrä	36	0	0
Wels	56	0	0
Hallstatt, M.*	24	2	8.3
Hallstatt, Ramsauer Excs.	980	165	16.8
Križna gora	153	10	6.5
Magdalenska gora, M. IV, VII, X	174	37	21.3
Stična, M. IV	50	16	32.0
Stična, other M.	98	35	35.7
Welzelach	56	2	3.6

*M. = Mecklenburg graves.

tance away. Among the regions where tin occurs that have been considered in discussions of prehistoric tin in central European bronze are Cornwall, the Erzegebirge of East Germany, Bohemia, central France, Brittany, and Iberia (Muhly 1973, pp. 248–261; Hencken 1974; Coghlan 1975, p. 23; Bankoff 1977, p. 14; Piggott 1977). However, in the present state of the research, we have no good evidence to suggest which ore sources were being exploited for the tin used in the East Alpine region.

Amber. Amber is rare in Late Bronze Age contexts in all of central Europe, including the East Alpine region (table 10). In part this rarity may have to do with the practice of cremation burial; amber may have been burned with the corpse. But since grave goods were often placed in the grave after the cremation, this explanation cannot account completely for the small amounts present. In the Early Iron Age amber is abundant in East Alpine graves, most particularly at the centers of Hallstatt in Upper Austria and those of Lower Carniola in Slovenia. The most common form of amber is that of beads, which occur in various shapes and sizes (see figures accompanying the catalogue of the Mecklenburg graves from Stična).

The graves at Stična excavated by the Duchess provide a good indication of the quantities of amber at some of the East Alpine centers. Of 148 reasonably well-documented graves, 51, or 34 percent, contained some amber. In the best-documented tumulus, Tumulus IV, 16 of the 50 "good" graves, or 32 percent, contained amber. The number of beads in these 16 graves ranges from one to 159, the weight per grave from 0.5 gm of amber to 159 gm, with a total of 738 gm in the 50 graves (see accompanying graph). At Stična and elsewhere in Slovenia, amber beads are usually associated in graves with arm and leg rings and glass beads, all characteristically (but not exclusively) women's grave goods. Among the Mecklenburg graves from Stična, amber never occurs with weapons, although it does in some other, exceptionally rich, men's graves elsewhere in Slovenia (e.g., Knez 1978).

Technical studies of amber recovered at Hallstatt and at the centers of Lower Carniola demonstrate that almost all, if not all, of it is "Baltic amber" (Beck and Sprincz, in press; see Beck's technical study in this volume, pp. 36–37). Classical writers such as Pliny consistently cite the Baltic as the source of amber imported to the Mediterranean world.

Most scholars agree that an overland route for the amber transportation from the Baltic to the East Alpine region is most likely (Strong 1966; Malinowski 1971; Bohnsack 1976). In present-day Poland several large hoards of raw amber have been found, which can be connected with loads of the material being transported south to the centers of east-central Europe (Malinowski 1971). It is unlikely that any one or several "amber routes" were consistently followed by those carrying the substance. As examples from historical times demonstrate (e.g., Klein 1950) routes used in long-distance trade are multiple and alternate, and the transporters choose one route or another depending upon immediate conditions of weather, warfare, tolls, or other variables.

The greatest quantities of amber in central Europe are found at the East Alpine centers, particularly those in Lower Carniola but also at Hallstatt. Several scholars have suggested that much of the amber in graves of west-central Europe was arriving via these commercial centers of the Eastern Alps (Kimmig 1975a, p. 201). It is very likely that the amber from Baltic Europe was transported to these centers, where some was put into local use and some traded on to Italy (Bohnsack 1976). Evidence for commercial interactions between Italy and the Eastern Alps is abundant (particularly at Hallstatt and at the Lower Carniola centers), and the amber trade was only a part of a larger system involving exchange of such materials as metals, foodstuffs, hides, and honey from the Eastern Alps for bronze ornaments, pottery, wine, and other materials from Italy (see below).

Some of the amber that was transported from the East Alpine centers to Italian workshops was re-exported northward in the form of carved ornaments. At Stična the amber ornament for a fibula bow from Grave VI/7 (fig. 137m), among other objects, may have been carved in a workshop in Etruria or northern Italy (see Massaro 1943).

Graphite. Graphite was used abundantly in the Early Iron Age for surface decoration of pottery, and the Mecklenburg graves from Hallstatt and Stična contain many examples of vessels with graphite coatings. Graphite has a limited distribution in nature, and occurs at a number of different locations within the East Alpine region (Kossack 1959, p. 71; Kappel 1969; *Atlas of the World's Resources*, vol. 2). On the basis of analyses of graphite on pottery from Hallstatt, Köhler and Morton (1954) conclude that the graphite came from both Alpine and Lower Austrian deposits. Modern studies of graphite source areas and trade in the Early Iron Age are lacking. In any case the common use of graphite on pottery throughout East Alpine Europe indicates substantial exploitation and trade of this material.

Salt. The evidence for production and export trade of salt at Hallstatt has been summarized above (pp. 7–12). As a water-soluble mineral, salt does not survive archaeologically on settlements, and the only evidence of its extraction and exportation is found in the prehistoric galleries and graves. The scale of this industry can be estimated from the cubic meters of salt and salt-clay mixture removed from the mountain (p.

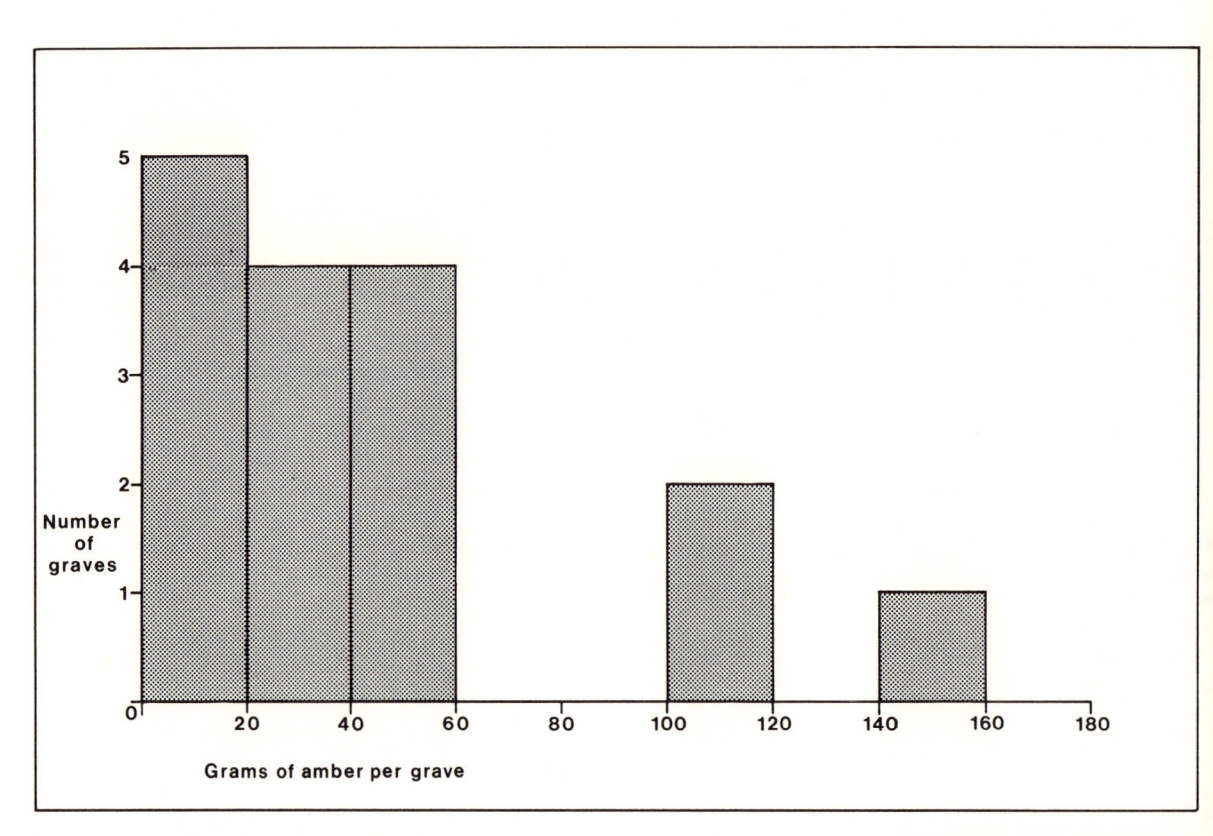

Text figure XXVI. Graph showing the quantities of amber in the well-documented grave groups from Tumulus IV at Stična. Amber beads were found in 16 of the 50 well-documented graves in this tumulus.

11), but this figure represents only a minimum, since it is derived from the galleries that have been discovered to date in modern mining operations.

The objects in the graves at Hallstatt indicate the parts of Europe with which the community was in commercial contact, that is to say, the parts to which it probably traded salt. More distant contacts are indicated by luxury products from northern Italy and Slovenia (see below) and by numerous small objects, such as fibulae, from different parts of central Europe. The amber at Hallstatt may reflect a trade of salt to northern parts of the continent, or the amber may have been arriving at Hallstatt from intermediary communities within the central European area. Closer and more regular contacts with communities of southern Bavaria, Upper Austria, and Lower Austria are suggested by the pottery and many of the jewelry objects in the Hallstatt graves (Pittioni 1976a, p. 257; Wells 1978b, pp. 86–88).

Because of its location in a steep, narrow valley surrounded by high Alps, the community of roughly 206 persons at Hallstatt was probably unable to produce all its own food (Kromer 1958, p. 39). The land is not fertile, and much of the ground lies in the shade of the high mountains even during the summer months. The community probably relied heavily upon imports of food, textiles, and other necessities from surrounding agricultural regions. The pottery and jewelry in the graves, with their close similarities to such materials in other parts of lowland Austria and Bavaria, may have been exchanged, along with foodstuffs and other substances that do not survive, for salt (Pittioni 1954, p. 643). The community at Hallstatt had to import copper and tin from outside, but was probably able to produce its own iron from small local surface deposits of the ore (p. 102).

There is some disagreement among scholars whether extra salt is required by persons with a mixed diet of vegetable and animal foods, but the prevailing opinion is that additional salt would probably not have been required by Early Iron Age peoples of central Europe (Multhauf 1978). Nonetheless salt was in great demand as a condiment and for use in preserving meat and fish (Pauli 1974, pp. 131–132; Carter 1975). Salt trade has been an important economic factor in many different contexts, and wars have been fought over salt deposits (Nenquin 1961; Bloch 1963). Duby (1974, p. 105) considers salt to have been the principal object of long-distance trade in early medieval Europe.

The wealth of grave goods in the cemetery at Hallstatt, greater than that in most cemeteries of Early Iron Age central Europe, attests to the material rewards of the salt trade. Besides the pottery, bronze, and iron objects characteristic of graves of the period, the graves at Hallstatt contain large numbers of objects that occur principally in rich graves elsewhere, such as swords, daggers, amber beads, and bronze vessels.

Iron. Trade in iron, like that in salt, is difficult to document in the East Alpine region in the present state of the research. Iron ore is abundant in Slovenia, Styria, and Carinthia in rich surface deposits (p. 102), and once the technology of its extraction and forging was introduced, iron metal was readily available to those communities in the region that had individuals versed in the techniques. The scale of iron smelting during the Early Iron Age is apparent in the great slag deposits on many of the settlements of the period in Slovenia (see p. 102) and in the large numbers of iron objects in the cemeteries.

Some regions neighboring the Eastern Alps were not as well endowed with iron ore, such as northeast Italy (Rieth 1942, p. 135). During the Roman period a large-scale trade in iron existed between the East Alpine iron-producing regions and northern Italy (Davies 1935, p. 173; Egger 1961; Alföldy 1974, pp. 111–114; Mócsy 1974, p. 31). Šašel (1977) argues that Strabo's (IV 6, 10–12, V 1, 8, VII 5, 2) description of trade between the regions, which mentions this trade in iron, refers to conditions of the Early Iron Age. There is abundant evidence for regular interactions between the peoples of the Eastern Alps and northeast Italy from the eighth century B.C. on (Frey 1966, 1969, 1974b; Kastelic 1965). Iron objects are well represented in the graves at Este (Frey 1969) and other sites in northeast Italy during the Early Iron Age, and these may have been produced of iron from the Eastern Alps. From the end of the sixth century B.C. iron from these sources may also have been supplying the Greek port cities of Adria and Spina (Alfieri and Arias 1958) in the Italian regions of the Head of the Adriatic. Technical analyses of iron objects from northeast Italy and of those in the graves in East Alpine regions and of slag associated with the Early Iron Age settlements may provide further evidence of this trade.

Many specialists in East Alpine prehistory have suggested that the development of the iron industry during this period was the basis of the cultural fluorescence of the centers in Slovenia (e.g., Müllner 1908, p. 31; Gabrovec 1966, p. 42, 1980, pp. 41–42; Pauli 1980, p. 276). I suggest that it was this export trade of iron from these regions that enabled some of the communities to acquire considerable wealth in imported goods, thereby stimulating further production which in turn led to the emergence of the manufacturing and commercial centers of the period (see below).

Glass. Little systematic work has been done to date on the subject of trade in glass, though the studies of Haevernick indicate some of the patterns apparent in the evidence. The glass bowls or cups, three of which have been found in the graves at Hallstatt and seven more in the burials at Most na Soči, are thought to have been manufactured at or near the latter site (Haevernick 1958). In her study of the glass beads from the graves at the Dürrnberg at Hallein, Haevernick identifies a large number of beads of Slovenian origin (1974b, p. 152). The large quantities of glass beads being produced at some of the centers in Slovenia were being traded as well as worn locally, but the scale and extent of the trade in glass still needs to be investigated.

Agricultural and Forest Products. Evidence for trade in these materials very rarely survives in the archaeological record. Even though prehistoric trade in such substances must usually remain hypothetical, it is nonetheless important to consider the likely commerce in such items, since trade in organic materials of these kinds was usually of much greater significance than that in the metal, ceramic, and glass products that survive. This point has been emphasized for both the classical (Will 1955–1956, pp. 157–159; Cook 1972, p. 276) and the medieval (Pirenne 1937, p. 157) contexts, as well as for agrarian societies in general (Cipolla 1970, p. 66).

In his discussion of trade between the region of Italy at the Head of the Adriatic and the East Alpine region, which Šašel (1977) believes to describe Early Iron Age circumstances, Strabo (IV 6, 10–12, V 1, 8, VII 5, 2) cites as products going from the Eastern Alps slaves, cattle, hides, resin, pitch, wax, honey, cheese, gold, and iron, and as products going from Italy eastward he mentions wine and oil. This list of items going from the Eastern Alps is similar to the list made by Polybius (IV 38, 4–5) of products traded from the lands north of the Black Sea to Greek colonists on the shores of that sea and conforms to a general pattern of agricultural, forest, and mineral products traded by peoples of inland Europe to merchants representing the more urbanized societies of the Mediterranean region (see e.g., Cary 1949; Semple 1931; Braudel 1972).

Even though at present we cannot demonstrate trade in these materials, we need to reckon with such a commerce, since it was probably of much greater economic significance to the communities concerned than the archaeologically obvious exchange of pottery and bronze ornaments.

Luxury Goods. I turn now to a much smaller group of luxury products that occur in archaeological contexts in the East Alpine region and that were imported in finished form. They originated principally in Italy and other parts of the Mediterranean world and are best represented at the major trade centers, at Hallstatt and in Lower Carniola. A few of the most important objects will be cited here.

Luxury products from Italy are well represented at Hallstatt. For example, the ornamented lids and probably their accompanying situlae from Graves 696 and 697 (Kromer 1959a, pls. 126, 1.3 and 128, 1.5–7) were most likely manufactured at or near Este in northeast Italy (Pittioni 1949, p. 117; Frey 1969, p. 52; Polenz 1978). The bronze "comb" helmet from Hallstatt, perhaps from Grave 49 of the Linz excavations, was also made in Italy (Egg 1978a). A variety of fine crafts products from Slovenia are present in the graves at Hallstatt, such as the three glass bowls from Graves 502 and 733 (Haevernick 1958) and several bronze helmets, as well as smaller items (Egg 1978b).

In Lower Carniola the site of Stična has yielded a number of imported fine crafts products. The decorated sheet bronze situla lid was probably made in the Este region of Italy (Ložar 1937a; Kastelic 1960, p. 19, pl. I,5; Frey 1969, pls. 54, 55,6). The ceramic oinochoe found in the same grave was most likely made in southern Italy (Jacobsthal 1956, p. 179; Gabrovec 1966, p. 33; Frey 1969, pp. 53–55, text pl. A,1). The ceramic "Apulian" craters, recovered at Stična (Kastelic 1960, p. 19 and pl. III,3) and other sites in Slovenia (Frey 1969, pp. 76–79, 114), also probably originated in southern Italy. Ceramic objects of southern Italian origin have also been found at Magdalenska gora and other sites (Frey 1969, p. 84, note 420). Probable Etruscan imports in Slovenia include several bronze figurines and the bronze tripod from Novo mesto (Gabrovec 1968; Staré 1975a). The ceramic rhyton in Stična Mecklenburg Grave IV/47 (fig. 101a) and the kylix in Grave II/7 (fig. 41) were most likely made somewhere on the east coast of the Adriatic, though their origins are uncertain in the present state of the research (see pp. 52, 66).

Imported objects from greater distances have also been recovered at Stična. The bronze bowl ornamented with palmettes in relief from the *Panzergrab* (Ložar 1937b; Jacobsthal 1956, pp. 178–179, figs. 582–584; Gabrovec 1966, p. 11, fig. 5,4) was probably made in a workshop at the eastern end of the Mediterranean. The polychrome glass bottle from Stična is believed to have originated in Egypt (Kastelic 1960, p. 19, and pl. III,2). The settlement excavations at Stična have yielded at least one sherd of what is probably Attic pottery (Gabrovec, Frey, Foltiny 1970, p. 32).

All of these luxury imports at Stična and other sites in Slovenia, and some at Hallstatt, are vessels for holding liquids. It is very likely that the principal communities were importing wine from Italy (Šašel 1977) and that these vessels arrived as part of the import trade in wine, much like the Attic pottery, ceramic amphorae, and Greek and Etruscan bronze vessels in west-central Europe during the Late Hallstatt period (Wells 1977, 1980a). These imported vessels at Hallstatt, Stična, and elsewhere are types associated with wine drinking in the Mediterranean world. The banquet scenes in the situla art strongly suggest the drinking of wine, and wine residue has been identified in the bronze flask of only slightly later date from the Dürrnberg (Specht 1972, p. 128).

To date, the number of such imported vessels found in the East Alpine region is much smaller than that of Attic pottery, ceramic amphorae, and bronze vessels found at settlements and in graves in west-central Europe (Wells 1977, 1980a). This difference may depend in part on the lack of extensive settlement excavation in the former region. Many of the investigated sites in west-central Europe, such as the Heuneburg (Kimmig 1975b), Mont Lassois (Joffroy 1960), the Britzgyberg (Schweitzer 1973), Château-sur-Salins (Dayet 1967), and Châtillon-sur-Glâne (Schwab 1975), have yielded Attic pottery and ceramic amphorae. At Stična the limited settlement excavations have yielded a single probable Attic sherd. As excavations continue at Stična and at other East Alpine sites, this picture will probably change. On the other hand, the graves are well known, and they have not yielded Attic pottery (as did the burial at Vix) nor many Greek or Etruscan bronze vessels which are so well represented in the rich burials of west-central Europe. Thus, there are major differences between East Alpine Europe and west-central Europe in the nature of trade relations with Mediterranean societies reflected in these different patterns of imports found. Future excavation of the settlements in the Eastern Alps will help to clarify the similarities and differences in the two, partly contemporaneous situations.

Mechanisms and Models. The definition of trade adopted above (p. 109) implies peaceful transmission of materials. It is unlikely that violent means, such as piracy or capture of booty in warfare (see Reinecke 1958; Grierson 1959), played a major role in the transmission of goods in the context under consideration here. The apparent regularity of movement of goods throughout the Early Iron Age suggests peaceful and organized trade systems.

Gift exchange is an important mechanism for the circulation of materials in traditional societies (Mauss 1967; Sahlins 1972a), and Fischer (1973) has argued for this mode of circulation in Late Hallstatt and Early La Tène west-central Europe. In the East Alpine region there are no extraordinary luxury imports of the character of the Vix krater and "diadem" (Joffroy 1954), the bronze cauldron and couch from Hochdorf (Biel 1978), or the tripod and sphinxes from Grafenbühl (Zürn 1970), all of which differ from the majority of Mediterranean imports in west-central Europe and probably constituted "political gifts," as Fischer suggests. The lack of such extraordinary imports in East Alpine contexts suggests a difference in the nature of the trade relations. Such objects as the situlae with ornamented lids in Hallstatt Graves 696 and 697 may have constituted "political gifts" of a sort, but they are in no respect as exceptional as the aforementioned objects in west-central Europe.

For the bulk materials, including copper and tin, graphite, amber, salt, and the probable exports of iron and agricultural and forest products, a highly organized trade system is likely, perhaps comparable to some in traditional societies documented historically and ethnographically (e.g., Sundström 1974; Curtin 1975). The quantities of these materials at sites in all parts of the East Alpine region throughout the Early Iron Age suggest that trade was regular and institutionalized. We do not know how and where the exchange transactions took place, nor the quantities of materials exchanged in transactions. It is unclear, for example, whether the producers of copper in the Tirol and Salzburg organized transport of the metal to the populous centers of Slovenia, or whether those latter communities sent individuals to the mining regions to trade for metal. The same question pertains to salt at Hallstatt, amber from the Baltic region, and to all the other products discussed above. Further excavation of the settlement sites may well provide evidence bearing on this problem, for example, in traces of foreign merchants residing at the centers.

The transport of all the bulk materials was probably accomplished principally with pack horses, which are well documented in these regions from ancient into modern times (Müllner 1908, p. 32; Klein 1950; Pauli 1980, pp. 222–224, 230–231). Wagons may also have been in use (Jankuhn 1969, pp. 97–98) and are mentioned in this region by Strabo (IV 6, 10, V 1, 8, VII 5, 2).

Organization of the circulation of materials is closely connected with social organization. In traditional societies, trade is usually controlled by the principal personage in each community, the senior man or woman of a family or the headman of a larger social unit. This individual regulates interactions between his community and the outside world and is also the coordinator of his community's economic activities, and thus acts as the economic focus for production and collection of materials for export and as the redistributor of imported materials (see Wells 1980a, pp. 5–8). Trade in the various materials discussed above in the East Alpine area was most likely in the hands of the principal heads of each community, who organized the production of materials for export and the distribution of goods coming in from outside. This model applies whether we consider the small, nuclear family-occupied farmsteads or the large centers, such as Hallstatt and Stična, whose social organization was that of an agglomeration of individual family units (see below).

In cultural contexts such as Early Iron Age Europe, in which a variety of different materials were being traded, different goods were transmitted through different mechanisms (see e.g., Herlihy 1971; Chang 1975). A detailed discussion of the various trade networks for the different materials is beyond the scope of this study, although the rich data base now permits such an analysis. For present purposes it will suffice to draw attention to three main aspects of the interconnected trade systems: (1) trade between East Alpine communities and regions outside of that area; (2) trade between communities in different parts of the East Alpine area; and (3) circulation between centers and smaller communities in their immediate vicinities (see text figs. XXVII–XXIX). These three trade systems were interdependent. The circulation of raw materials and probably foodstuffs from the small communities to Stična allowed that community to specialize in manufacturing, and thus to increase the quantities of materials, such as bronze objects and glass beads, that could be traded with communities elsewhere. Products obtained by the community at Stična from other regions, such as amber and salt, could then be exchanged with the smaller communities. Thus these three levels of trade networks were interrelated, and all operated together as part of a single, multifaceted system.

SOCIAL ORGANIZATION

The changes that took place at the start of the Early Iron Age can be understood only in terms of the social organization of the communities involved. I use the term "social organization" here to mean simply the organization of relations between people. The archaeological data do not provide direct evidence about so-

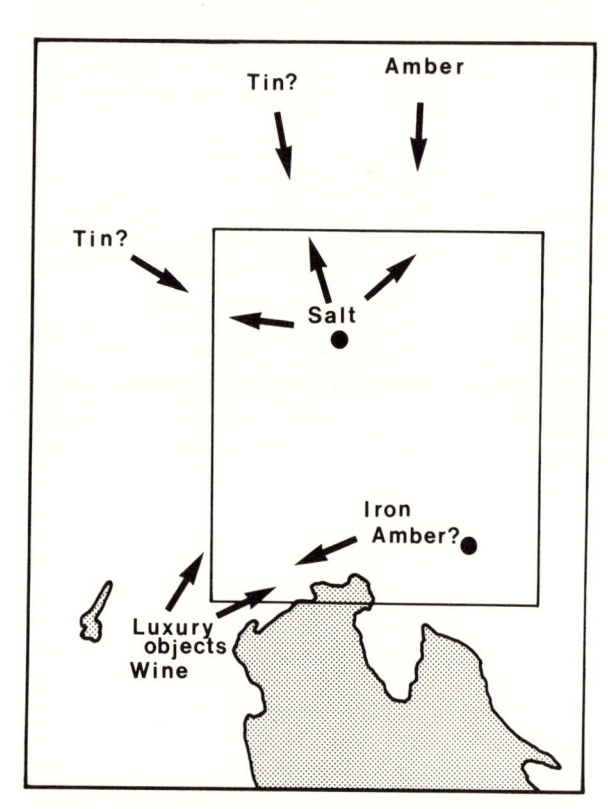

Text figure XXVII. Schematic representation showing a few of the materials traded between communities in the East Alpine region and other parts of Europe. The communities at Hallstatt and Stična probably played a major role in the importation of products from outside the region, as is suggested by the quantities of such imports (especially amber and luxury objects) in the graves at these sites.

Text figure XXVIII. Representation showing several of the materials traded between communities in different parts of the East Alpine region. Trade within the region is well attested by a variety of different kinds of materials in the cemeteries, for example, objects from Lower Carniola in graves at Hallstatt (Egg 1978b) and at the copper-mining cemetery of Uttendorf (Moosleitner 1977, p. 117).

cial organization; but the scale of the settlements, the nature of the economies, and the burial patterns provide partial sources of information from which to propose models for social organization in this context. The principal source of information in East Alpine Europe is that of the graves.

The issue of extracting data about social organization from burials has been much discussed in the literature (see references in Wells 1980a, pp. 47–48). Briefly, although the relationship between social patterns and burial practices is complex, ethnographic and historical burial data demonstrate that certain connections can usually be drawn between the material evidence of graves and the social patterns they reflect. Burial evidence incorporates much potential information about social organization that can be extracted by the archaeologist (see e.g., Rathje 1970; Pauli 1972; Christlein 1973; Kossack 1974; Shennan 1975).

Patterns in the Evidence

Late Bronze Age (Hallstatt A and B, roughly 1200 to 750 B.C.). Burial during this period was characteristically by cremation, the cremated remains being placed in an urn which was buried in a small pit in the ground, usually without any kind of tumulus over it. There is considerable variation, both regionally and within single cemeteries, in the form and structure of the pit and in the number and location of grave goods. Sizes of cemeteries vary greatly, from very small ones of just a few graves to great urnfields comprising many hundreds.

The most common grave good is pottery. The majority of graves of the period contain a ceramic urn, and many contain additional ceramic vessels of various forms and sizes as further grave offerings. Bronze objects occur in graves as well, but much less frequently and in smaller numbers than pottery; iron is rare. The most common bronze objects are garment pins and ring jewelry, both of which usually are found singly. Fibulae occur occasionally, and bronze knives are often represented in a few graves in each cemetery. Less common are other bronze objects, including needles, awls, and belt hooks. All of these objects are small, incorporating little metal. More elaborate items, such as weapons and vessels, are very rare. Also rare are exotic substances such as glass, amber, and gold.

Table 11 indicates the percentages of graves in each cemetery containing any metal objects and weapons. All of the cemeteries have some graves that contain bronze objects, but in no instance do more than half of them. Only one weapon is present in any of the cemeteries—at Dobova. Neither gold nor amber is present, and only a single glass bead occurs in one grave at Dobova and in one at St. Andrä (see tables 8, 10).

In cemeteries of the Late Bronze Age in the East Alpine region, as in other parts of central Europe, there is little differentiation among the graves with respect to the burial goods. Most variation is in the numbers of ceramic vessels and the presence or absence of one or a few bronze objects. A very small number of exceptionally rich graves are known in all of central Europe, such as the one at Hart an der Alz in Upper Bavaria (Müller-Karpe 1955), containing the cremated remains of an individual together with a wagon with bronze fittings, a bronze sword, three bronze vessels (bucket, sieve, cup), and a spiral ring of gold wire. As Peroni points out (1979, p. 13), such burials are very exceptional and are to be regarded as isolated instances rather than as parts of a consistent pattern of cultural significance.

On the basis of population estimates, it is apparent that Late Bronze Age settlements were occupied by

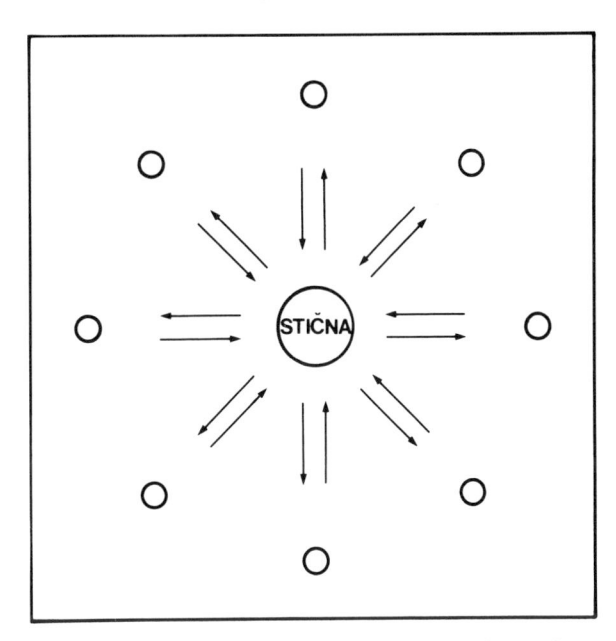

Text figure XXIX. Representation of circulation between centers and smaller communities, using the example of Stična. The community at Stična was probably actively engaged in commerce with the smaller settlements of the region, including both sites such as Šmarjeta and Libna and individual farmsteads, which are little known archaeologically at the present. On the basis of the evidence from cemeteries at sites such as Šmarjeta and Libna and related situations elsewhere (see Wells 1980a), it can be hypothesized that Stična traded manufactured goods (bronze ornaments, iron tools and weapons, glass beads) and imported substances (amber, graphite) in exchange for raw materials, foodstuffs, and other plant and animal products (such as textiles and leather) generated by the smaller communities.

Table 11. Percentages of graves containing metal and weapons.

Cemetery	No. reliable graves	% graves with metal	% graves with weapons
Dobova	310	31.6	0.3
Hadersdorf	125	16.0	0
Novo mesto	44	11.4	0
Pobrežje	134	42.5	0
Ruše	206	29.1	0
St. Andrä	36	55.6	0
Wels	56	44.6	0
Hallstatt, M.*	24	87.5	12.5
Križna gora	153	60.8	2.0
Magdalenska gora, M. IV, VII, X	174	79.9	33.3
Stična, M. IV	50	76.0	18.0
Stična, other M.	98	77.6	17.3
Welzelach	56	64.3	23.2

*M. = Mecklenburg graves.

small groups: nuclear families, extended families, or several extended family units. Cemetery sizes suggest that the settlements were for the most part single farmsteads, hamlets, and very small villages (see p. 99).

Early Iron Age (Hallstatt C and D, roughly 750 to 400 B.C.). It is well to remind ourselves that the concepts of Late Bronze and Early Iron Age, as well as the Hallstatt phases A to D, are all artificial constructs imposed upon a fluid and continuous series of cultural developments. These constructs are useful for comparing earlier and later configurations in the patterns of the evidence.

Beginning during the eighth century B.C., changes took place in burial patterns in East Alpine Europe, as well as in other parts of central Europe. Burials in tumuli became the predominant form, replacing flat graves in most regions. Other changes were a general increase in wealth in graves and the appearance of a small number of graves more richly outfitted than the majority.

The general increase in wealth in Early Iron Age graves, apparent in tables 7 to 11, is a reflection of the increase in production, trade, and material well-being during this period as compared with the Late Bronze Age. An instructive comparison can be made between the bronze objects of the two periods.

As table 9 shows, Early Iron Age graves contain substantially greater quantities of bronze objects than do Late Bronze Age ones. If comparison of cemeteries were made on the basis of weight of bronze metal, instead of simply numbers of objects, the difference would be more striking. (Extensive data on weights of objects in the graves are not available at present.) Whereas in the earlier period almost all of the objects are small jewelry pieces and knives, in the Early Iron Age many larger items occur in the graves, such as axes (e.g., fig. 17i), vessels (fig. 38f), and armor (figs. 85c–e, 144c).

Besides containing larger quantities of the metal, the Early Iron Age graves contain a much wider range of bronze objects than Late Bronze Age graves. The most common bronze objects in Early Iron Age graves are of the same kinds as those in the graves of the preceding period—ring jewelry, fibulae, buttons, and various types of ornamental rings (see table 6). But Early Iron Age graves contain a number of categories of bronze objects very rarely appearing in Late Bronze Age burials. These include offensive weapons (swords, axes), defensive weapons (cuirasses, helmets, pectorals, phalerae), and vessels (situlae, ribbed buckets, cauldrons, sieves, cups). Many of these special items occur in the richest graves, but they also occur in graves that are not otherwise distinguished by exceptional grave goods (see e.g., among the Mecklenburg Stična Graves IV/15, V/14, V/15, V/18, and VIII/2).

Among the more richly outfitted burials are the sword graves at Hallstatt (Kromer 1958, p. 50), the earlier series of wealthy graves at Stična (Gabrovec 1966, pp. 10–13) and Novo mesto (Gabrovec 1960), the five at Kleinklein (Schmid 1933), and the "warrior's grave" at Villach (Müller-Karpe 1952). Most of these burials share in common the presence of a sword, usually of bronze but occasionally of iron (table 12). In Late Bronze Age graves weapons are very rare (table 11), thus this appearance of swords in a series of well-outfitted graves throughout the East Alpine region marks a significant new pattern in the eighth and seventh centuries B.C. This series of well-equipped graves contains other objects that are rare in Late Bronze Age burials, such as bronze vessels and defensive armor of bronze. Table 12, indicating some of the categories of objects in a selection of these graves, draws attention to the similarities of the burial assemblages in different parts of the area.

After about 600 B.C., changes occur in the patterns of weapons placed in the graves, although in other respects the trends developing in the early part of the Early Iron Age continue. Swords in graves are replaced at Hallstatt and elsewhere north of the Alps by daggers, and south of the Alps in Slovenia by spears and battle-axes, while bronze helmets continue to appear in the latter region. The proportion of graves containing weapons increases during the two centuries after 600 B.C. These changes in the character and quantity of weaponry in graves have been connected with changes in fighting techniques, with organized units of well-armed troops replacing limited combat by the individual leaders of the earlier communities (Kossack 1959, pp. 93–99; Kromer 1964, pp. 95–96; Frey 1973; Wells 1978a, pp. 225–226), which in turn can be related to the growing populations of settlements in the East Alpine region and to the concomitant growth in complexity of social organization.

The rich graves of this phase, of which Novo mesto Grave IV/3 (Knez 1978) and Magdalenska gora Grave V/6-7-7a (Hencken 1978, pp. 30–31, 143–147, figs. 108–112) and Grave V/29 (Hencken 1978, pp. 36–38, 160–171, figs. 135–149) are prime examples, are characterized by the same kinds of objects as the rich graves of the first half of the Early Iron Age. These include offensive and defensive weapons (iron spears and battle-axes, bronze helmets), bronze vessels (situlae, including those with relief figural decoration, cauldrons, and ribbed buckets), and a range of bronze ornaments consisting of personal jewelry and belt parts. This later series of rich graves bears the same relation to the plain graves as those of the 750 to 600 B.C. period.

Like the earlier rich graves, these are also in the same tumuli as the plain ones and are not distinguished topographically from them (see e.g., Knez 1978, p. 127, fig. 1). This pattern is in marked contrast to the contemporaneous situation in west-central Europe, where a single rich grave was often situated at the center and base of a mound, and subsequent, poorer graves were placed concentrically around it (see Zürn 1970 on Grafenbühl and Spindler 1975 on the Magdalenenberg). As in the earlier instance, while the richer graves are distinguished by a combination of relatively infrequent objects, particularly defensive weapons and bronze vessels, these objects do also occur singly in other, not so distinguished graves. The rich graves also contain assemblages of the bronze, glass, and amber jewelry and of the pottery common to the plain graves.

Interpretation

The basic units of social organization in most preindustrial societies are those of the family, nuclear and extended. This pattern is widely documented in worldwide ethnographic contexts and in specifically European historical and ethnographic studies (Firth 1961; Diaz and Potter 1967; Homans 1942). Family groups are also the basic units of economic organization, usually with all members of the family taking active part in the economic activities of the group (Firth 1961, p. 88; Diaz and Potter 1967, pp. 155–156; Fél and Hofer 1969, pp. 94–112). One individual, a senior man or woman, heads the family, directs the efforts of the other members, and represents the family in interactions with the outside world. This individual usually possesses the highest status and authority within the family group.

I believe that the most productive approach to

Table 12. Some objects in richer graves in East Alpine Europe.

Grave	Offensive weapons (sword/dagger/spear/axe)	Defensive weapons (cuirasse/chest protector/helmet)	Bronze vessels
Hallstatt 573	2		1
Hallstatt 504	1 1		5
Hallstatt 697	1 1	3	4
Hallstatt 469	1 3 2	1 3	
Hallstatt 507	1		7
Hallstatt 696	1		4
Hartnermichelkogel	1 1		2
Pommerkogel	* 1 1 1	1	27
Kröllkogel	1 6	1 1	26
Stična, Panzergrab	1 1	1 6	1
Novo mesto, Panzergrab	2	1 1	

*Kleinklein group.

the issues of social organization of the Early Iron Age communities in East Alpine Europe is in terms of such family units, rather than in terms of the larger integrative units of bands-tribes-chiefdoms-states (Service 1962). Models based on the latter scheme have been applied recently to later prehistoric central Europe, but I find that viewing organization in terms of the smaller family units provides a better scheme for the purposes of this study. During the Late Bronze and Early Iron Ages (1200 to 400 B.C.), the most common form of settlement in central Europe was very small (see p. 99). In the well-documented context of southern Germany, Kossack has discussed the probable family basis of the settlement patterns (1972, p. 92), and Kilian-Dirlmeier (1974) has demonstrated the applicability of the family model to the cemetery at Mühlacker in northern Württemberg (see also Krämer 1964 on the slightly later cemetery at Nebringen). In each case, the excavated cemeteries show a mix of male and female graves, and those of children, corresponding to what would be expected of family-based residence. In the Early Iron Age contexts of southern Bavaria Kossack (1972, pp. 90, 92) has called attention to the one or two graves containing swords in many small cemeteries and suggests that these are the graves of individuals of status and authority in the family.

In limited parts of central Europe larger communities developed during the Early Iron Age. In the Eastern Alps such centers emerged at Hallstatt and in parts of Slovenia. Some of these communities had populations in the hundreds. Stična's population was probably as high as 400 to 500 (p. 99). Although these communities differed greatly in scale from the farmsteads and hamlets, persistence of the family units in the social organization is still clear in the burial patterns (Kilian-Dirlmeier 1971; Gabrovec 1974, pp. 180–182; Urleb 1974, pp. 83–88). To judge by the numbers of graves associated with each family group and by the character of the grave goods, these units were similar in size and organization to those represented in the smaller community cemeteries. Thus, we can view the social organization of the larger communities in terms of the same nuclear and extended family groups constituting the communities at the smaller settlements, a pattern consistent with ethnographic studies of larger communities in traditional societies (e.g., Homans 1942; Fél and Hofer 1969). There is no evidence that the family units were greatly transformed by incorporation into larger communities.

Most investigators believe that the tumuli of Lower Carniola were burial places for individual family groups through time (Filip 1961, p. 295; Gabrovec 1974, 1980, p. 44). The tumuli at Stična, Magdalenska gora, and other sites contain graves of different periods, often indicating that they were used for burial throughout the Early Iron Age. The Great Tumulus at Stična, recently excavated by the Narodni muzej of Ljubljana, contained graves dating from the earliest phase of the Early Iron Age, Podzemelj I, through the Negau Period at the end of the Early Iron Age. The tumuli excavated by the Duchess at Stična show the same extended time of use, as do those excavated by her at Magdalenska gora (Hencken 1978). Many different tumuli were being used for burial at the same time at each settlement. The grave contents show that the tumuli were not sex specific, male and female burials occurring roughly equally in each mound. Nor is there any clear relation between grave wealth and tumulus, most tumuli containing graves of all degrees of wealth. Similarly, weapon graves occur in almost all of the tumuli at the principal sites and are not restricted to a limited number of mounds, as table 13 shows for the tumuli excavated by the Duchess at Stična. There is at present no evidence to suggest any criterion on which graves were grouped together in tumuli other than that of family membership. Further supporting this suggestion is the fact that the number of graves in the tumuli in relation to the length of time represented corre-

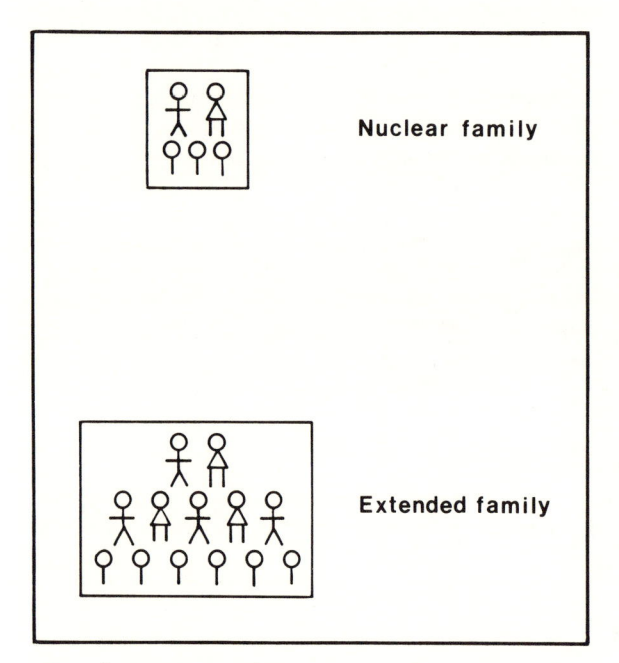

Text figure XXX. Schematic representations of nuclear and extended family units, such as probably inhabited the small settlements of the Late Bronze and Early Iron Ages. Individual farmsteads might have been occupied by either a nuclear or extended family, while other small settlements, such as those represented in the cemeteries at St. Andrä and Welzelach, may have been occupied by single extended families or by two family groups.

ponds to the expected attrition of members of single families.

For the flat grave cemeteries there is also evidence for burial in family units (for Hallstatt see Kilian-Dirlmeier 1969, 1971; for the Dürrnberg at Hallein see Maier 1974, pp. 337–338, note 45; Pauli 1978, pp. 505–512; for Križna gora see Urleb 1974, pp. 83–88). Like the tumuli at Stična, in these flat grave cemeteries the groups of graves interpreted as those of families extend through time and comprise roughly equal numbers of male and female burials. In none of these instances is there clear evidence that the individuals buried in one group of graves were of substantially higher status or greater wealth than those in others.

If the evidence of physical anthropology were better developed in these contexts, we might be able to study relationships of individuals in these hypothetical family groupings on the basis of the skeletal remains. Unfortunately, the skeletal remains are generally poorly preserved, and in those instances in which they were recovered more or less intact, they have often not fared well since their excavation (see Trinkaus report, pp. 30–36; Angel 1968).

The fact that the rich graves at the various centers of Lower Carniola are not concentrated in one or two tumuli and the rich graves at Hallstatt are not situated in a single precinct of the cemetery suggests that the individuals buried in the richer graves were not far removed from the others in status (see Christlein 1973 for a case of the opposite). The same point is suggested by the fact that the rich graves contain no, or very few, objects that are restricted to the richest burials. Bronze vessels are a feature of the richest graves, but they also occur in otherwise plainly equipped burials (e.g., Mecklenburg Stična Graves IV/15, VIII/2). Bronze defensive weapons are characteristic of the richest graves, yet elegant helmets also occur in less distinguished ones (e.g., Mecklenburg Stična Grave VI/30). At Hallstatt Hodson (1977) has demonstrated a continuum of grave wealth between the poorest and richest, with no sharp breaks in the continuum.

The rich graves at Hallstatt, Stična, and other sites in the Eastern Alps can be contrasted with those of Late Hallstatt west-central Europe, where burials such as Vix (Joffroy 1954), Grafenbühl (Zürn 1970), and Hochdorf (Biel 1978) are distinct from nearby plain graves topographically, have exceptional grave structures, and contain objects that never occur in graves not otherwise sumptuously outfitted. Such objects include the krater, "diadem," and Attic kylikes at Vix; the tripod and sphinxes and the ivory, bone, and amber furniture accessories in the Grafenbühl grave; and the bronze couch, bronze cauldron, and lavish gold ornaments at Hochdorf. The evidence suggests a very different kind of relation between the people buried in the rich graves and those buried in the plain ones in East Alpine Europe and in the west-central European region.

Working with the model of family units comprising the communities at the centers of East Alpine Europe, the occurrence of rich graves in different tumuli at Stična and other sites of Lower Carniola and in different areas of the cemetery at Hallstatt can be interpreted to indicate that the individuals represented in the rich graves were members of the various different families. In the evidence presently available, there is no clear pattern of any one rich grave being richer than others at any of these sites, nor of one tumulus (in Lower Carniola) or group of graves (at Hallstatt) containing graves richer than the others. At the Dürrnberg at Hallein, a very well-investigated site, a priority of rich graves or families is similarly lacking (Pauli 1978, pp. 505–516).

There are some differences between the rich graves, but the significance of them is unclear at present. For example, the *Panzergrab* at Stična (Gabrovec 1966, pp. 10–13) is richer in several respects than other published graves from Stična and might be interpreted

Table 13. Graves at Stična containing weapons.

Tumulus	No. graves	No. graves with weapons	% graves with weapons
I	7	1	14
II	16	1	6
III	13	0	
IV	57	9	16
V	20	3	15
VI	32	4	13
VII	7	0	
VIII	2	0	
Vas Vir	27	6	22
Vas Pece	2	0	
Vas Glogovica	3	1	33

as that of an individual who was at one time the principal leader of the community, but any such suggestion must await further research in the tumuli. It would be interesting and productive to examine comparative wealth of burial assemblages in several different tumuli in order to try to identify relative material wealth of different family units. At present, the sample of well-documented tumuli from any of these sites is too small to provide an adequate data base.

If the tumuli represent family burial places, then using the formula on page 98 we can calculate that the Great Tumulus at Stična, with 183 graves spanning the Early Iron Age, represents a living community with an average population of about 19 individuals. Tumulus IV excavated by the Duchess would have served a group of six individuals, on the average. Other, smaller tumuli would have served families with smaller average numbers, or perhaps families that had distinct tumuli only for a part of the Early Iron Age. These numbers are only very rough indications of the scale, because they represent averages for 350 years and do not take account of fluctuations or growth over time. Ideally, the chronology for each tumulus and each grave should be worked out, and from such data a detailed pattern of population changes could be proposed (as done by Kilian-Dirlmeier 1974). Until more complete data become available, these rough figures at least provide a picture of the possible size of these groups.

On present evidence it does not appear that any one family group at Hallstatt, Stična, or other sites was wealthier or of higher status than any other. If this impression is confirmed by future investigation, we might hypothesize that no single leading family had emerged at these centers, but that community leadership shifted from the head of one family to that of another, depending upon such factors as ability and political prowess in the community.

Finally, we need to consider the subject of sociopolitical connections between communities. In the present state of the research, there is little good evidence for a hierarchy of centers. Hallstatt, as a specialized salt-mining community, is exceptional and cannot be compared with the agriculturally based centers of Slovenia. In Lower Carniola, the site of Stična stands out from the rest in having the largest hillfort area (Frey 1974a) and probably the largest number of associated tumuli. Stična may well have been the most populous community in the region. Stična is also distinguished among other sites of the area in having substantially greater quantities of glass (of local production) and amber (imported) in its graves and having quantities of extraordinary local products (such as bronze cuirasses) and luxury imports (p. 114). The evidence available at present suggests that Stična was both the largest community of Lower Carniola and the principal center of industry and trade. The character of economic and sociopolitical relations between Stična and other, smaller sites remains to be investigated, as more archaeological evidence from the region becomes available. It is likely that the workshops at Stična were producing goods for a wide area and that the site served as a focus for different trade networks. Stična's role in the sociopolitical organization of its region was probably similar to its role in the economic configurations, and the nature of this role will become clearer as the data base grows.

A MODEL FOR THE CHANGES

Any explanation of changes in society and economy must deal first with the issue of social organization, since the organization of the relations between people determines how changes occur (Firth 1961; Rogers and Shoemaker 1971; Cowgill 1975, p. 515). Except in cases in which some catastrophic event, such as plague, natural disaster, or invasion, causes havoc in the societal system, change can be best viewed in terms of choices made by individuals who are in a position to effect change (Barnett 1953; Firth 1961; Rogers and Shoemaker 1971).

The settlement system and social organization of communities in East Alpine Europe at the start of the last millennium B.C. have been outlined above, and it is in terms of the models set forward there that an explanation of the changes will be offered.

Pittioni and his colleagues investigating the prehistoric copper mines of the Salzburg and Tirol regions of Austria cite evidence indicating an increase in the quantities of copper being mined during the Late Bronze Age (p. 104). Yet there is archaeological evidence that strongly suggests that there was a shortage of bronze metal during the Late Bronze Age, indicating that the higher rate of production of copper was not enough to satisfy the even more rapidly growing demand. (Since we know very little about the production of tin, we cannot say anything about the quantities of that metal involved.)

Bronze is represented in graves of all, or most, cemeteries of the Late Bronze Age in the East Alpine region, though not nearly as often as in Early Iron Age graves (table 9). Bronze objects in Late Bronze Age graves are generally small (p. 117). Larger objects, incorporating greater quantities of metal, are rare in the graves. We know that larger objects were being manufactured and used, since fragmentary, and occasionally complete, sickles, axes, spearheads, swords, bronze vessels, and other items are well represented in the hoards of the period (table 14; Müller-Karpe 1959, pls. 128–139). Their general absence from graves suggests a reluctance to remove so much metal from circulation.

The Late Bronze Age hoards are also an important indication of metal shortage. Hoards of the same character are rare in the preceding Middle Bronze Age and the succeeding Early Iron Age, and their presence in the Late Bronze Age suggests particular conditions of the period with respect to the supply of bronze. Most of the hoards in this region contain primarily fragmentary objects, including weapons (swords, daggers, spears, axes), tools (sickles, knives, chisels, razor knives), jewelry, and vessels. These hoards can best be interpreted as deposits of scrap metal collected by smiths or metal peddlers to be remelted and recast into new objects. Especially significant is the frequency of large objects among the tools and weapons, such as rarely turn up in graves. Instead of burying large objects with the deceased, as was often done in the Early Iron Age, Late Bronze Age communities were recycling the metal in order to produce more objects from it (see p. 127).

At the same time that this shortage of bronze was developing, iron was beginning to come into use. During the period 1000 to 800 B.C. iron was being worked in different parts of central Europe and used as decorative inlay in bronze objects and in the form of iron blades for composite tools with bronze handles, especially swords and knives (see p. 102). Objects made entirely of iron are rare before about 800 B.C. in the East Alpine region. Thus, it is apparent that some few individuals in East Alpine Europe knew the techniques of producing and forging iron from about 1000 B.C. on, although iron did not begin to replace bronze as the principal material for tools and weapons for another two centuries. The fact that the bronze objects with iron inlay and the composite tools are forms characteristic of the areas in which they are found shows that the objects were manufactured locally rather than being imported from outside.

An explanation for the processes of change can be offered in terms of the three conditions existing in East Alpine Europe in the period 1000 to 800 B.C.: (1) the shortage of bronze metal relative to demand; (2) the presence of small-scale ironworking technology; and (3) an abundance of easily accessible and metal-rich iron ore (p. 102). An individual who perceived a solution to the problem of the shortage of bronze metal in the possibilities of developing iron as a replacement and was able to implement this idea would have stood to gain greatly in wealth and personal status. Such an individual would have had to have been knowledgeable in the working of iron himself, or else have been in a position to organize individuals with that knowledge.

The importance of considering the role of individual initiative in studying prehistoric change has been brought into discussion recently (e.g., Deetz and Dethlefsen 1967; Cowgill 1975, pp. 514–515; Frankenstein and Rowlands 1978; Wells 1980a, pp. 97–102). Although in prehistoric contexts we cannot identify specific individuals, we can nonetheless assume that persons in the past behaved in ways similar to individuals in the ethnographic and historical present. As Firth points out (1961, pp. 83, 85), it is the individuals in a society who bring about change, in ways circumscribed by their background, experience, and social roles (see also Barnett 1953). In all communities some individuals are more ambitious and imaginative than others, and given the opportunity such persons can bring about changes not only in their own situations but also in their communities. Barth and his col-

Table 14. A selection of Late Bronze Age hoards in the Eastern Alps.*

Location	Weapons (sword/dagger/spear/axe)				Tools (sickle/chisel/knife)			Jewelry	Vessels
Augsdorf	+**		3	+	+			1	3
Bruck a.d.M.	+		+		7+			1	+
Cermožišče	+		+	+	+	2	3	4	1
Črmošnjice	1	1	2	3	+	3		2	1
Haidach		1	1	3	1	5	1	1	1
Hallstatt	+		+	+	+				
Jurka vas	1	1	1	2	1		2		
Mixnitz			1		+	1	1	11+	
Špure	+	1	4	+	+	1		+	
Strassengel	2	1	2	1	+		2	6	1

*For literature, see Müller-Karpe 1959; on Hallstatt see Reitinger 1968, pp. 128–129. Only the principal categories of objects occurring in the hoards are included here.
**"+" indicates that more than one of that kind of object was present in the hoard, but that the exact number of objects is uncertain.

leagues (1963) and Strickon (1979) provide instructive studies of the role of "entrepreneurs" in bringing about cultural change.

In the present case, the initiative for change may well have come from an enterprising family or community head. Three conditions would have had to have been satisfied. First, he or someone in his community had to be familiar with the techniques of smelting and forging iron. Second, he had to perceive some advantage to encouraging the development of greater iron production. Third, he had to be able to rally the support of his community in order to substantially increase the production of the new metal.

The iron objects and parts of composite objects in contexts dating between 1000 and 800 B.C. make it apparent that some individuals in the East Alpine region knew the techniques of working iron. The very small number of iron objects from this period suggests that the number of persons familiar with the techniques was also very small.

In discussing social change, Firth writes (1961, p. 86), "The essence of the dynamic process lies in the continuous operation of the individual psyche, with its potential of unsatisfied desires—for more security, more knowledge, more status, more power, more approval—within the universe of its social system." There is no reason to believe that individual motivations were any different in later prehistoric Europe than they are today in the modern world and in the ethnographic present (Homans 1967; Cowgill 1975, p. 515). Persons who possessed the power, status, or freedom to do so are likely to have seized any opportunity of perceived advantage to themselves.

Ethnographic examples abound of the mechanisms by which individuals can rally the support of their families and fellow community members to help them achieve a desired goal. In most instances, the help required involves a temporary sacrifice on the part of the family or community members (collecting foods for a feast, producing goods for trade), and then a subsequent reward to them for their efforts through some form of redistribution (see Sahlins 1972b for examples). In the present case, the support needed by the enterprising individual would have been in the increased production of food and other necessities by members of his community, in order that other individuals could be maintained as full-time ironworking specialists. In the framework of a typical community of the period 1000 to 800 B.C. the maintenance of such a full-time specialist would constitute a substantial change in the organization of the community. The small farmsteads and hamlets of that period most probably did not support full-time specialists of any kind, and the bronze that came into the communities was probably either imported in finished form from outside or produced by wandering metalsmiths bringing metal with them.

Once this change—the supporting of a full-time ironworker—was made by one community, a series of other changes could follow. A community of the scale of those of the period 1000 to 800 B.C. would have quickly had its own needs of metal satisfied by a full-time smelter and smith, particularly with the abundance of metal-rich ore available in the East Alpine regions. Once those needs were satisfied, the community could produce iron for trade with other groups. Since all of the East Alpine region (as well as other parts of Europe) was apparently experiencing a shortage of bronze during this period, other communities would have been interested in acquiring the new metal. The techniques of smelting and forging iron may have been closely guarded secrets for a time. If the community that was producing iron could exchange products of the metal for foodstuffs, clothing, and other necessities, then it could further specialize, reducing the amount of agricultural production in which it engaged, and putting more manpower into ironworking (text fig. XXXI). Individuals in the iron-producing

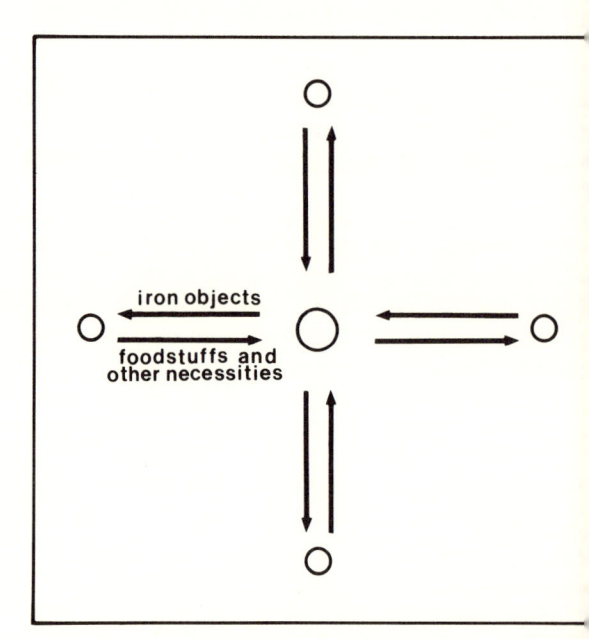

Text figure XXXI. Diagram representing the exchange of iron objects by a community developing iron metallurgy for foodstuffs and other necessities from surrounding communities in need of metal products. Establishment of such an exchange system could provide the first community with the necessities of life, permitting its members to specialize further on iron production. It could thus increase its output of the metal and extend its trade of iron products to other communities requiring metal.

community would gain materially from the trade goods that would come in in exchange for the iron exported, in the same way that the salt miners at Hallstatt and the copper miners at Welzelach became well-to-do through their enterprising efforts. Thus, in the model iron-producing community everyone gained by the production and exportation of iron, and hence supported the effort.

This community could develop into a much larger one. As surrounding groups were eager to trade for the new metal, perhaps already much less costly than bronze because it was produced of ores abundant in the region, it was in the interest of the head and his community to continue to increase the quantities of iron produced. In order to do so, more specialist ironworkers would have been needed, and in order to support them, more primary food producers would have been required. New members of the community would have been attracted by the material wealth available there (text fig. XXXII). Thus attempts to continue increasing the amounts of iron being produced would have tended to increase the sizes of communities. This continuing process can account for the emergence, in the eighth century B.C., of the principal centers such as Stična in the iron-rich regions of the Eastern Alps.

As community size increased, the status of the head of the community also increased. The larger communities of the Early Iron Age, such as Stična, with populations in the hundreds, were probably still organized on the basis of family units, as is apparent in the burial patterns. One of the family heads served as head of the community as a whole. There is no evidence to suggest a ruling family at Stična, but rather a range of families of greater or lesser status in the community. As communities grow in size, social complexity increases, and the status of the head increases as well. One way of viewing the change is that with increasing complexity of society, greater energy must be invested in structure and organization (Gall and Saxe 1977). This pattern is represented archaeologically in the richer graves at the Early Iron Age sites. The increase in size and in manufacturing and commerce brought greater material wealth to the community as a whole, and proportionately more to the head of the community. In any community, a range of statuses can be identified, and the range of burial wealth in the graves at Hallstatt, Stična, and other centers of the Eastern Alps probably corresponds roughly to the pattern of status of the individuals buried (p. 117). As noted above, there is no sharp break in location, grave character, or burial goods between the richest graves and the plain ones, but rather a continuum.

Increased community size, including larger numbers of primary producers, and greater material wealth made possible the support of more specialized industries, such as those in glass and in fine sheet bronze work producing helmets, cuirasses, and vessels.

Among these changes in the degree of industrial specialization is an increase in the amounts of bronze available to these iron-producing communities over the quantities available in the Late Bronze Age (p. 110 and table 9). Hoards are very rare in this later period, suggesting less of a concern for recycling bronze metal than during the preceding period.

The reason for the increase in quantities of bronze probably has to do with changes in the organization of production and trade. The dispersed character of Late Bronze Age society, organized in small community units, hindered the organization of supply systems to maintain large numbers of miners and processors of the copper. Thus communities of miners such as that represented at Kitzbühel (Eibner, Plank, Pittioni 1966) had to remain small. To judge from the cemeteries most of these were of the same scale as the farmsteads and hamlets in the agricultural regions. When the centers of ironworking developed, the much larger communities could generate greater surpluses

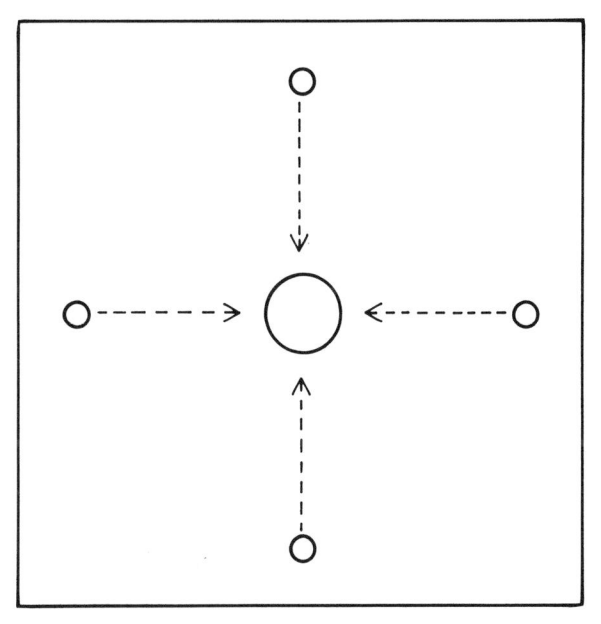

Text figure XXXII. Through the export of iron products, members of the iron-producing community acquire considerable material wealth. This wealth attracts persons from other communities in the surrounding areas, who come to work as food producers, craftsmen, and perhaps as metalsmiths and traders. This influx of new individuals attracted by the increasing wealth of the community causes it to grow in population and enables it to support more specialists in ironworking and in other crafts.

and means of transporting them to copper-mining communities, thus making possible the growth of larger groups producing copper metal such as those at Welzelach and Uttendorf.

The same applies to the large, highly specialized community of salt miners at Hallstatt. Although radiocarbon dates from the mines indicate mining at Hallstatt before 750 B.C. (Barth, Felber, Schauberger 1975), no evidence has been found to suggest the existence of a large, long-term community at the site before the Early Iron Age. The maintenance of this community of some 200 persons was probably also accomplished through supply systems based upon the larger-scale production of foodstuffs, metals, and other materials which developed in the Early Iron Age as part of the changes outlined here.

While discussion here centers around changes in industrial and trade systems, it is important to remember that most communities, including the centers of activity such as Stična, were still agrarian in base and probably no more than 5 percent of their populations, at the most, were full-time specialists in activities other than food production. (The situation with the mining communities such as Hallstatt and Welzelach was, of course, different.) When I speak of sites such as Stična as centers of industry and trade, I do not mean that a large part of the populace was directly involved in any aspect of these processes beyond household needs. But in these communities for the first time we find evidence that at least a small proportion of the population was directly involved in manufacturing and trade activities well beyond the needs of the community. The larger communities that developed after 750 B.C. in the Eastern Alps could generate surpluses of agricultural produce and of manufactured goods (including iron products) much more efficiently than could the smaller communities of the preceding period, because with larger community size came more energy and attention devoted to organization (Gall and Saxe 1977). With better coordination of different individuals' and groups' efforts, foodstuffs and manufactured goods could be produced more efficiently. It is also likely that as iron metallurgy developed, more metal tools became available which contributed to the increase in efficiency in agricultural production. This aspect is difficult to document because of the paucity of iron agricultural implements that survive archaeologically from this period. In the Late Bronze Age bronze implements such as sickles and axes are well represented in the hoards (table 14) but not in graves.

I have mentioned several interrelated changes that would have occurred along with the development of iron metallurgy by a community in the Eastern Alps. These include growth of an export trade in iron, growth in community size, changes in social organization accompanying growth in size, and development of other specialized industries. As I have tried to show, these changes were mutually reinforcing. Numerous other related changes can be identified but are beyond the scope of this study.

A principal element in the change scenario outlined here is the shortage of bronze during the Late Bronze Age. The question might be asked, why could not the bronze producers increase their output, thereby increasing the supplies of the metal to East Alpine communities and at the same time increasing their own wealth? Why did the new source of metal have to be a different one, iron? The principal reason lies in the nature of the copper deposits. Copper occurs in relatively inaccessible regions of the Alps, and the communities living and working at the copper deposits were able to maintain themselves only by keeping their numbers small enough so that the limited land could provide enough sustenance for them, with some additional supplies being brought in from the outside. If such communities were to increase their productivity substantially, they would require a broad economic base, particularly an expandable subsistence system, as was possible in the fertile valleys of Lower Carniola. Because of the limitations of the land near copper sources, such expansion was impossible.

Iron ore, on the other hand, occurs in abundance in the Eastern Alps in areas which also offer rich, well-watered farmland and fertile pasturage, as at Stična. In such locations it was possible for the size of communities to increase because of the rich natural environment and the broad subsistence base (p. 97).

I have left the issue of population growth till last. Although there is good archaeological evidence to suggest that the population of the East Alpine region was increasing during the Late Bronze and Early Iron Ages (Čović and Gabrovec 1971, p. 327; *Arheološka Najdišča Slovenije* 1975; Peroni 1979, pp. 7–8), I agree with Cowgill's assertion (1975) that archaeological evidence for population change is too complex and elusive to be used by prehistorians in explaining change. Thus, I have chosen to explain the changes apparent in the evidence without reference to regional population growth, although I believe that such growth was occurring and was contributing to the changes. For example, population increase would have contributed to the shortage of bronze during the Late Bronze Age. A general increase in population would also have contributed to the rapid growth of the larger communities, once iron production was getting under way.

The changes discussed here did not stop in the Early Iron Age. Culture is always changing (see e.g., Linton 1936; Clarke 1968, pp. 50–52 for discussions from different perspectives), although at some stages of change the results are materially more obvious than at others. The processes of change outlined above continued to operate after the development of the economic centers of East Alpine Europe.

Compared with the situation in the Early Iron Age, during the Late Bronze Age little metal was being taken out of circulation, suggesting that in the Early Iron Age much more bronze metal was being produced than in the preceding period. These different patterns of production and consumption can be represented diagrammatically (text fig. XXXIII).

Why did communities of the Early Iron Age bury much larger quantities of metal in graves than their predecessors? Increasing the quantities of metal in graves both implies and necessitates an increase in production, and there is a systemic connection between removing material from circulation and increasing the production of that material (Flannery 1968, pp. 107–108). I have suggested above that the larger, more productive communities at the Early Iron Age centers were able to support larger groups of copper miners and thus to increase production of bronze objects. With such an increase, if some bronze had not been removed from circulation, the needs of the community would have become satisfied, and production would have slowed. If, however, bronze was removed regularly from circulation, then production had to remain high to satisfy the needs of the living. In the expanding economic systems each aspect of production and trade played an important role, and increase in each aspect stimulated increase in every other one. The change in burial practice to incorporate larger quantities of bronze in the graves was an adaptive strategy, however conscious or unconscious, to assure a continuing high level of metal production and trade, the economic basis of the centers. The same principle applies to iron, glass, and amber, and their inclusion in graves.

As the scale of iron production grew in the eighth, seventh, and sixth centuries B.C., iron probably became an export product of some significance. The East Alpine region was the first area of non-Mediterranean Europe to develop substantial iron production during the eighth and seventh centuries B.C. Although relevant technical analyses of iron objects are lacking, there is good evidence to suggest export trade of iron from Carinthia and Slovenia to northeast Italy (p. 113). Šašel (1977) argues that Strabo's description of trade between Slovenia and the lands at the Head of the Adriatic (IV 6, 10–12, V 1, 8, VII 5, 2) refers to a period well before the time that he was writing (around the birth of Christ), specifically to the Early Iron Age. Šašel suggests that Strabo's discussion refers to specific known Early Iron Age centers (see also Kahrstedt 1927). Among the trade products that Strabo mentions as coming from the East Alpine area is iron.

Trade in iron from the East Alpine region, including Carinthia and Slovenia, to northeast Italy is well documented during the Roman period and subsequent ages (Müllner 1908, p. 32; Alföldy 1974, pp. 111–

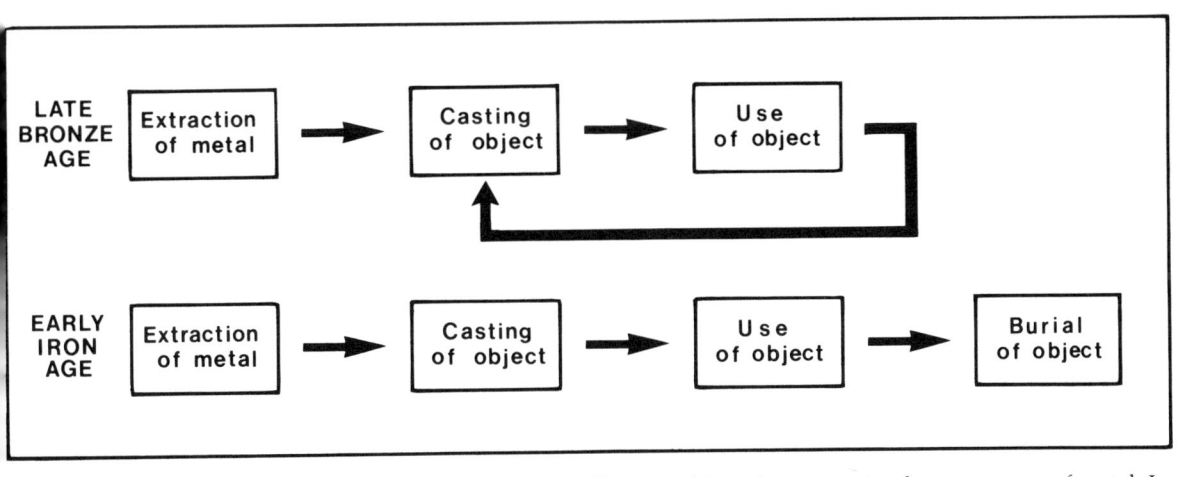

Text figure XXXIII. Diagram illustrating the life-course of bronze objects incorporating large amounts of metal. In the Late Bronze Age generally only small objects of bronze were placed in graves, while large ones were recycled and made into new ones. Such large objects, broken and destined for the caster's crucible, are well represented in the hoards of the period (table 14), and they are very rare in graves. In the Early Iron Age, on the other hand, large bronze objects, including vessels, offensive weapons, and armor, frequently occur in graves. Some bronze metal was probably remelted and recast during the Early Iron Age as well, but hoards are rare in this period. During the Early Iron Age much greater quantities of bronze metal were being removed from circulation, implying that the level of production of the metal must have been much higher than that during the Late Bronze Age, in order to maintain the supply of bronze objects for the living.

114; Mócsy 1974, p.31). Numerous inscriptions dating from the latter half of the last century B.C. and the first half of the first century A.D. at the Magdalensberg near Klagenfurt in Carinthia provide names of Italian customers purchasing iron products, names of their cities of origin, and lists of quantities of various objects obtained (Egger 1961). The objects are mostly of iron—rings, anvils, axes, picks, and hooks, but also include copper and brass vessels. Quantities of the various items listed are generally in the hundreds. The metal goods traded at the Magdalensberg were produced not only there, but throughout the surrounding lands (how far afield is unclear). Egger notes that the production of these trade goods was done exclusively by native metalworkers and not by individuals coming from Italy. Similar patterns of trade, on a smaller scale, are likely for the Early Iron Age.

An export trade in iron with regions outside the East Alpine sphere would have contributed to the ongoing changes. Strabo cites wine and olive oil as exchange products from northeast Italy to the East Alpine region (V 1, 8). The banquet scenes in the situla art suggest the presence of wine, and wine has been attested analytically from a bronze vessel of slightly later date at the Dürrnberg (Specht 1972, p.128). Some of the luxury imports discussed above (pp. 114–115) may have arrived in exchange for iron, though they may have come into the East Alpine area via personal relations as described by Fischer (1973). Whatever its mechanisms, exchange in such luxury products as well as in finished objects such as fibulae, though very apparent archaeologically, was probably of minor scale and importance compared to that of bulk goods such as iron and wine (see p. 114).

The importation of wine, olive oil, and manufactured goods from northeast Italy meant the arrival of new, exotic, and probably much sought-after items into the material cultural system of East Alpine Europe. Availability of such new and desired luxury goods would have profoundly affected iron production. External demand for a product encourages greater production of that product, usually resulting in substantial changes in the organization of a society's economy (examples in Firth 1929, pp. 476–482; Walker 1972). The availability of wine, oil, and other items from Italy is likely to have encouraged the production of greater quantities of iron for exchange.

I have brought into the foregoing discussion only some of the aspects of change indicated by the archaeological evidence. As I have argued, we can view the development of the cultural system characteristic of the Early Iron Age in East Alpine Europe as the result of a series of interrelated and mutually-reinforcing changes in different economic and social aspects of the communities, changes initiated by enterprising individuals responding to the need for more metal in a region in which iron was readily available and the technology of its production already present in an incipient stage. The result of these changes was the emergence of the industrial and commercial centers of the East Alpine region, the precursors of the west-central European centers of the Late Hallstatt Period and of the oppida of the Late Iron Age.

Afterword

The second part of this volume has presented a discussion of industrial activity, trade systems, and social patterns in Early Iron Age East Alpine Europe and has proposed one model to account for the changes leading to the emergence of the principal centers of economic activity. It should be clear to the reader that, although we have some good evidence bearing on these issues, there are many directions for future research which will help to develop the picture outlined very roughly here. The most pressing need in East Alpine Europe, as throughout later prehistoric Europe, is for large-scale settlement excavation, such as that being carried out at the Heuneburg. Such investigations of settlements in the East Alpine region would vastly increase our information about industry, trade, and social organization. The recent researches by Gabrovec, Frey, and Foltiny (1970), Pertlwieser (1969, 1970), Svoljšak (1974), and Guštin (1976) on settlements of the period have produced important results and great hopes for future investigations.

Quantitative studies of the various categories of objects from the graves would also be of great use to further studies along the lines of the present one. I have tried to indicate the value of weights of materials—bronze objects, glass beads, amber beads—as indicators of the quantities of them at different sites and in different periods, but so little quantitative data of this kind is recorded in the published reports that the basis for comparison is very small.

Technical analyses of bronze and iron objects would contribute to our understanding of the production and trade systems, as Pittioni (1949) and others have already demonstrated. Further such analyses, particularly if done as part of a large-scale program involving studies of materials at different sites of the period, should shed much new light on the questions, as Beck's work has done for amber.

Besides excavation of the settlement centers, we need research into the smaller community sites in order to develop a full picture of the economic systems of the period. The inhabitants of the economic centers like Hallstatt and Stična must have interacted with small communities in their vicinities, probably exchanging manufactured products (such as bronze jewelry, iron tools, and glass beads) and imported luxury materials (for example, amber beads) for such items as foodstuffs, textiles, and various raw materials. These interactions are important to any complete understanding of the economic systems at the centers. Ongoing investigations at the small settlement of Hascherkeller in Lower Bavaria, at the northwestern corner of the region under consideration here, are indicating the kinds of data which can be recovered relevant to the problems of the economic systems operating on the larger scale at the time (Wells 1979, 1980b).

One of the principal aims of this study is to draw attention to some of the major questions whose answers can help us to better understand the processes of change which led to the development of towns and urban centers of later prehistoric Europe. Ongoing research by scholars in Austria, Yugoslavia, and elsewhere is constantly added to our knowledge of this rich and important context.

Figures

The drawings are at scale of 1:2, unless otherwise indicated.

HALLSTATT 133

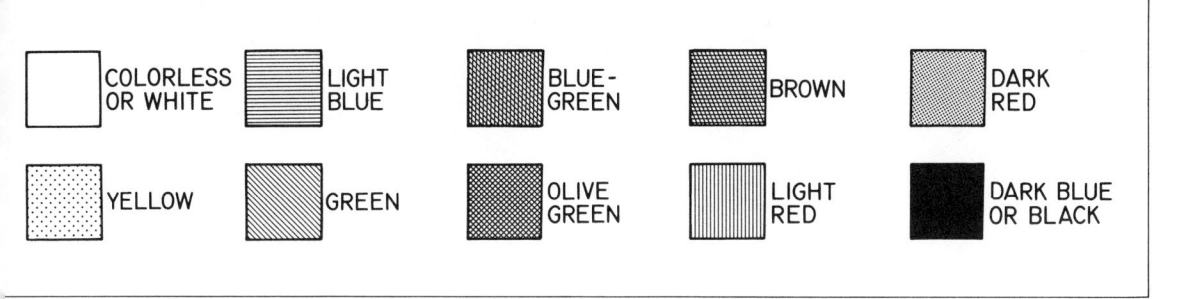

COLORLESS OR WHITE	LIGHT BLUE	BLUE-GREEN	BROWN	DARK RED
YELLOW	GREEN	OLIVE GREEN	LIGHT RED	DARK BLUE OR BLACK

Schematic color chart for glass beads illustrated in the following figures.

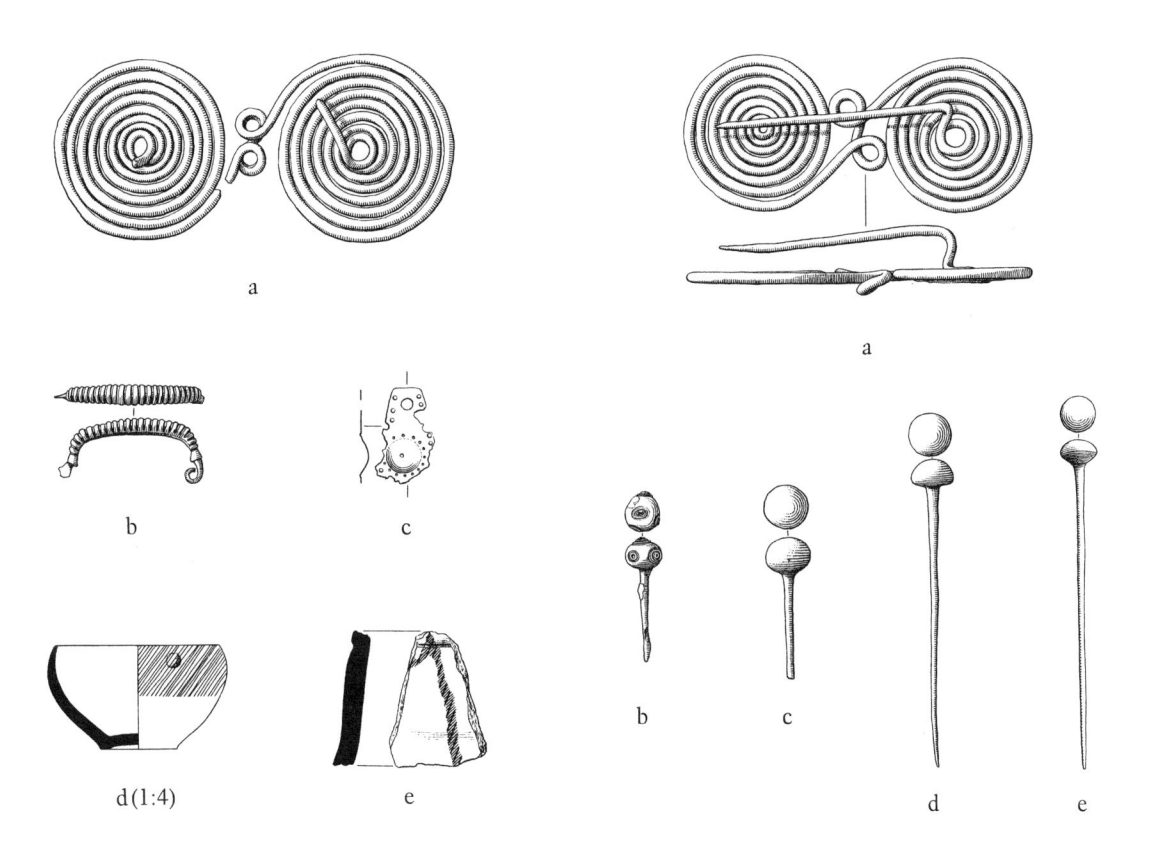

Figure 1. Grave 1a.

Figure 2. Grave 1b.

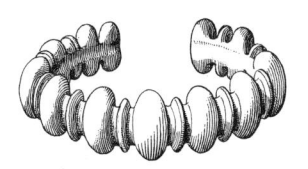

Figure 3. Grave 2.

134   HALLSTATT

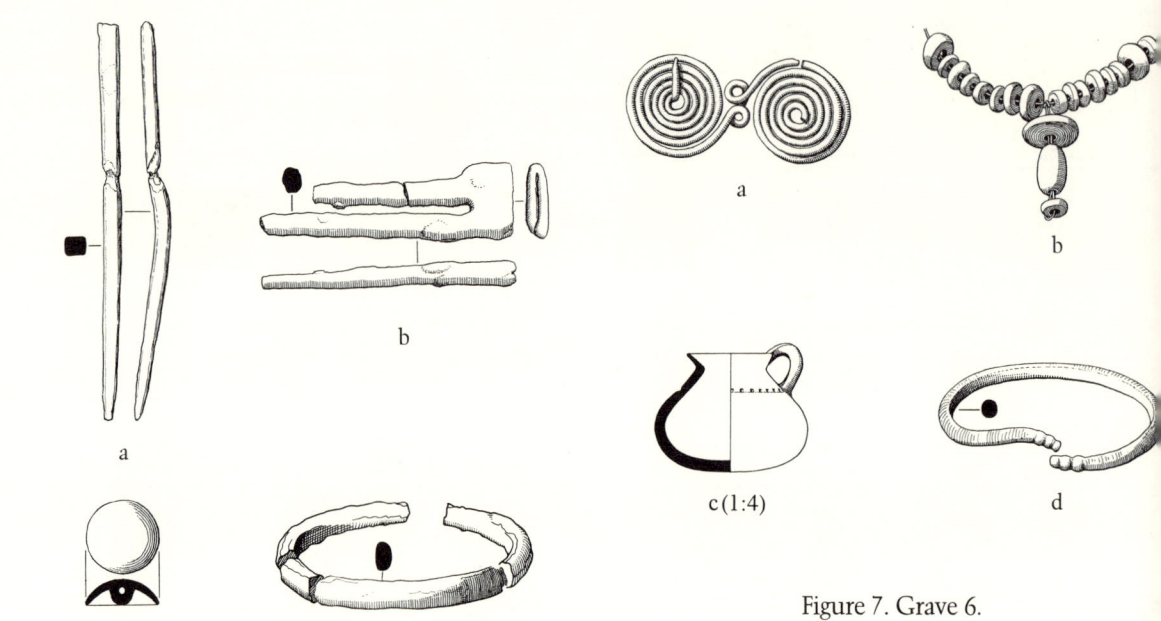

Figure 4. Grave 3.

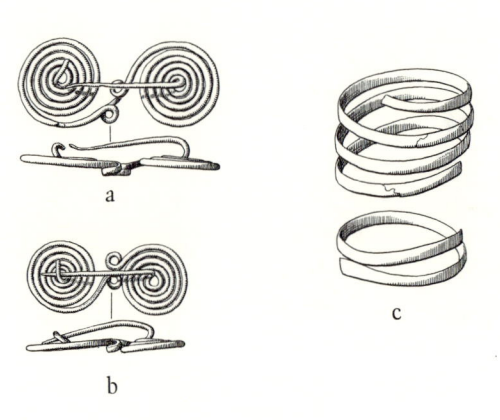

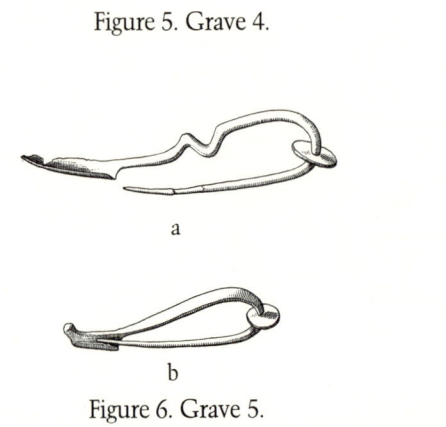

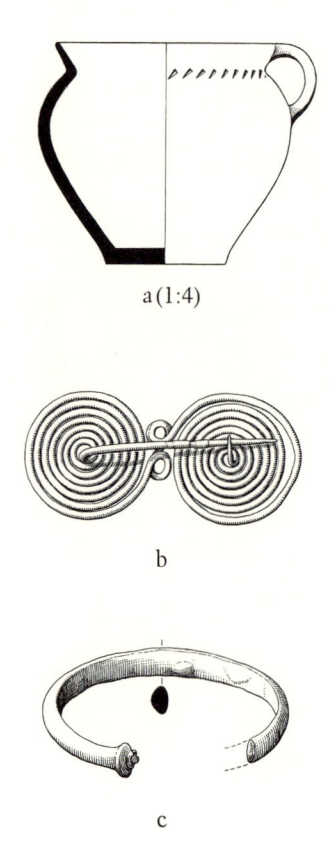

Figure 5. Grave 4.

Figure 6. Grave 5.

Figure 7. Grave 6.

Figure 8. Grave 7.

HALLSTATT 135

d(1:4)

b

c

e(1:4)

f

a

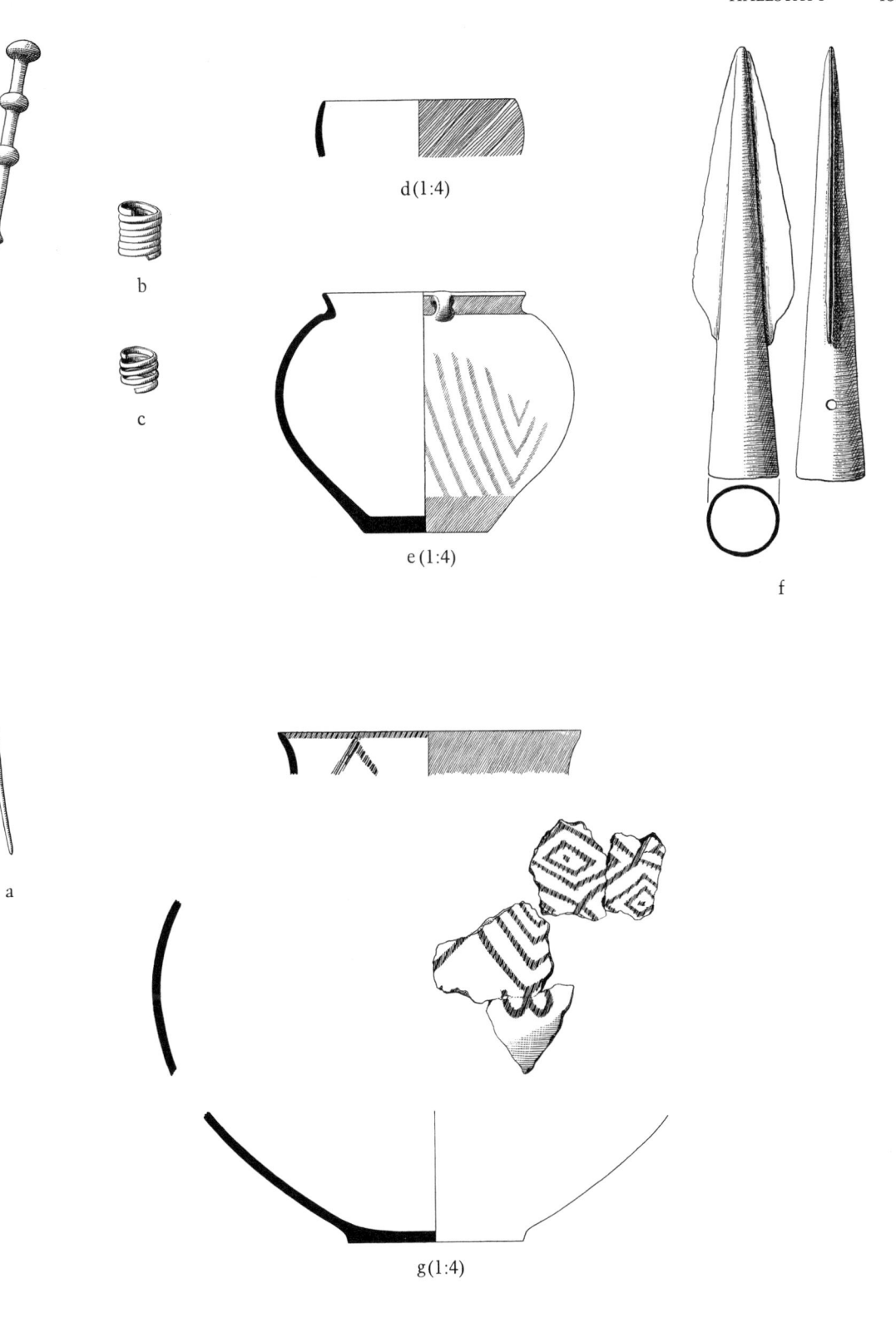

g(1:4)

Figure 9. Grave 8.

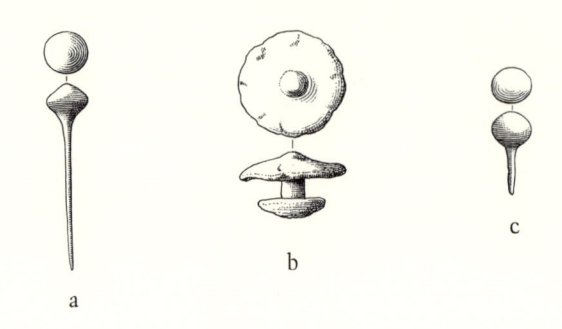

Figure 10. Grave 9.

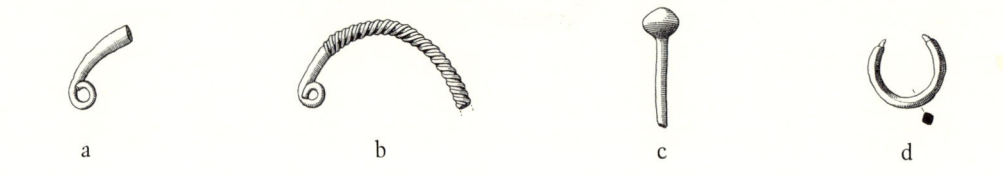

Figure 11. Grave 10.

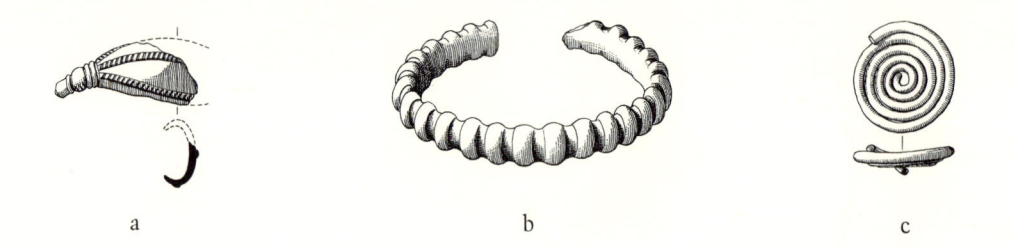

Figure 12. Grave 11.

HALLSTATT 137

a

b

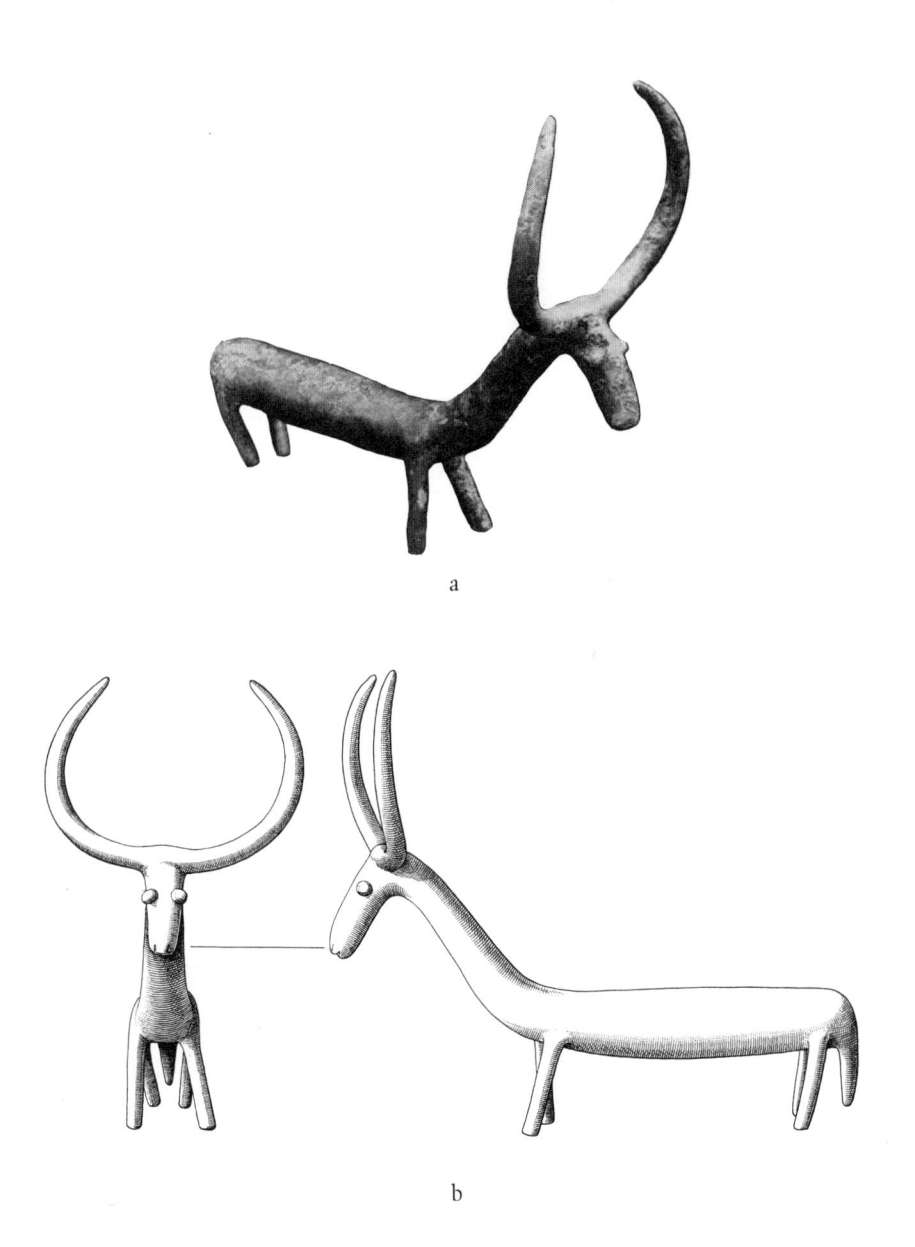

Figure 13. Grave 12.

138   HALLSTATT

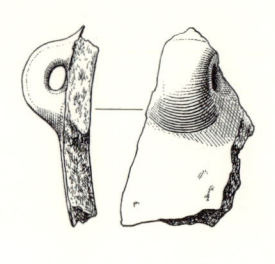

Figure 14. Grave 13.

a

b

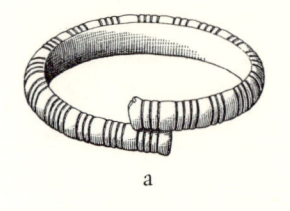

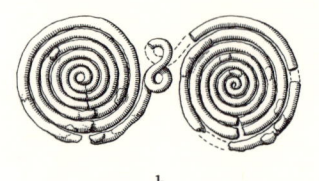

Figure 16. Grave 15.

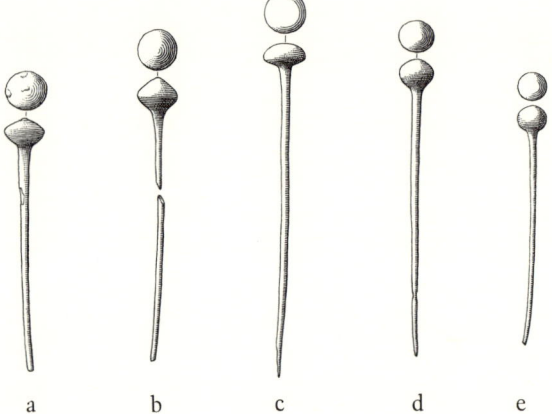

a   b   c   d   e

a(1:4)

f

g

h

i

j

k

b

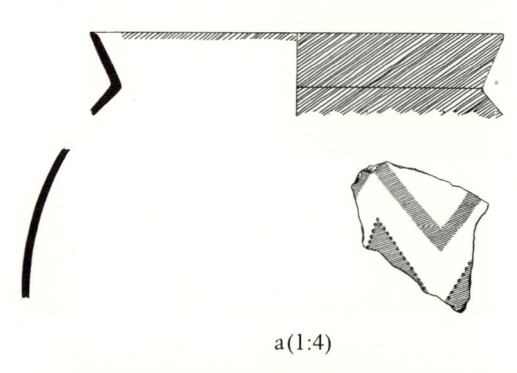

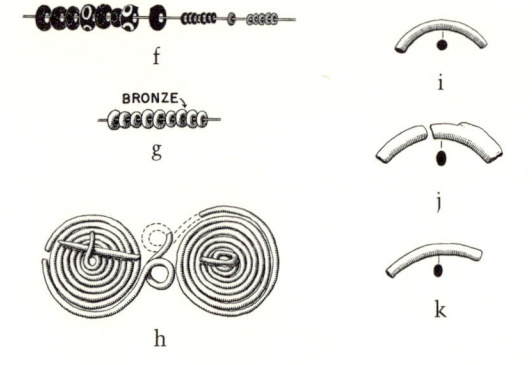

Figure 15. Grave 14.

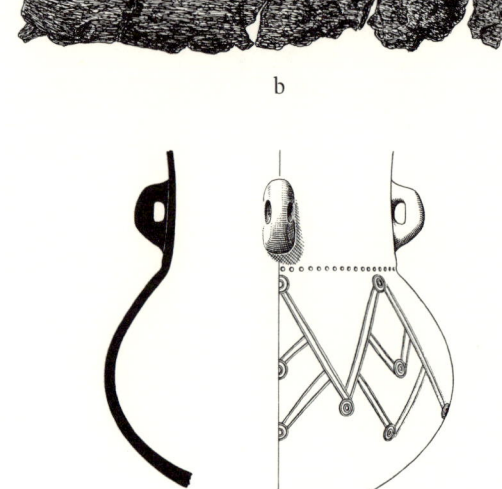

c(1:4)

Figure 17. Grave 16.

HALLSTATT 139

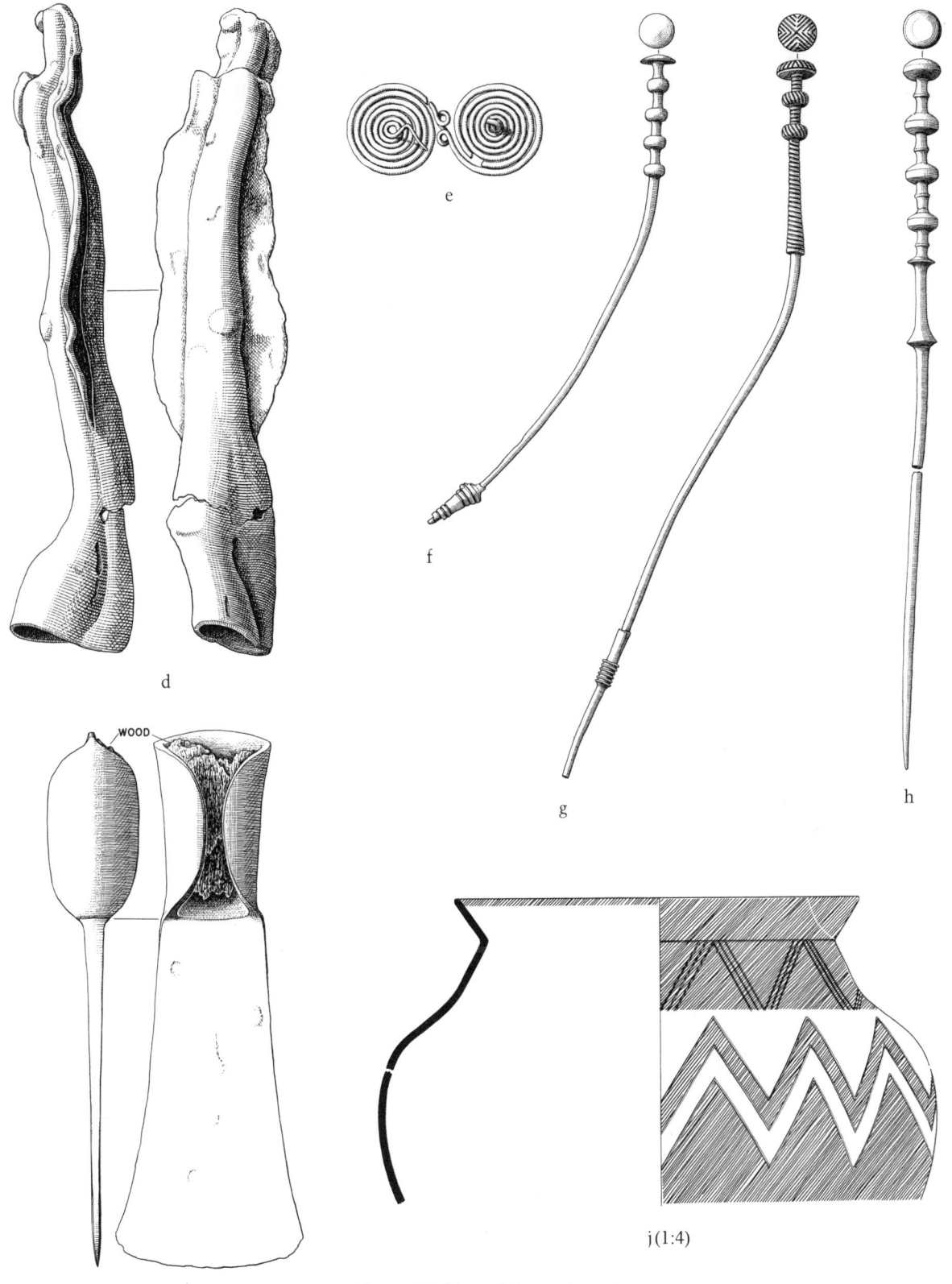

Figure 17. Grave 16, continued.

140   HALLSTATT

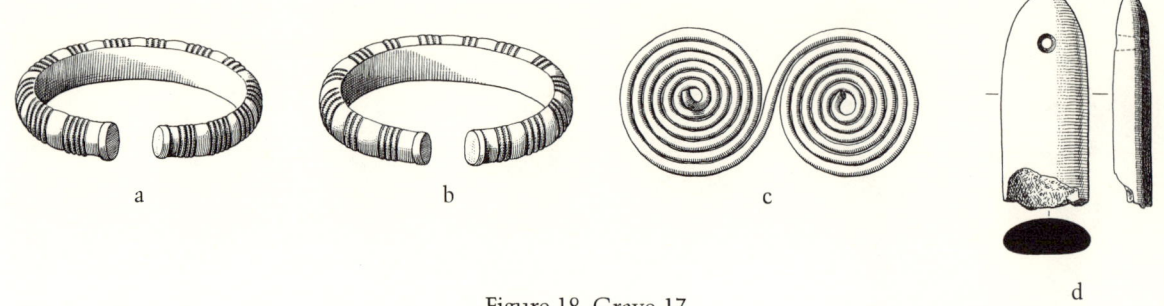

Figure 18. Grave 17.

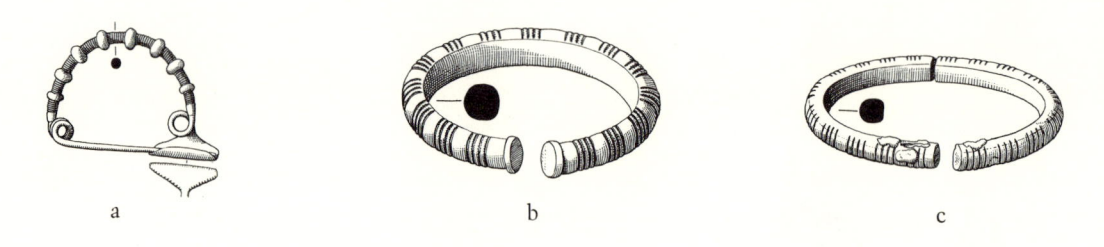

Figure 19. Grave 18.

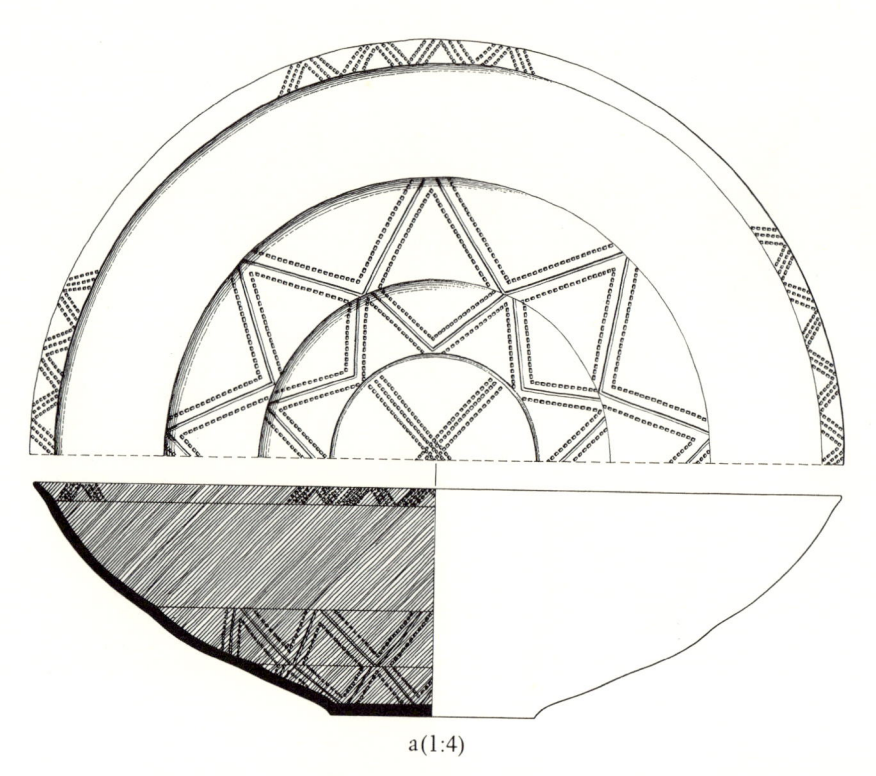

a(1:4)

Figure 20. Grave 19.

HALLSTATT 141

b (1:4)

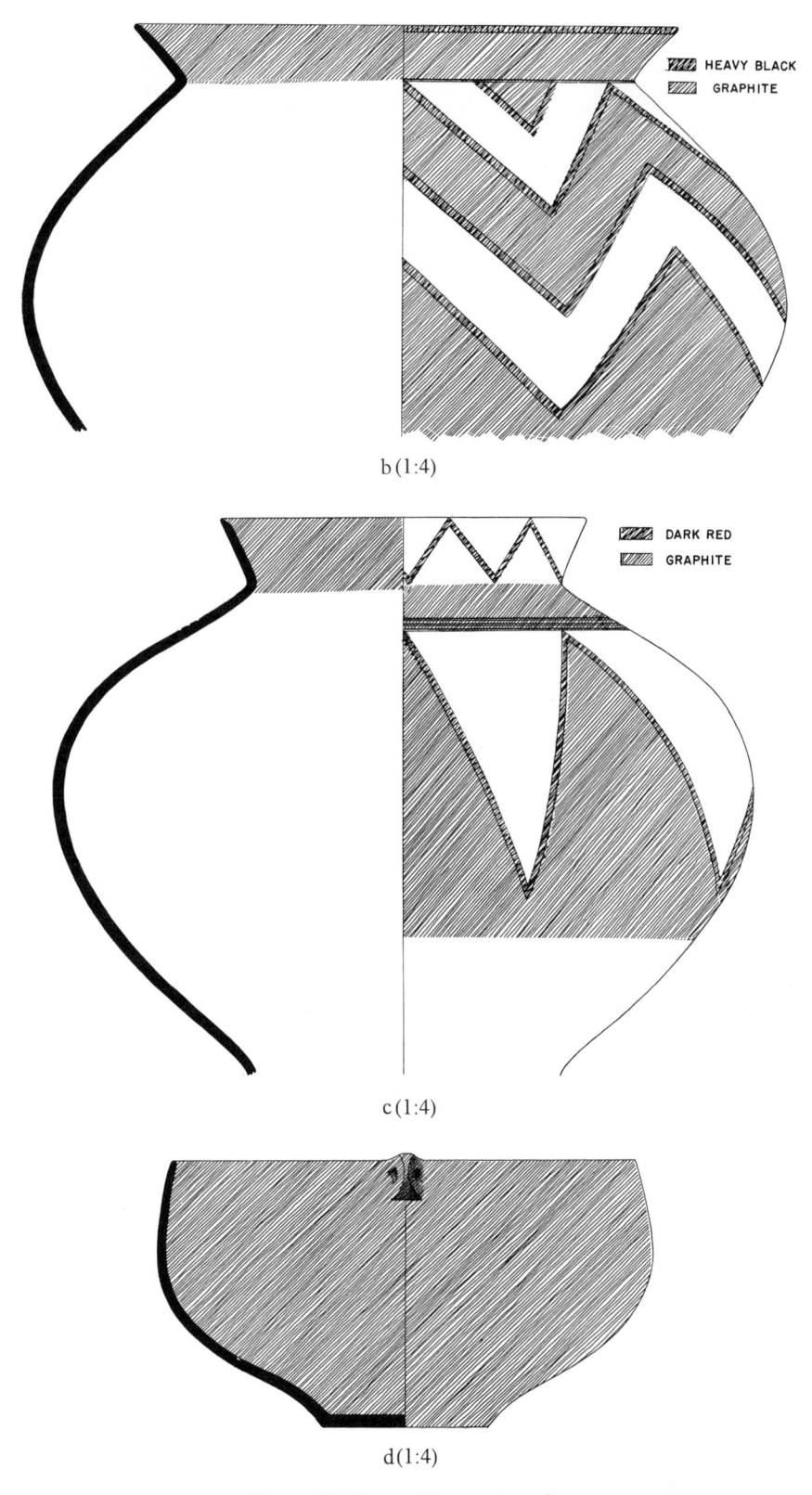

HEAVY BLACK
GRAPHITE

c (1:4)

DARK RED
GRAPHITE

d (1:4)

Figure 20. Grave 19, continued.

142   HALLSTATT

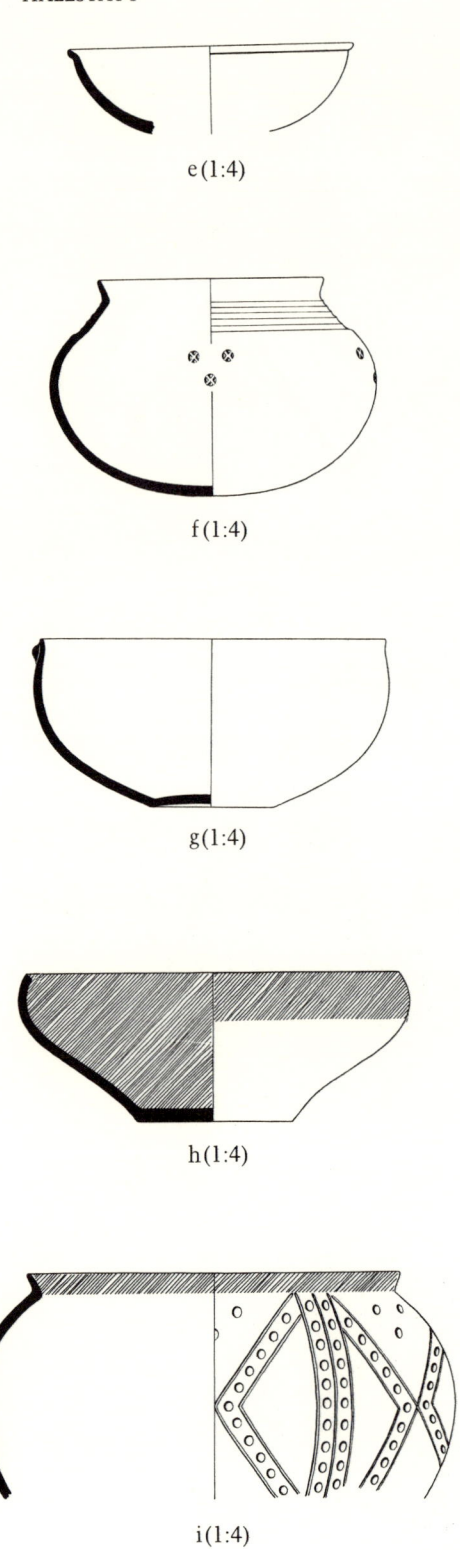

e (1:4)

f (1:4)

g (1:4)

h (1:4)

i (1:4)

Figure 20. Grave 19, continued.

a (1:4)

b (1:4)

c

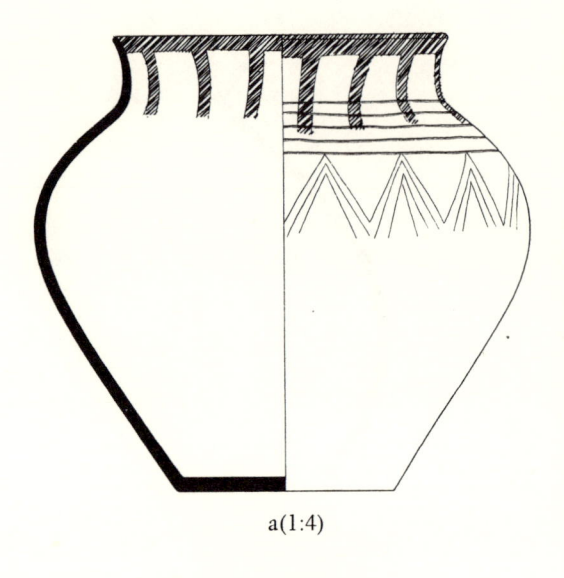

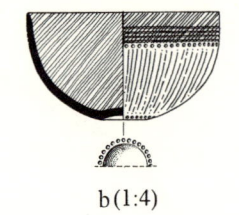

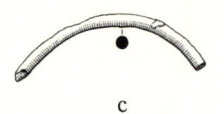

Figure 21. Grave 20.

HALLSTATT 143

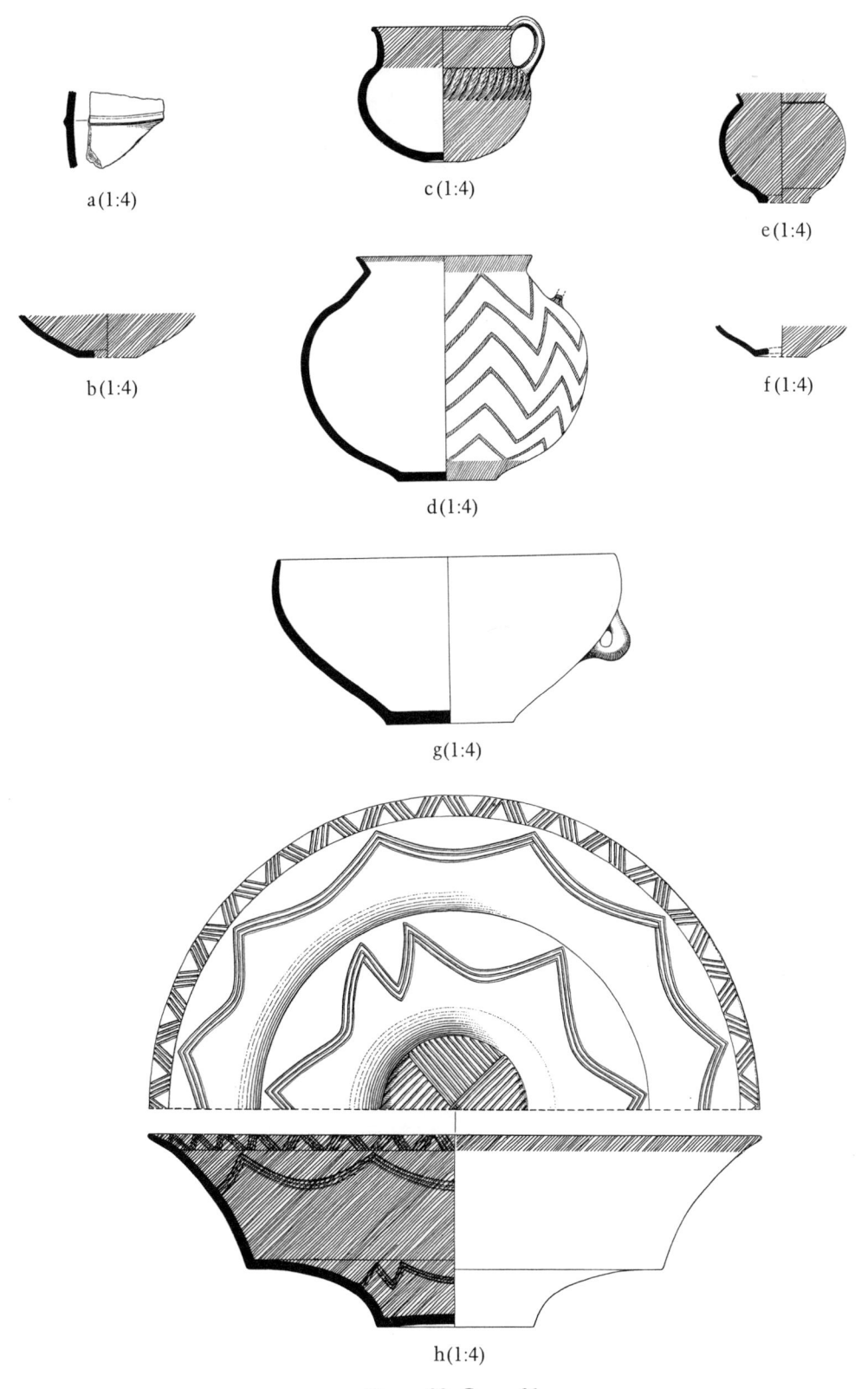

a(1:4) c(1:4) e(1:4)
b(1:4) d(1:4) f(1:4)
g(1:4)
h(1:4)

Figure 22. Grave 21.

144　HALLSTATT

a(1:4)　　　　b(1:4)　　　　c(1:4)

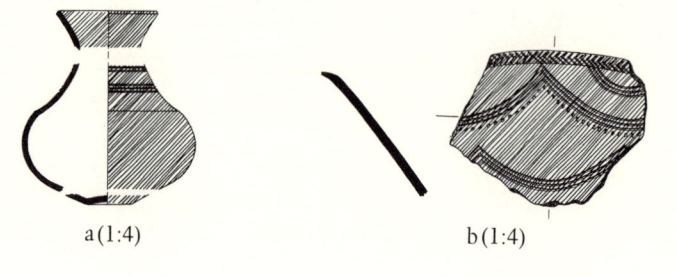

Figure 23. Grave 22.

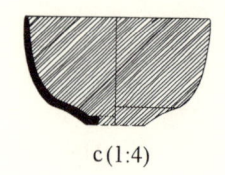

a(1:4)　　　　b(1:4)　　　　c(1:4)

d(1:4)

e(1:4)

f　　g　　h　　i

j

k

l(1:4)

m

Figure 24. Grave 23.

HALLSTATT 145

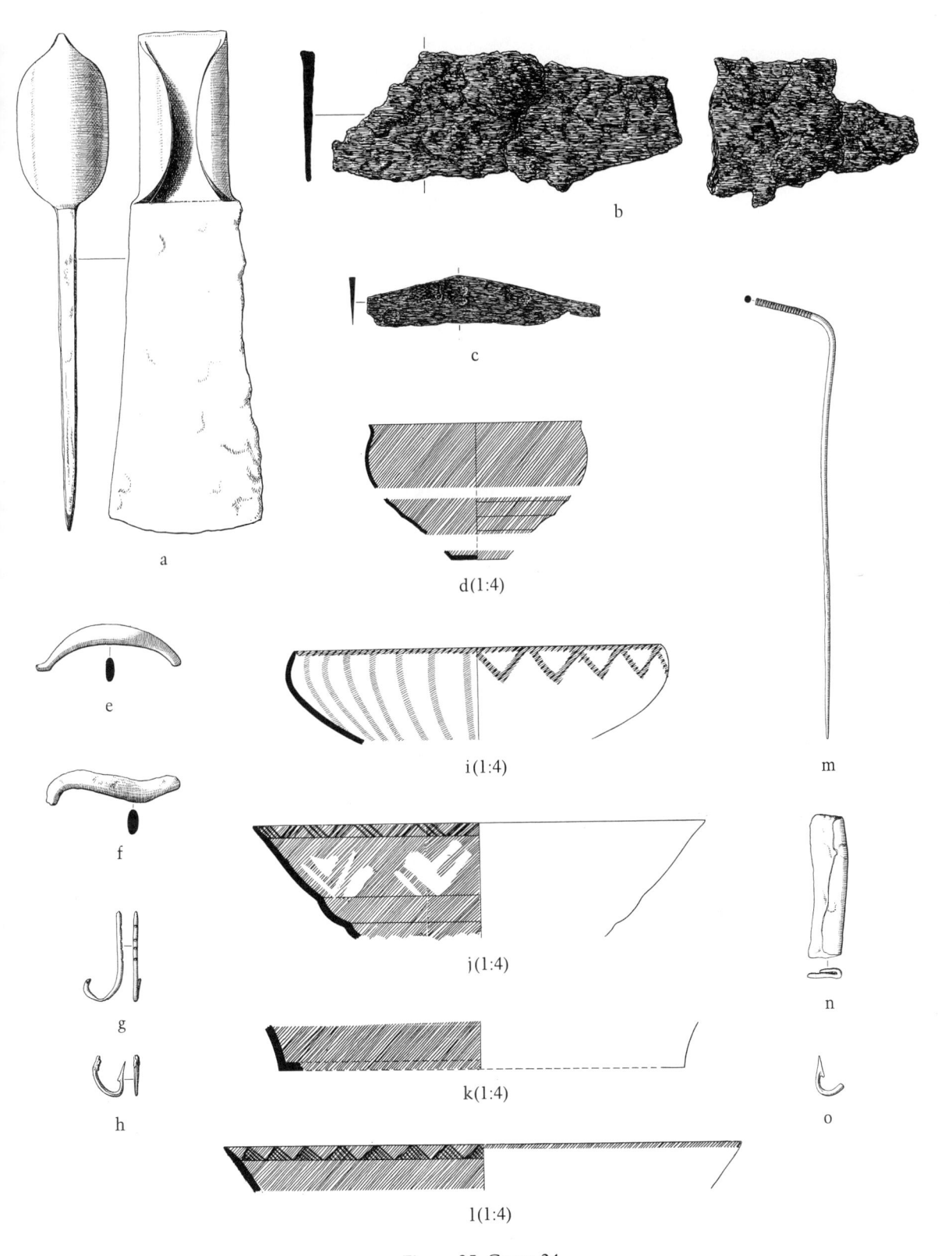

Figure 25. Grave 24.

146   HALLSTATT

a

b

c

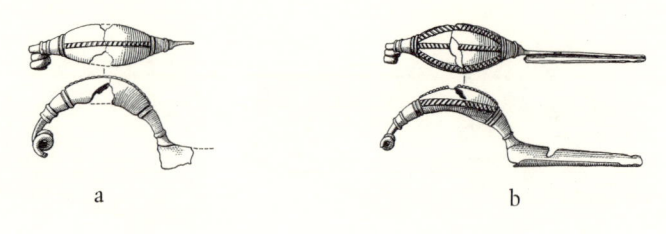

Figure 26. Grave 25.

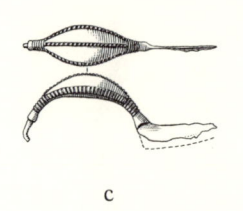

a

b

c

d

e

f

g

Figure 27. Isolated finds.

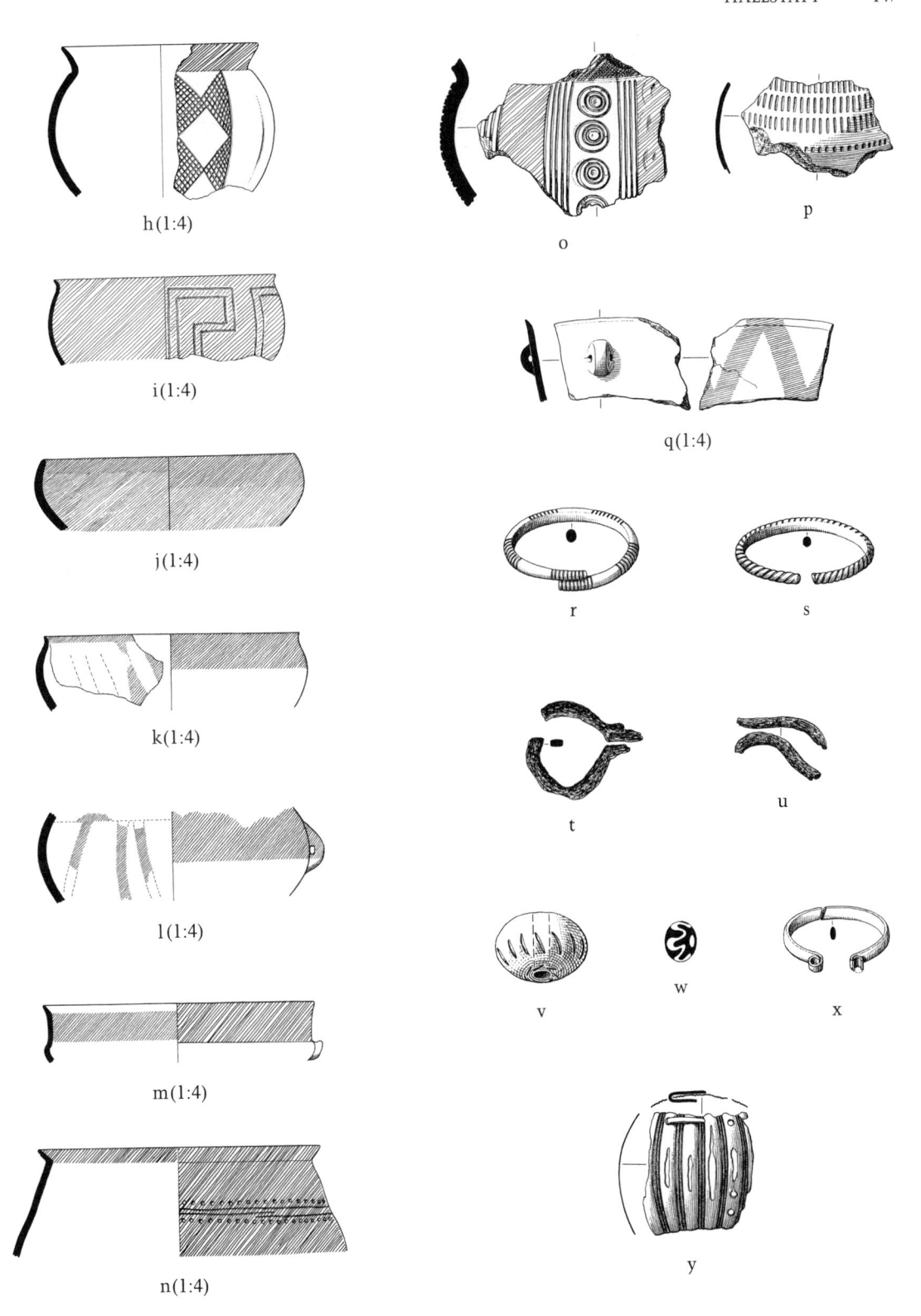

Figure 27. Isolated finds, continued.

STIČNA: TUMULUS I 149

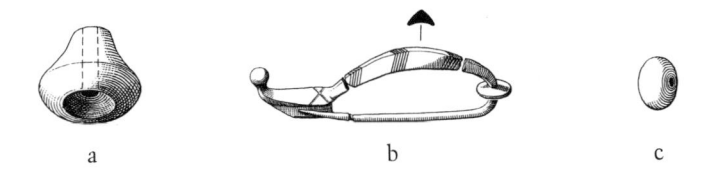

a b c

Figure 28. Tumulus I, Grave 1.

a

b

c (1:4)

d

e

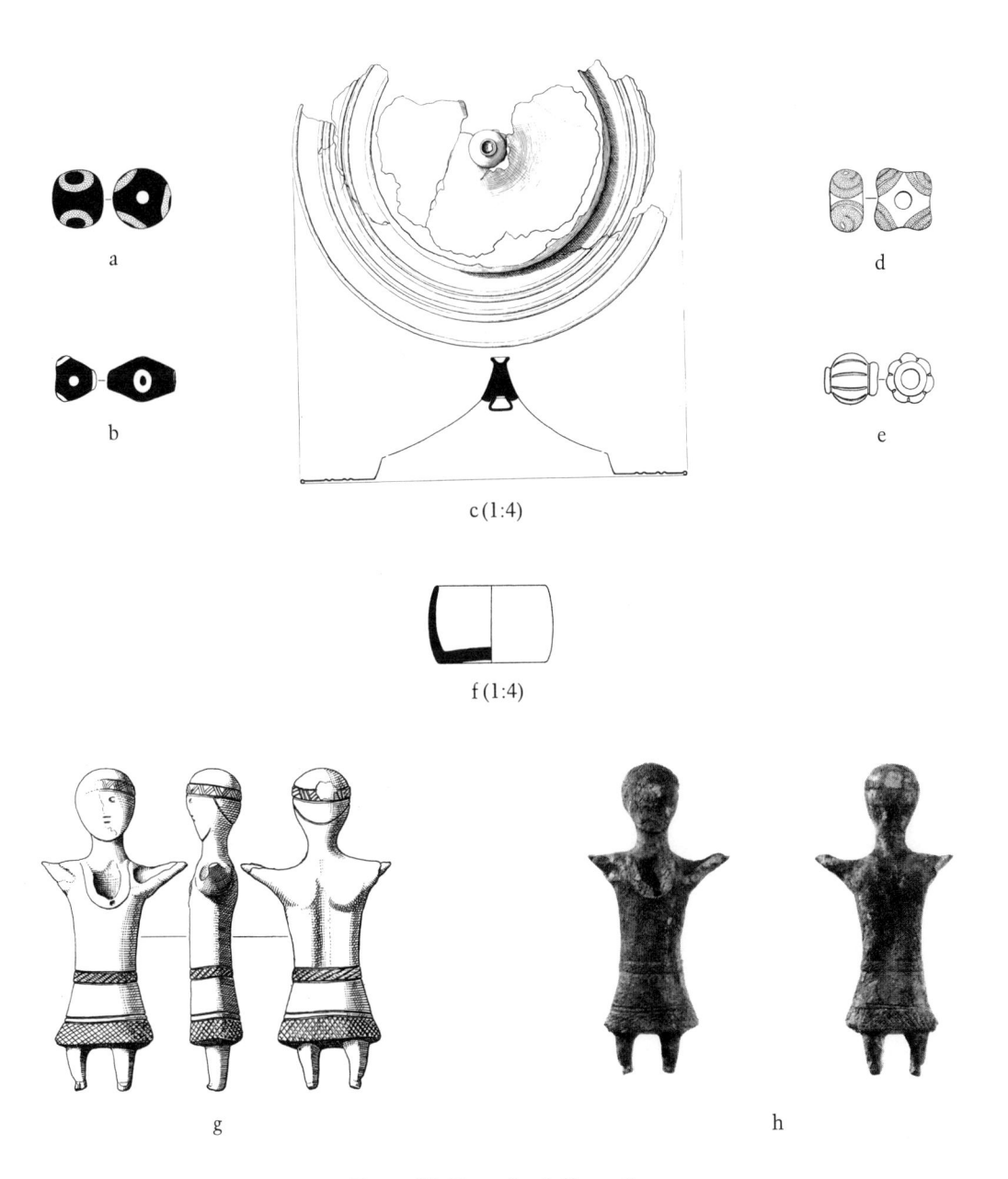

f (1:4)

g h

Figure 29. Tumulus I, Grave 2.

150 STIČNA: TUMULUS I

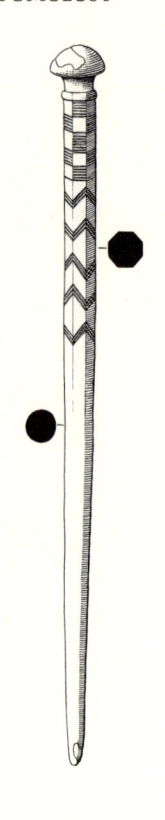

Figure 30. Tumulus I, Grave 3.

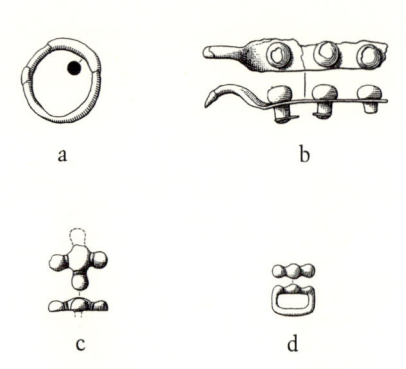

Figure 31. Tumulus I, Grave 4.

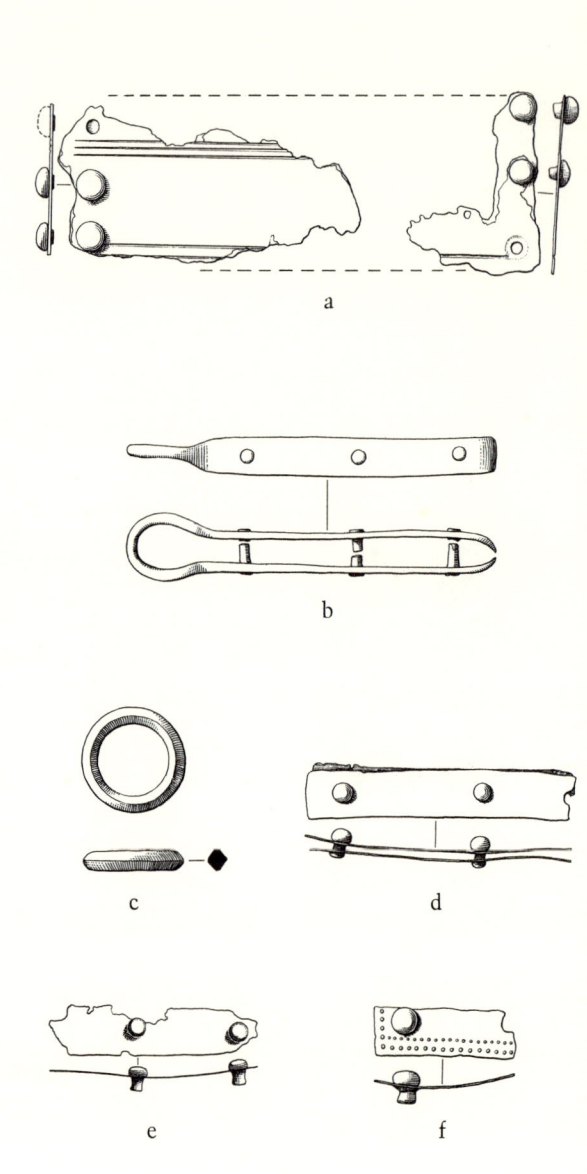

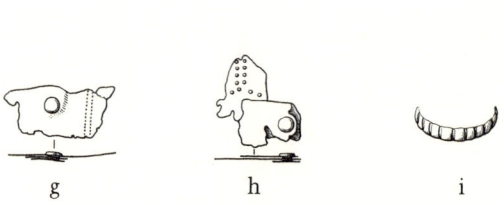

Figure 32. Tumulus I, Grave 5.

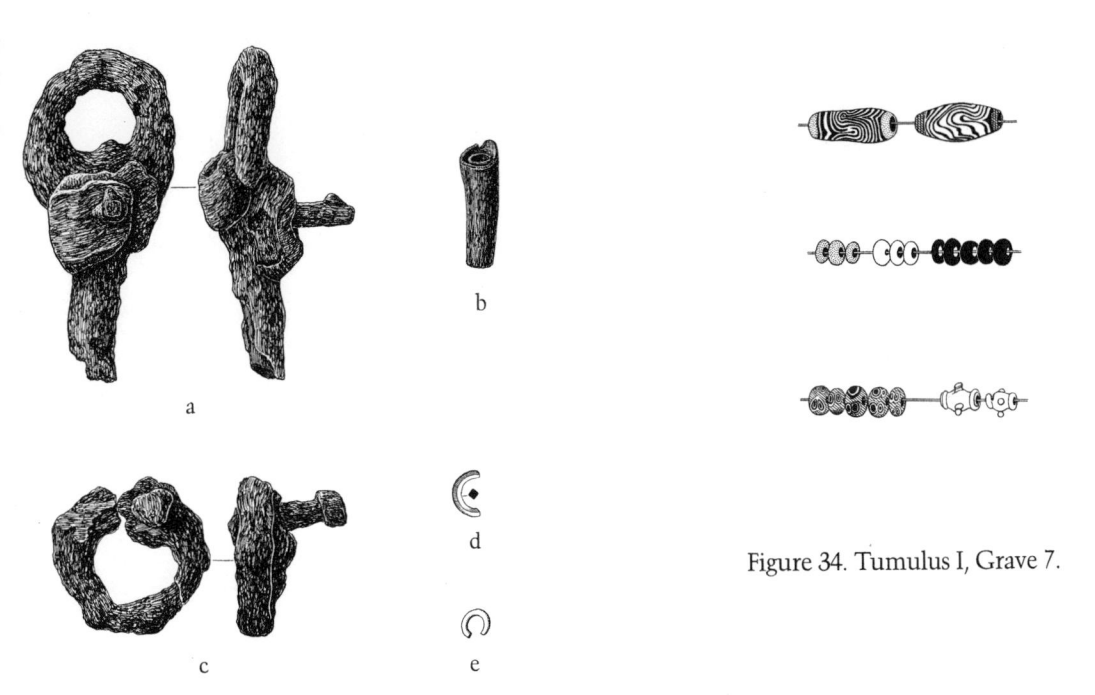

Figure 33. Tumulus I, Grave 6.

Figure 34. Tumulus I, Grave 7.

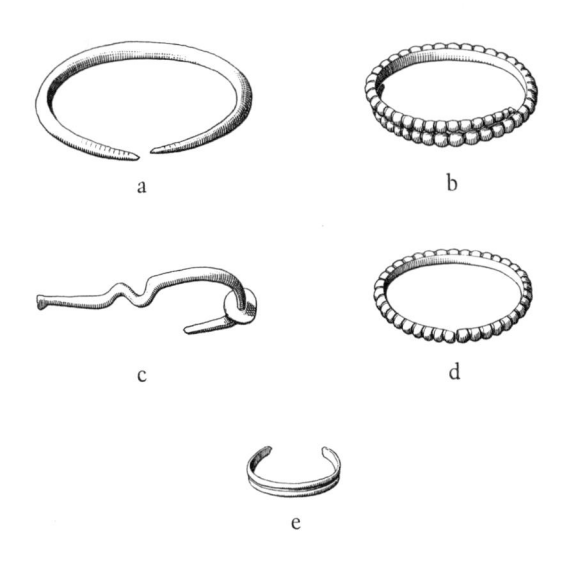

Figure 35. Tumulus I, isolated finds.

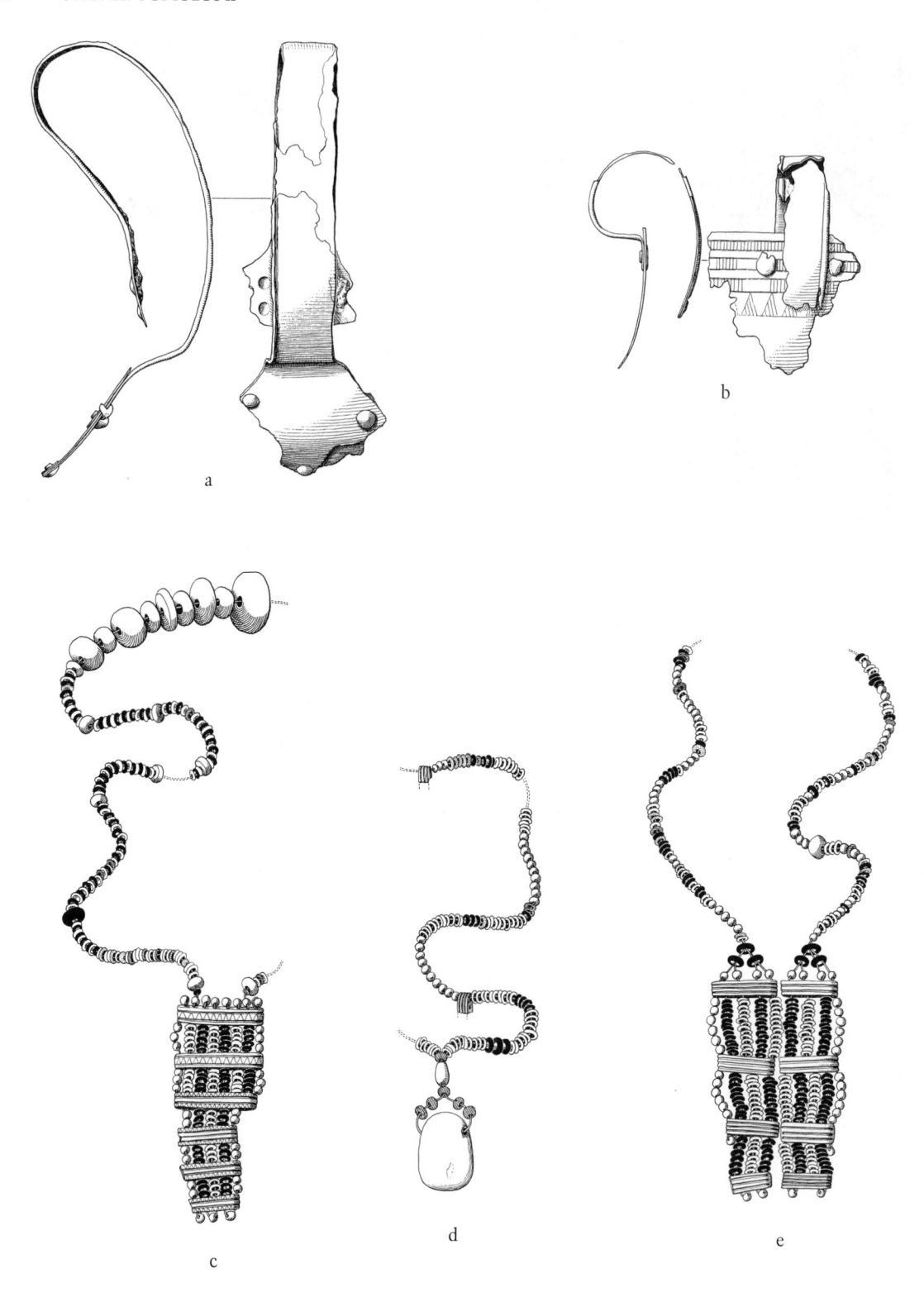

Figure 36. Tumulus II, Grave 2.

STIČNA: TUMULUS II 153

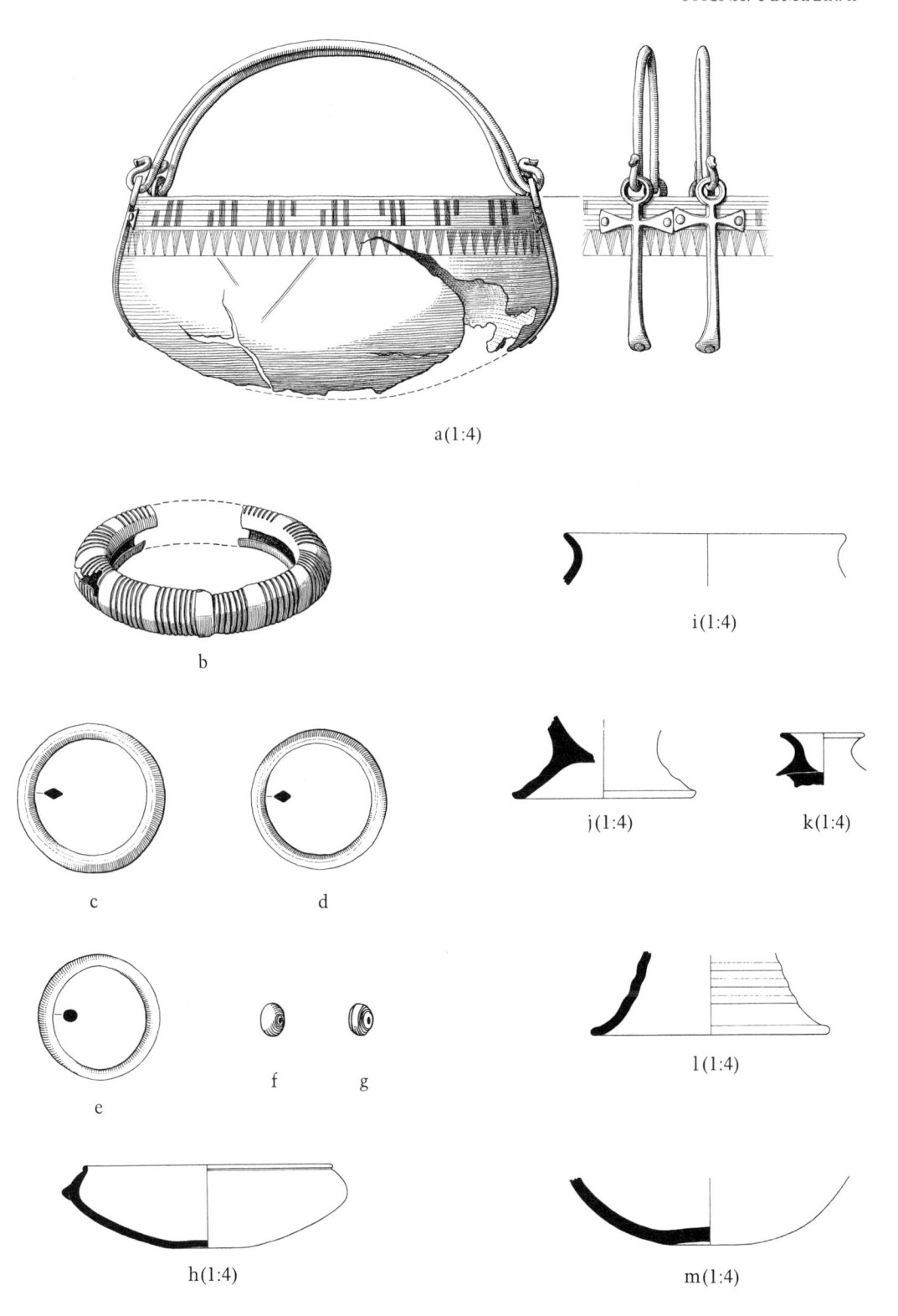

Figure 37. Tumulus II, Grave 3.

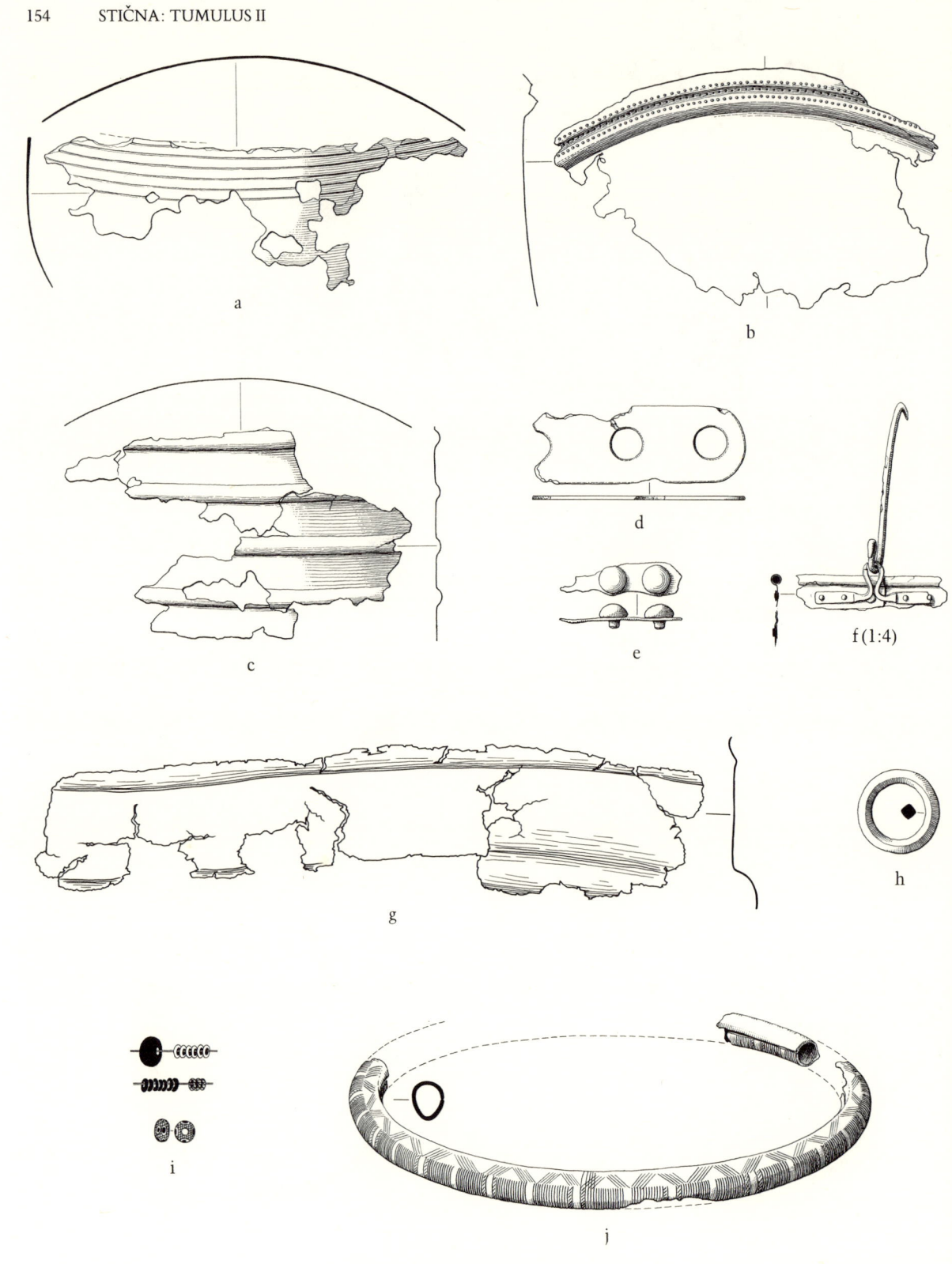

Figure 38. Tumulus II, Grave 4.

STIČNA: TUMULUS II   155

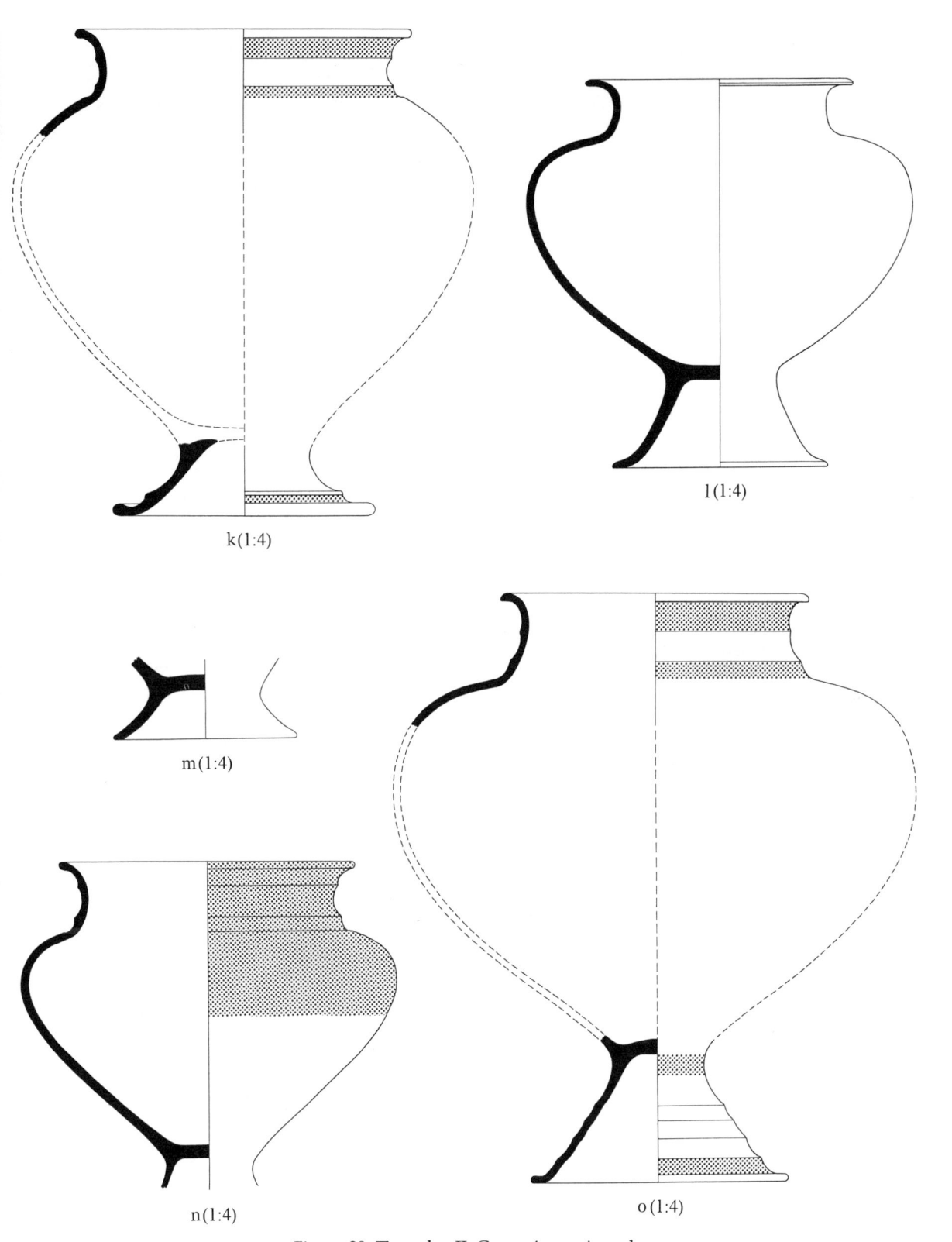

k(1:4)

l(1:4)

m(1:4)

n(1:4)

o(1:4)

Figure 38. Tumulus II, Grave 4, continued.

156   STIČNA: TUMULUS II

a(1:4)

b(1:4)

c(1:4)

d(1:4)

e

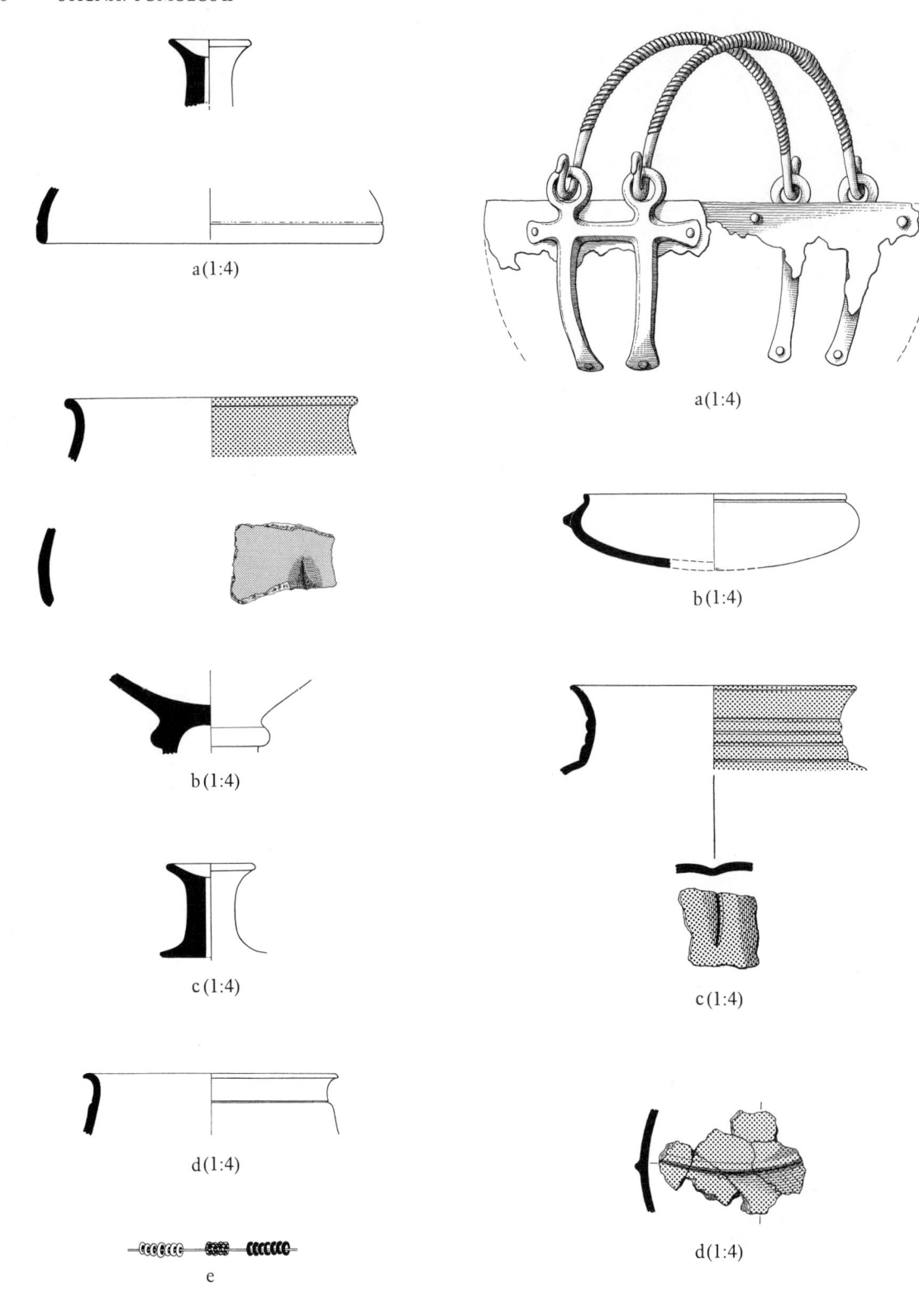

Figure 39. Tumulus II, Grave 5.

a(1:4)

b(1:4)

c(1:4)

d(1:4)

Figure 40. Tumulus II, Grave 6.

STIČNA: TUMULUS II 157

Figure 41. Tumulus II, Grave 7.

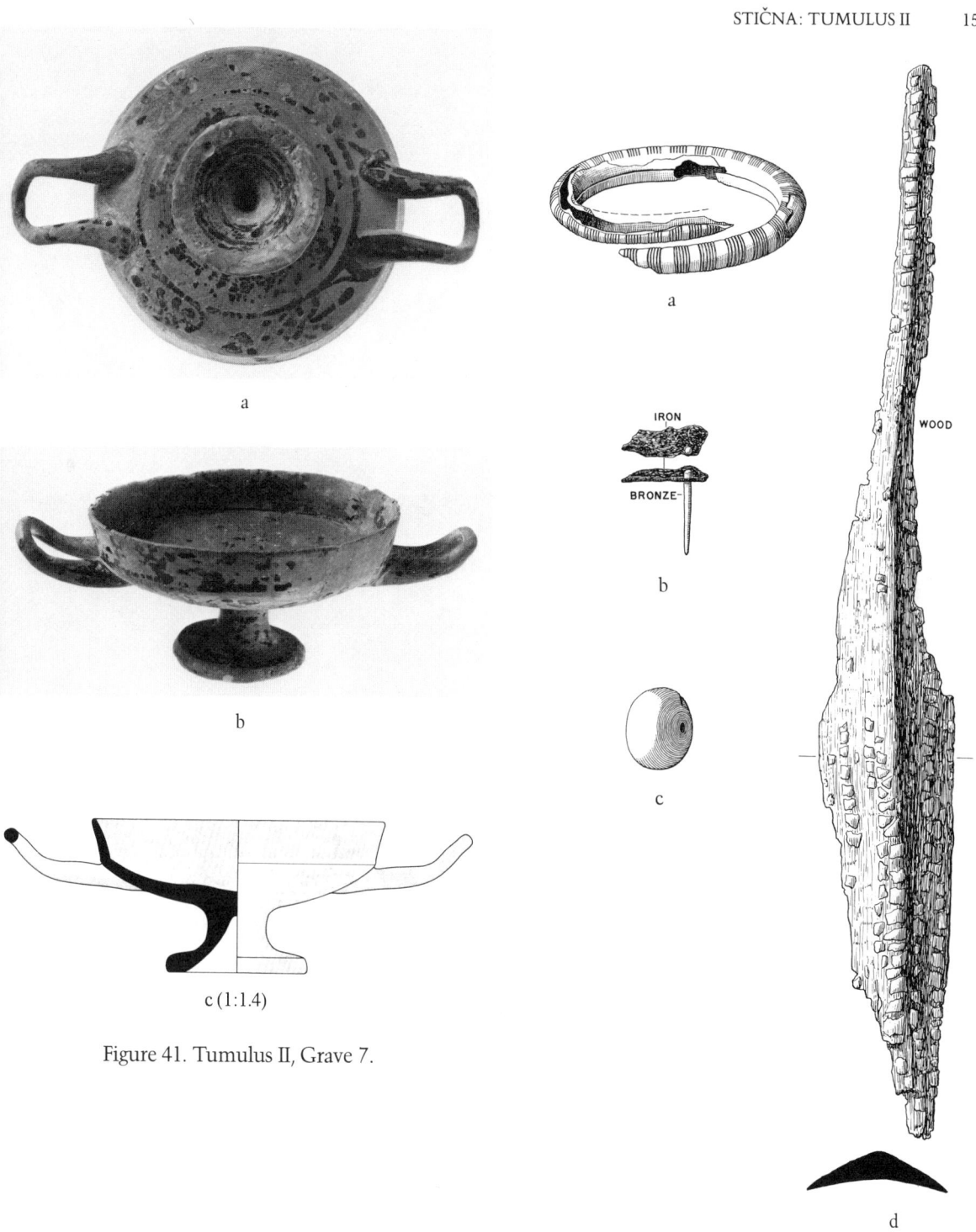

Figure 42. Tumulus II, Grave 9.

158　STIČNA: TUMULUS II

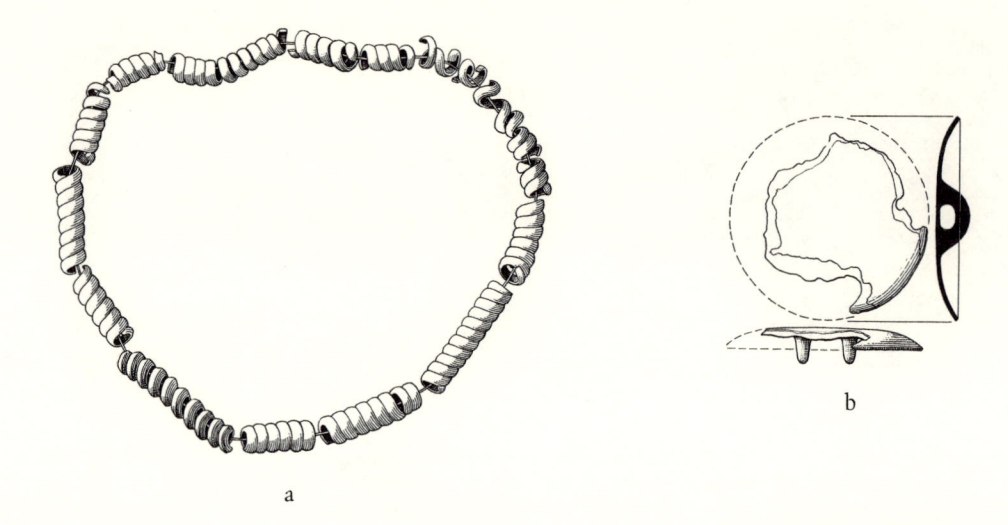

Figure 43. Tumulus II, Grave 14.

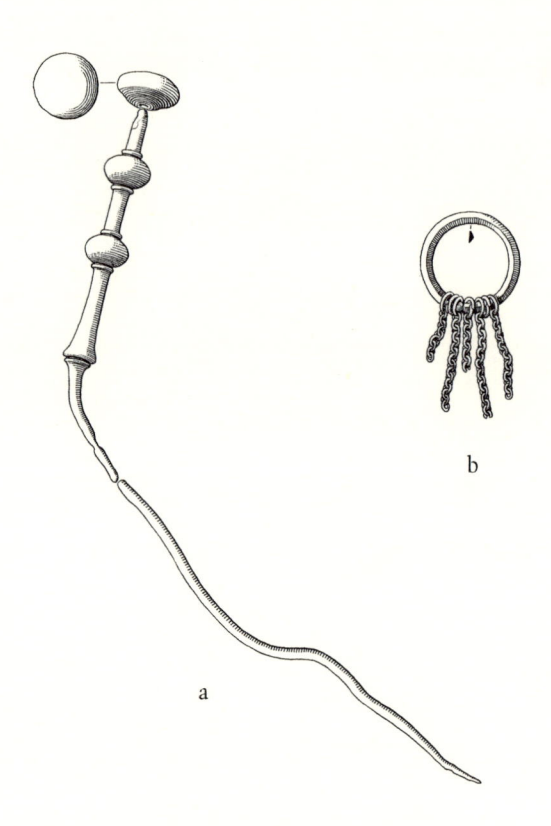

Figure 44. Tumulus II, Grave 15.

STIČNA: TUMULUS II 159

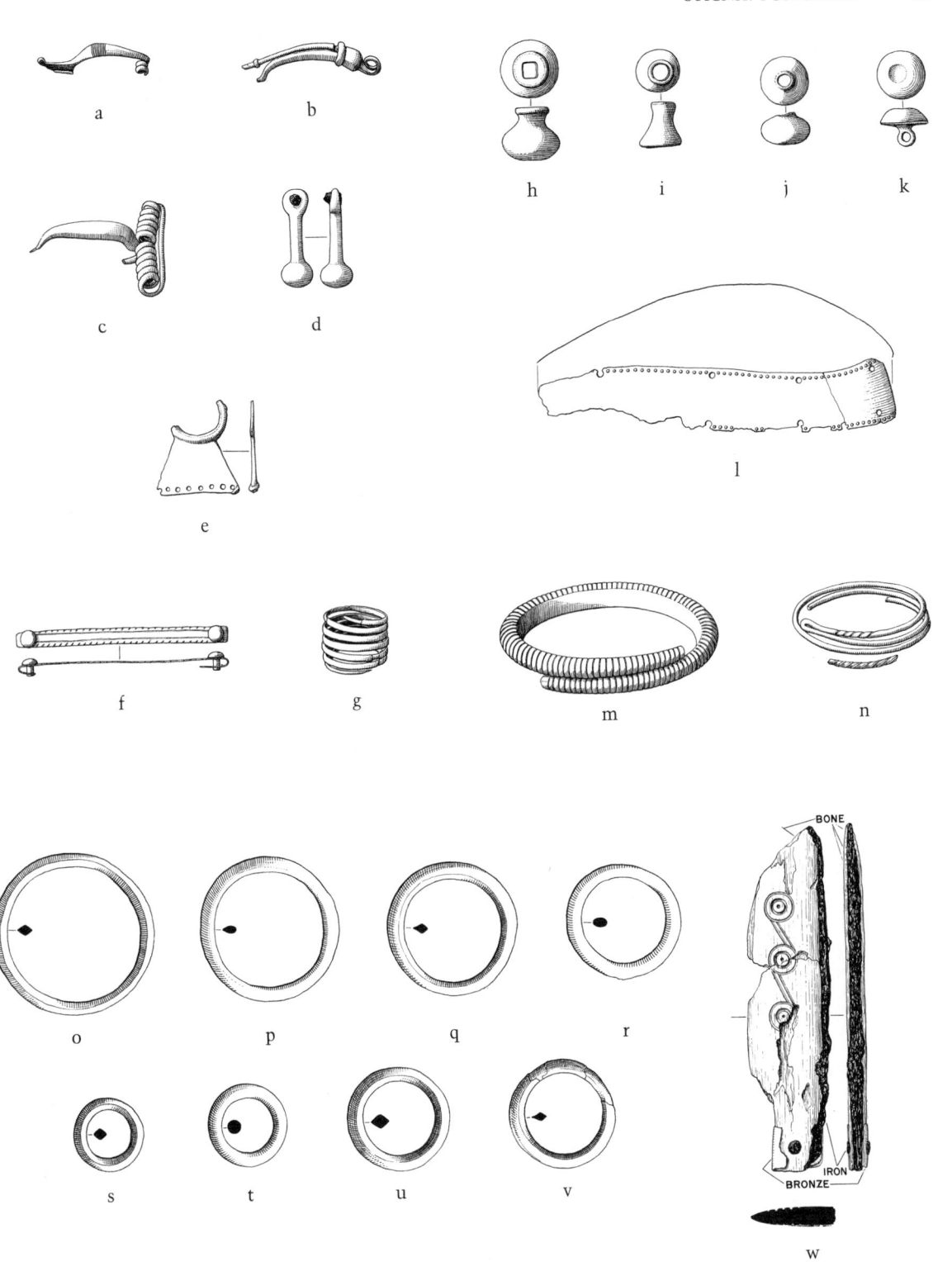

Figure 45. Tumulus II, isolated finds.

160 STIČNA: TUMULUS II

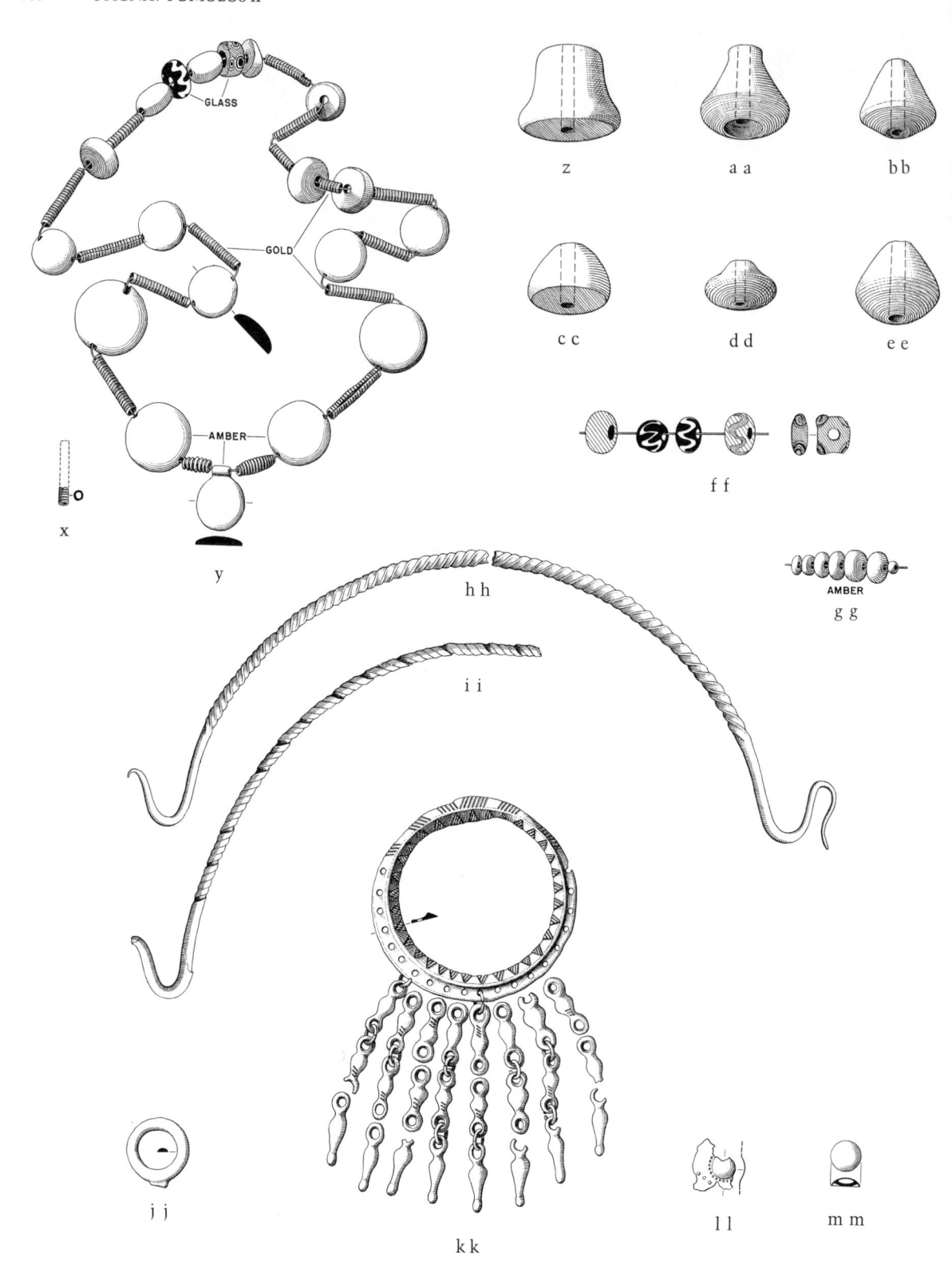

Figure 45. Tumulus II, isolated finds, continued.

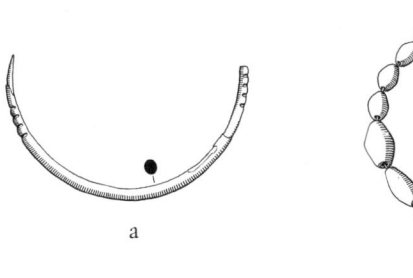

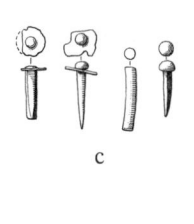

Figure 46. Tumulus III, Grave 1a.

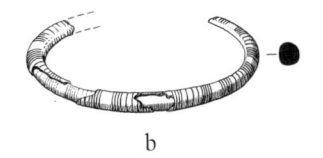

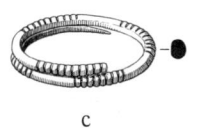

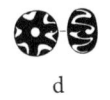

Figure 47. Tumulus III, Grave 2a.

Figure 48. Tumulus III, Grave 2c.

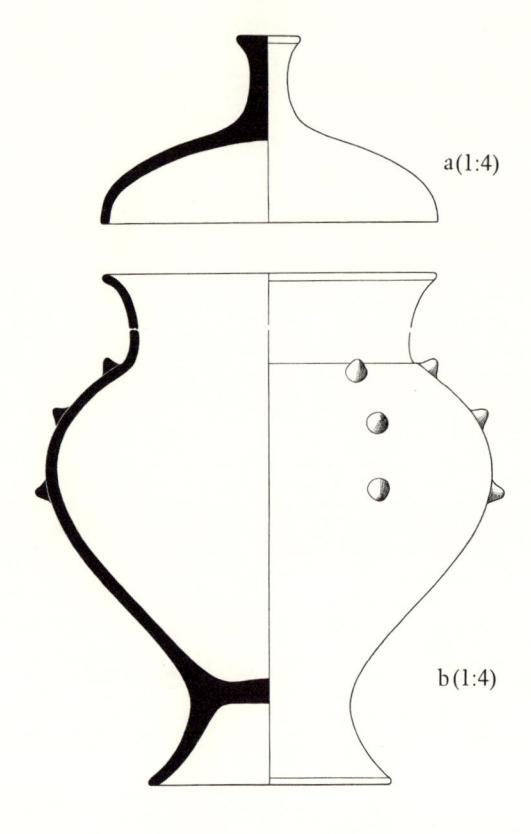

Figure 49. Tumulus III, Grave 6.

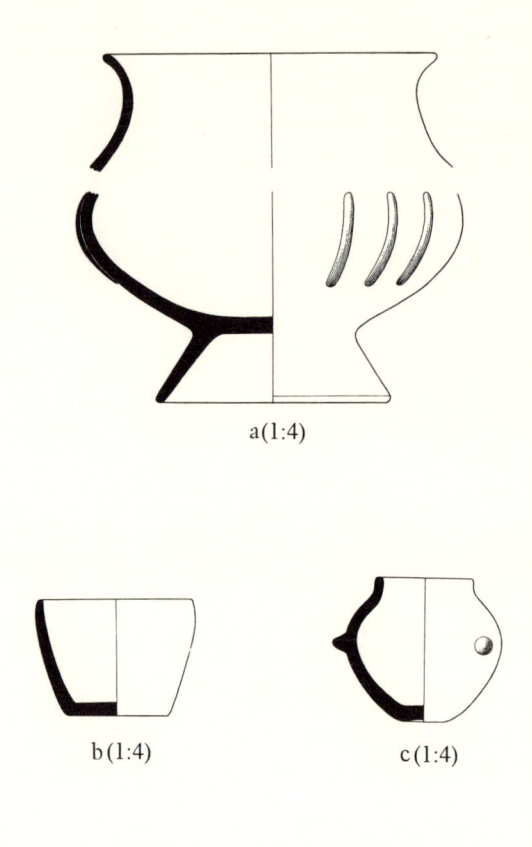

Figure 51. Tumulus III, Grave 8.

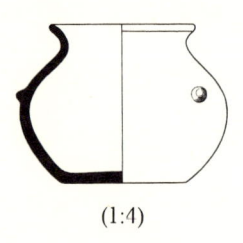

Figure 50. Tumulus III, Grave 7.

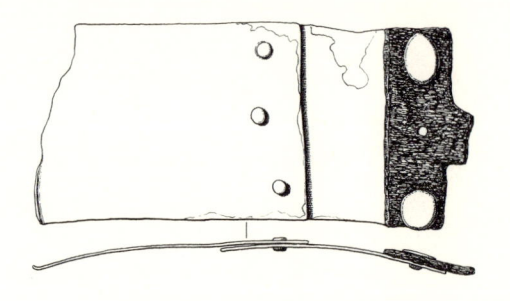

Figure 52. Tumulus III, Grave 9.

STIČNA: TUMULI III AND IV   163

Figure 53. Tumulus III, Grave 10.

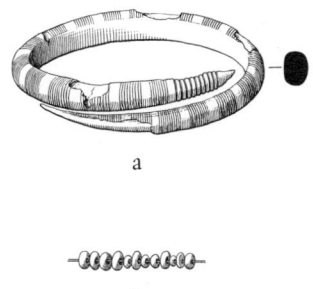

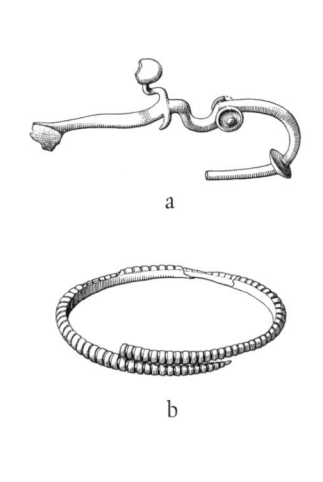

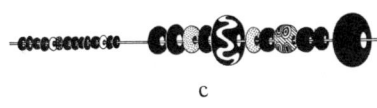

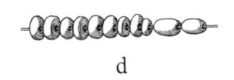

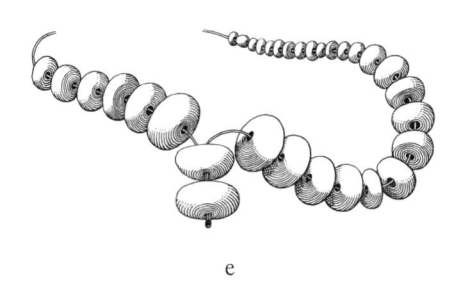

Figure 54. Tumulus III, isolated finds.

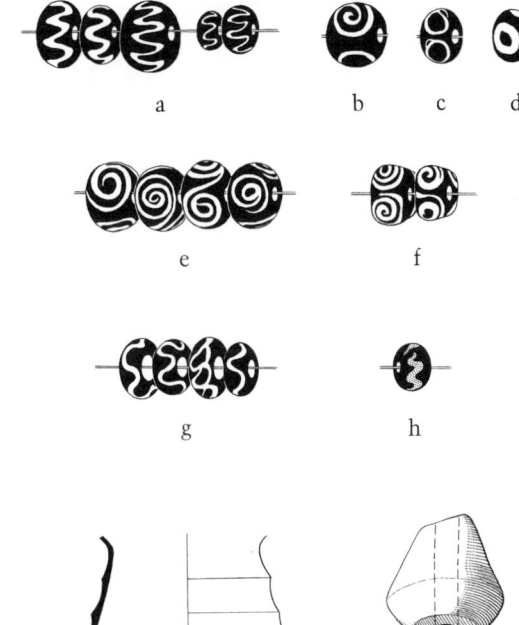

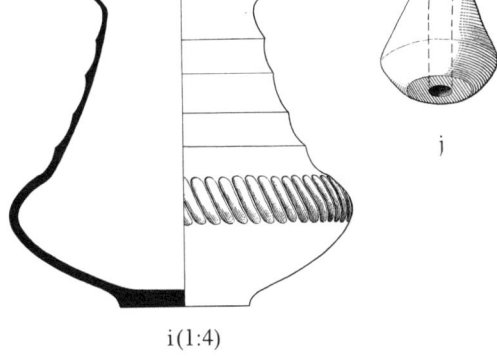

Figure 55. Tumulus IV, Grave 1.

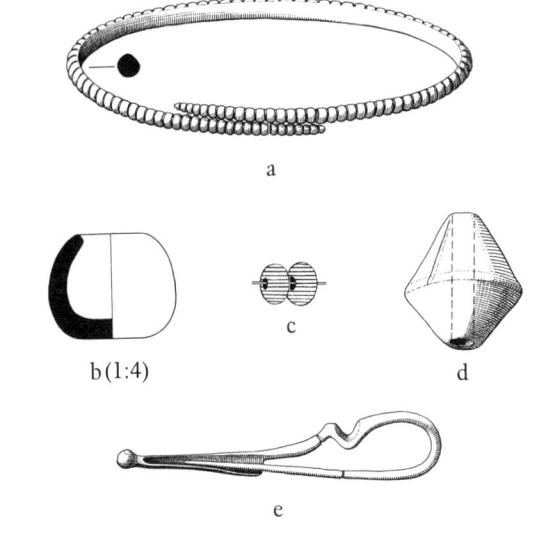

Figure 56. Tumulus IV, Grave 2.

a(1:4)

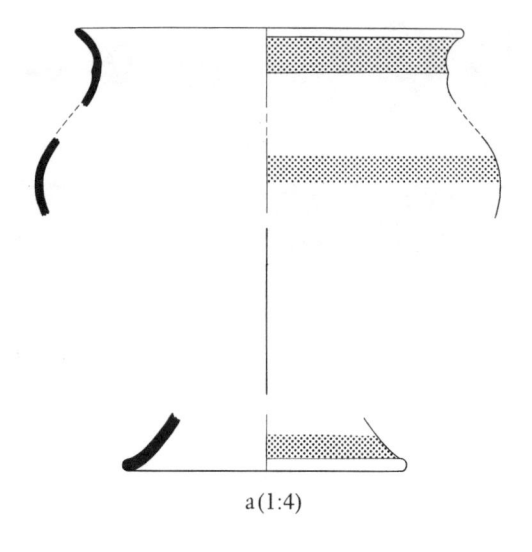

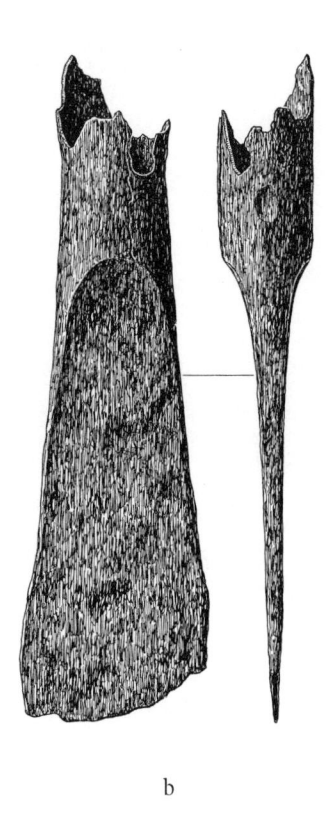

Figure 57. Tumulus IV, Grave 3.

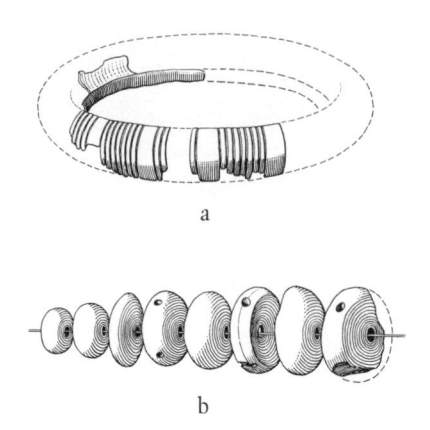

Figure 58. Tumulus IV, Grave 4.

a(1:4)

b(1:4)

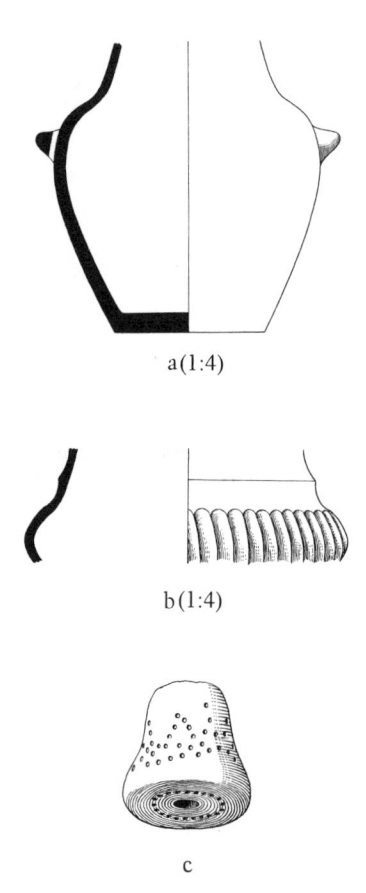

Figure 59. Tumulus IV, Grave 5.

STIČNA: TUMULUS IV   165

Figure 60. Tumulus IV, Grave 6.

a

b   c

a

b

c

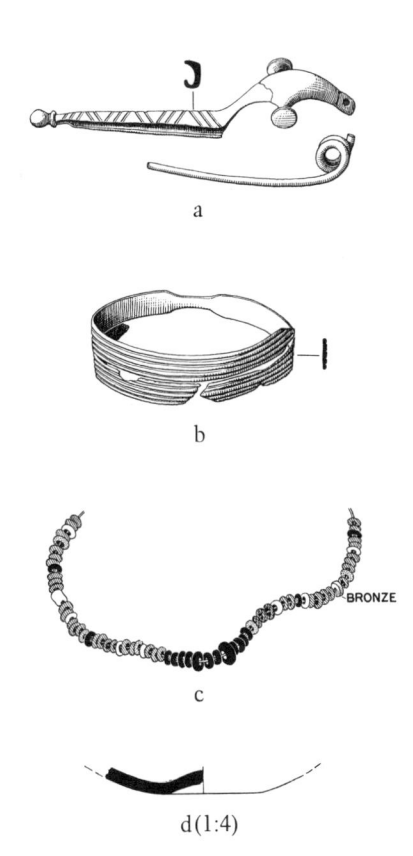

d(1:4)

d(1:4)

e(1:4)

Figure 61. Tumulus IV, Grave 7.

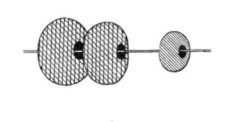

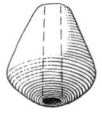

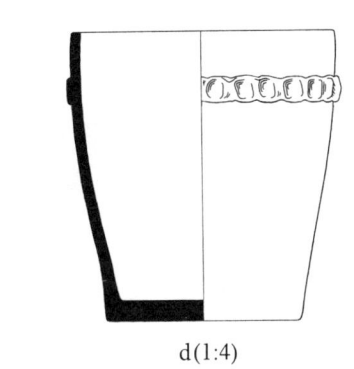

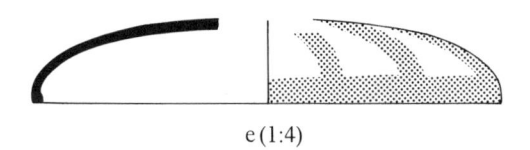

Figure 62. Tumulus IV, Grave 8.

166　STIČNA: TUMULUS IV

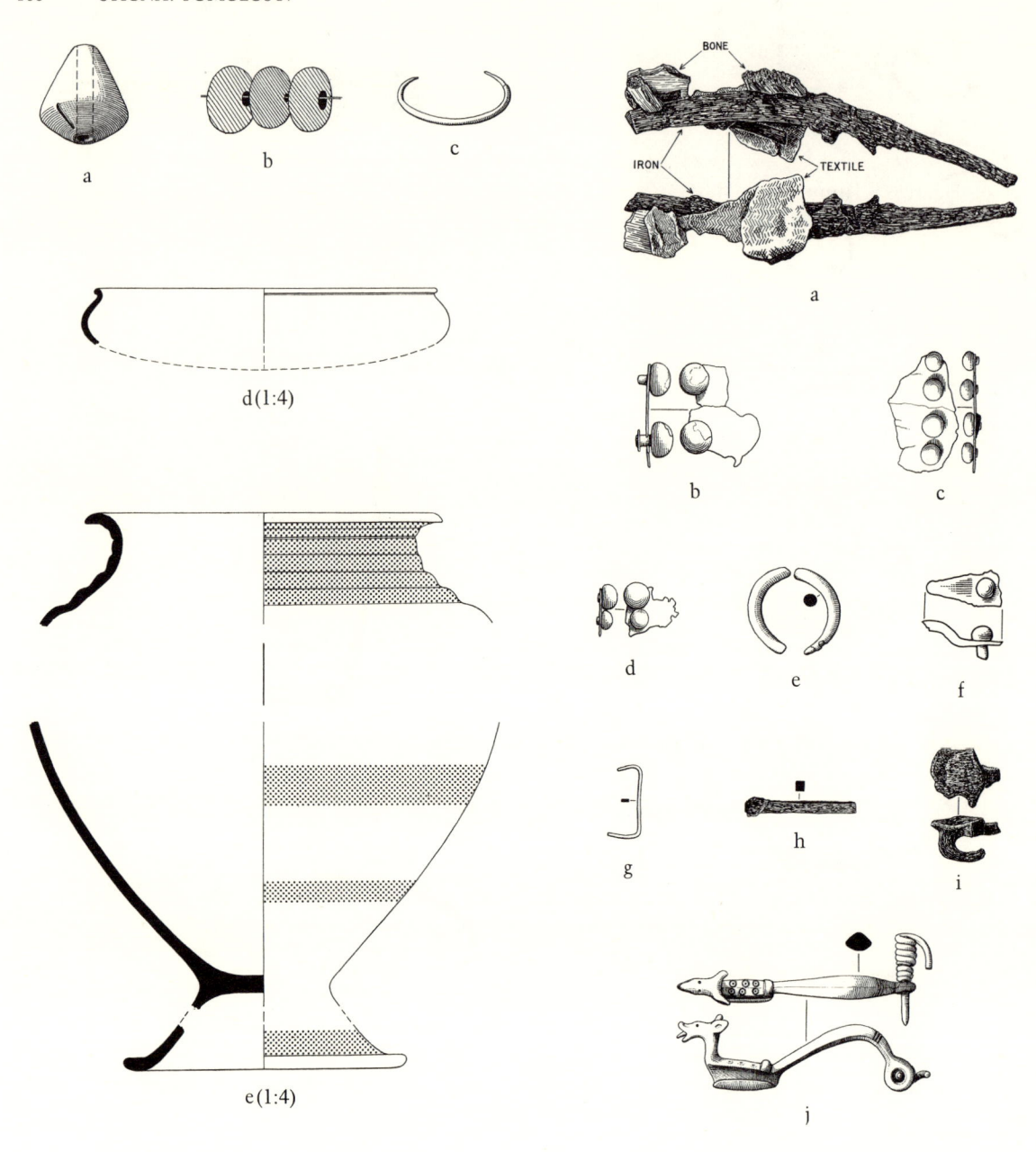

Figure 63. Tumulus IV, Grave 9.

Figure 64. Tumulus IV, Grave 10.

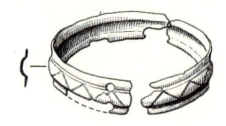

Figure 65. Tumulus IV, Grave 10a.

STIČNA: TUMULUS IV 167

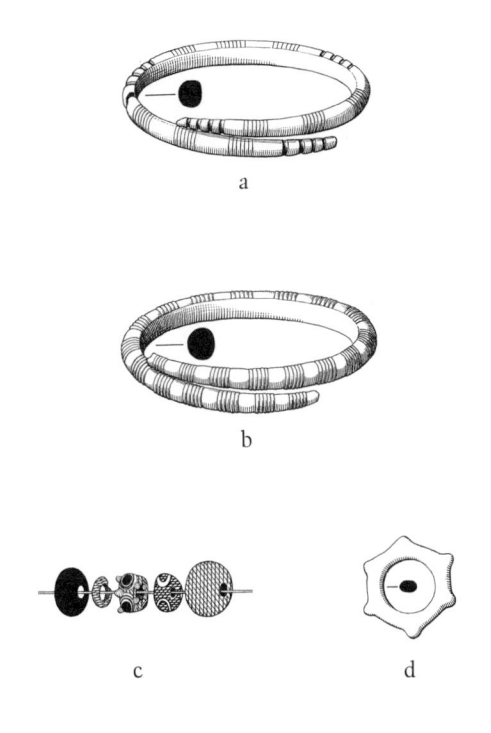

Figure 66. Tumulus IV, Grave 11.

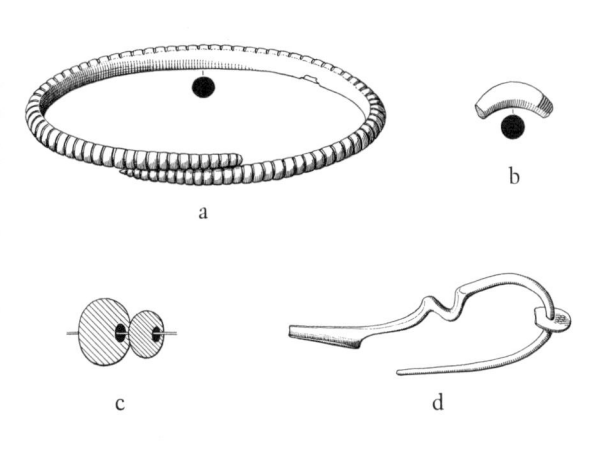

Figure 67. Tumulus IV, Grave 12.

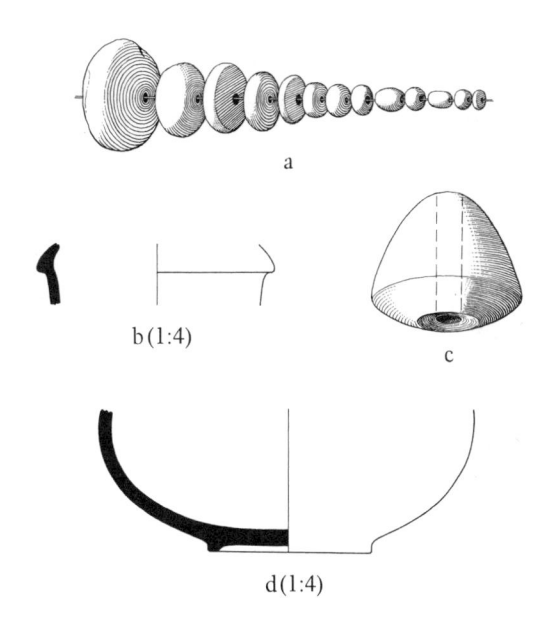

Figure 68. Tumulus IV, Grave 14.

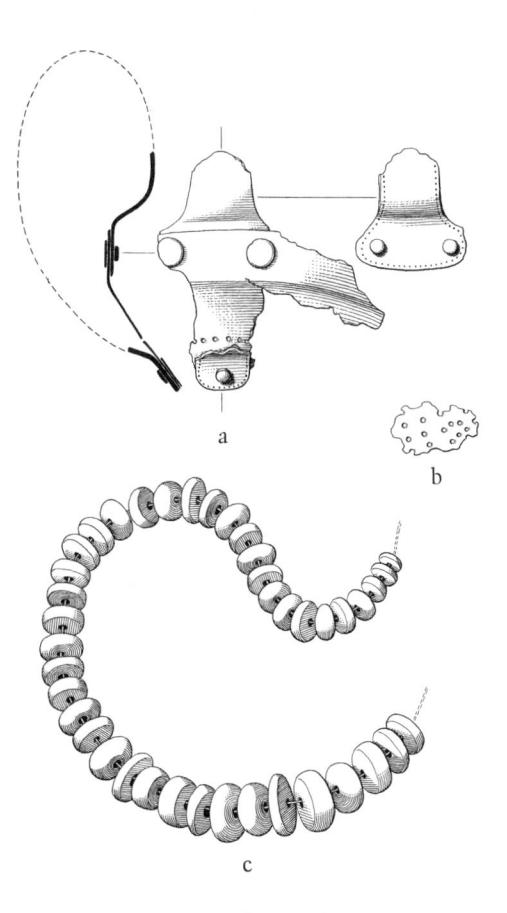

Figure 69. Tumulus IV, Grave 15.

a b c d e

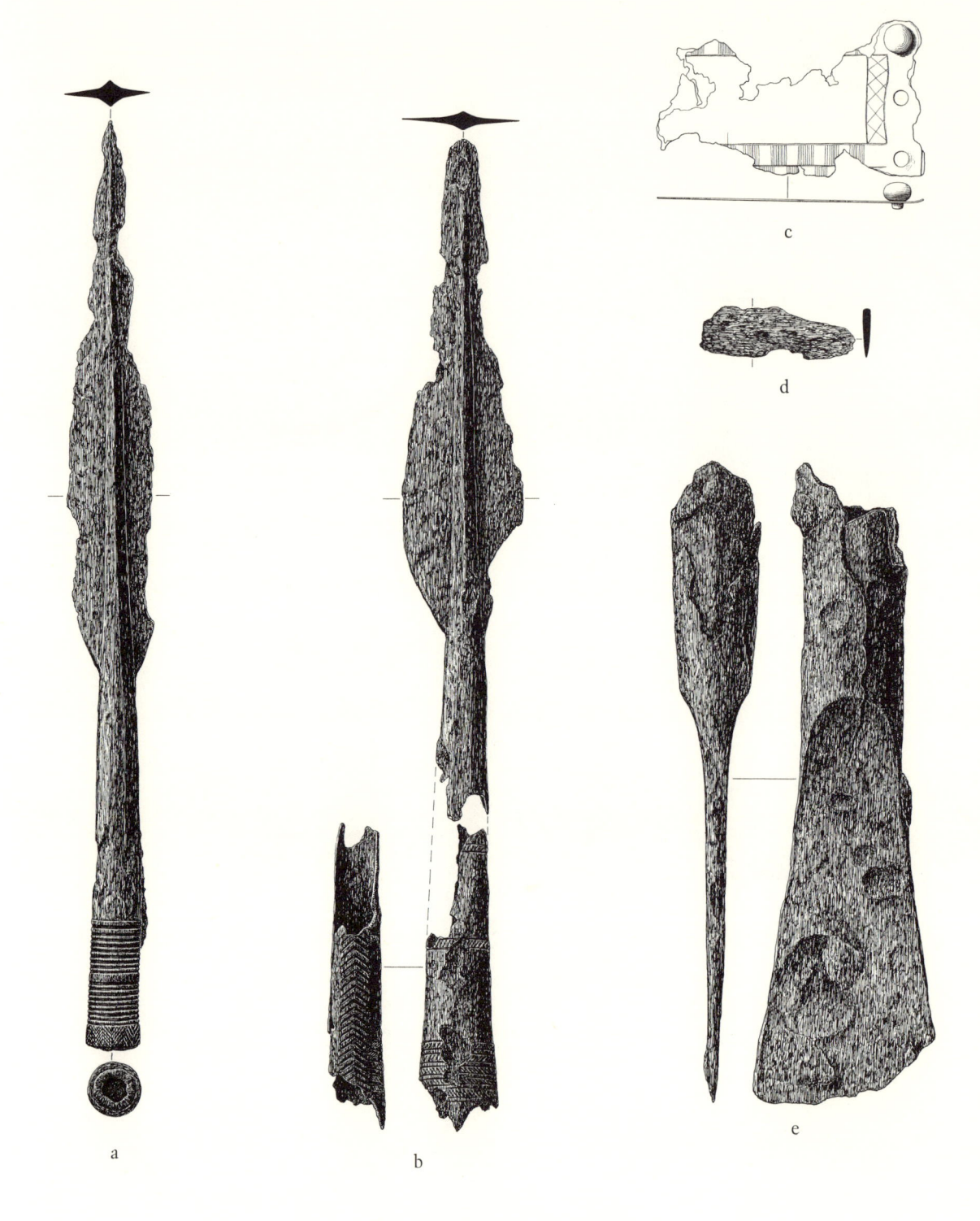

Figure 70. Tumulus IV, Grave 16.

STIČNA: TUMULUS IV   169

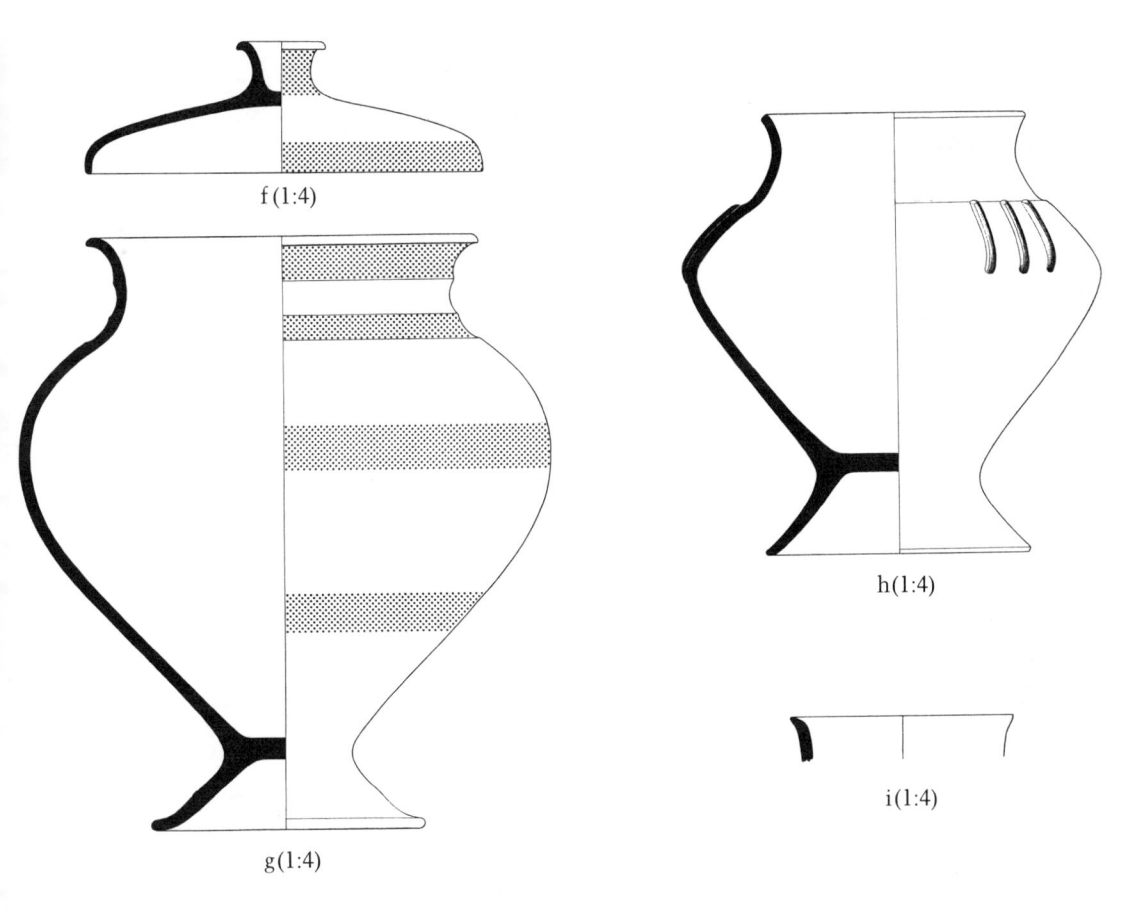

f (1:4)

g(1:4)

h(1:4)

i(1:4)

Figure 70. Tumulus IV, Grave 16, continued.

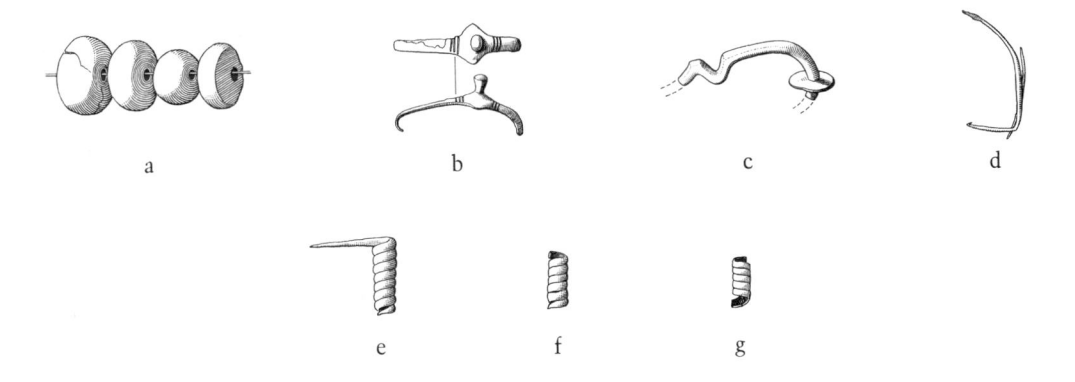

a   b   c   d

e   f   g

Figure 71. Tumulus IV, Grave 17.

170 STIČNA: TUMULUS IV

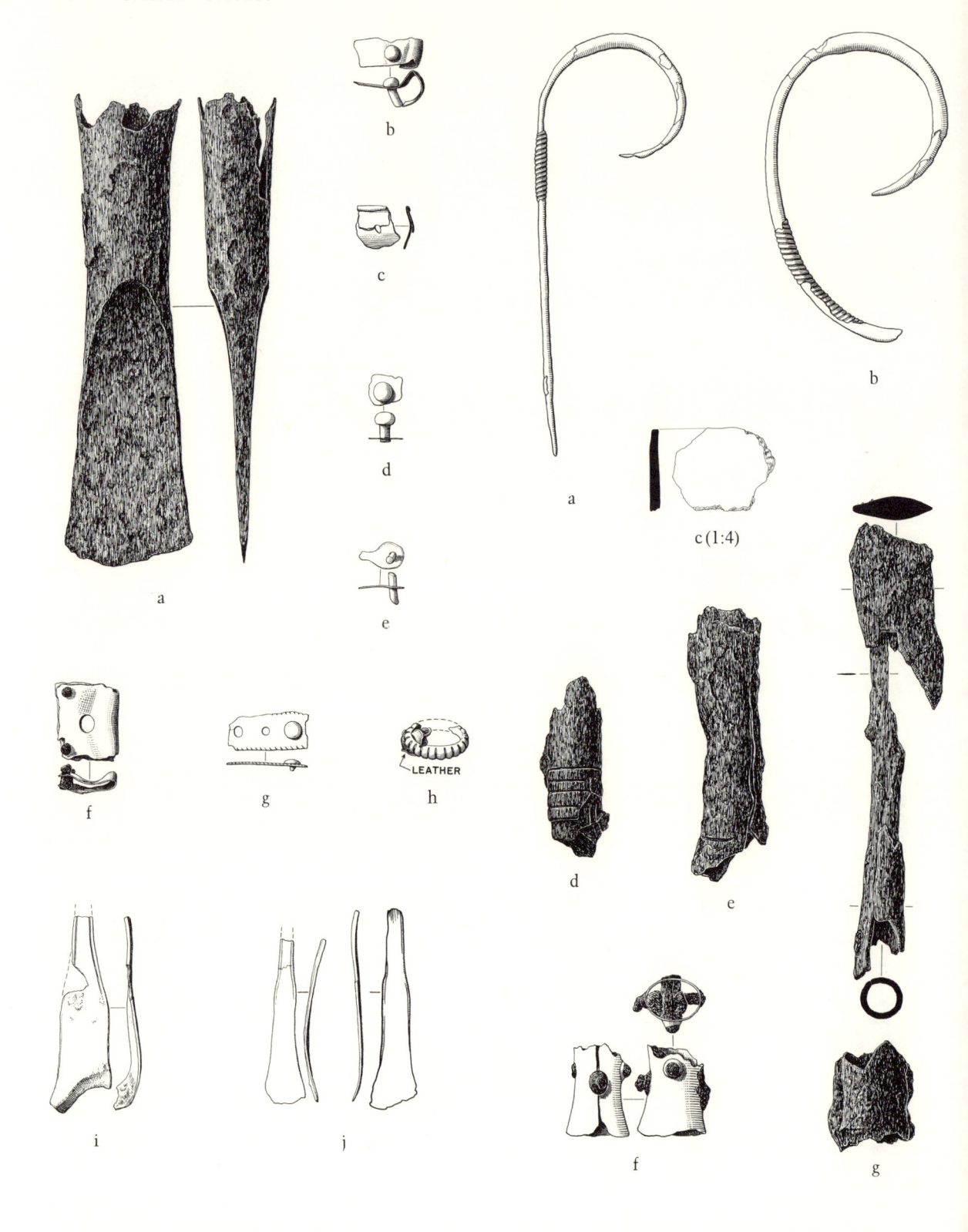

Figure 72. Tumulus IV, Grave 18.

Figure 73. Tumulus IV, Grave 19.

h(1:4)

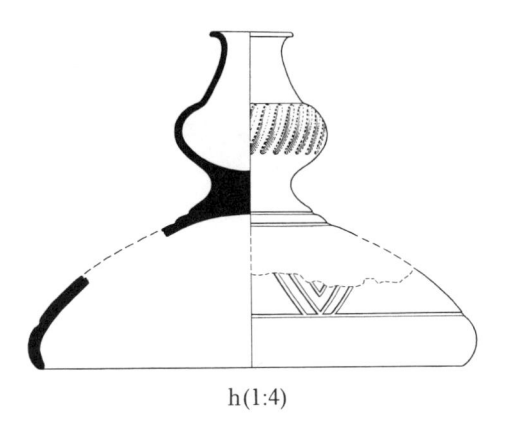

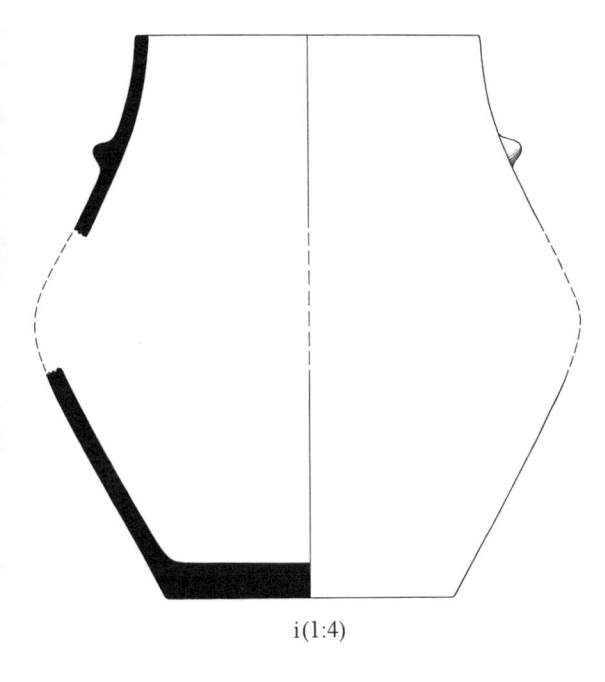

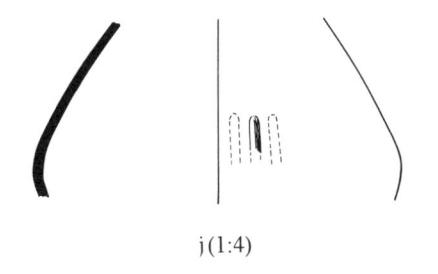

i(1:4)

j(1:4)

Figure 73. Tumulus IV, Grave 19, continued.

STIČNA: TUMULUS IV   171

a

AMBER

b

GOLD

c

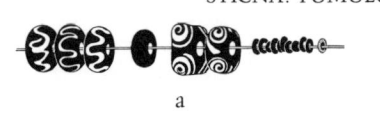

Figure 74. Tumulus IV, Grave 19a.

a

b

c

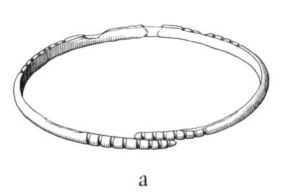

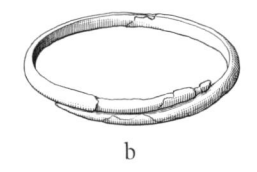

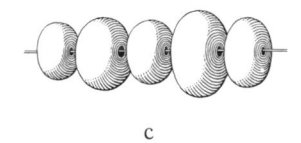

Figure 75. Tumulus IV, Grave 20.

172　STIČNA: TUMULUS IV

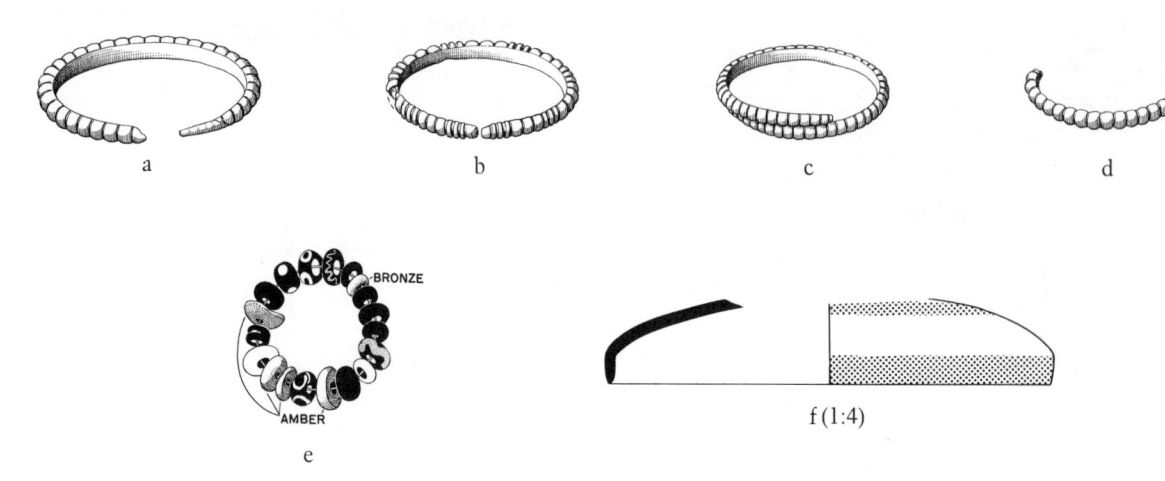

Figure 76. Tumulus IV, Grave 21.

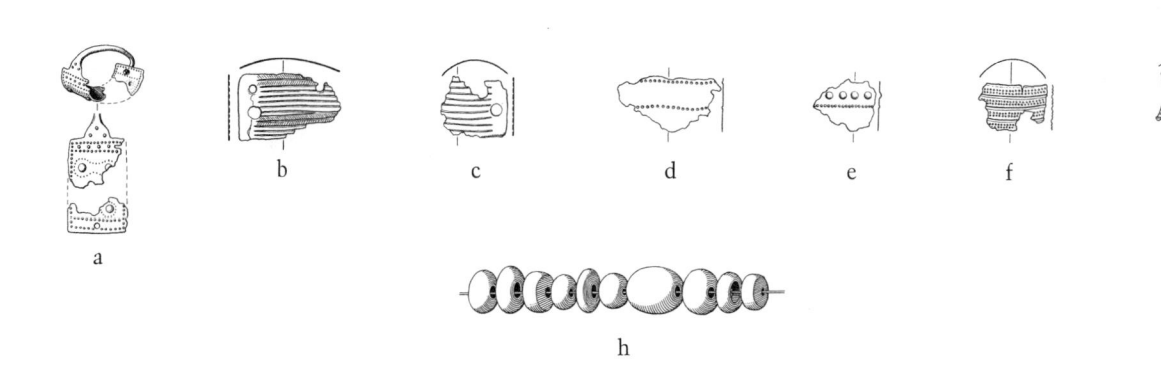

Figure 77. Tumulus IV, Grave 22.

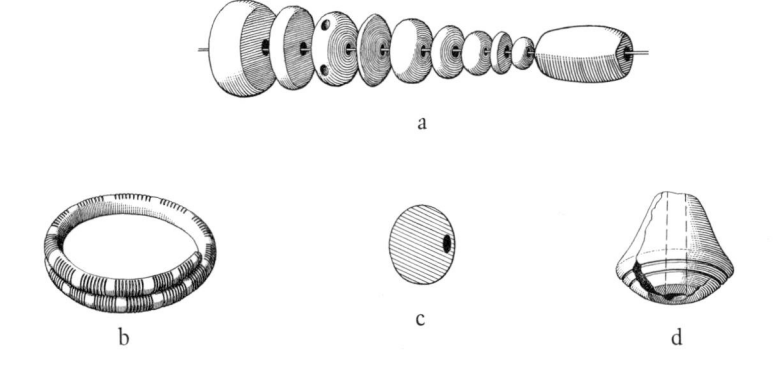

Figure 78. Tumulus IV, Grave 23.

STIČNA: TUMULUS IV 173

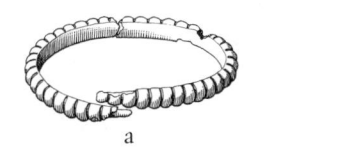

Figure 80. Tumulus IV, Grave 25.

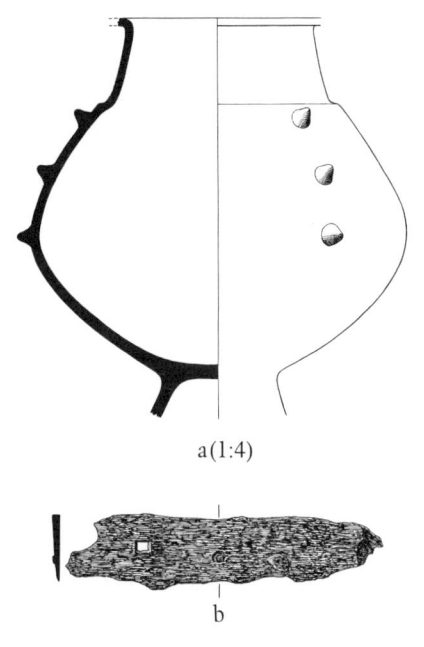

Figure 79. Tumulus IV, Grave 24.

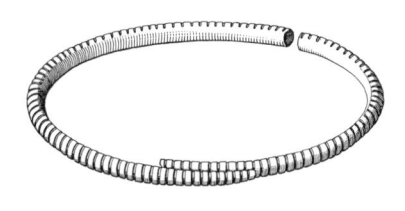

Figure 81. Tumulus IV, Grave 26.

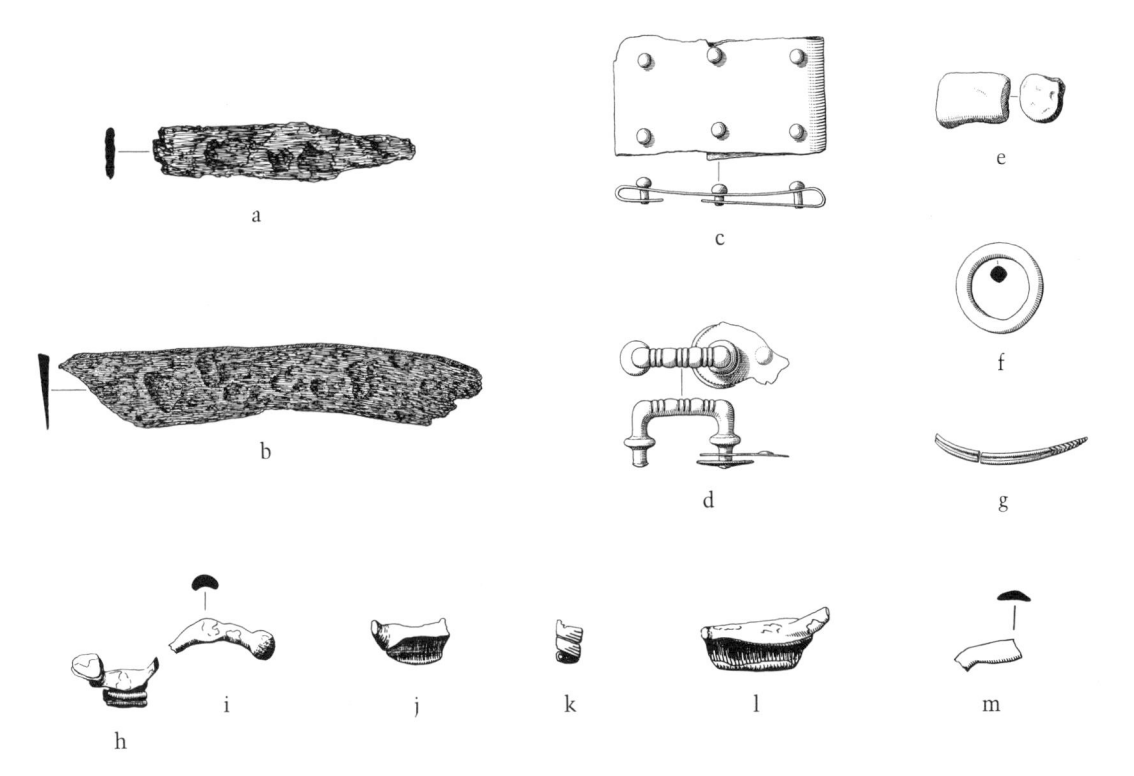

Figure 82. Tumulus IV, Grave 27.

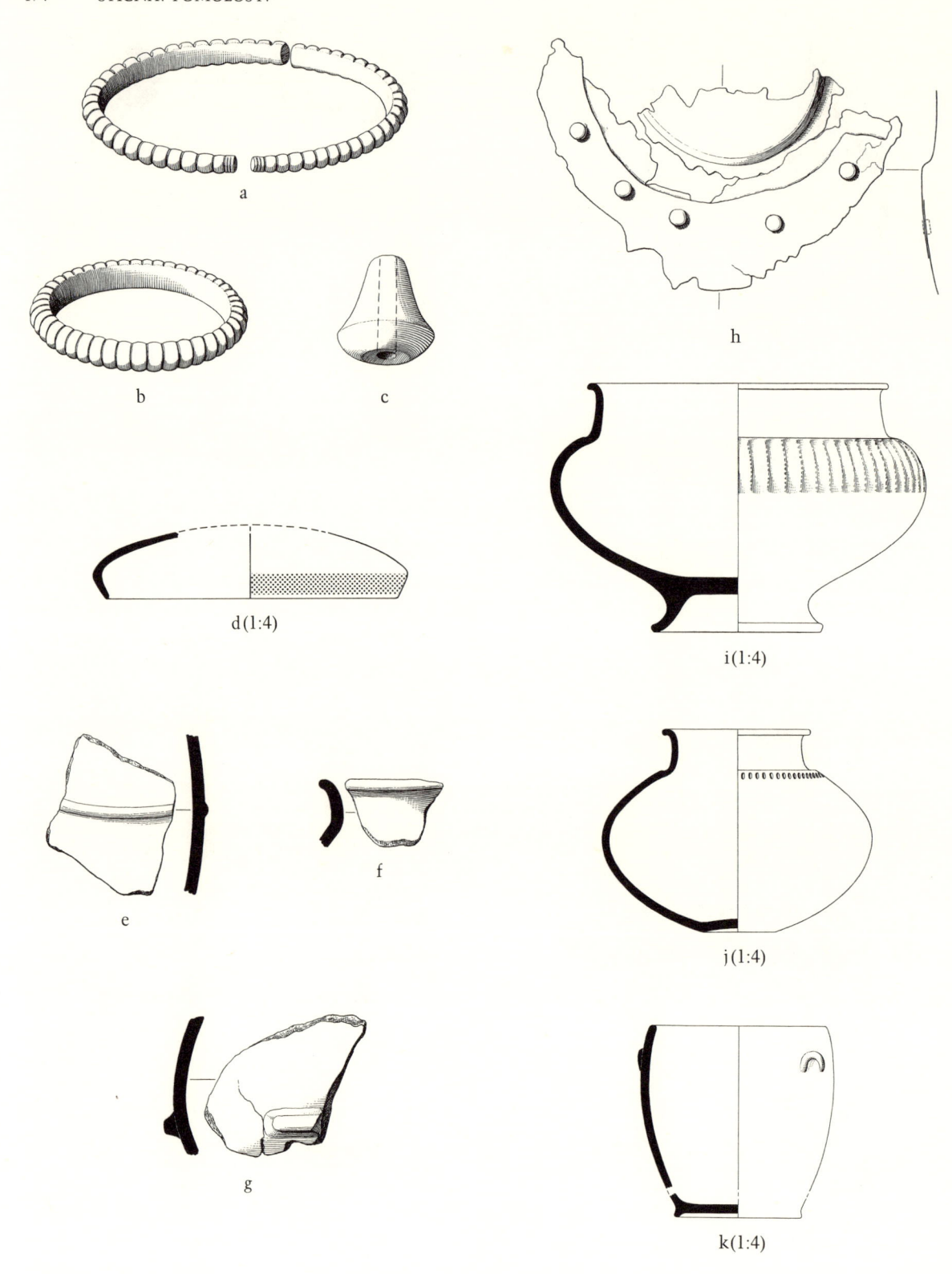

Figure 83. Tumulus IV, Grave 28.

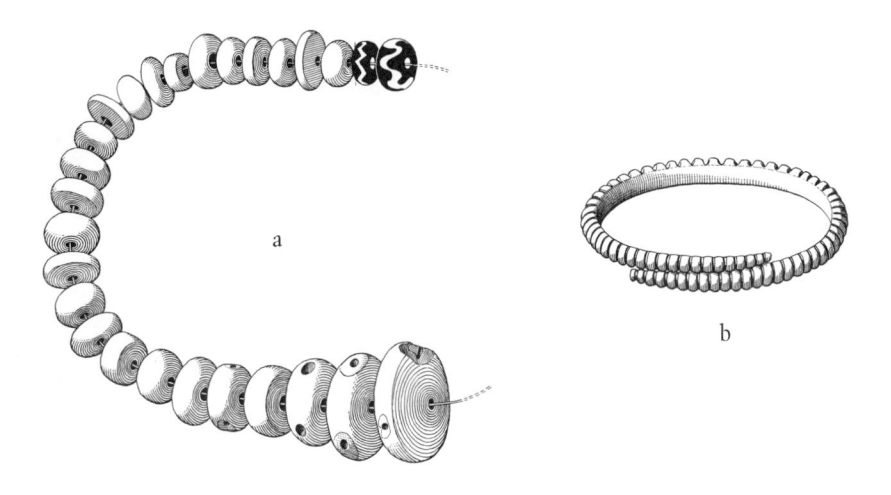

Figure 84. Tumulus IV, Grave 29.

Figure 85. Tumulus IV, Grave 30. a. The Duchess standing next to the partly opened grave. b. The Duchess excavating the grave. Visible are the bronze cuirasse (c–e) and the ceramic vessel with raised spiral decoration and four little vessels on the shoulder (n–p). c–e. Three views of the cuirasse, probably taken shortly after excavation. n–p. Photograph and drawings courtesy of Dr. Adolf Mahr, Staatliche Museen, Berlin.

176　STIČNA: TUMULUS IV

c

d

e

f

g

h(1:4)

i(1:4)

j(1:4)

k(1:4)

l

m

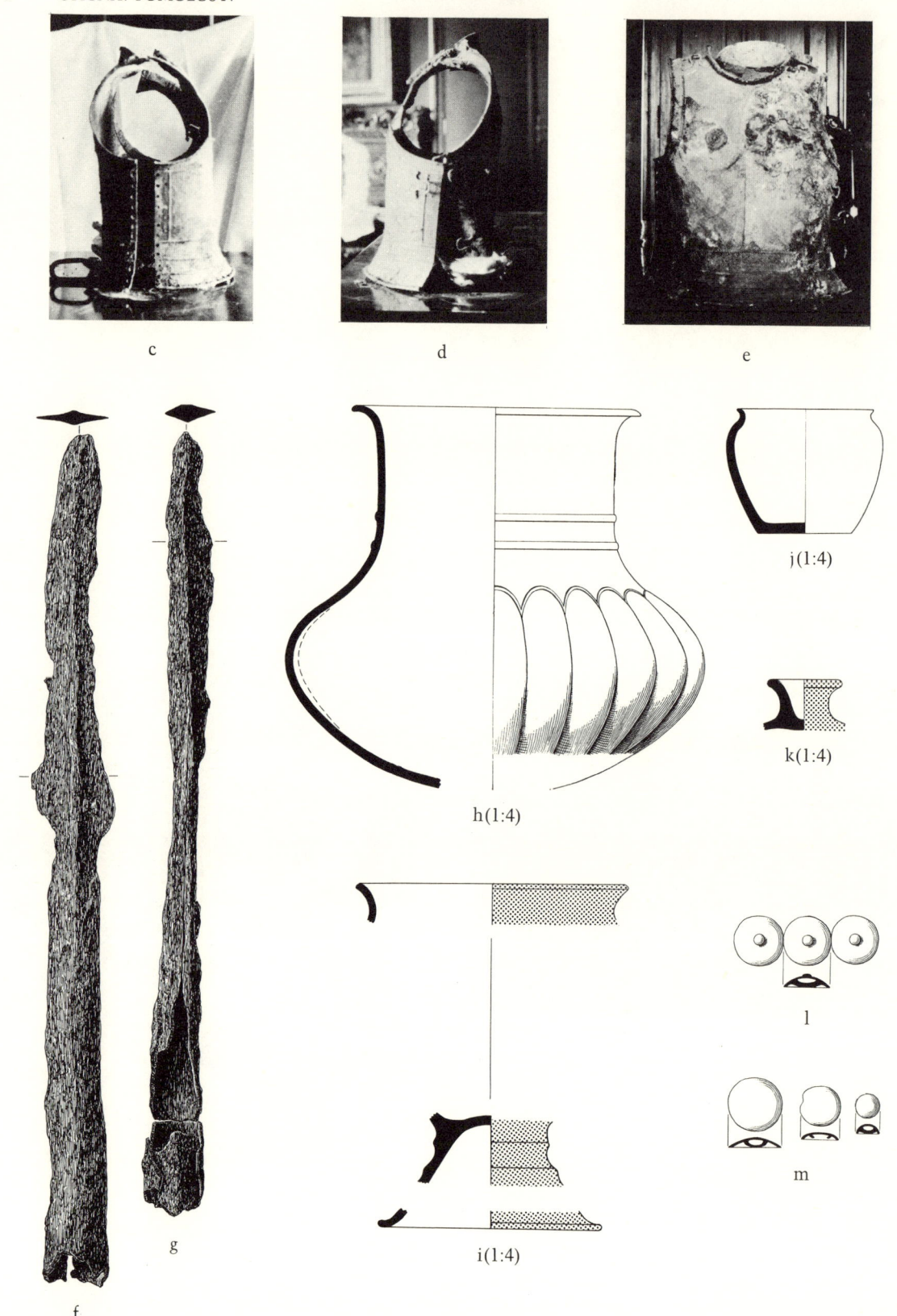

Figure 85. Tumulus IV, Grave 30, continued.

STIČNA: TUMULUS IV 177

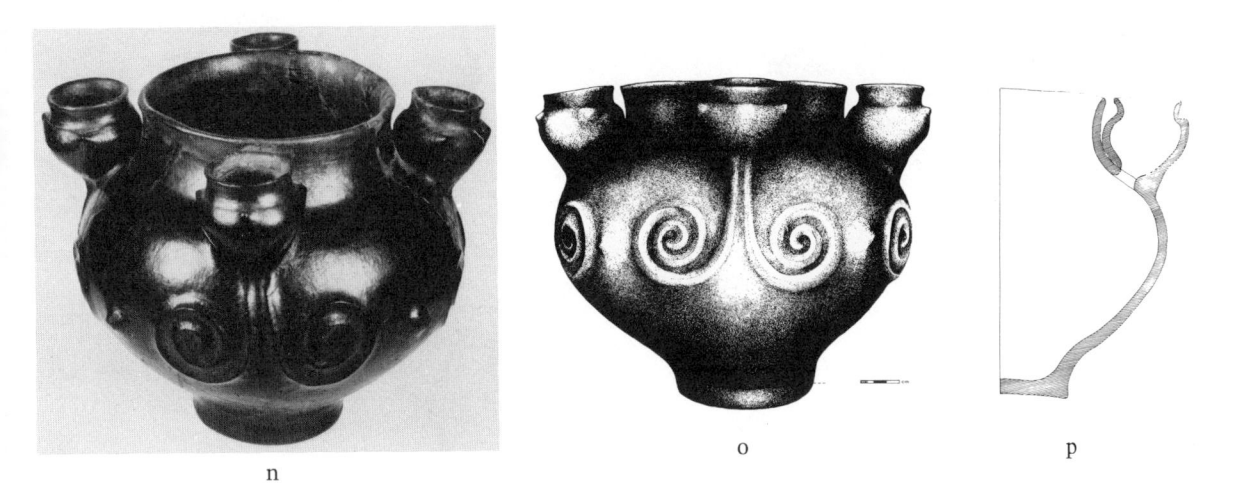

Figure 85. Tumulus IV, Grave 30, continued.

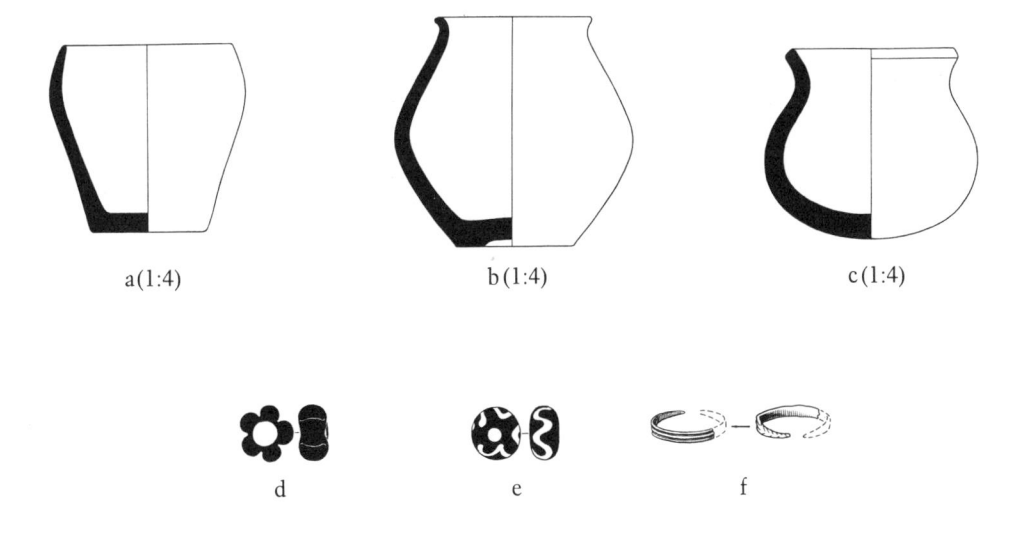

Figure 86. Tumulus IV, Grave 31.

178　STIČNA: TUMULUS IV

Figure 87. Tumulus IV, Grave 32.

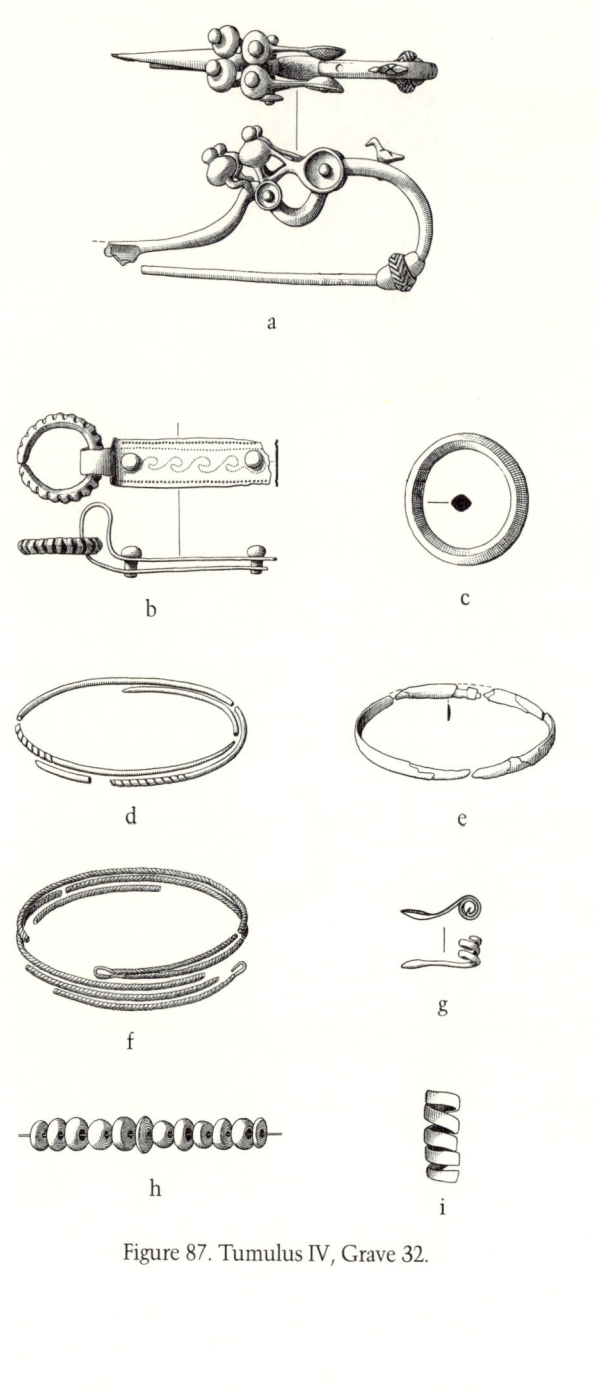

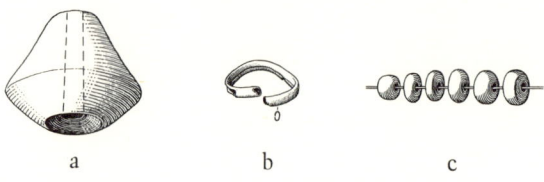

Figure 88. Tumulus IV, Grave 33.

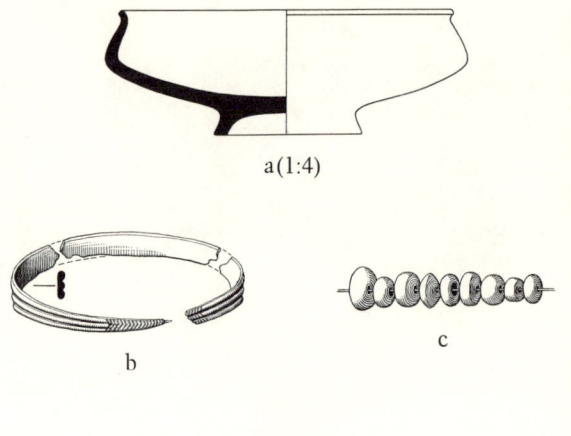

Figure 89. Tumulus IV, Grave 35.

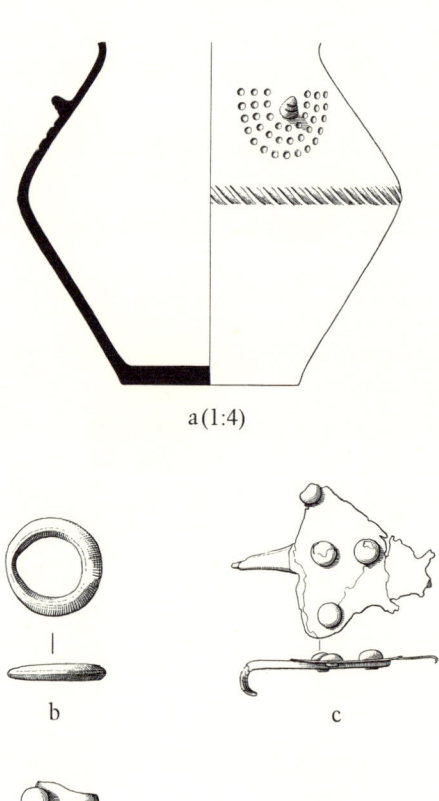

Figure 90. Tumulus IV, Grave 36.

STIČNA: TUMULUS IV 179

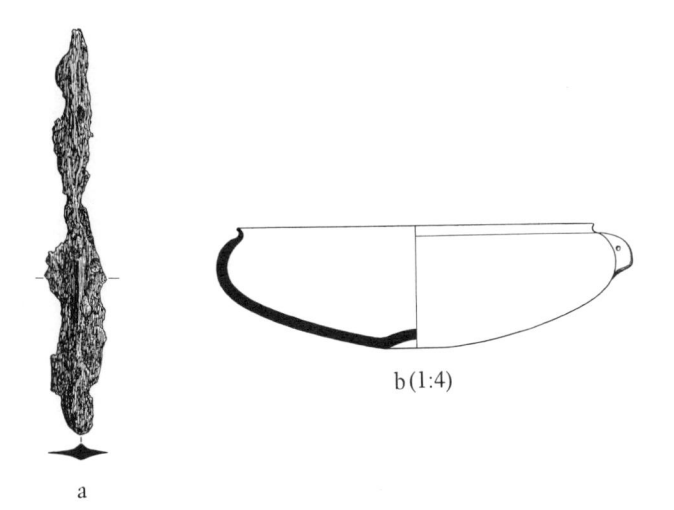

Figure 91. Tumulus IV, Grave 37.

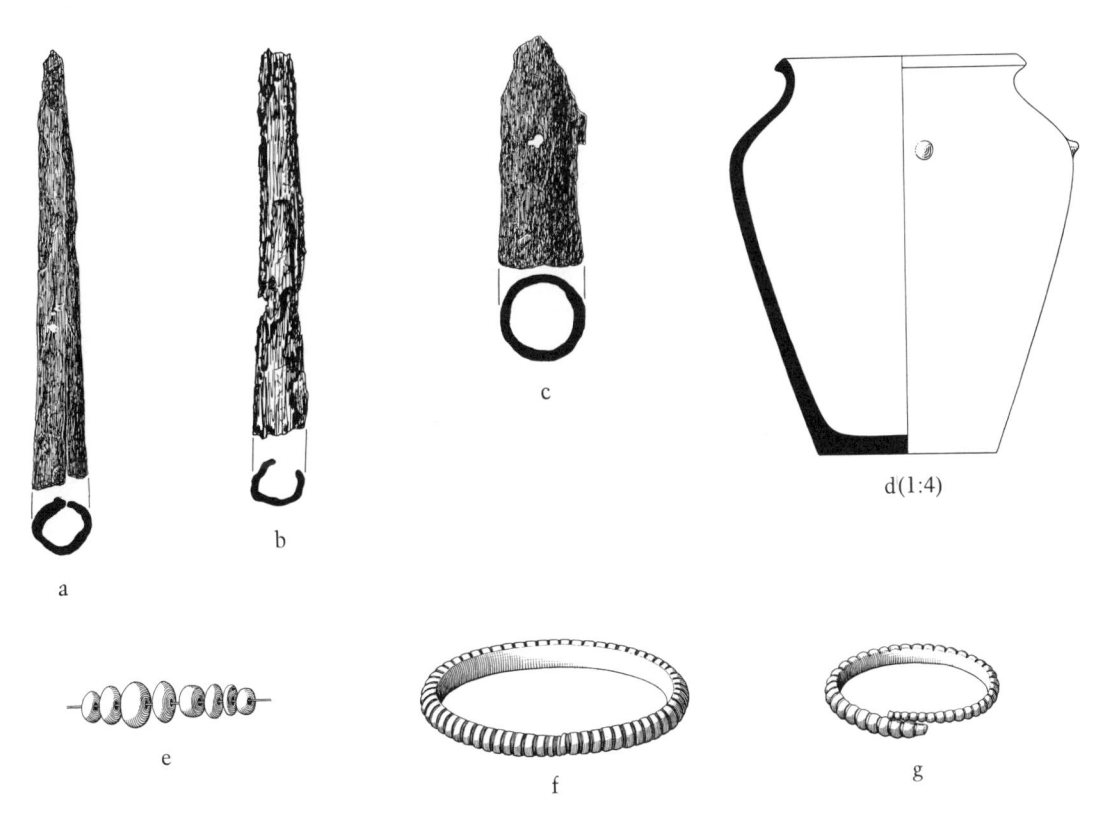

Figure 92. Tumulus IV, Grave 38.

180 STIČNA: TUMULUS IV

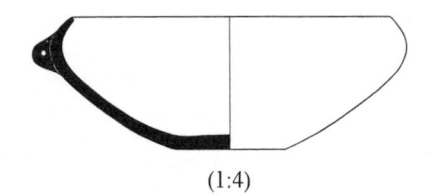

(1:4)

Figure 93. Tumulus IV, Grave 39.

a(1:4)

b(1:4)

c(1:4)

d(1:4)

e

f

g

h

i

j

k

l

m

n

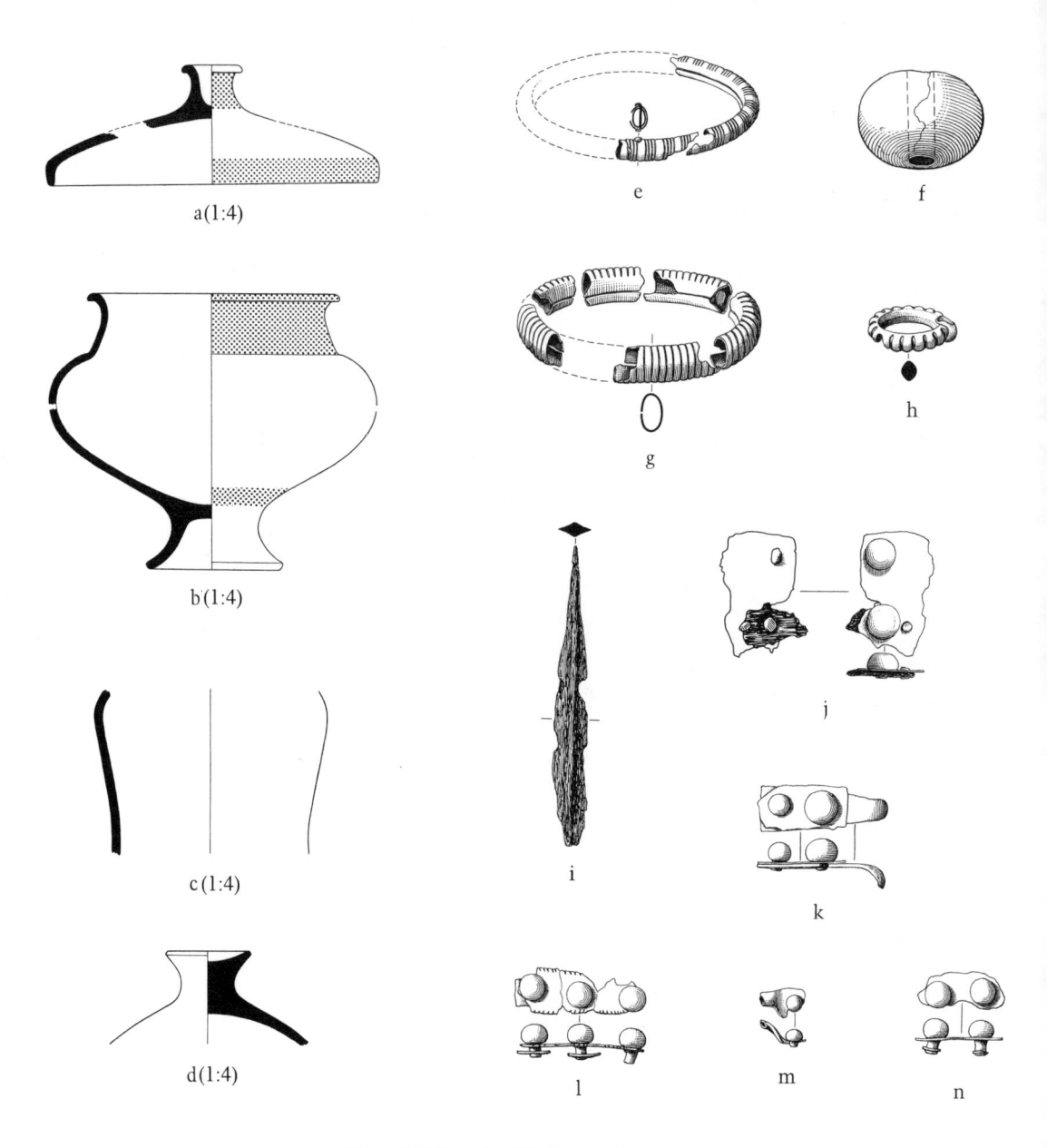

Figure 94. Tumulus IV, Grave 40.

STIČNA: TUMULUS IV 181

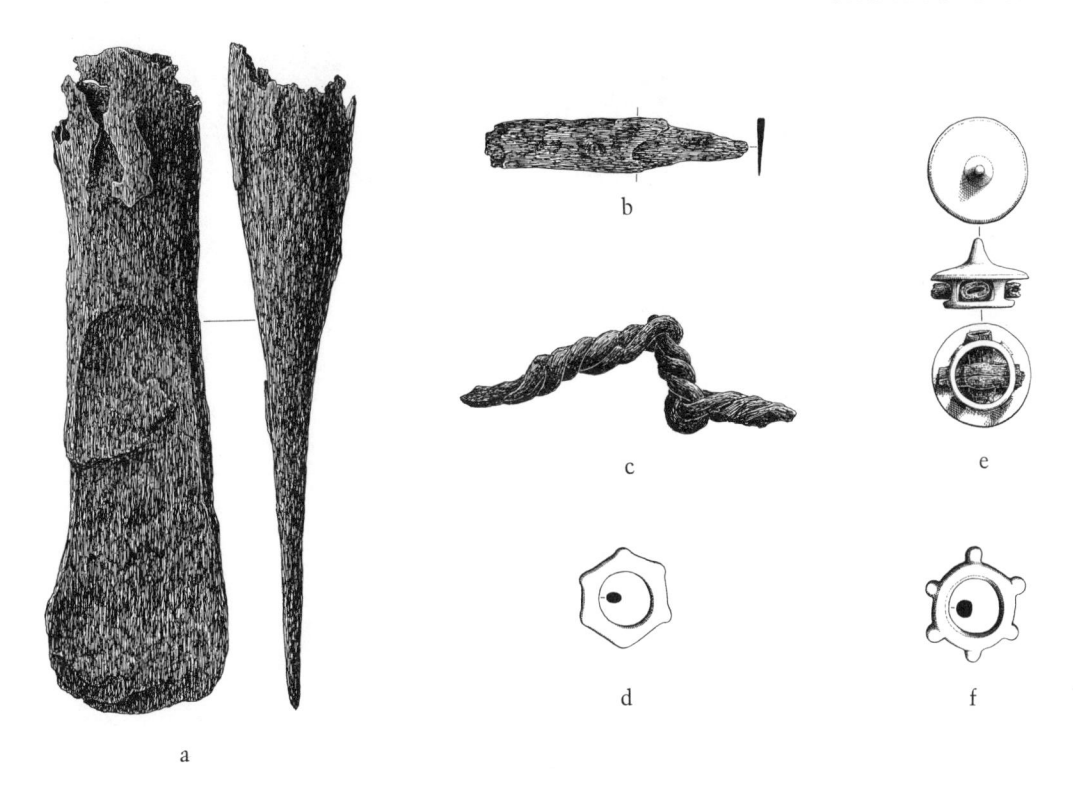

Figure 95. Tumulus IV, Grave 41.

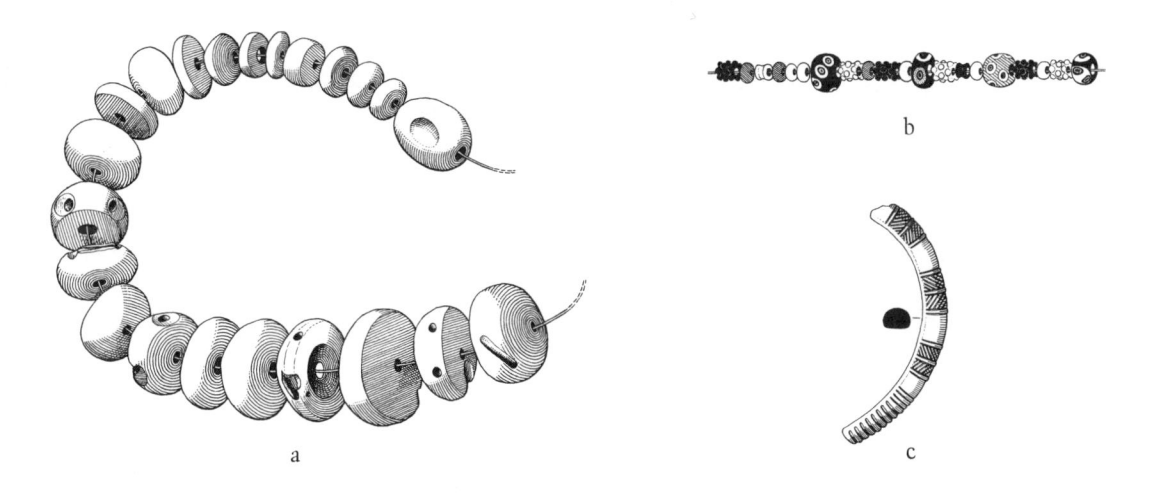

Figure 96. Tumulus IV, Grave 41a.

182   STIČNA: TUMULUS IV

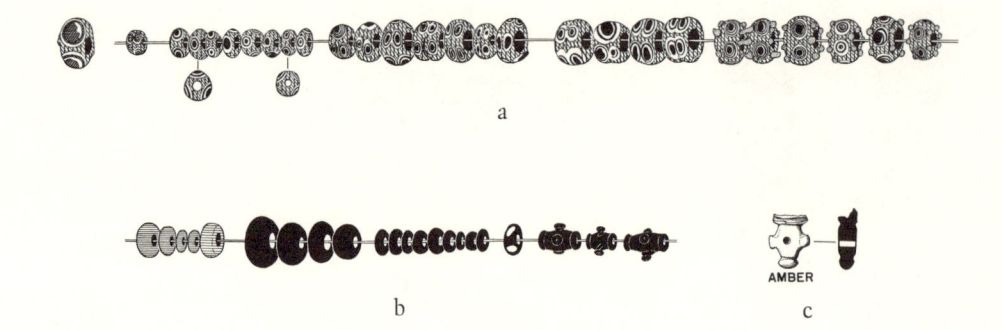

Figure 97. Tumulus IV, Grave 42.

Figure 98. Tumulus IV, Grave 43. a. Photograph showing the two ceramic vessels and the two bronze rings.

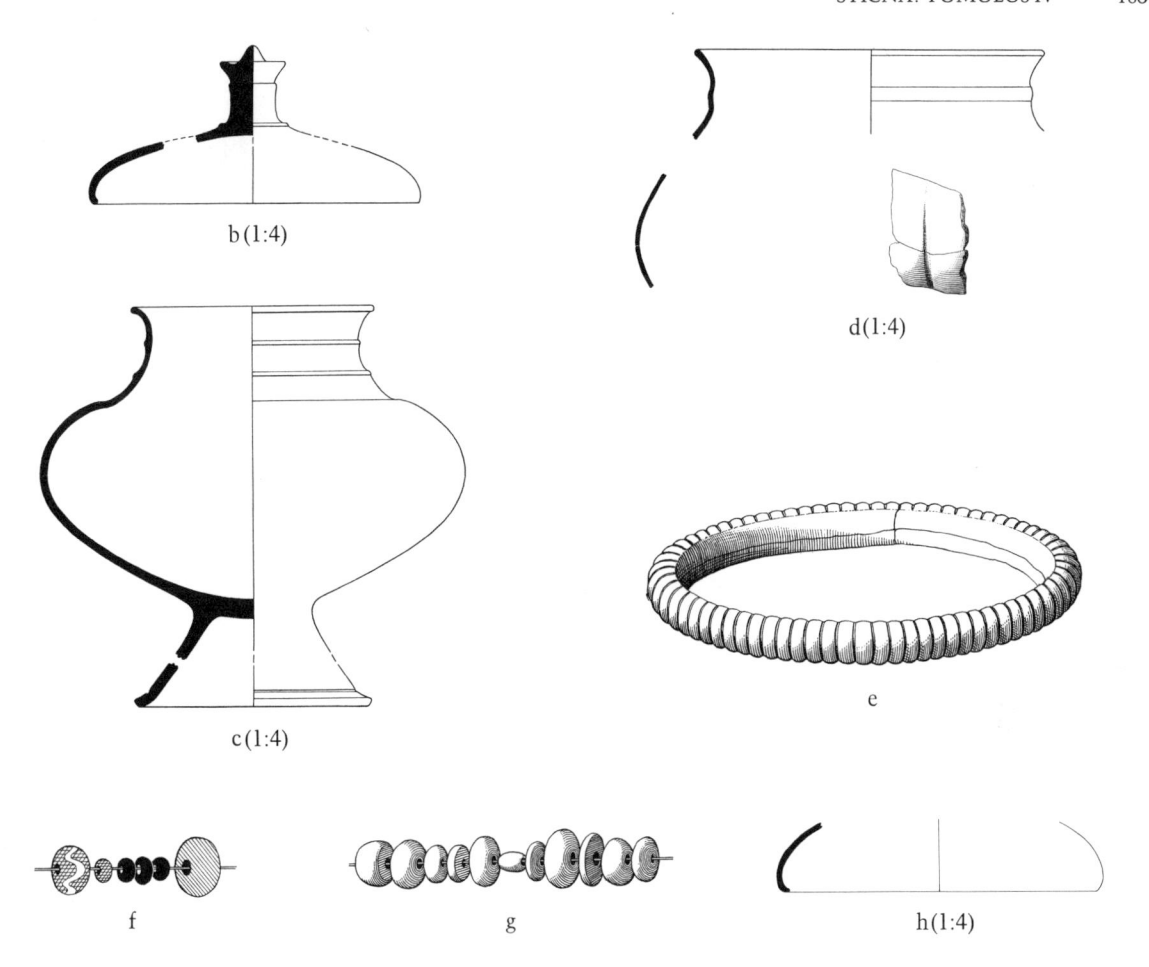

Figure 98. Tumulus IV, Grave 43, continued.

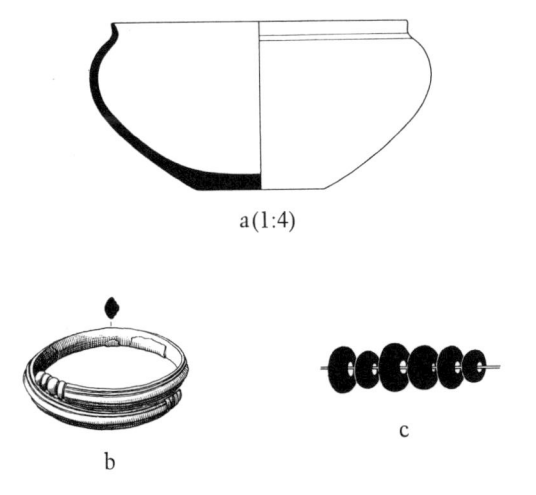

Figure 99. Tumulus IV, Grave 45.

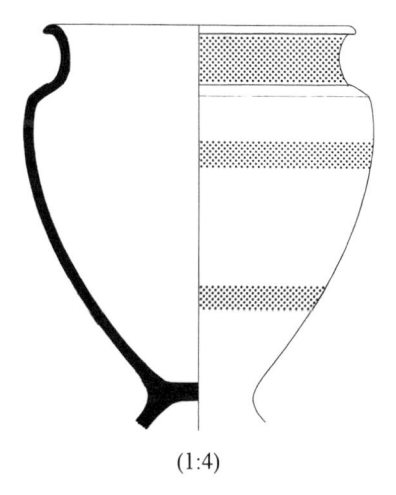

Figure 100. Tumulus IV, Grave 46.

184   STIČNA: TUMULUS IV

a(1:4)

b

c

d   e

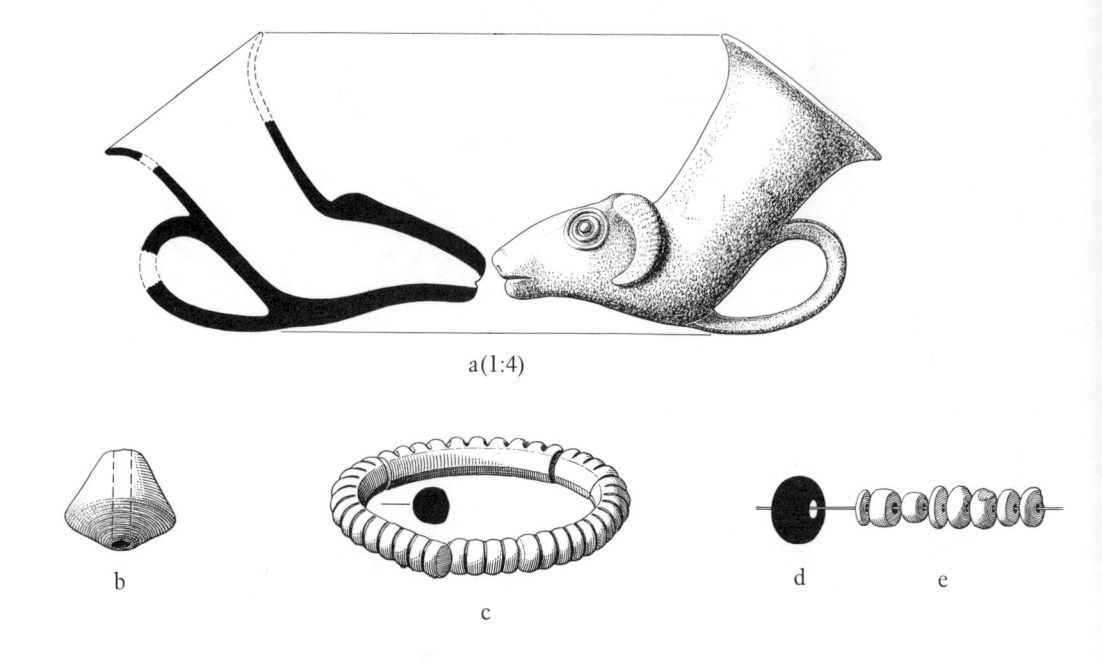

Figure 101. Tumulus IV, Grave 47.

a(1:4)

b

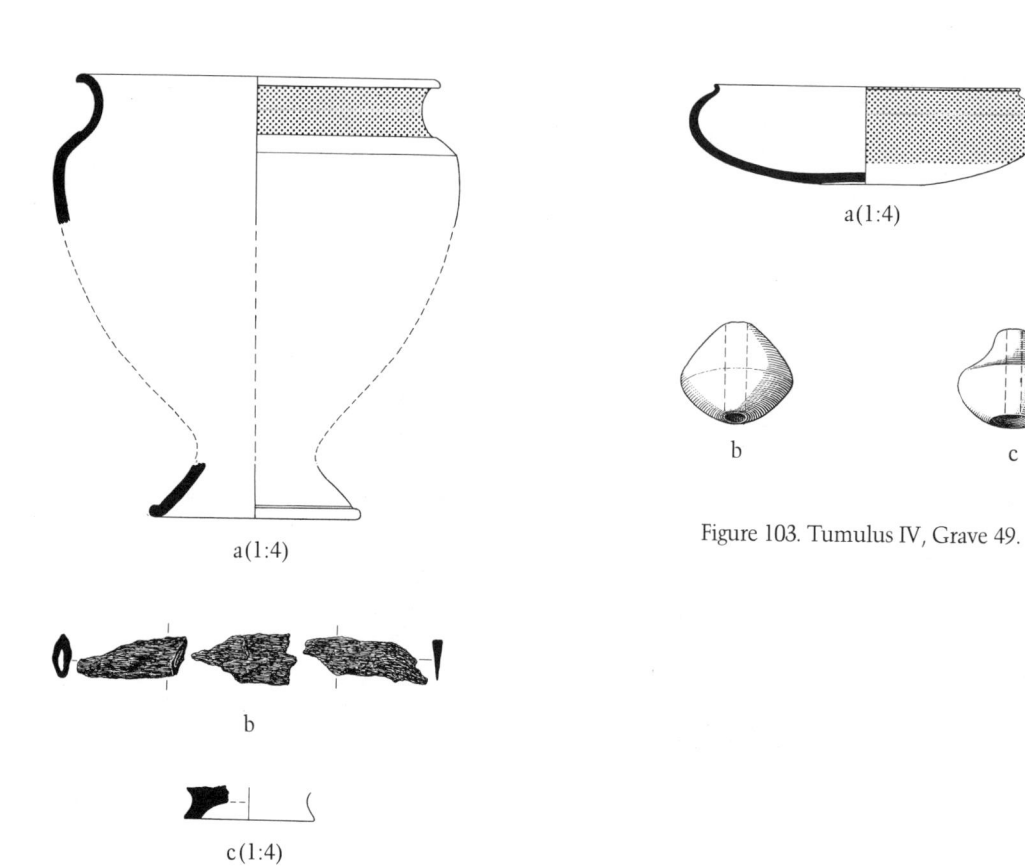

c(1:4)

Figure 102. Tumulus IV, Grave 48.

a(1:4)

b   c

Figure 103. Tumulus IV, Grave 49.

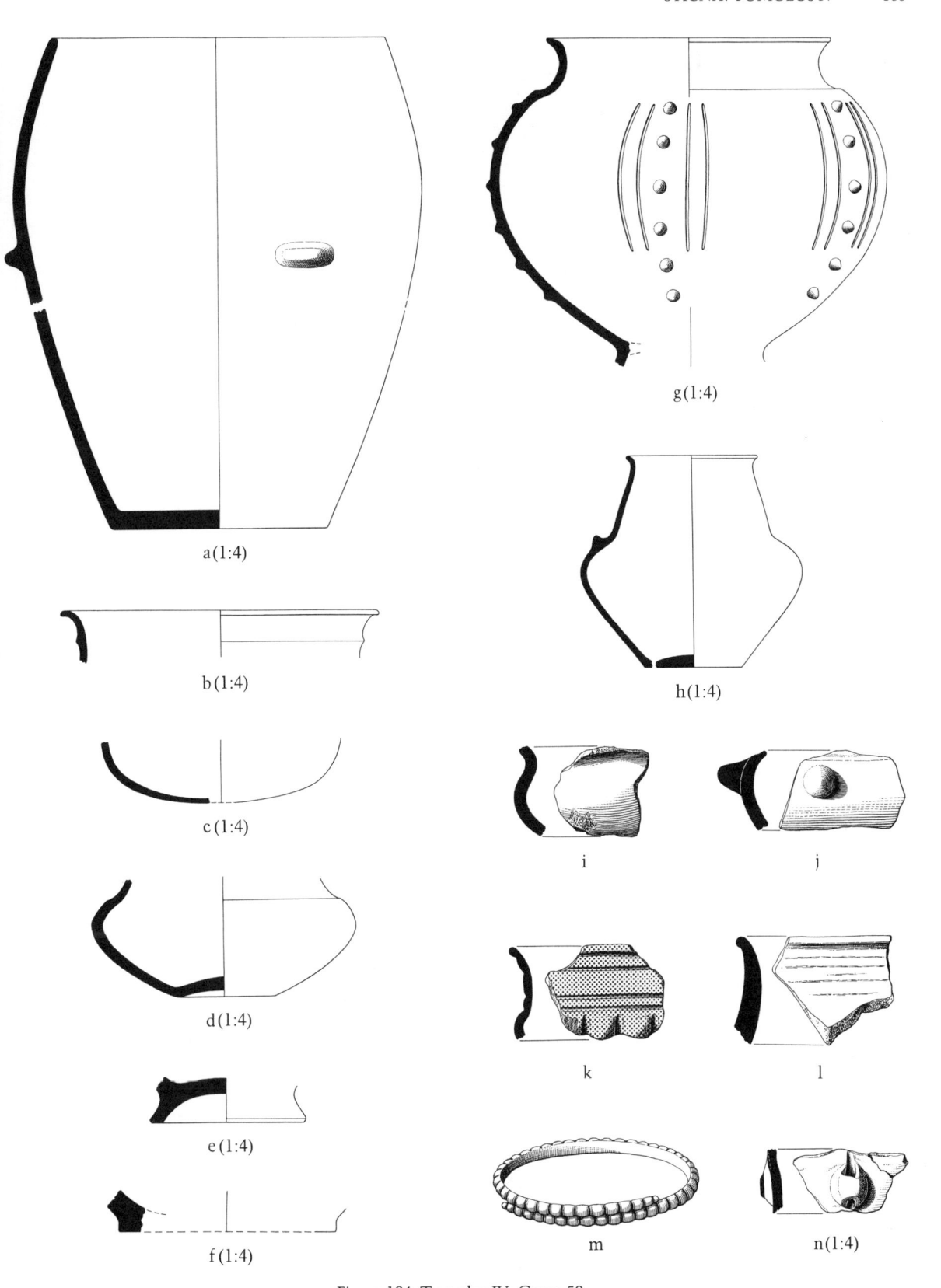

Figure 104. Tumulus IV, Grave 50.

186   STIČNA: TUMULUS IV

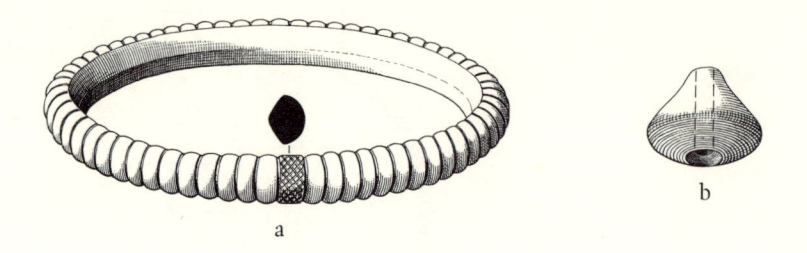

Figure 105. Tumulus IV, Grave 51.

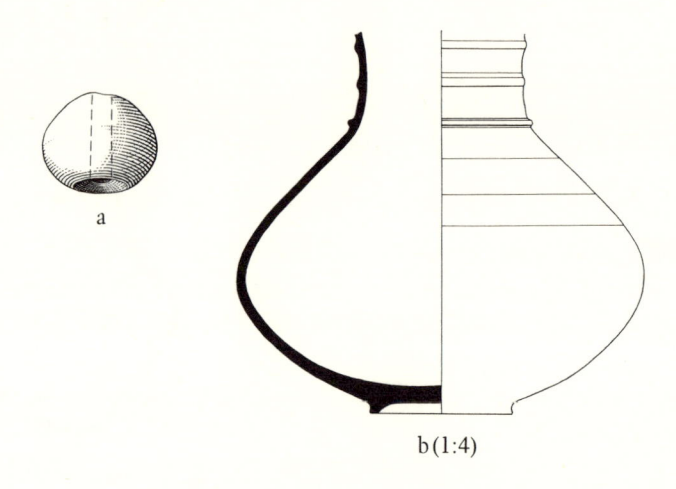

Figure 106. Tumulus IV, Grave 52.

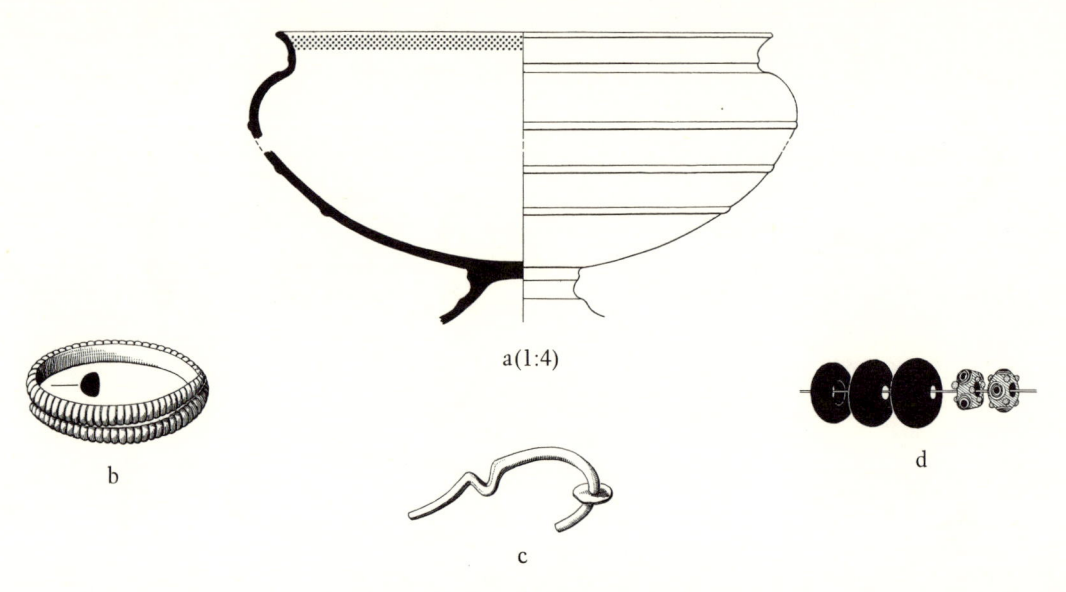

Figure 107. Tumulus IV, Grave 53.

STIČNA: TUMULUS IV   187

a (1:4)

b (1:4)

c (1:4)

d

e

Figure 108. Tumulus IV, Grave 54.

a

b

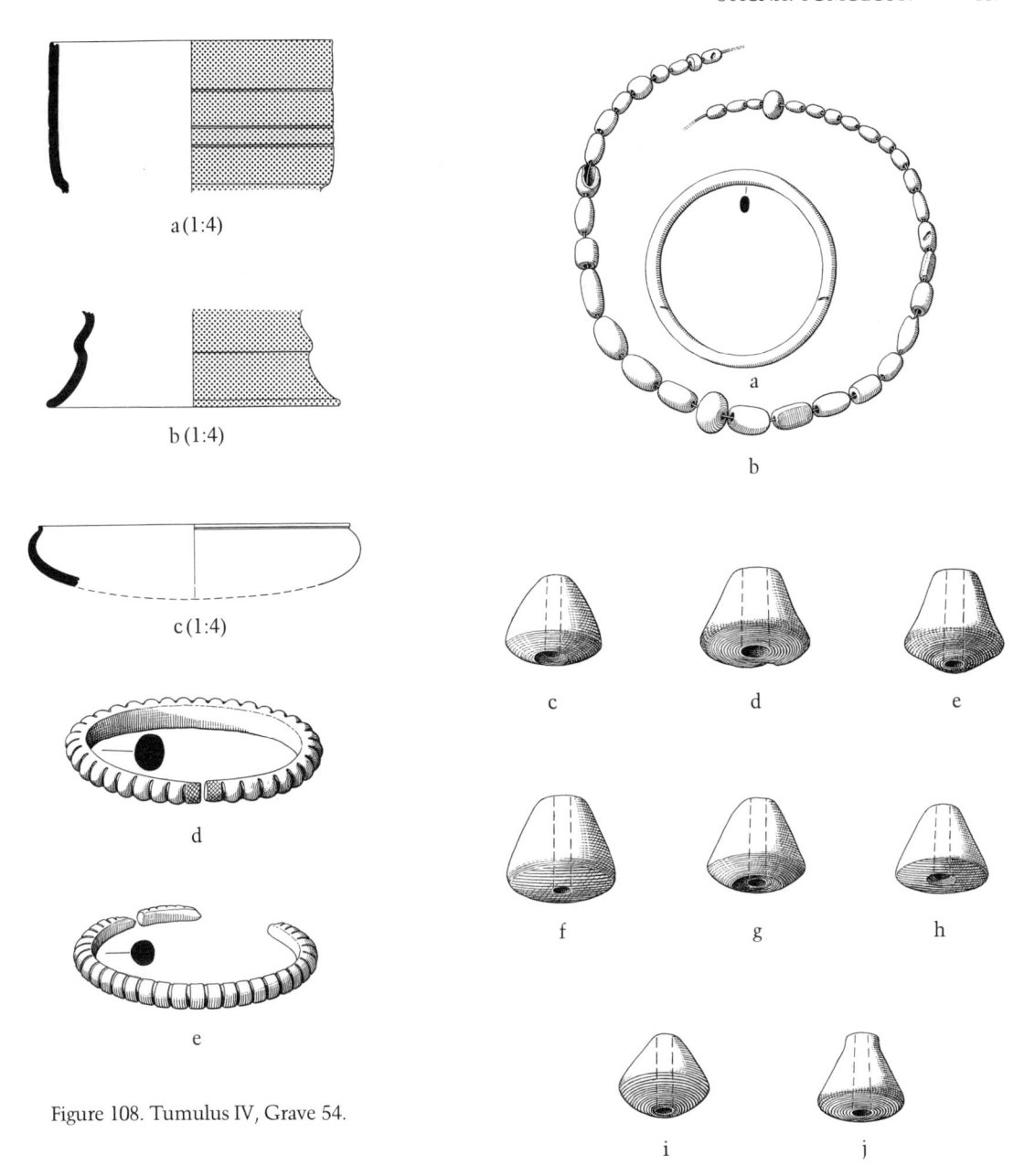

c   d   e

f   g   h

i   j

Figure 109. Tumulus IV, Grave 55.

188 STIČNA: TUMULI IV AND V

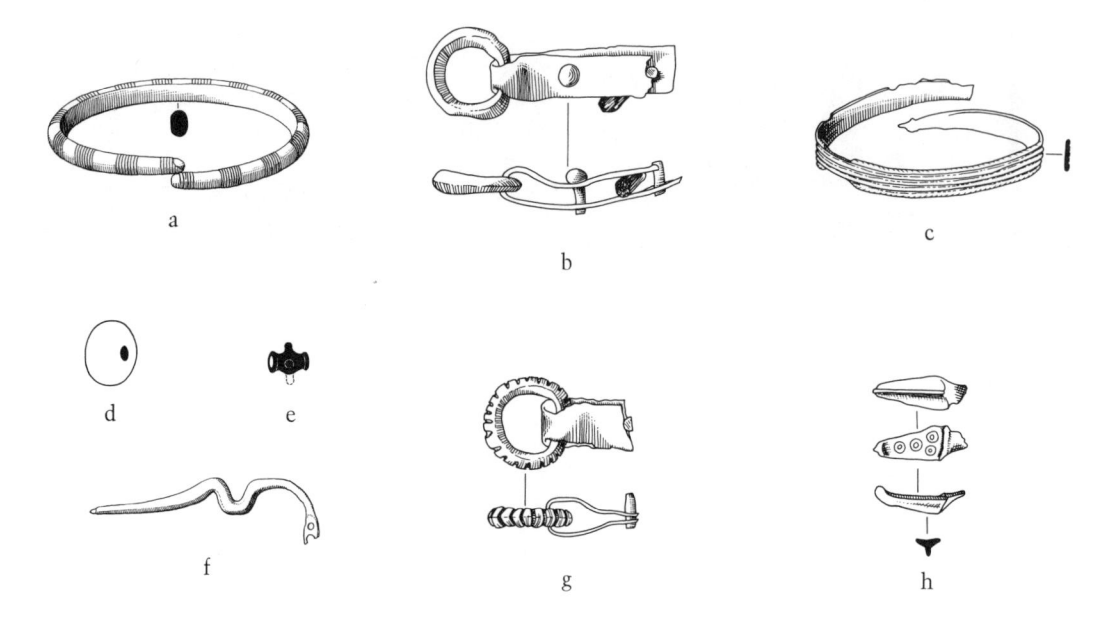

Figure 110. Tumulus IV, isolated finds.

Figure 111. Tumulus V at the beginning of excavation.

Figure 112. Tumulus V in the course of excavation. To the right of the Duchess stands Oscar Montelius, who was visiting the excavations.

Figure 113. Tumulus V in the course of excavation.

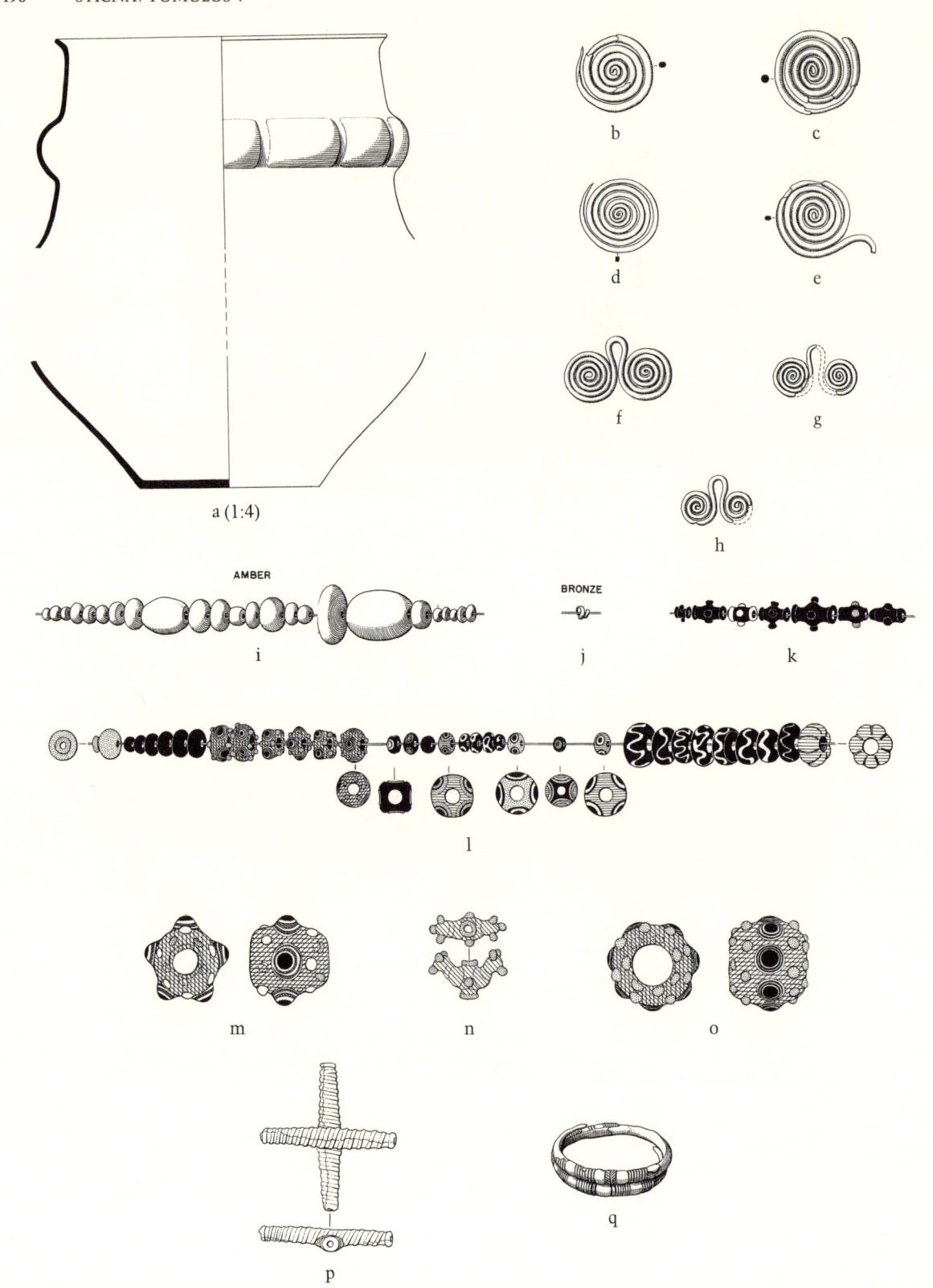

Figure 114. Tumulus V, Grave 2.

STIČNA: TUMULUS V 191

a (1:4)

b (1:4)

Figure 115. Tumulus V, Grave 3.

Figure 116. Tumulus V, Grave 5.

Figure 117. Tumulus V, Grave 6.

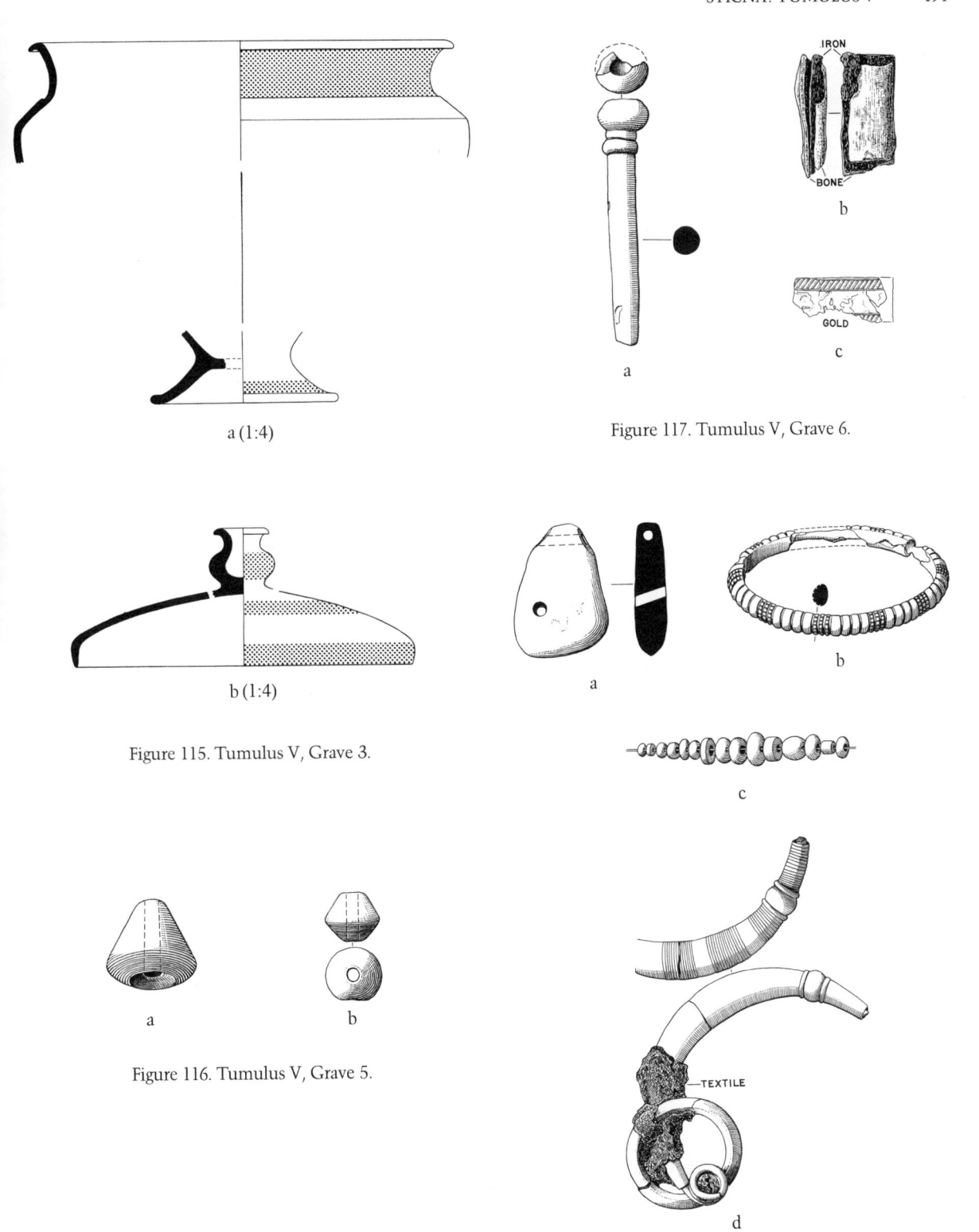

Figure 118. Tumulus V, Grave 7.

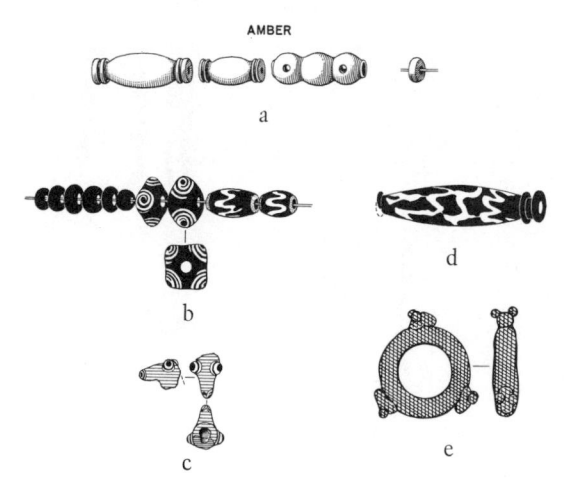

Figure 119. Tumulus V, Grave 8.

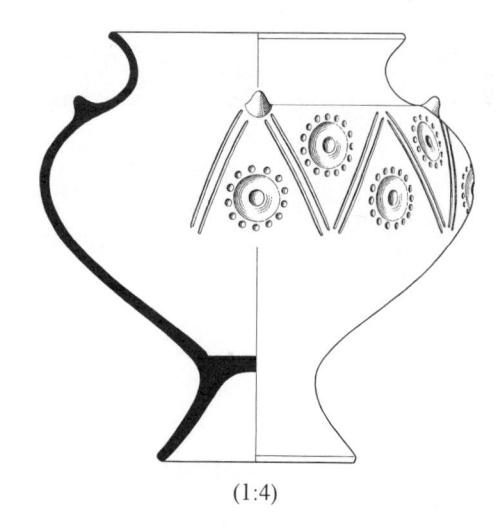

Figure 120. Tumulus V, Grave 9.

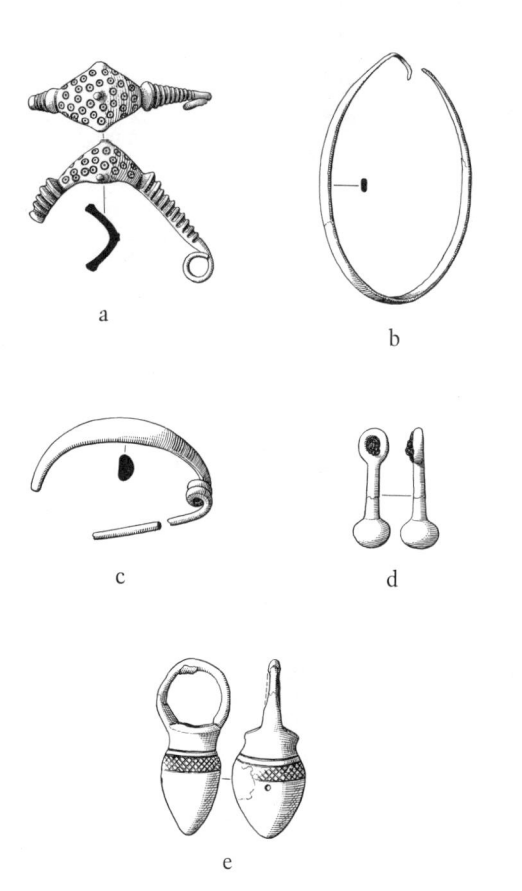

Figure 121. Tumulus V, Grave 10.

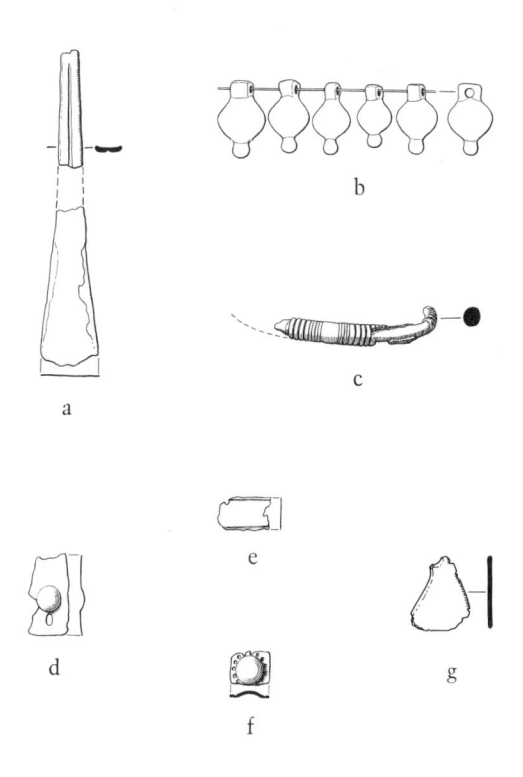

Figure 122. Tumulus V, Grave 11.

STIČNA: TUMULUS V 193

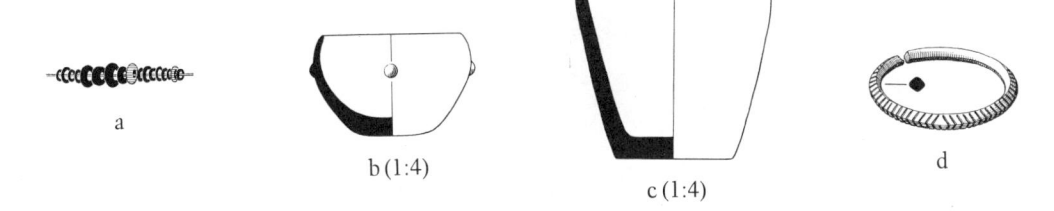

Figure 123. Tumulus V, Grave 13.

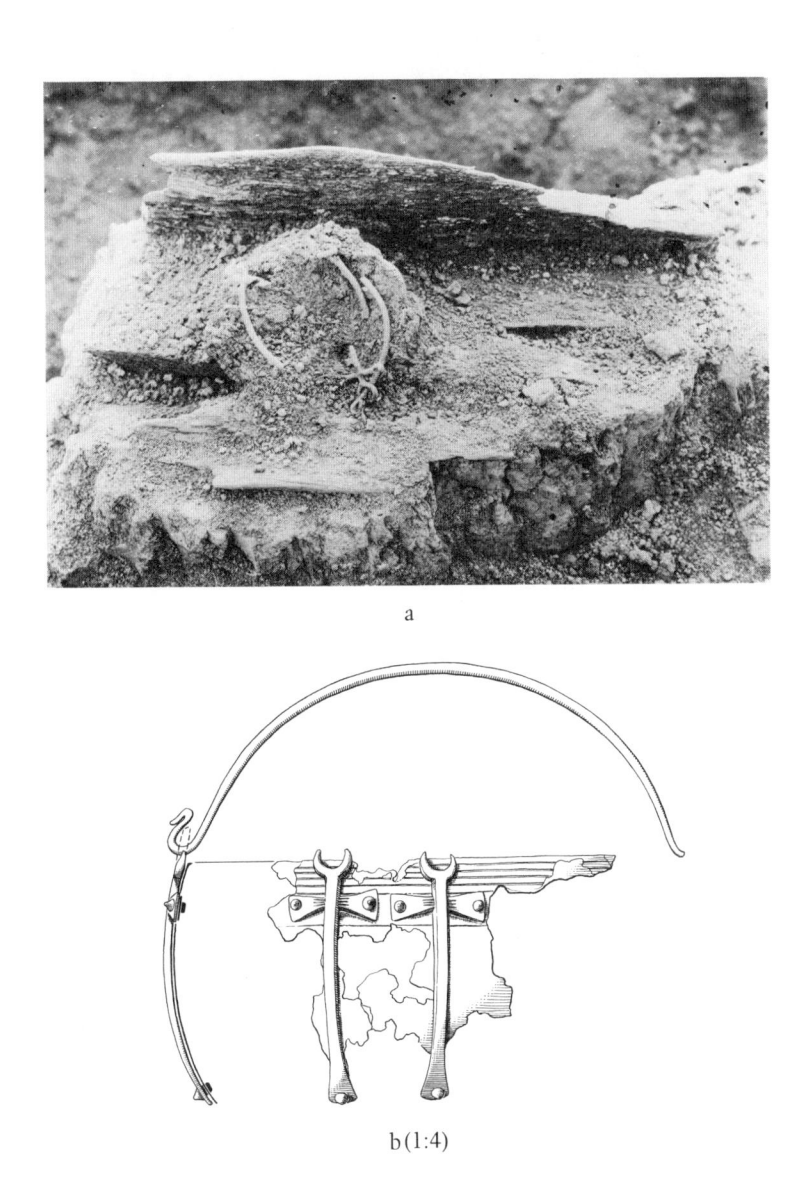

Figure 124. Tumulus V, Grave 14. a. Photograph showing the remains of the bronze cauldron resting on a large fragment of wood.

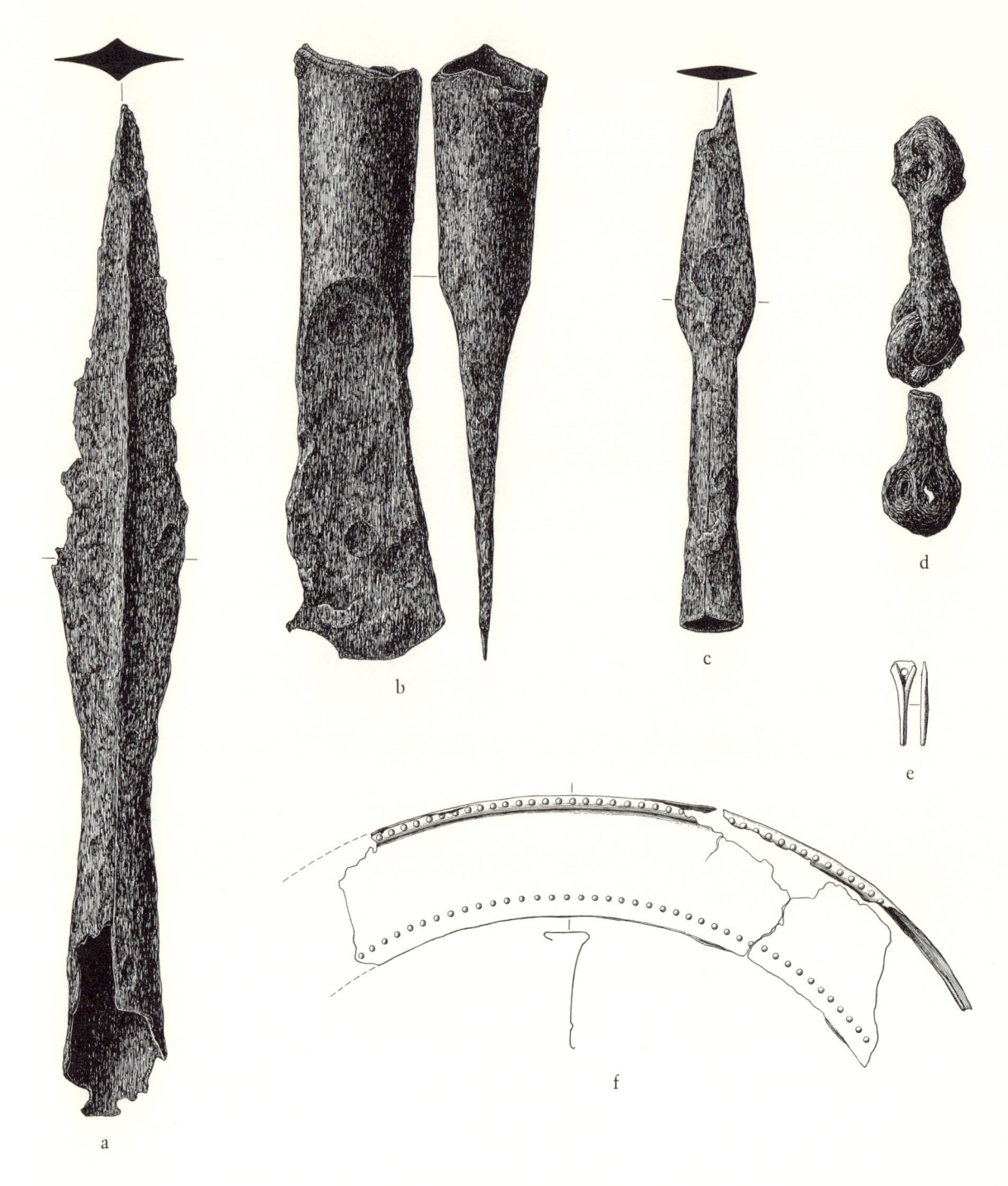

Figure 125. Tumulus V, Grave 15.

STIČNA: TUMULUS V 195

Figure 126. Tumulus V, Grave 16.

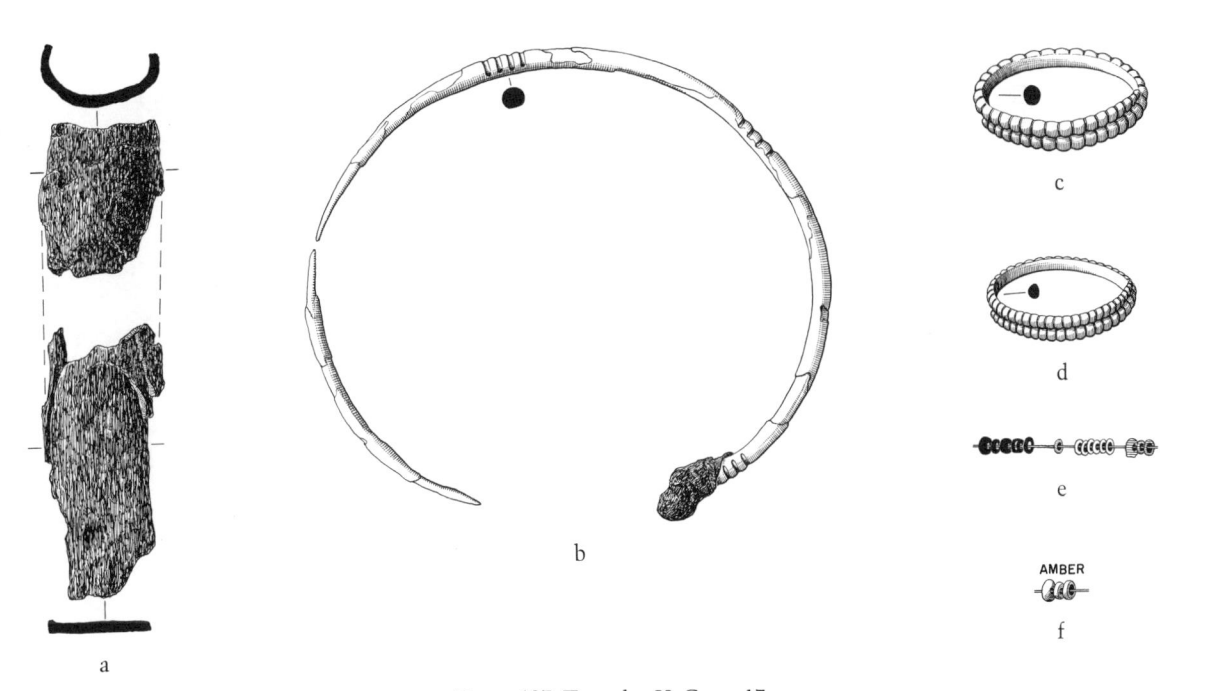

Figure 127. Tumulus V, Grave 17.

b (1:4)

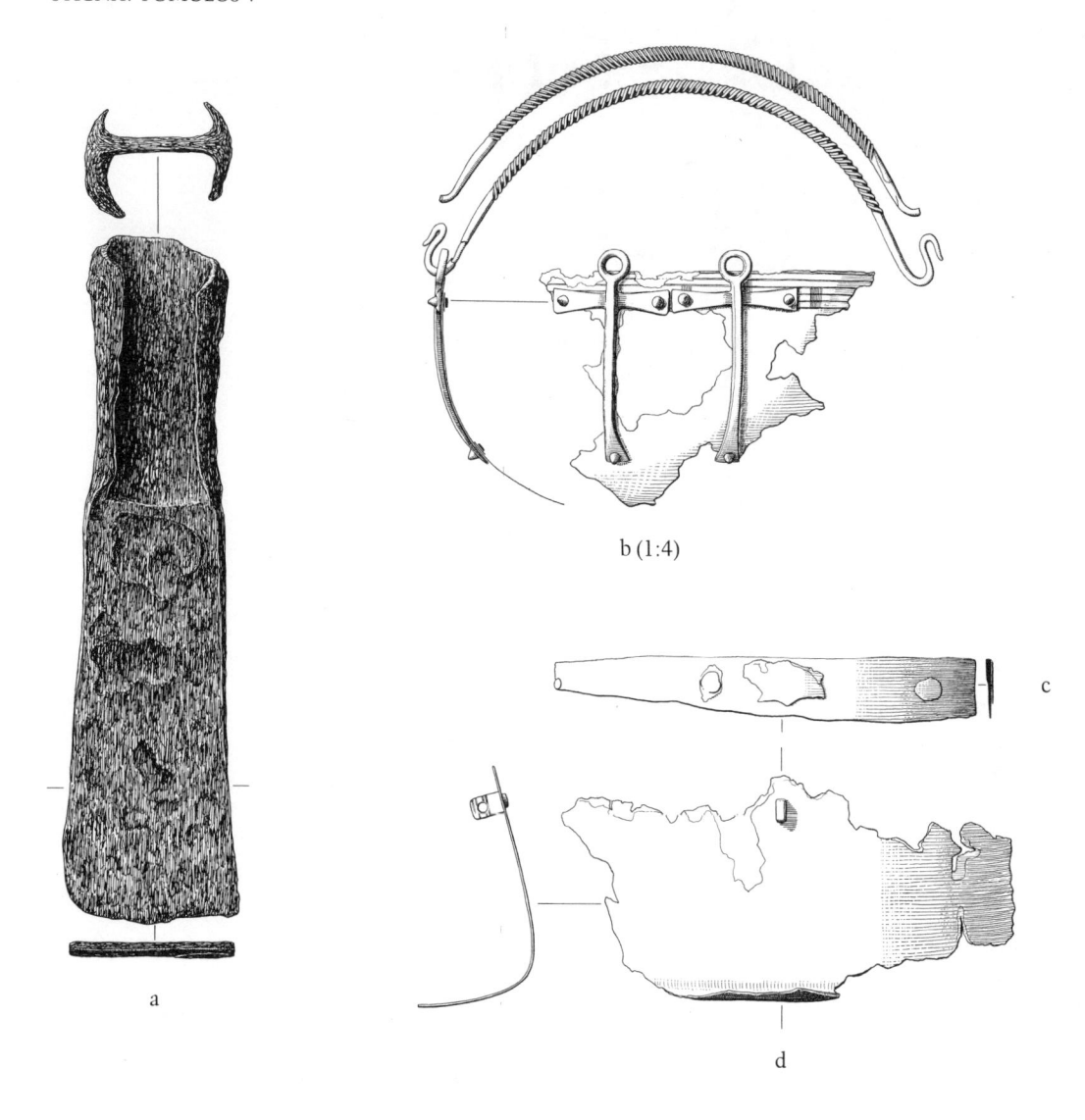

Figure 128. Tumulus V, Grave 18.

Figure 129. Tumulus V, Grave 19. The Duchess (left) and the stone packing covering the grave.

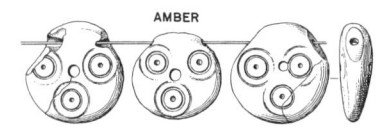

Figure 130. Tumulus V, Grave 20.

Figure 131. Photograph taken on December 22, 1913, showing the Duchess's winter camp during the excavation of Tumulus VI.

198 STIČNA: TUMULUS VI

Figure 132. Tumulus VI, Grave 1.

a (1:4)

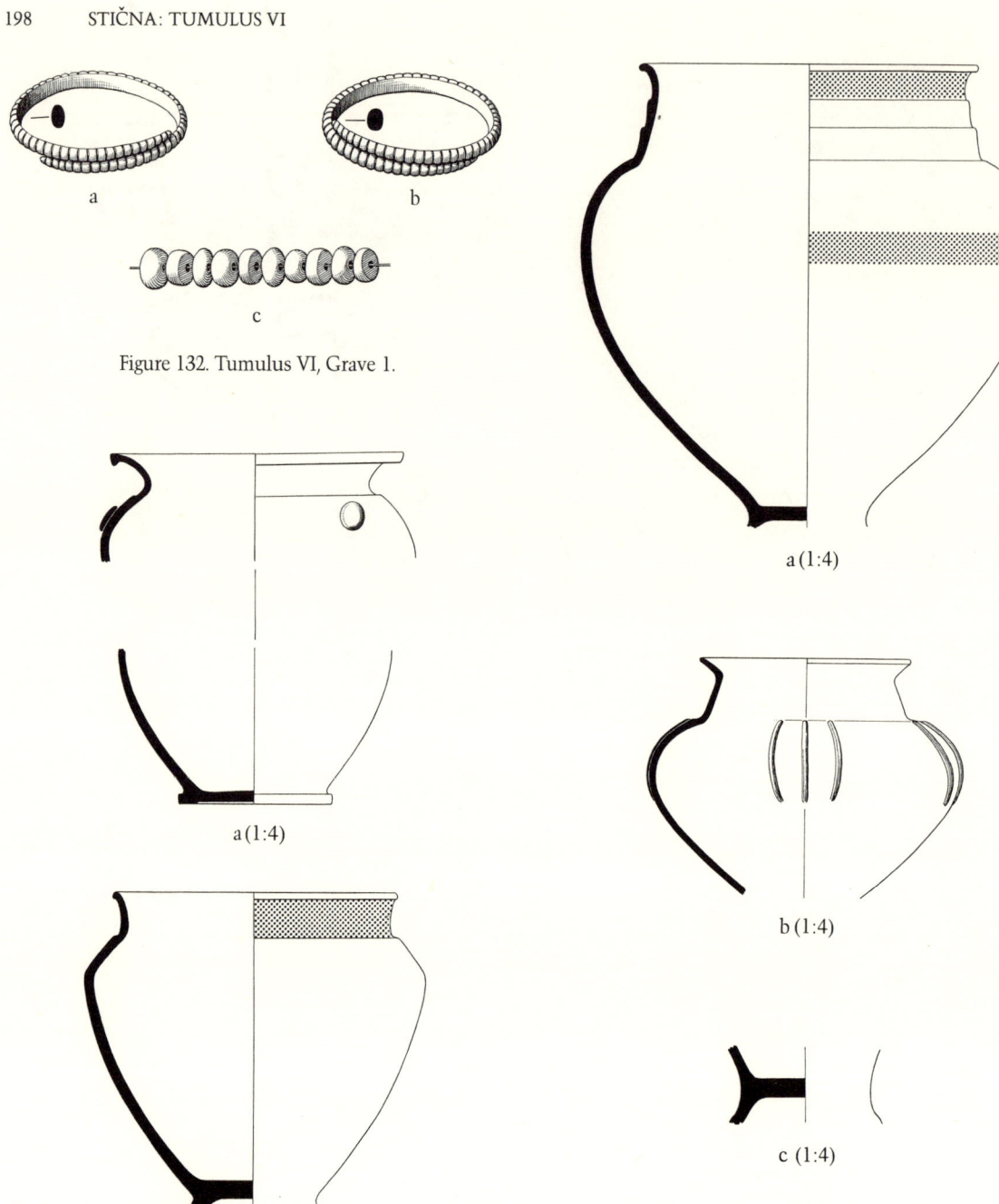

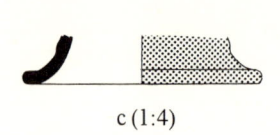

b (1:4)

c (1:4)

Figure 133. Tumulus VI, Grave 2.

a (1:4)

b (1:4)

c (1:4)

d

Figure 134. Tumulus VI, Grave 3.

(1:4)

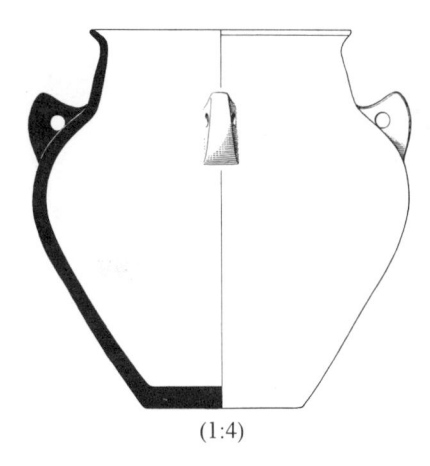

Figure 135. Tumulus VI, Grave 4.

Figure 136. Tumulus VI, Graves 5, 6, and 7.

200   STIČNA: TUMULUS VI

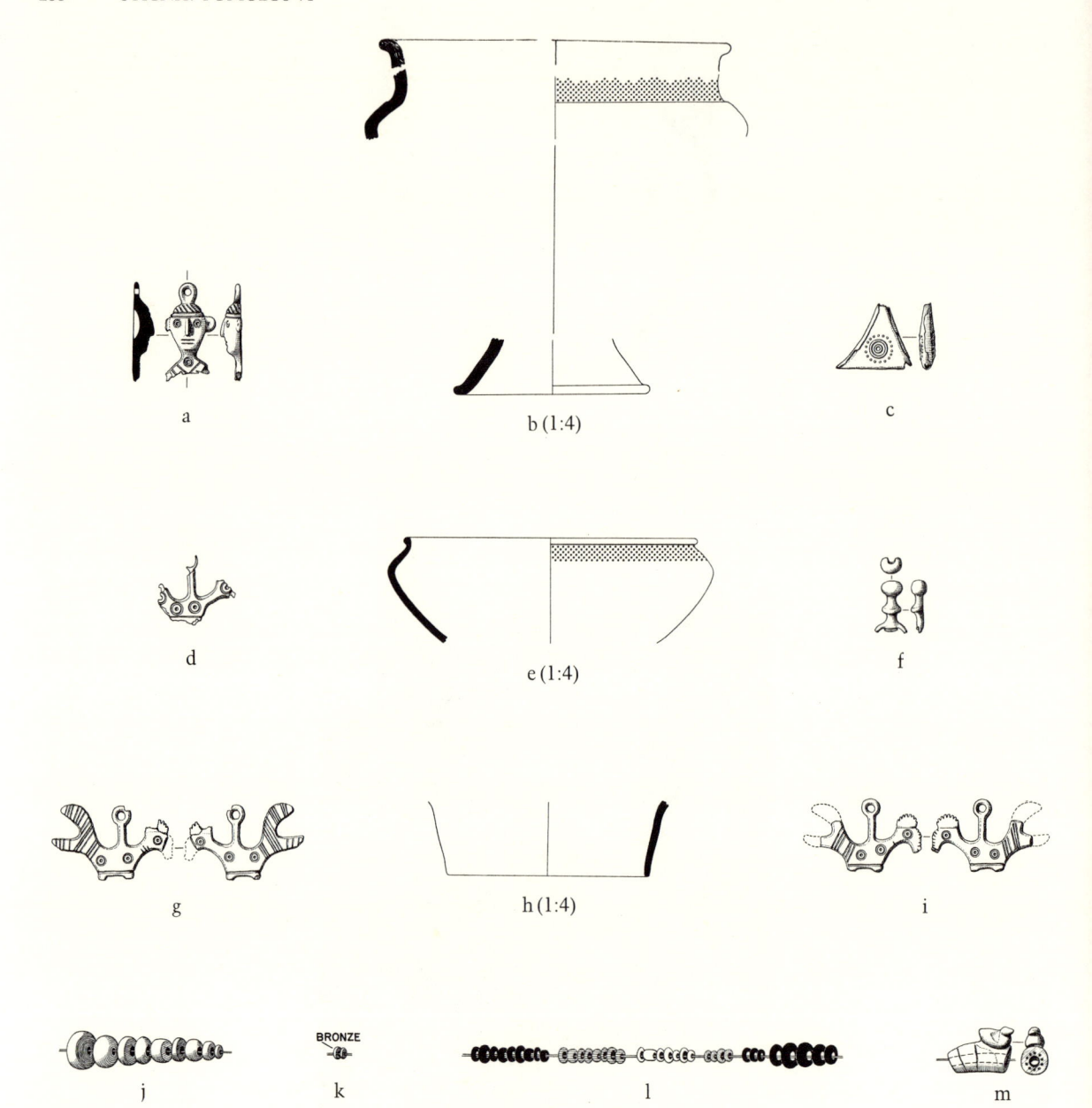

Figure 137. Tumulus VI, Grave 7.

a (1:4)

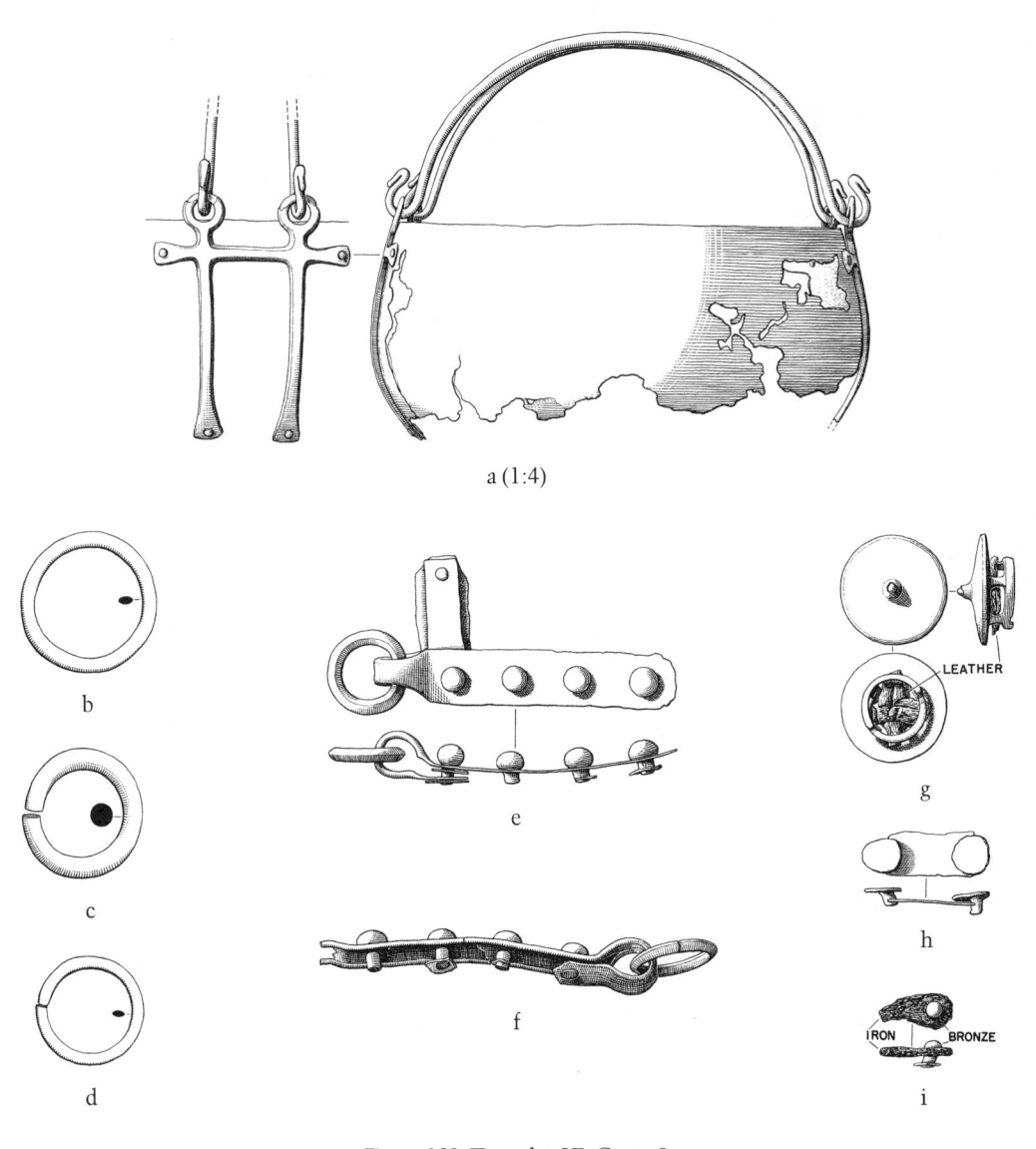

Figure 138. Tumulus VI, Grave 8.

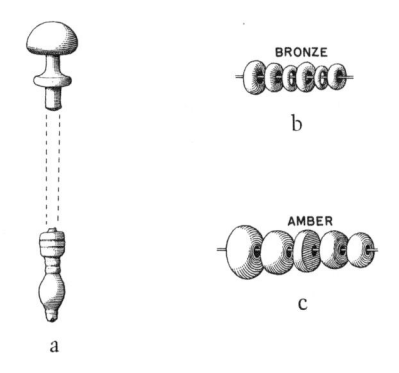

Figure 139. Tumulus VI, Grave 9.

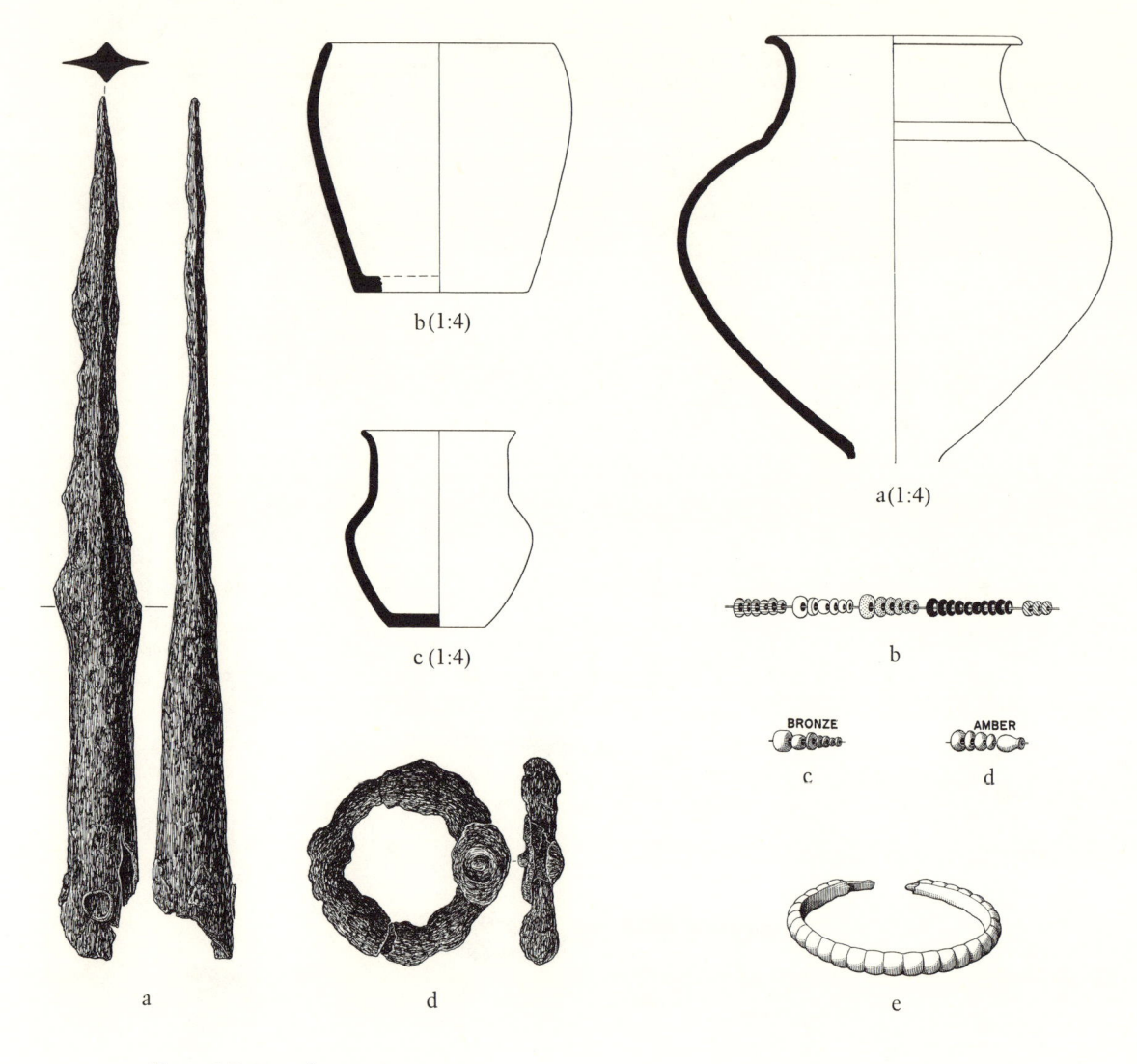

Figure 140. Tumulus VI, Grave 10.

Figure 141. Tumulus VI, Grave 11.

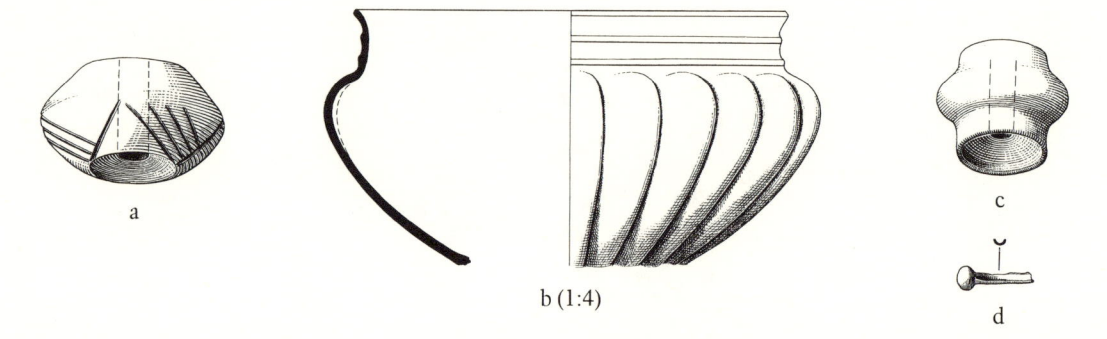

Figure 142. Tumulus VI, Grave 12a.

STIČNA: TUMULUS VI 203

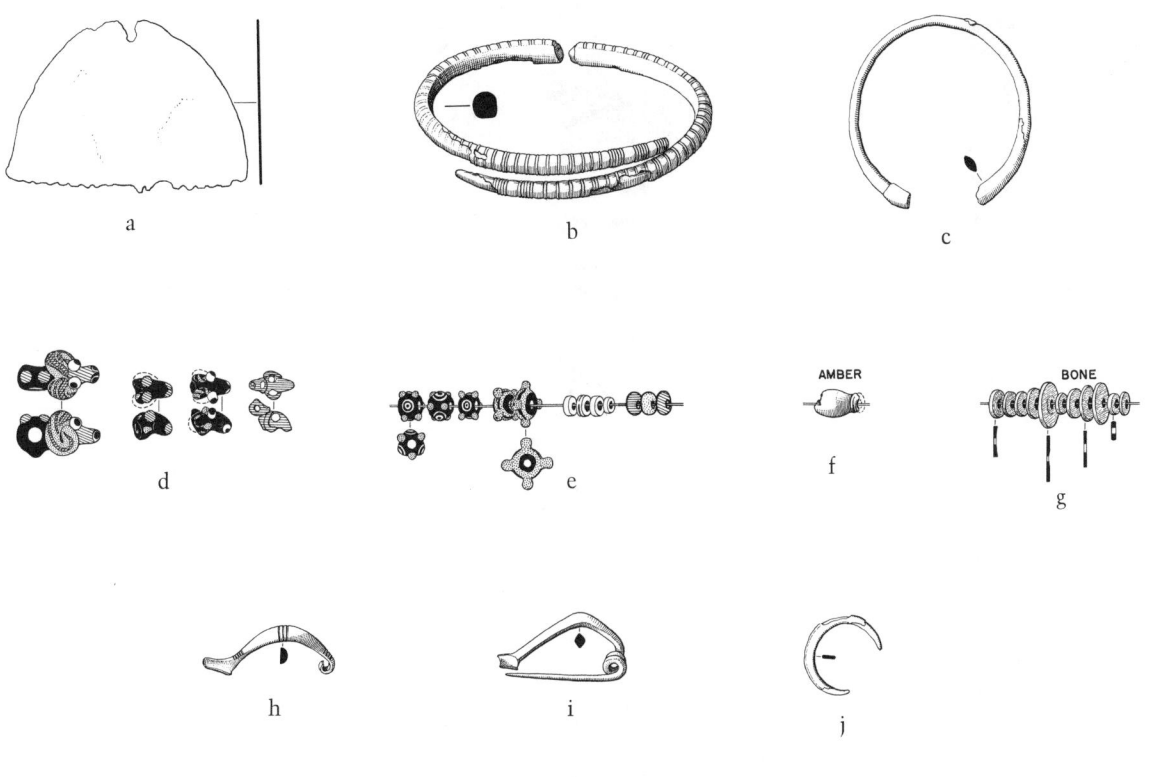

Figure 143. Tumulus VI, Grave 12b.

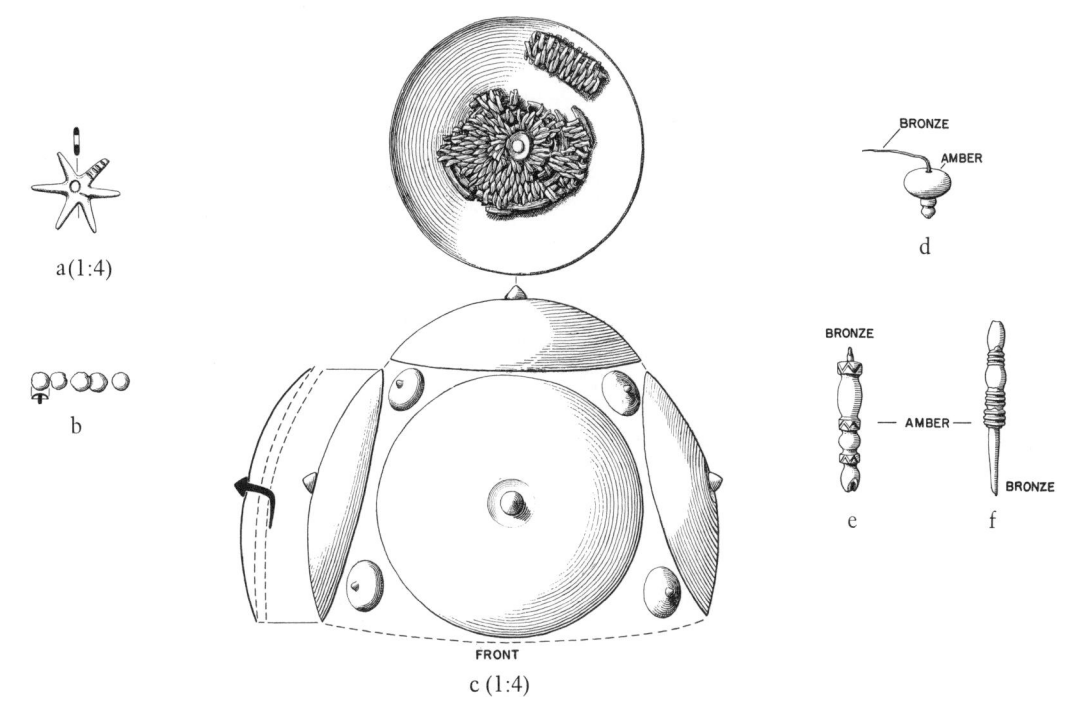

Figure 144. Tumulus VI, Grave 13.

204 STIČNA: TUMULUS VI

i (1:4)

h

g

—BRONZE

Figure 144. Tumulus VI, Grave 13, continued.

a

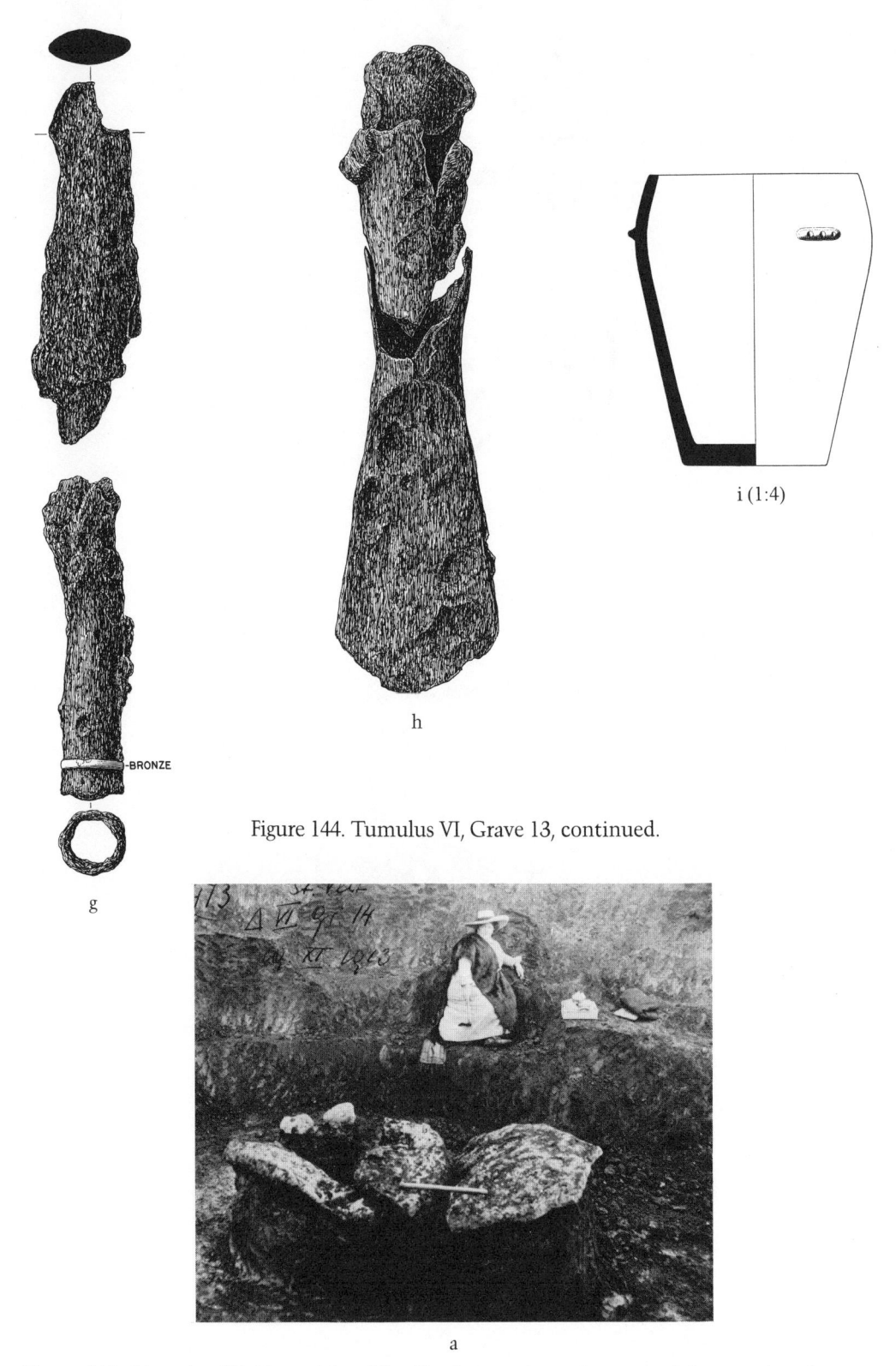

Figure 145. Tumulus VI, Grave 14. a. The Duchess next to the stone slabs covering the grave.

STIČNA: TUMULUS VI 205

b

c (1:4)

d

e (1:4)

f (1:4)

g

h (1:4)

i

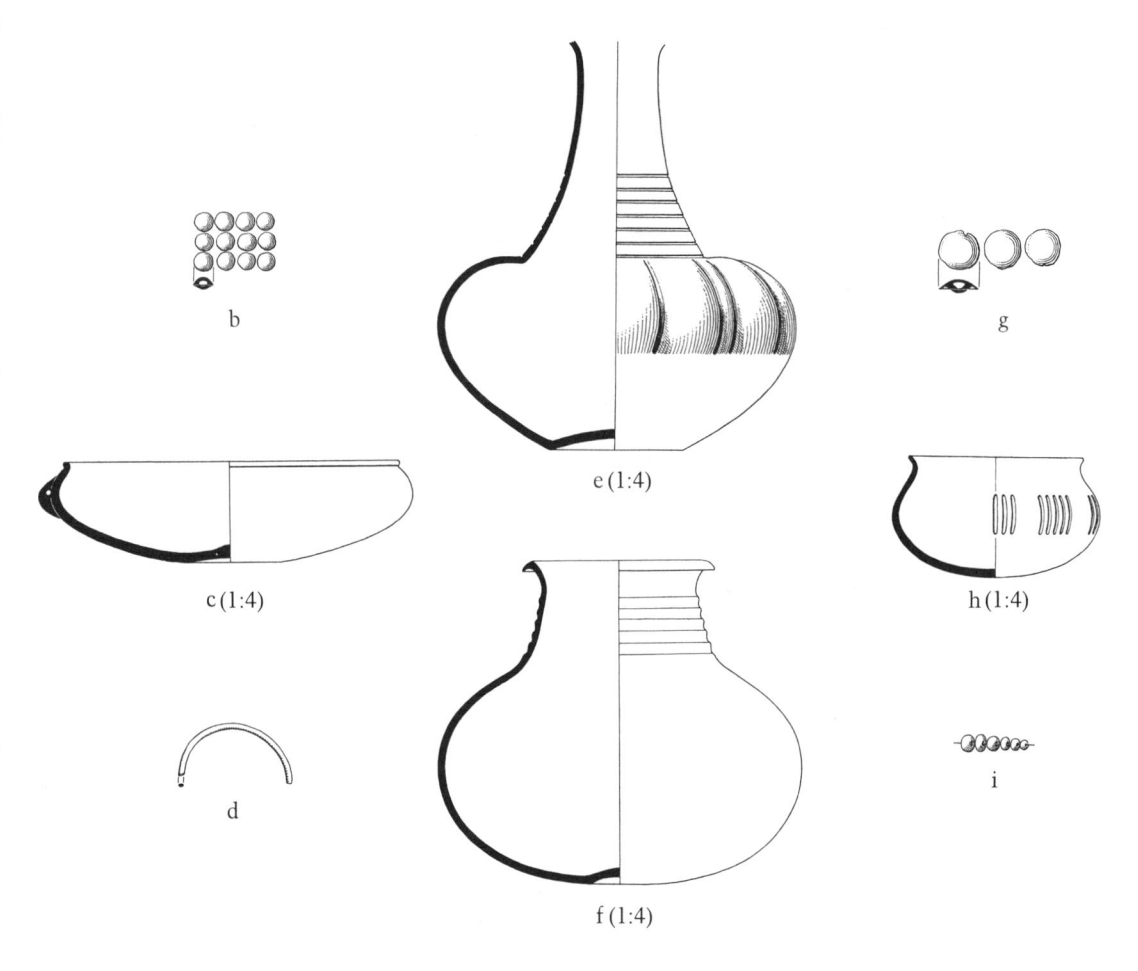

Figure 145. Tumulus VI, Grave 14, continued.

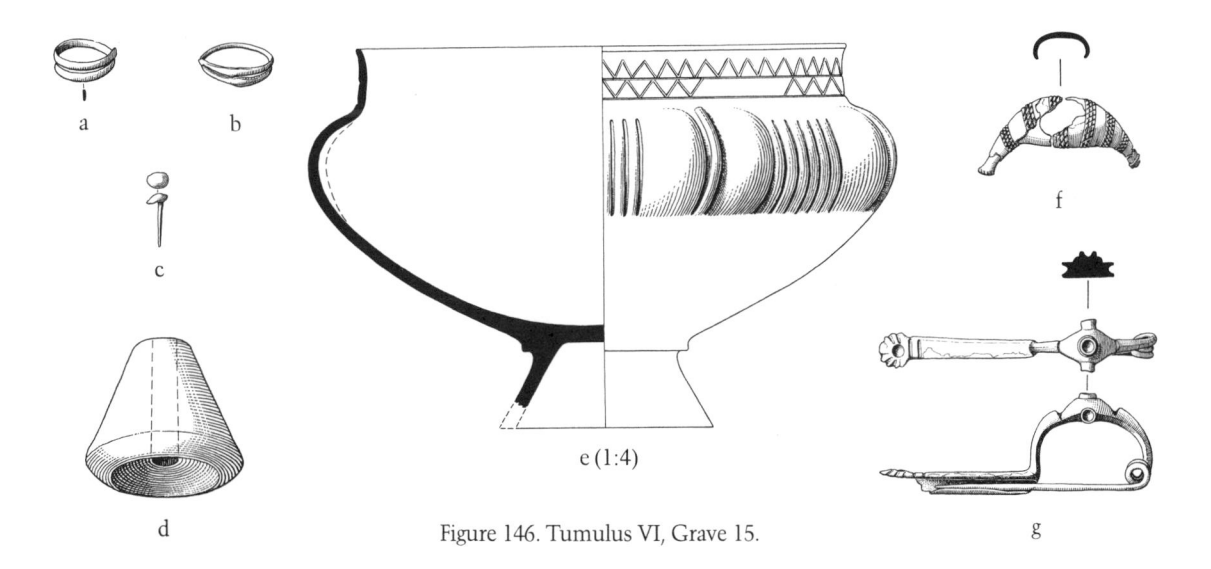

a

b

c

d

e (1:4)

f

g

Figure 146. Tumulus VI, Grave 15.

206 STIČNA: TUMULUS VI

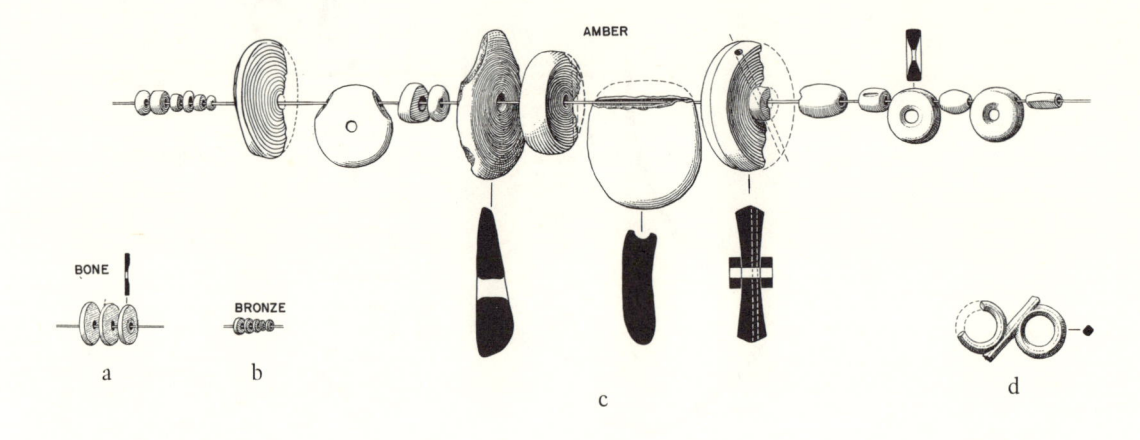

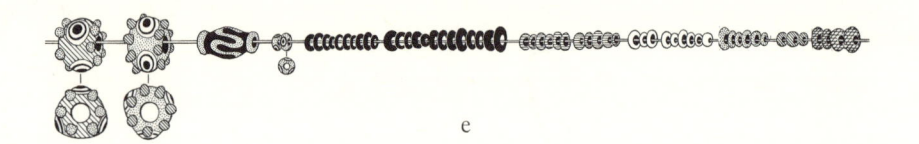

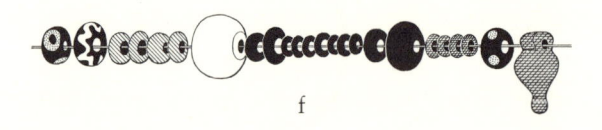

Figure 147. Tumulus VI, Grave 16.

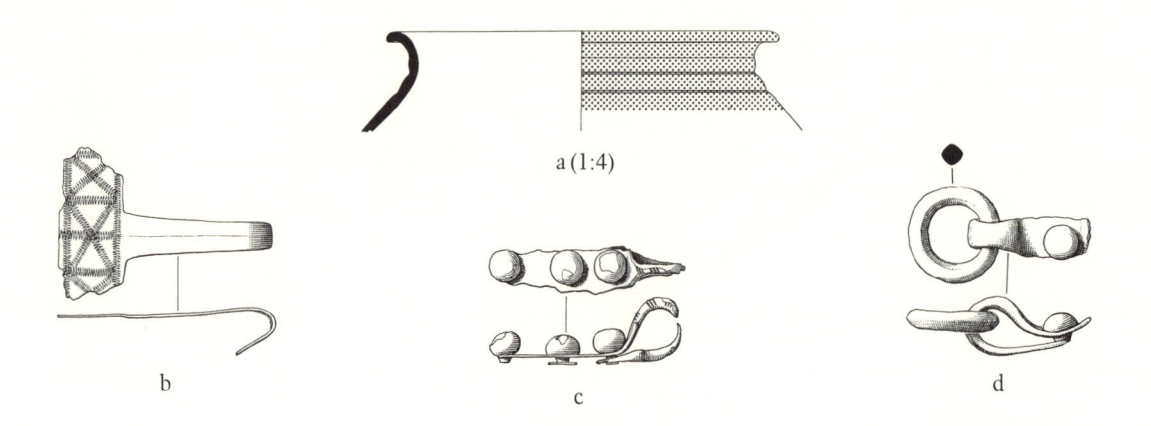

Figure 148. Tumulus VI, Grave 17.

STIČNA: TUMULUS VI 207

c (1:4)

d (1:4)

SIDE

TOP

END
e

f

g

b (1:4)

h

i

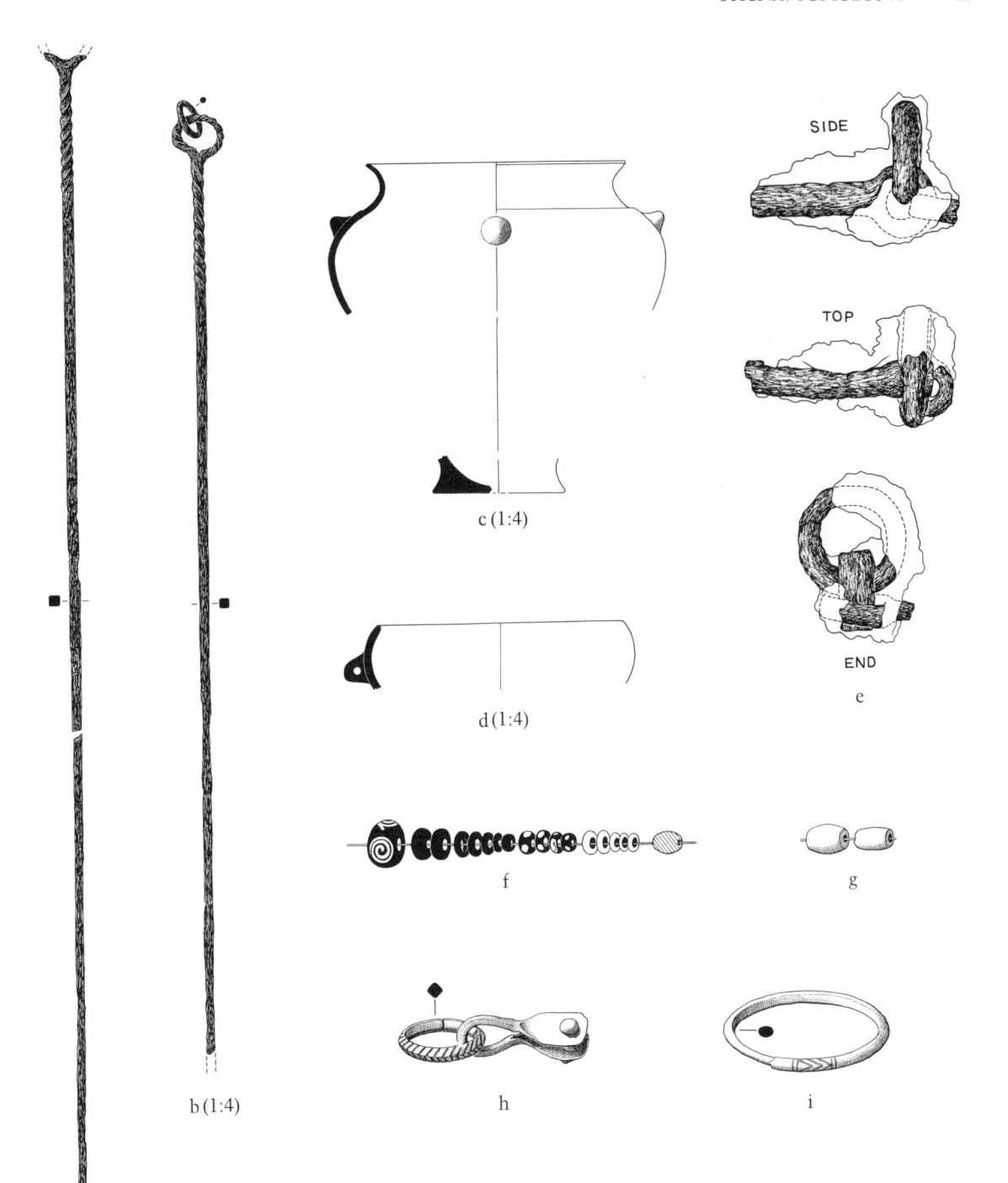

a (1:4)

Figure 149. Tumulus VI, Grave 18.

208   STIČNA: TUMULUS VI

a

b

c

d (1:4)

e (1:4)

f (1:4)

g

h

i

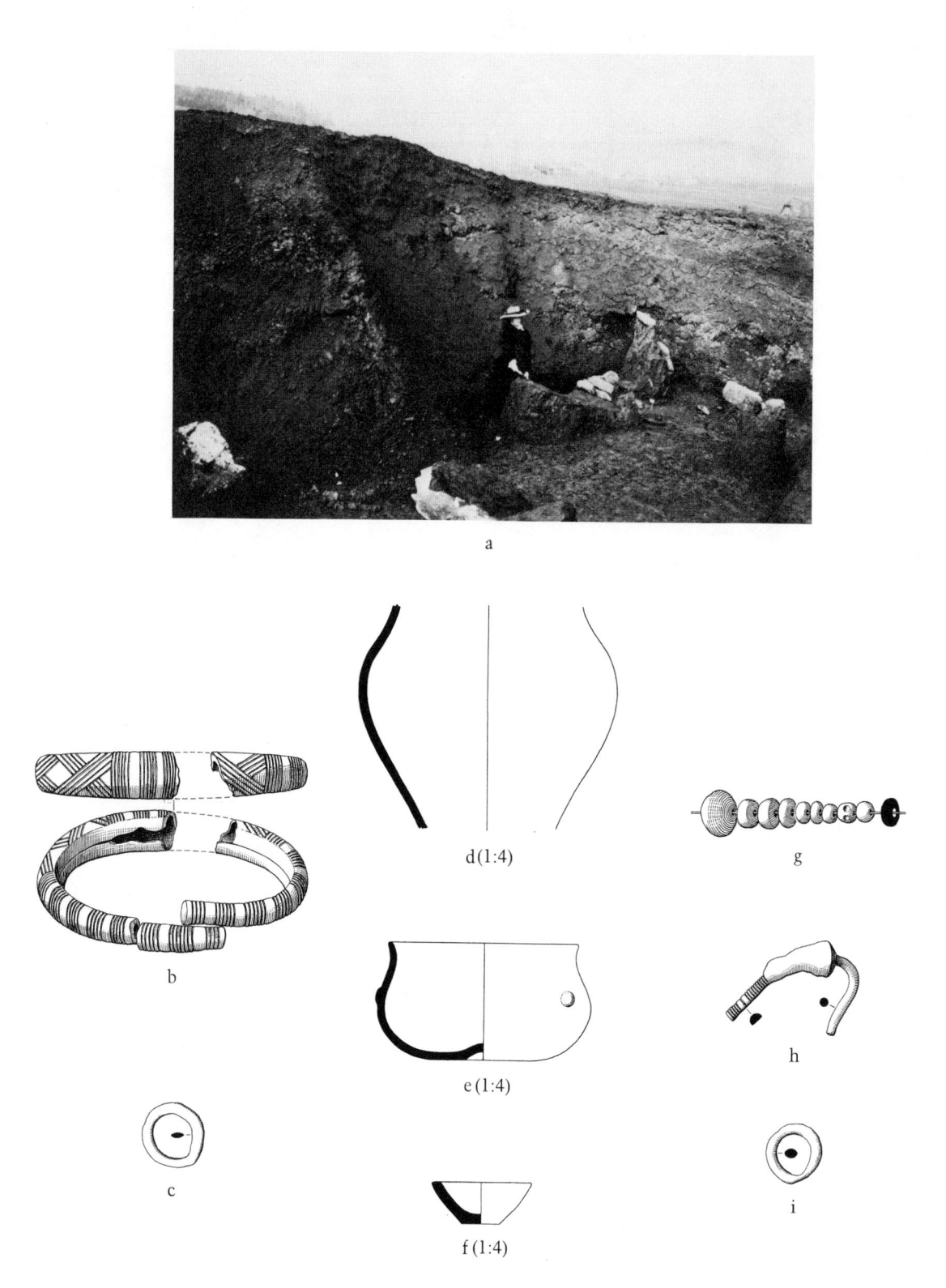

Figure 150. Tumulus VI, Grave 19. a. The Duchess standing next to Grave 19, with remains of other graves in the foreground and right of the picture.

STIČNA: TUMULUS VI 209

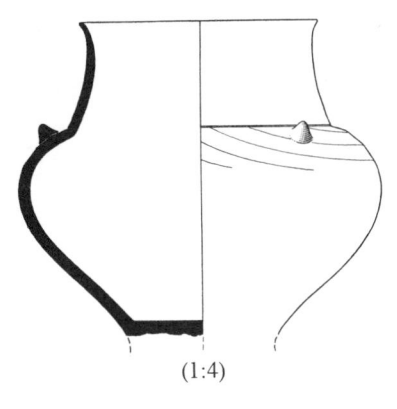

(1:4)

Figure 151. Tumulus VI, Grave 20.

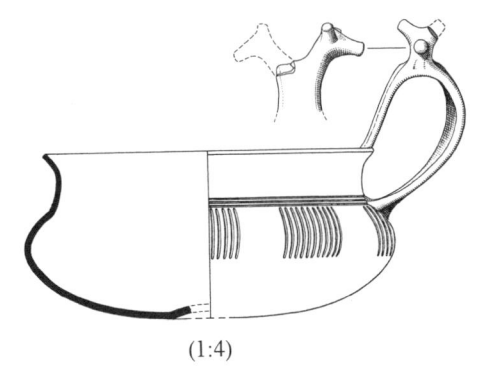

(1:4)

Figure 152. Tumulus VI, Grave 21.

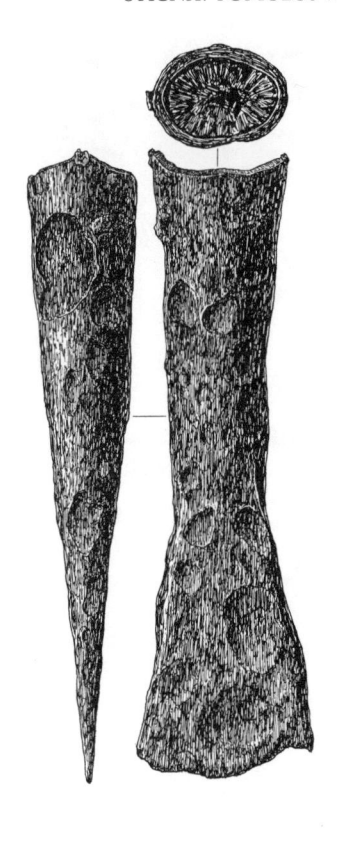

Figure 153. Tumulus VI, Grave 21a.

Figure 154. Tumulus VI, Graves 22, 23, and 24. The three graves are marked by the three groups of stone slabs in the center of the picture. There is no surviving record of which grave is which.

210   STIČNA: TUMULUS VI

a (1:4)

b (1:4)

c (1:4)

d

e (1:4)

Figure 155. Tumulus VI, Grave 23.

a (1:4)

b (1:4)

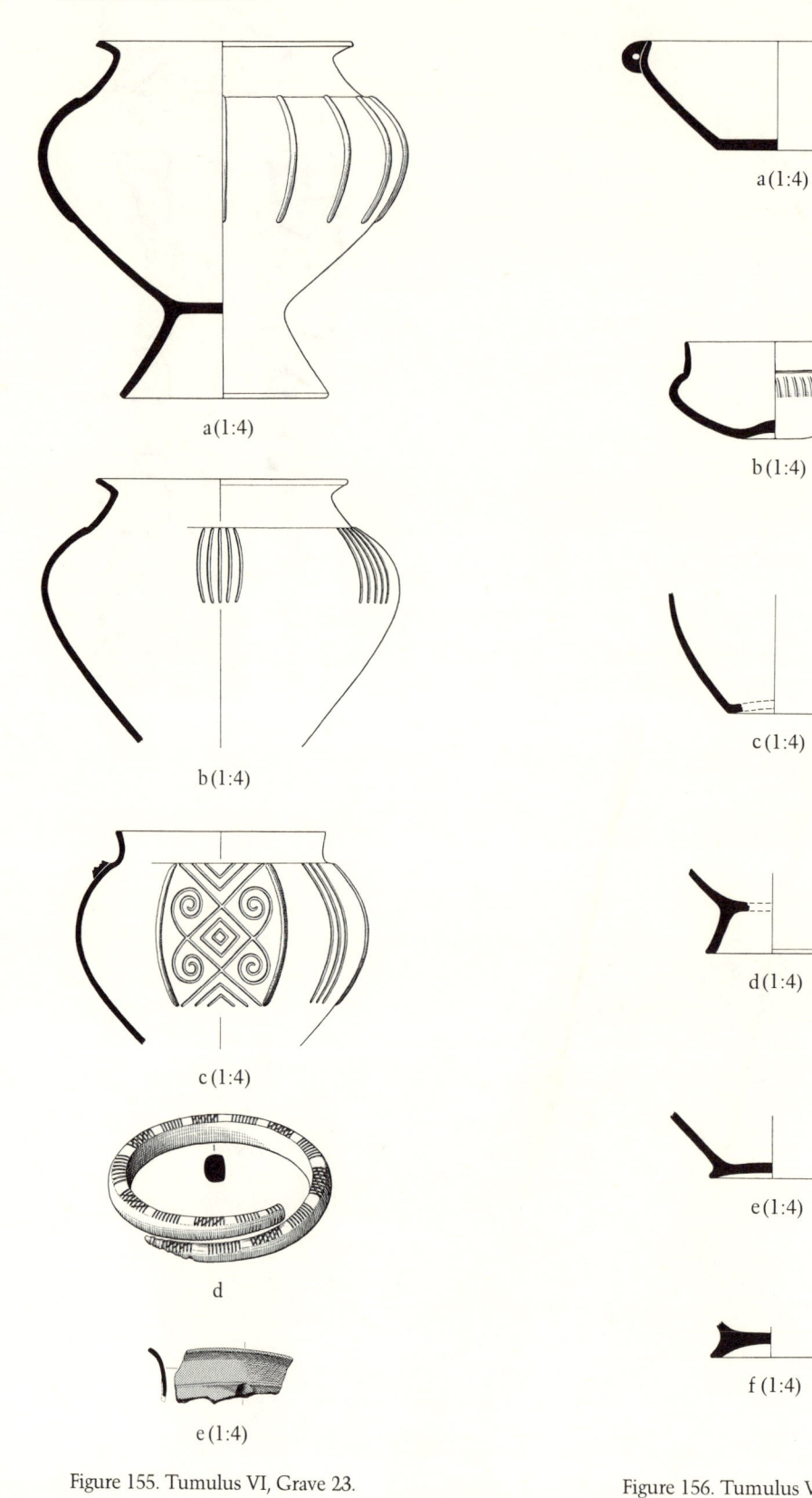

c (1:4)

d (1:4)

e (1:4)

f (1:4)

Figure 156. Tumulus VI, Grave 24.

STIČNA: TUMULUS VI   211

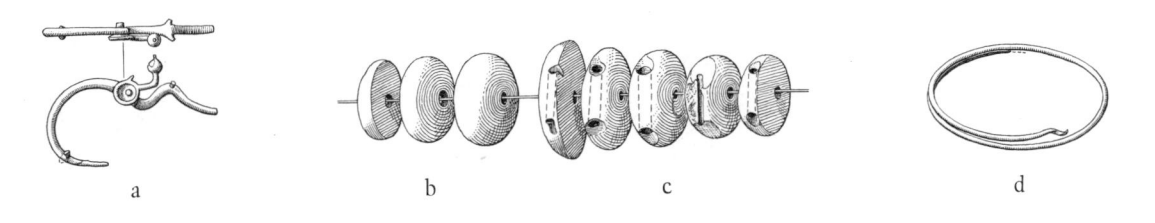

a   b   c   d

Figure 157. Tumulus VI, Grave 25.

a

b (1:4)

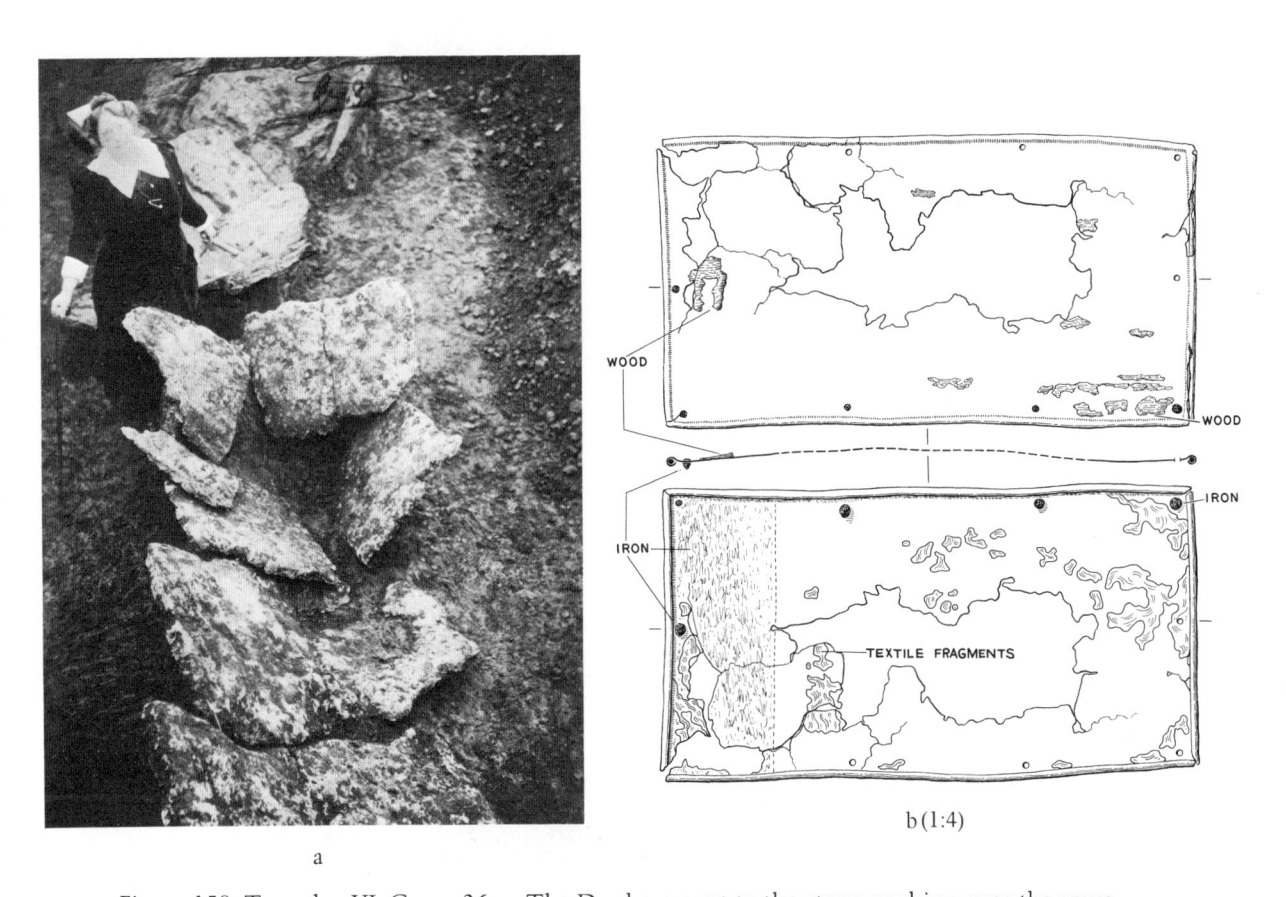

Figure 158. Tumulus VI, Grave 26. a. The Duchess next to the stone packing over the grave.

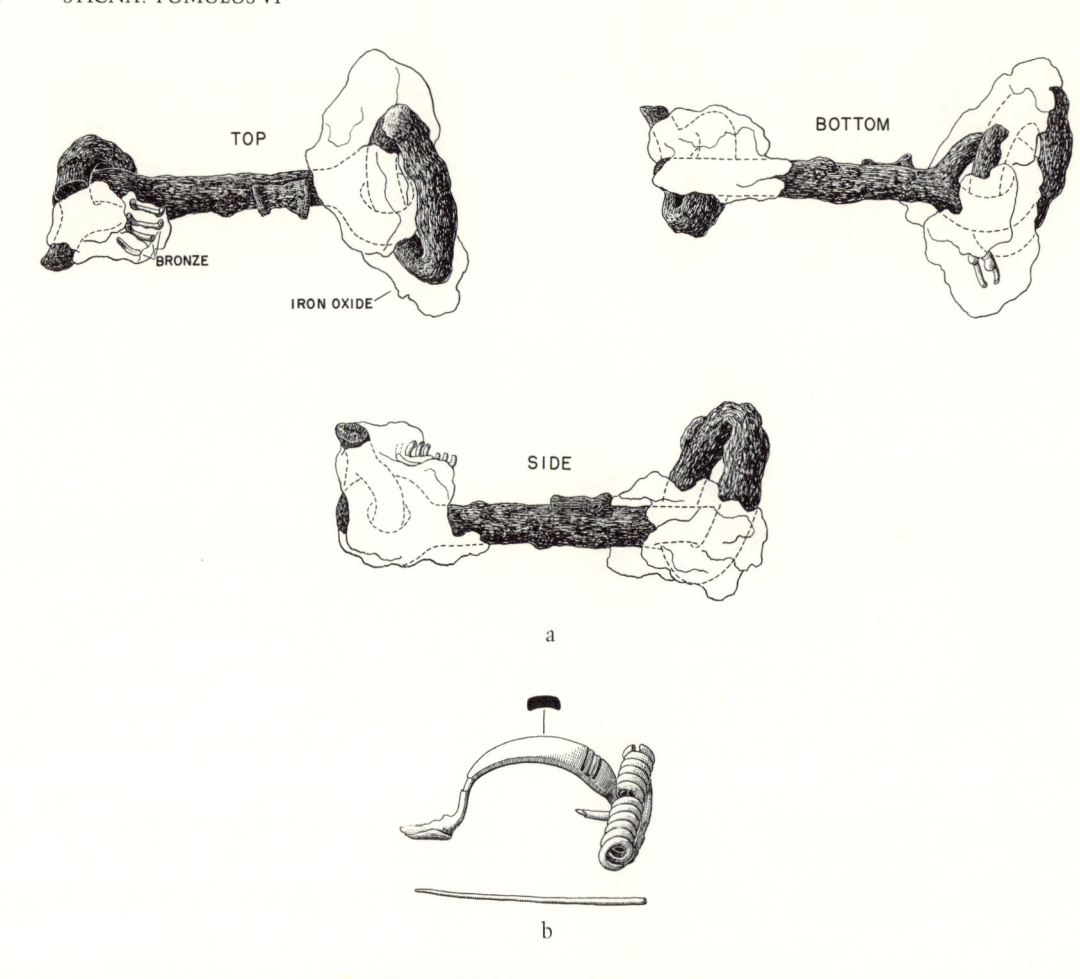

Figure 159. Tumulus VI, Grave 29.

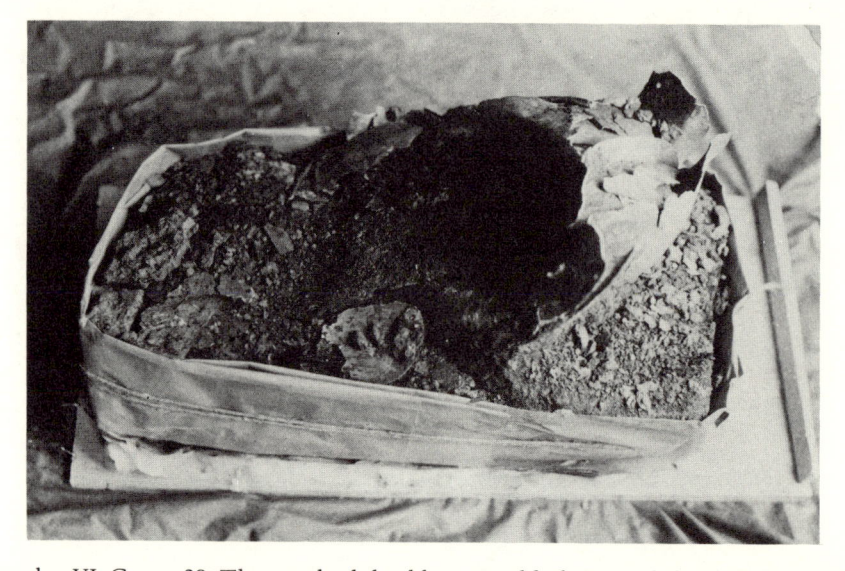

Figure 160. Tumulus VI, Grave 30. The crushed double-crested helmet and the disk from the grave, still partly in soil and in a packing box.

STIČNA: TUMULUS VI 213

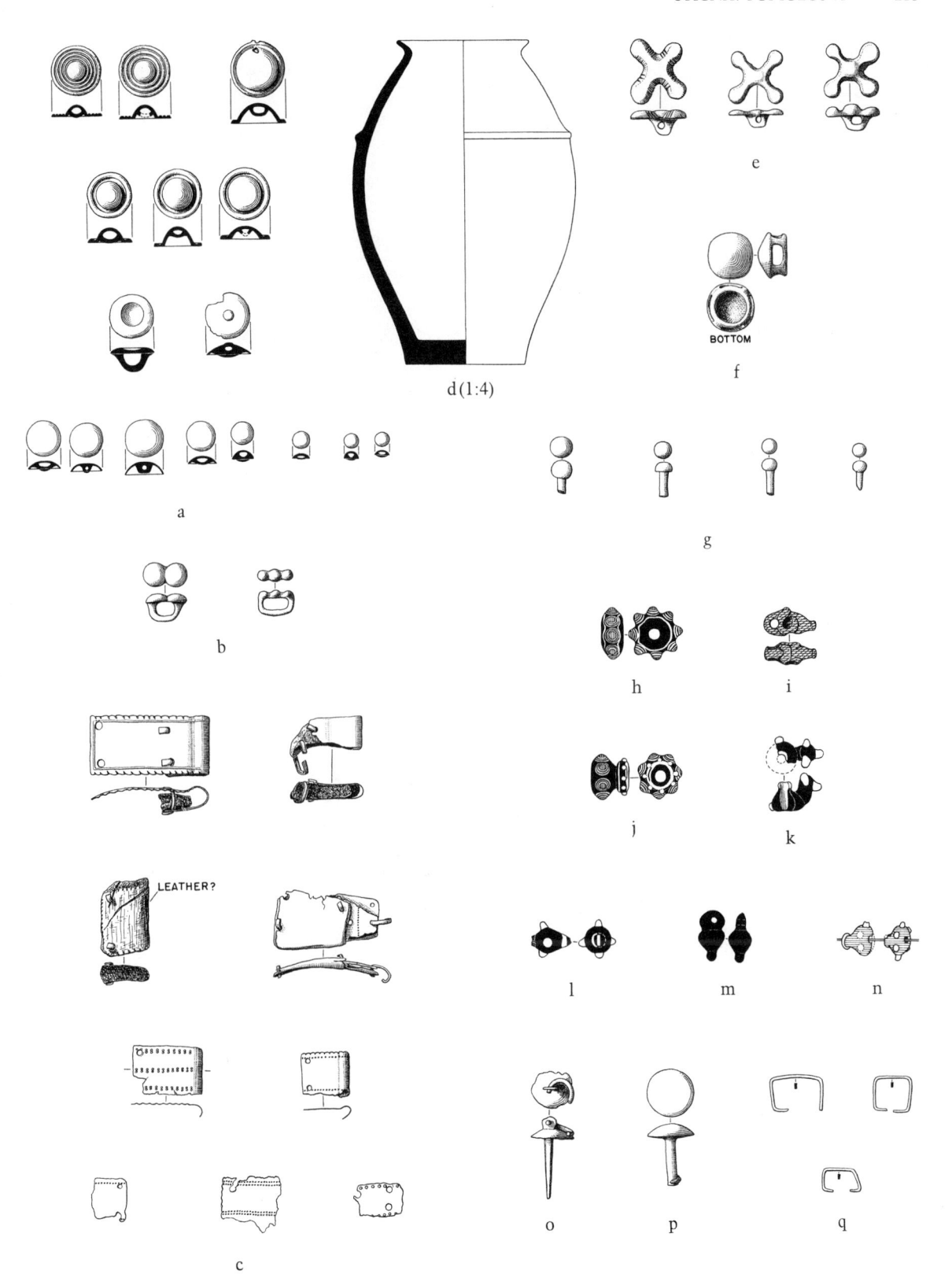

d(1:4)

Figure 161. Tumulus VI, isolated finds.

Figure 162. Tumulus VII. a and b. Two views of the tumulus during excavation.

STIČNA: TUMULUS VII 215

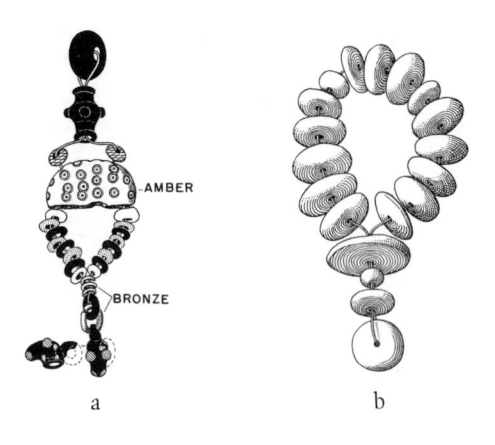

Figure 163. Tumulus VII, Grave 1.

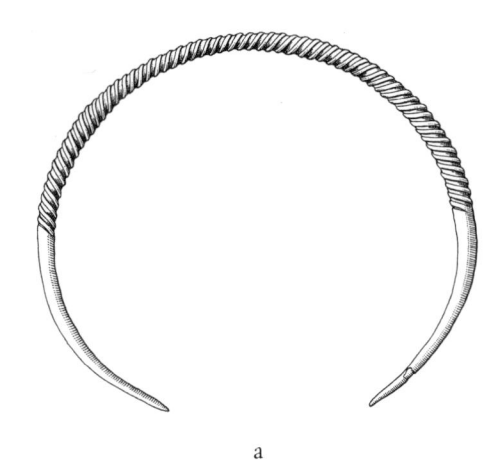

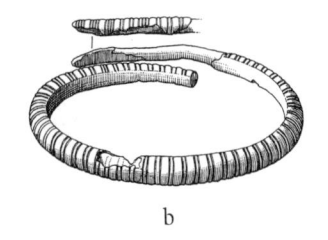

Figure 165. Tumulus VII, Grave 3.

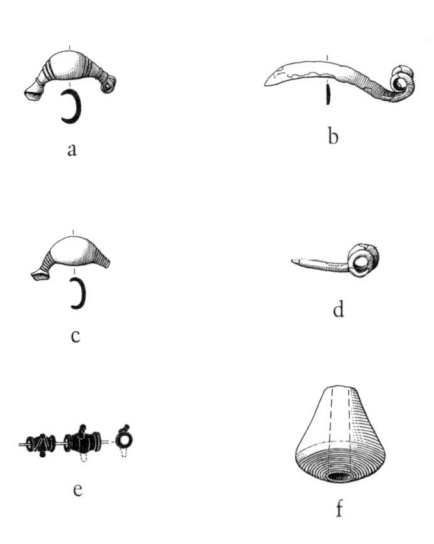

Figure 164. Tumulus VII, Grave 2.

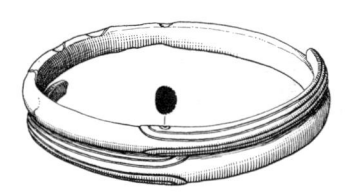

Figure 166. Tumulus VII, Grave 7.

Figure 167. Tumulus VII, isolated finds.

216 STIČNA: TUMULUS VIII

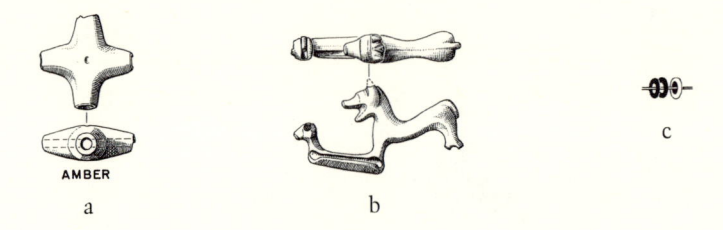

Figure 168. Tumulus VIII, Grave 1.

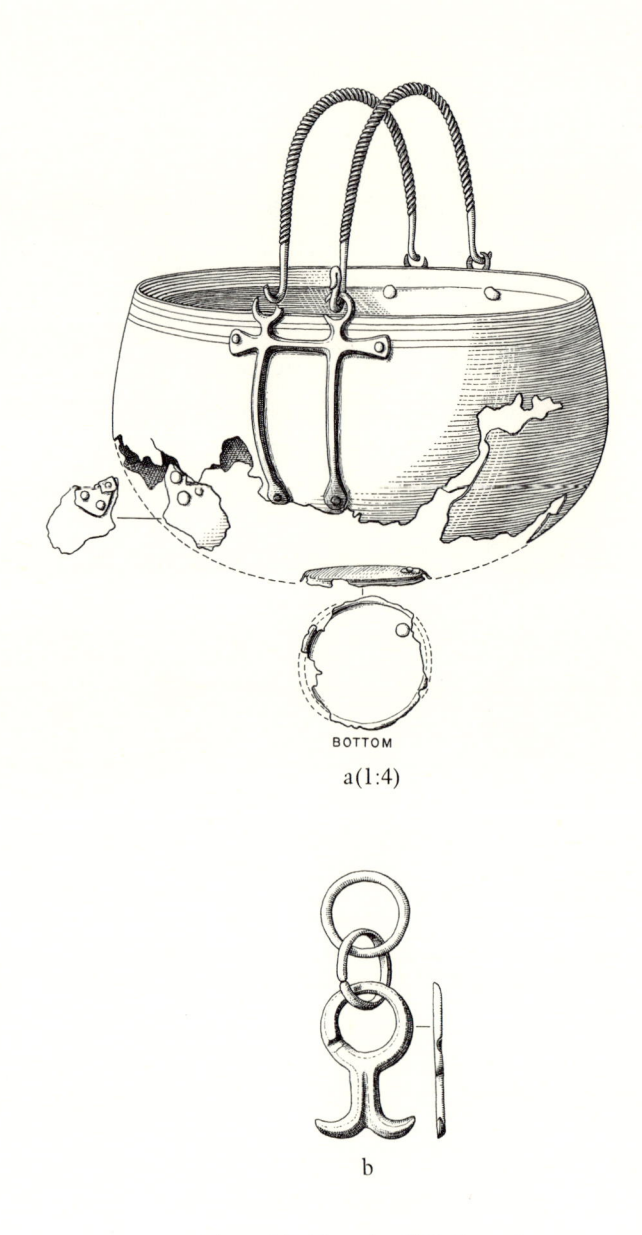

a(1:4)

Figure 169. Tumulus VIII, Grave 2.

STIČNA: VAS VIR 217

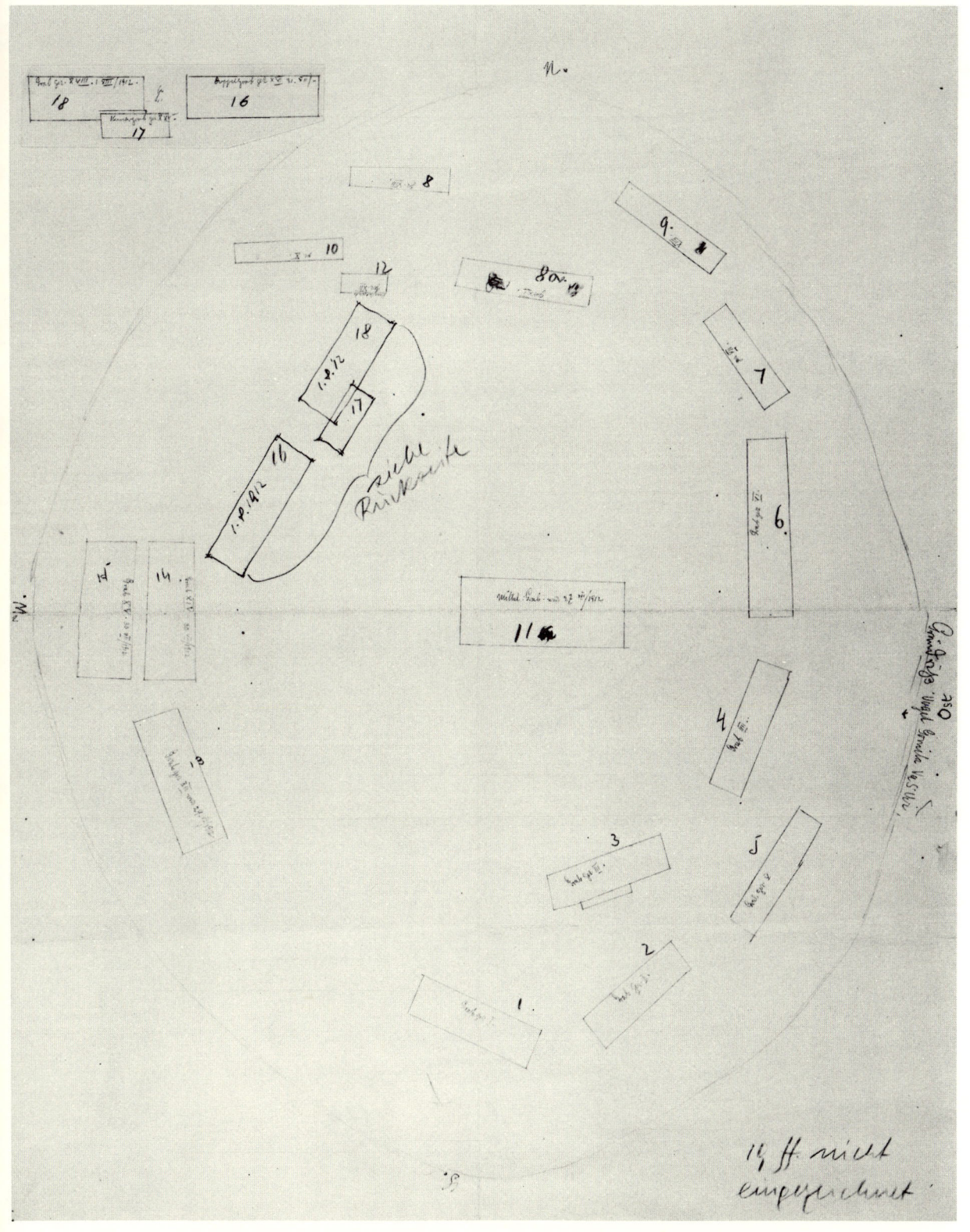

Figure 170. Vas Vir. The surviving plan of the Vas Vir tumulus.

218 STIČNA: VAS VIR

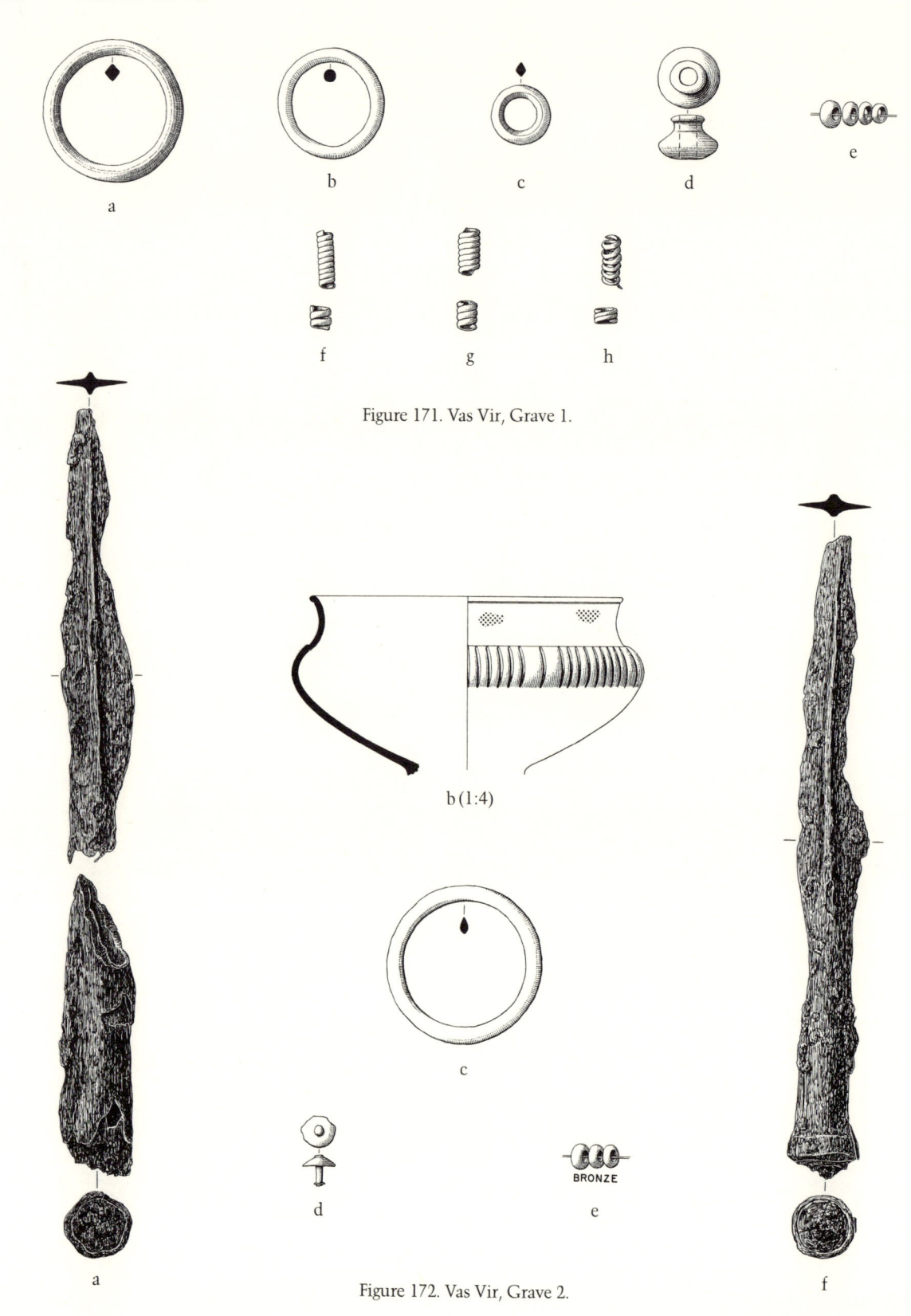

Figure 171. Vas Vir, Grave 1.

Figure 172. Vas Vir, Grave 2.

STIČNA: VAS VIR 219

a (1:4)

b

c (1:4)

d

e

f

g

h

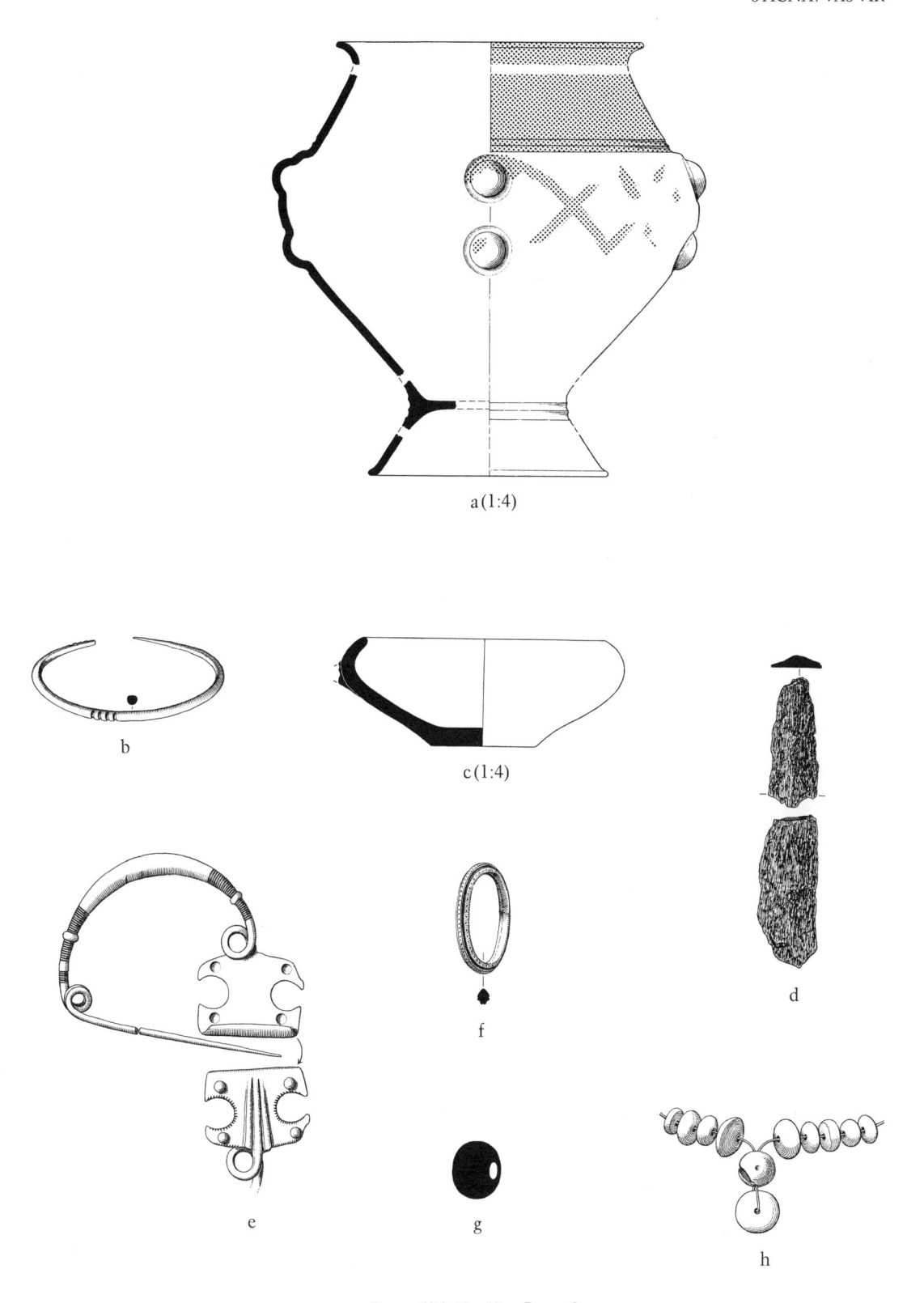

Figure 173. Vas Vir, Grave 3.

220　STIČNA: VAS VIR

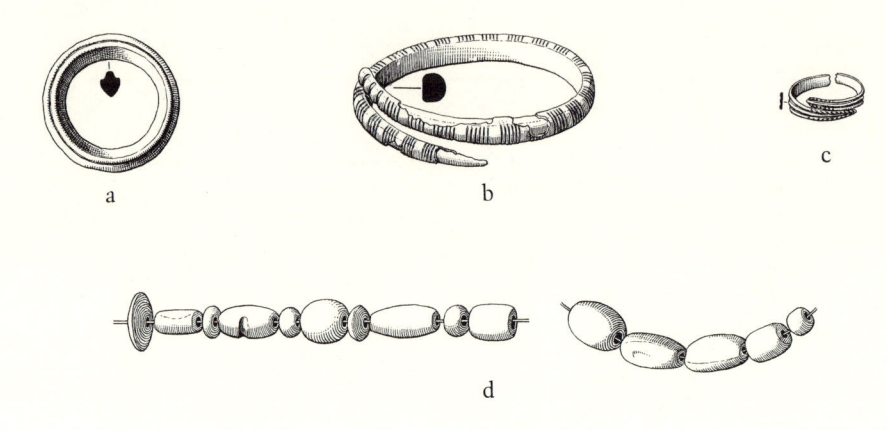

Figure 174. Vas Vir, Grave 4.

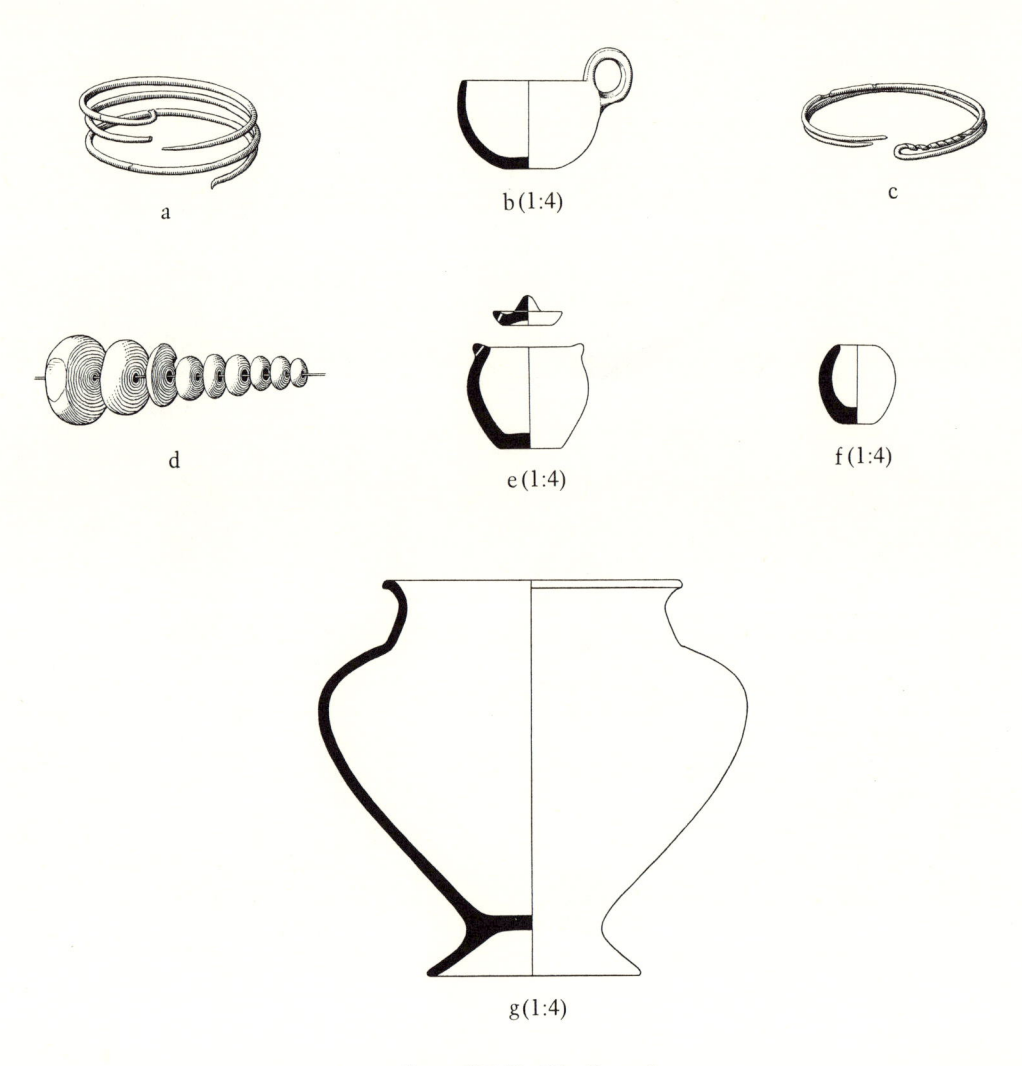

Figure 175. Vas Vir, Grave 5.

STIČNA: VAS VIR 221

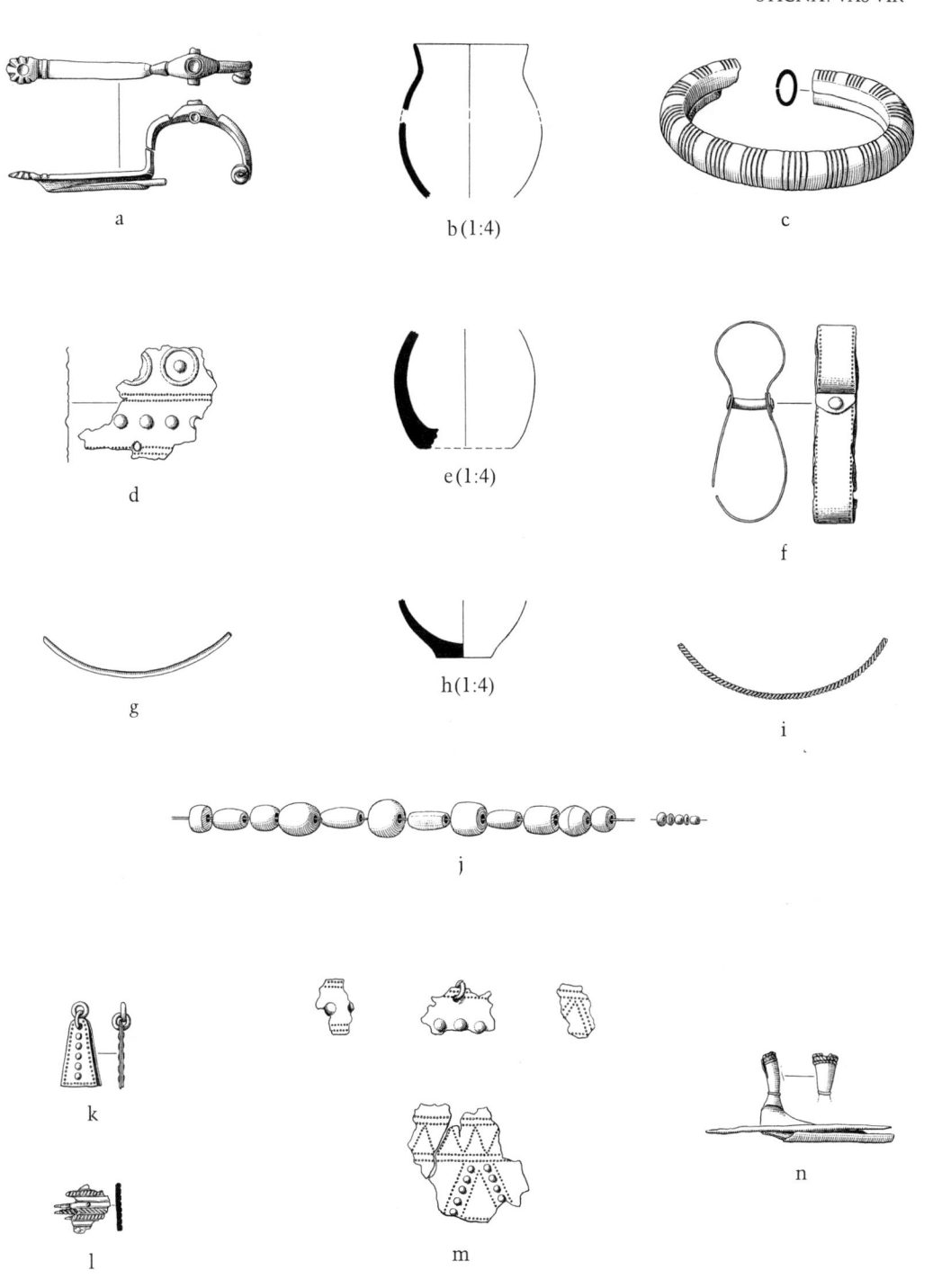

Figure 176. Vas Vir, Grave 6.

222   STIČNA: VAS VIR

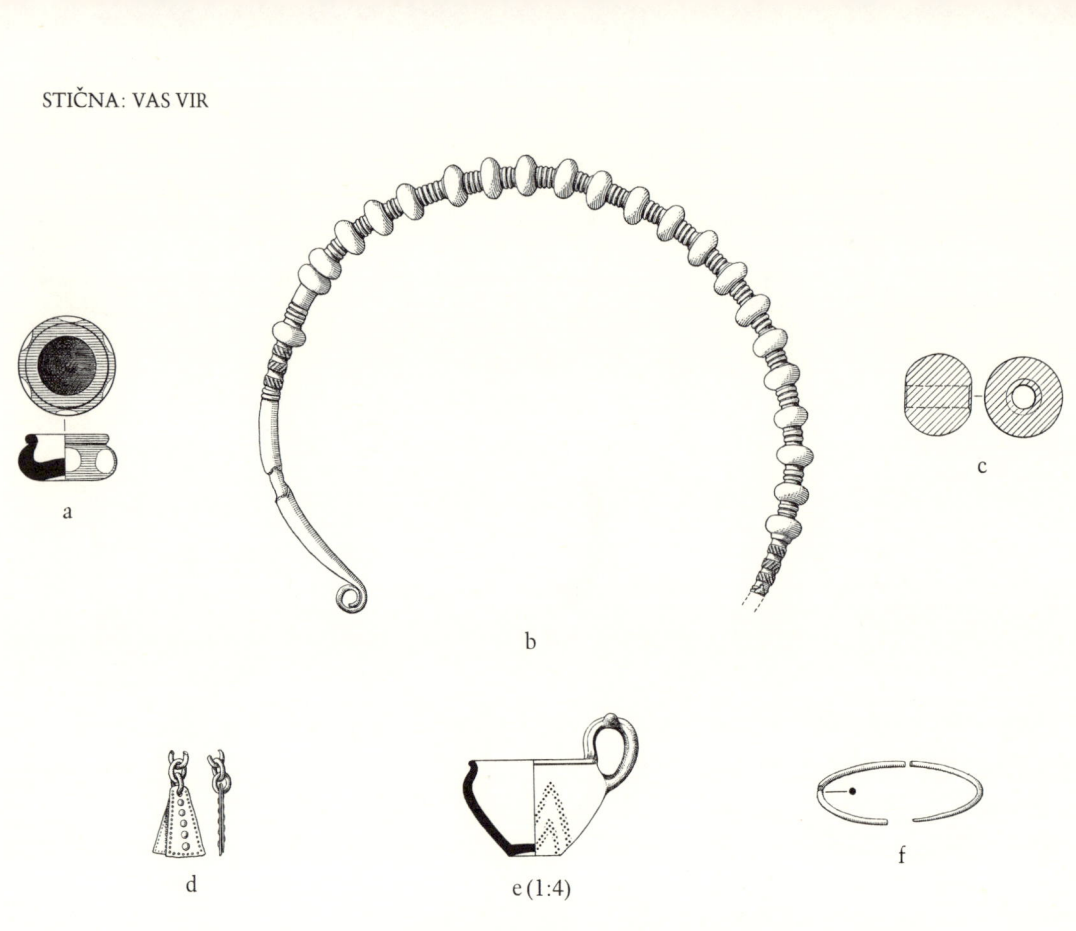

Figure 177. Vas Vir, Grave 7.

Figure 178. Vas Vir, Grave 8.

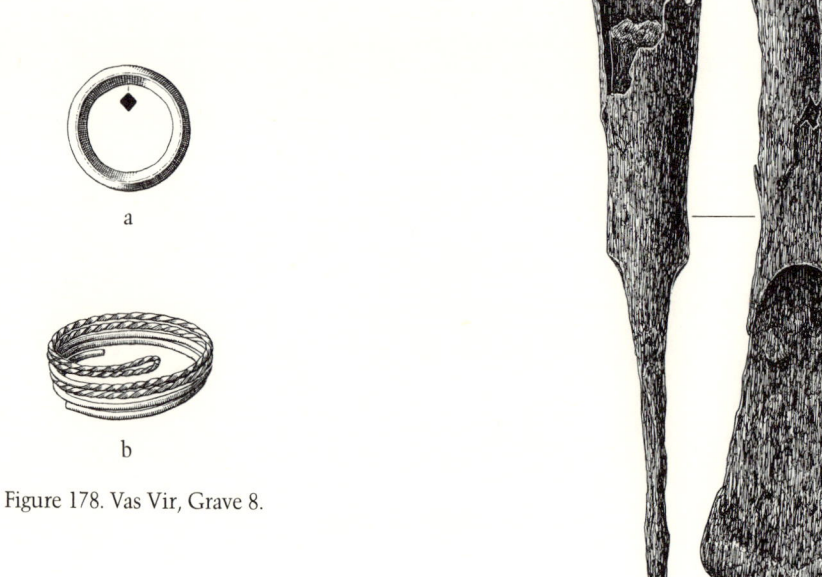

Figure 179. Vas Vir, Grave 8a.

STIČNA: VAS VIR 223

a(1:4)

b(1:4)

Figure 180. Vas Vir, Grave 9.

b(1:4)

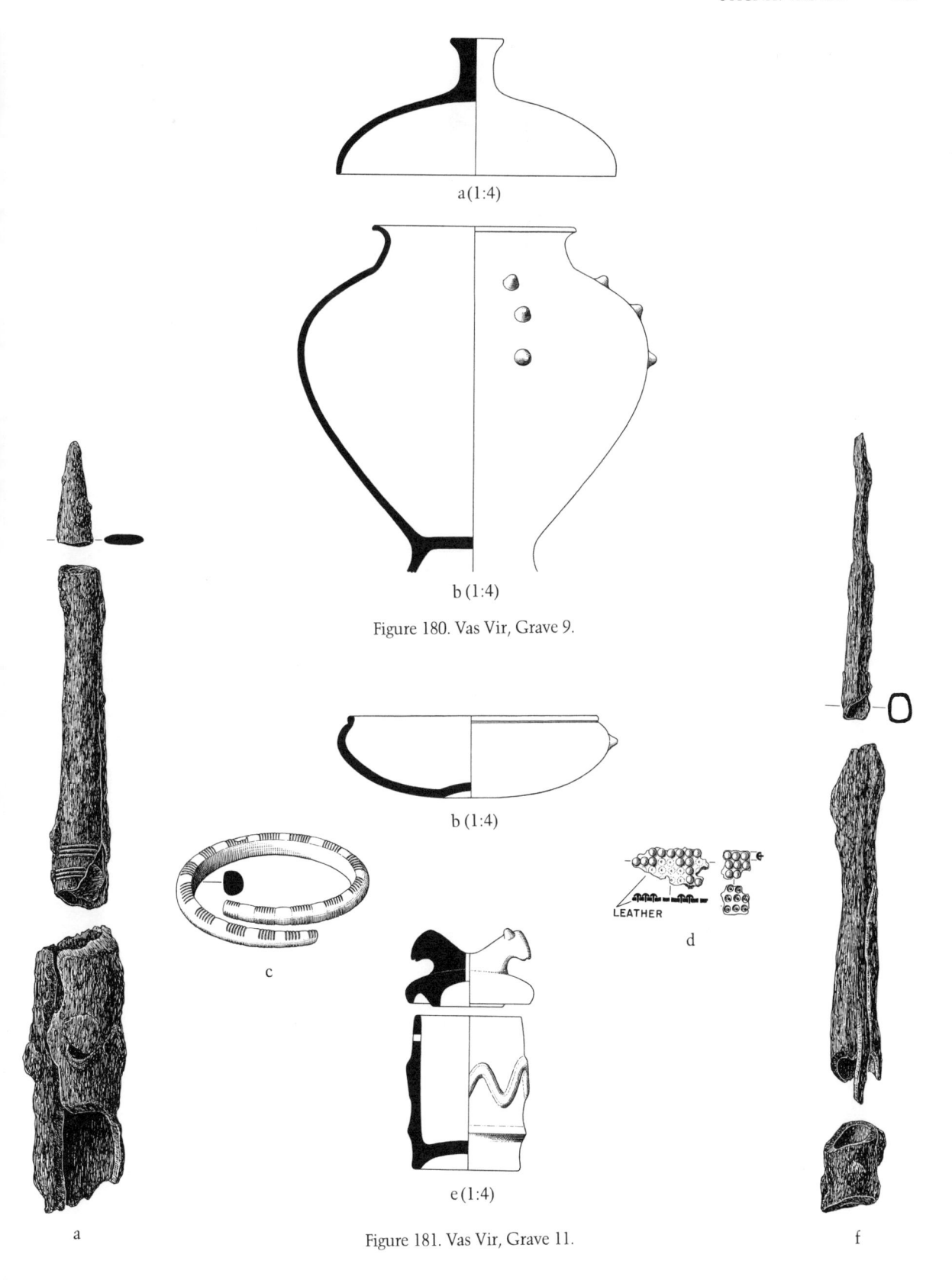

e(1:4)

Figure 181. Vas Vir, Grave 11.

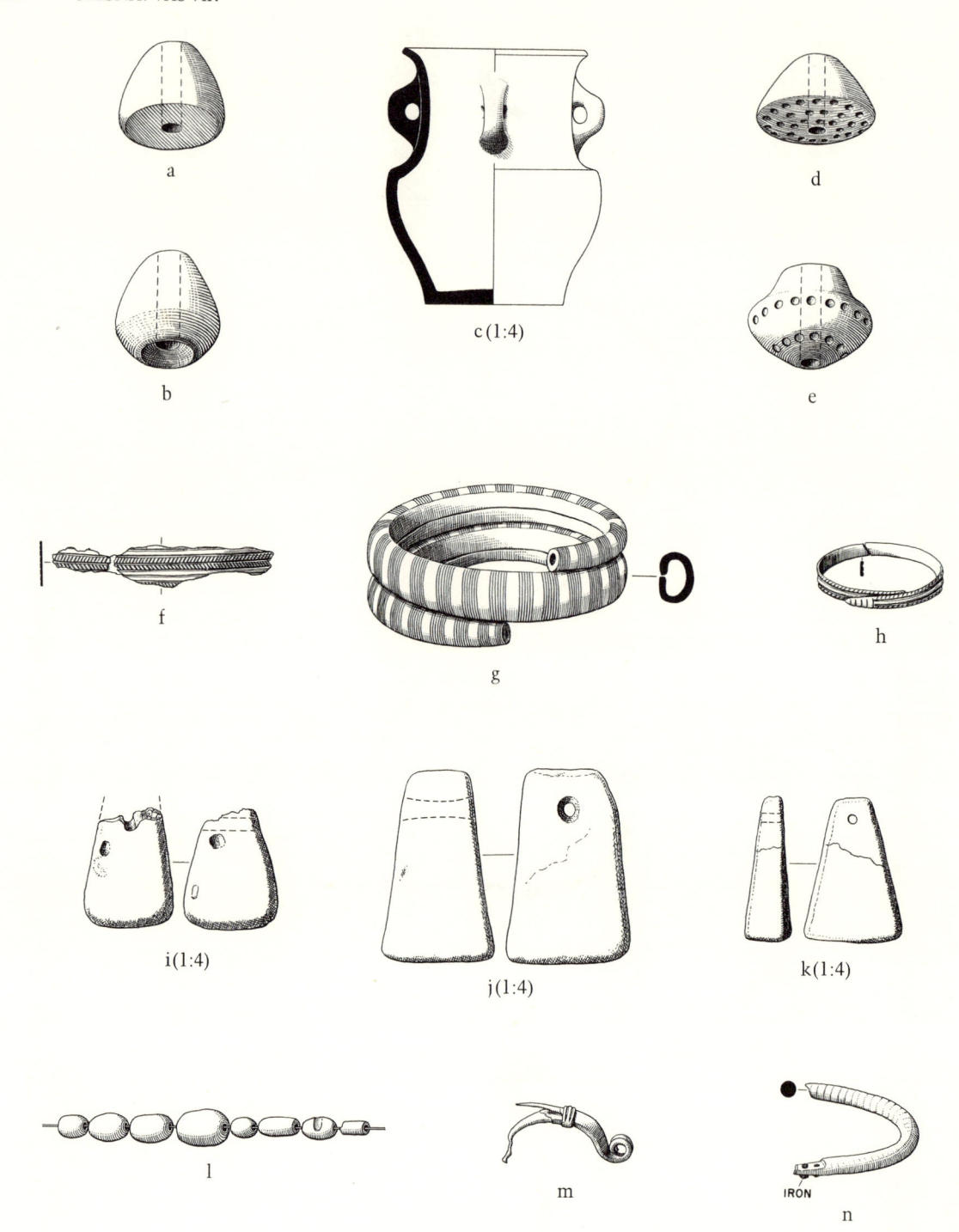

Figure 182. Vas Vir, Grave 12.

STIČNA: VAS VIR 225

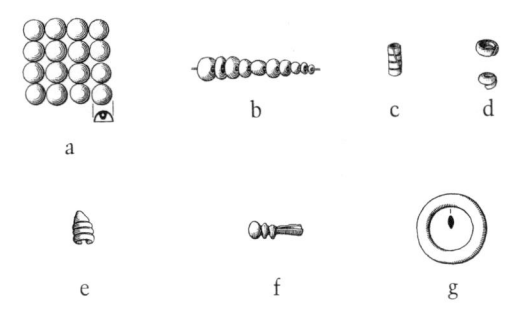

Figure 183. Vas Vir, Grave 16.

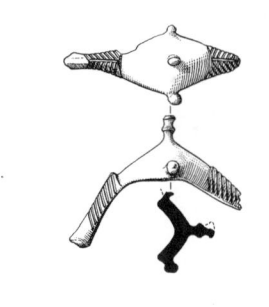

Figure 185. Vas Vir, Grave 19.

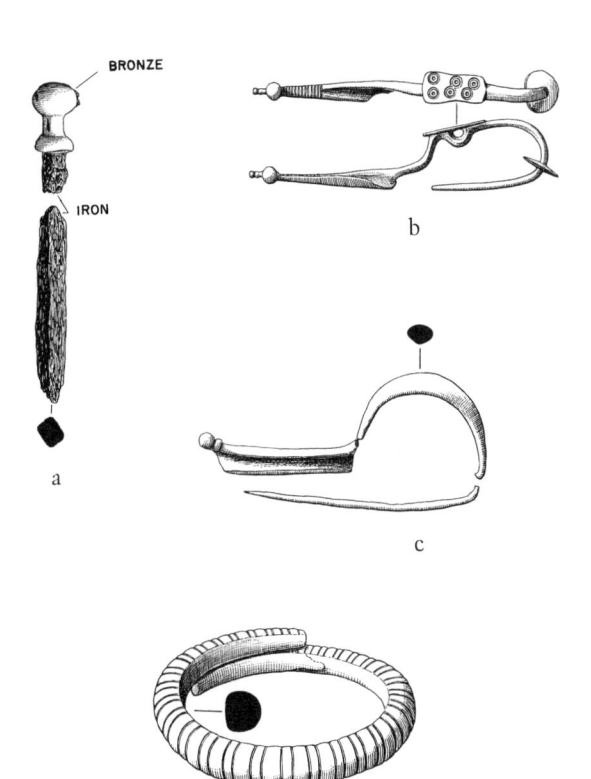

Figure 184. Vas Vir, Grave 18.

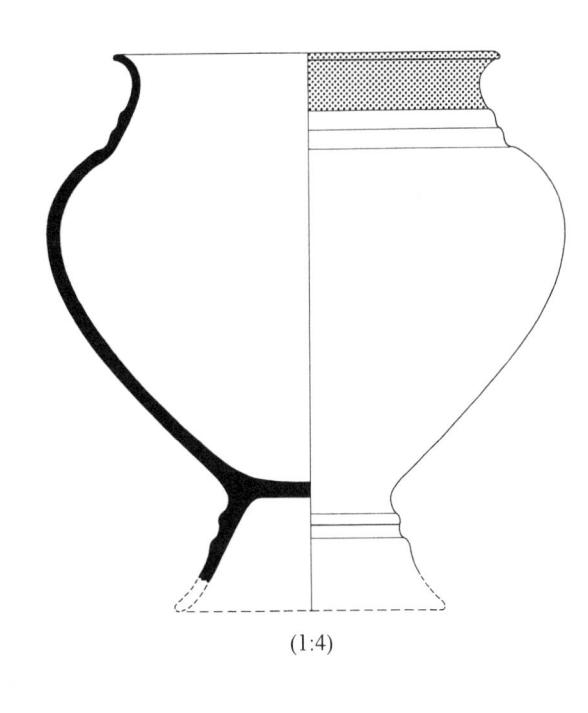

Figure 186. Vas Vir, Grave 22.

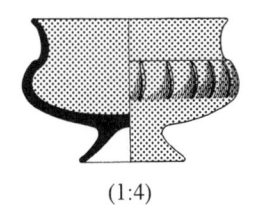

Figure 187. Vas Vir, Grave 26.

a   b   c   d

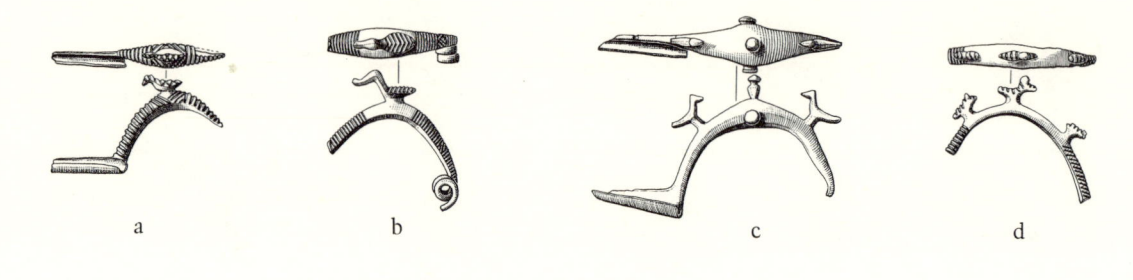

Figure 188. Vas Vir, isolated finds.

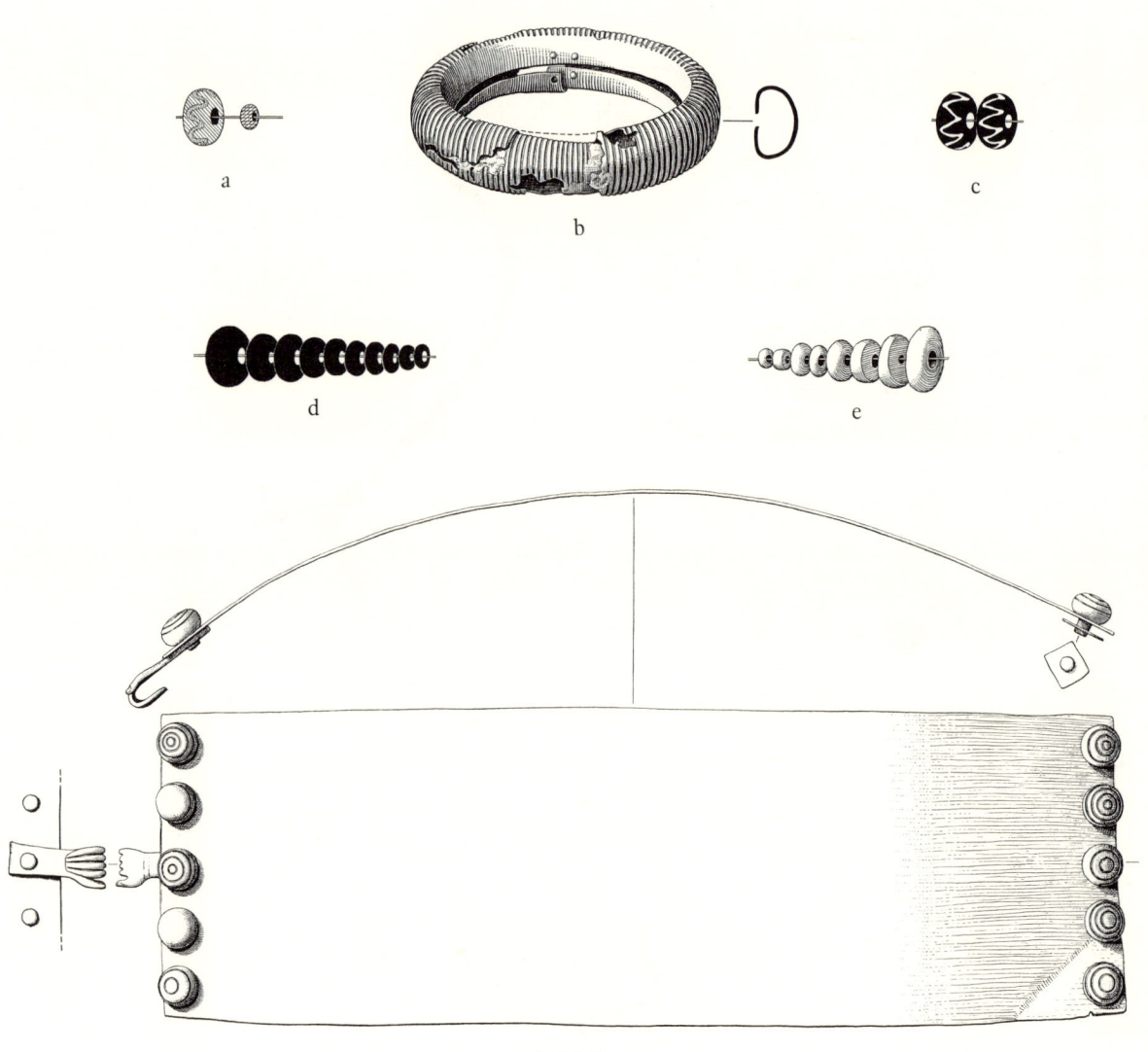

a   b   c

d   e

f (1:1.1)

Figure 189. Vas Pece, Grave 1.

STIČNA: VAS PECE   227

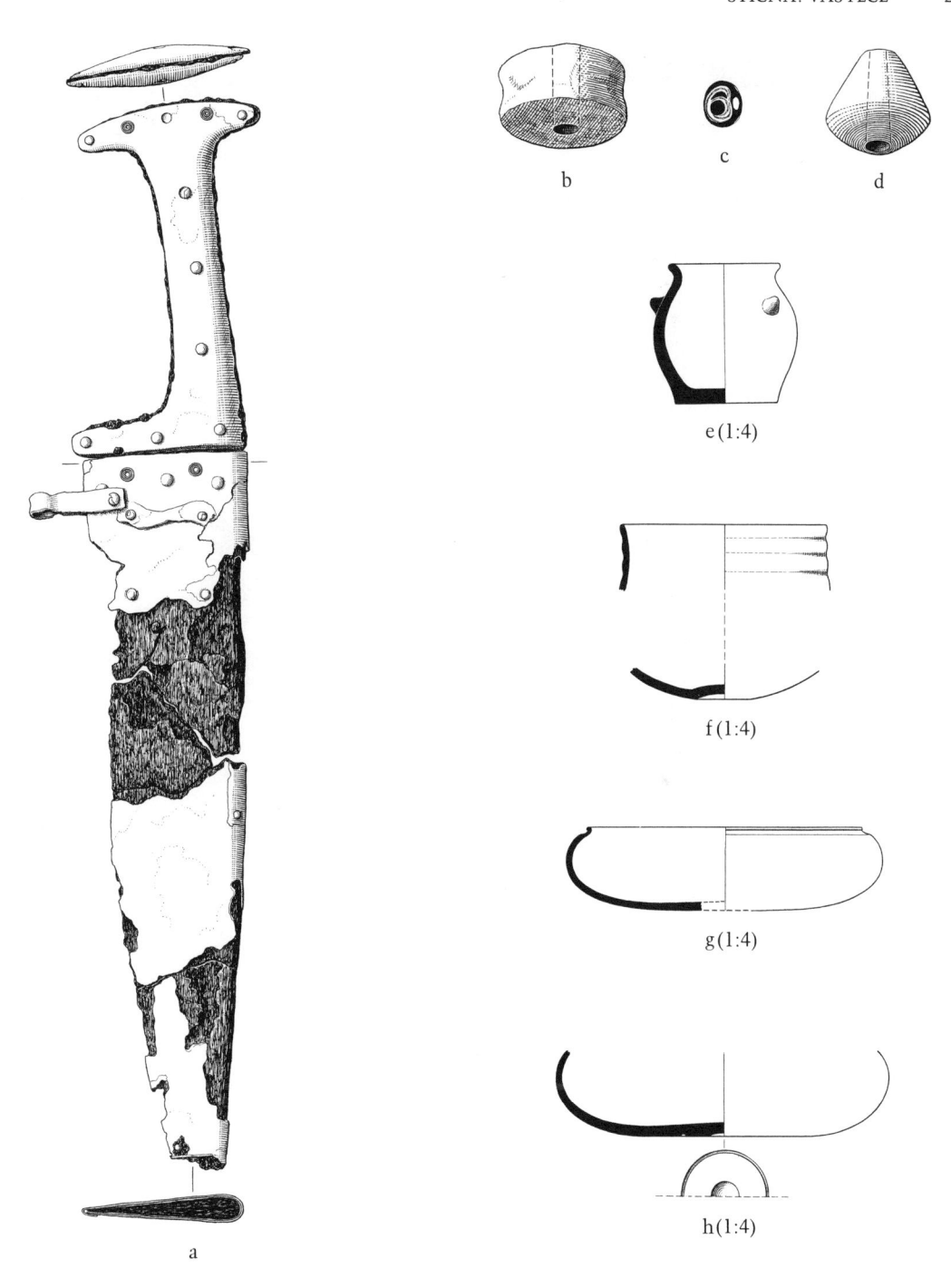

Figure 190. Vas Pece, Grave 2.

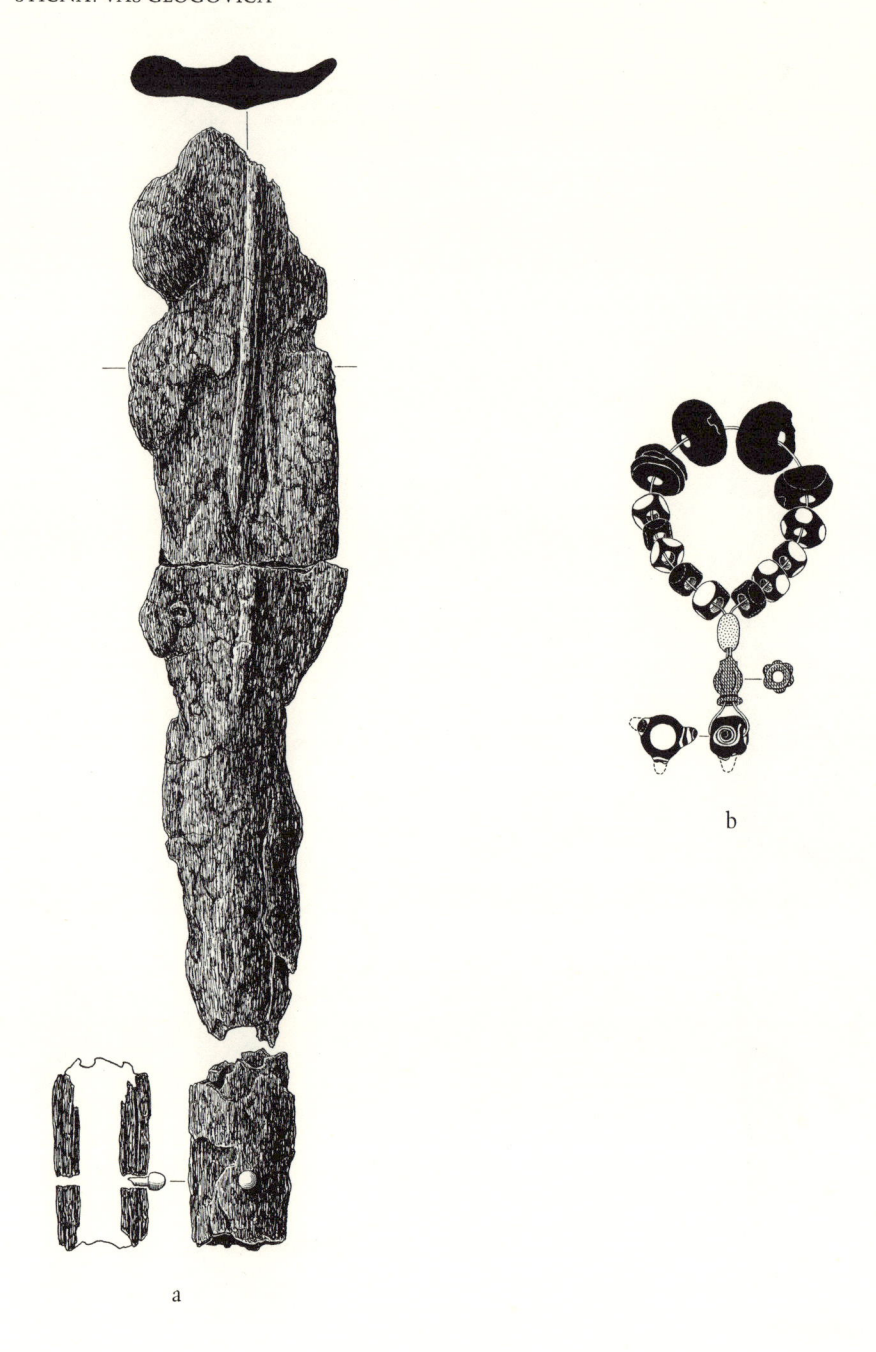

Figure 191. Vas Glogovica, Grave 2.

a(1:4)　　　　　　　b

Figure 192. Vas Glogovica, Grave 3.

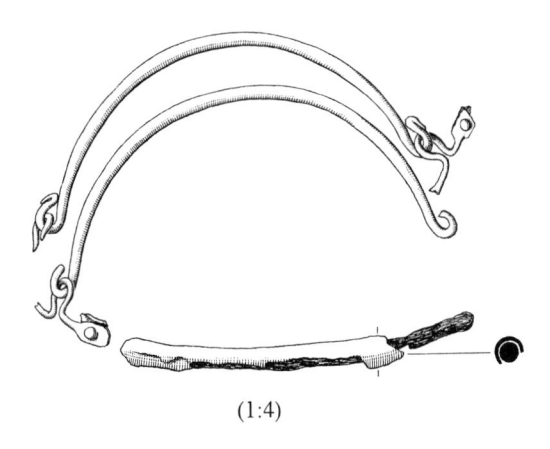

(1:4)

Figure 193. "St. Vid."

References

For those articles published in Slavic languages having summaries in German or English, the main article title is listed first, with the title of the summary immediately following in brackets.

Acsádi, G., and J. Nemeskéri
   1970 *History of Human Life Span and Mortality.* Akadémiai Kiadó, Budapest.

Alfieri, N., and P. E. Arias
   1958 *Spina.* Hirmer, Munich.

Alföldy, G.
   1974 *Noricum.* Routledge and Kegan Paul, London.

Amschler, J. W.
   1949 "Eisenzeitliche und römerzeitliche Tierreste aus Hallstatt, Oberösterreich," *Archaeologia Austriaca,* vol. 3, pp. 36–46. Vienna.

Angel, J. L.
   1968 "Human Skeletal Material from Slovenia," in H. Hencken (ed.), *Mecklenburg Collection, Part I.* American School of Prehistoric Research, Bulletin 25, pp. 73–108. Peabody Museum, Harvard University, Cambridge, Mass.

Angeli, W.
   1970 "Die Erforschung des Gräberfeldes von Hallstatt und der 'Hallstattkultur'," in *Krieger und Salzherren: Hallstattkultur im Ostalpenraum,* pp. 14–39. Römisch-Germanisches Zentralmuseum, Mainz.

Arheološka Najdišča Slovenije
   1975 Izdala Slovenska Akademija Znanosti in Umetnosti Inštitut za Arheologijo, Ljubljana.

Aspöck, H., F. E. Barth, H. Flamm, and O. Picher
   1973 "Parasitäre Erkrankungen des Verdauungstraktes bei prähistorischen Bergleuten von Hallstatt und Hallein (Österreich)," *Mitteilungen der Anthropologischen Gesellschaft in Wien,* vol. 103, pp. 41–47. Vienna.

Atlas of the World's Resources, vol. 2: *The Mineral Resources of the World*
   1952 Prentice-Hall, New York.

Bankoff, H.A.
   1977 "Metal Ores and Trade on the Middle Danube," in V. Markotic (ed.), *Ancient Europe and the Mediterranean,* pp. 13–16. Aris and Phillips, Warminster.

Barnett, H. G.
   1953 *Innovation: The Basis of Cultural Change.* McGraw-Hill, New York.

Barth, F. (ed.)
   1963 *The Role of the Entrepreneur in Social Change in Northern Norway.* Norwegian Universities Press, Bergen.

Barth, F. E.
   1969 *Die hallstattzeitlichen Grabhügel im Bereiche des Kutscher bei Podsemel (Slowenien).* Habelt, Bonn.
   1970a "Salzbergwerk und Gräberfeld von Hallstatt," in *Krieger und Salzherren: Hallstattkultur im Ostalpenraum,* pp. 40–52. Römisch-Germanisches Zentralmuseum, Mainz.
   1970b "Neuentdeckte Schrämspuren im Heidengebirge des Salzberges zu Hallstatt, Oö.," *Mitteilungen der Anthropologischen Gesellschaft in Wien,* vol. 100, pp. 153–156. Vienna.
   1970c "Ein prähistorisches Signalhorn aus dem Salzbergwerk in Hallstatt," *Mitteilungen der Anthropologischen Gesellschaft in Wien,* vol. 100, p. 157. Vienna.
   1971 "Funde aus dem Ender-Werk des Salzberges zu Hallstatt. Aufsammlung 1899/1900," *Mitteilungen der Anthropologischen Gesellschaft in Wien,* vol. 101, pp. 37–40. Vienna.
   1973 "Versuch einer typologischen Gliederung der prähistorischen Funde aus dem Hallstätter Salzberg," *Mitteilungen der Anthropologischen Gesellschaft in Wien,* vol. 102, pp. 26–30. Vienna.

1976a Review of L. Pauli, *Die Gräber vom Salzberg zu Hallstatt* (1975), *Archaeologia Austriaca*, vol. 59–60, pp. 475–478. Vienna.
1976b "Ein prähistorischer Salzbarren aus dem Salzbergwerk Hallstatt," *Annalen des Naturhistorischen Museums Wien*, vol. 80, pp. 819–821. Vienna.
1976c "Weitere Blockbauten im Salzbergtal bei Hallstatt," *Archaeologia Austriaca*, supplement 13, vol. 1, pp. 538–545. Vienna.
1978–79 "Eine neue Quelle zur Dokumentation der historischen Grabungen im Gräberfeld Hallstatt," *Schild von Steier*, vol. 15–16, pp. 33–41. Graz.
1980a "Das prähistorische Hallstatt," in *Die Hallstattkultur*, pp. 67–79. Oberösterreichischer Landesverlag, Linz.
1980b "Neue archäologische Forschungen im Salzbergwerk Hallstatt," *Oberösterreich*, vol. 30, no. 1, pp. 17–19. Linz.

Barth, F. E., H. Felber, and O. Schauberger
1975 "Radiokohlenstoffdatierung der prähistorischen Baue in den Salzbergwerken Hallstatt und Dürrnberg-Hallein," *Mitteilungen der Anthropologischen Gesellschaft in Wien*, vol. 105, pp. 45–52. Vienna.

Barth, F. E., and F. R. Hodson
1976 "The Hallstatt Cemetery and Its Documentation: Some New Evidence," *Antiquaries Journal*, vol. 56, pp. 159–176.

Beck, C. W.
1970 "Amber in Archaeology," *Archaeology*, vol. 23, no. 1, pp. 7–11. New York.

Beck, C. W., A. B. Adams, G. C. Southard, and C. Fellows.
1971 "Determination of the Origin of Greek Amber Artifacts by Computer-Classification of Infrared Spectra," in R. H. Brill (ed.), *Science and Archaeology*, pp. 235–240. The MIT Press, Cambridge, Mass.

Beck, C. W., and E. Sprincz
In press "The Origin of Amber Found at Hallstatt," *Acta Archaeologica*. Budapest.

Beck, C. W., E. Wilbur, and S. Meret
1964 "Infrared Spectra and the Origin of Amber," *Nature*, vol. 201, pp. 256–257. London.

Beck, C. W., E. Wilbur, S. Meret, D. Kossove, and K. Kermani
1965 "The Infrared Spectra of Amber and the Identification of Baltic Amber," *Archaeometry*, vol. 8, pp. 96–109. Oxford.

Bittel, K., and A. Rieth
1951 *Die Heuneburg an der oberen Donau*. Kohlhammer, Stuttgart.

Biel, J.
1978 "Das frühkeltische Fürstengrab von Eberdingen-Hochdorf, Landkreis Ludwigsburg," *Denkmalpflege in Baden-Württemberg*, vol. 7, pp. 168–175. Stuttgart.

Bloch, M. R.
1963 "The Social Influence of Salt," *Scientific American*, vol. 209, no. 1, pp. 88–96. New York.

Boardman, J., and F. Schweizer
1973 "Clay Analysis of Archaic Greek Pottery," *The Annals of the British School at Athens*, no. 68, pp. 267–283. London.

Bökönyi, S.
1968 "Data on Iron Age Horses of Central and Eastern Europe," in H. Hencken (ed.), *Mecklenburg Collection, Part I*. American School of Prehistoric Research, Bulletin 25, pp. 1–71. Peabody Museum, Harvard University, Cambridge, Mass.
1974 *History of Domestic Mammals in Central and Eastern Europe*. Akadémiai Kaidó, Budapest.

Bohnsack, D.
1976 "Bernstein und Bernsteinhandel," in J. Hoops (ed.), *Reallexikon der Germanischen Altertumskunde*, 2nd ed., vol. 2, pp. 290–292. Walter de Gruyter, Berlin.

Brandford, J. S.
1978 "The Textiles," in H. Hencken, *The Iron Age Cemetery of Magdalenska gora in Slovenia*. *Mecklenburg Collection, Part II*. American School of Prehistoric Research, Bulletin 32, pp. 301–310. Peabody Museum, Harvard University, Cambridge, Mass.

Braudel, F.
1972 *The Mediterranean and the Mediterranean World in the Age of Philip II*. Harper and Row, New York.

Carter, C. O.
1975 "Man's Need of Salt," in K. W. de Brisay and K. A. Evans (eds.), *Salt: The Study of an Ancient Industry*, p. 13. Colchester Archaeological Group, Colchester.

Cary, M.
1949 *The Geographic Background of Greek and Roman History*. Clarendon, Oxford.

Chang, K. C.
1975 "Ancient Trade as Economics or as Ecology," in J. A. Sabloff and C. C. Lamberg-Karlovsky (eds.), *Ancient Civilization and Trade*, pp. 211–224. University of New Mexico Press, Albuquerque.

Christlein, R.
1973 "Besitzabstufungen zur Merowingerzeit im

Spiegel reicher Grabfunde aus West- und Südwestdeutschland," *Jahrbuch des Römisch-Germanischen Zentralmuseums*, vol. 20, pp. 147–180. Mainz.

Cipolla, C. M.
1970 *The Economic History of World Population*, 5th ed. Penguin, Harmondsworth.

Clarke, D. L.
1968 *Analytical Archaeology*. Methuen, London.

Coghlan, H. H.
1975 *Notes on the Prehistoric Metallurgy of Copper and Bronze in the Old World*, 2nd ed. Pitt Rivers Museum, Oxford.
1977 *Notes on Prehistoric and Early Iron in the Old World*, 2nd ed. Pitt Rivers Museum, Oxford.

Collis, J.
1975 *Defended Sites of the Late La Tène in Central and Western Europe*. British Archaeological Reports, Supplementary Series, vol. 2. Oxford.

Cook, R. M.
1972 *Greek Painted Pottery*, 2nd ed. Methuen, London.

Čović, B., and S. Gabrovec
1971 "Age du Fer," in A. Benac, M. Garašanin, and N. Tasić (eds.), *Epoque préhistorique et protohistorique en Yougoslavie*, pp. 325–349. Comité National d'Organisation du VIIIe Congrès International des Sciences Préhistoriques et Protohistoriques, Belgrade.

Cowgill, G. L.
1975 "On Causes and Consequences of Ancient and Modern Population Changes," *American Anthropologist*, vol. 77, pp. 505–525. Washington, D.C.

Cunliffe, B.
1978 "Settlement and Population in the British Iron Age," in B. Cunliffe and T. Rowley (eds.), *Lowland Iron Age Communities in Europe*, pp. 3–24. British Archaeological Reports, International Series, vol. 48. Oxford.

Curtin, P. D.
1975 *Economic Change in Precolonial Africa*. University of Wisconsin Press, Madison.

Davies, O.
1935 *Roman Mines in Europe*. Clarendon, Oxford.

Dayet, M.
1967 "Recherches archéologiques au 'camp du Château' (Salins) (1955–1959)," *Revue archéologique de l'Est et du Centre-Est*, vol. 18, pp. 52–106. Dijon.

Deetz, J., and E. Dethlefsen
1967 "Death's Head, Cherub, Urn and Willow," *Natural History*, vol. 76, pp. 29–37. New York.

Dehn, W., and O.-H. Frey
1979 "Southern Imports and the Hallstatt and Early La Tène Chronology of Central Europe," in D. and F. R. Ridgway (eds.), *Italy Before the Romans*, pp. 489–511. Academic Press, New York.

Diaz, M. N., and J. M. Potter
1967 "The Social Life of Peasants," in J. M. Potter, M. N. Diaz, and G. M. Foster (eds.), *Peasant Society*, pp. 154–168. Little, Brown, Boston.

Donat, P., and H. Ullrich
1976 "Bevölkerungszahlen: Archäologie," in J. Hoops (ed.), *Reallexikon der Germanischen Altertumskunde*, 2nd ed., vol. 2, pp. 349–353. Walter de Gruyter, Berlin.

Drescher, H.
1958 *Der Überfangguss*. Römisch-Germanisches Zentralmuseum, Mainz.
1980 "Zur Technik der Hallstattzeit," in *Die Hallstattkultur*, pp. 54–66. Oberösterreichischer Landesverlag, Linz.

Drobne, K.
1973 "Favna koliščarskih naselbin na Ljubljanskem barju" [Fauna der Pfahlbautensiedlungen auf dem Moor von Ljubljana], *Arheološki Vestnik*, vol. 24, pp. 217–224. Ljubljana.

Duby, G.
1974 *The Early Growth of the European Economy*. Cornell University Press, Ithaca.

Dular, J.
1978 *Podzemelj*. Narodni muzej, Ljubljana.

Egg, M.
1978a "Ein italischer Kammhelm aus Hallstatt," *Archäologisches Korrespondenzblatt*, vol. 8, pp. 37–40. Mainz.
1978b "Das Grab eines unterkrainischen Kriegers in Hallstatt," *Archäologisches Korrespondenzblatt*, vol. 8, pp. 191–201. Mainz.

Egger, R.
1961 *Die Stadt auf dem Magdalensberg, ein Grosshandelsplatz: Die ältesten Aufzeichnungen des Metallwarenhandels auf dem Boden Österreichs*. Österreichische Akademie der Wissenschaften, Philosophisch-Historische Klasse, Denkschriften, vol. 79. Vienna.

Ehgartner, W., and A. Kloiber
1959 "Das anthropologische Material," in K. Kromer, *Das Gräberfeld von Hallstatt*, pp. 29–33. Sansoni, Florence.

Eibner, C.
1974 *Das späturnenfelderzeitliche Gräberfeld*

von *St. Andrä v. d. Hgt. P. B. Tulln, NÖ.* Archaeologia Austriaca, supplement, vol. 12. Vienna.

Eibner, C., L. Plank, and R. Pittioni
1966 "Die Urnengräber vom Lebenberg bei Kitzbühel, Tirol," *Archaeologia Austriaca*, vol. 40, pp. 215–248. Vienna.

Fél, E., and T. Hofer
1969 *Proper Peasants: Traditional Life in a Hungarian Village.* Wenner-Gren, New York.
1972 *Bäuerliche Denkweise in Wirtschaft und Haushalt.* Schwarz, Göttingen.

Filip, J.
1961 "Rod a rodina v předkeltském a keltském prostředí" [Sippe und Familie in der vorkeltischen und keltischen Umwelt], *Památky Archeologické*, vol. 52, pp. 282–296. Prague.

Firth, R.
1929 *Primitive Economics of the New Zealand Maori.* Routledge, London.
1961 *Elements of Social Organization*, 3rd ed. Beacon Press, Boston.

Fischer, F.
1973 "ΚΕΙΜΗΛΙΑ: Bemerkungen zur kulturgeschichtlichen Interpretation des sogenannten Südimports in der späten Hallstatt- und frühen Latène-Kultur des westlichen Mitteleuropa," *Germania*, vol. 51, pp. 436–459. Berlin.

Flannery, K. V.
1968 "The Olmec and the Valley of Oaxaca: A Model for Inter-Regional Interaction in Formative Times," in E. P. Benson (ed.), *Proceedings, Dumbarton Oaks Conference on the Olmec*, pp. 79–117. Dumbarton Oaks, Washington.

Foltiny, S.
1958 *Velemszentvid, ein urzeitliches Kulturzentrum in Mitteleuropa.* Veröffentlichungen der Österreichischen Arbeitsgemeinschaft für Ur- und Frühgeschichte, vol. 3. Vienna.

Frankenstein, S., and M. J. Rowlands
1978 "The Internal Structure and Regional Context of Early Iron Age Society in South-Western Germany," *Institute of Archaeology Bulletin* 15, pp. 73–112. London.

Frey, O.-H.
1966 "Der Ostalpenraum und die antike Welt in der frühen Eisenzeit," *Germania*, vol. 44, pp. 48–66. Berlin.
1969 *Die Entstehung der Situlenkunst.* Walter de Gruyter, Berlin.
1971 "Hallstatt und die Hallstattkultur," *Mitteilungen der Österreichischen Arbeitsgemeinschaft für Ur- und Frühgeschichte*, vol. 22, pp. 110–116. Vienna.
1973 "Bemerkungen zur hallstättischen Bewaffnung im Südostalpenraum," *Arheološki Vestnik*, vol. 24, pp. 621–636. Ljubljana.
1974a "Bericht über die Ausgrabungen im Ringwall von Stična (Slowenien)," in *Symposium zu Problemen der jüngeren Hallstattzeit in Mitteleuropa*, pp. 151–162. Vydavateľstvo Slovenskej Akadémie Vied, Bratislava.
1974b "Schwarz-rot gebänderte Keramik in der Zone südlich der Alpen," *Hamburger Beiträge zur Archäologie*, vol. 4, pp. 97–100. Hamburg.

Frey, O.-H., and S. Gabrovec
1971 "Zur Chronologie der Hallstattzeit im Ostalpenraum," *Actes du VIIIe Congrès International des Sciences Préhistoriques et Protohistoriques*, vol. 1, pp. 193–218. Belgrade.

Friedrich, O. M.
1958 "Das Gebiet der alten Goldwäscherei am Klienigbach bei Wiesenau, Kärnten," *Archaeologia Austriaca*, supplement, vol. 3, pp. 108–115. Vienna.

Gabrovec, S.
1960 "Grob z oklepom iz Novega mesta" [Panzergrab von Novo mesto], *Situla*, vol. 1, pp. 27–79. Ljubljana.
1962–63 "Halštatske čelade jugovyhodnoalpskega kroga" [Die hallstättischen Helme des südostalpinen Kreises], *Arheološki Vestnik*, vol. 13–14, pp. 293–347. Ljubljana.
1966 "Zur Hallstattzeit in Slowenien," *Germania*, vol. 44, pp. 1–48. Berlin.
1968 "Grob s trinožnikom iz Novega mesta" [Das Dreifussgrab aus Novo mesto], *Arheološki Vestnik*, vol. 19, pp. 157–188. Ljubljana.
1970 "Dvozankaste ločne fibule" [Die zweischleifigen Bogenfibeln], *Godišnjak*, vol. 8, pp. 5–65. Sarajevo.
1971 "Stična," in A. Benac, M. Garašanin, and N. Tasić (eds.), *Epoque préhistorique et protohistorique en Yougoslavie*, pp. 230–232. Comité National d'Organisation du VIIIe Congrès International des Sciences Préhistoriques et Protohistoriques, Belgrade.
1973 "Začetek halštatskega obdobje v Sloveniji" [Der Beginn der Hallstattzeit in Slowenien], *Arheološki Vestnik*, vol. 24, pp. 338–385. Ljubljana.
1974 "Die Ausgrabungen in Stična und ihre Bedeutung für die südostalpine Hallstattkultur," in *Symposium zu Problemen der jüngeren Hallstattzeit in Mitteleuropa*, pp.

163–187. Vydavatel'stvo Slovenskej Akadémie Vied, Bratislava.
1976 "Zum Beginn der Hallstattzeit in Slowenien," *Archaeologia Austriaca*, supplement 13, vol. 1, pp. 588–600. Vienna.
1980 "Der Beginn der Hallstattkultur und der Osten," in *Die Hallstattkultur*, pp. 30–53. Oberösterreichischer Landesverlag, Linz.

Gabrovec, S., O.-H. Frey, and S. Foltiny
1970 "Erster Vorbericht über die Ausgrabungen im Ringwall von Stična (Slowenien)," *Germania*, vol. 48, pp. 12–33. Berlin.

Gall, P. L., and A. A. Saxe
1977 "The Ecological Evolution of Culture," in T. K. Earle and J. E. Ericson (eds.), *Exchange Systems in Prehistory*, pp. 255–268. Academic Press, New York.

Gersbach, E.
1971 "Vorläufige Ergebnisse der Ausgrabungen im Bereich der Südostecke der Burg 1959–1969: Die Siedlungsstadien der Periode IV," in W. Kimmig and E. Gersbach, "Die Grabungen auf der Heuneburg 1966–1969," *Germania*, vol. 49, pp. 61–91. Berlin.

Grierson, P.
1959 "Commerce in the Dark Ages," *Transactions of the Royal Historical Society*, ser. 5, vol. 9, pp. 123–140. London.

Guštin, M.
1976 *Libna*. Posavski muzej, Brežice.
1978 "Gradišča železne dobe v Sloveniji" [Typologie der eisenzeitlichen Ringwälle in Slowenien], *Arheološki Vestnik*, vol. 29, pp. 100–112. Ljubljana.
1979 *Notranjska*. Narodni muzej, Ljubljana.

Haevernick, T. E.
1958 "Hallstatt-Tassen," *Jahrbuch des Römisch-Germanischen Zentralmuseums*, vol. 5, pp. 8–17. Mainz.
1974a "Zu den Glasperlen in Slowenien," *Situla*, vol. 14–15, pp. 61–65. Ljubljana.
1974b "Die Glasfunde aus den Gräbern vom Dürrnberg," in F. Moosleitner, L. Pauli, and E. Penninger, *Der Dürrnberg bei Hallein II*, pp. 143–152. Beck, Munich.
1978 "Urnenfelderzeitliche Glasperlen," *Zeitschrift für Schweizerische Archäologie und Kunstgeschichte*, vol. 35, pp. 145–157. Basel.
1979 "Die Glasperlen der Býcî Skála-Höhle," *Mitteilungen der Anthropologischen Gesellschaft in Wien*, vol. 119, pp. 113–119. Vienna.

Hampl, F.
1976 "Die bronzezeitliche Kupfergewinnung in Niederösterreich," *Archaeologia Austriaca*, supplement, vol. 14, pp. 58–67. Vienna.

Härke, H. G. H.
1979 *Settlement Types and Patterns in the West Hallstatt Province*. British Archaeological Reports, International Series, vol. 57. Oxford.

Häusler, A.
1968 "Kritische Bemerkungen zum Versuch soziologischer Deutungen ur- und frühgeschichtlicher Gräberfelder—erläutert am Beispiel des Gräberfeldes von Hallstatt," *Ethnographisch-Archäologische Zeitschrift*, vol. 9, pp. 1–30. East Berlin.

Hedinger, A.
1903 *Die vorgeschichtlichen Bernsteinartefakte und ihre Herkunft*. Trübner, Strassburg.

Hell, M.
1948 "Hausformen der Hallstattzeit aus Salzburg-Lieferung," *Archaeologia Austriaca*, vol. 1, pp. 57–71. Vienna.

Helm, O.
1877 "Notizen über die chemische und physikalische Beschaffenheit des Bernsteins," *Archiv der Pharmazie*, vol. 211, pp. 229–246. Berlin.

Hencken, H.
1968 "Introduction," in H. Hencken (ed.), *Mecklenburg Collection, Part I*. American School of Prehistoric Research, Bulletin 25, pp. v–vi. Peabody Museum, Harvard University, Cambridge, Mass.
1974 "Bracelets of Lead-Tin Alloy from Magdalenska gora," *Situla*, vol. 14–15, pp. 119–127. Ljubljana.
1978 *The Iron Age Cemetery of Magdalenska gora in Slovenia. Mecklenburg Collection. Part II*. American School of Prehistoric Research, Bulletin 32. Peabody Museum, Harvard University, Cambridge, Mass.

Herlihy, D.
1971 "The Economy of Traditional Europe," *Journal of Economic History*, vol. 31, pp. 153–164. New York.

Hildebrand, H.
1876 "Sur les commencements de l'âge de fer en Europe," *Compte Rendu, 7. Congrès International d'Anthropologie et d'Archéologie Préhistorique*, pp. 592–601. Stockholm.

Hodson, F. R.
1977 "Quantifying Hallstatt," *American Antiquity*, vol. 42, pp. 394–412. Menasha, Wisconsin.

Hoernes, M.
1905 "Die Hallstattperiode," *Archiv für Anthropologie*, vol. 31, pp. 233–281. Braunschweig.
1921 *Das Gräberfeld von Hallstatt, seine Zusam-*

mensetzung und Entwicklung. Kabitzsch, Leipzig.

Hoffmann, H.
1966   *Tarentine Rhyta*. Zabern, Mainz.

Hollstein, E.
1974   "Jahrringkurven aus dem prähistorischen Salzbergwerk in Hallstatt," *Archäologisches Korrespondenzblatt*, vol. 4, pp. 49–51. Mainz.

Holste, F.
1938   "Hügelgräber von Lochham, BA. München," in E. Sprockhoff (ed.), *Marburger Studien*, pp. 95–104. Wittich, Darmstadt.
1953   *Die Bronzezeit in Süd- und Westdeutschland*. Walter de Gruyter, Berlin.

Homans, G. C.
1942   *English Villagers of the Thirteenth Century*. Harvard University Press, Cambridge, Mass.
1967   *The Nature of Social Science*. Harcourt, Brace and World, New York.

Howells, W. W.
1973   *Cranial Variation in Man*. Peabody Museum Papers, vol. 67. Cambridge, Mass.

Hundt, H.-J.
1959   "Vorgeschichtliche Gewebe aus dem Hallstätter Salzberg," *Jahrbuch des Römisch-Germanischen Zentralmuseums*, vol. 6, pp. 66–100. Mainz.
1960   "Vorgeschichtliche Gewebe aus dem Hallstätter Salzberg," *Jahrbuch des Römisch-Germanischen Zentralmuseums*, vol. 7, pp. 126–150. Mainz.
1961   "Neunzehn Textilreste aus dem Dürrnberg in Hallein," *Jahrbuch des Römisch-Germanischen Zentralmuseums*, vol. 8, pp. 7–25. Mainz.
1967   "Vorgeschichtliche Gewebe aus dem Hallstätter Salzberg," *Jahrbuch des Römisch-Germanischen Zentralmuseums*, vol. 14, pp. 38–67. Mainz.
1970   "Gewebefunde aus Hallstatt: Webkunst und Tracht in der Hallstattzeit," in *Krieger und Salzherren: Hallstattkultur im Ostalpenraum*, pp. 53–71. Römisch-Germanisches Zentralmuseum, Mainz.

Jacobsthal, P.
1956   *Greek Pins*. Clarendon, Oxford.

Jankuhn, H.
1969   *Vor- und Frühgeschichte vom Neolithikum bis zur Völkerwanderungszeit*. Ulmer, Stuttgart.

Joffroy, R.
1954   *Le trésor de Vix (Côte-d'Or)*. Presses Universitaires de France, Paris.
1960   *L'oppidum de Vix et la civilisation hallstattienne finale dans l'Est de la France*. Bernigaud, Dijon.

Kahrstedt, U.
1927   *Studien zur politischen und Wirtschafts-Geschichte der Ost- und Zentralalpen vor Augustus*. Nachrichten von der Gesellschaft der Wissenschaften zu Göttingen, Phil.-Hist. Klasse, vol. 1, pp. 2–36.

Kappel, I.
1969   *Die Graphittonkeramik von Manching*. Steiner, Wiesbaden.

Kastelic, J.
1960   "Nov tip halštatskega diadema v Sloveniji" [A New Type of the Diadem from the Hallstatt Period in Slovenia], *Situla*, vol. 1, pp. 3–26. Ljubljana.
1965   *Situla Art*. McGraw-Hill, New York.

Kerchler, U.
1976   "Urzeitliche Kupferschmelzplätze im Gebiet des Kulmberges, in der Umgebung von Sieding und im Höllental, Niederösterreich," *Archaeologia Austriaca*, supplement, vol. 14, pp. 89–99. Vienna.

Kilian-Dirlmeier, I.
1969   "Studien zur Ornamentik auf Bronzeblechgürteln und Gürtelblechen der Hallstattzeit aus Hallstatt und Bayern," *Berichte der Römisch-Germanischen Kommission*, vol. 50, pp. 97–189. Berlin.
1971   "Beobachtungen zur Struktur des Gräberfeldes von Hallstatt," *Mitteilungen der Österreichischen Arbeitsgemeinschaft für Ur- und Frühgeschichte*, vol. 22, pp. 71–75. Vienna.
1973   Review of A. Lippert, *Welzelach. Jahrbuch des Römisch-Germanischen Zentralmuseums*, vol. 20, pp. 216–218. Mainz.
1974   "Zur späthallstattzeitlichen Nekropole von Mühlacker," *Germania*, vol. 52, pp. 141–146. Berlin.

Kimmig, W.
1964   "Seevölkerbewegung und Urnenfelderkultur," in R. von Uslar and K. J. Narr (eds.), *Studien aus Alteuropa*, vol. I, Bonner Jahrbücher, supplement, vol. 10/1, pp. 220–283. Cologne.
1969   "Zum Problem späthallstättischer Adelssitze," in K.-H. Otto and J. Herrmann (eds.), *Siedlung, Burg und Stadt*, pp. 95–113. Deutsche Akademie der Wissenschaften zu Berlin, Sektion für Vor- und Frühgeschichte, vol. 25. East Berlin.
1975a   "Die Heuneburg an der oberen Donau," in *Ausgrabungen in Deutschland 1950–1975*,

vol. I, pp. 192–211. Römisch-Germanisches Zentralmuseum, Mainz.
1975b "Early Celts on the Upper Danube: Excavations at the Heuneburg," in R. Bruce-Mitford (ed.), *Recent Archaeological Excavations in Europe*, pp. 32–64. Routledge and Kegan Paul, London.
1979 "Buchau," in J. Hoops (ed.), *Reallexikon der Germanischen Altertumskunde*, 2nd ed., vol. 4, pp. 37–55. Berlin.

Kimmig, W., and O.-W. von Vacano
1973 "Zu einem Gussform-Fragment einer etruskischen Bronzekanne von der Heuneburg a.d. oberen Donau," *Germania*, vol. 51, pp. 72–85. Berlin.

Klein, H.
1950 "Der Saumhandel über die Tauern," *Mitteilungen der Gesellschaft für Salzburger Landeskunde*, vol. 90, pp. 37–114. Salzburg.

Knez, T.
1966 "Žarno grobišče v Novem mestu" [Das Urnengräberfeld in Novo mesto], *Arheološki Vestnik*, vol. 17, pp. 51–101. Ljubljana.
1974 "Halštatski zlati diadem iz Novega mesta" [Ein hallstattzeitliches Golddiadem aus Novo mesto], *Situla*, vol. 14–15, pp. 115–118. Ljubljana.
1978 "Ein späthallstattzeitliches Fürstengrab von Novo mesto in Slowenien," *Germania*, vol. 56, pp. 125–149. Berlin.

Köhler, A., and F. Morton
1954 "Mineralogische Untersuchung prähistorischer Keramik aus Hallstatt im Zusammenhang mit der Frage nach ihrer Herkunft," *Germania*, vol. 32, pp. 66–72. Berlin.

Koreisl, W.
1934 "Speisebeigaben in Gräbern der Hallstattzeit Mitteleuropas," *Mitteilungen der Anthropologischen Gesellschaft in Wien*, vol. 64, pp. 229–264. Vienna.

Kossack, G.
1959 *Südbayern während der Hallstattzeit*. Walter de Gruyter, Berlin.
1970 *Gräberfelder der Hallstattzeit an Main und Fränkischer Saale*. Lassleben, Kallmünz.
1972 "Hallstattzeit," in O. Kunkel (ed.), *Vor- und frühgeschichtliche Archäologie in Bayern*, pp. 85–100. Bayerischer Schulbuch-Verlag, Munich.
1974 "Prunkgräber," in G. Kossack and G. Ulbert (eds.), *Festschrift J. Werner*, pp. 3–33. Beck, Munich.

Krämer, W.
1964 *Das keltische Gräberfeld von Nebringen (Kreis Böblingen)*. Silberburg, Stuttgart.

Kromer, K.
1958 "Gedanken über den sozialen Aufbau der Bevölkerung auf dem Salzberg bei Hallstatt, Oberösterreich," *Archaeologia Austriaca*, vol. 24, pp. 39–58. Vienna.
1959a *Das Gräberfeld von Hallstatt*. Sansoni, Florence.
1959b *Brezje*. Narodni muzej, Ljubljana.
1963 *Hallstatt: Die Salzhandelsmetropole des ersten Jahrtausends vor Christus in den Alpen*. Naturhistorisches Museum, Vienna.
1964 *Von frühem Eisen und reichen Salzherren: Die Hallstattkultur in Österreich*. Im Wollzeilen, Vienna.

La Baume, W.
1935 "Zur Naturkunde und Kulturgeschichte des Bernsteins," *Schriften der naturforschenden Gesellschaft in Danzig*, n. s. vol. 20, pp. 5–48. Danzig.

Langer, G.
1936 "Der prähistorische Bergmann im Hallstätter Salzberge," *Berg- und Hüttenmännisches Jahrbuch*, vol. 84, no. 4, pp. 149–170. Vienna.

Laslett, P.
1973 *The World We Have Lost*, 2nd ed. Charles Scribner's Sons, New York.

Lehr, R.
1978 *Das Salzbergwerk Hallstatt*. Generaldirektion der Österreichischen Salinen, Bad Ischl.

Linton, R.
1936 *The Study of Man*. Appleton-Century, New York.

Lipp, F. C.
1976 "Hallstatt-Blockhaus und Dachstein-Almhütten," *Archaeologia Austriaca*, supplement, vol. 13, pp. 611–633. Vienna.

Lippert, A.
1970 "Früheisenzeitliche Funde aus Zedlach, K. G. Matrei, p. B. Lienz, Osttirol," *Archaeologia Austriaca*, vol. 48, pp. 8–18. Vienna.
1972 *Das Gräberfeld von Welzelach (Osttirol)*. Habelt, Bonn.

Ložar, R.
1934 "Predzgodovina Slovenije, posebej Kranjske, v luči zbirke Mecklenburg" [Die Vorgeschichte Sloweniens, insbesondere Krains, im Lichte der Sammlung Mecklenburg], *Glasnik muzejskega društva za Slovenijo*, vol. 15, pp. 5–91. Ljubljana.
1937a "Situla iz Griz pri Stični" [Eine neue Situla aus Krain], *Glasnik muzejskega društva za Slovenijo*, vol. 18, pp. 1–14. Ljubljana.
1937b "Bronasti oklep z Vrhpolja pri Stični," *Glas-*

nik musejskega društva za Slovenijo, vol. 18, pp. 73–86. Ljubljana.

Lucke, W., and O.-H. Frey
1962 *Die Situla in Providence (Rhode Island)*. Walter de Gruyter, Berlin.

Mahr, A.
1925 *Das vorgeschichtliche Hallstatt*. Österreichische Bundesverlag, Vienna.

Mahr, A. (ed.)
1934 *Treasures of Carniola: The Unique Collection of Prehistoric Antiquities Excavated by H. H. The Late Duchess Paul Friedrich of Mecklenburg*. American Art Association, New York.

Maier, F.
1974 "Gedanken zur Entstehung der industriellen Grosssiedlung der Hallstatt- und Latènezeit auf dem Dürrnberg bei Hallein," *Germania*, vol. 52, pp. 326–347. Berlin.

Malinowski, T.
1971 "Über den Bernsteinhandel zwischen den südlichen baltischen Ufergebieten und dem Süden Europas in der frühen Eisenzeit," *Praehistorische Zeitschrift*, vol. 46, pp. 102–110. Berlin.

Martin, R.
1928 *Lehrbuch der Anthropologie*, 2nd ed. Fischer, Jena.

Massaro, D.
1943 "Le ambre di Vetulonia," *Studi Etruschi*, vol. 17, pp. 31–45. Florence.

Mauss, M.
1967 *The Gift: Forms and Functions of Exchange in Archaic Societies*. Norton, New York.

McEvedy, C., and R. Jones
1978 *Atlas of World Population History*. Penguin, Harmondsworth.

Medwenitsch, W.
1954 "Die Geologie von Hallstatt," in F. Morton, *Hallstatt: Die letzten einhundertfünfzig Jahre des Bergmannsortes*, pp. 124–130. Musealverein, Hallstatt.

Meyer, A. B.
1885 *Das Gräberfeld von Hallstatt*. Hoffman, Dresden.

von Miske, K.
1929 "Bergbau, Verhüttung und Metallbearbeitungswerkzeuge aus Velem St. Veit (Westungarn)," *Weiner Prähistorische Zeitschrift*, vol. 16, pp. 81–94. Vienna.

Mócsy, A.
1974 *Pannonia and Upper Moesia*. Routledge and Kegan Paul, London.

Modrijan, W.
1957 "Das hallstattzeitliche Gräberfeld von Frög, Kärnten," *Carinthia I*, vol. 147, pp. 3–42. Klagenfurt.
1963 "Das hallstattzeitliche Gräberfeld von Leoben-Hinterberg," *Schild von Steier*, vol. 2, pp. 3–15. Graz.

Molnar, S.
1971 "Human Tooth Wear, Tooth Function and Cultural Variability," *American Journal of Physical Anthropology*, vol. 34, pp. 175–189. Philadelphia.

Moosleitner, F.
1977 "Hallstattzeitliche Grabfunde aus Uttendorf im Pinzgau (Österreich)," *Archäologisches Korrespondenzblatt*, vol. 7, pp. 115–119. Mainz.

Morton, F.
1949 "Zur Frage der Grubenarbeit im Hallstätter Salzbergwerk," *Archaeologia Austriaca*, vol. 2, pp. 68–75. Vienna.
1951 "Analyse einer hallstattzeitlichen Eisenschlacke aus Hallstatt," *Germania*, vol. 29, pp. 70–71. Berlin.
1953 *Hallstatt und die Hallstattzeit*. Musealverein, Hallstatt.
1954 *Hallstatt: Die letzten einhundertfünfzig Jahre des Bergmannsortes*. Musealverein, Hallstatt.
1956 *Salzkammergut: Die Vorgeschichte einer berühmten Landschaft*. Musealverein, Hallstatt.
1959 "Die 'Hallstatt'," in K. Kromer, *Das Gräberfeld von Hallstatt*, pp. 3–6. Sansoni, Florence.

Müller-Karpe, H.
1952 "Das Kriegergrab von Villach," in *Festschrift R. Egger*, vol. I, pp. 104–113. Geschichtsverein für Kärnten, Klagenfurt.
1955 "Das urnenfelderzeitliche Wagengrab von Hart a.d. Alz, Oberbayern," *Bayerische Vorgeschichtsblätter*, vol. 21, pp. 46–75. Munich.
1959 *Beiträge zur Chronologie der Urnenfelderzeit nördlich und südlich der Alpen*. Walter de Gruyter, Berlin.

Müllner, A.
1908 *Geschichte des Eisens in Innerösterreich von der Urzeit bis zum Anfang des XIX Jahrhunderts*. Part I: *Krain, Küstenland und Istrien*. Von Halm and Goldmann, Vienna.

Muhly, J. D.
1973 *Copper and Tin*. Connecticut Academy of Arts and Sciences, Transaction 43. New Haven.

Multhauf, R. P.
1978 *Neptune's Gift: A History of Common Salt*.

Johns Hopkins University Press, Baltimore.

Mutton, A. F. A.
- 1961 *Central Europe: A Regional and Human Geography*. Longmans, London.

de Navarro, J. M.
- 1934 "The Finds from Hallstatt in the Mecklenburg Collection," in A. Mahr (ed.), *Treasures of Carniola*, pp. 69–72. New York.

Nebehay, S.
- 1980 "Hallstatts zweite Ausgrabung," *Oberösterreich*, vol. 30, no. 1, pp. 29–36. Linz.

Nenquin, J.
- 1961 *Salt: A Study in Economic Prehistory*. De Tempel, Brugge.

Neuninger, H., and R. Pittioni
- 1959 "Woher stammen die blauen Glasperlen der Urnenfelderkultur?" *Archaeologia Austriaca*, vol. 26, pp. 52–66. Vienna.
- 1961 "Nachtrag zu den blauen Glasperlen der Urnenfelderkultur," *Archaeologia Austriaca*, vol. 30, pp. 150–151. Vienna.

Neuninger, H., R. Pittioni, and E. Preuschen
- 1969 *Salzburgs Kupfererzlagerstätten und Bronzefunde aus dem Lande Salzburg*. Archaeologia Austriaca, supplement, vol. 9. Vienna.

Pahič, S.
- 1957 *Drugo žarno grobišče v Rušah* [Das zweite Urnenfeld in Ruše]. Slovenska Akademija Znanosti in Umetnosti, Ljubljana.
- 1972 *Pobrežje*. Narodni muzej, Ljubljana.
- 1973 "Najdišča starejše železne dobe v Podravju" [Fundstätten der frühen Eisenzeit im slowenischen Drauland], *Arheološki Vestnik*, vol. 24, pp. 521–543. Ljubljana.

Pauli, L.
- 1972 *Untersuchungen zur Späthallstattkultur in Nordwürttemberg*. Helmut Buske, Hamburg.
- 1974 "Der Goldene Steig: Wirtschaftsgeographisch-archäologische Untersuchungen im östlichen Mitteleuropa," in G. Kossack and G. Ulbert (eds.), *Studien zur vor- und frühgeschichtlichen Archäologie, Festschrift J. Werner*, pp. 115–139. Beck, Munich.
- 1975a *Die Gräber vom Salzberg zu Hallstatt*. Philipp von Zabern, Mainz.
- 1975b *Keltische Volksglaube*. Beck, Munich.
- 1978 *Der Dürrnberg bei Hallein III*. Beck, Munich.
- 1979 "Blockwandhäuser am Hallstätter Salzberg?" *Archäologisches Korrespondenzblatt*, vol. 9, pp. 81–86. Mainz.
- 1980 *Die Alpen in Frühzeit und Mittelalter*. Beck, Munich.

Peroni, R.
- 1973 *Studi di cronologia hallstattiana*. De Luca, Rome.
- 1979 "From Bronze Age to Iron Age: Economic, Historical and Social Considerations," in D. and F. R. Ridgway (eds.), *Italy Before the Romans*, pp. 7–30. Academic Press, New York.

Pertlwieser, M.
- 1969 "Die hallstattzeitliche Höhensiedlung auf dem Waschenberg bei Bad Wimsbach/Neydharting, Politischer Bezirk Wels, Oberösterreich: Part I: Die Anlage," *Jahrbuch des Oberösterreichischen Musealvereins*, vol. 114, pp. 29–48. Linz.
- 1970 "Die hallstattzeitliche Höhensiedlung auf dem Waschenberg bei Bad Wimsbach/Neydharting, Politischer Bezirk Wels, Oberösterreich: Part II: Die Objekte," *Jahrbuch des Oberösterreichischen Musealvereins*, vol. 115, pp. 37–70. Linz.

Petersen, W.
- 1975 "A Demographer's View of Prehistoric Demography," *Current Anthropology*, Vol. 16, pp. 227–237. Chicago.

Phillips, P.
- 1972 "Population, Economy and Society in the Chassey-Cortaillod-Lagozza Cultures," *World Archaeology*, vol. 4, pp. 41–56. London.

Piaskowski, J.
- 1970 "The Achievements of Research Carried Out in Poland on the History of Early Technology of Iron," *Archaeologia Polona*, vol. 12, pp. 187–215. Warsaw.

Piggott, S.
- 1977 "A Glance at Cornish Tin," in V. Markotic (ed.), *Ancient Europe and the Mediterranean*, pp. 141–145. Aris and Phillips, Warminster.

Pirenne, H.
- 1937 *Economic and Social History of Medieval Europe*. Harcourt, Brace, New York.

Pittioni, R.
- 1949 "Spektralanalytische Untersuchungen von Bronzen aus Hallstatt, O.-Ö.," *Mitteilungen der Prähistorischen Kommission der Akademie der Wissenschaften*, vol. 5, no. 4, pp. 101–125. Vienna.
- 1951 "Prehistoric Copper-Mining in Austria," *Institute of Archaeology Bulletin* 7, pp. 16–43. London.
- 1952 "Das Brandgrab vom Lebenberg bei Kitzbühel, Tirol," *Archaeologia Austriaca*, vol. 10, pp. 53–60. Vienna.

1954 *Urgeschichte des Österreichischen Raumes.* Franz Deuticke, Vienna.

1976a "Bergbau: Salz," in J. Hoops (ed.), *Reallexikon der Germanischen Altertumskunde,* 2nd ed., vol. 2, pp. 256–258. Walter de Gruyter, Berlin.

1976b "Bergbau: Kupfererz," in J. Hoops (ed.), *Reallexikon der Germanischen Altertumskunde,* 2nd ed., vol. 2, pp. 251–256. Walter de Gruyter, Berlin.

Pleiner, R.

1962 *Staré Evropské Kovářství* [Alteuropäisches Schmiedehandwerk]. Československá Akademie Ved, Prague.

1968 "Schmiedetechnik der Hallstattzeit im Lichte der Untersuchung des Hortfundes von Schlöben," *Archeologické Rozhledy,* vol. 20, pp. 33–42. Prague.

1980 "Early Iron Metallurgy in Europe," in T. A. Wertime and J. D. Muhly (eds.), *The Coming of the Age of Iron,* pp. 375–415. Yale University Press, New Haven.

Plöckinger, E.

1976 "Untersuchungen an hallstattzeitlichen Eisenwerkzeugen," *Archaeologia Austriaca,* supplement, vol. 14, pp. 142–152. Vienna.

Polanyi, K.

1944 *The Great Transformation.* Rinehart, New York.

1957 "The Economy as Instituted Process," in K. Polanyi, C. M. Arensberg, and H. W. Pearson (eds.), *Trade and Market in the Early Empires,* pp. 243–270. Free Press, New York.

Polenz, H.

1978 "Einige Bemerkungen zum figuralverzierten Bronzedeckel aus Grab 697 von Hallstatt," *Mitteilungen der Anthropologischen Gesellschaft in Wien,* vol. 108, pp. 127–139. Vienna.

Polybius

  The Histories. Translation by W. R. Paton. Harvard University, Cambridge, Mass. (1954)

Pounds, N. J. G.

1969 *Eastern Europe.* Longmans, London.

Prag, A. J. N. W., F. Schweizer, J. Ll. W. Williams, and P. A. Schubiger

1974 "Hellenistic Glazed Wares from Athens and Southern Italy: Analytical Techniques and Implications," *Archaeometry,* vol. 16, pp. 153–187. Oxford.

Presslinger, H., C. Eibner, G. Walach, and G. Sperl

1980 "Ergebnis der Erforschung urnenfelderzeitlicher Kupfermetallurgie im Paltental," *Berg- und Hüttenmännische Monatshefte,* vol. 125, pp. 131–142. Vienna.

Puš, I.

1971 *Žarnogrobiščna nekropola na dvorišču SAZU v Ljubljani* [Nekropole der Urnenfelderkultur im Hof der Slowenischen Akademie der Wissenschaften und Künste in Ljubljana]. Slovenska Akademija Znanosti in Umetnosti, Ljubljana.

Quillian, C. C.

1980 "The Plant Remains at Hascherkeller, an Early Iron Age Settlement in Bavaria." Senior Honors Thesis, Department of Anthropology, Harvard University, Cambridge, Mass.

Rathje, W. L.

1970 "Socio-political Implications of Lowland Maya Burials," *World Archaeology,* vol. 1, pp. 359–374. London.

Read, C. H., and R. A. Smith

1916 "On a Collection of Antiquities from the Early Iron Age Cemetery of Hallstatt," *Archaeologia,* vol. 67, pp. 145–162. London.

Redfield, R.

1953 *The Primitive World and Its Transformations.* Cornell University Press, Ithaca.

Reinecke, P.

1900 "Brandgräber vom Beginne der Hallstattzeit aus den östlichen Alpenländern und die Chronologie des Gräberfeldes von Hallstatt," *Mitteilungen der Anthropologischen Gesellschaft in Wien,* vol. 30, pp. 44–49. Vienna.

1958 "Einführgut oder Beutegut?" *Bonner Jahrbücher,* vol. 158, pp. 246–252. Bonn.

Reitinger, J.

1968 *Die ur- und frühgeschichtlichen Funde in Oberösterreich.* Oberösterreichischer Landesverlag, Linz.

1969 *Oberösterreich in ur- und frühgeschichtlicher Zeit.* Oberösterreichischer Landesverlag, Linz.

Ridgway, F. R.

1979 "The Este and Golasecca Cultures: A Chronological Guide," in D. and F. R. Ridgway (eds.), *Italy Before the Romans,* pp. 419–487. Academic Press, London.

Rieth, A.

1942 *Die Eisentechnik der Hallstattzeit.* Barth, Leipzig.

Rogers, E. A., and F. Shoemaker

1971 *The Communication of Innovations.* Free Press, New York.

von Sacken, E.

1868 *Das Grabfeld von Hallstatt in Oberösterreich und seine Altertümer.* Braumüller, Vienna.

Sahlins, M.
1972a "The Spirit of the Gift," in *Stone Age Economics*, pp. 149–183. Aldine, Chicago.
1972b *Stone Age Economics*. Aldine, Chicago.

Šašel, J.
1977 "Strabo, Ocra and Archaeology," in V. Markotic (ed.), *Ancient Europe and the Mediterranean*, pp. 157–160. Aris and Phillips, Warminster.

Schauberger, O.
1960 *Ein Rekonstruktionsversuch der prähistorischen Grubenbaue im Hallstätter Salzberg*. Anthropologische Gesellschaft, Vienna.
1976 "Neue Aufschlüsse im 'Heidengebirge' von Hallstatt und Dürrnberg/Hallein," *Mitteilungen der Anthropologischen Gesellschaft in Wien*, vol. 106, pp. 154–160. Vienna.

Scheibenreiter, F.
1954 *Das hallstattzeitliche Gräberfeld von Hadersdorf am Kamp, N.-Ö.* Urgeschichtliche Arbeitsgemeinschaft, Vienna.

Schiek, S.
1959 "Vorbericht über die Ausgrabung des vierten Fürstengrabhügels bei der Heuneburg," *Germania*, vol. 37, pp. 117–131. Berlin.

Schmid, W.
1933 "Die Fürstengräber von Klein Glein in Steiermark," *Praehistorische Zeitschrift*, vol. 24, pp. 219–282. Berlin.

Schuchhardt, C.
1935 *Vorgeschichte von Deutschland*, 3rd ed. R. Oldenbourg, Munich.

Schultz, M.
1978 "Pathologische Veränderungen an den Dürrnberger Skeletten," in L. Pauli, *Der Dürrnberg bei Hallein III*, pp. 583–600. Beck, Munich.

Schumacher, E.
1978 Review of R. Peroni, *Studi di cronologia hallstattiana*. *Germania*, vol. 56, pp. 269–280. Berlin.

Schwab, H.
1975 "Châtillon-sur-Glâne," *Germania*, vol. 53, pp. 79–84. Berlin.

Schweitzer, R.
1973 "Le Britzgyberg," *Bulletin du Musée Historique de Mulhouse*, vol. 81, pp. 43–64. Mulhouse.

Semple, E. C.
1931 *The Geography of the Mediterranean Region: Its Relation to Ancient History*. Henry Holt, New York.

Service, E. R.
1962 *Primitive Social Organization*. Random House, New York.

Shennan, S.
1975 "The Social Organization at Branč," *Antiquity*, vol. 49, pp. 279–288. Cambridge.

Sherratt, A. G.
1972 "Socio-Economic and Demographic Models for the Neolithic and Bronze Ages of Europe," in D. L. Clarke (ed.), *Models in Archaeology*, pp. 477–542. Methuen, London.

Simony, F.
1851 *Die Altertümer vom Hallstätter Salzberg und dessen Umgebung*. Akademie der Wissenschaften, Vienna.

Specht, W.
1972 "Der Inhalt der Flasche," in E. Penninger, *Der Dürrnberg bei Hallein I*, pp. 124–128. Beck, Munich.

Spindler, K.
1975 "Grabfunde der Hallstattzeit vom Magdalenenberg bei Villingen im Schwarzwald," in *Ausgrabungen in Deutschland 1950–1975*, vol. I, pp. 221–242. Römisch-Germanisches Zentralmuseum, Mainz.

Starè, F.
1954 *Ilirske najdbe zelezne dobe v Ljubljani* [Illyrische Funde aus der Eisenzeit in Ljubljana]. Slovenska Akademija Znanosti in Umetnosti, Ljubljana.
1955 *Vače*. Narodni muzej, Ljubljana.
1975a *Etruscani in jugovzhodni predalpski prostor* [Die Etrusker und der südöstliche Voralpenraum]. Slovenska Akademija Znanosti in Umetnosti, Ljubljana.
1975b *Dobova*. Posavski muzej, Brežice.

Stare, V.
1973a *Prazgodovina Šmarjete*. Narodni muzej, Ljubljana.
1973b "Kultne palice iz Šmarjete" [Kultstäbe aus Šmarjeta], *Arheološki Vestnik*, vol. 24, pp. 730–743. Ljubljana.

Stjernquist, B.
1967 *Cista a Cordoni*. Habelt, Bonn.

Strabo
The Geography. Translation by H. J. Jones. Harvard University, Cambridge, Mass. (1917).

Strickon, A.
1979 "Ethnicity and Entrepreneurship in Rural Wisconsin," in S. M. Greenfield, A. Strickon, and R. T. Aubey (eds.), *Entrepreneurship in Cultural Context*, pp. 159–189. University of New Mexico Press, Albuquerque.

Strong, D. E.
1966 *Catalogue of the Carved Amber in the De-*

partment of *Greek and Roman Antiquities*. British Museum, London.

Sundström, L.
1974 *The Exchange Economy of Pre-Colonial Tropical Africa*. St. Martin's Press, New York.

Svoljšak, D.
1974 "Raziskovanje prazgodovinske naselbine na Mostu na Soči" [Research of the Prehistorical Settlement at Most na Soči (St. Lucia)], *Goriški Letnik: Zbornik Goriškega Muzeja*, pp. 5–32. Nova Gorica.

Szombathy, J.
1890 "Urgeschichtliche Forschungen in der Umgebung von Wies in Mittel-Steiermark. VI: Schlussbemerkungen," *Mitteilungen der Anthropologischen Gesellschaft in Wien*, vol. 20, pp. 170–196. Vienna.
1937 "Altertumsfunde aus Höhlen bei St. Kanzian im österreichischen Küstenlande," *Mitteilungen der Prähistorischen Kommission der Akademie der Wissenschaften*, vol. 2, pp. 127–190. Vienna.

Teržan, B.
1978 "O Halštatski noši na Križni gora [Über das Trachtzubehör auf Križna gora], *Arheološki Vestnik*, vol. 29, pp. 55–63. Ljubljana.

de Tompa, F.
1934 "The Cemetery at Št. Vid pri Stični (St. Veit near Sittich)," in A. Mahr (ed.), *Treasures of Carniola*, pp. 57–62. American Art Association, New York.

Tylecote, R. F.
1976 *A History of Metallurgy*. The Metals Society, London.

Ucko, P.
1969 "Ethnography and Archaeological Interpretation of Funerary Remains," *World Archaeology*, vol. 1, pp. 262–280. London.

Urleb, M.
1974 *Križna gora pri Ložu*. Narodni muzej, Ljubljana.

Vogt, E.
1949–50 "Der Beginn der Hallstattzeit in der Schweiz," *Jahrbuch der Schweizerischen Gesellschaft für Urgeschichte*, vol. 40, pp. 209–231. Zurich.

Walker, D. E. (ed.)
1972 *The Emergent Native Americans*. Little, Brown, Boston.

Wankel, H.
1882 *Bilder aus der Mährischen Schweiz*. Holzhausen, Vienna.

Waterbolk, H. T.
1964 "The Bronze Age Settlement of Elp," *Helinium*, vol. 4, pp. 97–131. Wetteren, Belgium.

Wells, P. S.
1977 "Late Hallstatt Interactions with the Mediterranean," in V. Markotic (ed.), *Ancient Europe and the Mediterranean*, pp. 189–196. Aris and Phillips, Warminster.
1978a "The Excavations at Stična in Slovenia by the Duchess of Mecklenburg, 1905–1914," *Journal of Field Archaeology*, vol. 5, pp. 215–226. Boston.
1978b "Twenty-Six Graves from Hallstatt Excavated by the Duchess of Mecklenburg," *Germania*, vol. 56, pp. 66–88. Berlin.
1978c "Eine bronzene Rinderfigur aus Hallstatt," *Archäologisches Korrespondenzblatt*, vol. 8, pp. 107–109. Mainz.
1978d "A Bronze Figure from Stična in Slovenia," *Archaeological News*, vol. 7, pp. 73–82. Tallahassee.
1979 "The Early Iron Age Settlement of Hascherkeller in Bavaria: 1978 Excavations," *Journal of Field Archaeology*, vol. 6, pp. 17–28. Boston.
1980a *Culture Contact and Culture Change: Early Iron Age Central Europe and the Mediterranean World*. Cambridge University Press, Cambridge.
1980b "The Early Iron Age Settlement of Hascherkeller in Bavaria: 1979 Excavations," *Journal of Field Archaeology*, vol. 7, pp. 313–328. Boston.

Werneck, H. L.
1961 "Ur- und frühgeschichtliche sowie mittelalterliche Kulturpflanzen und Hölzer aus dem Ostalpen und dem südlichen Böhmerwald," *Archaeologia Austriaca*, vol. 30, pp. 61–117. Vienna.
1969 *Pflanzenreste aus der Stadt auf dem Magdalensberg bei Klagenfurt in Kärnten*. Landesmuseum für Kärnten, Klagenfurt.

Will, E.
1955-56 "Archéologie et histoire économique," *Etudes d'Archéologie Classique*, vol. 1, pp. 149–166. Paris.

Willvonseder, K.
1950 "Das Urnenfeld von Wels (O.-Ö.)," *Archaeologia Austriaca*, vol. 7, pp. 16–56. Vienna.

Wurmbrand, G.
1879 "Das Urnenfeld von Maria Rast," *Archiv für Anthropologie*, vol. 11, pp. 231–280, 399–440. Braunschweig.

Wyss, R.
1969 "Wirtschaft und Technik," in W. Drack (ed.), *Ur- und frühgeschichtliche Archäologie der Schweiz, II: Die Jüngere Stein-*

zeit, pp. 117–138. Schweizerische Gesellschaft für Ur- und Frühgeschichte, Basel.
1971 "Siedlungswesen und Verkehrswege," in W. Drack (ed.), Ur- und frühgeschichtliche Archäologie der Schweiz, III: Die Bronzezeit, pp. 103–122. Schweizerische Gesellschaft für Ur- und Frühgeschichte, Basel.

Zürn, H.
1970 "Der 'Grafenbühl' bei Asperg, Kr. Ludwigsburg," in Hallstattforschungen in Nordwürttemberg, pp. 7–51. Müller and Gräff, Stuttgart.

Index

The index includes principal sites mentioned in the text, some categories of objects important to the discussion in Part II, and major topics covered in that section.

Adria, 113
Amber, 19, 20, 26, 28, 36–37, 48, 49, 50, 52, 53, 54, 55, 56, 58, 59, 60, 62, 63, 64, 65, 66, 68, 69, 70, 71, 72, 73, 74, 75, 76, 77, 79, 80, 81, 82, 83, 84, 85, 86, 87, 88–89, 108, 111–112, 113, 115, 116, 117, 119, 121, 122, 127. *See also* trade
Attic pottery, 52, 114, 115, 121
Augsdorf, 123
Axe, 21, 23, 24, 26, 28, 49, 54, 56, 58, 59, 64, 65, 71, 75, 78, 82, 83, 84, 86, 88–89, 103, 104, 107, 109, 118, 119, 122, 123, 126
Brezje, 71, 94, 95, 99, 109
Bronze production. *See* manufacturing; mining; trade
Bruck an der Mur, 123
Burgstall at Wies, 95, 96, 99, 101
Býcî Skála, 103
Cermožišče, 123
Change, culture, 93, 101, 116, 118–120, 122–128
Chronology, 2, 12, 30, 45, 47
    absolute, 2, 12, 30
    radiocarbon dates, 10–11, 42, 126
Copper. *See* mining; trade
Craft specialization, 105, 107, 108, 109, 124, 125, 126
Črmošnjice, 123
Cuirasse, 62, 89, 104, 105, 110, 118, 119, 122, 125
Dagger, 86, 113, 119, 123
Demography. *See* population
Dobova, 95, 101, 104, 106, 110, 111, 117, 118
Dürrnberg, 2, 18, 29, 43, 95, 108, 114, 115, 121, 128
Este, 113, 114
Etruscan imports, 112, 114, 115
Frög, 95, 99, 100
Gift exchange, 115, 128
Glass
    beads, 20, 25, 26, 28, 48, 49, 50, 51, 53, 54, 55, 56, 57, 58, 60, 61, 62, 63, 65, 66, 67, 68, 69, 70, 71, 73, 74, 75, 76, 77, 80, 81, 82, 83, 86, 87, 88–89, 93, 105–106, 107, 109, 116, 117, 119, 122, 125
    vessels, 114
    See also manufacturing; trade

Gold, 28, 51, 53, 59, 63, 69, 73, 89, 93, 106, 108, 109, 114, 117, 121
Grafenbühl, 108, 115, 119, 121
Graphite. *See* trade
Hadersdorf, 95, 101, 102, 104, 106, 110, 111, 118
Haidach, 123
Hallstatt, *passim*
Helmet, 12, 71, 75, 80, 84, 104, 105, 109, 110, 114, 118, 119, 121, 125
Heuneburg, 93, 105, 115
Hoard, 97, 110, 111, 122, 123, 125, 126, 127
Hochdorf, 108, 115, 121
Hohenasperg, 93
Individual as agent of change, 122, 123–124, 128
Iron. *See* manufacturing; mining; trade
Jurka vas, 123
Kitzbühel, 95, 102, 104, 105, 125
Kleinklein, 95, 100, 118, 119
Križna gora, 95, 101, 104, 106, 110, 111, 118, 121
Kuffarn, 29
Lebenberg (Kitzbühel), 102, 105, 109, 125
Libna, 94, 95, 96, 99, 100, 106, 109, 117
Magdalenenberg, 119
Magdalensberg, 128
Magdalenska gora, 1, 2, 13, 47, 94, 95, 98, 99, 100, 101, 102, 104, 106, 110, 111, 114, 118, 119, 120
Manufacturing, 101–109
    bronze, 103–105, 126–127
    glass, 105–106, 109, 127
    gold, 106
    iron, 96, 101–103, 107, 108–109, 123–126, 127, 128
    models for organization of, 107–109, 124–127
Mining, 107–109
    copper, 103–105, 107–109, 110, 122, 126
    iron, 102–103, 108–109
    salt, 7, 10–11, 12, 107–109
    models for organization of, 107–109
Mitterberg, 95, 104
Mixnitz, 123
Mont Lassois, 93, 115

Most na Soči, 94, 95, 96, 114
Mühlacker, 99, 120
Novo mesto, 95, 101, 104, 106, 110, 111, 114, 118, 119
Oil. *See* trade
Oppida, 93, 128
Pliny, 111
Pobrežje, 95, 101, 104, 106, 110, 111, 118
Podzemelj, 94, 106
Polybius, 114
Population, 93–94, 97–101, 108, 109, 117–118, 119–120, 122, 125, 126
Ruše, 95, 101, 102, 104, 106, 110, 111, 118
Salt, 7, 25, 39, 112–113. *See also* mining
St. Andrä, 2, 95, 99, 100, 101, 102, 104, 106, 110, 111, 117, 118, 120
Situla, 12, 29, 97, 109, 114, 115, 118, 119, 128
Škocjan, 95, 102
Slavery, 108
Šmarjeta, 94, 95, 100, 106, 117
Social organization, 12, 94, 108, 115, 116–122, 124–126
Spear, 19, 21, 26, 28, 30, 50, 54, 56, 58, 59, 62, 63, 64, 71, 74, 75, 80, 82, 83, 84, 86, 88–89, 103, 104, 105, 107, 109, 119, 122, 123
Spina, 113
Špure, 123
Stična, *passim*
Strabo, 113, 114, 115, 127, 128
Strassengel, 123
Subsistence, 96–97, 113
Sword, 23, 24, 26, 28, 30, 102, 103, 104, 105, 108, 110, 113, 117, 118, 119, 120, 122, 123

Tin. *See* trade
Toplice, 102
Trade, 109–116, 124–128
  agricultural and forest products, 114, 115, 117, 124
  amber, 12, 111–112, 113, 115, 116, 117
  bronze objects, 116, 117
  copper, 110, 115, 116
  glass, 106, 113–114, 116, 117
  graphite, 112, 115, 117
  iron, 113, 114, 115, 116, 117, 124–125, 126, 127–128
  luxury goods, 113, 114–115, 116, 122, 128
  oil, 114, 128
  salt, 112–113, 115, 116
  tin, 105, 110–111, 115, 116, 122
  wine, 114, 116, 128
  models for organization of, 115–116
Transport of trade goods, 111, 115
Uttendorf, 95, 105, 107, 109, 116, 126
Vače, 13, 29, 47, 94, 95, 99, 100, 102
Velem Szentvid, 105
Villach, 95, 118
Vinica, 1, 13, 72
Vix, 108, 115, 121
Waschenberg, 95, 96, 102–103
Wealth in graves, 28, 96, 107–108, 109, 113, 117–122, 125
Wels, 95, 101, 104, 106, 110, 111, 118
Welzelach, 2, 95, 96, 99, 100, 101, 104, 105, 106, 107, 108, 109, 110, 111, 118, 120, 125, 126
Wine. *See* trade
Zedlach, 105, 107

ISBN 0-87365-536-2

Basic Technical Reporting

Herman M. Weisman
Fellow, Society for Technical Communication

Prentice Hall
Englewood Cliffs, New Jersey   Columbus, Ohio

Library of Congress Cataloging-in-Publication Data

Weisman, Herman M.
  Basic technical reporting / Herman M. Weisman.
    p.   cm.
  Includes bibliographical references and index.
  ISBN 0-13-349689-9
  1. Technical writing.   I. Title.
T11. W42   1996
808'.0666—dc20   95-17215
                                                                   CIP

Cover photo: P. Kresnan/H. Armstrong Roberts
Editor: Stephen Helba
Production Editor: Julie Anderson Tober
Production Management: Betsy Keefer
Cover Designer: Brian Deep
Production Manager: Patricia A. Tonneman
Marketing Manager: Debbie Yarnell
Illustrations: The Clarinda Company

This book was set in Palatino by The Clarinda Company
and was printed and bound by Quebecor Printing/Book Press.
The cover was printed by Phoenix Color Corp.

© 1996 by Prentice-Hall, Inc.
A Simon & Schuster Company
Englewood Cliffs, New Jersey 07632

All rights reserved. No part of this book may be reproduced,
in any form or by any means, without permission
in writing from the publisher.

Credits: pages 56–58 and 67, extracts courtesy of Factory
Mutual Engineering; page 179, Figure 7.2, courtesy of Ken Cook Product
Support Systems; page 181, Figure 7.6, courtesy of Westinghouse Electric
Corporation.

Printed in the United States of America

10 9 8 7 6 5 4 3 2 1

ISBN: 0-13-349689-9

Prentice-Hall International (UK) Limited, *London*
Prentice-Hall of Australia Pty. Limited, *Sydney*
Prentice-Hall of Canada, Inc., *Toronto*
Prentice-Hall Hispanoamericana, S. A., *Mexico*
Prentice-Hall of India Private Limited, *New Delhi*
Prentice-Hall of Japan, Inc., *Tokyo*
Simon & Schuster Asia Pte. Ltd., *Singapore*
Editora Prentice-Hall do Brasil, Ltda., *Rio de Janeiro*

*To Margaret, Harlan, Lise, Abbi, Sally, Stanley, Mike,
and to Jason, Sara, Daniel, Nathan, and Jennifer
for all your support*

Preface

Basic Technical Reporting (BTR) is a derivative of *Basic Technical Writing*, Sixth Edition (Prentice Hall, 1992). The material in the present text, updated and revised, concentrates on the requirements for developing and producing a technical report. Technical reports play an essential role in today's information age in helping the progress of not only science and technology, but also business and industry. The purpose of *BTR* is to provide you, the student, with learning experiences in the craft of technical report writing. I have designed the text to help you understand the fundamental principles and techniques of technical writing by practicing the preparation of a technical report.

BTR will take you through a step-by-step sequence of instructions on methods for developing a report, beginning with the role the Problem plays both in the investigation and in the organization of the report's data. You will examine methods for conducting primary and secondary research, performing information-gathering tasks, doing data analysis, organizing data, using graphics to present and explain data, and completing the phases of the writing process and the production of the report.

Here are some key features of *Basic Technical Reporting:*

- Direct, clear, readable text and illustrations
- Logical organization and breadth of coverage
- Relevance of material to student experience
- Use of examples and illustrations, many taken from student writings, to support the presentation of principles and techniques
- Step-by-step guidance of principles and techniques
- Summaries of guidelines and principles at end of subject sequences and/or chapters

- Sound and effective instructional treatment

    Chapters begin with chapter objectives, followed by identification of chapter's focus

    Chapters end with a review paragraph and identification of chapter focal points

- Computer technology interwoven in the text in such matters as

    Literature searching

    Using databases to obtain information

    Hypertext

    Word processing and editing the report's text

    Graphics

    E-mail and other uses of electronic technology in correspondence

    Desktop publishing

- Examples and discussions of technical correspondence

    Letter and memo requirements

    Employment letters and resumes

    Requests for information

    Claim letters

    Letters of instruction

- Oral presentations
- Exercises at the end of each chapter

    Class discussion to ensure understanding of principles and techniques

    Assignments to put principles and techniques into practice

- Reading lists
- Reference Index and Guide to Grammar, Punctuation, and Style
- Updated bibliography
- Glossary of Computer Terminology

I want to acknowledge my gratitude to authors and copyright holders for permission to reprint their material and share their insights with readers of *BTR*.

I would also like to thank the reviewers of this text, Barry Batorsky, DeVry Institute of Technology—Woodbridge; Patricia Evenson, North Central Technical College; Helene Lamarre, DeVry Institute of Technology—Lombard; Stephen O'Neill, Bucks County Community College; George Stanton, East Tennessee State University; David K. Vaughan, Air Force Institute of Technology; Jackie Zrubek, Texas State Technical College—Waco.

Last but not least, I want to mention the following persons, listed alphabetically, who gave me special help in producing *Basic Technical Reporting:* Dr. Lise Duran, Steve Helba, Betsy Keefer, Julie Tober, Pat Tonneman, Abbi J. Weisman, Harlan F. Weisman, M.D., and Sally Weisman. They all have my deepfelt gratitude.

—H.M.W.

Contents

1
Technical Writing—How We Transfer Factual Information   1

Role of Technical Communication Today   2
What Is Communication?   2
How Communication Works   3
Meaning   4
What Is Technical Writing?   6
Technical Writing—Communication of Factual Experience   7
    Problems in Factual Communication   9
Ethical and Legal Considerations   10
    Professional Considerations   10
    Moral Considerations   11
    Legal Considerations   11

2
Technical English, Technical Style   15

Qualities of Technical Style   16
    Clarity and Precision   16
    Conciseness and Directness   17
    Objectivity   17
    When to Use Active and Passive Voices in Technical Writing   19

Elements of Style   21
    Types of Sentence Structure and Their Capacity for Expression   21

The Paragraph—The Basic Unit in Writing 24
    The Topic Sentence   24
    Structural Paragraphs   26
    Paragraph Principles Summarized   27

Reader Analysis—How to Write for Your Reader 27
    Focussing on the Reader   28

Making Writing More Readable 30
    Factors to Improve Readability   34

Some Advice on Style 34

3
Basic Expository Techniques in Technical Writing   41

The Nature of Definitions 42

Methods of Developing Definitions 42
    The Formal Definition   42
    The Informal Definition   43
    Defining by Using Synonyms and Antonyms   44
    Defining by Stipulation   45
    The Operational Definition   45
    The Expanded Definition—Amplification   46
    General Principles of Definition   47

Technical Descriptions 48
    Describing a Mechanism or Organism   48
    Guidelines for Organizing the Written Description of a Mechanism or Organism   49
    Example of a Technical Description   50
    Description of an Organism   52

Describing a Process 53

Guidelines for Organizing the Description of a Process 54
    Introduction   54
    Main Steps   55
    Concluding Section   55
    Use of Illustrations   56
    Style Considerations   56

Examples of Processes 56
    Principles of Explaining a Process   58

Analysis 62

Classification 63
    Using Classification as an Expository Technique   63
    Guidelines for Classification   63

Partition 64
    Guidelines for Partitioning   65

Achieving Interpretation Through Analysis and Synthesis 66

Example of Classification   67

Example of Partition   68

Summary of Analysis   69
    Style in Technical Descriptions   70
    Use of Illustrations in Technical Descriptions   70

4
Report Writing—Reconstruction of an Investigation   75

Report Writing—Reconstruction of an Investigation   76
    The Significance of the Problem Concept   76
    Types of Problems   76
    Apprehending the Problem   77
    The Hypothesis—A Tentative Solution to the Problem   78
    How to Use the Hypothesis to Help Solve the Problem of the Investigation   78

Relationship of Research to Report Writing   79

Decision Making—The Role Reports Play in Science, Technology, and Industry   79

What Is a Report   79
    Facts—The Basic Ingredients   80
    Forms Reports Take   80
    Major Types of Reports   81

Steps in Report Writing   82
    Selecting a Problem for Investigation   83

Prewriting—Strategies, Analysis, and Planning   84

Investigative Procedures   86
    Searching the Literature   86
    Catalog of Holdings   87
    Computerized Databases and Information Services   91
    Suggestions for Literature Searching   97
    Hypertext   98
    Preparing a Bibliography   98
    Taking Notes   99
    Plagiarism   100

Observation—Examining the Actual Situation, Condition, or Factors of the Problem   101
    How to Conduct Observations   102

Experimenting   102
    Planning Experiments   103
    Rules of Experimental Research   104
    Keeping Records   105

Interviewing and Discussing with Experts or People Qualified to Give Required Data   105
    How to Interview   106

Using Questionnaires   107

Systematizing, Analyzing, and Interpreting the Data   109
    How to Systematize the Data   109
    How to Analyze and Interpret the Data   110

5
Report Writing—Organizing the Report Data   115

How to Develop the Report's Thesis Sentence   116

Guidelines for Organizing the Report Structure   118

Patterns for Organizing the Report's Data   118
    Logical Method of Organization   119
    The Psychological Pattern of Organization   121

The Outline—A Guide to the Writer and Reader   122
    The Topical Outline—The "Laundry List"   122
    The Detailed Topical Outline   123
    The Sentence Outline   123
    The Decimal Outline   128
    The Format and Organization of the Outline   128
    Storyboarding as an Outline Technique   128
    Computer Outliners   130
    Organizing the Outline Material—Introduction, Body, and Terminal Section   130
    Checking Outline Requirements   130

6
Report Writing—Writing the Elements of the Report   135

How to Develop the Structural Elements of the Report   136
    The Front Matter   137
    The Letter of Transmittal   137
    The Cover and Title Page   137
    The Abstract   139
    The Executive Summary   139
    The Table of Contents   141
    Writing the Report Text—The Introduction and Its Elements   141
    Writing the Report Text—The Body of the Report and Its Elements   149
    Writing the Report Text—The Terminal Section   150
    Back Matter   150
    The Index   152
    The Distribution List   152

Final (Completion) Reports   152

7
How to Write, Edit, and Produce the Report   169

Writing the First Draft   170

The Revision and Editing Process   171
    The First Reading—The Revision/Editing Process   171

   The Second Reading—The Revision/Editing Process 171
   The Third Reading—Organization, Language, and Style 172
   Revising and Editing with a Word Processor 174

Producing and Printing the Report 176

How to Use Graphic Aids 177
   Photographs 177
   Drawings/Diagrams 178
   Graphs 178
   Tables 181
   Checklist for Constructing Tables 184
   How to Handle Equations 185
   How to Handle Headings 186

Documenting Your Report's References 187
   Why Documentation Is Necessary 187
   A Simple Documentation System 188
   Using Footnotes 189
   Bibliography 190

Proofreading 192

8
Technical Correspondence **199**

Role of Correspondence in Industry and Technology 200

Psychology of Correspondence 200

Prewriting—Determining Your Purpose 201

Organizing Your Letter—Role of the Paragraph 201

Format of the Letter 202

Mechanical Details 206
   Stationery 206
   Framing a Letter on the Page 207
   The Heading 207
   The Date Line 207
   The Inside Address 208
   The Attention Line and Subject Line 208
   The Salutation 210
   The Body of the Letter 211
   The Complimentary Close 211
   The Signature 211
   Enclosures 212
   Copy Notations 212
   The Postscript 212
   Second and Succeeding Pages 212

The Memorandum 213
   Purpose and Format 213

Employment Letters—How to Apply for a Job 216
    Job Stategy 218
    Self-Appraisal 219
    Preparing a Dossier 219
    Researching Job Possibilities 220
    Job Analysis 220
    Developing a Resume 221
    Types of Resumes 222
    Preparing the Resume 222
    Basic Resume Ingredients 223
    Writing the Resume 226
    Writing a Cover Letter 228
    How to Attract Favorable Attention 229
    How to Describe Your Qualifications 231
    Securing Action 232
    Writing an Executive Briefing 242
    Guidelines for Preparing Resumes 242
    The Job Interview 244
    Writing a Post-Interview Letter 246
    Acceptance and Refusal Letters 246

How to Write Inquiries 248
    Answers to Inquiries 252

How to Write Claim Letters 255
    The Adjustment Letter 255

The Letter of Instruction 257

Computer Technology in Correspondence 259
    Electronic Mail 263
    Electronic Bulletin Boards 263
    Facsimile (FAX) 263

9
Short Report Forms   271

The Letter Report 272

The Memo Report 272

Recommendation Reports 277

Progress Reports 280

10
Oral Reports   287

Types of Oral Reporting Situations 289
    Informal, Impromptu Oral Reports 289
    Extemporaneous, Semiformal Reports 290
    Formal Reports 290
    The Poster Board 290

Prespeaking—Preliminary Analysis and Planning 292

Gathering the Information 292

Organizing the Information 292

Composing the Oral Presentation 293
    The Beginning or Introduction 293
    Body/Middle 293
    Conclusion/Close 294

Practicing the Delivery 294

Delivering the Oral Report 295

Audiovisual Aids in Oral Presentations 297
    Using Audiovisual Aids 298

Guidelines for Oral Report Presentation 298

Reference Index and Guide to Grammar, Punctuation, Style, and Usage   301

Discussion Questions and Assignment Exercises in Grammar and Usage   337

Glossary of Computer and Desktop Publishing Terms   347

Selected Bibliography   363

General References 363

Technical Report Writing 365

Graphics and Production 366

Business Communication 367

Computers and New Information Technology 368

Oral Communication 369

Index   371

1
Technical Writing—How We Transfer Factual Information

Chapter Objective

Provide an understanding of the communication process and its role in technical writing.

Chapter Focus

- How the communication process works
- How meaning takes place
- What technical writing is and does
- Problems in the communication of factual information
- Ethical and legal considerations

Role of Technical Communication Today

Samuel Johnson, the irascible eighteenth-century author and dictionary maker, once remarked that he could not understand why anyone wrote except to make money. Implied in his witticism is the lamentably obvious truth that the writing process is so difficult and painful that unless a person is amply paid for the effort, she should not attempt it. Dr. Johnson's wisdom is still applicable. Today, much of your professional success depends on your ability to communicate about your work activities. Effective writing pays well, but effective writing is not easy. This book is intended to help make the writing process easier. Yes, writing can be made easier but never easy. Now, let's examine how we can make the process easier. First, we need to understand how communication works.

What Is Communication?

Communication is the means by which two or more human beings share one another's thoughts, ideas, feelings, insights, and information. The transfer of meaning is always involved. As a process, communication is dynamic. Many factors act upon the process and, of course, on the communicator and the communicatee. As the process operates, each factor in the communication event acts upon the other factor and is consequently changed in the process. Because these explanatory words may sound like double-talk, let's pause and examine communication more fully. The word *communication* can be traced to the Latin *communis*, which means commonness. When people communicate, they establish and share a commonality. Dictionaries define the process as "the giving and receiving of information or messages by talk, writing, gestures, and signals."

Sociologists tell us that the communication process is basic to the development of the individual, to the formation and healthy existence of groups, and to the functioning interrelations among groups, organizations, cities, and nations. Communication links person to person, every person to a group, and every group to a larger social structure.

To understand this dynamic and complex process, we must break it down and examine its ingredients. If we base our analysis on the definition of communication, we will come up with the following components:

1. The *source*, or *sender* of the message
2. The *message* being sent
3. The method of the sending, or *channel*
4. The obstacles in the way—interference, or *noise*
5. The *receiver*, or *destination* of the message
6. The *effect* produced in the receiver by the message
7. The *feedback*, or *reaction* by the sender to the effect of the message on the receiver
8. The *frame of reference*, or *background factors*, in which the process is taking place

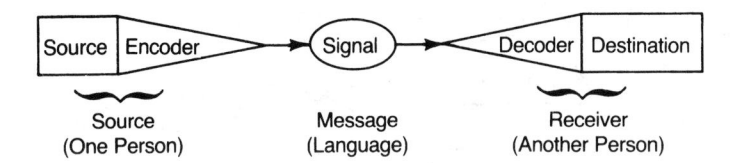

Figure 1.1 The three basic elements in the human communication system — source, message, receiver.

and the influence of that environmental setting on the sender, the message, the channel, the noise, and the receiver

With eight ingredients or variables involved in the interaction, the process is so complicated that it seems a wonder that communication ever takes place. However, it does take place. Let us see how.

How Communication Works

What happens when communication takes place? The answer is diagramed in Figures 1.1, 1.2, and 1.3.[1] The source receives a stimulus by means of his perception apparatus. Reacting to the stimulus, the source formulates a message—that is, takes the information or thought or idea to be shared, and encodes or expresses it in a form that can be transmitted. The encoding process is the thinking that takes place in the mind of the source. The message is the thought, coded in a language and format that can be transmitted—spoken, hand-written, drawn, or keyboarded—through words, pictures, or gestures. The receiver can understand the message only within the framework of his own stockpile of experience and knowledge. The source can formulate messages and the receiver can decode them only within the experience each has had. If there is no commonality of experience or adequate empathy, then the communication is difficult or impossible.

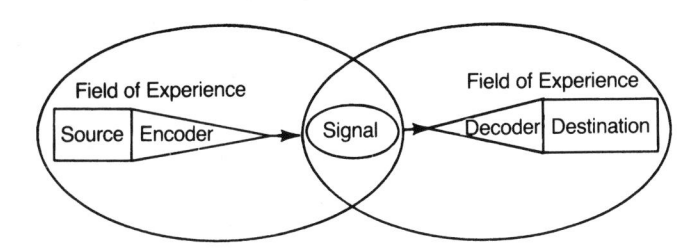

Figure 1.2 Commonness of experience is requisite for communication.

---

[1] Figures 1.1, 1.2, 1.3, and 1.4 are based on diagrams in Schramm's excellent article cited in reference B.8.

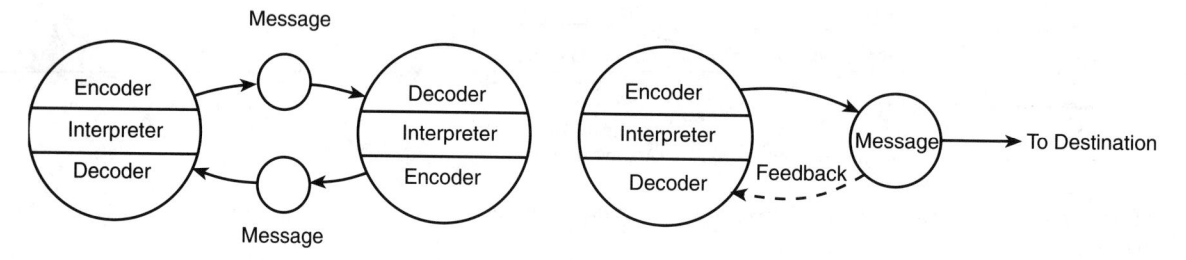

Figure 1.3 Communicators get feedback of their own messages by listening to their own voices as they talk or by reading their own messages as they write.

Meaning

When we communicate, we are trying to establish a commonality with someone—we are trying to share an experience, a thought, an idea, a feeling, or information. Therefore, when communication takes place, *there has been a transference of meaning.* Three elements involved in the conveyance of meaning are:

1. a person having thoughts,
2. a symbol,
3. a referent.

These three elements are frequently represented by three corners of a triangle, as in Figure 1.4.

The symbols or words have no direct relationship to their referents and can be identified only indirectly with the physical fact that they symbolize through the reader's mental processes. Line AC of the triangle becomes a direct relationship only after the reader pronounces the word symbols denoting the fact; the symbolization (the sentence, "Acid turns blue litmus paper red") becomes identical (means the same thing in the mind of the reader) with the fact that it repre-

Figure 1.4 Triangle of meaning operating in the mind of the encoder of a communication message.

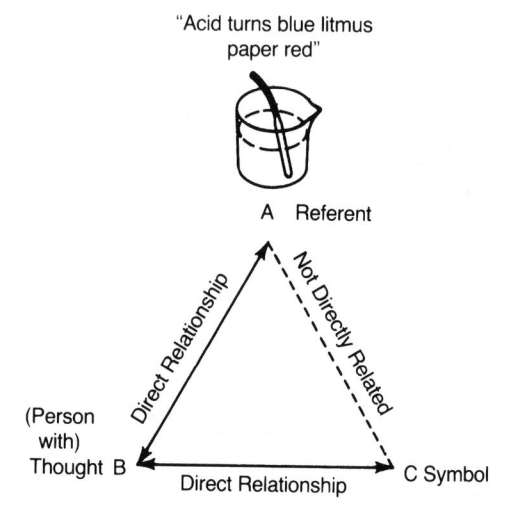

Figure 1.5 Simple idea.

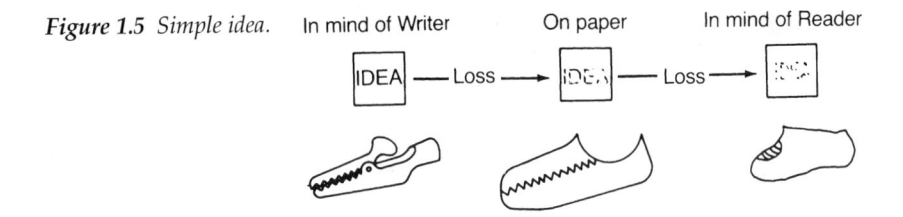

sents. The receiver's meaning emerges from the operations illustrated in Figures 1.2 and 1.4.

However, we need to recognize that there are three types of meaning:

1. what the communicator (source) intends to indicate,
2. what is suggested to the receiver (destination) by the message, and
3. the more or less general usage a symbol has that indicates a given connotation.

What a communicator intends and what a receiver understands depend heavily on meaning number 3, which is influenced by the frame of reference or context in which the words are used.

What occurs when a source successfully or unsuccessfully sends a message to a receiver? Some diagrams will help. Figure 1.5 represents the attempt to communicate a simple idea. By substituting the alligator clip for the square, you can see the extent of loss that can occur in a communication situation. Figure 1.6 represents the extent of loss in the communication of a complex idea.

Now, let us imagine a situation in which the source begins with a vague or confused idea. While the source formulates the idea, the encoding process starts to shape the message, during which some details of the idea achieve clarity. The **receiver,** using his experience, knowledge, and associations and stimulated by the symbols sent, organizes the symbols through his cerebral process to make some meaningful sense of the message, as might be indicated by the requirements of the message situation (see Figures 1.7 and 1.8). *Such a gain process is not usual, often rare.*

Language usage is both the occupational providence and hazard of the technical writer, who must communicate knowledge clearly and precisely. Language is the link between the outside world and the concepts or thoughts in people's minds. Everyone's nervous system is distinct; each of us may see reality differ-

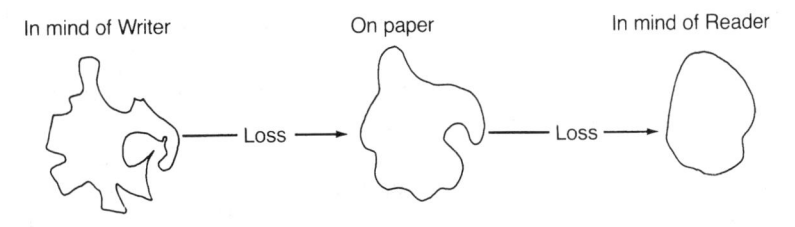

Figure 1.6 Complex idea.

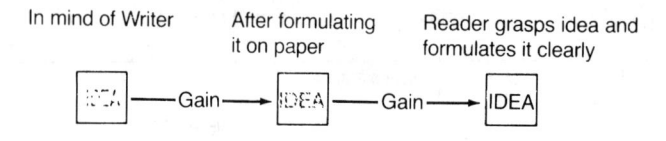

Figure 1.7 Simple idea.

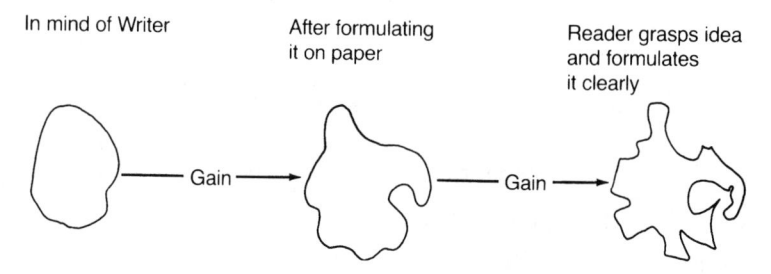

Figure 1.8 Complex idea.

ently. This can cause problems as illustrated in Figure 1.9 or present the providential opportunity shown in the previous Figures 1.7 and 1.8.

What Is Technical Writing?

Let's now turn to the encoding or preparation of messages in the process of communication. Our concern will focus on *technical writing,* a very old and common field of communication whose objective is to convey scientific, technical, and other specialized information and ideas accurately and effectively for the purpose of informing, instructing, and persuading.

Humanlike creatures have inhabited our planet for over a million years. For most of the time, they lived like other animals. It is only in the last 25,000 years that we have seen civilization and progress. The invention of writing contributed immeasurably to this advance. Writing gave us the ability to record and communicate our experiences and knowledge. Each generation thereafter did not have to begin all over again. The recordings of predecessors became an available source of information and ideas that stimulated further thought and progress. It took us over a million years to arrive at the agricultural revolution; only 25,000 years to get to the industrial revolution; a mere 150 years to come to the space age; and but 1 year to bring azidothymidine (AZT) from idea to research stage, to commercial production and sale. The process of technical writing has given continuity to human efforts and has accelerated the tempo for increasing knowledge and progress.

However, *technical writing* as a term has not found its way into the dictionary. The words *technical* and *writing* are defined separately. Webster's *New World Dictionary* defines *technical* as "having to do with the practical, industrial, or mechanical arts or the applied sciences." *Writing* is defined as "the occupation of the writer . . . the practice of composition" (the encoding process). We might combine

Thing or Event	![tree]	![chip]	![flag]
Symbol	Tree	Chip	Freedom
Thought or Concept			

Figure 1.9 How each person sees reality differently.

these two definitions as "writing about science and technology." People in the profession might want to restate the definition: "Technical writing is a specialized field of communication whose purpose is to convey technical and scientific information and ideas accurately and efficiently for the purpose of informing, instructing, or persuading the receiver."

Not only the physical and life sciences and their technologies, but also the social sciences, business, and the humanities require the services of technical writers. For example, a discussion of suprasegmental phonemes or metathesis in linguistics or an explanation of the vagaries of the business cycle or the economics of technological obsolescence can become very "technical," as can the problem and demands involved in constructing and explaining a sociogram of an individual's interaction with other consort group members. Demography offers a variety of technical aspects involving complex statistical data and mathematical formulas, such as cohort analysis and racial typology. In psychology, the physiology of stimulus-response and of memory; the techniques of reading faster; and analyses of processes such as association, cognition, and simplification. Such problems are similar to those facing the writer in explaining scientific processes such as laser radiation or genetic replication.

Technical Writing—Communication of Factual Experience

Some observers believe that the information manipulation capabilities of the computer such as hypertext, desktop publishing E-mail, Usenet, and Internet have the

IEEE Transactions on Professional Communication
The Journal of Business and Technical Communication

B. **Books and Essays**

1. Brockman, John, and Fern Rook, eds. *Technical Communication and Ethics.* Arlington, Va.: Society for Technical Communication, 1989.

2. Chase, Stuart. *Power of Words.* New York: Harcourt, Brace and Company, 1954.

3. DeGeorge, Richard T. *Business Ethics.* 3d ed. New York: Macmillan Publishing Company, 1990.

4. Haldane, J. B. S. "Communication in Biology." In *Studies in Communication.* London: Martin Secker and Warburg, 1955.

5. Huxley, Aldous. *Words and Their Meaning.* Los Angeles: The Ward Ritchie Press, 1940.

6. Lee, Irving J. *Language Habits in Human Affairs.* New York: Harper and Brothers, 1941.

7. Schiller, F. C. S. *Logic for Use.* New York: Harcourt, Brace and Company, 1930.

8. Schramm, Wilbur. "The Nature of Communication Between Humans." In *The Process and Effects of Mass Communication.* Rev. ed., ed. Wilbur Schramm and Donald F. Roberts. Urbana, Ill.: University of Illinois Press, 1971.

9. Sinclair, W. A. *An Introduction to Philosophy.* London: Oxford University Press, 1944.

10. Urban, Wilbur M. *Language and Reality.* New York: Macmillan Publishing Company, 1951.

11. Whorf, Benjamin Lee. "Linguistics as an Exact Science." In *Language, Thought and Reality, Selected Writings of Benjamin Whorf,* edited by John B. Carroll. New York: John Wiley and Sons and Massachusetts Institute of Technology Press, 1956.

2
Technical English, Technical Style

Chapter Objective

Provide guidance on the stylistic qualities and elements of technical writing.

Chapter Focus

- Qualities of technical style
  Clarity and precision
  Conciseness and directness
  Objectivity
  Voice
- Elements of technical style
  Sentences
  Paragraphs
- Reader analysis and readability

To write effectively about technical matters, we need to know how to use our language, English. Technical English is not a substandard form of expression. Technical writing meets the conventional standards of grammar, punctuation, and syntax. Technical style may have its peculiarities—in vocabulary and at times in mechanics—but it is, nevertheless, capable of effective expression and graceful use of language. The purpose of this chapter is to examine the characteristics of good technical style.

Jonathan Swift said that the "proper words in the proper places" make for style. Seneca and Lord Chesterfield said that style is the "dress of thoughts." Expressed simply, **style** is the way a person puts words together into sentences, arranges sentences into paragraphs, and groups paragraphs to make a piece of writing express thoughts clearly. Technical style, then, is the way you write when you deal with a technical or scientific subject.

Technical style can be described by the richness or poverty of vocabulary, by the syllabic lengths of words, by the relative frequency of sentences of various lengths and types, by grammatical structure, by pictorial representation and tabular matter integrated with text. The style varies with the writer and subject matter. Nevertheless, it has certain basic characteristics.

Qualities of Technical Style

By tradition, technical style is plain, impersonal, and factual. It is characterized by a calm, restrained tone; an absence of any attempt to arouse emotion; the use of specialized terminology; the use of abbreviations and symbols; and the integrated uses of illustrations, tables, charts, and diagrams to help explanation. Technical writing is characterized by exactness rather than grace or variety of expression. Its main purpose is to be informative and functional rather than entertaining. Thus, the most important qualities of technical style are clarity, precision, conciseness, and objectivity.

Clarity and Precision

Clarity and precision are frequently interdependent. Clarity is achieved when the writer has communicated meaning fully to the reader. Precision occurs when the writer attains exact correspondence between the matter to be communicated and its written expression.

Faults in clarity and precision result when the following occur:

1. The writer is not familiar enough with the subject matter to write about it.
2. The writer, though generally familiar with the subject, cannot distinguish the important from the unimportant. (The essence of the subject matter has escaped the writer.)
3. The writer has a thorough mastery of the subject matter but is deficient in communication techniques.
4. The writer is unfamiliar with the reader and has not directed the communication to the desired level of audience understanding.

Conciseness and Directness

Concise writing saves the reader time and energy because meaning is expressed in the fewest possible words and readability is thereby enhanced. Directness also increases readability; it eliminates circumlocutions (roundabout expressions involving unnecessary words) and awkward inversions. Take this example:

> An important factor to be cognizant of in the relation to proper procedures along the lines necessary is to consider first and foremost in connection with the nature of the experiment that effectuation is dependent on a fully and complete darkened interior enclosure.

The following sentence says the same thing more concisely, directly, and clearly:

> The experiment requires a completely darkened room.

Objectivity

Scientific style is characterized by objectivity. Personal feelings are excluded; attention is concentrated on facts. Furthermore, the use of the passive voice and the third person point of view is a long-established tradition in technical writing. The feeling is that the exclusion of personal pronouns produces a style consistent with objectivity and the use of the passive voice places emphasis on the subject matter. As a result, technical writing is much more impersonal and much drier than it has to be. True, directions for assembling a ceiling fan are quite different from explanations of basic research. It is also true that much "literary" writing is as guilty of mechanical, lifeless expression as is much technical writing. Still, a major complaint is that research is reported in such a cut-and-dried manner as to drive all interest and excitement from it. The personalness, directness, and thoroughly human qualities that emerge clearly from the explanations of Harvey, Newton, Huxley, or Watson make for fascinating and comprehensible reading; whereas much current scientific research is reported in such an impersonal manner as to be as dull and lifeless as a telephone book.

Opinion differs as to whether impersonality in scientific and technical writing requires the third person and passive voice. Writing for the general or less knowledgeable reader requires the frequent use of devices to inveigle interest. The first person point of view and the active voice help to create interest. Informative and functional technical writing can be objective and still include personal pronouns. Many successful technical writers establish effective rapport with readers by playing an active role in their narration as if they were the principal actors involved. Readers often allow themselves to be involved in exposition if it is made interesting for them by the actual participation of a human being elaborating on data that could otherwise be as foreign and dry to them as a lobster's tail. This is exactly what Huxley did, and it was Huxley who did more to popularize science than any other person at a time when scientific activity was beginning to expand and was in need of public support.

18   *Technical English, Technical Style*

Two excerpts from Huxley's writing follow. Both exemplify excellent scientific style and effective communication. Each is aimed at a different audience. The first example is aimed at an intelligent, but uneducated audience.

The Lobster's Tail

Note the use of the first person pronoun, I. Huxley uses excellent psychology to involve the uninformed reader immediately by asking a question about the matter he will be explaining: "What do you think is the most characteristic aspect of the lobster?" Its tail, of course. Huxley, speaking in the first person, involves the reader in examining the special physiological components of the lobster's tail. He has the reader examine, as he does in his explanation, the separate parts of the tail. Notice how he explains the technical, anatomical term homologue, *an organ or part of the animal (lobster) similar to another part. Huxley maintains interest by involving the reader in the examination and asking questions that the uninformed would ask, and then answering the questions.*

I have before me a lobster. When I examine it, what appears to be the most striking character it presents? Why, I observe that this part which we call the tail of the lobster, is made up of six distinct hard rings and a seventh terminal piece. If I separate one of the middle rings, say the third, I find it carries upon its under surface a pair of limbs or appendages, each of which consists of a stalk and two terminal pieces. So that I can represent a transverse section of the ring and its appendages upon the diagram board in this way.

If I now take the fourth ring, I find it has the same structure, and so have the fifth and the second; so that, in each of these divisions of the tail, I find parts which correspond with one another, a ring and two appendages and in each appendage a stalk and two end pieces. These corresponding parts are called, in the technical language of anatomy "homologous parts." The ring of the third division is the "homologue" of the ring of the fifth, the appendage of the former is the homologue of the appendage of the latter. And, as each division exhibits corresponding parts in corresponding places, we say that all the divisions are constructed upon the same plan. But let us consider the sixth division. It is similar to, and yet different from, the others. The ring is essentially the same as in the other divisions; but the appendages look at first as if they were very different; and yet when we regard them closely, what do we find? A stalk and two terminal divisions, exactly as in the others, but the stalk is very short and very thick, the two terminal divisions are very broad and flat, and one of them is divided into two pieces. I may say, therefore, that the sixth segment is like the others in plan, but that it is modified in its details. [3:21]

The other example from Huxley's technical writing is an excerpt from a textbook intended for advanced students of zoology. Note that the first person is entirely missing and that most of the sentences are structured in the passive voice. Recall the use of nontechnical terms in the first passage and compare the use of technical terminology in the one below, where the details are more complete, the approach is more formal, and the sentences are much longer.

The Abdomen of the English Crayfish

Here the reader is a college student. Huxley uses some scientific terms without definition. Students of an advanced course in zoology are expected to know what morphological unit, exoskeleton, transverse section, ganglion, extensor muscles, *and so forth, mean. However, note that Huxley will define a term that is new to the student; for example, "the* cephalon *or head." His*

The body of the crayfish is obviously separable into three regions—the *cephalon* or head, the *thorax*, and the *abdomen*. The last is at once distinguished by the size and the mobility of its segments. And each of its seven movable segments, except the telson, represents a sort of morphological unit, the repetition of which makes up the whole fabric of the body.

The fifth segment can be studied apart. It constitutes what is called a *metamere;* in which are distinguishable a central part termed the *somite*, and two appendages.

In the exoskeleton of the somites of the abdomen several regions have already been distinguished; and although they constitute one continuous whole, it will be convenient to speak of the *sternum* (Fig. 36, st. XIX), [These are call outs in the drawing of a transverse section through the fifth abdominal somite.] the *tergum* (t. XIX) and the *pleura* (pl. XIX), as if they were separate parts, and to distinguish that portion of the sternal region, which lies between the articulation of the appendage and the pleuron, on each side, as the *epimeron* (ep. XIX). Adopting the nomenclature, it may be said of the fifth somite of the abdomen, that it consists of a segment of the exoskeleton, divisible into tergum, pleura, epimeron, and sternum, with which two appendages are articulated; that it contains a double ganglion (gn. 12), a section of the flexor (f.m.) and extensor (e.m.) muscles, and of the alimentary (h.g.) and vascular (s.a.a., i.a.a.) systems. [4:141]

explanation of new terms considers the intelligence and knowledge of the reader. For instance, all he needs to do to explain metamere *is to say it is the fifth segment of the abdomen of the crayfish (English lobster).*

Notice how Huxley's organization of the description of the abdomen fits the principles of the written technical description explained in Chapter 7. In this excerpt, Huxley deals with an anatomical part of the crayfish, the abdomen. He identifies the segments of this anatomical division, tells what each is, its purpose, appearance, shape, and how each interrelates.

When to Use Active and Passive Voices in Technical Writing

In grammar, *voice* is the term used for a form of a verb to show connection between the subject and the verb. The voice of a verb tells the reader whether the subject performs an action (active voice) or receives an action (passive voice). In active voice construction, the subject is the doer of the action or is the condition varied by the verb:

>   The canal starts at Whalen Dam.
>   Man bites dog.
>   Vertebrates learn mazes readily.
>   A radiometer detected the electromagnetic radiation.

When the subject of a verb receives the action, the verb is in the passive voice:

>   The canal at Whalen was built many years ago.
>   The dog was bitten by a man.
>   Mazes are learned readily by vertebrates.
>   The electromagnetic radiation was detected by a radiometer.

The passive voice form is used in all tenses. It usually consists of a form of the verb *to be*, but the past tense of the verbs *to get* and *to become* also is sometimes used to form a passive:

>   The component became overheated.
>   The traveling wave tube is to be used in the circuit.
>   During mitosis, the heterochromatic segments get stained more strongly than the euchromatic regions.

Much technical writing is concerned with the description of work so objective that the reader does not care who did it. The reader is interested solely in the work itself and is not at all interested in the agency or agent involved. The conventional, impersonal passive construction is suitable for this kind of subject. Compare the next two sentences with the two that follow:

> The other end of the tie beam was connected to an anchor pile by a bolt of 2½" diameter, inserted through an opening in the pile.
>
> As the experiment progressed, additional water was added to equal the amount lost from evaporation.
>
> I connected the other end of the tie beam to an anchor pile, using a bolt of 2½" diameter which I inserted through an opening in the pile.
>
> As I went on with the experiment, I decided to add water equal to the amount I determined was lost through evaporation.

A comparison shows the third person passive construction to be more objective and efficient than the first person active example.

But compare this sentence:

> It is desired to ascertain how the success was achieved in increasing the yield of Russian wild rye.

with this one:

> We want to know how you increased the yield of Russian wild rye.

and this sentence:

> The agglutination is caused by substances analogous to antibodies that are present in the serum.

with this one:

> Substances analogous to antibodies present in the serum caused the agglutination.

or the following:

> It is believed that the city should increase its reserve water supply.

with this sentence:

> We believe the city should increase its reserve water supply.

Active verbs are more lively than passive verbs and call for simpler sentence structure. Usually, therefore, they are more efficient and writers should prefer them. However, let us remember that passive verbs are as grammatically correct as active verbs and that there are instances when the passive voice is to be preferred:

1. When the doer of an action is not known to the writer or when the writer does not want to be identified:
   a. In 1947, when this site was selected, the water table was low and pump irrigation was necessary in many areas of the valley.
   b. The decision was made against the employee.

2. When the writer desires to place the emphasis on the action or on the doer at the end:
   a. The mineral is mined in Wyoming.
   b. The research was carried out by the director.

In normal usage, nonetheless, passive constructions are considered weak because they have actionless verbs, invert the natural word order, and require additional phrasing.

Some publications and organizations have a specific policy forbidding the use of *I* or *we*. In writing for such a publication or organization, live with its rules unless you have achieved the position and skill of a Thomas Huxley. Then you can change the rules.

Elements of Style

So far I have been discussing qualities of style. Qualities are overall impressions or characteristics. They result from the writer's typical or individual use of the elements of style: grammatical construction, diction, phrasing, sentence length, and figures of speech. **Sentence structure** and **diction** (choice of words) are two of the major concerns of the technical writer.

Types of Sentence Structure and Their Capacity for Expression

The technical writer should understand the capacity of the sentence for expressing simple and complex relationships. This understanding is valuable to the technical writer in formulating observations, generalizations, and conclusions.

Simple Sentence

For stating an uncomplicated, unqualified observation, a **simple sentence** is used:

> Lavoisier, the great French chemist, named the new gas oxygen.
> Honesty is the best policy.
> Fill the test tube with water.
> The child patted the dog.
> Light is absorbed in the retina by a pigment called visual purple or rhodopsin.

Compound Sentence

The **compound sentence** expresses coordinate ideas in balance or in contrast:

> "And there was evening, and there was morning, one day" (Genesis 1:51—RSV).
> The flow is dark brown and blocky on the surface, but it continues to steam from hot viscous lava beneath.

"Science is nothing but trained and organized common sense, differing from the latter only as a veteran may differ from a raw recruit; and its methods differ from those of common sense only as far as the guardsmen's cut and thrust differ from the way in which a savage wields his club" (Thomas H. Huxley).

Complex Sentence

In the **complex sentence,** dependent clauses are used to express ideas subordinate to the thought of the main clause. The word *complex* is derived from Latin. It does not mean difficult, but literally "woven into." The dependent clause (an incomplete thought having a subject and predicate that modify or support in some way a word or sentence element of the whole sentence) is woven into the design:

The dependent clause, which would really take its place, *is not of equal rank to the independent clause, a* substitute for wood has not been developed. *It provides an explanation of the main thought.*	A substitute for wood, which would really take its place, has not been developed.
When you would come *tells the reader the necessary information about what the main thought,* we wondered, *is concerned.*	We wondered when you would come.
If you use sufficient patience and don't go into unnecessary detail *explains why* any sentence can be analyzed, *the major thought in the sentence.*	Any sentence can be analyzed if you use sufficient patience and don't go into unnecessary detail.
Read the directions *is the important thought in this sentence, but it is meaningless unless it is explained by the descriptive qualifier,* when all else fails.	When all else fails, read the directions.
If the revised process is to succeed *is a dependent clause that explains (modifies or describes) the two independent clauses connected by the coordinating conjunction* but, *which connects the two statements actually in opposition to each other,* the first stage may be completed under the careful supervision of the shop personnel *contrasted with* the second stage must be directed by high-level engineers.	If the revised process is to succeed, the first stage may be completed under the careful supervision of the shop personnel, but the second stage must be directed by high-level engineers.

Uniformity in report writing undoubtedly has some advantages, but when the uniformity results in dull and difficult reading, I seriously question its value.

The value of the thought expressed in the independent clause, uniformity in report writing undoubtedly has some advantages, *is clarified by the qualifying dependent clause,* but when the uniformity results in dull and difficult reading. *The opposing thought expressed in the independent clause,* I seriously question its validity, *provides the intended meaning.*

Complex-Compound Sentence

A **complex-compound sentence** contains two or more independent clauses (expressing coordinate ideas in balance or in contrast) and at least one dependent clause expressing a thought(s) subordinate to the main clause it modifies.

Professional writers today use about 50 percent complex sentences, 35 percent simple sentences, and only about 15 percent compound sentences, compound-complex sentences, and fragmentary sentences. (A fragmentary sentence actually is not a sentence, but a phrase or dependent clause, expressing an incomplete thought.) Out of twenty sentences, three are compound; seventeen are either simple or complex. The most frequently written sentence in current English is a complex sentence from twelve to thirty-six words long.

Which type of sentence to use depends mainly on the thought to be communicated. Other factors pertinent to the communication are the purpose of the communication and the reader of the message. Efficient technical writing depends on clarity, precision, conciseness, and objectivity in the composition. For the sake of example and analysis, let us examine the sentence below. At first, it seems to express an uncomplicated thought concisely and clearly.

> A heavy object will sink readily.

On closer examination, the thought of the sentence is not as clear as it might be. The meaning of the modifiers *heavy* and *readily* is vague. Heavy and readily are subjective judgments. The sentence, though a short one, does not express a clear, precise, objective thought. Shortness is not the equivalent of conciseness. Conciseness requires succinctness and clarity. Let us try rewriting the sentence to communicate the thought more clearly and efficiently.

> An object of great density will sink very quickly.

The new attempt, also a simple sentence, is an improvement. Though the word *density* carries a certain factual significance in the rephrased thought, the adjective *great* reflects subjectivity, as does the intensive *very*. *Quickly*, while having an aspect of subjectivity, is a more appropriate word than *readily* because it suggests an inherent capability for speed of action; whereas *readily* suggests speed in compliance or response. Let us try again. This time let us aim for adequate expression no matter how many words or clauses are to be used in the sentence.

> A heavy object is defined as one whose density is such that it will not displace its own weight when placed in water, and, therefore, it will sink quickly.

This twenty-nine word complex-compound sentence has achieved objectivity. Its heavy-handed structure is frequently seen in current technical writing. It can be improved:

> An object that does not displace its weight in water will sink quickly.

Both the critical qualities of the weight factor, which causes the object to sink, and the manner of sinking are clearly, objectively, precisely, and concisely expressed in the complex sentence. The complex sentence is effective in technical writing because the dependent clause can be a modifier of exacting precision and clarity.

The Paragraph—The Basic Unit in Writing

Every serious piece of writing has a structural design. Many professional writers develop an outline for that purpose. The outline (which I will discuss in detail in Chapter 5) helps the writer subdivide and arrange the subject matter into related units or topics. In the composition (encoding) process, each topic becomes the structural basis of a paragraph. A **paragraph** is a group of related sentences that a writer presents as an organized unit in development of the subject. Technically, then, the function of the paragraph is to break the text into readable units. It has two principal uses:

1. It holds together thoughts or statements that are closely related.
2. It keeps apart thoughts and statements that belong to different parts of the subject.

The Topic Sentence

A **topic sentence** expresses the main idea developed by a paragraph. Writing a paragraph has been compared to sorting material into labeled baskets: The material is the sentences conveying ideas or information; the label on the material is the topic sentence. The topic sentence can be a generalization that summarizes what the paragraph is about—its central thought—or a statement that tells what the paragraph is to do or indicates the direction the discussion will take. Grammarians call this latter type a **pointer** sentence, since it points or guides the reader in the direction the paragraph is to develop. Often a paragraph with a beginning pointer sentence will have a summarizing topic sentence at its close.

By steering the design of its paragraph, the topic sentence controls the text. It provides:

unity (its material is related),

coherence (its material is connected),

emphasis (its important material is strategically positioned or given graphic prominence), and

proportion (its material is balanced and it has harmony in the amount of information it has positioned).

The first sentence of this paragraph is both a topic and a pointer sentence.

The italicized words provide details—four specifics on how the topic sentence "steers" the design of the paragraph. The indentations and italics provide emphasis and give the text graphic prominence.

The indentation also provides special balance to the material of the paragraph as well as to supplemental details.

The final sentence summarizes the central idea of the paragraph.

The topic sentence is usually, though not always, placed at the beginning of the paragraph. It may appear at any position in the paragraph, depending on the factors indicated. If you compose your topic sentence with care, you will not only help your reader grasp the meaning of the paragraph, but also help yourself by providing the necessary information that supports and clarifies your intended meaning.

If you are an inexperienced technical writer, you would do well to begin your paragraphs with a topic sentence. It is a useful technique that helps set the flow of necessary information on paper. A good procedure for developing paragraphs is to ask yourself two questions:

1. What is the main point of this paragraph?
2. What must I tell my reader to support, explain, clarify, or accept it?

Expository devices, such as examples, analogies, analyses, comparisons or contrasts, explications, and details, are used to develop the topic sentence.

A few examples can illustrate how the reader's expectations are satisfied by the development of the topic sentence:

> It is a commonplace fact that scientific discoveries are a function of methods used.

The reader's natural question is why is it a commonplace fact? The writer has an obligation to give the reasons in the rest of the paragraph.

> Several occurrences during the experiment confirmed this opinion.

The reader logically expects specific instances to confirm the opinion of the writer.

> "In certain other aspects, especially its spatio-temperal aspects as revealed by the theory of relativity, nature is like a rainbow." [6:3]

The reader is interested in knowing how the analogy applies. The writer (in this case, Sir James Jeans) elaborates an effective explanation of his analogy.

> The rattle is the most characteristic feature of the rattlesnake and is one of the most remarkable structures in nature.

The reader expects an explanation to answer the question "Why?"

Operation of an autopilot may be seen from the diagram in Figure 12.

The rest of the paragraph becomes supplemental to the diagram in the explanation of how an autopilot operates. Graphic illustrations are used with great effect in technical writing to aid the development of the topic sentence of a paragraph. Frequently, they are the most important substantiating details in such development.

What causes wind shear?

A question and its response can be a useful technique for organizing diverse aspects of information. To answer the above question, the various types of turbulence that cause wind shear are identified and elucidated. If the elucidation requires much informational material, each item in the answer may become a paragraph and each separate item becomes the topic sentence of that paragraph.

Test your paragraphs by these criteria:

1. What is the central idea?
2. What details are needed to support or explain the central idea for the reader?
3. Is there anything in the paragraph not related to that idea?
4. Are the sentences organized in a sequence that is sufficiently logical to support or explain the topic sentence clearly?

Structural Paragraphs

There is considerable similarity between the topic sentence of a paragraph and the first paragraph of a section. Both are necessary to summarize, preview, and connect—to orient the reader and offer a proper perspective. Furthermore, closing paragraphs of sections often summarize the contents of that section and show their significance to the whole.

Structural paragraphs are commonly placed between the major heading and the first subheading of the section. Such paragraphs usually point both backward and forward. Their primary purpose is to introduce the subject to be discussed. Like a road map, their function is to help the reader as she moves along from one phase of the presentation to the next. This type of paragraph prods her to look back to where she has been and to look ahead to where she is going. The technique is simple: The writer tells the reader briefly the major points covered and then indicates what is coming next. The structural paragraph serves as a connecting link for the topics, sections, and chapters of information you present to your reader.

An example of such a paragraph is the one that begins Chapter 6 of Dewey's book, *How We Think:*

We have in previous chapters given an outline account of the nature of reflective thinking. We have stated some reasons why it is necessary to use educational means to secure its development and have considered the intrinsic resources, the difficulties, and ulterior purpose of its educational training—the formation of disciplined logical ability to think. We come now to some descriptions of simple genuine cases of thinking, selected from the class papers of students. [1:91]

Sentence 1 recaps the previous chapters. Sentence 2 gives the major thesis of those chapters. Sentence 3 indicates what we will read next—examples of what was discussed in previous chapters.

A well-organized paper has structural paragraphs that have duties of introduction, transition, review, and summarization. Like headings, they keep the reader informed of the design of the whole composition; in addition, they connect the larger parts of the report. They are an aid to readability and comprehension.

Paragraph Principles Summarized

In writing, the paragraph is the basic unit in the development of a subject. The paragraph's basic developmental unit is the topic sentence. The topic sentence provides unity, coherence, and proportion to the material of the text. If you are to meet your reader's needs efficiently, you must discuss one thing at a time. Keep things together that *belong* together. Make clear relationships among the ideas of your paragraph with reference words, repetition, connectives and relative words, phrases, and clauses. Indicate important ideas by properly subordinating the unimportant ones. Finally, help your reader make transitions from one idea to the next, one subject to the next, or one section to the next by using linking words, sentences, and paragraphs.

Reader Analysis—How to Write for Your Reader

In every English composition class that you have had, you've been told that you need to pay attention to your reading audience, otherwise your message will not get through. In Chapter 1, we learned how communication works. When we communicate, we are trying to establish a commonality with someone. To communicate, then, a writer needs to establish a common frame of reference with the reader. In the human communication system, as we have seen, there is a *source*, a *message*, and a *receiver*. Inexperienced writers, often unwittingly, are self-centered and more concerned with themselves (the source) and their message than with the recipient of the message. They forget that the message they want to transmit must be encoded (written) within the framework of the experience and outlook of the receiver (reader). To be comprehended and accepted, messages must be structured to meet the needs, desires, interests, and background of the reader.

Your writing experience—like that of most students—has usually been limited to the classroom. Your intended reader has been your instructor, who supposedly knows more about the subject than you do. The objective of your written assignment often is academic. Its purpose is to demonstrate that you can write adequately, if not competently, and coherently about the subject, thus proving you have mastered the assignment. In the real world of professional activity, your readership varies. Some readers, like your supervisor, will know a good deal about your subject; some will know nothing at all. However, most readers will not know what you know or what your considered judgment is about the subject. If you have done your job well, you will have brought a sharp focus on the problem of interest. That is why your message is or should be important to the reader.

Professionals write to people within and outside their organizations. Although their documents may be directed to a specified reader-client, they may yet have to meet the needs of many groups:

- Readers within their own groups, for example, supervisors and colleagues
- Readers within the organization with a specialized need to know, e.g., upper management personnel, the legal office, the public relations office, the advertising office, and so on
- Readers outside the organization with a specialized interest in the subject, the most prominent being the client; such outside readers may lie in the expert class or may range from persons with little formal education to experts in fields other than the subject matter

You can see that a document may have to serve the needs of many different kinds of readers. A good example is a report on hazardous waste leaks or spills. The effects of hazardous chemical effluence on a community like Love Canal in Niagara Falls, New York, or on Times Beach, Missouri, are of interest to a wide variety of readers: all levels of the Environmental Protection Agency (EPA), other concerned federal agencies, the governors, mayors, legislators of the states and communities directly and potentially concerned, the mass media, environmental scientists and professionals in related disciplines, public safety personnel, the organizations or persons said to be responsible for the effluence, the medical profession, public spirited and concerned citizens, the legal profession, members of the community directly and indirectly affected, and many others too numerous to list.

To prepare a document relevant to such a diverse universe of needs is not easy—certainly not for the inexperienced writer. Our purpose in this text is to lessen the pitfalls and to make the task easier. (Notice, I said again *easier*—not easy.) With the guidance of experience, many writers have learned to meet successfully the needs of such a wide universe of readers. Our purpose in this section is to provide you with the thinking and guidance to analyze your reader requirements and to offer helpful instruction on the means to reach your readers.

Focussing on the Reader

If we stop to think a minute about what is involved in analyzing the readers of our writing, certain obvious things are clear. You can list them as well as I:

> Who is the primary reader? (The primary reader will use the writing to act on the information it contains.)

Who is the secondary reader? (These are readers who could be directly affected by the document or by the uses their organization may make of it.)

Who is the immediate reader? (The immediate reader is the formal transmitter of the document or of its information.)

You will certainly list other specifics to help characterize your reader or readers:

What is the reader's job or role?
What is the reader's background, education, technical knowledge, and experience?
What are the reader's chief responsibilities, concerns, needs, and desires?
What does the reader know about the matter or problem the writing deals with?
What are the concerns and requirements of the reader's organization?
What are the political realities of the situation or problem, and how can you best meet them?
What personal characteristics does the reader have that affects the comprehension, reception, and acceptance of the document?
What attitudes, preconceptions, biases, or misinformation does the reader bring to the problem?
Who, if anyone, will be offended or pleased by the document?
How will the reader use the document?

- as a guide for immediate action?
- as background for future action?
- as a reference?
- as an archival document?

Such prewriting, planning, and thinking, you'll find, will help because you will be able to:

- identify your reading audience;
- determine the purpose and scope;
- organize your facts and ideas to meet the purpose of your study and needs of your reader(s);
- keep your writing on track from the introduction section to the body to the conclusion section.

Your introduction indicates immediately for whom the writing is intended, what the writing addresses, and the reason it was prepared. (See chapters 5 and 6 for further elaboration.) When a reader is motivated and understands why she is supposed to read, she is more receptive to investing her reading time. To maintain that interest, you will remind her from time to time where your information has taken her and where she will be going. Such transition devices, as we saw in our discussion of structural paragraphs, keep the reader oriented and economize on her attention and time.

Making Writing More Readable

Research has been going on since the early 1920s to find a formula for more readable writing. One of the prominent **readability** researchers, Rudolf Flesch, a consultant for the Associated Press, various newspapers, and many corporations, was responsible for making their printed communications, annual reports, and other writing more readable. According to Flesch, writing has more "reading ease" if sentences are short—an average of not more than 19 words each; if sentences have short words—not more than 150 syllables per 100 words; and if the writing has liberal use of words and sentences possessing human interest—that is, liberal use of personal pronouns. [2]

Parents who have looked at the reading books their children bring home know that a page made up of short, simple sentences—even with personal pronouns—is dreadfully monotonous. Variety in sentence length—change of pace—helps sustain reader interest. How short is a "short" sentence? What does *readable* mean? Shortness and readability are, of course, relative terms. A person's concept of sentence length changes with age, education, and reading experience. One study has shown that sentences written by schoolchildren increase in length from an average of 11.1 words in the fourth grade, to 17.3 in the first grade of high school, and 21.5 in the upper college years. [10:180]

A sentence that looks long to the fourth grader may look short to the college junior. A person whose only readings are Andy Capp, tabloid headlines, and TV program captions will find a sentence long that looks short to the student of literature.

A story for children has sentences averaging less than fifteen words, whereas sentences for educated adult readers may average between twenty and thirty words. A higher or lower average indicates that a writer should examine his sentences critically, but *it does not necessarily mean* that anything is wrong. Variety, type, construction, and length, on the whole, are more important than the average number of words.

A long sentence is suited to grouping a number of related details clearly and economically. Thus, the writer of a newspaper story answers in her first sentence the six essential questions: Who? What? Where? When? Why? How? Causes and reasons, lists, results, characteristics, and minor details may all be expressed tersely and clearly in long sentences. One of the most effective sentences in the English language is eighty-two words long:

> It is rather for us to be here dedicated to the great task remaining before us—that from these honored dead we take increased devotion to that cause for which they gave the last full measure of devotion—that we here highly resolve that these dead shall not have died in vain—that this nation, under God, shall have a new birth of freedom—and that government of the people, by the people, for the people, shall not perish from the earth. [Lincoln, *Gettysburg Address*]

Readability formulas may be used as diagnostic instruments. They are not a quick and easy answer to making your writings more readable. The chief ingredient for readability is within the definition of communication: the establishment of a common interest between writer and reader. Readability formulas will not guarantee comprehension. Consider the following typical sentence from Gertrude Stein's "Four Saints in Three Acts"

> Short longer longer shorter yellow grass Pigeons large pigeons on the shorter longer yellow grass alas pigeons on the grass. [11:533]

Or, the opening paragraph of Franz Kafka's enigmatic novel, *The Metamorphosis:*

> As Gregor Samsa awoke one morning from uneasy dreams he found himself transformed in his bed into a gigantic insect. He was lying on his hard, as it were armor-plated, back and when he lifted his head a little he could see his dome-like brown belly divided into stiff arched segments on top of which the bed quilt could hardly keep in position and was about to slide off completely. His numerous legs, which were pitifully thin compared to the rest of his bulk, waved helplessly before his eyes. [7:1432–33]

Both of these excerpts would score higher in readability formulas than Lincoln's *Gettysburg Address* but would prove confusing to many readers. Readability formulas do not measure content, organization, or cogency, since these characteristics cannot be measured quantitatively; nor will readability formulas improve the writer's style in a written communication. However, formulas do point out certain qualities in written communication pertaining to comprehension. Therefore, they may be helpful if discriminatingly used.

Research on how learning takes place has contributed significant insights into readability. Certain writing techniques, researchers have found, help the reader to receive and comprehend information. Such techniques include:

> advance organizers,
> overviews,
> inserted questions,
> prompting clues, and
> graphic aids.

Advance Organizers

Headings (as we shall see in Chapter 7) are the best examples of advance organizers. They are road signs telling the reader the text territory to be visited.

Introductory text material also prepares and helps the reader organize and bridge from section to section the elements the document deals with. For example:

> This report will present a comparative cost analysis of high pressure hot water (HPHW) and steam systems as heat transfer media for a four-building complex at Boeing Company's Transport Division plant at Renton, WA. First, the report will describe the HPHW system in two of the buildings and the steam system servicing the other two structures. Cost for labor, materials, and maintenance will then be examined and analyzed. Conclusions and recommendations based on the cost efficiency of the system most practical for the Renton facilities will complete the report. A timetable to implement the recommendations is also provided.

Overviews

Similar to advance organizers, *overviews* give the reader a quick glance at the subject of the writing plus an indication of its significance. This technique whets the interest of the reader because it reveals at once the importance of the topic. For example:

In an article entitled "Food and Drug Interactions," appearing in the *FDA Consumer,* there is an overview above the article that begins:

> *If you're taking a drug, the food you eat could make it work faster or slower or even prevent it from working at all. Eating certain foods while taking drugs can be dangerous. And some drugs can affect the way your body uses food.* [9]

Overviews, like this one, are usually set off by italics, boldface typography, indentions, or by other graphic embellishments to catch the reader's eye. The purpose of the overview is to grab the reader's attention and arouse interest with the promise of details contained in information to come. The reader will then want to read the entire material. The hints provided in the overview help the reader to follow the details.

Inserted Questions

If you are asked a question, you pause to think whether you know the answer or you become curious to learn the answer. A writer can take advantage of our innate inquisitiveness by devising a question or set of questions that epitomize the topic or any of its aspects. For example, in the article just mentioned, "Food and Drug Interactions," the writer begins with several questions, which immediately grab the reader's attention and lead to the point of the article, that eating certain foods while taking certain drugs can be dangerous:

> Would it occur to you not to swallow a tetracycline capsule with a glass of milk? Or avoid aged cheese and Chianti wine if you are taking a certain medicine to combat hypertension? Or to eat more green leafy vegetables if you are on the pill? Probably not. Yet the effects foods and drugs have on each other can determine whether medications do their job and whether your body gets the nutrients it needs. [9]

Prompting Clues

Giving the reader a clue about the significance of the content to be presented helps the understanding and makes the details easier to follow. The simplest form of clue is typographical: use of italics, boldface, or underlining. Color and illustrations can also be used. Rhetorical devices such as examples, analogies, or comparisons can be effective. They prepare the reader for the substance and particulars because such prompting devices have made the path to comprehension more familiar and comfortable. Note in the example below how the metaphoric use of *pump, duplex apartment,* and *pipes* as well as italics enables a lay reader better to understand how the heart works and what happens in a heart attack:

To understand what happens in a heart attack, we have to think of the heart, a muscle, as a pump (Figure 2.1). Blood from the body enters the right side of the heart. The heart has four chambers, which have special roles in the pumping process. The upper chambers are called the *auricles;* the lower chambers, the *ventricles*. The auricle and ventricle on each side form an independent part of the heart somewhat like rooms in a duplex apartment; in effect they make up a "right heart" and a "left heart." There is no connection for the blood to flow between right and left hearts; they are separate "duplexes." Each pumps its own circuit; the right side sends blood under low pressure into the lungs where it is combined with oxygen. From the lungs, the left ventricle pumps blood under relatively high pressure to the rest of the body, supplying oxygen and nutrients to the tissues. So the heart is like a pump, squeezing and forcing blood throughout the body. The most important part of the heart is the middle muscular layer of the heart wall, the *myocardium*. Like all muscles in the body, the myocardium must have oxygen and nutrients to do its work. Unfortunately, the myocardium cannot use oxygen and nutrients directly from the blood within the chambers of the heart. Nutrients and oxygen are furnished by blood vessels outside the heart. The two most important vessels are the right and left coronary arteries or veins that begin at the base of the *aorta,* the large artery that carries blood from the heart to other parts of the body.

As a person grows older, the coronary arteries are sometimes narrowed by fatty deposits or *plaque*. This process is called *atherosclerosis*. The narrowing is no different than the accumulation of "gook" in old pipes, which impedes or stops the liquid from flowing through. When such deposits occur, the heart cannot always pump enough blood through the arteries. When one of the coronary vessels is blocked completely, even for a short time, part of the heart may die and scar tissue may form. This injury is called a heart attack. Scarring is bad because any injured area causes the heart to lose its effectiveness as a pump; there is less muscle to contract to force blood out.

Figure 2.1 A normal heart.

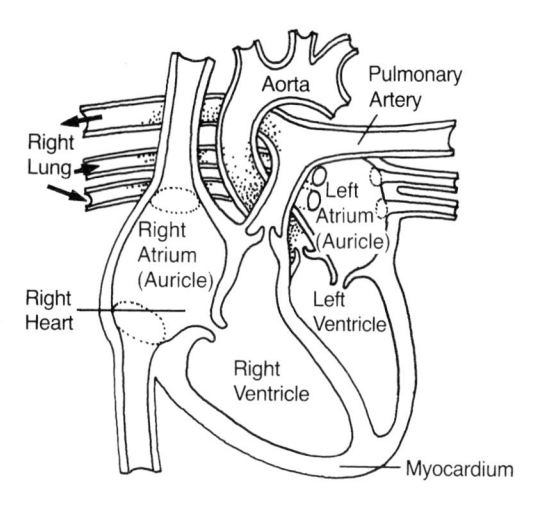

Graphic Aids

Graphic aids are lists, tables, photographs, drawings, diagrams, graphs, charts, flow sheets, and editorial devices. These help the reader to digest, think about, and visualize facts and ideas. Graphics help the reader to organize details and see them in relationships. This was seen in the drawing of the heart, Figure 2.1, in the previous example. Strategic use of space, movement, emphasis, color, shades, and highlights in graphic aids lend truth to the old saying that a picture is worth a thousand words in promoting readability.

Factors to Improve Readability

A number of factors will aid readability of written communications:

1. A thorough knowledge of the matter to be communicated
2. A knowledge of the reader
3. Organization of the text to lead the reader to the thesis sentence (see Chapter 5)
4. Use of format devices such as display heads, enumerations, uncrowded spacing, and margins
5. Use of illustrations, tables, and other graphic devices to supplement the text
6. Use of topic sentences in paragraphs
7. Use of structural paragraphs, sentences, and words and phrases
8. Use of advance organizers
9. Use of overviews, if appropriate
10. Use of prompting clues
11. Inserted questions, as appropriate
12. Variety in sentence type and length
13. A clear, concise, direct, and objective style of writing
14. Relegation of long derivations, computations, and highly technical matter to the appendix

Some Advice on Style

Style is the way you put your thoughts into words, sentences, paragraphs, and groups of paragraphs to convey information to your reader. Effective technical style consists of these elements:

1. Clarity
2. Precision
3. A logical construction of words into sentences, paragraphs, sections, and chapters
4. Directness in statements of thought

To achieve these ends, you must do the following:

a. Balance the length and type of your sentences (using more complex than simple or compound sentences).
b. Select, whenever appropriate, the simple word rather than the obscure, the familiar term rather than the unfamiliar. (However, if complex and unfamiliar terms are necessary to meaning, logic, and clarity of the thought to be communicated, you should use them—with appropriate definitions or explanations.)
c. Maintain a balance of active verbs with passive verbs. (Explanation depends on facts. Verbs express the relationship among facts. When the action is more important than the actor, you should use the passive construction. Active verbs give more force, directness, and clarity to expression. However, your reader is the determining factor. If you know the reader prefers an impersonal style, let your writing reflect it. If you have a choice, use a more personalized approach. By doing so, you will be more concise and to the point because you are expressing yourself in a style that is you, not in the style you think you ought to use.)
d. Finally, make sure that every word, sentence, and paragraph you write is not merely capable of being understood but incapable of being misunderstood.

No one, least of all the technical writer, should be open to the criticism Alice in Wonderland received:

> "Speak English!" said the Eaglet. "I don't know the meaning of half those long words, and what's more, I don't believe you do either."

Chapter in Brief

We have examined the definition of and the characteristic qualities and elements of technical style. In the process, we analyzed the use of the active and passive voice, types of sentences and their capacity for expression, the design of paragraphs, and the role of the topic sentence. We turned next to reader analysis and the factors that improve readability.

Chapter Focal Points

- Technical style
- Clarity and precision
- Objectivity
- Active and passive voice
- Sentence types
- The paragraph
- The topic sentence
- Reader analysis
- Readability

Questions for Discussion

1. Locate two technical articles on a subject of interest. Each article should be directed to an audience with a different level of understanding of the subject matter. Prepare to analyze these articles on the basis of the following questions:
   a. What similarities in style and what differences do you find in the two articles?
   b. What audience is each trying to reach?
   c. Is each successful in the factor of readability for the intended audience? Why and how?
   d. Does each article achieve its purpose?
   e. What writing devices do the authors use to achieve or attempt to achieve their purpose?
   f. Are there differences in terms used? Average length of sentences? Paragraphs? Use of personal pronouns? Use of abbreviations? Article organization? Format?
   g. What graphics help maintain readability and interest?
   h. How successful is each article in achieving its purpose? (Do you know at the end what the author has attempted to communicate?)

2. Classify the following titles as to the level of intended readership: general reader, technical specialist, executive.
   a. Engineering Tomorrow's Dinner
   b. Embryogenesis in Carrot Culture
   c. Coal in the United States: A Status Report
   d. The Architecture of Cognition
   e. Carbon Dioxide and Our Changing Climate
   f. Corporate Computing from the Top Down
   g. Software That Helps Homework
   h. How to Win the Budget Battle
   i. Fourier Transform Infrared Spectrometry
   j. Detecting Deception From Verbal, Visual, and Paralinguistic Cues

3. From any of your textbooks or professional periodicals, locate four paragraphs that have the following:
   a. The topic sentence at the beginning of the paragraph
   b. The topic sentence at the end of the paragraph
   c. The topic sentence in the middle of the paragraph
   d. No topic sentence within the paragraph (the topic sentenced is inferred)
   e. A pointer sentence
   f. Both a topic sentence and a pointer sentence

   Which paragraph construction do you find easiest to follow? Why?

4. Read the four paragraphs aloud in class. Which constructions do your classmates find the clearest to understand?

5. Locate a passage of bureaucratic writing—regulations of various types, leases, laws, legal agreements, insurance policies, bank documents, and so forth. Analyze the charac-

teristics that interfere with the flow of the message. Identify the stereotypical phrases and gobbledygook words the passage contains. In what voice is it written? Any personal pronouns? Any ungrammatical constructions? Does the punctuation help or hinder readability and understanding?

6. Locate a paragraph that you feel uses the passive voice structure effectively. Try to rewrite the passage in the active voice. Bring the two versions to class and have the class judge their effectiveness. Opinions should be substantiated.

7. How would you rewrite the following announcement?

> The Student Chapter of the Society for Technical Communication is an organization of interested students in college or in a university dedicated to development of further knowledge about careers in technical writing enhancement of necessary technical writing and computer skills and further contacts for the beginning careerist. The student chapter is now open to accepting applications for new memberships. Application forms are obtainable from any present member. Dues are modest for students in this prestigious organization.
>
> The meeting will be on October 1, at seven o'clock PM in Room 17 the Student Center. An interesting program is being planned with Montgomery F. Blakestaff of and also president, Blakestaff & Associates main speaker with a very interesting topic. Interested students are invited to attend and questions are permitted.

Assignments

1. The sentences or paragraphs below lack clarity, precision, directness, and balance. Rewrite them in accordance with the principles in this chapter.

   a. The purpose of this report is to offer the State of Ohio ways and resources to assist those in charge of developing procedures to increase the effective utilization of computer-based information system.

   b. Beginning management accountants may often advance to chief plant accountant, chief cost accounting, budget director, or manager of internal auditing though starting as ledger accountants, junior internal auditors, or trainees for technical accounting positions with salaries just as good as engineers starting out.

   c. It is concluded that the use of flexitime scheduling by companies will continue to bring about an increase in productivity by increasing employee morale and job satisfaction, the quality of labor, organization of work, and less absenteeism. Although drawbacks were mentioned about flexitime scheduling the rate of success and positive points clearly outnumber the problems or drawbacks. We will continue to see flexitime scheduling in the future because young workers of today want individual say and input into the company and by implementing flexitime scheduling this will be made possible.

   d. On any given day, one can turn on the "idiot tube" (television) and be assaulted by any number of twenty- to sixty-second messages and longer which preach of the unfulfillment in our life because the lack of a specific product or service.

   e. Adults, humans who have accrued a certain number of years of existence, must do all that they can to inform children in the area of sexual behavior and protect them from future problems.

f. As you requested here is the report on the problems faced by book and clothing buyers of retail and wholesale firms. These buyers also provided me with a number of solutions to these problems. I have included them also, as you requested. This paper will be limited to the major problems of book and clothing buyers and will not include specific details of individual situations faced by book and clothing buyers such as the management situation at their firms.

g. A clothing buyer must be able to work together with her store-department coordinators. The buyer should show them how to coordinate outfits for display. The perspective customer needs to know how the outfits go together. A clothing buyer spends a great deal of time working on advertisements for the items he has purchased. People need pictures to entice them to buy clothes if they're expensive, so the buyer must work up lay-outs of the different items he has purchased. He or she should also work up layouts for the floor of the store.

h. A 20 milliamp (ma) signal shall be available to control the additive system pumps from the control panel, automatically, or with a manual override.

i. A surgically implanted device devised to normalize the rhythm of a patient's failing heart will significantly reduce the death of high risk cardiac patients is called an implantable automatic defibrillator because it prevents sudden death caused by VA's (ventricular arrhythmias), which are rapid erratic heartbeats that cripple the heart.

j. Each pump's fabrication shall consist of ASTM 316 stainless steel where in direct contact with chemical additives and all piping connections shall be flanged to conform to ANSI Standard B16.5 to joint with interface connections.

2. a. Lawyers are the worst offenders in the use of a very specialized professional language in their writings. The writing of most lawyers is shackled by the gobbledygook of legal terminology and by the use of the third person and passive voice. Below is an example of an article a lawyer wrote in an engineering magazine. How would you rewrite the excerpts to make sense for a reader? Keep in mind that the qualities of technical style are clarity, precision, conciseness, and objectivity.

> The argument has been made that the contractor is a third party beneficiary of the promise of the engineer or architect to the owner that he, the architect, will act in a certain way with respect to the contractor, such as, for example, timely approval of plans. . . .
>
> Another interesting possibility presents itself with respect to the plaintiff contractor's problem of avoiding the exculpatory and notice provisions of a construction contract. These are the "fine print" clauses that attempt to shift onto the contractor all responsibility for everything that does or does not happen. Such provisions, either by terms or because a plaintiff contractor fails to comply with them, often effectively deprive a plaintiff contractor of the fruits of what otherwise could have been a successful suit against the owner. It has been suggested that when the actions of the engineer or architect have given rise to the cause of action, and the owner has protected himself as noted, there may exist enforceable legal liability against the engineer or architect independently of the owner under conditions where the architect will not receive the benefit of the protection afforded the owner. [5:49–50]

b. If possible, check your revision with a lawyer to see whether your rewriting is accurate and conforms with the legal nuances in the original. Obtain the lawyer's opinion about the specialized terminology of the legal profession. Is there anything wrong in the original quotation? What is the lawyer's opinion of legal writing when done by lawyers for laypersons as well as by lawyers for lawyers?

    c. Locate a Supreme Court decision and compare its writing style and clarity with that in the quoted material. An alternative reference might be the decision of U.S. District Court Judge John M. Woolsey lifting the ban on the book *Ulysses* by James Joyce. [8:ix–xiv]

3. Locate and read a short article in a professional journal of your field that you find easy to read and understand. Analyze the paragraph and sentence structure. How many simple sentences does it contain? How many complex? How many compound? How many complex-compound? Does it have any fragmentary (incomplete) sentences? Are there any ungrammatical sentences? Note how the construction leads you to the point of the thesis of the article. See how the relationship between sections, paragraphs, and sentences is handled. First, go through the article paragraph by paragraph and underline the thesis sentence. Second, draw a box around the transitional paragraph. Then circle each transitional sentence or phrase. Are there places in the article in which transitions are missing—where the flow of information stops? Or did the logic of the construction move the information unimpeded in that instance? What insights about writing for the reader did you gain from this exercise?

4. Find a paragraph in one of your texts that you find difficult to understand—not because of its technical substance but because of its expression. What readability principles did it violate? Rewrite the paragraph to make it more readable.

5. Write your instructor an autobiographical letter. The purpose of this assignment is to help open communication channels. Include details on not only your background and ambitions but also your feelings about writing. Let your hair down so you can be helped. Let your instructor know the following:

    a. You enjoy writing or you hate it, you are afraid of writing, or you haven't thought much about it.

    b. You would like to be able to write better, but you recognize you have certain problems. (Identify them.)

    c. You are taking this course because it's required, you recognize you need it, or the computer scheduled you in it.

    d. How do you feel about being in the tech reporting course?

    e. Have you given any thought to the reader of your writing? Do you think the reader should influence your writing? Why?

    f. How long do you spend on your writing assignments? Do you plan ahead or do you wait until the last minute? Do you feel pressure about writing? More or less than from assignments in other classes?

    g. About your writing assignments: Do you worry about them? Do you spend more time worrying than writing?

    h. Do you get writing blocks? What do you do about writing blocks? Are you aware that professional writers get writing blocks and they worry about them—even more than most students?

    i. Do you write at one sitting? Or do you doodle around? Do you try to write sections you are most comfortable with, or do you try to follow the logical sequence of the subject?

j. Have you had other classes in writing? Other than Freshman Composition? Have they helped? How, if you answer yes? Why not, if you answer no?
k. What do you want this class to do for you?
l. How can your instructor help you?

References

1. Dewey, John. *How We Think.* Lexington, Mass.: D.C. Heath, 1923.
2. Flesch, Rudolf. *The Art of Readable Writing.* New York: Harper and Brothers, 1949.
3. Huxley, T. H. *Essays.* New York: Macmillan and Company, 1929.
4. Huxley, T. H. *An Introduction to the Study of Zoology.* New York: D. Appleton, 1938.
5. Jarvis, Robert B. "The Engineer and Architect—As Defendants." *Civil Engineering,* April 1961.
6. Jeans, Sir James. *The New Background of Science.* Cambridge: Cambridge University Press, 1933.
7. Kafka, Franz. "The Metamorphosis." In *World Masterpieces,* vol. II, revised, edited by Bernard M. W. Knox. New York: W.W. Norton, 1965.
8. Joyce, James. *Ulysses.* New York: The Modern Library, 1940.
9. Lehmann, Phyllis. "Food and Drug Interactions." *FDA Consumer,* April 1988.
10. Perrin, Porter G. *Writer's Guide and Index to English.* 3d ed. Glenview, Ill.: Scott, Foresman, 1959.
11. Stein, Gertrude. "Four Saints in Three Acts." In *This Generation,* revised ed., edited by George K. Anderson and Eda Lou Walton. Glenview, Ill.: Scott, Foresman, 1949.

3
Basic Expository Techniques in Technical Writing

Chapter Objective

Provide guidelines for and proficiency in the expository processes of definition, description, and analysis.

Chapter Focus

- Definitions
  Formal and informal
  Synonyms and antonyms
  Illustration
  Stipulation
  Operational
  Extended
- Descriptions of mechanisms and organisms
- Description of processes
- Analysis
  Classification
  Partition
- Synthesis and interpretation

Writing that primarily is intended to inform and instruct is called *expository*. Its purpose is to increase a reader's understanding of a subject or situation. The expository techniques of technical writing may be grouped into three major categories: definition, description, and analysis. In explaining facts and ideas of a specific or technical nature, the technical writer uses these methods more often in combination than separately. However, for purposes of illustration and understanding, we will examine these methods individually.

The Nature of Definitions

A **definition** is an explanation of an object or idea that distinguishes it from all other objects or ideas. Definition is basic to knowledge. Infants, for example, learn about their environment by gradually defining the objects in it. A mother points to herself and says, "Mama." After a time, the infant will begin, in imitation and understanding, to point and say, "Mama." Using this process, the parent will teach by definition through pointing to the infant's food, to common articles of usage, and to common experiences. Certain dangerous or delicate articles become "no-no's"; others are "nice-nice." Through this rudimentary instructional process, infants begin to perceive and define their environment.

Similarly, adults attach importance to the names of objects and ideas in their environment. We seem to understand what we are familiar with and what we can name. Anthropologists tell us that our belief in the potency of names was one of our earliest human traditions. As a new activity achieves maturity, it also attains a nomenclature. Systematically, every component is named. In order for technicians, engineers, or scientists to understand a mechanism, they usually must know the names of its various parts.

However, we should not oversimplify. Understanding an instrument, species, or concept is more than just being able to give it a name or list its parts. We must be able to relate it to similar classes of instruments, species, or concepts and distinguish it by those significant characteristics that make it different from other members of its class. Through the process of definition, we become more aware of the exact nature of things that exist or could exist in our world.

The derivation of the word *definition* will help us understand it. The Latin word *definire* is its origin; *de* means "from," and *finire* means "to set a limit to" or "to set a boundary about." To define, then, is to delimit the area of meaning of a word, term, or concept. Definitions are verbal maps that indicate or explain what is included within a term and what is excluded. The latter is often communicated by implication.

Methods of Developing Definitions

The Formal Definition

A definition is **formal** when it has a prescribed form consisting of three parts. The first part is the *term*—the word, object, idea, or concept to be defined. The second is the *genus*—the class, group, or category in which the term belongs. The third part is the *differentia*—the characteristics that distinguish the term from other members of the genus. The differentia excludes all other members of the genus except the term being defined.

1. A *rectangle* is a four-sided figure having all its angles right angles and, thus, its opposite sides equal and parallel.

    "Rectangle" is the term; *"four-sided figure" is the* genus; *"having all its angles right angles and, thus, its opposite sides equal and parallel" is the* differentia.

2. A *mouse* is an electronic device that looks like a small box and plugs into the computer operating system to allow the user to interact with the information on the screen without using the keyboard.

    "Mouse" is the term; *"electronic device" is the* genus; *"that looks like a small box and plugs into the computer operating system to allow the user to interact with the information on the screen without using the keyboard" is the* differentia.

The formal definition is not an academic exercise. It is closely related to the scientific process of classification. It utilizes a logical method of analysis to place the subject to be defined into a general class (genus) and then differentiates it from all members of its class. The term to be defined should not be repeated in the genus or differentia. For example, to define chess as a game played on a chessboard tells the reader very little about the game. To be satisfactory, the genus must identify the term precisely and completely. If the genus is too general, it complicates the identification because the differentia must be expanded. The differentia must be broad enough to include everything the term covers and specific enough to exclude everything that the term does not cover. It fences in the meaning of the term by listing qualities, giving quantities, making comparisons and/or itemizing elements.

Definitions should be stated in simpler or more familiar language than the term itself; otherwise the purpose of the definition is lost. A classic example of this fault is Samuel Johnson's definition of a cough: "A convulsion of the lungs, vellicated by some sharp serosity." Also, definitions should not be phrased in obscure or ambiguous language. Definitions should be impersonal, objective, and should *describe*, not praise or condemn, the matter being defined. Johnson's definition of oats as "a grain eaten by horses and in Scotland by the inhabitants" reflects a personal bias. These stated principles apply, of course, not only to the formal but also to all methods of definition that follow.

The Informal Definition

The strict format of the formal definition is not appropriate or efficient in all situations. The **informal definition** uses the shortest and simplest method for identifying or explaining the matter to be defined. The method may involve substituting a short, more familiar word or phrase for the unfamiliar term or using special expository devices, such as antonyms or illustrations, that give the reader a quick recognition of the term. Informal definitions are used in less formal writing—for the general public, not for the technical specialist.

Defining by Using Synonyms and Antonyms

If you were asked, "What is a microbe?" you probably would answer, "a germ." *Germ* means the same as *microbe*. The two words are used interchangeably. They are **synonyms.** *Double* means "twice;" *paleography* means "ancient writing;" *helix* means "spiral." A known word is substituted for an unknown word in definition by *synonym*.

Closely associated with this technique is the use of an **antonym** for aiding definition. *Down* is the opposite of *up*. *Abstruse* means "not obvious"; *indigenous* means "the opposite of foreign"; *empirical* means "not theoretical."

Both synonyms and antonyms are simplified forms of definitions that frequently set rough, approximate boundaries of meaning rather than complete and exact limits. They are techniques more appropriate for impromptu and informal situations than for more formal requirements. Children or laypersons do not usually require the complete and specialized details for their understanding. For example, if a child asks, "What is penicillin?" her informational needs would be satisfied with "a substance that kills germs." She might actually be confused by technically more accurate information such as:

> Penicillin is an antibacterial substance produced by microorganisms of the Penicillium chrysogenum group, principally penicillium notatum NRRL832 for deep or submerged fermentation and NRRL 1249, B21 for surface culture. Penicillin is antibacterial toward a large number of gram positive and some gram negative bacteria and is used in the treatment of a variety of infections. [9:1206]

Consequently, definitions by synonyms and antonyms frequently are used in the technical article aimed at the general reader.

Defining by Illustration

Offering an illustration is a primary means for defining an unfamiliar thing or concept. We saw at the beginning of this chapter that adults use pointing as an effective way of explaining things to children: "*This* is an oak leaf." "*This* is a Phillips screwdriver." "*This* is a ten-penny nail." Definition by pointing or illustrating makes the task easier for both adult and child.

Dictionaries, too, resort to definition by illustration. For instance, in defining *emu*, the dictionary says it is "a large, nonflying Australian bird, like the ostrich, but smaller." Included is a drawing of the bird that gives the reader details of the bird's appearance. The dictionary defines the *trapezium* as a "plain figure with four sides, no two of which are parallel." Again, an illustration is included and shown in Figure 3.1.

Figure 3.1 A trapezium.

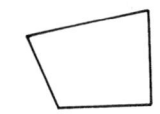

Defining by Stipulation

In Chapter 6 of Lewis Carroll's *Through the Looking Glass,* Humpty Dumpty announces:

> "There's glory for you!"
> "I don't know what you mean by 'glory'," Alice said.
> Humpty Dumpty smiled contemptuously. "Of course you don't—till I tell you. I mean 'there's a nice knockdown argument for you.'"
> "But 'glory' doesn't mean 'a nice knockdown argument,'" Alice objected.
> "When I use a word," Humpty said in rather a scornful tone, "it means just what I choose it to mean—neither more or less." [2:214]

Humpty Dumpty is using definition by **stipulation**—that is, he attributes to a word or term a specific meaning he wants it to have. Stipulative definitions are common practice in all spheres of activity to enable a reporter to convey a necessary meaning. Reports and papers frequently will say, "When the term x is used in this report, it means such and such." In contracts, legal documents, and specifications, it is not only convenient but often necessary to establish definition by stipulation, as for example:

> The term, *special tooling,* as used in this clause, includes all jigs, dies, fixtures, molds, patterns, special taps, special equipment and manufacturing aids acquired or manufactured by the Contractor for use in the performance of this contract. The term does not include: (a.) items of tooling or equipment heretofore acquired by the Contractor; (b.) items of tooling or equipment for performance of services which are not peculiar to the needs of this contract; or, (c.) general or special machine tools or similar capital items.

The Operational Definition

In the scientific and technical fields, the **operational definition** has become a useful technique. It offers meaning of a term, not by classifying it into a genus and then isolating its distinguishing characteristics from other members of its class, but by describing the activities, procedures, or operations within which the term operates.

Rapoport, in an article called "What is Semantics?" explains this approach:

> An operational definition tells *what to do* to experience the thing defined. Asked to define the coefficient of friction, the physicist says something like this: "If a block of some material is dragged horizontally over a surface, the necessary force to drag it will, within limits, be proportional to the weight of the block. Thus the ratio of the dragging force to the weight is a constant quantity. This

quantity is the coefficient of friction between the two surfaces." The physicist defines the term by telling how to proceed and what to observe. The operational definition of a particular dish, for example, is a recipe. [6:128–29]

The Expanded Definition—Amplification

Sometimes a synonym, antonym, or formal definition adequately explains the meaning of a thing or idea. At other times, especially if an idea or a complex object is being explained, the definition must be developed by the use of details, examples, comparisons, and other explanatory devices. The **expanded definition** is frequently an amplification of the formal definition. How it is developed depends on the nature of the concept and the writer's approach to it. Most expanded definitions follow the structure of the paragraph. They will begin with a topic sentence, structured as a formal definition or as a statement of the topic for discussion. Some expanded definitions are **no** longer than a paragraph; some may require several hundred or several thousand words.

There are several methods for developing expanded definitions. Among them are the following.

Analogy is a comparison of two things that are alike in certain aspects. Analogies are particularly useful in defining an unfamiliar object, idea, or process by comparing it to a more familiar one, as for example, comparing Internet, the global data system with the U.S. national highway system. You should use analogies with care because a superficial or unknowledgeable reader will not discern likeness in objects, ideas, or processes.

Explication is an explanation or interpretation of terms used in a definition:

> The rather odd term, "optical pumping", means just what it says. In general, "pumping" is a process of raising matter from a lower to higher energy. For example, raising the potential energy of water by moving it from an underground well to an elevated tank. In this article, we shall be concerned with the pumping of individual atoms from lower to higher energy states of internal energy. The word, "optical," refers to the light energy that is the source of power in the pump. [1:72]

Derivation helps explain the meaning of a term by examining its etymological origin, this was the approach I used in the beginning of my discussion of definition as an expository technique.

Use of an *example* is a method closely related to definition by illustration. In the scientific and technical fields, examples often are necessary to bring understanding to the uninformed. They are especially useful in explaining abstract and conceptual matters. In his book *Electrons, Waves, and Messages*, Pierce uses some everyday experiences to exemplify and quickly define some very abstract processes:

> If you touch a steam radiator, your hand is heated by *conduction*; if you hold your hand over the hot air arising from the hot air register, your hand is heated by *convection*; if you hold your hand in the beam of heat from a reflector-type electric heater, your hand is heated by *irradiation*; it is warmed despite the fact that the air surrounding it is cool. [5:181–82]

History. By providing the history of a subject, you enable a reader to get a deeper understanding of the term and the context of its operation.

Analysis. You can give a reader a better grasp of a complex subject if you break it up into component parts, enabling him to digest one portion before proceeding to the next. You will find this approach effective in defining various steps in a process, especially if succeeding steps increase in complexity.

Comparison and Contrast. What is difficult to comprehend often can be effectively explained by comparing and/or contrasting it to something less difficult or more familiar.

Distinction. An essential of definition is differentiation, so an extended definition may be composed entirely by identifying the distinguishing characteristics of the subject.

Elimination. In some instances, you may develop a definition effectively by the process of elimination—demonstrating what something is by enumerating what it is not.

Combination of Methods. The more complicated a term or concept is, the more involved the explanation must be. In that instance, you will find, no one type of definition is adequate; it will be necessary to use a combination of several techniques.

You can see that there are many methods for achieving definition. The effective writer does not choose his method haphazardly, but he chooses a method appropriate to bringing understanding to the reader. In report writing, as in other types of writing, definitions are most often placed in the introductory section so the reader can better understand and follow the main body of the written work.

General Principles of Definition

1. Definitions are needed when an unfamiliar term is used; or a familiar term is given a specialized meaning; or a term is given a stipulated meaning.
2. Definitions should include everything the term means and exclude everything the term does not mean.
3. Definitions should not include the term being defined or any variant form of it in the genus (class or family to which it belongs) or in its distinguishing qualities or traits.
4. Definitions should include the essential qualities of the term defined.
5. Definitions of terms in which magnitudes are the essential differentia should provide the essential measurable quantities involved.
6. Definitions not measurable by quantities but limited or bounded by other terms that are closely related should include essential similarities and differences of the term defined and the terms bordering it.
7. Definitions should be stated in simpler or more familiar language than the term being defined.
8. The audience for whom the definition is intended should determine the definitional approach to be taken.

9. An expanded definition should employ expository devices such as examples, comparisons, contrasts, details, distinction, analysis, analogy, history, and so forth to promote clarity, meaning, and interest. Each expanded definition should contain a logical or formal sentence definition of the term being amplified.
10. When appropriate, illustrations should be used to promote clarity and help the reader visualize the subject being defined.
11. Definitions should not be phrased in obscure or ambiguous language.
12. Definitions should describe, not praise or condemn, the matter being defined.
13. Definitions may appear anywhere in the text, as a footnote, in a glossary at the end of a text, in an appendix, or in a special section of the introduction to a document. Where it appears depends on its importance to the text and on the knowledge of the intended reader.

Technical Descriptions

A primary concern of the technical writer is to achieve exactness in the representations of phenomena. To achieve exactness, the technical writer often uses drawings so the reader can visualize what is being described. However, drawings and photographs cannot give complete representations. Although they help the reader see what something looks like, they cannot answer certain questions:

1. What is it?
2. What is it for?
3. What does it do?
4. How does it do it?
5. What happens after it does it?
6. What is it made of?
7. What are its basic parts?
8. How are they related to make it do what it does?

To answer these questions fully, technical writers must be able to visualize clearly the thing or process being described. They must have a thorough command of the appropriate nomenclature. They must know the components and their interrelationships and proportions. Finally, they must know the "why": the purpose of the thing or organism in question, the end it serves.

Describing a Mechanism or Organism

Complete knowledge of the thing described is fundamental to writing a technical description. Being able to draw the matter to be described indicates ability to visualize it completely and comes only with intimate familiarity and understanding. Nomenclature is important and inherent in technical descriptions. Every part has a name and should be correctly labeled. Part identification is best accomplished through labeling on the drawing. However, mere drawing is not full description because the sketch or diagram cannot indicate many essentials and attributes, nor can it always show relationships or structure.

It should be apparent that you, the technical writer, need to have the subject before you. Drawings are two-dimensional; descriptions need to be three-dimensional. You must be concerned not only with proportions but also with shapes, materials, essences, finishes, connections, relationships, purposes, and actions of the various components. Size, proportions, materials, finishes, and compositions of essences are fairly straightforward. Connections and relationships, however, need precise definition. How an element is fastened or connected needs to be examined very carefully. Is one component riveted, bolted, screwed, coupled, molded, wired, and so forth to another?

The precise location of components in relation to each other is important. At what angle is one element joined to another? Is it under or above? Inside or outside? Beside, parallel to, diametric to, and so forth? These details are significant to the *what* and *how* of the matter described.

In such analysis, one other element remains: the *why*, or the purpose. What does the thing or organism do? How and why does it do it? What is the significance of its action? The combination of the *what, how,* and *why* becomes the complete technical description.

Guidelines for Organizing the Written Description of a Mechanism or Organism

After becoming familiar with the mechanism or organism, your task is to organize the data into a written description. Written description usually falls into an arrangement of major sections. Section I is the introduction; it consists of a general description of the mechanism, phenomenon, or organism. Section II contains the main functional divisions of the subject, its main parts, and the principle under which they operate. Section III, the concluding section, shows how the subject operates by taking it through a cycle of operation.

The Introduction

Technical descriptions usually begin with a formal definition of the matter to be described. The definition is followed with a statement of the purpose or use of the matter and then with a very general description of its appearance. This initial description is general; its purpose is to give the reader a visual image of the subject by describing its size, shape, and appearance. An analogy can help readers understand something that might not be familiar to them. The major parts or assemblies of the subject are then listed. This listing leads readers to the middle portion of the report.

Major Divisions and the Principle of Operation

A technical description of more complex devices often includes the principle or theory of operation. The description of the major components can be arranged in three ways. One arrangement may follow the order in which a viewer's eye might see the matter described. For example, in the case of a claw hammer, the viewer might first see the head, then the peen, the face, the neck, and finally the handle. Each part, then, would be described in the sequence from which it is viewed.

Another way of arranging the description of the parts may be according to the sequence in which the parts are assembled. For example, a car door lock cylinder might be described in the order in which its various parts are arranged in the car door: the retaining clip, the pawl, the cylinder housing, the lock cylinder, the cylinder cap springs, the cylinder cap, and the cylinder housing scalp.

A third method of arrangement that might be appropriate is the order in which the parts operate. Which type of description to use depends on the reader's requirements. If the reader is interested only in a general knowledge and understanding, the first arrangement—according to the visual perspective—would be appropriate. If the reader needs to assemble the object, the second order should be used. If the reader needs to know how to operate the mechanism, obviously the third order is called for.

Terminal Section

After fully describing all the parts, your next step is to explain how the complete unit functions by taking it through a cycle of operation. This element is the concluding section. It should show how each assembly and/or part achieves its purpose. Emphasis is placed on the action of the parts in relation to one another. Special applications, variations, and other pertinent details are appropriate for this terminal section. A major consideration is completeness and clarity. Drawings and photographs can help to indicate the precise size and shape of parts and assemblies and should be integrated with the text.

Keep your intended readership in mind. Are you writing for experts, for well-informed individuals, or for the general public? Do readers need to know in a general way what the matter described looks like and how it functions? Or do they need to know how to operate the device or how to fabricate it? Your purpose is going to determine the organization and the amount of detail necessary. In a generalized approach, features are fewer and not as exacting. Even drawings are generalized. However, if a reader is to be intimately involved with the mechanism, you must make the details specific and precise.

Example of a Technical Description

The following description of the venturi carburetor by a student in a technical writing class is an example of an effective technical description, meeting, on the whole, the requirements set forth in this chapter.[1]

---

[1] "The Simple Venturi Carburetor" by Joe Marcus was written to meet an assignment for writing a technical description.

The Simple Venturi Carburetor

The simple venturi carburetor is used primarily as a fuel metering device for small, internal combustion engines such as are found on modern, self-powered lawn mowers. This type of carburetor, which is only remotely similar to a complicated automotive carburetor, consists basically of a venturi, a fuel supply line and needle jet, a butterfly valve, and sufficient mounting lugs so that the unit may be adequately secured to the engine on which it is to be used.

The Main Casting

The main casting, the diagonal pattern area [Figure 3.2a], which is formed of 195-TS-62 aluminum, is 5 inches in length, and has machined surfaces on all of the inner areas. The venturi entrance angle 0 is 5.38 degrees and the throat exit angle α is 7.12 degrees. The mounting flange is ¼-inch thick, and two ⁵⁄₁₆-inch diameter holes are drilled in this area for mounting bolts, as shown in [Figure 3.2b]. Butterfly shaft holes are drilled to a size of ⅛-inch in diameter, and are located in the unit's central, vertical plane, ¾ of an inch inward from the flange mounting surface. The fuel pick-up tube mounting hole is ⅛-inch in diameter and is also located in the central, vertical plane of the carburetor. This hole is drilled through the bottom of the casting at the mid-point of the throat section. The needle jet hole is radially drilled into the pick-up tube mounting lug, as shown in [Figure 3.2b]. This hole, which is ⁷⁄₃₂-inch in diameter, is then threaded with a ¼-inch National fine tap which corresponds to the needle jet's adjustment threads.

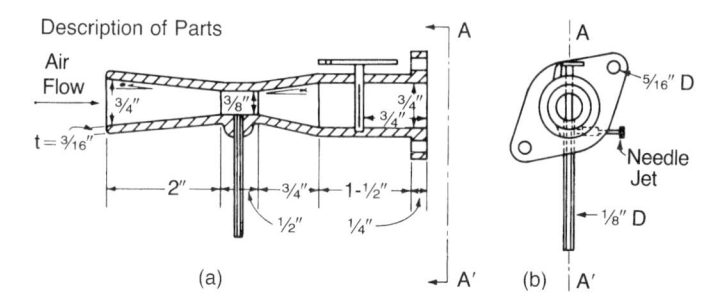

Figure 3.2

The Pick-up Tube

This unit is a ⅛ + 0.001 inch diameter (outside) brass tube which is two inches long, and is press fit into the casting due to the 0.001 inch interference. The inside diameter is ¹⁄₁₆-inch, and a ¹⁄₃₂-inch diameter hole is drilled radially through one wall of the tube ⁷⁄₁₆ of an inch down from the top surface which eventually is flush with the inside surface of the throat. This hole is the one through which the needle jet point protrudes so that the air-fuel mixture may be altered.

The Needle Jet

The needle jet, as shown in [Figure 3.3], is formed of brass material employing the dimensions shown. The threads indicated are ¼-inch fine to correspond with the threads cut in the main casting needle jet hole.

Figure 3.3

The Butterfly Valve

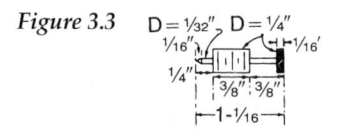

The butterfly valve consists of a ⅛-inch diameter by 1¼-inch long brass shaft with a diametral slot cut in the location shown. This slot and the circular butterfly plate are 0.020 inch thick and ¾ of an inch in height and diameter respectively. A hole [Figure 3.4a] is drilled after the shaft is installed in the main casting, and it corresponds with the hole in the butterfly plate. A rivet then joins the plate and shaft, employing this hole, which is ¹⁄₁₆-inch in diameter. A small shank is machined in the shaft which provides a retaining shoulder for the throttle linkage, [Figure 3.4c]. The stub extending from this shank is ¹⁄₁₆ of an inch in diameter and ⅛ of an inch tall; it is used as a rivet to secure the throttle linkage to the shaft. This throttle linkage plate is ¹⁄₁₆-inch thick steel plate 1-inch long and ¼-inch wide. Holes *(1)* and *(2)* are ¹⁄₁₆-inch in diameter, and are used for throttle rod attachment and mounting to the shaft respectively.

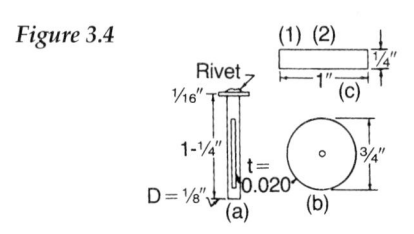

Figure 3.4

The Mechanism in Use

The nature of the engine with which this fuel metering device is to be used is such that a flow of air will almost continuously be drawn through the carburetor's throat. The amount of flow entering the carburetor is also a function of how much the butterfly valve has been opened. From fluid mechanics it can be shown that as a fluid (gas or liquid) passes through a venturi, its velocity increases: but its pressure decreases to some value below atmospheric. This negative pressure is greatest at the point in the throat where the fuel pick-up tube is located. This differential pressure, P (atmospheric) minus P (throat), will cause the gasoline, into which the tube has been submerged, to be forced up the tube and into the air stream. The needle jet, previously described, is used to accurately control the amount of gas flow through the pick-up tube. As the gasoline enters the air stream, it is vigorously mixed with the air flow and is therefore made compatible with combustion requirements.

Description of an Organism

The guidelines for describing an organism are similar to those for describing a mechanism. The following excerpt and illustrations [Figure 3.5] from a National Cancer Institute publication are an example of a description of an organism. [10:2–3]

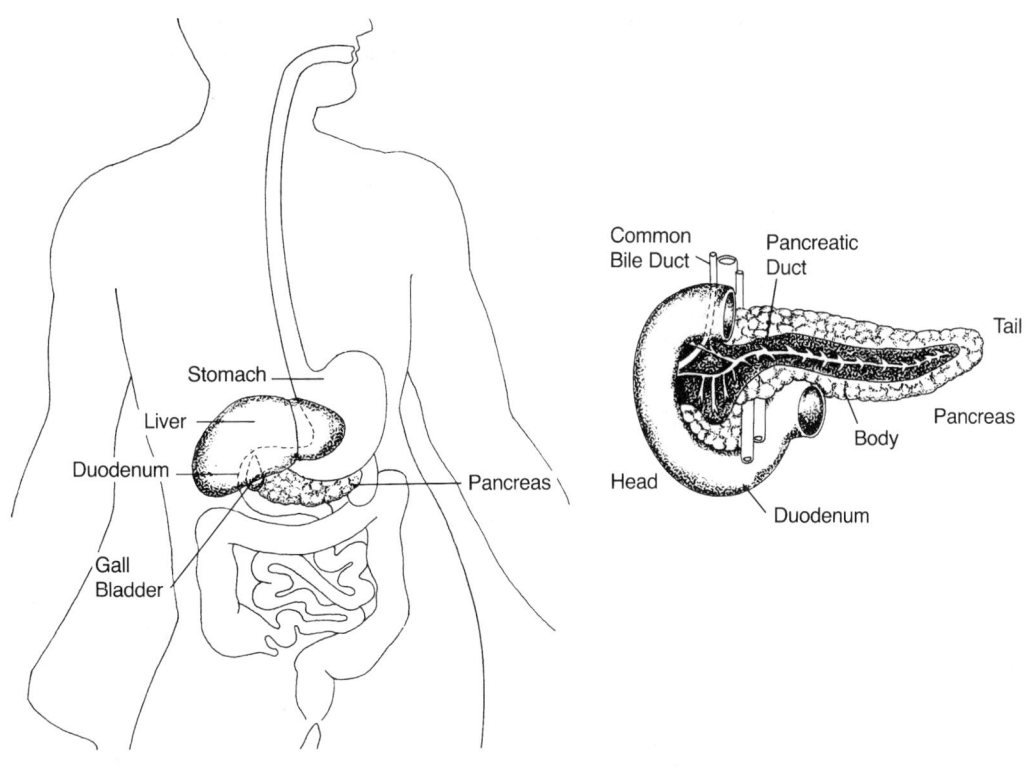

Figure 3.5

The Pancreas

The pancreas is a thin, lumpy gland about six inches long that lies behind the stomach. Its broad right end, called the head, fills the loop formed by the *duodenum* (the first part of the *small intestine*). The midsection of the pancreas is called the body, and the left end is called the tail. (See illustration, Figure 3.5).

The pancreas produces two kinds of essential substances. Into the *bloodstream* it releases *insulin,* which regulates the amount of sugar in the blood. Into the duodenum it releases *pancreatic juice* containing *enzymes* that aid in the digestion of food.

As pancreatic juice is formed, it flows through small ducts (tubes) into the main pancreatic duct that runs the full length of the gland. At the head of the pancreas, this main duct joins with the *common bile duct,* and together they pass through the wall of the duodenum. (See illustration.) The common bile duct carries *bile* (a yellowish fluid that aids in the digestion of fat) from the *liver* and *gallbladder* to the duodenum.

Describing a Process

Explaining a process is describing, narrating, or instructing how something is done, how an occurrence has happened, or how an effect has taken place. Certain events or activities are connected in a significant sequence and create an observable or measurable effect that, if repeated with the same quantitative and qualitative ingredients and in the same sequence, should produce the same or similar results. Some **processes** are due to natural—physical and biological—factors, some are due to societal—political, sociological, economic—forces, and some are due to psychological factors. There are processes resulting directly from human participation in scientific, technological, and industrial activities, as well as those resulting from commonplace tasks. All of these processes result from the procedures, or sequence of events, by which products are made, occurrences take place, or results are achieved. Technicians, engineers, computer systems analysts, biologists, physicians, farmers, geologists, social scientists, home economists—practically everyone—are concerned daily with processes. On occasion all of us must explain procedures so that others may reproduce the same result, occurrence, or product.

Guidelines for Organizing the Description of a Process

The explanation of a process in which the reader must take part requires more specific details than the explanation of an activity or occurrence in which the reader does not take part but needs to understand the occurrence. In other words, the written description of the process depends, as does every type of writing, on the intended reader's requirements. For readers who must perform the process, the technical writer will need to include every detail. If the reader needs only a general knowledge of the principles involved and will not need to perform the process or to supervise its performance, the writer need not go into specific details that may only confuse the reader. Instead, the technical writer should emphasize the broad principles and give a generalized account of the steps and sequences.

Intimate knowledge of the process to be described is fundamental. This involves not only complete understanding of how the process works or an ability to perform it but also a knowledge of the appropriate terminology and a logical organizational plan for the explanation.

Introduction

An introduction serves to define what is being done or what happens. Inherent within it are such questions as:

What is the process?
Who performs it?
Why is it performed? or
How does it happen?[2]
What are the chief elements or steps in what happens or in what results?
What is the consequence or result of the process?

---

[2]For processes occurring without human intervention.

Not all of the questions need to be answered, nor is the order of the listing significant. Reader level and reader requirements determine the depth of detail used or omitted.

As in the case of the description of a mechanism or organism, the explanation of the process may begin with a definition; then it is followed by a generalized description to give the reader an immediate visual image of the nature of the process.

The introduction should include any special circumstances, conditions, and personnel requirements. Frequently, it is necessary to explain why the process is being described. Sometimes the reason is contained in the definition. Sometimes the purpose is so obvious that it is unnecessary to explain, for example, the opening of a jar of pickles or the stapling of a sheaf of papers.

The introduction might also include the necessary materials, tools, and apparatus required for the process. The tabular form lends convenience and clarity. It is helpful to the reader to get a bird's-eye view of the general procedure before getting into the details. The introduction, accordingly, will end with a listing of the chief steps in the process.

In an explanation of a simple process, the introduction may consist of no more than a paragraph or two. In a complex process, the principle of operation or theory may occupy several hundred words. Drawings are frequently used to help explain what tools, instruments, or materials are used.

Main Steps

The main body of the explanation may have a paragraph of details for each major step. Each step is taken in sequential or chronological order, defined, described, and explained. Steps may be arranged as a list in which each item is preceded by graphic bullets, sequential numbers, or letters; or they may be written or keyboarded in sentence form with or without graphics, numbers, or letters. Whether in an itemized list or in sentence form, steps are listed in parallel grammatical structure and in correct sequence for the process. Materials, conditions, tools, and apparatus necessary in the performance are included in the explanatory unit of each step. Each descriptive unit has a topic sentence indicating the subject of the step. The details clarify the action in their relation to the process as a whole. All essential details of action should be included in the explanation. Whenever a nut and bolt are removed, the explanation must be complete enough to show their replacement. Each essential action should be specified in the terms of who, what, when, why, and how. Each substep within a major step constitutes a process within itself. Substeps should be properly introduced, and, if necessary, subdivided so that the reader will understand and will be able to perform the entire action. In the description of any action, the reader needs to understand and to visualize the activity. Qualitative conditions as well as precise quantitative factors are essential to obtain the required result.

Concluding Section

After the step-by-step explanation of the process is completed, you should summarize the whole process so the reader can see the activity as a whole and not as a series of separate steps. Requirements of the reader may necessitate additional information, such as an evaluation of the process, a discussion of its importance, an underscoring of important steps, equipment, materials, and precautions to consider, and, if appropriate, alternative steps that might be taken if certain difficulties are encountered.

Use of Illustrations

The reader will frequently be helped by drawings that show different stages of the process. Drawings can verify relationships and show shapes, which can be difficult to describe precisely in language. Dimensions are most conveniently indicated in a drawing. In complex processes or those in which several steps or actions are going on simultaneously, a flow diagram will be necessary to show the relationship of the several phases. Drawings must be integrated with the text and referred to specifically by figure number and with callouts to help the reader follow the complete process in text and illustration.

Style Considerations

The style considerations discussed in Chapter 2 are applicable and should be followed in explaining a process. Depending upon the point of view and the formality of the writing situation, processes may be explained in the first, second, or third person, and in the active or passive voice. Many processes are described for the express purpose of directing others to replicate the particular activity. In those instances, the active voice and imperative mood are required. However, the style must be consistent. If the explanation of the process is part of a larger report or a handbook of instructions, it must be integrated stylistically with the larger work.

Examples of Processes

Two examples of process descriptions follow. The first example is from a commercial technical manual explaining the process of removing a sample of a steel roof deck from an existing roof for calorimeter fire hazard evaluation. The process, though not complex, involves critical details. The explanation is intended to instruct safety or maintenance personnel who may or may not have professional technical training. Its details are very specific and precisely enumerated. The illustration is integrated into the text and adds clarity to the explanation of a critical step in the process. Note the conformity of this process explanation to the guidelines in this chapter.

Steel Roof Deck Sample for Calorimeter Evaluation

It is sometimes necessary to remove a steel roof deck sample from an existing roof for calorimeter fire hazard evaluation.

The following materials, equipment, and tools are necessary for removing one sample.

Materials

2–4½ ft. × 5-ft. × ¾-in. sheets of plywood (half table tennis size).
4–½ × 7-in.-long (minimum) carriage bolts with nuts and washers (7 in. is a minimum length for 1½ in. deep deck. For a deeper deck, increase the bolt length by the increase in deck depth over 1½ in.).

Equipment

Staging to support roof sample.
Waterproof coverings.

Tools

1 Heavy duty saber saw with 7-in. (min.) metal cutting blade.
1 Crescent wrench (8 or 10 in.).
1 Heavy duty drill with ⁹⁄₁₆ in. bit.
1 Ruler.

Sample Area

When selecting a sample area, make certain that it is between roof supports so that the sample will not be fastened to the supporting steel.

After the sample area has been chosen, remove any stock or equipment from the area immediately below and for a 10-ft. radius of the area. Equipment that cannot be moved should be covered with waterproof covers.

Wrap the sample (including the bolted-on plywood) to protect it from the weather and ship to the following address:

Chief Materials Engineer
Factory Mutual Research Corporation
1151 Boston-Providence Turnpike
Norwood, Massachusetts 02026
Note: Deliver to Bldg. 14

Place one sheet of plywood over the other and drill four ⁹⁄₁₆ in. holes through both sheets 12 in. in from each corner measured diagonally (Figure 3.6).

Leave one piece of plywood in the building; take the second piece to the roof. The tools and materials should be brought to the roof at this time also.

Attaching and Cutting the Sample

1. At the point on the deck from where the sample is to be taken, place the 4½-ft. × 5-ft. sheet of plywood. Make certain the 5-ft. dimension is parallel to the ribs of the steel deck.
2. Using the plywood as a template, drill four ⁹⁄₁₆-in. holes through the roofing and steel deck.
3. Place the bolts through the plywood and holes.

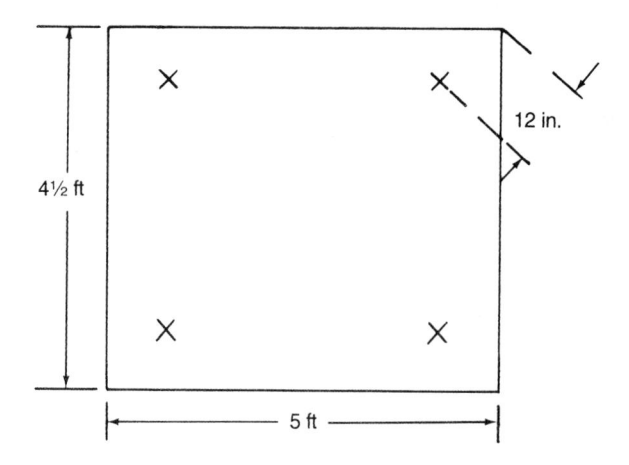

Figure 3.6

4. From the underside, place the second piece of plywood over the bolts and tightly fasten with the washers and nuts.
5. Provide support for the sample from the underside so that when the roof sample is cut, there will be no collapse.
6. Cut around the full perimeter of the plywood with the saber saw.
7. Remove the sample carefully so as not to disturb any of the components. Roof repair work should be started as soon as the sample has been removed to avoid the possibility of water damage.

This data sheet does not conflict with NFPA standards. [7:1–2]

The second sample process explanation, written by a student in a technical writing class, exemplifies the guidelines for the process description. See Figure 3.7.

Principles for Explaining a Process

The explanation of a process, especially one that involves the fabrication of a product or the conducting of an experiment or activity that leads to a specific result, should include the following information:

1. The definition of the process
2. A description of the time, setting, performers, equipment, materials, and preparations
3. An indication of the principles behind the operation
4. The listing of the major steps in sequential order
5. A step-by-step account of every action and, if appropriate, inclusion of description of apparatus, materials, and special conditions
6. Details under major steps, arranged in sequential order

>
> How to Obtain a Velocity Profile of
> Water Flowing in a Pipe
>
> The process of obtaining a velocity profile of water flowing in a pipe consists of taking velocity measurements by means of a U-tube manometer at specified distances across the pipe. The velocity is measured by a pitot tube. This is a tube which is situated in the pipe so that it is pointing in the direction of flow. The flowing water is brought to a stop in front of the tube. This results in an increase in pressure of the fluid in the tube. This increased pressure is transmitted inside a rubber tube in a U-tube manometer where the pressure differential pushes the water level down one leg and up in the other. The difference in the height of these columns of water in the U-tube manometer is an indication of the velocity of the water in the pipe.
>
> The process of measuring the velocity of water flowing in a pipe requires the use of the following pieces of equipment:
>
> U-tube manometer
>
> Rubber tubing
>
> Pitot tube assembly with adjustment screw, pointer and scale
>
> Pipe flanges
>
> Rubber gaskets
>
> Wrenches
>
> Data paper and pencil
>
> French curve
>
> Scale
>
> The steps to be followed are: (1) placing the pitot tube assembly in the pipe, (2) assembling and checking the equipment, (3) taking the velocity data, (4) plotting the results.

Figure 3.7 Sample explanations of technical processes.

Figure A
Pitot Tube Assembly Installed in Pipe

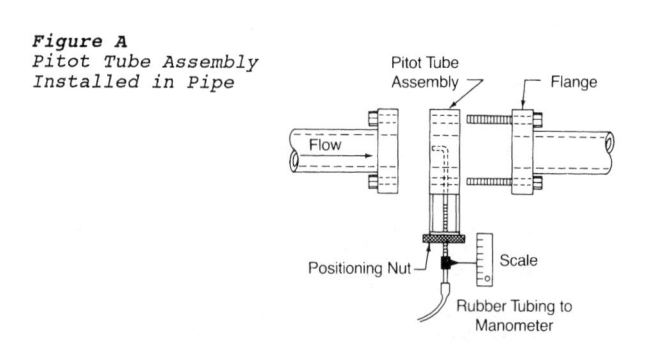

Placing the Pitot Tube Assembly in the Pipe

1. Choose a joint in the pipe and screw the pipe flanges on the pipe at this point. Bolts through the flanges will hold the pipe together with the pitot tube assembly between them.

2. Insert the pitot tube assembly in the pipe making sure that the pitot tube is pointed upstream. See Figure A.

3. Slip the bolts through the holes in the flanges and pitot tube assembly. See Figure A.

4. Place rubber gaskets between the pipe flanges and pitot tube assembly, then screw on the nuts and tighten them with a wrench. Care must be taken here to be sure that the rubber gaskets do not slip and cause a leaky joint.

Assembling and Checking the Equipment

1. Select a U-tube manometer with two foot legs and a scale between them. This size of manometer will permit a large range of flow rates. See Figure B.

2. Fill the manometer legs with water until the top of the meniscus in both legs is at the zero mark of the scale.

Figure B
U-Tube Manometer

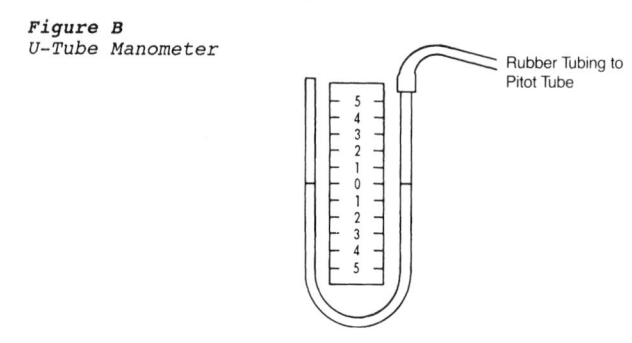

Figure 3.7 (continued)

3. Attach one end of the rubber tubing to a leg of the manometer, and the other end to the pitot tube assembly.
4. Select a flow rate and allow water to flow in the pipe.
5. Check the equipment for plugged lines and leakage by turning the screw clockwise to advance the pitot tube into the stream flow.
6. Check that the pointer indicates zero on the scale when the pitot tube is against the near side of the tube.

<u>Taking the Readings</u>
1. Observe and record the difference in levels of the liquid in the manometer when the pitot tube pointer indicates zero. There will be a slight difference in levels indicated since the pitot tube has the same diameter and will project into the flow area.
2. Advance the pointer by turning the screw clockwise to 0.05 inches and read, then record the difference in levels in the manometer liquid again. The difference will be greater since the velocity is greater in this part of the pipe.
3. Continue taking readings every 0.05 inches across the diameter of the pipe.
4. Repeat the process of determining the velocity by the difference of liquid levels in the manometer every 0.05 inches on the return trip through the pipe. This procedure will give two values at each point and their average will give a more representative value.

<u>Plotting the Results</u>
1. Determine the average of the pressure difference at corresponding points in the pipe.
2. Set up a Cartesian coordinate system with the difference in levels of the manometer (Δ_η) as abscissa and the distance from zero (Δ_x) as ordinates. See Figure C.
3. Plot the points and connect with a smooth curve. This curve represents the velocity profile of the water in the pipe. See Figure C.

As may be seen in Figure C, water does not flow at a constant speed across the diameter of a pipe. The velocity is zero at the inner edge of the pipe and maximum in the center of the pipe. This can be explained by the fact that there is relative motion between the water and the wall of the pipe. The water must therefore shear and the velocity profile shown indicates the symmetrical distribution of shear stress and velocity.

Figure C

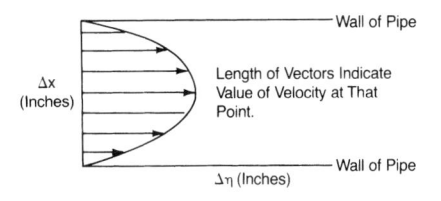

Δx (Inches)

Wall of Pipe

Length of Vectors Indicate Value of Velocity at That Point.

Wall of Pipe

$\Delta \eta$ (Inches)

Figure 3.7 (continued)

7. Drawings to aid the explanation of crucial steps of an action
8. A concluding section, which may be a summary or an evaluation of the process

The major elements in the organization of the description of a process are:

1. The introduction (items 1–4),
2. A step-by-step description of actions taken by the performer, or the steps in the development of the process (items 5–7), and
3. The conclusion, which summarizes the process and comments on its importance or usefulness (item 8).

Analysis

Dictionaries define **analysis** as a systematic and logical process of separating or breaking up a whole into its parts to determine their nature, proportion, function, or relationship. The word is derived from the Greek, *lyein,* meaning "to loosen," and the Greek prefix, *ana-,* meaning "up." To analyze, then, is to loosen or break up a subject into its logical entities.

The process of analysis is fundamental to all scientific and technical activity and to reporting and communicating such activity. It is the process of dividing a problem into its component parts. In chemistry, analysis plays an important role in the separation of compounds and mixtures into their constituent substances to determine the nature or the proportion of the constituents. In mathematics, the process is used to aid in solving problems by means of equations and to examine the relation of variables, as in differential and integral calculus. In medicine, analysis of symptoms plays an important part in the proper diagnosis of a disease. In logic, analysis is used to trace things to their source and to resolve knowledge into its original principles. Analysis aids clarity of thought by breaking down a complex whole into as many carefully distinct parts as possible and helps determine how the parts are related within the whole. In technical writing, the process of analysis helps writers understand the subject under investigation. It enables them to see component parts and identify the relationship of those parts to each other and to the whole. Analysis helps writers to distinguish and group together related things; to select data essential to the subject and problem; to select out of a mass of data the relevant material and to eliminate the irrelevant. In short, analysis is the process that helps writers understand their material and organize it into a logical order for efficient communication.

The basic operational element in analysis is division. When a heterogeneous assortment is divided into categories or classes, the process is known as **classification.** When a whole is divided into its parts, the process is called **partition.**

Classification and partition are closely related to definition. Definition is actually a form of analysis that resolves a subject into its component parts by (1) identifying the class to which a subject belongs and (2) differentiating the characteristics by which the subject is set apart from other members of its class. To define is partly to classify and partly to partition. Analysis by classification examines one arm of definition—the genus or class. To *classify* is to determine the whole of which the subject is part. Analysis by partition examines the other arm of definition—the differentia or distinguishing elements. To *partition* is to determine the parts of which the subject is a whole. Classification defines a subject by revealing its essence through comparison; partition defines a subject by listing the details or parts of its essence.

Classification

Any group of things that has a defined characteristic in common is called a *class*. Examples are compounds containing carbon, things made of iron, substances that are transparent, compatible computer systems, coordinate numbers, and scientific theories. It should be noted that membership in a class does *not* imply being *exactly* like all members of the class but being alike only with respect to the *specific* quality or characteristic on which the classification is based. One object can be a member of a large number of different classes, one for each of the qualities it possesses. For example, a dog is a member of the Vertebrata, the Mammalia, the Carnivora; it is furbearing, friendly to children, and vicious to intruders, and if the dog is young enough, it can be taught new tricks. Fogs may fit the classification of a colloid, a liquid, a gas, water, air, and, at times, ice crystals. Classifications can be structured in an infinite number of ways. The basis for the classification is always the practical consideration—the use to which it will be put.

Using Classification as an Expository Technique

Classification is a useful technique in exposition. It enables writers to systematize widely diverse facts for presentation in an orderly arrangement so readers can follow easily and understand the relationship of these facts. Classification may occupy an entire volume, as a textbook on botany or on types of motors, or it may form a chapter, a section of a chapter, or a paragraph in a chapter. Whenever writers must answer the question, Where does this species or this idea belong? they classify. The analytical process of classification helps writers organize their material for logical presentation. It enables them to examine their material in proper proportion: to differentiate the important from the unimportant, to give proper weights and values to items within the material, and to structure the presentation in parallel fashion or in subordinate fashion. In short, the process of classification helps the mind to interpret facts and data through inference.

Guidelines for Classification

1. Know your subject.
2. Define the term (subject) to be classified. The purpose of classification is to bring clarification and order to a number of elements that are diverse and perhaps confused in the reader's mind. Grouping things together may be meaningless to a reader unless he understands what you are talking about in the first

place. This requires careful identification and definition of the term. It may also mean sufficiently limiting the term so that it is useful to the purpose of the reader.

3. Select a useful and logical basis for the classification.
4. Keep the same basis for all of the items within a grouping. Changing the basis invites confusion. For example, a division of the cat family into lions, tigers, leopards, lynxes, pumas, jaguars, and cats friendly to children does not follow a consistent principle of grouping.
5. Keep groupings, though related, distinct. Classes must not overlap. Classification of a technical report as examination, investigation, recommendation, research, or formal indicates overlapping because a single report could easily fit all the listed categories at the same time.
6. Be sure to include all members in the classification. In other words, the classification should be complete. If incomplete, it does not serve as the "umbrella" to cover every member that logically belongs under it. For example, a classification of semiconductors would be incomplete if it did not contain thermisters.
7. Have at least two classes on each level of division. Since classification entails the breaking down of a grouping into its member parts on a logical basis, there must be at least two member parts in any such breakdown.
8. Arrange classifications in a logical order that is convenient for the reader to follow. Two formats lend themselves to such a presentation—tabular and outline. Tables facilitate classification of data. Outlines enable readers to see relationships and help reveal how subspecies are related to the parent genus.

Partition

Partition is a form of analysis. It is the division of a whole into parts. It is exactly the process used by an automobile mechanic in taking a motor apart, by a chemist in breaking down a substance into its components, and by a biophysicist in breaking down the cell into its minute elements.

For example, a typical microcomputer system has the following components:

Basic computer (containing the microprocessor and primary storage)
Keyboard
Disk drives
Monitor (display screen for soft copy output)
Printer (for hard copy output)
Serial or parallel interface card (to permit printer, modem, and other peripheral connections)
Connecting cables (to connect hardware components)
Software (for operation and application)
Modem (for telephone telecommunication)

The vertebrate eye may be partitioned into the conjunctiva, aqueous humor, pupil, lens, iris, cornea, vitreous body, layer of rods, optic nerve, retina, pigment layer, choroids, and sclera.

A formal report has a cover, a title page, an abstract or an executive summary, a table of contents, an introduction, a body, a terminal section, a bibliography, and, frequently, appendixes.

Partition, although employing a logical division, is not the same as classification. Within the process of partition, a complete entity is broken up into its components. Within classification, a general group is logically divided into the various species that make up the class. For example, mollusks, arthropods, and vertebrates all have eyes or visual organs. The eyes are quite different types of sensory organs, but they perform the seeing function for the animal of which they are a part. However, when an eye is partitioned, any of its parts—whether the pupil, lens, iris, retina, vitreous body, or optic nerve—is not, of itself, the eye.

Partition may be applied to abstract concepts as well as to physical entities. In communication theory, for example, the abstract concept of the communication unit is divided into the source, transmitter, receiver, and destination. The practice of psychiatry might be divided into the prevention, diagnosis, treatment, and care of mental illness and mental defects. The study of color divides into shade, hue, and intensity.

Guidelines for Partitioning

1. Be consistent in your approach or viewpoint in dividing your subject. Your viewpoint should be made clear to your readers. A logical approach to the partition might (as in the description of a mechanism) be from the viewpoint of the observer's eye, from the sequence by which the various parts are arranged, or from the way the parts function.
2. Separate and define clearly each part of the division. Parts should be mutually exclusive.
3. List all parts or explain any incompleteness. Within a generalized description—one representative of a class—partition may be limited to major, functional parts. In such a situation, the partition must be preceded by a qualifying statement such as "the chief functional parts are. . . ."
4. Check your stated partition for unity. The mechanism, organism, thing, or concept must be properly introduced and defined. The point of view from which the partitioning is approached must be explained. The analysis follows with a logical listing, description, and explanation of parts and their relationship. The concluding element of analysis by partition will show how the various parts relate to each other and to the whole.

Partition as an expository technique may comprise an entire monograph, or it may be included as a section or a chapter in a book or a paragraph or two within a larger piece of writing. Maintenance manuals are characterized by their numerous uses of the partition explanatory technique.

In summary, classification is a means of analyzing or explaining a plural subject. It examines relationships by determining similarities within the various species of its subject. Partition, on the other hand, analyzes and explains a single subject by examining its various components. The analytical approach used in partitioning is similar to that used in classification.

Both classification and partition are obviously related to formal logic. Classification uses reasoning from the particular to the general (induction); partition uses reasoning from the general to the particular (deduction). The identity of a class can be established by examining and grouping particulars together on the basis of a common element. The entity of particulars can be established by showing that the particulars belong to a class whose identity has been established. Often deduction (partition) is possible only after the identity of a class has been established by a previous induction (classification). In practice, this interrelationship is exemplified by a physician who diagnoses a disease by classifying the symptoms, then detects other diseases through the deduction of the diagnosis.

Achieving Interpretation Through Analysis and Synthesis

Synthesis is the antonym of **analysis**; it puts together parts or elements to form a whole. While opposed to analysis, the process of synthesis is frequently complementary to it. This is borne out graphically in the science of chemistry, which utilizes both processes of taking apart and putting together. Analysis and synthesis help in arriving at interpretation. Analysis breaks data down and arranges them into the logic demanded by the situation. The scientist or the technical writer may rearrange or recombine the various elements of the data in order to arrive at the meaning or explanation of the data through inductive and deductive inferences. **Interpretation** affords explanations, meaning, and conclusions regarding problems associated with the data. Analysis and synthesis provide a logical process for achieving appropriate insights, conclusions, and generalizations.

In his book, *How We Think,* Dewey shows how interpretation evolves through the operation of analytic and synthetic thought:

> Through judging [judgment], confused data are cleared up, and seemingly incoherent and disconnected facts are brought together. This clearing up is *analysis.* The bringing together, or unifying is *synthesis.* . . .
>
> As analysis is conceived to be a sort of picking to pieces, so synthesis is thought to be a sort of physical piecing together. . . . In fact, synthesis takes place wherever we grasp the bearing of facts on a conclusion or of a principle on facts. As analysis is *emphasis,* so synthesis is *placing;* the one causes the emphasized fact or property to stand out as significant: the other puts what is selected in its *context,* its connection with what is signified. It unites it with some other meaning to give both increased significance. When quicksilver was linked to iron, tin, etc., as a *metal,* all these objects obtained new intellectual value. Every judgment is analytic in so far as it involves discernment, discrimination, marking off the trivial from the important, the irrelevant from what

points to a conclusion; and it is synthetic in so far as it leaves the mind with an inclusive situation within which selected facts are placed. . . .

The analysis that results in giving an idea the solidity and definiteness of a concept is simply emphasis upon that which gives a clew for dealing with some uncertainty. . . .

Synthesis is the operation that gives extension and generality to an idea, as analysis makes the meaning distinct. Synthesis is correlative to analysis. As soon as any quality is definitely discriminated and given a special meaning of its own, the mind at once looks around for other cases to which that meaning may be applied. As it is applied, cases that were previously separated in meaning become assimilated, identified, in their significance. They now belong to the same kind of thing. . . . When anyone carries over any meaning from one object to another object that had previously seemed to be of a different kind, synthesis occurs. . . . It is synthesis when things themselves as different as clouds, meadow, brook, and rocks are so brought together as to be composed into a picture. It is synthesis when iron, tin, and mercury are conceived to be of the same kind in spite of individual differences. [3:126; 129–30; 157–59]

Example of Classification

Types of Fault Movement in Earthquakes

Most but not all earthquakes are associated with observed faults. A fault is a fracture zone along which the two sides are displaced relative to each other. Most faults are readily recognizable by trained geologists. Not all faults are active, but there is considered to be no satisfactory method of predicting the probable future activity of a given fault in a precise sense.

Displacement along a fault may be vertical, horizontal, or a combination of both. Movement may occur very suddenly along a stressed fault, producing an earthquake, or it may be very slow, or what is called "creep," unaccompanied by seismographic evidence. Permanent displacement of ground during an earthquake might be several inches, or it might be tens of feet.

Types of fault movement [are shown in Figure 3.8]. a) Names of some of the components of faults. b) Normal fault, in which the hanging wall has moved down relative to the foot wall. c) Reverse fault, sometimes called thrust fault, in which the hanging wall has moved up relative to the foot wall. d) Lateral fault, sometimes called strike-slip fault, in which the rocks on either side of the fault have moved sideways past each other. It is called left lateral if the rocks on the other side of the fault have moved to the left, as observed while facing the fault, and right lateral if the rocks on the other side of the fault have moved to the right, as observed while facing the fault. e) Left lateral normal fault, sometimes called a left oblique normal fault. Movement of this type of fault is a combination of normal faulting and left lateral faulting. f) Left lateral reverse fault, sometimes called a left oblique reverse fault. Movement of this type is a combination of left lateral faulting and reverse faulting. Two types of faults not shown are similar to those shown in e and f. They are a right lateral normal fault and a right lateral reverse fault (a right oblique normal fault and a right oblique reverse fault, respectively). [8:1–2]

This example on fault movement follows the principles of classification and offers an interesting and frequently used technique in technical writing—illustration. Sentence 1 sets the background for the subject to be classified. Sentence 2 defines the subject. The rest of the text and caption provide background information, but the illustration explains graphically and effectively the similarities and differences.

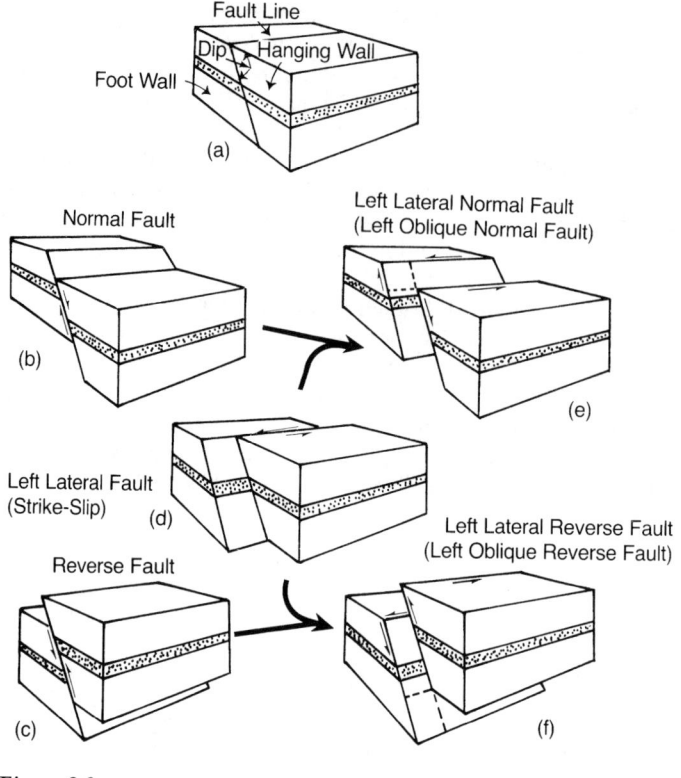

Figure 3.8

Example of Partition

This is an interesting example in that it is the basis of a definition of the planet earth, employing the techniques of explication and partition. The terms within the definition in the first paragraph are explicated by the explanations organized in partitioned components of the earth.

Crust of Earth

As it presents itself to direct experience, the earth can be physically described as a ball of rock (the lithosphere), partly covered by water (the hydrosphere) and wrapped in an envelope of air (the atmosphere). To these three physical zones it is convenient to add a biological zone (the biosphere).

The *atmosphere* is the layer of gases and vapor which envelopes the earth. It is essentially a mixture of nitrogen and oxygen with smaller quantities of water vapor, carbon dioxide and inert gases such as argon. Geologically, it is important as the medium of climate and weather, of wind, cloud, rain and snow.

The *hydrosphere* includes all the natural waters of the outer earth. Oceans, seas, lakes and rivers cover about three-quarters of the surface. But this is not all. Underground, for hundreds and even thousands of feet in some places, the pore spaces and fissures of the rocks are also filled with water. This ground water, as it is called, is tapped in springs and wells, and is sometimes encountered in disastrous quantities in mines. Thus there is a somewhat irregular but nearly continuous mantle of water around the earth, saturating the rocks, and over the enormous depressions of the ocean floors completely submerging them. If it were uniformly distributed over the earth's surface, it would form an ocean about nine thousand feet deep.

The *biosphere*, the sphere of life, is probably a less familiar conception. But think of the great forests and prairies with their countless swarms of animals and insects. Think of the tangle of seaweed, of the widespread banks of mollusks, or reefs of coral and shoals of fishes. Add to these the inconceivable numbers of bacteria and other microscopic plants and animals. Myriads of these minute organisms are present in every cubic inch of air and water and soil. Taken altogether, the diverse forms of life constitute an intricate and ever-changing network, clothing the surface with a tapestry that is nearly continuous. Even high snows and desert sands fail to interrupt it completely, and lava fields fresh from the craters of volcanoes are quickly invaded by the presence of life outside. Such is the sphere of life, both geologically and geographically it is of no less importance than the physical zones.

The *lithosphere* is the outer solid shell or crust of the earth. It is made of rocks in great variety, and on the lands it is commonly covered by a blanket of soil or other loose deposits, such as desert sands. The depth to which the lithosphere extends downward is a matter of definition: it depends on our conception of the crust and what lies beneath. It is usual to regard the crust as a heterogeneous shell, possibly about twenty to thirty miles thick, in which the rocks at any given level are not everywhere the same. Beneath the crust, in what may be called the *substratum*, or *mantle*, the material at any given level appears to be practically uniform, at least in those physical properties that can be tested. [4:29–30]

Summary of Analysis

1. Analysis requires thinking. It is the systematic and logical process of separating a whole entity into its component parts.
2. The basic operation in analysis is division. When an assemblage of things, ideas, people, or processes is divided into categories, the operation is known as *classification*.
3. When a whole is divided into its parts, the process is called *partition*.
4. Classification defines a subject by revealing its essence through comparison.
5. Partition defines a subject by listing and explicating the details or parts of its essence.
6. Tables, charts, and illustrations are effective aids in showing comparisons, similarities, differences, and component parts in the classification and partitioning processes.
7. Analysis helps writers to organize their subject matter into a rational order for more effective communication.
8. In technical writing, analysis helps both writers and readers to understand a subject; the process helps both to see and understand the ingredient parts and the relationship of those parts to each other and the whole.

Style in Technical Descriptions

The two major requirements in a technical description are completeness and clarity. The requisites of technical style discussed in Chapter 2 are certainly necessary. Conciseness, precision, and objectivity are the keystones. Description of an existing mechanism or organism is usually written in the present tense. On occasion, a more appropriate tense is the future or the past, but whatever tense is used, it should be consistent and logical throughout the description. A writing pitfall in taking a mechanism or organism through a cycle of operation is lack of parallel grammatical structure (see pages 326–327 in the Reference Index and Guide to Grammar, Punctuation, Style, and Usage). Finally, always keep in mind the reading audience. Are you writing for experts? For well-informed individuals? For the general public? Do the readers need to know only in a general way what the matter described looks like and how it functions, or do they need to be taught how to manufacture or operate the device? Your purpose is going to determine the organization and the amount of detail necessary. In a generalized approach, for example, the organizational divisions of the text are going to be the same as in a specific approach, but the details are going to be fewer and not as exacting. Drawings will be generalized and functional rather than specific and detailed.

Use of Illustrations in Technical Descriptions

Drawings and photographs can indicate precisely the size and shape of things. They need to be integrated with the text. The following suggestions will be helpful:

1. All drawings should be made to scale and fully dimensioned.
2. All illustrations should be properly numbered, and each should have its own captioned title.
3. Even where there is only one illustration, it should have a title.
4. Text matter in the illustration should be kept to a minimum.
5. Descriptive matter needed to explain an illustration should be incorporated.
6. Standard abbreviations should be used.
7. Where space permits, words should be spelled out completely.
8. Reference letters or numbers in illustrations make it easier for the reader to correlate the drawing with the text.
9. When the purpose of a technical description is to enable the reader to reproduce or fabricate a device, complete dimensions should be indicated in drawings and critical dimensions given in the text description.

Chapter in Brief

We examined the basic expository techniques that characterize technical writing, concentrating on the role and methods for writing definitions; how to write descriptions of mechanisms and organisms; how to describe processes; how the processes of analysis, classification, and partition help writers to understand the substance of their data; and how to organize the data for more effective communication. Synthesis and interpretation, the processes for achieving insights and conclusions, were also examined.

Chapter Focal Points

- Definition
- Description of mechanisms and organisms
- Description of processes
- Analysis—classification and partition
- Synthesis and interpretation

Questions for Discussion

1. Find five formal definitions in any of your textbooks. Chart the definitions into their three parts.
2. Locate and discuss examples of classification and partition in two of your textbooks that cover different subject areas.

Assignments

1. Write expanded definitions of 100–200 words for any of the terms below:
   a. gimlet (hand tool)
   b. gimlet (cocktail)
   c. file (handtool)
   d. file (for data or information)
   e. Oedipus complex
   f. herbicide
   g. solar cell
   h. host (biology)
   i. joystick (airplane)
   j. joystick (computer game)
   k. scroll (religious document)
   l. scroll (computer)
   m. chip (poker)
   n. chip (computer)
   o. chip (a small piece of something [keep it clean])
   p. chip (flaw)
   q. chip (fragment)
   r. fault (geologic)
   s. depression (mental illness)
   t. depression (economic)
   u. depression (meteorological)

2. Choose any of the common objects listed below and write a paragraph description of 100–250 words that enables the reader to accurately visualize the subject; include a drawing.
   a. flattop Phillips screw
   b. hair curler
   c. dendrite
   d. grapefruit knife
   e. diskette
   f. QWERTY keyboard
   g. cell (biology)
   h. whistling tea kettle

  i. hand calculator   k. carpenter's hammer
  j. human eye   l. stapler

3. Write a detailed explanation of an experiment you have performed. In writing your exposition, use the first person active voice. Consider the following questions:
   a. What was the experiment or process you performed?
   b. Why did you perform it?
   c. What tools or instruments did you use?
   d. What materials did you use and where did you get them?
   e. How did you proceed? What steps did you follow?
   f. What was the result of your work?

4. Write a description of a process within your field of professional interest whose occurrence is the result of a natural, psychological, sociological, political, or human interaction factor. Follow the organizational guidelines in this chapter. You may choose from any process listed below or any your instructor may assign.
   a. volcanic eruption
   b. home equity loan
   c. how a space rocket works
   d. perception of depth
   e. homogenization (physical or social)
   f. role relationship with a group
   g. NOW bank checking account
   h. photosynthesis
   i. operant conditioning
   j. electrical storm
   k. city manager form of government

5. Write a classificatory analysis of one of the following topics:
   a. grasses
   b. pets
   c. psychosomatic illnesses
   d. cells
   e. drugs
   f. insurance
   g. games people play
   h. forms of government
   i. software for computers
   j. punishments

6. Prepare an expository partition of one of the following:
   a. dwelling you live in
   b. ten-speed bicycle
   c. beef Wellington
   d. management information system
   e. rattlesnake
   f. sundial
   g. heat pump
   h. your university/college
   i. rosebush
   j. economic recession

References

1. Bloom, Arnold M. "Optical Pumping." *Scientific American* (October 1960).
2. Carroll, Lewis. *The Complete Works of Lewis Carroll.* New York: Random House [n.d.].
3. Dewey, John. *How We Think.* New York: D.C. Heath, 1923.
4. Holmes, Arthur. "Interpretation of Nature." In *The Crust of Earth,* edited by Samuel Rappaport and Helen Wright. New York: Mentor Books, 1955.
5. Pierce, John R. *Electrons, Waves, and Messages.* Garden City, NY: Hanover House, 1956.

6. Rapoport, Anatol. "What Is Semantics?" *American Scientist* (January 1952).
7. "Steel Roof Deck Sample for Calorimeter Evaluation," *Factory Mutual System Loss Prevention Data* (July 1972).
8. "Types of Fault Movement." *Factory Mutual Loss Prevention Data* (November 1973).
9. *Van Nostrand's Scientific Encyclopedia.* New York: D. Van Nostrand Company, 1960.
10. *What You Need To Know About Cancer of the Pancreas.* Washington, D.C.: National Cancer Institute, 1979.

4
Report Writing—Reconstruction of an Investigation

Chapter Objective

Provide the prewriting background for the preparation of a technical report.

Chapter Focus

- Role of the problem in research
- The hypothesis
- Definition of a report
- Types of reports
- Prewriting strategies
- How to search the literature
- Computerized on-line services
    Hypertext
- Research—observation
- Research—experimentation
- Research—interviews and discussions
- Research—questionnaires
- Systematizing, analyzing, and interpreting data

Report Writing—Reconstruction of an Investigation

The Significance of the Problem Concept

From earliest history, one of our greatest urges has been to *know*. The deep impulse to learn and to share knowledge with others has been one of the most potent factors in our rise from primitive caves to travels in space.

What are the lights in the sky? What makes grass grow? Why is grass green? How long is a river? How deep is the sea? How far away is the moon? These questions were probably asked by our earliest ancestors. The basics of "new" science are found in primitive people's ability to identify and articulate the unknowns of life and in their crude attempts to find solutions to such questions. Primitive savages' recognition of an obstacle, difficulty, or problem and the urge to find answers started them on their way to civilization.

As a primitive people conquered obstacles, difficulties, and problems, they told others in the tribe about their experiences and successes. This communication helped the tribe. The more "research minded" the primitive clan, the greater its prospects for survival. Therefore, civilization grew as humans observed the phenomena of their world, recognized and isolated their problems, investigated them, and arrived at answers. When approaching more difficult obstacles, they had to encourage others to cooperate with them as a team. One person might not be able to get a large log across a raging stream, but two, three, or four might be able to do it. The clan could then cross the stream safely.

Recognizing the role of the problem is the starting point of inquiry. In *Logic: The Theory of Inquiry,* Dewey states that "a problem well put is half solved" [3]. In *An Introduction to Logic and Scientific Method,* Cohen and Nagel point out the following:

> It is an utterly superficial view that the truth is to be found by "studying the facts." It is superficial because no inquiry can even get underway until and unless *some difficulty is felt* in a practical or theoretical situation. It is the difficulty, or problem, which guides our research for *some order among facts* in terms of which the difficulty is to be removed. [2:199]

The problem helps researchers decide what direction they must take in their investigation. It is their criterion for what is relevant and what is not; it guides them in selecting the data appropriate to the end result—the answer to the problem.

Types of Problems

Problems fall into three major categories: problems of fact, problems of value, and problems of technique.

Problems of fact seek answers to what the facts are. Is the earth flat or round? At what temperature will water freeze at an altitude of 10,000 feet? What causes cancer? How much salinity is in Farmer Brown's well? How effective is interferon against viral infections? Problems of fact involve questions of what happens, when it happens, how it happens, and why it happens.

Problems of value deal with what is more valuable, what is preferable, or what ought to be the case (rather than what is the case). Problems of value are involved in setting up standards or criteria. Examples of problems of value that affect scientific research are the determination of criteria or standards of safety, health, efficiency, tolerance, economy, and so forth, within a particular situation. Many problems of value are related to problems of fact.

Problems of technique concern the methods for accomplishing a desired result. How, for example, can a space station be launched in the mesosphere? Problems of technique are usually the concern of applied science or engineering. These problems combine elements of fact and value. Solving a significant problem frequently entails all three categories. For example, in conquering polio, there was first a problem of fact—what causes polio? After discovering that a virus was the cause, the problem of value arose—what known techniques of immunology against viruses are effective against polio? After Salk perfected his vaccine, there arose a technical problem—how to manufacture the vaccine in adequate amounts to supply the need.

Apprehending the Problem

Every field and activity have problems requiring investigation. The researcher or student who decides to investigate a problem because it interests her has a natural incentive to find the answer. An academic advisor or a supervisor may suggest something that opens the researcher's eyes to new possibilities. Here are some guides to help you define and formulate your problem:

1. Can the problem be stated in question form? Stating your problem as a question is an excellent way to make your problem clear and concise. Stated in question form, your problem obviously requires a specific answer. Finding the answer then becomes the objective of the study.

2. Can the problem be delimited? By deciding in advance the boundaries and considerations of your problem, you will save yourself much useless work.

3. Are resources of information available and the state of the art practical? The previous two points become immaterial if the present state of knowledge is inadequate or the means for research is unavailable. For example, certain research material in the field of aerodynamics may not be available to a researcher because of its classified nature. Government security restrictions may prevent a researcher from obtaining all necessary resources of information for the investigation.

4. Is the problem important or significant? Your problem need not be earthshaking in its importance, but the question should be worthwhile for the expenditure of time, energy, and funds involved. No one in our day can afford to pursue the problem, as did medieval scholars, of how many angels can dance on the head of a pin!

The Hypothesis—A Tentative Solution to the Problem

The observation that leads a scientist to recognize a problem also suggests the tentative answer. This answer is called a *hypothesis,* or a working guess. A hypothesis, therefore, is an explanation placed under the known facts of the problem to account for and explain them. Recognizing and stating the problem clearly move the researcher along the path where the answer may lie. Identifying clues and recognizing road signs of the problem point toward an answer. The hypothesis is tested by following the directions and picking up the clues. Traveling the road of the hypothesis, the researcher finds out facts about the problem. Some facts do and some facts do not corroborate the hypothesis. Constant examination along the way enables revision to correspond with the facts of the researcher's investigation.

How to Use the Hypothesis to Help Solve the Problem of the Investigation

1. The investigator, after gathering data or evidence and analyzing it, uses inductive reasoning to see what the data, evidence, and clues add up to. The provisional answer or hypothesis is the first or trial hypothesis.
2. With this trial hypothesis in the background, the researcher next uses deductive reasoning to decide what kind of data, evidence, or fact she will need to test the trial hypothesis. In other words, the researcher determines what should follow logically from the provisional conclusions being tested.
3. From this analysis, the researcher proceeds to apply her hypothesis. She gathers all possible data and tests them to see whether the actual accumulated evidence agrees with her hypothesis.
4. If the evidence fails to support the hypothesis, the investigator either rejects it or modifies it to conform with the evidence she has. If she rejects it, she will analyze the facts and search further until arriving at a second hypothesis. She will test the second hypothesis by comparing it to the new total evidence amassed.
5. In a search that calls for finding facts or information alone, there may be little use for a hypothesis. For example, if the search is historical in nature or if the search is a request for information—i.e., What industries in the United States use robotics? What is the number of robotics in use in the United States?—then a hypothesis is rarely necessary. However, most legitimate research involves interpretation of facts. For example, the knowledge of the number of robots in use in the United States may raise the problem, Why isn't the robot our company manufactures in greater use? After the facts have been discovered, they must be analyzed to find out what they mean, what conclusions should be drawn, and what should be done about those facts. The conclusions and recommendations are usually the chief object of such research.

Relationship of Research to Report Writing

Report writing is the reconstruction of a purposeful investigation of a problem in written form. As Bloomfield and Whorf have noted, scientific research begins with a set of sentences pointing the way to certain observations and experiments the results of which do not become fully scientific until they have been turned back into language yielding again a set of sentences that becomes the basis for further exploration into the unknown [5:220].

Decision Making—The Role Reports Play in Science, Technology, and Industry

Our society depends on cooperation. The range of knowledge within the last few generations, and most of all within our own life span, has increased faster than humans are able to assimilate and understand it. No one person, even within the narrowest field, can grasp all there is to know about that field. Today's knowledge and experience represent a coordinated effort. Efficient communication, therefore, has become an important process in the standard operating procedure of every human activity. Today's scientific genius does not work in an ivory tower laboratory. What the scientist does depends on the efforts of the other fine workers. In turn, her efforts influence the efforts of others. Scientists of various countries are researching energetically for a cure for cancer, but every competent scientist knows that individual efforts alone are not enough. The researcher must acquire and use the knowledge, experience, and help of others by knowing what they are doing and the significance of what they are doing. The role of reports and technical papers is to relay this information.

Here is where you and I come in. Some of us may be engaged in reporting to the boss how many nuts and bolts are left in the storage bin. However, all of us are concerned with organizing the facts of an experience we are engaged in because the facts are important for someone to know. A decision or action may wait upon these facts. The decision may be as commonplace as ordering more nuts and bolts or as dramatic as finding out which carcinogen causes which type of cancer.

What Is a Report?

One of my colleagues, a teacher of literature, tells an appropriate story. He was lecturing on Scott's poem, *The Lady of the Lake*, which begins "The stag at eve had drunk his fill. . . ." Halfway through the poem, he paused in his enthusiasm to notice that one student looked puzzled. He decided to take more time in his explanation, but no matter how carefully he pointed out the poet's technique, skill, and meaning in each successive line, the puzzled look on the student's face remained.

He finally stopped and asked the student, "Is there anything in the last few lines that you don't understand?"

"It's not the last few lines," said the perplexed student. "It's way back at the beginning. What's a stag?"

What's a report?

The origin of the word tells us much about its meaning and function. *Report* comes from the Latin *reportare,* meaning "to bring back." A working definition of a report might be: *organized, factual, and objective information brought by a person who has experienced or accumulated it to a person or persons who need it, want it, or are entitled to it.* Reports contain opinions, but the opinions are considered judgments based on factual evidence uncovered and interpreted in the investigation.

Facts—The Basic Ingredients

The basic ingredients of a report are facts. A **fact** is a verifiable observation. Webster says: a fact is "that which has actual existence; an event." Facts are found through direct observation, survey techniques, experiment, inspection, and through a combination of these processes as they occur in the research situation. A fact is different from an opinion. An **opinion** is a belief, a judgment, or an inference—a generalization that is based on some factual knowledge.[1] An opinion is not entirely verifiable at the time of the statement. Sometimes opinions are little more than feelings or sentiments with a bit of rational basis. *Opinion* and *judgment* are synonyms and are frequently used interchangeably. Judgments imply opinions based on evaluations, as in the case of a legal decision. Neither opinions nor judgments are facts and must be distinguished from facts in technical writing and reports. Since facts are verifiable observations, a direct investigation is inherent in their disclosure.

Another point that should be emphasized is that facts, the chief ingredient of reports, are expressed in unambiguous language. The purpose of every technical communication is to convey information and ideas accurately and efficiently. That objective, therefore, demands that the communication be as clear as possible, as brief as possible, and as easy to understand as possible.

Forms Reports Take

Information and facts dealing with a simple problem or situation may be reported simply. Thus, if your supervisor tells you, "Joe, find out how much it will cost to replace the compressor on the number 2 pump," all that is necessary for the most efficient reporting of the information called for, after you have found the answer, is to pick up the telephone or pencil a note on a memo pad and say, "Boss, a new compressor costs $256.28."

However, if your supervisor's supervisor wants to know the cost, you may have to "dress up" your penciled note in the form of a typed memo in several

---

[1] An *inference* is a conclusion derived deductively or inductively from given data. However, an inference is considered a partial or indecisive conclusion. The term *conclusion* is reserved for the final logical result in a process of reasoning. A conclusion is full and decisive.

copies with additional information to provide the background for the statement that a new compressor costs $256.28. If customers or clients get involved, the note may have to be enlarged to include comparative costs of several makes of compressors. And if the same pump has given you trouble for the last two years, you may have to dig up more facts and information—perhaps to find the reasons for the continued difficulty or whether another type of pump or a different system is called for. Then the matter begins to become more complex, and the complications become sections of information and facts to be reported. Recommendations, what to do about it, become the most important part of your report. Also, when a customer is involved, instead of using a memo form, you report in a letter. If a situation gets fairly complicated, requiring extensive investigation and reporting, the report becomes more formal and many of its elements receive formal structuring, format, and placement. You may end up having a letter of transmittal, an abstract, a table of contents, a list of illustrations, an executive summary, the report proper divided into formal sections, an appendix, bibliography, and perhaps an index, with the whole thing bound in a hard cover. In other words, the report writer designs her report for the particular use and particular reader it will have. However, we are getting a little ahead of ourselves.

Because of the many and complex circumstances that call for reports, it is difficult to classify reports rigidly. In some organizations, little formality is attached to report writing. Each writer puts down what she has to say, often haphazardly. In other organizations, particularly large ones, numerous and often elaborate forms are devised and given names, as for example, record report, examination report, operations report, performance report, test report, progress report, failure report, recommendations report, status report, accident report, sales report, and so forth. Given five minutes, you probably could think of at least thirty different types of reports you have come across.

Actually, the facts and analyses marshaled to meet a certain reporting situation take many forms. There is no universal "right" form to clothe all reports. "Form," a learned colleague once said, "is the package in which you wrap your facts and analysis. Choose (or design) a package that is suitable for your material, your purpose, and your reader" [1:6].

Major Types of Reports

There are many bases for classifying reports: subject matter, function, frequency of issuance, type and formality of format, length, and so forth. A traditional classification divides reports into two descriptive categories:

1. Informational
2. Analytical

The Informational Report

The *informational report,* as the term implies, presents information without criticism, evaluation, or recommendations. It gives a detailed account of activities or conditions, making no attempt to give solutions to problems but confining itself to past and present information. Many informational reports, nevertheless, contain inferences, which suggest the conclusions the writer would like the reader to reach, for example, There are fourteen nuts and bolts in the storage bin. *Inference:* We should order another train load. In this category belong the routine daily, weekly, or monthly reports on sales, inventory, production, or progress. Often such reports are mere tabulations and follow a definite pattern or have a preprinted form requiring fill-ins. The best-known example of the informational report is the annual report of a corporation to its stockholders.

The Analytical Report

The *analytical report* goes beyond the informational report since it presents an analysis and interpretation of the facts in addition to the facts themselves.

The conclusions and recommendations are the most important and interesting parts of the report. The analytical report serves as a basis for the solution of an immediate problem or as a guide to future happenings. It is a valuable and frequently used instrument in all types of activity. Emphasis in this text is on the analytical report because the techniques applying to it apply equally well to the informational types of report.

Steps in Report Writing

Report writing is the reconstruction in written form of a purposeful investigation of a problem. Whereas most technical writers do not engage in research, many are assigned to a research team or project to serve as interpreters or communicators of the investigation. The technical writer, therefore, must understand investigative methods and procedures and be intimately conversant with the research she is reporting. Frequently, the writer assigned to reconstruct the investigation by means of a report is in a position to help digest and find meaning in the mass of data the investigation reveals.

Within the writing process itself, the writer follows steps analogous to those followed by the experimental scientist. Just as a scientist observes and hypothesizes, so, by analogy, the technical writer examines the mass of data, reads it initially for meaning, tries to determine the readership, and tries to make sense of the data by establishing important ideas. In a second or succeeding phase, the scientist proceeds to experiment. Again by analogy, the technical writer organizes the material and sets up an initial order of continuity of data; she may find upon closer scrutiny that such an organization is not effective and may proceed to rearrange and reshuffle the data to make them more logical and understandable. In this way, the writer is *experimenting* with the data.

This chapter begins a four-chapter instructional sequence on report writing. The approach we are taking assumes that your instructor assigns you to write a formal report, preferably on an investigation of a research problem you are conducting or one with which you are associated. In this context, and with your instructor's approval, you have selected a problem for research. You will identify the question (problem) to be investigated in accordance with the guidelines for selecting a research problem discussed previously on page 77.

For convenience, let us review the guidelines:

1. The problem can be isolated and stated in question form. (Finding the answer becomes the objective of your research.)
2. The problem can be delimited to meet the circumstance of your research situation.
3. The resources for the data and information required to find the answer are practically available to you.
4. The problem is purposeful enough to make your effort worthwhile.

Selecting a Problem for Investigation

As some of you review the guidelines, you may be troubled. "How do I find a problem to write about?" you may ask yourself. I understand your quandary. The guidelines are helpful, but only to a point; they are meant only to make your selection of a problem more manageable. You still may need help to find a problematic subject area. It's time to do some brainstorming.

Brainstorming is exploring what is already in your mind. The technique is easy: You list information about a topic in any order as it comes to your mind, writing it down quickly, *uncritically* in list form. You record what you think at the moment without heckling your brain about the worth of the thought. You go on this way until your brain is "stormed out." The result is a series of jottings that may help you select a subject area, which you may then localize further by using the guidelines.

Perhaps, after consideration, you are not too enthused with the first topic you brainstormed. Simply brainstorm again, this time listing subjects you are interested in (or could be interested in, with some background research). The subject should meet the following criteria:

1. The subject is interesting to you.
2. The subject is related to your major field of study.
3. The subject is one you already know enough about to research intelligently.
4. The subject falls within the guidelines.

If you come up with more than one research topic, ask your instructor to help you make your final selection. Now you can be on your way.

The purposeful reconstruction of an investigation involves four major steps, which follow very closely the experience of the investigation:

1. Prewriting—strategies, analysis, and planning
2. Gathering the data—investigating the problem or situation
3. Organizing the data
4. Writing the report

The report writer, whether the original investigator or the interpreter or communicator of the original investigation, must follow the procedures the researcher followed in arriving at a solution to the problem.

Prewriting—Strategies, Analysis, and Planning

You, the report writer, like the researcher, must ask yourself a number of questions: What is the purpose of the investigation? Who needs the answer to the problem? How will the answer be used? From the writer's standpoint, you must know the answers to such questions because the effectiveness of your communication depends on the answers. You may have to rephrase the questions to: What information is wanted? Who will read the report? For what purpose will it be used? What problem or problems am I expected to solve? These four questions resolve the larger question, What is the purpose of my proposed report?

As the writer, you must be careful to distinguish between the purpose of the research and the problem studied in the research. The purpose of a research project is generally understood as the reason why the investigation has been undertaken; whereas the problem is what the researcher specifically hopes to solve. In considering the purpose of a research project, you should regard it as the explanation of the possible uses to which the results of a study may be put. Purpose concerns the probable value of the study. It offers the explanation of why the research was undertaken. In short, the problem concerns the *what* of the study, and the purpose concerns the *why*. When you, the writer, can formulate the purpose in your mind—actually write it down clearly and distinctly—you have started on the right road to answering your problem.

Once the purpose has been determined, the next step is to define scope. It, too, is not to be confused with purpose. Purpose defines goals to be reached. Scope determines the boundaries of the ground to be covered. Scope answers the questions relating to what shall be put in and what shall be left out. (Scope is sometimes indicated by a client, if the investigation has been contracted for, but it is usually left to the judgment of the researcher.)

Having problem, scope, and purpose in mind, you are now ready to start on the next important step in your prewriting, analysis, and planning stage: blocking out a plan of procedure. Always keep in mind that the writing of a report is a reconstruction activity. You must go back to the equivalent investigative point where the problem was defined in a clear-cut interrogative statement. With the problem defined, the purpose clarified, and the scope clearly set, you are ready to begin the work of solving the problem. The next step consists of breaking the problem or situation into its component parts. Again, ask yourself questions: What are the elements that make up the problem? Which elements are fundamental? Which are secondary? (Figure 4.1) You, the writer, might set down on paper an outline or a procedural plan to follow. This outline might have the following scheme:

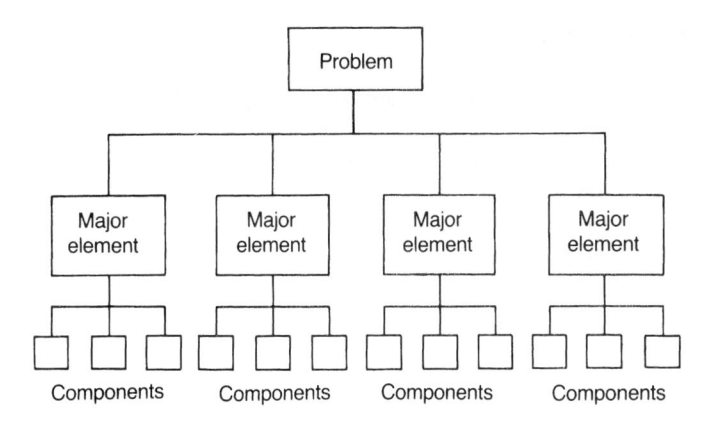

Figure 4.1 Block diagram showing analysis (breakdown of problem into its major elements and constituent components).

1. Statement of the problem in question form
2. Purpose or objective of the investigation
   a. Primary purpose
   b. Secondary purpose
3. Major elements
   a. First major element
      1. Component
      2. Component
      3. Component
   b. Second major element
      1. Component
      2. Component
      3. Component
   c. Third major element
      1. Component
      2. Component
      3. Component
   d. Additional major elements, and so forth
4. Correlation of all elements into a final combination that constitutes the problem

The purpose of this type of analysis is to (1) help clarify the problem and what composes it; (2) check and define the scope; and (3) help formulate the task of the research. The analysis should lead to the provisional hypothesis that sends the research on its proper way.

If the problem is a new one, you may have to feel your way at first. As facts accumulate and you reason about the various elements of the problem, you begin to see a logic to them and can arrange them in accordance with the logic of the problem.

In the prewriting analysis stage, no part—purpose, scope, plan of procedure—is final. In the course of the investigation, something unexpected may call for readjusting your approach in any or all of the previous elements. The prewriting analysis has revealed the direction for the writer to follow. You, the writer, gather your information accordingly or according to any necessary revision in recognition of unexpected turns in the investigation.

Investigative Procedures

There can be no real report without facts. Facts are garnered through research. Research falls into two categories, primary and secondary. *Primary* research is based on an original, firsthand investigation of a problem or situation. *Secondary* research is based on information published by primary researchers. This does not mean that secondary research is necessarily stale, warmed-over information. New, incisive insights on a problem frequently are garnered from published information. Most working research is based on both primary and secondary sources. Ideas, conclusions, evaluations, and recommendations must derive from facts.

Before the writer can begin to organize and construct her report, she must first gather and assemble the facts—her data. Information may be gathered by several methods:

1. Searching all available recorded—electronic or printed—information related to the problem or situation
2. Observing and critically examining the actual situation, condition, or factors of the problem
3. Experimenting (observation carried out under special conditions that are controlled and varied for specific reasons)
4. Interviewing and discussing with experts or persons qualified to give needed data
5. Using questionnaires when interviews are impractical

Searching the Literature

Searching the literature is the method used to learn new facts and principles through the study of documents, records, and the literature of the field. This type of research is used extensively in history, literature, linguistics, and in the humanities. Because it is almost the exclusive research technique used by historians, it is sometimes called the historical method of research. This research method is valuable in all fields whenever knowledge and insights into events of the past are required.

Human knowledge is a structure, which grows by the addition of new material to the store that previously has been gained. An investigator has little chance of making a worthwhile new contribution if she is completely ignorant of what is already known about a problem. Before beginning an investigation, the investigator must find out what has been written thus far about the problem. Six hours fruitfully spent in a library or in searching an automated database may save six months in a laboratory.

There are two goals in literature searching:[2]

1. To find out if the information that is the object of the proposed research is already available
2. To acquire a broad general background in the area of research

The major secondary research tool available to college students is the library. Efficient literature searching depends on a researcher's knowledge of library reference materials and available automated data and information systems. Library resources include:

Catalog of holdings
The stacks (books on the shelves)
Periodical holdings
Reference books and materials
Literature guides, indexes, and abstract journals
Government documents
Popular press
Audiovisual materials
Computerized databases and information services
Computer software, such as hypertext

Let us now examine some of these resources.

Catalog of Holdings

The catalog is the key to a library's collection of published materials, audiovisuals, and computerized databases. You probably are familiar with the card catalog. It cross-indexes the library's holdings by author, title, and subject. Many libraries now produce their catalog listings by computer. It is called a *COM* catalog system, an acronym for *computer output microform*. **Microform** is the librarian's term for text material greatly reduced on microfilm or microfiche. Microfilm is stored on a reel; **microfiche** is a transparent sheet that may hold images of about 200 or more pages. To read microfilm or microfiche requires special equipment. COM catalogs, like card catalogs, may be searched by author, title, or subject. You read a COM entry the same way you read a card catalog entry. Some libraries have on-line

---

[2]This statement excludes the historical method of research, which employs literature searching as its investigative technique. The historical researcher puts together in a logical way evidence derived from documents, records, letters, papers, literature, and appropriate electronically stored data, and from that evidence forms conclusions that either establish facts hitherto unknown or offer new insights and generalizations about past or present events, human motives, characteristics, and thoughts.

catalogs that can be accessed from a distance by modem, a device that connects computers over telephone lines. (On-line refers to the linkage capability of one computer for communicating with another.)

Some libraries make computer terminals with printout facilities available to students. Entering a subject heading into the system produces a hard-copy list of holdings on that subject. The library may charge for this type of service. When holdings on a subject are simply displayed on a screen, you must copy them yourself, though, of course, this allows you to eliminate entries you deem irrelevant.

Literature Guides and Sources of Published Materials

As an aid to finding bibliographic and other reference materials in a field, guides to the literature of a subject area have been prepared for students and research workers. Sheehy's *Guide to Reference Books* is an excellent first source for finding listings of literature guides, reference works, handbooks, encyclopedias, yearbooks, and so forth on any given subject field. Another good source is Walford's *Guide to Reference Material.* For technical subject areas, *Scientific and Technical Information Sources* by Chen covers the full range of reference sources in biological, physical, and engineering sciences. These three sources can help you identify the literature guides for your subject area of interest. Some examples to be found include:

Durbin, Paul, T., ed. *The Reader's Advisor, a Layman's Guide to Literature.* 13th ed. New York: R. R. Bowker Co., 1988.

Lesko, Mathew. *Lesko's Info-Power.* Detroit, Mich.: Visible Ink Press, 1994. (Desciptive list of 45,000 free and low-cost sources of information.)

Schwarzkopf, L. C. *Government Reference Books.* Littleton, Colo.: Libraries Unlimited, published bi-annually.

Smith, Roger C., and Malcolm Reid. *Guide to the Literature of the Life Sciences.* Minneapolis: Burgess, 1972.

U.S. Government Printing Office. *Monthly Catalog of United States Government Publications.*

White, Carl M. *Sources of Information in the Social Sciences.* Chicago: American Library Association, 1973.

Bibliographies

Publication details of the literature for a subject area have been assembled and published in bibliographies. Examples include:

DeGeorge, Richard T. *A Guide to Philosophical Bibliography and Research.* New York: Apple-Century-Crofts, 1971.

Irwin, Leonard B. *A Guide to Historical Reading.* Brooklawn, N.J.: McKinley, 1970.

Mellon, M. G. *Chemical Publications.* 4th ed. New York: McGraw-Hill, 1965.

Scientific and Technical Books and Serials in Print. New York: R. R. Bowker Co., published annually.

Handbooks

Handbooks are compact reference manuals containing state-of-the-art data and information on particular subjects. Examples include:

Hardie, Edward, T.L., and Vivian Neou, eds. *Internet: Mailing Lists.* Englewood Cliffs, N.J.: SRI Internet Information Series. PTR Prentice Hall, published annually.

Lide, David R., ed. *CRC Handbook of Chemistry and Physics.* Boca Raton, Fla.: CRC Press, Inc., published annually.

Hoover's Handbook of American Business. Austin, Texas: The Reference Press, Inc., 1994.

Jacobs, Sheldon, editor-in-chief. *The Handbook for No-Load Fund Investors.* 13th ed. Irvington-on-the-Hudson, New York: The No-Load Fund Investors, Inc., 1993.

Lathrop, James, K. *Life Safety Code Handbook.* 5th ed. Quincy, Mass.: The National Fire Protection Association, 1991.

Perry, Robert, and Don Green, eds. *Perry's Chemical Engineer's Handbook.* 6th ed. New York: McGraw Hill Book Co., 1984.

Encyclopedias

An encyclopedia is a volume or a set of volumes giving information on one special field or all branches of knowledge. Editors and contributors are specialists within specific subject areas. Examples are:

Clark, Robert E., and Judith Clark. *The Encyclopedia of Child Abuse.* New York: Facts on File, 1984.

Corsini, Raymond. *Encyclopedia of Psychology.* 2nd ed. New York: John Wiley & Sons, 1994.

Edmonds, Robert A. *The Prentice Hall Encyclopedia of Information Science.* Englewood Cliffs, N.J.: Prentice Hall, 1987.

Encyclopedia of Material Science and Engineering. 8 vols. Cambridge, Mass.: MIT Press, 1986.

Kirk-Othmer Encyclopedia of Chemical Technology. 3rd ed. 24 vols. New York: Wiley-Interscience, 1984.

McGraw-Hill Encyclopedia of Science and Technology. New York: McGraw-Hill, 1982.

Shepard, Leslie. *Encyclopedia of Occultism and Parapsychology.* Detroit, Mich.: Gale Research Co., 1978.

Ralston, Anthony, and Edwin D. Reilly, eds. *Encyclopedia of Computer Science.* 3rd ed. New York: Van Nostrand Reinhold, 1993.

Way, James, ed. *Encyclopedia of Business Information Sources.* 9th ed. Detroit, Mich.: Gale Research, Inc., 1992.

Books

Reference books and textbooks provide basic material. Monographs are books, articles, or papers written about a narrow, specialized technical area with an in-depth treatment of a subject. Searching the subject card index of a good library and then browsing the library shelves can be helpful in locating pertinent books. There are a number of useful publications listing scientific and technical books:

Books in Print is a listing of books currently available in print, arranged by both subject areas and authors, published by R. R. Bowker Co., New York.

The Cumulative Book Index, List of Books in the English Language. This list is issued monthly and then cumulated in semiannual volumes published by the H. W. Wilson Company, New York.

Scientific, Medical and Technical Books Published in the United States of America. Washington, D.C.: National Research Council.

The United States Catalog. This is a comprehensive list of books printed in English, arranged by title, author, and subject.

Abstracting and Indexing Journals

Journals that abstract and index publications within a field are the main reliance of investigators seeking papers on scientific topics. These journals provide researchers with an important way of keeping abreast of scientific progress and furnish the investigator with an overview of published material on a given subject by a particular author under specific titles. Indexes usually provide no more than bibliographic references, but abstracts provide a digest or synopsis of the listed literature. Some better-known examples are:

Applied Science and Technology Index covers monthly and cumulatively industrial and trade subjects and provides an annotated description of articles appearing in trade publications.

Biological Abstracts provides worldwide publications coverage of research in the life sciences.

Business Periodical Index is a monthly subject index to all fields of business.

Chemical Abstracts covers worldwide publications; lists by author, subject, and chemical formula. *CA* also includes patents in the chemical field.

Computer Periodical Index is a quarterly index to basic articles in the field.

Congressional Record Abstracts records and updates weekly congressional activities regarding bills and resolutions, committee and subcommittee reports, public laws, executive communications, speeches and inserted material in the *Congressional Record*.

Economic Abstracts International provides coverage of the world's literature on markets, industries, country-specific data, and research in the fields of economic science and management.

The Engineering Index is a monthly listing of published engineering subjects with brief annotations.

Excerpta Medica provides abstracts and citations of biomedical journals published worldwide.

The New York Times Index is a monthly index to news stories appearing in that newspaper.

Psychological Abstracts covers the world's literature in psychology and related disciplines in the behavioral sciences.

Readers Guide to Periodicals Index is an index of general subjects, listing articles from a great number of sources. It has a broad subject coverage of articles appearing in popular publications.

Sociological Abstracts covers the world's literature in sociology and related disciplines in the social and behavioral sciences.

Science Abstracts appears monthly in two sections. Section A, *Physical Abstracts*, covers mathematics, astronomy, astrophysics, geodesy, physics, physical chemistry, crystallography, geophysics, biology, techniques, and materials. Section B, *Electrical Engineering Abstracts*, covers generation and supply of electricity, machines, applications, measurements, telecommunications, radar, television, and related subjects.

World Textile Abstracts covers the world literature on the science and technology of textiles and related materials.

Yearbooks

Yearbooks are annual publications reporting or summarizing events, achievements, and statistics for a specific year. Some, like yearly almanacs, are general; others are specific to a subject. Examples include:

Communication Yearbook
The Europa World Yearbook
Facts on File, cumulated yearly
New International Yearbook
UNESCO Statistical Yearbook
World Almanac
The Yearbook of Agriculture
Yearbook of Astronomy
Yearbook of Drug Therapy
Yearbook of Education
Yearbook of Forest Products
Yearbook of Labor Statistics
Yearbook of World Affairs

Computerized Databases and Information Services

So much information is currently generated about everything and anything that we speak of an "information explosion." This explosion has resulted in such a mass of published materials that anyone trying to find information by using traditional methods, such as card catalogs, literature guides, or subject area indexes, often is frustrated by this time-consuming and seemingly endless task. Fortunately, most libraries, including those in colleges and universities, have become computerized. Many college libraries are network members of the On-Line Computer Library Center (OCLC) located in Columbus, Ohio. By using the member library's computer terminal, the student has recourse to the holdings of the entire OCLC network, and the student's own library can order any of these holdings through the Interlibrary Loan System.

Using an on-line computer database requires some training. Your college librarian may either conduct the computer search for you or train you to use the system. The librarian establishes contact with the database via modem by entering the library's identity code and then enters the keywords describing the type of information you want. The computer responds on screen or with a printout of the titles of the documents filed under your key terms.

There are several thousand commercial computer information services and databases in the United States as well as bases operated by professional societies, industry associations, government agencies, and corporations. They cover every field, discipline, subdiscipline, and specialized interest groups and subgroups. Below are some of the more prominent systems, listed by field, title, and responsible agency or operator.

Agriculture: AGRICOLA, National Library of Agriculture

Biological Sciences: BIOSIS PREVIEWS, Biosciences Information Services

Business: ABI/INFORM, Data Courier, Inc.

Chemistry: CA SEARCH, Chemical Abstract Service, American Chemical Society

Education: ERIC (Educational Resources Information Center), National Institute of Education

Engineering: COMPENDEX (Computerized Engineering Index), Engineering Information, Inc.

Environment: ENVIROLINE, Environment Information Center, Inc.

Geosciences: GEO-REF, American Geologic Institute

Government research and development reports: NTIS (National Technical Information Service), Department of Commerce

Law: LEXIS, Mead Data Central

Mathematics: MATHFILE, American Mathematical Society

Mechanical Engineering: ISMEC, Data Courier, Inc.

Medicine: MEDLINE, National Library of Medicine

Metallurgy: METADEX, American Society of Metals

Physics: SPIN, Physics Information Notices, American Institute of Physics

Pollution and Environment: POLLUTION ABSTRACTS, Cambridge Scientific Abstracts

Psychology: PSYCINFO, American Psychological Society

Science Abstracts: INSPEC, Institution of Electrical Engineers
Science and Technology: SCISEARCH, Institute of Scientific Information

Among the more prominent commercial information/database systems covering a wide spectrum of subjects are America Online; CompuServe Information Services; Prodigy; The Information Bank of the *New York Times;* the Bibliographic Retrieval Services (BRS); DIALOG; and Knowledge Index, an after-hours service offered by DIALOG at a lower cost. Of DIALOG's 320 databases, Knowledge Index offers the 80 most often used. Using simpler operation commands, it is designed for persons with little or no information retrieval skills. BRS also has a reduced service called After Dark, with about 40 databases available on weekends and evenings.

The commercial databases provide instructions in their printed catalogs as well as on-line indexes to help you select the information appropriate for your needs. Once the database is selected, you enter the search terms of interest. *Search terms* are keywords or phrases to be searched for in the database that identify pertinent documents and information.

Most databases use Boolean algebra to eliminate specific terms or topics and to combine search terms. The major Boolean algebra operators are AND, OR, NOT, IF, THEN, EXCEPT. They designate logical relationship among search terms. For example, to search for information on spaceship disasters, you might use the terms *spaceship* and *disaster*. A search of *spaceship* OR *disaster* would find all references that contain the word *spaceship,* all that contain the word *disaster,* and all that contain both words. The search would find a mountain of irrelevant information using the OR operator. A search of *spaceship* NOT *disaster* would locate all references containing the word *spaceship*. In this run, you would also find an overwhelming amount of general information on *spaceships.* By searching *spaceship* AND *disaster,* only the references containing both search terms will be identified. The use of the operator, AND, in this instance provides the best search choice for locating the literature for your topic.

Among DIALOG's special offerings is the complete database of the National Technical Information Service (NTIS). This database contains about 2,000,000 citations and is updated twice a month. NTIS is the federal government's central technical and scientific service, which provides access to the results of U.S. and foreign government sponsored research and development as well as other types of engineering and scientific activities. It announces annually more than 150,000 summaries of completed and ongoing federal and foreign-sponsored research, and provides complete technical reports for most of the results it announces. DIALOG also offers CD-ROMs (**compact disk,** read-only memory)[3] of the NTIS Bibliographic Data Base as well as NTIS-created CD-ROMs for AGRI-

---

[3]Compact disks provide information bases on many subjects. A single optical compact disk, can store the entire *Encyclopaedia Brittanica*. Using a computer, you can access any topic of an encyclopedia within seconds. Many commercial databases are providing specialized subject information on CD-ROMs to customers. Some libraries subscribe to disk-based information and indexing services.

A Typical Dialog Search

Shown below is a suggestion of the kind of conversation you might have with DIALOG during a typical search. On the facing page is a replica of the actual printout that would be generated at your computer terminal during the search.

From start to finish the search took less than three minutes. During that time more than 15,000 documents were examined and the seven pertinent ones were identified.

PURPOSE OF THE SEARCH: You want to find the sources of recent articles on *the effect of stress on executives*.

WHICH DATABASE TO SEARCH? DIALINDEX, the online subject index, shows you that File 15 ABI/INFORM contains information about articles on business and management.

Here, in effect, is what takes place at your computer terminal.

What you say to Dialog	How Dialog responds
1 I'd like to search your Business/Eonomics File 15, please	What would you like me to find for you?
2 Do you have any articles that include the word *stress* or the word *tension*?	Yes, I have 997 that refer to *stress* and 259 that include a reference to *tension* for a total of 1178 documents that mention either or both terms.
3 How many articles do you have that mention *executives* or *managers* or *administrators*?	I have the following references: *executives*—5,349; *managers*—10,253; *administrators*—648, for a total of 14,962.
4 How many of those articles or documents contain the terms *stress* or *tension* AND ALSO the terms *executives* or *managers* or *administrators*?	Only 311.
5 I'm interested only in *recent* articles. How many of those 311 were published during 1995?	Seven.
6 I'd like the following information about the first of those seven documents: record number, title, journal title, date, pages, and an abstract on the article if available.	Title of the article is "Learning to Handle Stress—A Matter of Time and Training." It's by Dennis R. Briscoe and appeared in *Supervisory Management* magazine, volume 25, number 2 on pages 35 to 38 of the February 1995 issue. An abstract of the article follows: (For complete text of the abstract please refer to the sample printout on the facing page.)
7 For the remaining six articles please give me only the basic information, no abstracts.	(For detailed response, see printout at right.)
8 Thank you, I'm finished. Please log me out and give me a record of this search and its cost.	This search was made on April 25, 1995 and completed at 3:15:44 P.M. The user's identification number is 3268. Cost for computer time was $3.30. Time required to conduct the search was 0.044 hours. The search was made in File 15. Six descriptive terms were used to make the search. Communications cost (TELENET) was $.22 and the total estimated cost was $3.52.

If you had wished to do so you could have requested that the references be printed offline and mailed to you, typically more cost effective if many references are desired.

Most databases contain abstracts or summaries of the original document such as that shown in our sample search. Often these abstracts provide enough information to answer your question. Should you decide that you want to order the full text of the article abstracted, you can do this easily while still connected to the DIALOG computer through Dial-Order, DIALOG's online ordering system. You simply type ORDER and just the record number from the upper left of each reference.

This search is an example of how simple yet powerful a DIALOG search can be. As you grow in familiarity with DIALOG you'll find yourself taking advantage of the many additional search capabilities that can improve speed, increase precision, or lower costs.

Figure 4.2 *How a literature search is conducted by an on-line database (DIALOG).*

1 File 15: ABI/INFORM 71-95/MARCH
(Copr. Data Courier Inc.)
   Set   Items   Description.

2 ? SELECT STRESS OR TENSION
            997   STRESS
            259   TENSION
   1   1178   STRESS OR TENSION

3 ? SELECT EXECUTIVES OR MANAGERS OR ADMINISTRATORS
            5349   EXECUTIVES
           10253   MANAGERS
            648   ADMINISTRATORS
   2   14962   EXECUTIVES OR MANAGERS OR ADMINISTRATORS

4 ? COMBINE 1 AND 2
   3   311   1 AND 2

5 ? SELECT S3 AND PY = 1995
            2347   PY =1995
   4   7   3 AND PY =1995?

6 ? TYPE 4/7/1   4/7/1   80005291
Learning to Handle *Stress*-a Matter of Time and Training
Briscoe, Dennis R.
Supervisory Mgmt   v25n2   35-38   Feb 1995

   Management jobs are becoming increasingly stressful. Considering the nature of managerial work today, people can survive only by learning to avoid the situations they find stressful or by adjusting to stress factors. Stress may be defined as the way that people react to the constant changes occurring in and around them. Some stress is used positively to develop abilities and skills, while other types and amounts of stress are dysfunctional. There are 3 important concepts to follow in training *managers* to cope with the stress of their jobs and all 3 must be used to optimize training results and minimize any dysfunctional reactions to stressors: 1. specificity of training, which requires that training be designed to increase the person's ability to manage, 2. magnitude of training, which forces adaptation or learning, and 3. gradual and continual intensification of training, with new levels of learning and adaptation building on prior levels.

7 ? TYPE 4/3/2-7   4/3/2   80005280
Managing Yourself
Kleiner, Brian H.
Management World   v9n2   17-18,36   Feb 1995

4/3/3   80004717
Managerial/Organizational Stress: Identification of Factors and Symptoms
Appelbaum, Steven H.
Health Care Mgmt Review   v5n1   7-16   Winter 1995

4/3/7   80003034
Getting Out of a Sales Slump
Anonymous
Small Business Report   v5n1   15-16   Jan 1995

8 LOGOFF
25apr95 15:15:44 User3268
   $3.30   0.044 Hrs File 15 6 Descriptors
   $ .22   Telenet
   $3.52   Estimated Total Cost

Figure 4.2 (*continued*)

COLA (the bibliographic research publication records of the U.S. Department of Agriculture) and the NIOSHTIC (database of the National Institute for Occupational Safety and Health).

A typical database search from DIALOG is reproduced as Figure 4.2. Note the use of Boolean algebra operators. You can see how simple, efficient, and inexpensive bibliographic searching by computer can be.

There are advantages and disadvantages to using computerized information services and databases. Among the advantages are:

1. Material related to your specific key term is accessed quickly and precisely from a great variety of databases.
2. Many indexing characteristics are available such as author, time frame, language, type of publication, and journal title.
3. Most human error (mistakes in copying, for example) is eliminated from data retrieved.
4. Current data are available. (Some databases are updated daily, some weekly, some monthly. Published sources take much longer to enter a system.)
5. Printouts are convenient and save time.

Disadvantages to be considered are:

1. Costs can be beyond student range, especially if selected key terms are general or vague. (Every second a database is used costs money.)
2. Chosen subject may lack a standardized indexing term. (It may not be recognized by the system.)[4]
3. Some subjects are difficult to reduce to precise component terms for retrieval (such as those dealing with relationships or ethical problems).
4. Some items within a database may be ten to twenty years old and the information may have become obsolete.
5. Historical information may be lacking. (Most databases go back only as far as the 1960s.)
6. You pay for irrelevant citations.
7. Browsing—randomly leafing through information—is difficult if not impossible and extremely expensive.
8. Thorough searches require the expertise of a librarian.

Costs for using a commercial information/data service are based on connect time (the time the terminal being used is connected to the database computer). Costs range from $15 to $200 an hour. To that, phone charges at the rate of about $10 an hour—the cost of calling coast-to-coast on a computer network, such as TELENET—should be added.

---

[4]An exception to this problem is the field of chemistry, which has universally adopted the Chemical Society's *Chemical Abstract Service* terminology. The *Chemical Abstract Service* assigns a unique identification number to every chemical substance. Other databases use these identification numbers when dealing with chemical substances.

Some universities provide these services to students without charge or at a very modest cost. A computer search provides a more comprehensive listing in a shorter period of time. Material uncovered by the information bases proves to be not only more extensive but also more pertinent if the research strategy is carefully formulated. Computer searches, however, can also produce an overwhelming amount of irrelevant information that is more confusing than useful.

Suggestions for Literature Searching

In the prewriting, planning stage, you have broken your problem down into its component parts. Next, to find the state of knowledge of the problem and to secure a good general background for pursuing your investigation, you might begin by reading the most general treatments of the problem first, as in, for example, an encyclopedia. This can be followed by a more detailed but still quite broad discussion in a handbook. Next it would be desirable to search the library catalog for books on the subject. If there is a recent monograph on your problem, the library search may end at this point because such specialized books often contain bibliographies sufficient for most purposes.

If you cannot find a book that is complete or entirely up-to-date, you might look for a survey or review article in the professional periodical or trade publication that specializes in the area of your problem. Then appropriate abstract publications should be searched by working backwards in time until the necessary coverage has been obtained or until the year is reached that has been adequately dealt with in a book. Technical and professional papers will usually contain references to earlier works, and in this way the researcher can be carried backward to pick up references formerly missed.

If you have a computerized information/database available to you, you might begin by querying it for the literature covering the keywords related to your topic or problem. The procedure for using DIALOG Information Retrieval Service described in Figure 4.2 is appropriate. To perform an effective computer search, you need to analyze your topic for terms and concepts that the computer can flag or lock into by searching the vast literature within its store. Be specific in identifying the key terms of your topic.

For example, let us say your research is investigating the role that nutrition plays in the IQ level of children. This problem contains three major concepts:

1	2	3
Nutrition	IQ	Children

Please note that the terms *role* and *level* are not included in your consideration. Why? At this point, they are too general and ambiguous. Their use would confuse the retrieval process by flagging a multitudinous quantity of extraneous literature unrelated to the problem. The exact effect they play in your problem is what is to be determined. The three concepts—nutrition, IQ, and children—form a relationship that lends itself to computer searching, as shown in Figure 4.3.

Figure 4.3

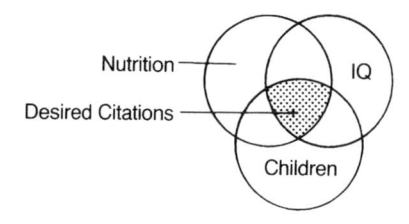

More effective retrieval can be achieved by expanding each concept with additional or synonymous terms that are relevant to the concept. Each of the concepts may be further expanded as follows:

1	2	3
Nutrition	IQ	Children
Diet	Intelligence	Boys
Food	Genius	Girls
Health	Heredity	Youngsters
Nourishment	Mental Age	Juveniles, etc.
Vitamins, etc.	Retardation	
	Imbecile	
	Moron, etc.	

Each group of terms can be used as a set of building blocks to effect the search. What you do is to instruct the computer, using the Boolean operator AND, to print out the citations wherein the three building blocks or concept terms intersect, that is, those citations having the three sets of terms in common. Depending upon what is available in your computerized information/database, you can ask for printouts of the pertinent bibliographic references, for abstracts, or for the full document.

Hypertext

Hypertext is a development in software technology designed to provide on-line nonlinear information. It is a computer system for linking or cross-referencing related text and graphic units into a new document. Some programs, such as **HyperCard** from Apple Computer, have the capability to include animation and sound segments in the document. A hypertext-produced document is not designed to exist as a printed text, although you can print text and graphic material you have browsed through and linked together electronically.

Preparing a Bibliography

One troublesome problem the researcher has is the recording of information acquired from reading and setting it up in accessible form. This involves keeping accurate and complete bibliography cards and note cards. Bibliography cards provide a complete record of the sources of information used in library searching. The first step in making a literature search is to check with a librarian for help in compiling a working bibliography—a list of possible sources of information. Most libraries have librarians trained in providing help in literature searching. Be sure to take full advantage of such an available aid. While searching through indexes, abstracts, card catalogs, and computerized information services, you should keep accurate and complete records of the sources of information. If you have recourse to the services of a computerized database, you can be ahead of the game by having your bibliography printed out automatically for you. In listing reference sources, the following elements are recorded:

1. Library call number, usually in the upper left-hand corner (if the literature is obtained from a library).
2. The author's name, last name first, or the editor's name followed by *ed*. If both the author and the editor are given, list the editor after the book title. The edition number, translator, and number of volumes are listed after the title, if applicable.
3. The title of the book underlined. The title of an article is in quotation marks, and the title of a magazine is underlined if the entry is an article.
4. Publication data:
   a. For a book or a report, record the place of publication, the publisher, and the year of publication.
   b. For a magazine article, record the name of the magazine underlined, the date, the volume, and the pages on which the article appears.
   c. For a newspaper article, record the name of the newspaper underlined, the date, and the page number.
5. Subject label placed at the top of the card to allow filing of several bibliography cards under one topic.

The abstract's literature provides a quick means for evaluating the potential usefulness of a source item. If available to you, examine the abstract first.

Taking Notes

Most professional research workers take notes on 3-by-5-inch or 5-by-8-inch cards because cards are flexible and easy to handle, sort, keep in order, and later to organize. Three essential parts of the contents of a note card are:

1. the material, the facts, and the opinions to be recorded (include diagrams, charts, and tables if these are the data to be noted);
2. the exact source, title, and page from which they are taken; and
3. the label for the card showing what it treats.

It is usually a waste of effort to try to take notes in a numbered outline form.

It is best to read the article or chapter through rapidly at first to see what it contains for your purposes and then go over it again and make necessary notes. Distinguish between the author's facts and opinions. Specific points, such as dates and names of persons, should be recorded with particular care. Notes may be recorded either in paraphrase, summary, or direct quotation from the source. The exact wording of the author should be recorded on the note card when the original wording is striking, graphic, or appropriate; when a statement is controversial or may be questioned; or when it is desirable to illustrate the style of the author.

In recording quoted matters, take care to copy accurately the words, capitalization, punctuation, and even any errors that may appear in the original. Use quotation marks to indicate exactly where the quoted passage begins and ends. Ellipsis may be indicated by the use of three dots (. . .) at the beginning or within the sentence, or four dots at the end of a sentence (. . . .). Before you return the reference source, be sure that your bibliography and note cards include every item of information you will need for use in your paper. Also note the library or source where the book or publication is obtainable.

In your library research, you should be concerned with the meaning, accuracy, and general trustworthiness of the material you are reading. In evaluating the reading matter, you should be asking yourself questions related to the author's competence and integrity. How good an observer is the writer? Did she have ample opportunity to observe and master the matters she writes about? Does the author have a reputation for authoritativeness in the field? How well does the author know the facts of the case? Was she personally interested in presenting a particular point of view? Is she prejudiced? Is the author trying to deceive? Are her observations made firsthand or did she receive information from others? Are there discrepancies in the writing that throw question on the reliability of the literature? Are the data sufficient to support the points the author is making? In short, are the data relevant, material, and competent?

Plagiarism

A cautionary word about plagiarism is necessary because student writers—and often professional writers—depend on printed material for much of the information they use. According to copyright law, plagiarism is illegal; it is theft. A writer who steals the substance or the actual expression of ideas from others is a plagiarist. Plagiarism is more obvious when the exact words of another writer are used as one's own.

If you use another person's words or ideas, according to law, you need to give that person credit for it. If you quote word for word 250 or more successive words from a published source, you must obtain formal permission to use that material.

Careless note-taking can often be the cause of plagiarism. Check your notes for phrases and sentences copied word for word. Groups of as few as five successive words from a source should be placed between quotation marks on your note cards. After each bit of information you have recorded on a note card, give the page reference and source from which it comes. Even if you paraphrase the original words, you are still making use of another writer's ideas. I am not suggesting that you should not paraphrase from the reference sources you use to write your report. Far from it: Changing another's words to meet the needs and context of your situation is frequently more appropriate and effective. However, the use of another's materials needs to be acknowledged. How you do this is explained under Documentation, Chapter 7.

As soon as the findings of other investigators are exhausted, it is time for you to do your own primary work. Procedure depends, of course, on the technical elements of your problem.

Observation—Examining the Actual Situation, Condition, or Factors of the Problem

A common and traditional means for conducting research is through direct observation—a cornerstone of the scientific method. Observation is careful examination of the actual situation, condition, or factors of the problem. If your problem requires you to use observation in its investigation, it is important to decide whether you will use selective sampling or whether you will cover the entire field.[5] Observation implies selection because our powers are limited. While we might want to make random observations, we do select the conditions of time and place. Frequently, we find it necessary to examine and observe only a small portion of a problem. Inherent in observation is the necessity for recording what we examine and perceive. Human memory is not to be trusted. Observation must be followed by description. Observation should be recorded in precise, exact, and objective language.

Another essential point is that scientific observation tends to be quantitative. Numbers are used as part of the description where possible: how many, at what rate, with what value? The use of numerical measures permits a more precise description and makes possible the application of mathematics. Of course, not all matter and phenomena that are observed are numerical. Qualitative statements have an important role. However, the observer must try to be objective and free of bias. Even though it is perhaps impossible for any observer to be free completely from preconceptions and prejudices, it is important to arrange the conditions of the observation so the observer's bias will not result in distortion. Therefore, your observation should be given to others for checking. If possible, allow another observer or several observers to make independent observations of the same phenomena.

That this is necessary is illustrated by an experiment frequently repeated by psychologists: A man suddenly rushes into a room chased by another man with a revolver. After a scuffle in the middle of the room, a shot is fired and both men rush out again with barely thirty seconds elapsing for the incident. The psychologists conducting the experiment will ask the group to write down an account of what they saw. These descriptions usually show that no two persons in a group will agree on the principal facts of the incident. A noteworthy feature is that over

---

[5]For academic purposes you will recall that we are assuming that you, the student technical writer, are conducting the research of the problem to be reported. This assumption is necessary so that students know the process in thought and activity that researchers experience.

half of the accounts include details that never occurred. These experiments illustrate that observers not only frequently miss seemingly obvious things but also, what is even more significant, often invent false observations. Therefore, in the research situation, the careful observer makes use of instruments wherever possible to aid the observation and promote greater accuracy and objectivity. Photography, the photoelectric cell, and the thermocouple are frequently substituted for direct vision. Sound vibrations are converted into electrical oscillations and are analyzed and measured by instruments having a range far beyond that of the human ear. Thermometers, thermocouples, and pyrometers replace the sense of touch in estimating warmth and coldness. Where a phenomenon occurs rarely, or only for a short time, as in solar eclipses or earthquakes, optical and recording instruments are substituted for direct visual observation. Although many natural phenomena can be observed with the naked eye, many more become accessible with microscopes, binoculars, telescopes, and other optical and measuring instruments. Simple instruments such as meters and stethoscopes aid in direct human observation.

How to Conduct Observations

Here are some helpful suggestions for conducting observations under actual or controlled conditions:

1. Have a clear conception of the phenomena to be observed.
2. Secure a notebook or note cards upon which the data are to be recorded.
3. Set up entries or headings on the note cards or notebooks to indicate the form and units in which the results of the observation are to be recorded.
4. Define the scope of the observations.
5. Use care in selecting the basis of sampling, should sampling procedure be used.

If your investigation requires a site or field visit:

1. Obtain permission beforehand from proper authorities or from the owner if the site is private property.
2. Arrange access for an appropriate length of time under the proper circumstances for your observations.
3. Take along a camera, sketch pad, and tape measure, and arrange before the visit for permission to photograph and to make sketches.
4. Take careful notes as you observe, and double-check any measurements you make.
5. At the end of the visit, thank the owner/host in person or by letter.

Experimenting

Experimentation is observation carried out under special conditions that are controlled and varied for specific reasons. In an experiment, an event is made to occur under known conditions. As many extraneous influences as possible are eliminated, and close observation is made possible so that relationships between phenomena can be revealed. The sequence of the experimental process begins with the observation of the problem or difficulty. The experimenter formulates a hypothesis to explain the difficulty then tests the hypothesis by the experimental techniques and draws a conclusion as to its validity.

Experimentation is not limited to scientific research; it can be applied effectively to business and ordinary pursuits. For example, the owner of a hardware store may use an experimental procedure to test the effectiveness of his show window in displaying a new power lawn mower. He might stand outside his store and count the number of persons who look at the show window and note how long they stop. He is merely observing, if he does just that. If he designs three different displays for his lawn mower, each installed for the same period of time on three successive days and, furthermore, if he not only records the number of people who stop to look at the display but also notes the number who enter his store on each occasion to inquire about the product, he is performing an experiment under varied and controlled conditions.

Planning Experiments

Before planning the actual experiment, the investigator should have an understanding of the nature of the problem and any relevant theory associated with it. The **theory** is the explanation of the problem. Of course, the theory or explanation is to be proved, but it serves as a guide to formulating a hypothesis for testing the answer to the problem. The experimenter should analyze the problem and put it into words that express it in its simplest form. Frequently, it is possible to break problems into parts that are more easily answered separately than together.

An experiment should not be conducted without a clear-cut idea in advance of just what is to be tested. The investigator should ask: Why am I doing this particular thing? Will it tell me what I need to know about my problem? The first thing in planning an experiment is to decide the kind of event to be studied and the nature of the variables that previous information suggests might be the controlling ones of the matter being tested. These variables may be divided into those that can be controlled and those that cannot. The ideal experiment is one in which the relevant variables are held constant except for the one under study. The effects are then observed.

If observations are to be useful, the matter immediately under consideration must be separated from any that may confuse the issue. In scientific experimentation, a device known as *control* is used to avoid such error. Controls are similar test specimens that, as nearly as possible, are subjected to the same treatment as the objects of the experiment, except for the change in the variable under study. Control groups correspond to the experimental groups at every point except the point in question. Controls are frequently used in medical research, as in the test of the polio vaccine where two groups of subjects were used. One group, the experimental one, was given the vaccine, and the other, the control group, was given a placebo—a pharmaceutical preparation containing no medication but given for its psychological effect.

The use of controls is not always sufficient to ensure correct results. A story is told of a test of a seasickness remedy in which samples of the drug were given to a sea captain to test on a voyage. The idea of control was carefully explained to him. When the ship returned, the captain was highly enthusiastic about the results of the experiment. Practically every one of the controls was ill and not one of the subjects had any trouble. "It is really wonderful stuff!" exclaimed the captain. The medical researcher was skeptical enough to ask how the sea captain chose the controls and how he chose the subjects. "Oh, I gave the seasickness pills to my seamen and used the passengers as the controls!"

Rules of Experimental Research

John Stuart Mill, the great English philosopher, set up five rules for evaluating data in experimental research. They are useful guides in the design and evaluation of experiments and serve as general principles to aid interpretation of data. The rules are:

1. Method of Agreement (Recognizing What Is Similar)

This rule states that if the circumstances leading to a given result have even one factor in common, that factor may be the cause. It is especially true if it is the only factor in common. This principle is universally used but in and of itself is seldom considered as constituting valid proof of cause because it is difficult to be sure that a given factor is the only common one.

The need for such caution is illustrated by the story of a young scientist who imbibed liberal quantities of Scotch and soda at a party. The next morning he felt rather miserable. That night he tried rye and soda, again in very liberal amounts. The following day he was again visited by a distressing hangover. The third night he switched to bourbon and soda, but the morning after was no more pleasant. Being a scientist, he analyzed the evidence. Making good use of the method of agreement, he concluded that thereafter he would omit soda from his drinks since it was the common ingredient in his three distressing instances.

2. Method of Difference (Recognizing What Is Different)

The second rule states that if two sets of circumstances differ in only one factor and the one containing the factor leads to the event and the other does not, this factor can be considered the cause of the event. A note of caution: It is evidence but does not conclusively prove the hypothesis. The result may have been due to other factors and circumstances.

3. Joint Method of Agreement and Difference (Recognizing What Is Similar and What Is Different)

This rule states that if in two or more instances in which a phenomenon occurs, one circumstance is common to all of those instances, whereas in another two or more instances in which a phenomenon does not occur that same circumstance is absent, then it might be concluded that the circumstance or factor present in all positive cases and absent in all negative cases is the factor responsible for the phenomenon.

4. Principle of Concomitance ("Guilt by Association")

Concomitance is a "hard" word meaning coexisting or occurring with something else. The rule states that when two things consistently change or vary together, either the variations in one are caused by the variations in the other or both are being affected by some common cause.

5. Method of Residue (Process of Elimination)

This rule recognizes that some problems cannot be solved by the techniques used in the previous four rules. The method of residue arrives at causes through the process of elimination. When a specific factor causing certain parts of a given phenomenon is known, this principle suggests that the remaining parts of the phenomenon must be caused by the remaining factor or factors (by the residue).

Keeping Records

Data should be entered in a laboratory notebook at the time of observation of the experiment. Among the most unforgivable practices are dishonesty or carelessness in recording the full procedures, materials, or special elements and factors of the experiment, or in neglecting to keep a record of everything done; or failure to take into account every small part of the components and every action of the apparatus. Without records, successes cannot be repeated and failures will not have taught any lessons.

The experimenter sometimes has difficulty finding or knowing what to record. Each record of an experiment should include the purpose of the experiment, the equipment used and how it was set up, procedures, data, results, and conclusions. Sketches, drawings, and diagrams are frequently helpful. It is important to record what is actually seen, including things not fully understood at the time. Poor or unpromising experiments should be fully recorded, even those felt to be failures. They represent an investment of effort that should not be thrown away because often something can be salvaged, even if it is only a knowledge of what not to do the next time. The data always should be entered in their raw form.

Complete records are beneficial because the mere act of putting down on paper the what, where, when, why, and how will generate ideas of how the work can be improved. Where patent questions might be involved, it is desirable to witness and even notarize notebook pages at intervals. The witness should be someone who understands the material but is not a co-investigator.

Interviewing and Discussing With Experts or People Qualified to Give Required Data

Although interactive discussion techniques are fourth on the list, you, the writer, may turn to them first. Having ascertained the problem, you may first need to determine what you already know about it. After clarifying your own thoughts, you may find it profitable to turn to other people who are working in the same field or on the problem. Frequently, valuable information and shortcuts may be discovered by discussion with experienced and knowledgeable people. If the problem is one that your organization has previously done work on, you would do well to consult the files of your organization or company. You might talk to colleagues and superiors who have had experience in this area. However, you must prepare yourself before beginning any interviews or discussions, especially if you go outside your own organization to obtain information.

How to Interview

The interview may be conducted by letter and by telephone as well as in person. Letter and telephone interviews are less satisfactory. Direct contact with an individual and a face-to-face relationship often provide a stimulating situation for both interviewer and interviewee. Personal reaction and interaction help not only in rapport but also in obtaining nuances and additional information by the reactions, which are more fully observed in a face-to-face relationship.

Adequate preparation for the interview is a "must." Careful planning saves not only time but also the energy of both parties concerned. The interview is used to obtain facts or subjective data such as individual opinions, attitudes, and preferences. Interviews are used when questionnaires that may have been used to obtain data need to be checked, when a problem being investigated is complex, or when the information needed to solve it cannot be secured easily in any other way. People will often give information orally but will not put it in writing.

Here are points to consider to promote the success of your interview:

1. Make a definite appointment by telephone or letter, explaining carefully the purpose of the interview, the type of information required, and—this is very important—the significance or importance of the contribution the interviewee will make.

2. Select the right person who is in a position to know and has the authority to give the information you need. Find out as much as possible about the person before the interview.

3. Tape the interview if possible. Taping your interview has the advantage of capturing exactly what your expert or respondent says; you are then able more conveniently to check the details and accuracy of the information you obtained. Taping cuts down on note-taking efforts. Be aware that some persons object to being taped, some freeze up, and some will not provide full or candid answers, especially on sensitive or controversial subjects. Always obtain permission for taping prior to the interview.

4. Prepare for the interview. Know the subject matter of the interview so that the interviewee does not feel she is wasting valuable time explaining basics that you should have known beforehand.

5. Arrive on time. Have questions prepared and lead the interview. Do not expect the person being interviewed to do your job for you by volunteering all

the information you may need or pointing out other matters you do not know about or have forgotten.
6. Do only as much talking as is necessary to keep the interviewee talking. Do not contradict or argue with the interviewee even if you know she is wrong. Sometimes erroneous information can be significant data. Be courteous. If there is a point requiring further explanation, ask a question that might uncover the other side to the problem.
7. If the interviewee gets off the subject, be ready with a question that will get her back on track.
8. When the session is not taped, and the person interviewed says something especially significant or expresses herself particularly well on some point, or if she offers statistics, figures, or mathematical formulas, or other matters that might require careful checking, ask permission to write down such statements.
9. Do not prolong your interview. If the originally allotted time passes, remind the interviewee of this fact. It is up to her to ask you to stay longer to finish the conversation.
10. Immediately after the interview, record the answers. At a later time, it is a matter of courtesy to send the interviewee a record of the interview to give her the opportunity to correct any errors you may have made or permit her to change her mind about anything she said. If you are planning to quote her, be sure that the interviewee is aware of this and gives you permission to do so.

The interview has the advantage that the interviewer can partially control the situation and can interpret questions, clear up misunderstandings, and get firsthand impressions, which might throw light on data. The interview is a valuable instrument in those situations in which the only data available are opinions.

Using Questionnaires

As a research tool, questionnaires require judicious handling. However, there are certain situations in which questionnaires must be used and can be used effectively. A much wider geographic distribution may be obtained more economically from a questionnaire. Certain groups within the population are frequently more easily approached through a questionnaire, for example, executives, high-income groups, and professional people. Questionnaires often allow for opinions from the entire family. A questionnaire can be filled out at the respondent's leisure and, therefore, more thought can be given to the response. Finally, by careful sampling methods, a representative sample of a study universe may be made. See Figure 4.4 for a sample questionnaire.

Like the interview, the questionnaire must have a reason for being used. It should be designed to require as little time as possible for completion. A cover letter that will motivate the reader to answer the questions should be included with

Dear Mr. Nagel:

May we have just a few minutes of your time and the benefit of your experience in answering a few questions pertinent to the development of a Suggestion System Program?

Your assistance will be especially useful in helping us to plan effectively for a suggestion program. We would greatly appreciate your answering the brief survey which is attached and returning it to us in the attached postage-paid envelope. If you would like the tabulated results of this survey, please sign your name so that we may direct the results to you personally.

Won't you help us benefit from your experience? If we can ever serve you in a similar way, please call on us.

Sincerely yours,

Please Answer All Applicable Questions

1. Age of Company: Less than 5 years _____, 5 to 10 yrs. _____, more than 10 years _____.
2. Approximate number of employees: Under 50 _____, 50–99 _____, 100–250 _____, 251–499 _____, 500 or more _____.
3. Do you have or have you had a Suggestion System in your Company? Yes _____, No _____.
4. Is it in operation now? Yes _____, No _____.
5. If answer in 4 is no, please indicate reasons by checking:
    a. Too costly
    b. Lack of interest of employees
    c. Management indifference
    d. Supervisory resistance
    e. Reward system inadequate or unsatisfactory
    f. Other
6. If you do not have a Suggestion System, do you have alternate means of eliciting employees' ideas? Please indicate _____
7. How long have you had your Suggestion System in operation? _____.
8. Does your program include participation by Engineers _____, Foremen _____, Middle Management (Department Heads) _____, Upper Management (Division Heads) _____?
9. Types of Awards Offered: Cash _____, Certificates _____, Other _____?
10. What is your maximum award _____; minimum award _____; average size of award _____?
11. Who administers your Suggestion System?
    a. Personnel Office
    b. Suggestion System Director
    c. Committee
    d. Other _____
12. Do you consider that your Suggestion System accomplishes its objectives? Yes _____, No _____.

COMMENTS: _____
_____
_____

Figure 4.4 Sample questionnaire.

a questionnaire. The letter should tell the use to be made of the answers. If possible, the writer should offer a copy of the summary of the results of the investigation and assure the reader that the task of answering will not require too much of his time.

The questions should be phrased in the form of a list, not in lengthy sentences or paragraphs. The wording must be structured with care to ensure clarity and completeness. Where possible, questions must be grouped into logical arrangements. The first few questions should be easy to answer and should be interesting to secure cooperation. One question should stimulate interest in the next. Questions should be arranged in an order that aids the respondent's memory. The most effective questionnaires are frequently those that are designed to provide a yes or no, one word, a checkoff, filling in a small circle, or pushing out a blank for the answers. They are best because they are easier for a respondent to reply to and they lend themselves to computer tabulation and analysis. Each question should contain one idea only. If the questionnaire becomes too long or involved, the reader may get discouraged and neither finish nor mail it. Questionnaires should include a self-addressed, stamped envelope for reply.

Much of the success of a mail questionnaire depends on its physical appearance, the arrangements of questions, the ease with which answers may be filled in, and the amount of space left for comments. A questionnaire of one page will bring more returns than one of two pages, and a postcard is frequently the most effective questionnaire instrument. The sending of questionnaires should be accurately timed so that they reach their destination at a time when favorable replies may be expected. As far as possible, select periods when data or information may be fresh in the mind or when interest in a subject is ripe. Avoid vacation periods, periods when reports are made, and the close or the beginning of the year.

Systematizing, Analyzing, and Interpreting the Data

The data you have obtained from your investigative techniques must be systematized, analyzed, and interpreted to answer your problem. The data you have accumulated must be evaluated to ascertain the degree of appropriateness, accuracy, and completeness. If gaps appear in the mass of data acquired, further steps may be needed to obtain the missing information.

How to Systematize the Data

After you have decided that the raw data are complete and satisfactory, the next logical step is clear, methodological arrangement. This means that your raw or basic data must be so organized they will lead you to the answer to your problem. This type of arrangement is done best by listing the elements of your problem on note cards and then arranging the raw data alongside the listed components of the problem. This systematization is chiefly a matter of linking the data or bases of evidence to the specific elements to which they relate. Make use of the block diagram in Figure 4.1.

How to Analyze and Interpret the Data

The previous step consisted of evaluating, sifting, and arranging the data in an orderly relation to the elements in the research problem. You may now find it desirable or necessary to recast your data in a more refined way to derive inferences or conclusions. This is done by tabulation and retabulation of the raw data. Averages in various forms—modes, medians, quartiles, deciles—may be used to obtain quantitative criteria of mass data.[6] Frequently, the complete meaning of mass data will only be comprehended by averages, and they may then reveal qualitative differences. Data may have to be refined in a statistical form to eliminate the influences of such factors as cyclical or seasonal fluctuations. Intricate relationships may be revealed by tabulating, graphing, and diagramming. This refinement often results in greater insight and suggestions of inferences that may answer the components of the problem. By use of inductive and deductive reasoning, conclusions or answers to the problem can be arrived at.

Interpretation, as was seen in Chapter 3 on pages 66–67, is the process of arriving at inferences, explanations, or conclusions by examining data and applying the process of logical analysis and thought to them. Interpretation is accomplished when phenomena are made intelligible by relating them to the requirements of the matter or problem being investigated. Individual facts and/or opinions are placed within a deductive or inductive system for inferential generalization. In short, interpretation, by use of observation, logical analysis, synthesis, experience, knowledge, and insight, arrives at explanations and answers to the questions the investigation must resolve.

Applying and organizing the interpreted data constitute the next step, which will be discussed in Chapter 5.

Chapter in Brief

We defined report writing as the reconstruction of a purposeful investigation of a problem in written form. Therefore, the role of the problem and hypothesis in report writing was examined first. The four steps in report writing were identified. We focused on a report's prewriting processes and examined the necessary strategies for planning and analysis required to reconstruct the investigation being reported. In addition, we explained the methods for conducting an investigation of a problem and discussed the contribution of computer technology to literature searching.

---

[6]*Mode* is the value or number that occurs most frequently in a given series; *median* is the middle number in a series containing an odd number of items (e.g., 7 in the series, 1, 3, 5, 7, 15, 21, 34); *quartile* is the designating of a point so chosen that three-fourths of the items of a frequency distribution are on one side of it and one-fourth on the other; *decile* is any of the values of an attribute that separate the entire frequency distribution into ten groups of equal frequency.

Chapter Focal Points

- Role of the problem in research
- Hypothesis
- Types of reports
- Prewriting strategies
- Investigative procedures
    How to search the literature, including computer information resources
    Observation
    Experimentation
    Interviews and questionnaires
- Systematizing, analyzing, and interpreting data

Questions for Discussion

1. What is a report? What role do reports play in present-day industry and scientific endeavor?
2. What sources of information are employed in the historical method of research? Its aspects of library searching are useful in what ways to other methods of research?
3. What is the role of the problem in the technical paper or report?
4. Locate and examine a report from business, from industry, from a private, government, or educational research laboratory, and from a university experiment station. What are their differences and similarities? What is their purpose? intended use? readership? Can you classify these four reports? How was the research carried out in each? What methods were employed? Note their format, organization, style of writing, use of illustrations, and appendixes, if any.
5. Discuss the four major steps in report writing. What inference is to be drawn from the fact that the writing process is the last step?

Assignments

1. Select a topic for an analytical, formal report in accordance with the precepts stated in this textbook. Preferably, your topic should be in your major field of study; however, you may select one of practical value affecting your college, community, or yourself. Your instructor must approve the topic you select. To help your thinking, I have listed below some suggestions for types of problems to consider:
    a. Should the Harmony Preschool invest in two computers for its classroom use or buy additional jungle gyms and sandboxes?
    b. How to design a unique anti-icing device for home concrete walks and driveways.
    c. When and how should your township increase its water supply?
    d. Should the mathematics department add five additional graduate assistants to meet the need for remedial assistance to freshmen students or invest instead in two computer-aided instruction machines?

e. Is high-pressure hot-water heating more economical than steam for heating a given complex of buildings in the university?

f. What is the effect of antihistamine on the antibody titer induced by influenza virus in mice?

g. What environmentally safe measures can be used for campus lawns, trees, and shrubs without resorting to pesticides?

h. What is the feasibility of instituting a child care center on campus for parent students and university employees?

i. Are there effective alternatives to dieting for lowering cholesterol?

j. In what university department can multimedia technology be an advantageous pedagogical tool?

k. What industrial training areas best lend themselves to the hypertext technology?

l. Should student fees be reduced for students not desiring to attend football and basketball games, play performances, musical recitals, and similar events?

2. After you have selected a topic, write your instructor a memo asking her approval for your research question. Specify both the audience for whom your report is being prepared and the use for which it is intended. Justify your topic selection by stating the reason for your interest and its importance to the intended reader. Identify what, if anything, you already know about the subject and what you need to learn. Indicate how you will go about obtaining and researching the information.

3. Develop a working bibliography on your topic by searching your library catalog, literature guides, and such reference sources as abstracting and indexing journals, subject bibliographies, handbooks, yearbooks, and, if possible, computer databases. Don't hesitate to seek help from the librarian. Use index cards for your bibliographic entries. Take notes on at least three reference sources. Turn them in to your instructor for comment.

4. You have chosen to write a report on the subject, Panic During Emergencies. In your research, you have come across an article by Thomas E. Drabek, "Shall We Leave? A Study on Family Reactions When Disaster Strikes." The article includes some key principles, which you want to include in your conclusions. As you know, plagiarism is using words, ideas, and thoughts you have learned from another source as your own. Dr. Drabek's principles are quoted below. How would you make use of his material without resorting to plagiarism? Whereas material that is considered common knowledge need not be documented, direct quotations exhibiting a particular style or choice of words that express ideas concisely and effectively require acknowledgment. Even paraphrasing of such material requires documentation.

Warning Responses: Eight Behavioral Principles. [4]

1. Disbelief, not mass panic, is the typical initial public response to disaster warning.

2. A siren—like any other noise—does not constitute a public warning; at best it may alert some, but many will ignore it.

3. Warning messages must include both threat information and directions for adaptive actions.

4. The greater the specificity of the information given, the more likely people are to believe it.

5. Community warning systems must accomplish seven key functions: (1) detection; (2) measurement; (3) collation; (4) interpretation; (5) decision to warn; (6) message content; and (7) dissemination.
6. There are patterned variations in response—women and children are more likely to believe; elderly and ethnic minorities, like males, take more convincing.
7. Warnings received from individuals perceived to be authorities—a uniformed police officer—are more likely to be believed than from other sources, e.g., a relative or a media representative.
8. Typically, groups—be they family or work—receive and process warning messages, not single individuals in total isolation from others.

For this assignment, include introductory material to your presentation of Dr. Drabek's principles.

5. You are working for your college Public Affairs Office. You receive an assignment to analyze some statistics based on a questionnaire sent to the students who graduated ten years ago. Of sixty-three responses from women graduates, twenty provided data on their present yearly earnings. These reveal:

Betty J,	$27,500.	Donna T,	$33,000.
Vera P,	$30,000.	Catherine P,	$40,000.
Elizabeth K,	$38,000.	Sherry H,	$33,000.
Mary T,	$22,000.	Nancy S,	$50,000.
Nora A,	$36,000.	Karen K,	$40,000.
Beatrice W,	$70,000.	Helen B,	$22,000.
Laura B,	$19,800.	Ginger R,	$100,000.
Madeline L,	$1,850,000.	Jean E,	$27,500.
Terry M,	$25,000.	Virginia T,	$20,000.
Holly G,	$27,000.	Lenore L,	$27,500.

When you totaled the yearly salaries, it came to $2,538,300. Then you divided that amount by 20 to arrive at a mean (average) of $126,915 earned by women ten years after their graduation from your college! This startling statistic could make a wonderful publicity story for your college. But how truthful is that statistic? To get a complete picture, what other factors need to be considered about the data in these returns? How should you handle the statistics to make a more factual and objective presentation? Write a 200–250 word article maintaining the integrity of your data without distorting their validity.

6. a. Prepare a set of questions for an interview with an "expert" on an aspect of the problem you are investigating and reporting.
   b. Design a questionnaire for your use in obtaining information on your problem or an aspect of it.
7. If you are conducting an experiment or are doing field work and observation to obtain a solution to your problem, keep a laboratory notebook or journal to record your data.
8. After you have identified the problem you are to investigate for your report in your preliminary analysis phase, build a block diagram like the one pictured in Figure 4.1.

Resolve or factor out the major elements of the problem and their components. Place these elements and components within their proper boxes. This type of block diagram analysis will be invaluable in the prosecution of your research and its reporting in the next stage.

9. Set up a work schedule listing the tasks and timetable for accomplishing the identification of your research problem, its investigation, organization, and analysis of data, and the writing of a report on the research.

References

1. Anderson, Chester R., Alta Gwinn Saunders, and Frances W. Weeks. *Business Reports.* 3d ed. New York: McGraw-Hill, 1957.
2. Cohen, Morris R. and Ernest Nagel. *An Introduction to Logic and the Scientific Method.* New York: Harcourt, Brace, 1934.
3. Dewey, John. *Logic: The Theory of Inquiry.* New York: Henry Holt, 1938.
4. Drabek, Thomas E. "Shall We Leave? A Study on Family Reactions When Disaster Strikes." *Emergency Management Review* (Fall 1983).
5. Whorf, Benjamin Lee. *Language, Thought and Reality, Selected Writings of Benjamin Whorf.* Edited by John B. Carroll. New York: John Wiley and the M.I.T. Press, 1956.

5
Report Writing—Organizing the Report Data

Chapter Objective

Provide guidelines for organizing the report's data and structure.

Chapter Focus

- Thesis sentence's role in structure
- Logical methods for organizing a report
- Psychological method for organizing a report
- Outlining

When the data for the report are in, we face the problem of organizing them into useful, functional form, interpreting and analyzing them to see what they mean. If your prewriting planning and analysis have been carefully done, the work at this stage is almost half accomplished. You ask yourself questions again:

What facts have I found that are significant to my problem?
What facts are most significant?
What is their significance?
How do these facts answer my problem?
What is the answer to my problem?

The answers to these questions become the basis for the organization of the main body of the report.

How to Develop the Report's Thesis Sentence

Having begun with a problem, the investigator has accumulated data for answering it. Raw data of themselves do not make a report. Raw data properly examined, analyzed, and interpreted through the methods of logical reasoning become the material out of which the report is designed. The first step in structuring a report is to develop a clear and concise statement of the answer. The answer may be positive or negative. The statement, explicitly and clearly stated, is the payload you are bringing to your reader. This payload often is called the **core idea** or **thesis sentence** (Figure 5.1). The thesis sentence is the answer to the problem or situation that you have investigated and are reporting. It is what you want your reader to know. The thesis sentence, or core idea, is a single, comprehensive statement in complete sentence form that synthesizes the complete report and presents the

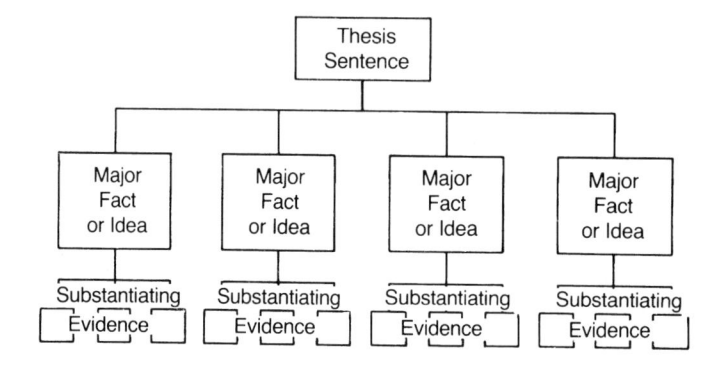

Figure 5.1 Each block of major fact or idea relates to and answers the block of the major element of the problem diagramed in Figure 4.1 (Chapter 4). Substituted for the block of the statement of the problem is that of the thesis sentence. Replacing the block of the major elements of the problem are the blocks of the major facts or ideas. The blocks of substantiating data or evidence replace the blocks of components of the earlier diagram.

problem's answer to the reader succinctly and clearly. A properly formulated thesis sentence is concrete evidence of how lucidly and simply you, the writer, see your subject. It is the backbone for unifying all of the elements of the report.

Adequate research requires the clarified statement of where the research has gone, what it has meant, and where it has led. Since clear thinking is the basis of clear writing, the writer must state the answer to the problem clearly and succinctly. Therefore, the first step in designing your report is to state distinctly and concisely the core idea, or thesis sentence.

For the sake of illustration, we might examine a few hypothetical problems and see how a thesis sentence might be structured from the data:

1. *Problem:* What causes the diurnal migrations of zooplankton?
   Thesis sentence: Migration of zooplankton is caused by an interplay of factors such as light, temperature, chemicals, and quest for food.
2. *Problem:* Could a light, single-engine, pontoon-type aircraft be used effectively for fire suppression in the lake states?
   Thesis sentence: The Beaver, a light, single-engine aircraft, could be used effectively for fire suppression in the lake states.
3. *Problem:* Are existing environmental conditions in Decatur County, Kansas, conducive to the propagation of bobwhites in sufficient numbers to support an annual hunting season?
   Thesis sentence: The environmental conditions in Decatur County, Kansas, are unfavorable to increased population of bobwhites.
4. *Problem:* Can implanted sex hormones in dairy heifer calves be used to promote maturity, better breeding efficiency, and greater udder development?
   Thesis sentence: Sex hormone implantation in dairy heifer calves is useless in promoting maturity and is detrimental to breeding efficiency and udder development.
5. *Problem:* Which of three wiring processes presently used in X Manufacturing Company is most efficient and best suited to the conditions of the factory?
   Thesis sentence: The printed circuit process is the most efficient and best suited for the special factory conditions of X Manufacturing Company.

The thesis sentence serves to keep you, the report writer, from exceeding your limits. It helps you follow consistently your objective, and in certain situations it suggests points for you to include and the arranged order of their sequence. The thesis sentence is the test of your mastery of your subject. Inability to formulate the thesis sentence is an indication that you either have not completed your investigation or have not been able to interpret and analyze logically the data accumulated in your investigation.

In purely informational types of reports, it might be difficult to synthesize the material of the investigation into the thesis sentence; here a summary statement is called for. But in all analytical types of reports, the thesis sentence is not only practical but also necessary.

Although the thesis sentence is necessary in the construction of the report, it may not be found verbatim anywhere in the report itself. It might be compared to a working sketch, which must be drawn (written) in order to point to the directions where the model or composition is going. The thesis sentence obviously cannot be written until all the research has been completed and all of the raw data analyzed in relation to the problem. How else is the answer derived? The answer to your problem becomes the core idea of your report. It is the dominant idea you want your reader to reach after he reads your report.

Guidelines for Organizing the Report Structure

Write the thesis sentence on a 3-inch-by-5-inch card, then set it on a table before you. A reconstruction process follows: Use other such cards and set down the major facts that have led you to the thesis sentence. Write each major fact or idea on a separate card. Place the card with your thesis sentence on it at the left of the table. Next, make a mental equal sign and arrange the major facts or ideas of the data of your investigation to equal your thesis sentence. What you have arranged before you is your thesis sentence = one major idea + another major idea + another major idea + . . . as many major ideas as are necessary to lead you to the answer to your problem.

The synthesizing process has been turned around. In actuality, the formula for the thesis sentence was derived from this sequence:

$$\text{major idea}_1 + \text{major idea}_2 \ldots + \text{major idea}_n \xrightarrow{\text{(yields)}} \text{thesis sentence}$$

In arriving at this formula, you may find it advisable to check on yourself by having each major fact on a separate card, followed by cards containing substantiating proof or data below it. Spread the cards out on a table and rearrange the cards into the best sequence for an outline, beginning with the most logical or valid fact or datum relevant to the answer. Follow sequentially in the order of the logic. The logic for the structuring will be discussed later in the chapter. The major facts become headings in your report. To identify their place in the outline, number each of them and number their substantiating matter.

Patterns for Organizing the Report's Data

I have just noted that the major facts and ideas and their substantiating data are to be organized in a logical sequence. Let us now see how the various kinds of content matter might lend themselves to effective arrangement for bringing the reader to the answer that you, the writer, have reached. In organizing the material of the investigation, you must keep in mind the purpose of the report and the purpose for which the answer to the problem will be used by the reader. A report's organization must be functional. You arrange your data so that they meet the reader's specific needs.

A number of approaches in the organization of the report are possible. The one you choose depends on such factors as these:

1. Purpose
2. Needs of the reader
3. Nature of the material

Temporarily, we are going to skip the elements of introduction and conclusion in the report and examine the part containing the main data, the *body* of the report. There are two major methods for organizing the data contained in the body of the report—the logical and the psychological.

Logical Method of Organization

The logical method builds its case step-by-step within the logical scheme of its pattern, leading to conclusions and possibly recommendations. Since problems and their investigations vary in nature, the logic to the organization of the data is going to be different in each report. Accordingly, in the logical method, there are a number of patterns to the organization of the main body of data.

1. Chronological Pattern

The chronological organization, sometimes called the narrative pattern, is the simplest and often the most obvious way of arranging the data of an investigation. It follows a time sequence. It is the pattern most frequently used in informational types of reports, particularly those of a historical nature. Chronological order may also be used in reports using other organizational patterns where the presentation of a sequence of doing a thing is important to the exposition. In a technical experiment, for example, conditions or results within a sequence must be presented as they occur; otherwise, the reader will be unable to duplicate the work. In an investigation of a historical nature, the chronology of events is of vital importance to the understanding of events; therefore, the presentation of data must follow the proper time sequence. This type of organizational approach does not lend itself well to either complex situations or those situations where nontemporal relationships and special emphasis are important. The chronological approach serves in simple, uninvolved situations where the time order is important and special emphasis on particular matters is not required.

2. Geographical or Spatial

Data may be presented or arranged according to geographical or spatial relationships. For example, a report to the president of a corporation on how to allocate space to the various departments of the corporation in a new building might logically begin with an assignment of the various wings moving east or west, as the case may be, or moving from the basement up to the various floor levels of the building. Or, in his State of the Union address at the start of a new Congress, the President of the United States might review the economic state of the country geographically, beginning with the northeastern states, working south and west across the country.

3. Functional

If you were reporting on the design of a new mechanism or instrument, a logical approach would be to examine each component or assembly by the function it performs in the working of the whole.

4. Order of Importance

It is sometimes appropriate to begin with the data most significant to the problem or situation, then move on to the next most significant, and so forth. This approach would be highly suitable in a situation where the researcher must find the best plan or procedure for accomplishing a certain end. Related to this pattern is the approach of putting first those phases of a project in which the greatest success was achieved and following sequentially to the least successful phase.

5. Elimination of Possible Solutions

Within this pattern, you would examine all possible solutions to a problem, beginning with the least likely and working toward the best possible solution. (This approach is opposite to that of number 4 above). This approach borrows from the narrative technique of building toward a climax.

6. General to Particular

The sixth structural pattern (deductive method) starts with discussion of general principles and then deduces the specific applications from them. In reporting on the efficacy of inaugurating a company training program, for example, you might first discuss the general benefits to be derived from a training program and then arrive at a specific benefit from a specific training such as report writing. You would then show how the class in report writing would add to the general benefits of a training program.

7. Particular to General

This pattern (inductive method) is the reverse of number 6. You might start with a specific training program—again, say, report writing—and then induce general benefits derived from such a specific program.

8. Simple to Complex, or Known to Unknown

This pattern of organization is appropriate to situations where it is advisable to begin with the simple case or known situation and then move to more and more complex or unfamiliar grounds.

9. Pro and Con

In the report that investigates whether to do or not to do something, the material on which an answer is based might appropriately be grouped into data for and data against, or advantages and disadvantages.

10. Cause and Effect

This approach is particularly useful in the exposition of problems that deal with questions like these: What is it? What caused it? or What are the effects of . . .? The writer may begin with a fact or a set of facts (cause or sets of causes) and proceed to the results or effects arising from them. Conversely, the writer may examine and report the causes from which effects arise.

These ten patterns are not mutually exclusive and are frequently used in combination.

The Psychological Pattern of Organization

With the psychological pattern of organization, the most important data of the report are arranged in the most strategic place—the beginning. The psychological method follows no order of time or sequence in which the data are collected. Usually the conclusions are placed first and the discussion second. This report pattern, sometimes known as the *double report*, originated in business and industry where busy executives prefer to conserve time and get to essential matters at once. When reading a report, they want to know quickly what the problem is, what the answers to the problem are, and how the answers were derived. The psychological pattern permits the conclusion to be seen first so the major issues can be apprehended immediately. The study of supporting data is usually left to subordinates. The organizational sequence of the psychological pattern is as follows:

A short introductory section states the problem. This is followed immediately by a section of conclusions and recommendations. Because executives reading the report may be interested in knowing how the conclusions were reached, the section on procedure then follows. Should they want to check points more carefully, they can continue to read the results based on the procedures. Then, if they want all the details, they can turn to the remaining section, the discussion.

In the psychological organizational pattern, the main body of the report does not contain "arithmetic" or other raw data. This material is put into the appendix. Busy executives want only the significant factors that have resulted in the generalizations making up the conclusions and recommendations. Technical subordinates will check the computations and the raw data in the appendix if the executives want full confirmation of the recommendations on which to act.

Just which of the two major methods of organization to use is determined by the writer after he considers all aspects of the purpose and nature of the report and the needs of the readers.

The Outline—A Guide to the Writer and Reader

The synthesizing approach we have been discussing in this chapter can conveniently take form first as an outline. The **outline** is a schematic road map of the report and shows the order of topics and their relationships. The outline makes the writing of your paper easier and more effective and enables you to write with confidence and to focus on one stage at a time. You can see how the whole will take shape, and you will not be distracted while writing by the question of whether to put a particular piece of information in here or reserve it for later. The outline, then, permits you, the investigator, to test the adequacy of your data. Subsequently, it offers the reader guideposts or road signs in the form of heads and subheads. The outline is the last step in the organization of the data for the writing of the report. Several types of outlines are used in practice. The simplest is the topical outline. Subjects or topics are noted in brief phrases or single words and numbered sequentially. Another type, the sentence outline, is more specific and provides a complete sentence about each topic.

The Topical Outline—The "Laundry List"

The topical outline is a useful device in thinking through the organization of the paper. To begin, you may want to jot down key ideas and data related to the material of your paper. For example, let us take the case of a geology student whose research problem is tracing the origins of the intrusive body of rocks in Big Thompson Canyon, Colorado. Initially, the student would write down the series of major facts and their components as follows:

1. Introduction
2. Historical background
3. The problem
4. Location and description of intrusive
5. Location and description of Silver Plume Granite outcrop
6. Specimen selection and field trimming
7. Microscopic analysis of specimens
8. The intrusive specimen
9. The Silver Plume specimen
10. Comparison of field and laboratory data
11. Conclusion
12. Recommendations

As you can see, topics are listed in a sequence without any indication of specificity, importance, or relationships, or any indication that some are topics subordinate to major subject heads. In early planning, this type of outline is useful; it sets down on paper matters to be considered for more detailed structuring.

The Detailed Topical Outline

The second phase of outlining would focus on greater specificity, subordination, and relationships. The analysis entailed would reveal a breakdown of greater detail. This phase of the outline might be structured as follows:

1. Introduction
    a. Significance of problem
    b. Scope
    c. Historical background
    d. Definitions
2. Analyzing the Problem
3. The Intrusive
    a. Location of intrusive
    b. Description of intrusive
4. The Silver Plume Granite Outcrop
    a. Location of the outcrop
    b. Description of the outcrop
5. Specimen Selection
6. Field Trimming
7. Microscopic Analysis of Specimens
    a. The intrusive specimen
    b. The Silver Plume specimen
8. Field and Laboratory Data
    a. Similarity of occurrence in field
    b. Comparison of laboratory data
9. Conclusion
10. Recommendations

The Sentence Outline

The detailed topical outline is an improvement over the first topical outline. It is more specific and it identifies relationships, allows some emphasis, and shows subordination of lesser items to more important ones. Nevertheless, it does little more than identify these matters. The writer still faces a painful task of thinking through the ideas and the status of the evidence to be presented. At some point in the compositional process, the writer will have to reason through all points and details of the report. Many writers accomplish this by a third phase of outlining—

the *sentence outline.* This form picks up the schematizing where the second phase left off. It places each topic within a complete sentence. Completing the thought of each topic enables the writer to test the context of the topic's environment. Such deeper thought not only reveals flaws in the data as heretofore seen by the writer but also permits deeper probings, examinations, analysis, and interpretation of major points and minor details. The result is clarification of aspects of the problem and derivation of insights not previously attained. A concurrent and important benefit is an improved, orderly outline in complete detail with properly designed relationships, emphasis, and subordination. Now examine the sentence outline for "A Preliminary Report on the Possible Origin of the Intrusive Bodies in the Big Thompson Canyon" (Figure 5.2).[1]

Ideas and information in a report should be presented in a steady progression so that the reader feels he is getting somewhere as he reads. The reader must have important data clearly pointed out to him. The topical outline does not provide any easy mechanics for this. The outline arranged to show relationships and subordination is an improvement. The sentence outline, because it has put the writer through the chore of clarifying his thoughts about the main facts and their substantiating details, promotes a more logical composition and a more readable and comprehensible report.

The sentence outline shown in Figure 5.2 reveals the conventional structuring of this form. It uses Roman numerals to designate the main divisions and capital letters to indicate major subdivisions under each division. Further subdivision makes use of Arabic numerals, and still further division makes use of lowercase letters. Each entry in the sentence outline is composed in a complete grammatical sentence. This is demanded not only for the Roman numeral headings but also for divisions and subdivisions within them. Since a topic is not divided unless there are at least two parts, logic demands that there be at least two subheads under any division. For any Roman numeral *I,* there should be a Roman numeral *II,* for every capital *A,* there should be a *B* in sequence. If only one point follows a main heading, make it part of the main heading:

I.
   A.
      1.
         a.
         b.
         c.
            1)
            2)
      2.
   B.
II.

---

[1]Check this outline with the student report based on it, Figure 6.10, Chapter 6.

```
            Sentence Outline for
      a Preliminary Report on the Possible
       Origin of the Intrusive Bodies in the
              Big Thompson Canyon
```

Thesis Sentence: The intrusive body in the Big Thompson Canyon, Colorado, is a recently exposed portion of a larger mass known as Silver Plume Granite which was intruded into the base of the Rocky Mountains in Pre-Cambrian times.

I. This investigation undertakes to trace the geologic origin of the intrusive bodies in Big Thompson Canyon, Colorado.

    A. The purpose of this investigation is to serve as a field analysis problem for beginning geology students in properly analyzing and identifying geologic features.

    B. The meaning of certain geological terms, though frequently used by students, is not always fully understood and should be defined.

        1. An intrusive body was once a molten lava, which cut across or was injected into overlying sedimentary or metamorphic rocks.

        2. An acidic rock, such as granite, is derived from a molten source that was high in silica content.

        3. A batholith is an igneous body more than forty square miles in area.

        4. A stock is an igneous body less than forty square miles in area.

        5. A dike is an igneous body that has cut across layers of sedimentary or metamorphic rock.

    C. Field work was conducted by the author and other students at the intrusive in Big Thompson Canyon and at an outcrop of Silver Plume Granite west of Horsetooth Reservoir.

        1. The intrusive in Big Thompson Canyon is located at the base of Palisade Mountain on State Highway 34.

        2. The location of the Silver Plume outcrop is midway between the west edge of Horsetooth Reservoir and the town of Masonville.

Figure 5.2 Example of a sentence outline.

D. Early preliminary observation and interpretation by geology students brought forth two varying opinions:

1. That the intrusive was a granite stock;

2. That the intrusive was a granite dike.

E. Extensive fieldwork and a library search have shown validity to both opinions.

1. Analyzed samples taken from the intrusive show that orthoclase feldspar, plagioclase feldspar, quartz, and biotite mica are present.

   a. Comparison of these constituents from a known outcrop of Silver Plume Granite shows that they are one and the same.

   b. Variations in color of the outcrops are due to magmatic differentiation.

2. The Silver Plume formation is composed of small batholiths and stocks.

   a. As the intrusive in question is relatively small in size, it can be assumed that it is an offshoot from a larger, underground body.

   b. Similar small intrusive bodies at other locations bear this out.

F. An analytical table of comparative mineral constituents and a map of the region validating this conclusion will accompany the report.

II. Field work and laboratory experiments combined with material gathered from a library search answered the question about the intrusive body.

A. Structurally, the intrusive and the outcrop of Silver Plume Granite are dissimilar, but of the same geologic period.

1. The intrusive is of a gray homogeneous granite with very little fracturing.

2. The Silver Plume Granite outcrop is flesh-colored with large, individual crystals.

3. Both of the bodies investigated were intruded into a Pre-Cambrian, metamorphic, country rock.

B. Hand specimens were taken from the site of the intrusive and the known Silver Plume outcrop.

1. A geology pick or prospector's hammer was used to break off good-sized rocks.

Figure 5.2 (continued)

2. The rocks were held in the hand and chipped to approximately 1" × 3" × 5".

3. The rocks were chipped in such a manner as to eliminate hammer bruises on the faces and also to expose only unweathered rock material.

C. The hand specimens, as observed under a microscope, were found to differ slightly in physical properties.

1. The specimen from the intrusive was found to be a granite.

a. The specimen from the intrusive contained orthoclase feldspar, 60 percent; plagioclase feldspar, 5 percent; quartz, 20 percent; and biotite mica, 15 percent.

b. The color of the intrusive specimen was gray.

c. The component grains of the specimen were one to five millimeters in diameter.

2. The specimen from the known outcrop of Silver Plume Granite was flesh-colored with grain sizes from 1 to 30 millimeters in diameter.

D. Comparison of field observations and laboratory data with information from T. S. Lovering's professional paper showed that the intrusive is a portion of Silver Plume Granite.

III. This preliminary research of the problem has led to a theory that may be fully validated following a more extensive investigation.

A. The intrusive in Big Thompson Canyon is a portion of Silver Plume Granite that was intruded into the roots of the Rocky Mountains during Pre-Cambrian times.

B. It is recommended that a more complete investigation be undertaken to determine definitively the relationship between the intrusive bodies in Big Thompson Canyon and that of the Silver Plume Granite.

(From a student report by Gerald L. Owens)

Figure 5.2 (continued)

The sentence outline enables you, the writer, to control the content and structure of your report to secure unity and coherence. Though more difficult to construct than the topical outline, the sentence outline is recommended because it forces you to think your points through more fully and to express them as whole units. Each sentence in the outline can become the topic sentence of a paragraph in the final writing.

The Decimal Outline

The decimal system of outlining uses decimals to show the rank of heads and subheads.

1. First main heading
   1.1 First subdivision of main heading
   1.2 Second subdivision of main heading
2. Second main heading
   2.1 First subdivision of main heading
   2.2 Second subdivision of main heading
      2.2.1 First subdivision of 2.2
      2.2.2 Second subdivision of 2.2
         2.2.2.1 First subdivision of 2.2.2
         2.2.2.2 Second subdivision of 2.2.2

The decimal system enables easier revisions and additions. It can be used with a sentence outline or with a topical outline.

The Format and Organization of the Outline

The outline may be single-spaced or double-spaced, or single-spaced within groups of headings and double-spaced between such groups. The writer should be consistent, however. A very short outline may be arbitrarily double-spaced to fill the page. All symbols, letters, and numbers should appear in a straight, vertical line throughout the whole. All capital letters should be indented the same distance, and all Arabic numerals the same distance, as should all lowercase letters. Three to five spaces for each level is conventional. Consistency in the amount of spacing will add neatness of layout and appearance. Excessive indention will look as unattractive as too little or none. (See Figure 5.2.)

Storyboarding as an Outline Technique

Based on film script preparation, the **storyboard** technique can be used to develop outlines for some reports. Films are a visual medium so the storyboard's narrative is designed via a series of drawings representing actions that advance sequences of a story being told. The drawings are captioned with appropriate text. See Figure 5.3.

A. Modulation

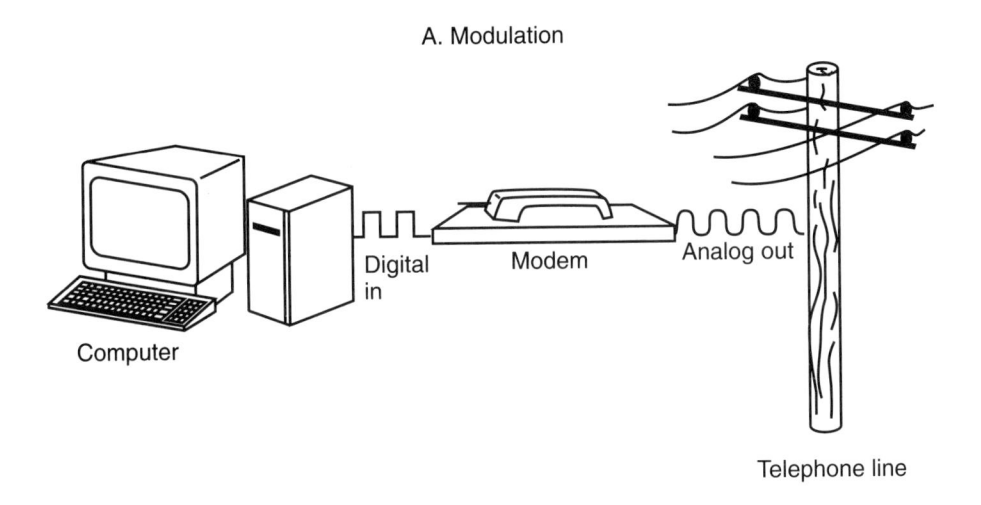

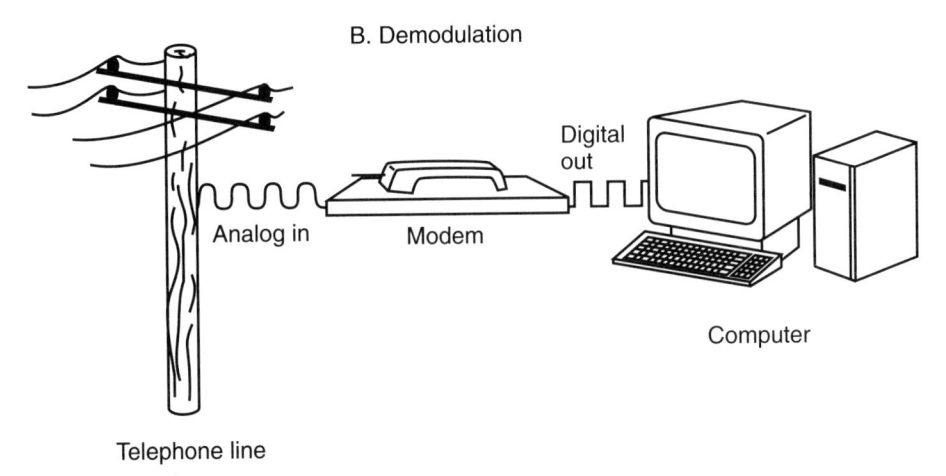

Computer — Digital in — Modem — Analog out — Telephone line

B. Demodulation

Telephone line — Analog in — Modem — Digital out — Computer

Figure 5.3 A storyboard sequence of panels for a report on the development of a data communication system. This sequence outlines how data are transmitted from one node of a network to another node by converting digital data to analog data and vice versa. Modulation is the conversion of a digital signal (1s and 0s) to an analog signal (voice). Demodulation is the conversion of a voice signal to a digital signal.

Similarly, the storyboard approach can be used to arrange the major facts and findings in a technical report of an investigation in which graphics play a prominent role in presenting the sequences of the data of the report. The block diagram, Figure 5.1 on page 116, on organizing the data of your investigation, lends itself to storyboarding. Using 3-inch-by-5-inch cards, you physically arrange the evidence, findings, facts, and ideas that lead to the thesis sentence, and, where appropriate, you use drawings to illustrate your findings.

Computer Outliners

Some computer software programs have a feature called an outliner, which will format spacing and place Roman and Arabic numerals in outline format. If you are developing your outline on a computer screen, the outliner feature gives you the convenience of entering your ideas as they occur and then enables you to organize and reorganize them as headings and subheadings until your outline reads the way you want it to. Furthermore, the outliner software allows you to break up headings so you can see only major topics or allows you to check a list of subtopics under a major head without the distraction of other heads or items diverting your view. At the proper point, the software enables you to convert the topical phrases into complete sentences with convenience.

Should your formal report be lengthy and require an index, you can mark key terms in your sentence outline for later retrieval in alphabetical order for index construction.

Organizing the Outline Material—Introduction, Body, and Terminal Section

The final draft of the outline can become the basis of the table of contents of your report. During the actual writing, the outline is used as the plan for composition. Structurally, the outline, like the report, has a beginning, middle, and end, or—to use the classical structural terms—an introduction, body, and conclusion. The introduction and conclusion are fixed points at the beginning and end of the outline. The experienced writer spends much time on the outline because it saves problems in the later writing of the paper.

Frequently, the body—which will begin with Roman numeral *II*, or if the decimal system is used, with number 2—may have two or three major divisions within it. The terminal section may be encompassed in one Roman numeral, although it is sometimes advantageous to separate the recommendations from the conclusions by creating another major heading preceded by a Roman numeral. This is appropriate if the recommendations are significant. Too many major heads could be symptomatic of inadequate analysis of the data.

Checking Outline Requirements

After you complete the outline, check it for sequence of major divisions. Are they in the right order? Look over your note material to be sure nothing important has been omitted. Check for duplication of headings. All main headings should add up to the thesis sentence. Are all main headings really main headings or should some of them be subheads? Check your subheads for proper subordination and sequence. Do all subheads within a major heading add up to the major heading? Should some of the subheads be promoted to main heads? Finally, check the wording of all divisions for clarity, correctness, and parallel construction. Usually, there are no more than four or five major heads. If a paper is to be long, the increased length should result from the use of more subheads rather than from an increase in the number of major headings. The outline should have no fewer than three and no more than five or six major heads, which are, in the conventional outline numbering system, preceded by Roman numerals.

The sentence outline forces you, the writer, to test the adequacy of your data. Not all data included are of equal significance. Evaluating facts correctly means giving them only as much weight as they have value in accomplishing the objectives of the report.

In summary, this type of planning gives the report coherence, continuity, and unity. By focusing on a central idea—the thesis sentence—you succeed in presenting ideas and information in a steady progression. As a result, the reader feels he is getting somewhere as he reads; everything in the report is pertinent to the problem. The outline has enabled you to achieve an overview of the report and to see relationships that are decisive in contributing to the objective. These factors can only help the reader.

Chapter in Brief

In this chapter, we discussed how to organize research data and analyses into a report. We stated that composing a thesis sentence, derived from the answer to the chosen problem, is critical to this organization process. The various patterns to organize the report material were presented, and we explained how to develop an outline, which serves as the skeleton of the report.

Chapter Focal Points

- Thesis sentence
- Guidelines for organizing the report
- Logical methods
    Chronological pattern
    Geographical or spatial
    Functional
    Order of importance
    Elimination of possible solutions
    General to particular
    Particular to general
    Simple to complex
    Pro and con
    Cause to effect
- Psychological pattern
- Outlining
    Topical
    Sentence
    Storyboard

Questions for Discussion

1. Explain how the thesis sentence is developed and discuss its role in focussing the report's material.
2. Interview two or more prolific researcher/writers on and off your campus. Ask them how they organize their research data for report or professional paper writing. Find out what system of outlining each researcher uses. Find out their reactions to the sentence outline. If a researcher does not use it, would he recommend it to a beginning research writer? Do these researchers use the device of a thesis sentence or core idea? Do they use computers in their research? Does the researcher use a computer for writing the report or professional paper? If so, does the researcher record his data and results on computer disk? Does the researcher convert any of the computer data and information into the report or paper? How? Do any of the researchers use hypertext techniques for their writing?
3. Analyze four of the reports you located for question 4 in Chapter 4 (page 111) as to the type of organizational patterns used by the report writers.
4. Your text claims that the process of outlining promotes coherence, continuity, and unity in your report. Defend or dispute this claim.

Assignments

1. Develop the thesis sentence for the report topic you selected in Chapter 4.
2. After you have derived the thesis sentence, construct a block diagram by using the major facts or ideas and their substantiating evidence within the blocks of the diagram. Use the structure recommended in this chapter.
3. Develop a sentence outline for your report by going through the three phases discussed in this chapter. The work you do in problem number 2, above, should simplify your task.
4. Evaluate, criticize, and rewrite the student sentence outline on sagebrush control (Figure 5.4, page 133). Lack of knowledge of the subject should not prevent you from correcting the faults in the outline.

Sagebrush Control

Thesis sentence: The most effective method of sagebrush eradication in western Colorado is either grubbing, railing, harrowing, blading, burning, plowing, or spraying.

I. The geographical area studied, species of sagebrush studied, and purpose of this research need to be explained.
   A. The area included in western Colorado is largely covered by big sagebrush (Artemisia tridentata).
      1. The area of western Colorado includes thousands of acres.
      2. This area of Colorado is typical sagebrush land in physical characteristics.
      3. Big sagebrush (Artemisia tridentata) is the dominant species in western Colorado.
   B. The purpose and object of this research are economic in nature.
      1. Valuable land is presently occupied by big sagebrush.
      2. With only moderate costs sagebrush can be eradicated by various methods.
   C. Past and present research in the field is inconclusive for western Colorado.
      1. Past research has been general.
      2. Present research is still inconclusive as applied to small areas.
   D. A restricted approach is taken toward the problem.
      1. The most effective method of eradication only is sought.
      2. Library research, interviews, and field work are the sources of information.
         a. Extensive library research is the basic source.
         b. Interviews with authorities in the field of range proves valuable.
         c. Verification of data through field investigation is necessary.

II. There are several different methods of sagebrush eradication.
   A. Grubbing is one method of sagebrush eradication.
      1. Advantages of grubbing are few.
      2. Disadvantages of grubbing are many.
   B. Railing is a method of sagebrush eradication.
      1. Advantages of railing are many.
      2. Disadvantages of railing are few.
   C. Harrowing is a method of sagebrush eradication.
      1. Advantages of harrowing are moderate in number.
      2. Disadvantages of harrowing are few.
   D. Blading is a method of sagebrush eradication.
      1. Advantages of blading are few.
      2. Disadvantages of blading are many.
   E. Burning is a method of sagebrush eradication.
      1. Advantages of burning are many.
      2. Disadvantages of burning are few.
   F. Plowing is a method of sagebrush eradication.
      1. Advantages of plowing are many.
      2. Disadvantages of plowing are few.
   G. Spraying is another method of sagebrush eradication.
      1. There are many advantages of spraying.
      2. The disadvantages of spraying are few.

III. The most effective method of sagebrush eradication in western Colorado is either grubbing, railing, harrowing, blading, burning, plowing, or spraying.

Figure 5.4

6
Report Writing—Writing the Elements of the Report

Chapter Objective

Provide the means for structuring the elements of the formal report.

Chapter Focus

- Constructing the organizational elements of the report
  Front matter
  Text of the report
  Back matter
- The final (completion) report

How to Develop the Structural Elements of the Report

So far, we have been examining the main discussion or body of the formal report. The formal report has other elements, usually arranged in a prescribed form. If you will recall, Chapter 4 stated that there is no universal "right" form governing the arrangement of a report's elements. Elements should be arranged in an order that promotes greatest convenience of use to, and understanding by, the reader. Reader requirements vary as reporting situations and problems vary. Many research and industrial organizations and government agencies have developed style manuals, guides, and specifications to ensure standards and promote effectiveness of reports. These guides prescribe forms and arrangements of report elements in keeping with the organization's needs.

Specific details of form and content may vary considerably, but generally elements of a report find arrangement in either the logical pattern of organization or the psychological pattern (the double report) as described in Chapter 5. The present chapter follows the logical method of organizing the report's elements because that approach is universal. Once you, the student, have mastered the ability to structure and arrange the data of the investigation and the elements of the report within the framework of the logical pattern, you will be able to meet the requirements of any type of report pattern and form.

The elements of the formal report are these:

A. Front matter
   1. Letter of transmittal
   2. Cover
   3. Title page
   4. Abstract
   5. Executive summary
   6. Table of contents
   7. List of tables and illustrations
B. Report text
   1. Introduction
   2. Body
   3. Terminal section
C. Back matter
   1. Bibliography
   2. Appendix
   3. Glossary
   4. Index
   5. Distribution list

Let us examine each of these elements.

The Front Matter

The **front matter** in a formal report includes the introductory elements that introduce, help explain, summarize, and assist the reader in locating the report's various sections.

The Letter of Transmittal

The major purpose of the letter or memo of transmittal is to present formally the report to the reader as a matter of record. The letter of transmittal indicates exactly how and when the report was requested, the subject matter of the report, and how the report is being transmitted—as an enclosure of the letter or under separate cover. Its length varies. Frequently, all that is necessary to say is, "Here is the report on. . . (the problem is indicated), which you asked me to investigate in your letter of December 21, 19___." If the report is sent to someone within one's own organization, the form used is a memo from the author to the recipient.

Letters of transmittal have been used occasionally to refer to specific parts of the report and to call attention to important points, conclusions, and recommendations. Some letters of transmittal may even go into certain elements that appear in the introduction, such as statements of purpose, scope, and limitations. The letter of transmittal may mention specific problems encountered in making the investigation. For example, a delay due to a strike or shortage of certain materials may have influenced the performance time but not the data and their results; this situation may be mentioned in the letter of transmittal. Some letters include acknowledgments.

The placement of a letter of transmittal varies in practice. It is sometimes bound within a report, or it may be placed within an envelope and attached to the outside of the package. In the latter case, the address on the letter envelope may serve as the address for the report packet itself. When the report is sent to the intended reader within one's own organization by hand, or through organization communication means, the memo of transmittal is frequently clipped to the outside cover of the report or placed within the cover for protection. Examine the sample letter in Figure 6.1.

The Cover and Title Page

The formal report usually is bound within a cover. Identifying information is listed on the cover page; this consists of the title of the report and its author. Occasionally, the recipient's name is also included in the cover information.

The purpose of the title page is to state briefly but completely the subject of the report, the name of the organization or person for whom the report is written, the name of the person and/or the firm submitting the report (frequently the address of the report's maker is included), and the date of the report. The title page may also have a number assigned to the report by the authorizing organization as well as the number of the project for which the report was prepared. The title page gives the reader first contact with the report. The various elements,

805 Remington Street
Fort Collins, Colorado 80521
December 5, 19__

Professor Daniel Weisman
Dept. of Physics
Colorado Polytechnic University
Fort Collins, Colorado 80521

Dear Professor Weisman:

In compliance with your request for a full report on the Power Calibration Curve for the CSU AGN-201 Reactor, this report is submitted.

This report defines the problem, develops the method, the theory for determining the power calibration curve, and discusses the results and conclusions of the experimental data.

The power calibration curve was found to be linear with the maximum power level of 101.5 milliwatts at 5×10^9 amps on channel 3 of the reactor control console. This compares favorably with 100 milliwatts determined by the Aerojet General Nucleonics Corporation.

It is recommended that in future experiments the data and data calculations be rounded off to less significant figures than those used in this report. This can be done with sufficient accuracy still maintained.

From the indications of the data in this report, an interesting experiment for determining the effect of foil thickness upon activity may possibly be incorporated in the Ph-124 Experiments in Nuclear Physics course.

Yours truly,

Nathan M. Duran

Encl.

Figure 6.1 Sample letter of transmittal.

therefore, should be arranged neatly and attractively on the page. (See Figure 6.7, page 155).

The Abstract

The abstract has a major role to play in the formal report. It has two important uses:

As Index and Announcement

Reports are frequently placed in the files of the organization's information system or in the information database of other information services, and they are published in abstract journals covering the latest literature of a field. To facilitate retrieval of the information of a report in a file, the document is first indexed; that is, the key topics discussed are identified. Many organizations require authors to provide **keywords,** which index or list the most important topics in their reports or papers. The keywords, usually limited from five to twelve in number, are arranged alphabetically and placed below the abstract.

As a Synopsis

The abstract is a brief factual version of the complete report. It provides the gist of essentials of the investigation. Included are an explanation of the nature of the problem; an account of the course pursued in studying it; the findings or results; and conclusions and recommendations of the investigation, which are summarized in the order of their importance.

Ideally, the abstract is no more than one typewritten page of about 100 to 250 words. It is placed first on a separate page following the title page to save a busy reader from wading through masses of technical data in search of answers to her questions (Figure 6.2).

The Executive Summary

The executive summary, a device based on the psychological pattern of organization (see Chapter 5), has become popular. The use of this element recognizes that busy administrators and decision makers will not wade through entire reports. Abstracts provide a bare inkling of the contents—not enough to base a decision. A synthesis or summary of the important issues is required. Furthermore, the report may be too massive or technically formidable. The *executive summary* recomposes the report into an abbreviated, reordered form that highlights the key factors of the investigation. Prerequisite information is provided. Included are purpose of the study; the nature and significance of the problem; the scope; an account of the investigation, its methods and materials; results obtained; conclusions about the results; and recommendations for a future course of action.

The executive summary adds to the usefulness of the report. It keys the reader to important issues; it enables the reader to comprehend and focus on the factors of the problem and the means for its solution. The highlights of the report as presented in the executive summary are more easily digested and remembered by the decision maker than is the report itself.

Abstract

An Examination of Some Methods Used by Hunters
for Care of Deer Meat

This paper examines some of the methods used by hunters for caring for deer meat. The objective was to determine just how a deer carcass was field-cared for. The data for the study were obtained by direct observations of deer carcasses and supplemented with questions asked hunters. An examination of 371 carcasses, over a two-week period, showed the methods of care given to deer carcasses to vary greatly. Search of the literature showed no similar study. The extremes of care varied from animals processed to those that were not field dressed. An average condition of care was determined. Many of the hunters live very close to the area sampled and do not take proper care of their deer, as they assume they will arrive home soon enough to care for it. Time, always a limiting factor, hurries a hunter in all of his procedures, including proper care of deer meat. Suggestions for proper care and a step-by-step procedure for field dressing a deer are presented. Ten recommendations to aid hunters in caring for deer are suggested. Nine bar graphs, located in the Appendix, diagram the data. A map of the area sampled and a form used for recording the data are also included within the Appendix. The most important recommendation for hunters is: Game should be treated like any good meat.

Key words: Deer, deer meat; field-care, carcasses; game; hunter.

(From a student report by Jack D. Cameron)

Figure 6.2 Sample abstract.

An example of an abstract and an executive summary of the same report are shown in Figures 6.3A and 6.3B.

The Table of Contents

The table of contents lists the several divisions and subdivisions of the report with their related page references in the order in which they appear. It is set on the page to make clear the relation of the main and subordinate units of the report. These units should be phrased exactly as are their corresponding headings in the text. A list of tables and/or illustrations follows the table of contents as in Figure 6.4.

Writing the Report Text—The Introduction and Its Elements

The elements discussed so far have been preliminary. The report itself begins with the introduction. The purpose of the introduction is to answer the immediate questions that come to the reader's mind: Why should I read the report? Who asked for the report? When? Where did the information come from? Why was this report written? What is the significance of this report for me?

The introduction gives the reader a first contact with the subject of the report. The introduction states the object of the report. It may be a restatement of the terms of the original commission either verbatim or as understood by the writer. It should give the background information necessary to understand the discussion that follows. The nature and amount of this information depend, of course, on the intended reader and the reader's knowledge of the subject. To follow the report, the reader must know this information:

1. *The purpose of the investigation*
2. *The nature of the problem*
   Here will be found the who, how, what, why, and when of the investigation. Some writers distinguish between *purpose* and *objective,* although the terms are often used interchangeably. If there are both immediate and ultimate goals, these must be identified. Either or both of these factors should be explained to the reader. The purpose and the objective concern the *why* of the study, and the problem concerns the *what* of the study. The nature of the problem and the purpose are often grouped together, but they are not the same, and this confusion should be carefully avoided.
3. *Scope, or the degree of comprehensiveness*
   Scope determines boundaries—what considerations are included and what are excluded. The delimitations of the investigation are carefully stated.
4. *Significance of the problem*
   The reader of a report consciously or subconsciously asks herself, "Why should I read this report?" The writer must answer this question in the introduction. She must tell the reader why the report is of significance to her. Needless to say, if the reader does not feel that the report holds any significance for her, she will not read it.

Abstract

The purpose of this report is to develop a guide for planning and selecting the site for the National Academy for Fire Prevention and Control. The investigation determined that the legislation, the Academy's mission, the nature of the training to be offered by the Academy, and the instructional technique to be used indicate the need for a national campus. The Academy may obtain its physical facilities by building a new structure or by adapting an existing federal, state, or privately owned facility to the Academy's purpose. Cost constraints favor the latter approach. Site selection criteria are developed and four categories of criteria factors are arranged in a matrix for possible use by the Site Selection Board.

Key words: National Academy for Fire Prevention and Control; Site Selection Board; site selection criteria; fire education and training.

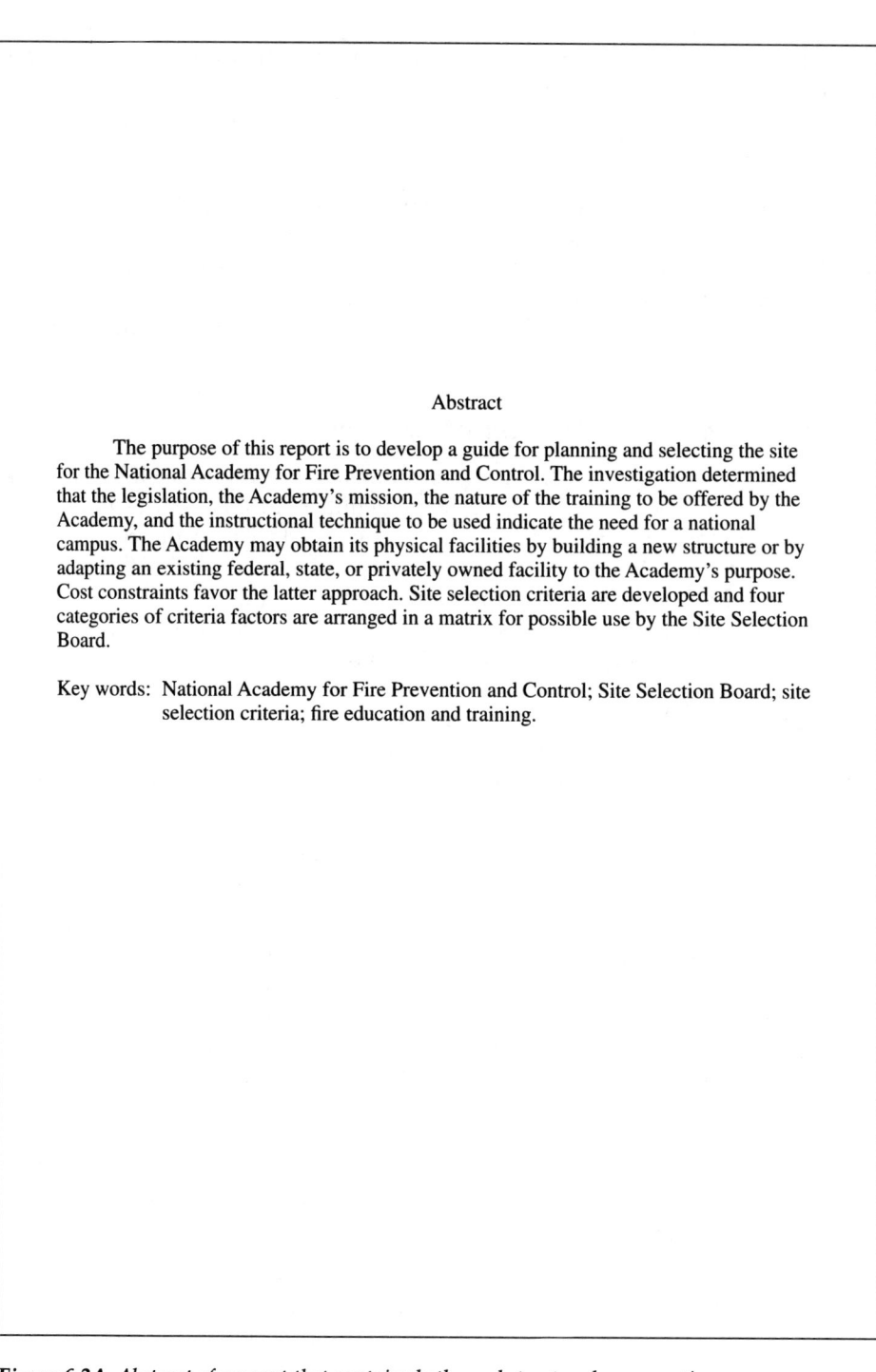

Figure 6.3A Abstract of a report that contains both an abstract and an executive summary.

Executive Summary

The National Fire Prevention and Control Administration (NFPCA) awarded a grant to the Academy for Educational Development, Inc. (AED), to develop site criteria and to outline procedures to be followed in selecting the site for the National Fire Academy. The result of AED's effort was to be a report that would serve as a planning document and as a guide to the Site Selection Board.

In preparing this report, AED was guided by the legislation, America Burning, position papers on the National Fire Academy, and other written documents. To determine additional views about the Academy, AED interviewed selected fire service personnel, educational leaders and authorities in the field of fire prevention and control, and others.

In the course of its investigation, AED found that the issues of program and site selection were strongly interrelated; and that the Academy's new site should be identified and designed to meet the Academy's program and operational needs. With this in mind, AED examined the Academy's program and concluded that it should consist of five major components:

1. Education and training that would focus on management with short-term courses lasting from several weeks to two or three months, and reaching as many as 400 persons at any one time and 12,000 over the course of a year at the national campus.

2. Curriculum development for education and training at the national campus and throughout the nation.

3. Information collection and dissemination, which includes the establishment of an educational research and reference center, including a first-rate library.

4. Technical and financial assistance to fire service personnel attending Academy courses and courses offered at other institutions, and to those attending fire education and training institutions and organizations, including colleges and universities.

5. Relationships with higher educational institutions, which would be concerned primarily with the Academy's accreditation of individual programs and with arranging for individual institutions to award credit for the Academy's programs.

Figure 6.3B *An executive summary of a report that contains both an abstract and an executive summary.*

AED further concluded that the legislation, the Academy's mission, the nature of the education to be offered by the Academy, and the instructional techniques to be used (such as simulation) indicated the need for a national campus facility. The Academy may obtain its physical facilities by adapting an existing federal, state, or privately owned facility to Academy purposes, or by building a new structure on land acquired for that purpose. Cost constraints seem to favor the former approach.

After developing space requirements in considerable detail, AED estimated that nearly 240,000 gross square feet of space would be required and that the size of the site should be approximately 100 acres distributed among built-up space, open space (landscaped and natural), a constructed outdoor recreation area, a reserved area for outdoor demonstration, and space for on-grade parking. The suggested facility plan provides for office space, an auditorium, classrooms equipped with audiovisual materials, seminar rooms, a library, an audiovisual distribution center, lecture and demonstration rooms, dining and residential facilities, indoor simulation facilities, health conditioning facilities, a close-circuit system for instruction, and adequate storage space.

In estimating the Academy's space needs, AED considered a planning option dependent on site location, the need for growth in the Academy's services, and the likelihood that the NFPCA and certain major programs—such as the National Fire Data Center, the Fire Safety Research Office, and the Office of Public Education—could be located in the Academy's national facility. The day-to-day interaction between the Academy, other NFPCA activities, and related activities of other federal agencies will require setting aside suitable space.

In reviewing and evaluating sites and making recommendations to the Secretary of Commerce, the Site Selection Board should, in AED's view, be guided by factors that fall in the following four groups:

A. Critical factors that provide indirect support to the Academy in the accomplishment of its mission. Group A factors indicate the Academy's relationship to professional and governmental activities, and proximity to a diversity of fire research and service activities (sixteen such factors are identified).

B. Physical and geographic factors. Included are access to public transportation arrangements, community support, and a moderate climate (six such factors are identified).

C. Factors related to the actual site of the Academy. Group C includes various land and environmental considerations (seven such factors are identified).

D. Mission accomplishments and support activities. These factors describe what the Academy is expected to accomplish over the years (twelve such factors are identified).

AED has developed a site and facility evaluation matrix that might be used by the Site Selection Board as a tool to determine how well each proposed site meets designated site factors. AED has also included, for the consideration of the Site Selection Board, a detailed checklist of commonly used factors to be used in reviewing specific sites.

The report concludes with a suggested list of eight steps to be followed by the Site Selection Board in making site recommendations.

Figure 6.3B (continued).

Table of Contents

Title Page	i
Abstract	ii
Table of Contents	iii
List of Illustrations	iv
Introduction	1
Purpose	1
Background	1
Nature and Significance of Problem	2
Object and Scope	3
Definition of Terms and Abbreviations	4
Personnel Involved	5
Planned Presentation	5
Investigation	6
Analysis of Transistor Operation	6
Analysis of Radio Frequency Signals	9
Experimental Investigation of Local Radio Frequency Signals	11
Analysis of the Voltage Quadrupler	15
Investigation of the Complete Bias Circuit	16
A Possible Single Bias Transistor Circuit	19
Results of Investigation	22
Conclusions and Recommendations	23
Conclusions	23
Recommendations	24
Appendix A	25
Appendix B	26
Bibliography	27

List of Illustrations

Figure 1—A Generalized Transistor Circuit	6
Figure 2—Characteristic Curves—2N358 Transistor	7
Figure 3—A Sinusoidally Modulated Radio Frequency Signal	9
Figure 4—The Spectrum of a Sinusoidally Modulated Radio Frequency Signal	10
Figure 5—A Schematic Diagram Showing a Series Resonant Circuit Coupled to an Antenna	12
Figure 6—The Carrier Signal of KCOL Measured Across the High Q Coil of the Series Resonant Tuned Circuit	13
Figure 7—A Voltage Quadrupler and Rectifier Circuit	15
Figure 8—The Complete Bias Circuit	16
Figure 9—Characteristics of 2N358 Transistor with Constant Bias Voltage	19
Figure 10—A Theoretical Schematic Diagram of the 2N358 with the Proposed Bias	20
Figure 11—A Possible Circuit Using the Proposed Bias	20
Figure 12—Transform Diagram at Resonance	25
Figure 13—Basic Rectifier Circuit with Smoothing Capacitor	26

Figure 6.4 Sample table of contents.

5. *Historical background* (review of the literature)
   The previous state of knowledge and the history of prior investigations on this subject are included. A review of the literature may be desirable to do the following:
   a. Give the reader confidence in the investigator's awareness of the state of the art of knowledge of the problem.
   b. Enable the reader to get the necessary background quickly.
   Only enough of the past should be included to make the present understandable. Some reports continue previous investigations; the report must then provide the historical background needed to orient the reader properly. In beginning a report, the reader may have the following questions in mind: What has given rise to the present situation? What occasions have given rise to similar situations? What significance has been attached to them in the past? Are there any conflicting views on this problem? A review of present conditions may also be necessary.
6. *Definitions are given of new or unusual terms or those having a specialized or stipulative meaning*
   Terms used only once are better defined in their context; those appearing constantly throughout the report should be defined in the introduction. If many such terms are to be used, you may include a glossary in the appendix.
7. *A listing of the personnel engaged in the investigation, together with a brief sketch of their background and duties*
   This will often give the reader more confidence in the data and conclusions obtained. The reader wants to know about the people who obtained the data and have assurance that they possess the requisite qualifications for working on the problem.
8. *The plan of treatment or organization of the report*
   This element gives the reader a "quick map" of the major points, the order in which they will be discussed, and perhaps the reason for the arrangement. It serves also as a bridge between the introductory section and the body and discussion sections.
9. *Methods and materials for the investigation*
   This item is included in the introduction only in reporting those investigations where procedures and materials are simple and inconsequential to the data obtained, as is illustrated in the sample introduction from a student report on how hunters field-care their deer meat (Figure 6.5). In this instance, the method of investigation is a simple interview and questionnaire, supplemented by observation. The materials were forms for recording the data, a clipboard, and a pencil. However, in those investigations in which the data obtained are directly related to laboratory or experimental methods, or are dependent on elaborate procedures and materials, this element is placed in the body section.

These eight or nine points are general to most formal reports although not absolutely necessary to all reports. There is no special significance in the order of their listing. Introductions may begin with the significance of the problem or with

I. Introduction

Objective and Scope

This paper examines some of the methods used by hunters for the care of deer meat. The objective was to determine just how a deer was field-cared for. The data for the study were obtained by direct observations of deer carcasses and supplemented with questions asked hunters at Ted's Place in the fall of 1986. Ted's Place is located at the junction of Highways 14 and 287 in North Central Colorado. A Colorado Game and Fish Department's permanent big game check station is located here. Since all hunters, successful or not, are required to stop, it is an ideal location for a study of this kind.

An examination of 371 carcasses, over a two-week period, showed the methods of care given deer to vary greatly. The procedure used in determination of the methods proved to be satisfactory; however, many limitations were encountered. The inability of one man to check all of the hunters and their deer during a rush period at the check station was the greatest difficulty encountered.

Also the great majority of the hunters shot their deer in the northeastern mountains of Colorado, game management units eight, nine, and nineteen. Therefore, this limited sample may be biased as only one location within the state was observed. However, the data will hold true for this specific northeastern area.

Time, as in the case of much research, was limited. However, 16 percent of the total deer checked through Ted's Place were observed. Since only 10 percent of a population is usually required for a statistical analysis, the data obtained were considered sufficient.

Review of the Literature

A thorough search of the literature uncovered many techniques and methods concerning the care of deer meat. However, this search showed no similar work on an actual examination of carcasses to determine the care given deer meat by hunters and the condition in which it was brought through a check station.

Much of the literature emphasized the great loss that occurs annually by improper care of game meat, but no specific study was found concerning examination of the field-dressed carcass.

At this date the author is unaware of any similar work in this specific field.

Methods and Materials

A direct observation of the deer carcasses and oral questions asked the hunter, make up the data presented. By the use of a prearranged form, as shown in the Appendix, the information desired could be readily recorded. All information, observations, and questions were recorded on the form. Columns on the form were arranged to facilitate recording maximum information in a minimum of time.

As a hunter's car approached the station the form was readied. While the Colorado Game and Fish employee was checking the license, most of the direct observations could be made and recorded. When the employee was finished, the hunter was asked the following questions:

1

Figure 6.5 Sample introduction.

1. Did you save the heart, liver or kidneys?
2. What method was used to bring your deer from the field to your vehicle?

Only when the carcass was obscured by camping equipment and tarps were additional questions needed. These would include questions concerning the following:

1. Sex
2. Appendage removal
3. Splitting of the pelvic and/or brisket bone
4. Tarsal and metatarsal gland removal

The majority of the carcasses were located so the flesh could be felt to determine coolness. Although this is a relative factor, 18 percent of the carcasses were not cooled as the flesh was still warm to the touch. Many of these instances were very recent kills.

Cooperation from the hunters was very satisfactory. Less than ten hunters were curious about the questioning and asked for an explanation. The other 360 hunters evidently took the questions for granted as they assumed the author to be a Colorado Game and Fish Department employee.

The only materials used in this study were forms for recording the data, a clipboard, and a pencil.

(From a student report by Jack D. Cameron. This paper was prepared as a class assignment in technical writing. All data presented are original.)

Figure 6.5 *(continued)*

the historical background. In certain situations where the problem may be new and complex, definitions of terms may begin the introductory section. These eight or nine elements (or those that are used) are frequently organized as subheadings within the introduction. The purpose of the introduction is to orient the reader. Placed within it is the information the reader needs to follow the main body of the report easily and confidently. See Figure 6.5.

Writing the Report Text—The Body of the Report and Its Elements

Although the term *body* as a heading is seldom used, it is the major section of the report that presents the data of the investigation. In its stead, words descriptive of the material contained in the section are used. The body section or sections include the theory behind the approach taken, the apparatus or methods used in compiling the data with necessary discussion, the results obtained from the procedure, and an analysis of the results. In a scientific or technical investigation, the theory determining the procedure is explained and the method of procedure is recounted in chronological order; apparatus, materials, setups, and so forth are described. The reader will place greater confidence in a report's conclusions if she knows how they were determined. Duties of the personnel are presented, and evidence is organized so the reader can follow the thinking in orderly fashion. These principles are illustrated in the "Preliminary Report on the Possible Origin of the Intrusive Bodies in Big Thompson Canyon," Figure 6.7 at the end of this chapter.

The body is usually the largest section of the report. The various organizational approaches for the body, which were determined when the outline was developed (see Chapter 5), were discussed earlier. The pattern of organization chosen depends, of course, on the nature of the problem. The reader is guided through the body of the report, which may be structured into more than one section, by the major and secondary headings as set down in the outline. These headings will indicate the relationship of the main and subordinate units of the organizational plan. They should be in agreement with the table of contents. Paragraphs, which represent units of the organizational plan and serve to bridge, introduce, and conclude topics, help to provide a coherent text leading the reader through the discussion of the investigation.

Examine the body sections of the report, "Possible Origin of the Intrusive Bodies in Big Thompson Canyon" in Figure 6.7. The writer reports on a field investigation. The chronological pattern of organization is the appropriate one for this situation. The report writer begins with a field description of the geologic formation being investigated. He then moves to examine and describe a nearby known outcrop. Specimens are selected from both the known and unknown formations. These are compared and analyzed. Analysis reveals some similarities. The structure of the body of this report follows the chronological sequence of the events of the investigation. The terminal section follows with the report writer's preliminary conclusions on the origin of the unknown outcrop and with the recommendation that further studies be made.

Writing the Report Text—The Terminal Section

The terminal section may be either a summary of major points of the body, if the report is purely informational, or conclusions based on analysis of the data, following logically from the evidence given in the body. The conclusions should, whenever appropriate, be listed numerically in the order of their presumed importance to the reader. Recommendations follow next. Conclusions and recommendations may be placed in one section or in separate sections. **Conclusions** deal with evaluations as to the past and present of a situation, whereas **recommendations** offer suggestions as to future courses of action. Recommendations are often the most important part of the report, and their adoption or rejection depends on how they are presented. Like the conclusions, they should be positive statements. They should suggest specific things to be done or a course of action to be followed and should, if appropriate, include an estimate of the cost involved. Some types of reports do not require recommendations, but usually the section on conclusions and recommendations is the most important part of the report. It is what the client is paying for. Turn to Figure 6.6 for an example of a conclusion and recommendations.

The Back Matter

The back matter is a descriptive term for the several supporting and ancillary data that supplement the report's information:

The **bibliography** is a list of references identifying literature that has contributed to your report. Its placement follows the report proper. It includes references to both published and unpublished material such as notebooks, reports, correspondence, and drawings. The items listed need not have been referred to in the text of the report. The conventional listing of the bibliography is alphabetical. The items should be numbered sequentially (see Chapter 7, pages 191–192 for examples).

The **glossary** is an alphabetical list of terms with their definitions, which are highly technical or which are used in a specialized way. A glossary is unnecessary if your report does not use highly technical terms or if your readers are familiar with the terms you use.

The **appendix's** chief purpose is to gather, in one place, all data that cannot be worked into the body without interrupting the flow of the report. If the body is self-contained, the detailed data in the appendix provide points of reference when questions arise. An appendix may not be necessary in a very short report. However, the appendix is indispensable to the type of report that uses considerable statistical information. Sometimes, all 8½-by-11-inch, or larger, charts, tables, diagrams, photographs, and other illustrations are placed in the appendix of a typed or photocopied report. The following items are usually saved for the appendix:

1. Charts
2. Tables
3. Computations and data sheets

Conclusions and Recommendations

Through the design and construction of the prototype model, it has been shown that an automatic parking lot attendant system is feasible. The prototype has been tested and operates as described in this report. The same circuits that operate the readout can be used to supply control information to the coin-operated gate. The finished model is a compact unit weighing approximately 30 pounds and measuring 18 x 11½ inches around the base. It is 10 inches high. For the proposed system to become operational, several difficulties present in the prototype must be eliminated. The prototype has no provision for altering the fee rate structure which is built into it. This could be accomplished by redesign of the printed circuit boards using removable jumper leads, whereby various combinations of digital readouts could be arranged. There are instances of price inequities in the present model such as in the example on page 11 of this report. In the prototype, a carry-over between rate change periods sometimes results in such a discontinuity of the accumulated fee. In the example given, the accumulated fee at 6:00 a.m. was 0.75. At the changeover to the day rates, this was picked up at 0.80 due to the fact that no 0.75 combination is available on the day rate photocell disk. Ideally, the card would have been picked up at 0.75 and continued from that point. These small inequities may or may not be considered serious. If the inequities are considered undesirable, it may be necessary to attack the method of decoding the card from a different viewpoint.

The handmade rotary stepping mechanism which moves the photocell disk is not completely positive in its action. There are commercial rotary stepping solenoids available on the market which should eliminate this problem, and it is recommended that such commercial components be used in the production system.

The author is of the opinion that the elimination of these difficulties may be accomplished in the production engineering phase and the system will be acceptable.

(From a student report by James B. Donnelly)

Figure 6.6 Sample conclusion and recommendations.

4. Diagrams and drawings
5. Exhibits, graphs, maps, photographs, letters, and questionnaires
6. Records of interviews and other similar matters serving as data that are not found in the literature or are not revealed through the methods and procedures of the investigation

The Index

An **index** is necessary only in voluminous reports where the alphabetical listing with page references of all topics, names, objects, and so forth is useful for ready reference. Normally, the table of contents performs this function adequately.

The Distribution List

The **distribution list** not only provides the names of persons and offices to receive the report but also serves as a control device to ascertain that the confidence of the sponsor or client is not violated. Distribution lists may be tacked to the inside of the front cover or placed at the very end of the report.

Figure 6.7 (pages 155–167) is an example of a student report on an investigation undertaken as a classroom assignment, containing report elements discussed in this chapter. The three outlines developed for organizing and writing this report appeared in Chapter 5, pages 122–127.

Final (Completion) Reports

When a project is completed, a final report documents the work concluded. It focusses on the results accomplished, identifies problem areas or matters still to be resolved, presents conclusions resulting from the work, and suggests recommendations on any follow-up work that might be necessary or desirable. Therefore, the purpose of the final report is not only to document the experience of the project for the record but also to serve as a reference point for any future work.

Final reports follow the substance and format of formal reports. Specific requirements include the following elements:

1. Cover
2. Title page (includes the title of the report; grant, contract, or project number; the performing organization, author, organization for whom the report was prepared; and the date)
3. Executive summary
4. Table of contents (including list of tables and illustrations)
5. Text of the report
    A. Introduction
        1. Purpose of the study
        2. Nature of the problem

3. Scope
   4. Significance of the problem
   5. Historical background (review of the literature)
   6. Definitions
   7. Personnel making the study
   8. Organization of the report
  B. Account of the study
   1. Methods and materials
   2. Theory (if appropriate)
   3. Problems
   4. Results obtained
   5. Discussion of reports
   6. Analysis and significance of results
  C. Conclusions
  D. Recommendations (include ways to utilize and diffuse results)
6. Bibliography
7. Appendix materials
8. Abstract (if needed for depositing report with the National Technical Information Service [NTIS])

Chapter in Brief

In this chapter, we learned how to write each element of the formal technical report.

Chapter Focal Points

- Letter of transmittal
- Cover and title page
- Abstract
- Executive summary
- Table of contents
- Report text—introduction, body, terminal section
- Bibliography
- Appendix
- Glossary
- Index
- Distribution list
- Requirements for final (completion) reports

Questions for Discussion

1. What is included in the front matter and what is the purpose of those elements?
2. What is an abstract? What is a synopsis? What is a summary? Answering these questions might require library searching. Why does a report require an abstract? Should the abstract of a report be composed primarily to follow the requirements of publication in an abstracts journal, or should your abstract be composed to meet the requirements of your intended reader?
3. Conclusions and recommendations are frequently grouped together within the terminal section of the report. Are they the same? What is their relationship? How are they derived?

Assignments

1. Write the first draft of the report on your chosen research problem, based on the outline(s) you prepared in assignment number 3, Chapter 5. Your instructor may wish to break this assignment into stages:
    a. First write the introduction to your report. Turn it in to your instructor for evaluation and comment.
    b. Write the body section(s) of your report. Your instructor may again offer comments on this stage of your report.
    c. Write the terminal section. Your instructor may again offer comments.
2. Prepare a letter of transmittal for your report; include reference to the commission of the investigation (by your instructor) and other pertinent details. Transmit your report to your instructor.
3. Write an abstract and executive summary for your report.

Classroom Project

Under the supervision of your instructor, exchange with your fellow students the first drafts of your reports, or any of their elements, for constructive comments and suggestions. Present these comments and suggestions orally in class. Your instructor may also ask you to write down these evaluations and turn them in.

422 West Laurel
Fort Collins, Colorado
November 30, 19__

Professor Weisman
Department of English
Colorado Polytechnic University
Fort Collins, Colorado 80521

Dear Professor Weisman:

In compliance with your term assignment to complete a technical paper, I hereby submit my report on the Possible Origin of the Intrusive Bodies in Big Thompson Canyon.

This report includes field work, description and location of the subject, laboratory research, and library research.

From research, laboratory, and field work, I found that the intrusive is an offshoot from a mass called Silver Plume Granite.

It is recommended that for additional study, thin sections of the intrusive should be used, thereby more accurately determining the percentage composition.

Sincerely yours,

Gerald L. Owens

Enclosure
GLO/lo

Figure 6.7 Sample student report.

Preliminary Report

on the

Possible Origin of the Intrusive Bodies

in

Big Thompson Canyon

Submitted to
Professor H. M. Weisman
of
Colorado Polytechnic University
Instructor
Technical Writing

By
Gerald L. Owens
Fort Collins, Colorado
November 30, 19__

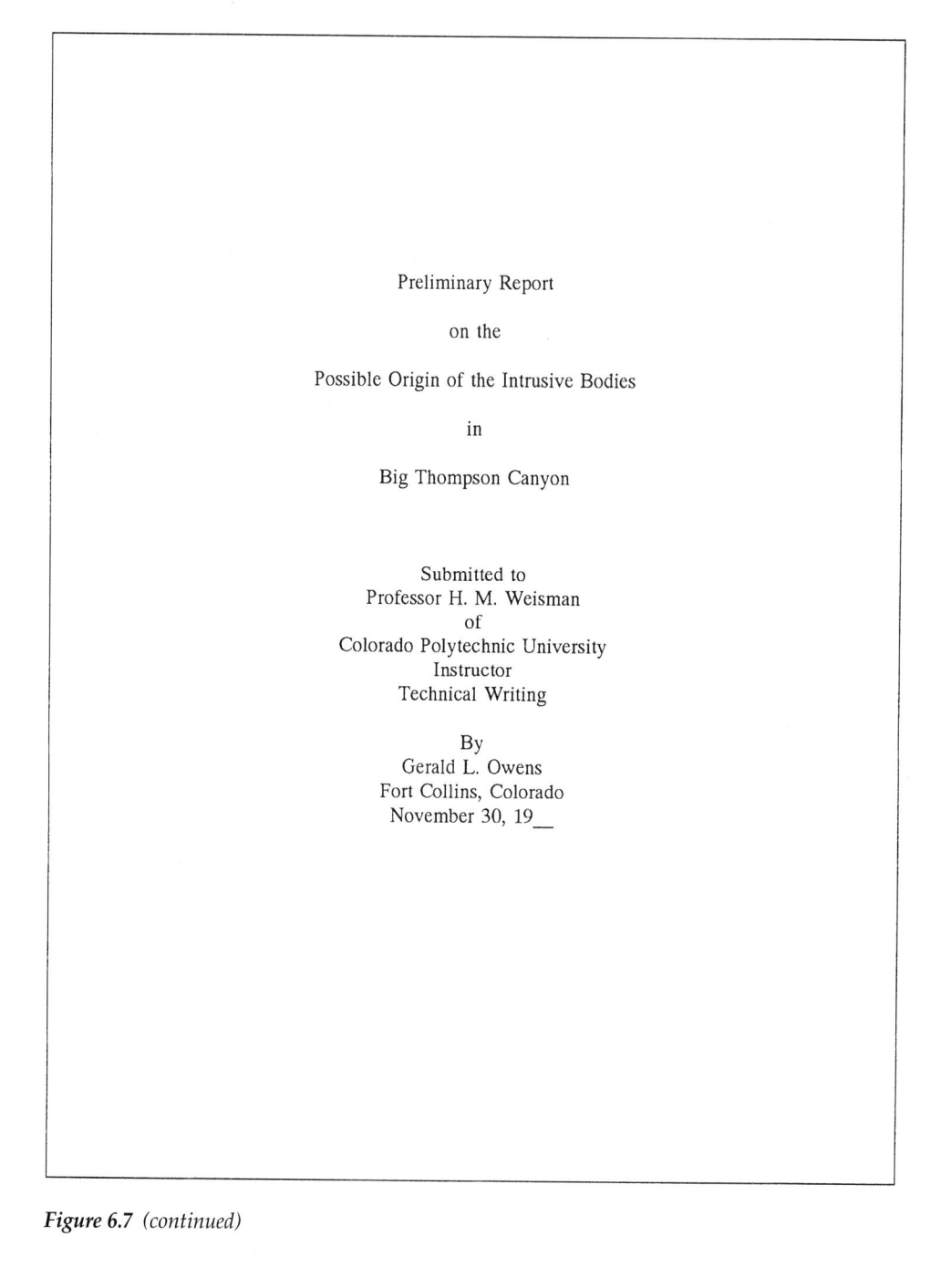

Figure 6.7 *(continued)*

Abstract

The intrusive body which lies at the base of Palisade Mountain on Highway 34 west of Loveland, Colorado, is an igneous mass that has been intruded into a metamorphic country rock. The country rock, which is essentially mica schist, covers a wide area with no other intrusives in evidence. How does this one small body of granite come to be in this location, and is it related in any way with known bodies of granite in the front range?

From the investigation, as to mineral constituents and structural correlation as compared with a known outcrop of Silver Plume Granite, it was found to be an offshoot from a main mass of Silver Plume Granite. The granite was intruded into pre-cambrian country rock during pre-cambrian times. Locally, the granite changes color due to varying percentages of mineral constituents. Individual crystal sizes depend on the rate of cooling in conjunction with the amount of mineralizers present.

For further study, it is recommended that thin-section studies be made of the intrusive in order to determine more accurately the percentage composition of the body.

Figure 6.7 (continued)

Table of Contents

INTRODUCTION	1
Significance of Problem	1
Scope	1
Historical Background	1
Definitions	1
Magma	1
Igneous Rocks	1
Intrusive Body	1
Acidic	1
Metamorphic Rocks	2
Country Rock	2
Stock	2
Batholith	2
Dike	2
Organization	2
ACKNOWLEDGMENTS	2
ANALYZING THE PROBLEM	2
LOCATION AND DESCRIPTION OF INTRUSIVE	2
Location of Intrusive	3
Description of Intrusive	3
LOCATION AND DESCRIPTION OF SILVER PLUME GRANITE OUTCROP	4
Location of the Outcrop	4
Description of the Outcrop	4
SPECIMEN SELECTION AND FIELD TRIMMING	4
Specimen Selection	4
Field Trimming	4
MICROSCOPIC ANALYSIS OF SPECIMENS	5
The Intrusive Specimen	5
The Silver Plume Specimen	5
COMPARISON OF FIELD AND LABORATORY DATA	6
Similarity of Occurrence in Field	6
Comparison of Laboratory Data	6
CONCLUSION	6
Recommendations	7
APPENDIX I	7
APPENDIX II	8
APPENDIX III	9
BIBLIOGRAPHY	9

Figure 6.7 (continued)

INTRODUCTION

West of the city of Loveland, Colorado, in the front range of the Rockies, lies the Canyon of the Big Thompson River. The river, while the mountains were being thrust upward, cut a narrow, deep canyon through the ancient metamorphic rock. At the base of Palisade Mountain, where construction work on Highway 34 exposed the flanks of the mountain, lies an area in which igneous material has been intruded.

An occurrence of this nature is not uncommon in a mountainous region. However, the fact that there are no other igneous bodies within miles led to the question of origin. Where did this lava originate? What were the factors of its intrusion into the metamorphic country rock? Could this body be correlated in any way with known igneous bodies in the front range? If there is a connection, would comparison of constituents of the two prove that they are of the same age?

SIGNIFICANCE OF PROBLEM

The problem and its solution is of most interest to geology students, for it will show them how important correlation and scientific investigation are to the study of geology. As in every unusual geologic feature, there is a subtle challenge to every geologist that says, "Come, find me out." The intrusive has, many times in the past, issued this challenge; but, due to other obligations, few students have tried to work it out. To benefit those who have the desire to know, but who do not have the time to spare, this report is submitted in hopes that it will give them insight into the processes of such an investigation.

SCOPE

Limited available laboratory time has necessitated investigation of only two major areas. One area deals with field observations in respect to correlation of the known and unknown bodies; and the other, in laboratory analysis of the hand specimens.

HISTORICAL BACKGROUND

There have not been any professional papers written on this particular intrusive body, but there are professional papers about the Silver Plume Granite formation. According to my advisor, Mr. Campbell of the Geology Department, there have been a few papers written about the intrusive by students in the past.

DEFINITIONS

The definition of terms in relation to description is a necessity for the non-technical as well as technical reader.

Magma—A magma is a naturally occurring molten rock mass in or on the earth which is composed of silicates, oxides, sulfides, and volatile constituents such as boron, fluorine, and water (1:177).
Igneous Rocks—Igneous rocks are those rocks which have formed in or on the earth's crust by solidification of molten lava (5:121).
Intrusive Body—An intrusive body is an igneous rock mass which has solidified within the earth's crust (1:31).
Acidic—Acidic refers to rocks which are very high in silica content (2:321).

Figure 6.7 (continued)

Metamorphic Rocks—Metamorphic rocks are rocks that were originally of igneous or sedimentary origin. Tremendous pressure and heat generated during mountain building transformed them into new minerals with a foliated outward appearance (3:35).
Country Rock—A country rock is defined as any rock that is penetrated by an intrusive, igneous body (5:92).
Stock—A stock is an intrusive body less than 40 square miles in area (3:77).
Batholith—A batholith is an intrusive igneous body more than 40 square miles in area (3:78).
Dike—A dike is a rock of liquid origin that intruded along faults and slips of a formation and cut across bedding planes (3:78).

ORGANIZATION

The manner in which material in this paper is presented will bear some explanation. In order for the reader to more fully understand the processes and geologic theories, it was necessary to include, at some points in the body of the report, certain evaluations of the material presented.

ANALYZING THE PROBLEM

The intrusive body in Big Thompson Canyon offered no tangible clues as to its origin. That it was a granite rock intruded into a metamorphic country rock was apparent, but how would this help? The only method to follow was to find out whether or not there were any known intrusive bodies in the area; and if there were, could they be correlated in any way?

From notes taken on a geological class field trip, it was found that there was a Silver Plume Granite outcrop near Masonville, Colorado. Although this was approximately 12 airline miles distant from the intrusive, it was the only one in the area that was positively known.

From this start it was decided that samples should be taken from both bodies and analyzed. Also, any material in the library that pertained to igneous rock in the front range should be studied.

With the thought that correlation between the two bodies might answer the question, work was begun.

LOCATION AND DESCRIPTION OF INTRUSIVE

In order for this report to be of value to those who wish to conduct subsequent studies or check the validity of the existence of the intrusive, direction will be given as accurately as possible.

2

Figure 6.7 (continued)

LOCATION OF THE INTRUSIVE

Starting from the south city limits of Fort Collins, Colorado, proceed south to Loveland, Colorado. At the junction of U.S. Highway 287 with State Highway 34, turn west on Highway 34. A general store is located near the entrance of Big Thompson Canyon called the "Dam Store." Check the mileage on the car's odometer at this point and proceed approximately eight miles west up the Canyon (see Appendix 1). On the north side of the highway stands a small white sign which reads "Palisade Mountain Elevation 8,258 Ft." (See Figure 1). At this point the small bodies which make up the intrusive extend parallel to the highway for a distance of 150 yards. The main intrusive is 15 feet to the northeast of the sign in Figure 1 and is readily identified by its clean, gray color.

Figure 1

DESCRIPTION OF THE INTRUSIVE

The larger of the four small intrusive bodies will be described as it is representative of the other three.

The intrusive extends vertically from the level of the highway approximately 25 feet to its uppermost contact with the metamorphic country rock. Horizontally, from contact to contact, the distance is 40 feet (see Figure 1, Appendix II).

Externally, the intrusive is a light-gray, fine-grained granite which lies in perfect contact with the dark-gray, foliated, micaceous schist (see Figure 2, Appendix II). Upon closer examination, small black books of biotite mica are seen to be incorporated into the mass. Cigar-shaped portions of the country rock, ranging from two to six inches long and one block three feet by six feet long, are evident in the mass, thus indicating that the intrusive cooled before complete melting had occurred. On a smaller intrusive, to the west, a pegmatic zone surrounds the intrusive at its contact with the country rock. The zonal growth of the large

3

Figure 6.7 (continued)

crystal grades inward for two feet where it again assumes the smaller size of crystals of the mass proper. This zone of pegmatite granite was the result of mineralizers, or volatile constituents, which were trapped in this area. The fluidity of the cooling mass was higher than normal for this particular intrusive; and, subsequently, crystal growth was quite rapid as proved by the large size of the individual crystals.

LOCATION AND DESCRIPTION OF THE SILVER PLUME GRANITE OUTCROP

For the reasons mentioned in "Location and Description of Intrusive," the following directions for finding the Silver Plume Outcrop will be given as accurately as possible.

LOCATION OF THE OUTCROP

Starting from the south city limits of Fort Collins, Colorado, proceed south on U.S. Highway 287 for three miles and then turn west on County Road Number 186, which goes to Masonville, Colorado. Upon reaching the location of the South Horsetooth Dam, check the odometer reading on the car and proceed for approximately four miles. At this point the road will be rising to the top of a narrow canyon. At the crest of the hill on the north side of the road lies a reddish-brown granite mass which has been partially exposed by construction work. This is the outcrop of Silver Plume Granite (see Appendix I).

DESCRIPTION OF THE OUTCROP

The outcrop is approximately 15 feet high by 50 feet long from east to west. Erosion has worn down the metamorphic rock into which the granite was intruded, but now a soil mantle covers it on the topside to a depth of several inches. Considerable chemical and mechanical weathering has taken place as the mass is fractured and crumbly in places. Also, a reddish film of iron has been deposited by circulating ground water.

Upon closer examination of a freshly chipped surface, crystal sizes appear to be fairly uniform with an occasional crystal approaching 15 millimeters in length by 10 millimeters in width. Color is pinkish-gray due to the flesh-colored feldspar and the black biotite crystals.

SPECIMEN SELECTION AND FIELD TRIMMING

SPECIMEN SELECTION

Specimens were taken from the intrusive and the known outcrop of Silver Plume Granite with an eye towards specimens that would be representative of the whole mass, as well as specimens that indicate unusual facets of its formation. Specimens were taken from the centers of the two bodies and also along the contacts with the country rock.

FIELD TRIMMING

It is sometimes necessary to use a three- to four-pound striking hammer to obtain rocks from a solid mass, or even to break up large chunks of rocks. However, there is generally enough rock material lying on the ground from which a specimen can be chosen. If possible, rocks should be chosen that approximate the

Figure 6.7 (continued)

3"x5"x1" size that hand specimens should be. In any event, a rock should be chosen that has at least one right angle and/or two flat sides.

A geology pick and a pair of heavy work gloves were used to chip the specimens down to size (see Figure 2). While holding the rock in one gloved hand, the geology pick was used to strike a glancing blow, making sure that the chips would fly away from the operator. This operation may be understood more readily with a diagram (see Figure 3). As indicated by the drawing, an imaginary line should be visualized down the center of the rock. Small fragments indicated by the dotted lines should be chipped off. The blows should be struck down and away so as not to crack the specimen in half. When one side has been trimmed off flat, the specimen should be turned over and chipped on the other side. Considerable patience is needed as these rocks are brittle and fracture very easily.

Figure 2

Figure 3

MICROSCOPIC ANALYSIS OF SPECIMENS

THE INTRUSIVE SPECIMEN

The specimen from the intrusive was observed under fifty power magnification. The predominant mineral was orthoclase feldspar with its white color and irregular grains showing many of the faces with nearly perfect right-angle cleavage. The next mineral, in order of abundance, was quartz. This mineral is the clear, colorless variety which has no crystal form as it was the last mineral to crystalize out in the cooling intrusive. It filled in all pore spaces left by the other crystals. Biotite mica, with its black, splendent luster and flexible folia, was regularly spaced in the matrix. The relatively small size of the crystals made them unnoticeable beyond a few feet. Infrequent, but quite large, crystals of plagioclase feldspar were observed. These were identified by their gray-white color and twinning striations on the cleavage surfaces. As evidenced by the high percentages of quartz, this rock can be termed acidic (see Table 1, Appendix III).

THE SILVER PLUME SPECIMEN

The specimen from the Silver Plume outcrop was also observed under fifty power magnification. The orthoclase feldspar was the most abundant mineral found. It varied from white to flesh-colored with euhedral, crystal faces. The quartz, next in abundance, which filled in the remaining spaces, was rose-colored to colorless. The color could have been imparted to the quartz by a minute quantity of cobalt. The biotite mica present was in small, black masses which were quite close together. A very small quantity of white plagioclase feldspar, showing excellent twinning striations, was present. This specimen represents a magma which was high in silica content. Therefore, this rock is also termed acidic (see Table 2, Appendix III).

Figure 6.7 (continued)

COMPARISON OF FIELD AND LABORATORY DATA

SIMILARITY OF OCCURRENCE IN FIELD

Comparison of the types of country rock penetrated by the respective bodies showed that they are of the same age and the same rock type. The country rock in both localities is a pre-cambrian, metamorphic rock called "mica schist." Both of the bodies are granite, varying only in percentages of minerals present, as well as in color. This follows quite well with T. S. Lovering's professional paper entitled <u>Geology and Ore Deposits of the Front Range</u>, U.S. Geol. Surv. Professional Paper, 223, page 28. The following is the section written on the Silver Plume Granite:

> In the front range are a large number of small stocks and batholiths generally intruded at the same time.... Most of the stocks and batholiths are pinkish-gray, medium-grained, slightly porphyritic biotite granite, composed chiefly of pink and gray feldspars, smoky quartz, and biotite mica; but muscovite is present in some facies.... The percentage of biotite varies from place to place....

The intrusive bodies are very small when compared to the size of a stock (3:77), or a batholith (3:78). They do, however, compare favorably with the definition for a dike (3:78). For the most part, dikes are rather small in a cross-sectional area but are known to extend up to 100 miles in length (3:78). For both of the bodies, which the author will call dikes, the rock that the molten lava passed through would have some bearing on the composition. This could be one of the reasons why there is a difference in color and percentage of composition. From this, then, it is logical to assume that both bodies are offshoots from a larger mass. They probably followed fractures or faults caused by crystal movements during the time of the pre-cambrian, metamorphic country rock.

COMPARISON OF LABORATORY DATA

The specimen of the intrusive, in comparison with that of the Silver Plume Granite, shows that they are very close in chemical composition. The intrusive specimen had 60% orthoclase in comparison with the Silver Plume's 40%. Quartz in the intrusive averaged 20%, while in the Silver Plume it was 30%. For biotite mica, the percentage was 15% in the intrusive and 25% in the Silver Plume. Both of the bodies had 5% plagioclase. For a better visual comparison, see Appendix III.

CONCLUSION

The intrusive bodies in Big Thompson Canyon are of the same geologic age as that of the Silver Plume Granite. They both were intruded into a pre-cambrian, metamorphic country rock during pre-cambrian times. The country rock, into which the granite was intruded, is a mica schist, which is quite common in the front range.

Figure 6.7 (continued)

Chemically, the intrusive and the Silver Plume Granite are the same. Although there is some variation in color and percentages of the constituents, this is within the somewhat broad range given for the Silver Plume Granite (4:28). Locally, the percentage can change due to an increase or decrease in amount of constituents. Color variations are due to minute inclusions of a metallic ion or molecule derived from the walls of the conduit or feeder pipe.

RECOMMENDATIONS

It is recommended that a larger number of Silver Plume Granite specimens be analyzed. These should come from different outcrops. Also, to more accurately determine the constituents and their percentages, thin-section studies of the specimens should be made.

APPENDIX I

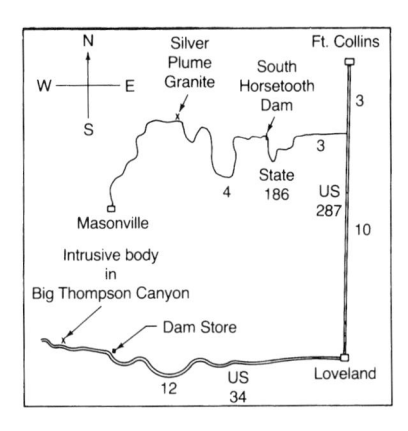

Figure 1
Illustrations Showing Work Sites (Not drawn to scale)

Figure 6.7 (continued)

APPENDIX II

Figure 1
Photo showing relative size
of intrusive in Big Thompson Canyon

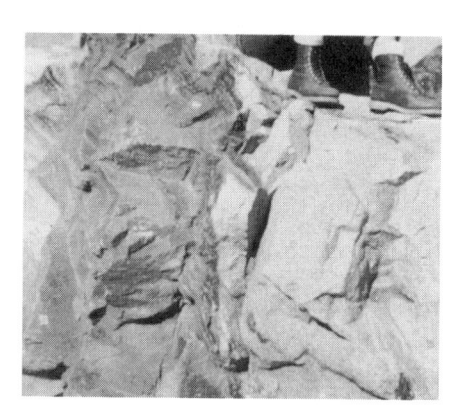

Figure 2
Photo showing contact between
country rock and granite intrusive

8

Figure 6.7 (continued)

APPENDIX III

Tables of Comparative Constituents

Table 1

Specimen From Intrusive

Mineral	Percentages	Color
Orthoclase Feldspar	60%	White
Quartz	20%	Clear, glassy
Biotite mica	15%	Black
Plagioclase Feldspar	5%	Gray-white

Table 2

Specimen From Silver Plume

Mineral	Percentages	Color
Orthoclase Feldspar	40%	Flesh-colored to white
Quartz	30%	Rose to clear, glassy
Biotite mica	25%	Black, vitreous
Plagioclase Feldspar	5%	White

BIBLIOGRAPHY

1. Bowen, N. L. (1922). "The Reaction Principle in Petrogenesis." Journal of Geology, Vol. 30, pages 177–98.
2. Grout, F. F. (1941). "Formation of Igneous Looking Rocks by Metasomatism. A Critical Review and Suggested Research." Bul. Geol. Soc. Am., Vol. 52, pages 1525–26.
3. Longwell, Chester R., and Flint, Richard Foster. Introduction to Physical Geology, New York: John Wiley and Sons, 1955, 432 pages.
4. Lovering, T. S. Geology and Ore Deposits of the Front Range, U.S. Geol. Surv., Professional Paper, 223, page 28.
5. Pirrson, Louis V., and Knolph, Adolph. Rocks and Rock Minerals, New York: John Wiley and Sons, 1957, 365 pages.

Figure 6.7 (continued)

7

How to Write, Edit, and Produce the Report

Chapter Objective

Instill students with confidence in their capability to write the formal report by taking them through the steps of the writing and editing processes, including the use of word processing technology.

Chapter Focus

- The first draft
- The revision and editing process—what to look for and do
- Revising and editing with a word processor
- Format and mechanics
- Headings
- Graphics
- Documentation
- Bibliography
- Proofreading

We can now turn to the encoding-composition process. The actual writing begins after you have completed your research, accumulated your data, and organized your work into an outline. Before beginning to write, you might profit from reviewing your outline. You will find that your concept of the report has been growing and ripening in the recesses of your mind, subconsciously, for the most part. A final review will increase your awareness and freshen your viewpoint. It will also test your outline. Your review may stimulate the check of a note here or datum there and perhaps the revision of a point here or there. You are likely to experience a certain stimulation and excitement as you prepare to do the actual writing. As you review, thoughts about various aspects of the report will come rapidly into your mind. You may want to jot these thoughts down. After you have reviewed the outline, data, and notes, you will be ready for the actual process of writing. Keep your outline before you and begin writing. (Professional writers are the first to admit that writing is never easy, but writing can become easier with proper preparation and experience.)

Writing the First Draft

Whether you use a pencil, typewriter, or word processor, your first draft should be written[1] in one sitting, if possible; so allow yourself at least several uninterrupted hours for this phase. Your report will have more life and will represent the sense of your material more closely if you write rapidly than it will if you pause to perfect each sentence before going on to the next. Save problems of spelling and grammar for the revision. To allow for revision, leave plenty of space in your rough draft between lines, between paragraphs, and in margins. If you follow a good outline that breaks your report up into logical stages, you will not be burdened by the strain of trying to keep a great deal of material in mind at one time. The outline permits you to concentrate on key aspects of your report. Some people find it is easier to write the body first and the introduction and the conclusion last. Others have a vivid interest in a certain aspect of the research and find they can "lick" an entire report by writing those parts first that come easiest to them. Thus, writing in stages is like hacking off small bits of a whole. Because of the outline, the writer can do this without losing continuity. It is probably better to make the first draft full and complete even though you may feel it is wordy, since it is always easier to scratch out material and explanations than it is to expand. Your rough draft is a production of ideas rather than a critical evaluation of those ideas. The logical flow of ideas will be interrupted if you try to evaluate your material critically as you write; punctuation, sentence form, and grammar also slow down the flow of writing. You should not worry about such mechanical details in the first draft. You will have time at a later stage to verify, check, correct, and revise. It is important that at first you write and write fully on all the aspects of the investigation that you have previously outlined.

---

[1]In computer terminology, the process of entering data is called either writing or inputting.

The Revision and Editing Process

Professional writers know that papers are rewritten, not written. After the rough draft has been completed, you ought to plan for a "cooling off" period. Plan for at least three readings of your draft for revision and editing.

The First Reading—The Revision/Editing Process

If possible, let at least two or three days elapse before you review your first draft. An interval of time allows you to approach what you have written, not from the closeness of the first heat of the writing, but from an objective distance. In this reading, take the viewpoint of your intended reader to see whether your report's objectives are being met and whether the problem is being answered. You should read your rough draft through from beginning to end without pausing for revisions. This first reading is necessary for an overview; it should not be used for checking details. You may note points by making marks in the margins of the draft for attention at a later time. At this reading, you should ask yourself questions such as these:

1. Does the thesis of the report come through clearly?
2. Have I covered all points essential to the objectives or purposes of the report?
3. Do they come through clearly?
4. Do the various parts of the report fit together smoothly?
5. Is the information adequate and arranged effectively for content and organization?
6. Does extraneous material confuse the issues?
7. Do my conclusions flow logically from my data?
8. Do my recommendations flow logically from my conclusions?

If your conclusion does not have the point you want your reader to get, or if the conclusion is not based on adequate and clear data, you will have to revise your report until its text provides the answers to the preceding questions. This brings us to the "second reading" phase.

The Second Reading—The Revision/Editing Process

The "second reading" is a figurative expression. This phase concentrates on the process of bringing clarity and cohesiveness to your report. You will be concerned with the *content matter*, its *organization*, and its *written expression*. Now is the appropriate time to pay attention to the items you have marked in the margins of your manuscript during the first reading.

The Content Matter

Here you are concerned with the eight questions you raised in your first reading phase. You sharpen your focus with questions such as these:

1. What additional information does the reader need to reach my conclusions and to accept my recommendations?

2. Is the information accurate, valid, or appropriate for my conclusions?
3. What information did I include that is not pertinent and that may confuse the reader?

In the heat of writing a first draft, it is not unusual for points or even topics—despite a good outline—to be left out. If the readings reveal that an explanation is inadequate, then you may need to provide:

a. additional data or examples to clarify or reinforce a point;
b. additional instructions, diagrams, or tables to visualize a point;
c. additional definitions; or
d. additional details on the who, what, when, where, why, or how of the situation.

You are responsible for the accuracy and validity of your information. Check the following:

Numerical data
Facts
Graphics
Quotations

Relate your conclusions to your data and information. Are your judgments based on solid facts and/or expert opinion? Are there contradictions in the evidence you have presented? If some of your data are based on interviews or references, have you provided the required documentation?

In the heat of the writing, we often empty ourselves on the page, setting forth everything we know. Aspects of the situation have been interesting for us, but details are not always pertinent or appropriate. If we include everything, if we do not sort out the extraneous, then the unimportant details clog the reader's mind and interfere with the important matter that leads to the conclusions and recommendations.

The thesis sentence is your test. You ask yourself: Does this item of information focus on or advance my thesis sentence? If it does, include it; if it does not, be ruthless—no matter how much you like the look of your sentences—and cross them out. Be careful to recognize not only what is superfluous but also what is redundant.

The Third Reading—Organization, Language, and Style

To check your report's organization, you need your outline in front of you. You have made revisions for content in your second reading phase. Now you are concerned with the arrangement of the details of your text material, with the emphasis not only on words, sentences, and paragraphs but also on sections and how they are connected or related to each other. The revisions made in the second reading phase affect arrangement of text within sections or subsections of your report. There should be little, if any, radical reorganization of the outline material. The cohesiveness of the report was implemented in the outlining stage of the writing.

Now you are mainly concerned with using the text to lead the reader through your investigative experience from its initiation through its various steps to the logic of your conclusion—the thesis sentence. Here are questions you should ask yourself about the overall organization:

1. Is my conclusion—thesis—logical, reasonable, substantiated?
2. Are my recommendations reasonable, practical?
3. Is the problem I am investigating clearly stated for the reader in the introduction?
4. Are the main sections of the report prepared for in the introduction? Are they inherent in the investigation of the problem or situation?
5. Are the main sections cohesive?
6. Does each section have a heading?

Here are questions you should ask yourself about the organization of each section:

1. Is the point of each section clearly indicated? (Each section, as your outline directs, has a thesis sentence.)
2. Are the subsections evident or announced?
3. Do I have a heading for each subsection?
4. Do I have connections between the subsections (transitional words, phrases, sentences)?
5. Do I have a summary at the end of the section in which the main point of the section is reaffirmed?

Language and Style

Your final concern in your "third reading" phase is language and style. You should review the material in Chapter 2 on style, sentences, and paragraphs. Now check for the following:

1. *Paragraphs.* Do the paragraphs hang together? Do all paragraphs have a topic sentence? Do the paragraphs have unity? Should any paragraphs be combined? Do any paragraphs need further development?
2. *Sentence structure.* Are all sentences complete grammatically? Do any sentences have to be reread for meaning? If so, break up or rewrite. Are sentences punctuated correctly?
3. *Style.* Is the style consistent and appropriate? Is the writing objective, concise, and clear?
4. *Word choice.* Can any deadwood be removed? Are the words as exact and meaningful as possible? Are there wrong, inexact, or vague words? Are there clichés, jargon, shoptalk? Are there any nonstandard abbreviations? Are there any inconsistencies in names, titles, symbols? Are words spelled correctly?

The writer's best tools in these matters are a dictionary and a good handbook of grammar. Consult the reference guide and index in the back of this text for more specifics on grammar, punctuation, style, and usage.

Revising and Editing with a Word Processor

If you have entered your report on a word processor, your revision and editing chores are simplified; nonetheless, the same factors and principles of grammar, logic, and composition apply. Certain time-consuming tasks are made easier because of the versatility of word processing programs. For example:

Delete and *insert* commands. By positioning the cursor under the exact place on the screen at which a revision is to be made and keying the appropriate command, you can delete a character, a word, a part of a line, an entire line, or a paragraph. With an insert command, you can similarly add material.

Macro. A **macro** is a sequence of keystrokes that you record and save in a file (computer memory) so you can use the sequence again whenever you wish, just by typing the "name" that you assigned to the sequence. The macro is simply a shortcut for entering frequently used data, commands, or a combination of the two. Macros range from very short, simple entries to elaborate chains.

Block moves and *block editing.* Block moves are useful commands that allow you to mark off a block of text ranging in length from one character to an entire document. You can mark a block as a separate unit to be saved in permanent memory, sent to the printer (of your computer), copied, deleted, moved to another location in the document, or converted from lowercase to uppercase, or given other enhancements such as italics or boldface.

Find and replace. This command allows you to search for and correct specific changes on command; for example, change all abbreviations of *NSF* to read *National Science Foundation.*

Merge. Merge means putting together data from two or more files in memory. For example, you may have entered data into memory in the form of charts or tables. By appropriate command, you can merge the charts and tables into the proper place in your report's text.

Formatting and reformatting. Rewriting with a typewriter because of changes due to revisions means retyping the entire report manuscript. Word processing saves you from this tedious job. It enables you to make revisions and format changes without having to retype the entire manuscript. Rewriting often involves changes not only in text but also in style and format. Style considerations include:

Capitalization
Italics
Boldface
Centering
Use of quotation marks

Format considerations include:

Margins: left, right, top, and bottom

Space between lines and between paragraphs

Space around illustrations and tables

Paragraph space indentation

Number of lines to a page

Widows and orphans on a page (**Widows** are the last line of a paragraph at the top of a new page; **orphans** are the first line of a paragraph isolated at the bottom of a page.)

Placement of page numbers

Placement of footnotes and headers (A **header** is a section heading that is repeated on consecutive pages.)

Word processing technology readily takes care of these formatting requirements, assists with other structural considerations, such as placement of graphics, and provides several convenient writing aids:

Grammar and style checkers. These programs help point out such problems as:

Faulty subject-verb agreements

Faulty pronoun-object agreement

Wrong number in predicate nominative

Incorrect formation of the possessive

Careless punctuation and proofreading such as missing periods and unpaired quotation marks

Clichés and hackneyed expressions

Confusion of words like *its* and *it's* and *whose* and *who's*

Prolix constructions like *all of the* instead of *all the*

Barbarisms like *irregardless*

Some grammar/style checkers keep track of statistics on average word and sentence length and readability formula computations. (See pages 30–31 for comments on readability formulas.) Actually, grammar checkers compare what you have written to a collection of rules to determine whether your writing disagrees with any of them, but style templates may not always be appropriate. For example, if you begin a sentence with *And,* it will be flagged as improper even though you may have purposely begun the sentence with the conjunction *And* for emphasis to suggest irony.

Dictionaries. Several dictionary publishers have computerized versions available that contain not only word meanings and synonyms, but also pronunciations and etymology. They also accept queries based on misspelled words.

Thesaurus. This is a dictionary program that suggests synonyms. When a writer is stumped for a word, the computerized thesaurus can help. By placing the cursor on the word to be replaced and making the appropriate keystrokes for the thesaurus software, a list of synonyms is presented on screen. Sometimes the synonyms have lists of synonyms.

Ideally, computerized writing aids would provide not only grammar and punctuation corrections, word spellings, and style improvements but also determine: whether a writer conveys the meaning intended; whether a writer provides a reader with a coherent logic in and flow of text; and whether a writer provides understandable descriptions and appropriate examples. Unfortunately, computers have not yet reached such analytical sophistication. However, they can provide the inexperienced writer with helpful aids to catch slips in expression and ungrammatical constructions.

Producing and Printing the Report

After the final revision process, writers using a word processor may have choices for the report's printing. The diskette may be sent to the print shop if it has the capability to use the electronic manuscript as direct input. If the computer you are using has a printer attached, you can print the report directly. If you or your organization has a laser printer, you have recourse to the desktop publishing route. Using appropriate graphic-oriented page composition software, you can convert the report manuscript into a handsomely printed formal report.

Format and Mechanics for the Typed Report

Most students depend on their typewriters for their written work. What follows are several standard format and mechanics considerations common to most formal reports. In general, these matters apply equally to typed and word processor-produced reports.

Use white, unruled 8½-by-11-inch bond paper of 20 pound, 25 percent cotton rag stock. Be sure to have sufficient copies made for filing and reference. The report should be typewritten or printed with a black-ink ribbon on one side of the page only. Leave ample margins on all sides of the page. Margins on the left should be no less than 1¼ inches, preferably 1½ inches to facilitate binding. Margins on the right should be no less than ¾-inch. The margin should be no less than 1 inch at the top. The bottom margin, including footnote space, if there are footnotes, should be no less than 1 inch, preferably 1¼ inches.

Manuscripts for publication are always double-spaced. Reports may be either double-spaced or single-spaced, depending on the conventions of your organization or specifications of your client. Any material that contains equations, superscripts, or subscripts is easier to read if it is double-spaced. Reports written as classroom assignments should be double-spaced to facilitate marking and correcting. If the typescript is single-spaced, use double spaces between paragraphs. Two spaces separate paragraphs of double-spaced copy. Paragraphs, whether single-spaced or double-spaced, are indented five spaces.

The appearance of your report page will be improved if you follow these rules:

1. Do not start the first sentence of a paragraph on the last line of a page.
2. Do not place a heading at the bottom of the page with less than two lines of text to follow.
3. Avoid placing the last line of a paragraph at the beginning of a page.

Text pages of the report are numbered with arabic numerals. The placing of numbers on the page should be consistent. They may be centered at the top or placed in the upper right-hand corner. Numbering at the bottom of the page, either in the center or at the lower left, should be avoided because these numbers may be confused with footnote material. Prefatory or preliminary pages of the report (Title Page, Abstract, Table of Contents, List of Illustrations, Foreword) are numbered with small Roman numerals. If blank pages are used for the sake of appearance, they are counted but not numbered. The Title Page is counted as the prefatory page (i) but is not numbered. Final assignment of numbers to pages might be delayed until all the pages are typed unless the exact numbers of illustrations and their placement are known and planned beforehand. However, tentative numbers could be written in the upper right-hand corners very lightly in pencil.

How to Use Graphic Aids

Visual aid material should be placed near the text matter it illustrates. This is not always possible in typewritten reports where several visual aids may be part of a discussion within a paragraph. If the visual aid is relatively small, it can be integrated into the page of the appropriate text paragraph. A full-page visual aid might be placed either facing or immediately after the page where it is discussed. Graphic material should not precede its discussion in the text because it may confuse the reader. In typed reports, illustrations that cannot be integrated within the text page are placed for convenience in a separate section, usually in the appendix. All visual aids—wherever they are placed—must be referred to in the text itself. The reader should be directed by explanatory sentences to the specific illustration or table for better understanding, interpretation, and correlation of the data being communicated. If an illustration or table supplements, clarifies, confirms, analyzes, or reveals conclusions, such explanations must be clearly stated in the text. The more complex the illustration, the more explanatory material is necessary. Directions for interpretation of illustrations may be included in the text or in captions below the graphic aid. Graphics need to be as simple as possible. Text matter and lengthy explanations are kept out of the illustration proper.

Photographs

Photographs offer realistic and accurate representations. Effective photographic illustrations require thoughtful planning and skill so that all desired details are shown at the most favorable angle (Figure 7.1). Callouts are frequently added to the photograph to identify distinctive details (Figure 7.2). In addition to photographs taken with a still camera, photographs can be taken by x-ray, electron microscope, telescope, or photo micrograph to provide impressive visuals (Figure 7.3). The airbrush is frequently used on photographs to provide highlights, to add emphasis and sharpness of detail, or to allow a de-emphasis of unimportant details.

Drawings/Diagrams

Drawings and diagrams can be made with pencil, pen, airbrush, or computer software. There are many types from simple freehand sketches to detailed engineering and architectural renderings with minutiae of detail. The more complex the subject matter, the greater is the necessity for callouts (Figure 7.4). Letter symbols with keys to identify the symbols are sometimes used to avoid clutter and confusion. Drawings also offer more flexibility than photographs for showing the inner movements of equipment, cross sections, and relationships (Figures 7.5 and 7.6).

Graphs

Graphs, curves, and *charts* are terms that are used interchangeably for diagraming, mapping, and presenting statistical information. These devices pictorially com-

Figure 7.1 *This photograph of the neutral beam injector apparatus at the Lawrence Berkley Laboratory provides the reader with an idea of the size of the apparatus.* [5]

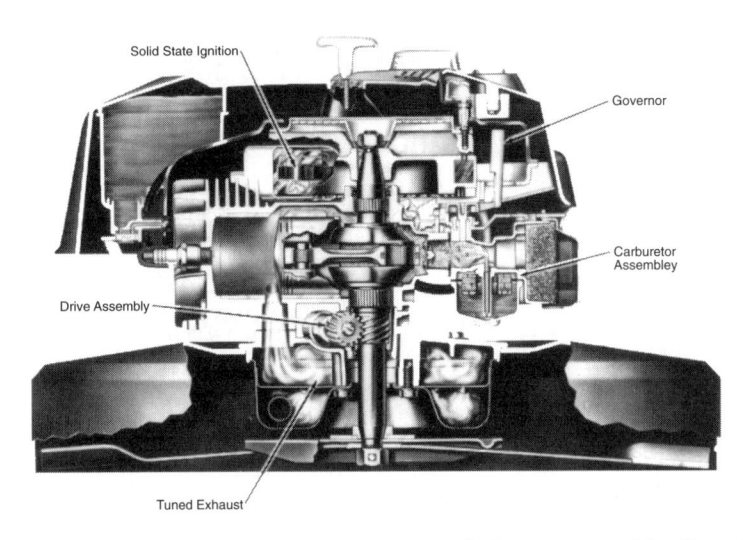

Figure 7.2 This photographic cutaway view of a lawn mower with callouts has benefited from an airbrush technique to provide highlights, emphasis, sharpness of detail, and de-emphasis of unimportant details. [2]

Figure 7.3 This is a photographic micrograph of canine tissue magnified 8,000 times. (N represents the nucleus; m are mitochondria.) [7]

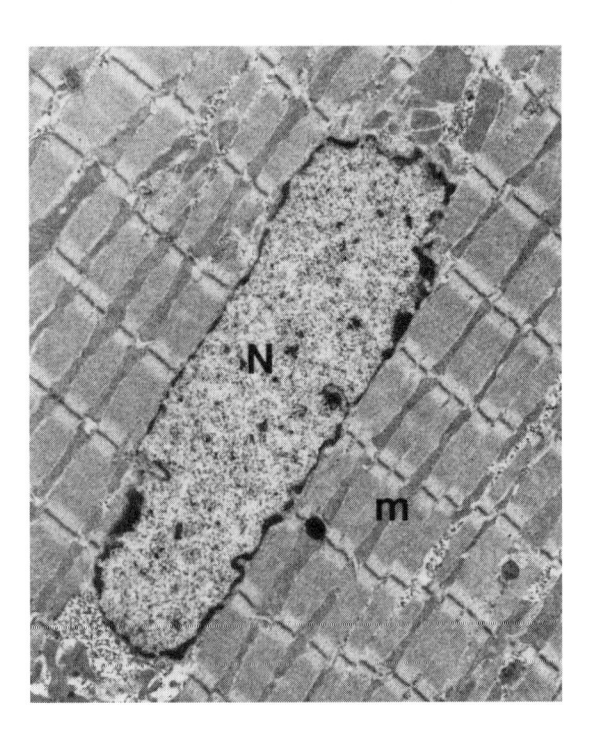

ADJUSTMENT DEVICES

FRICTION RELIEF HANDCRANK
The handcrank can be provided with an adjustable friction drive, by using a cup spring (or a helical spring) to apply pressure upon a gear bearing against a wood or composition disk. Adjustment of a clamp nut provides the means of varying the pressure to obtain the degree of friction required. If pressure becomes greater than the friction imposed upon it, the gear will slip and protect associated gearing from strain or damage.

ADJUSTABLE HOLDING FRICTION
The same handcrank may be provided with cork disks, a collar, and a bushing. This assembly puts a drag on the handcrank, keeps it positioned, and prevents motion from backing out through the handcrank.

POSITIONING PLUNGER
We can carry the design of the handcrank still further and add a plunger for the purpose of holding the shaft in either of two positions: an IN position and OUT position. In changing position, the shaft and the drive gear move in relation to the adapter housing. The plunger is pulled out and the handcrank pushed or pulled to its new position. When released, the plunger is returned by a spring and enters a hole in the bushing, locking the assembly in a particular position.

Moving the handcrank to the in or out position will cause it to engage or become disengaged, or this arrangement can be used to drive one or the other mechanism. By using a wide gear, this drive can be kept in engagement all the time, the in and out position being to control the drive of another gear. Thus, it is possible to drive one gear at all times, alone, or in conjunction with another. Further, we would include a switch actuated by the in or out position of the shaft.

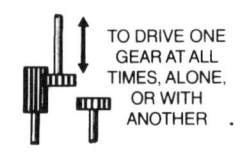

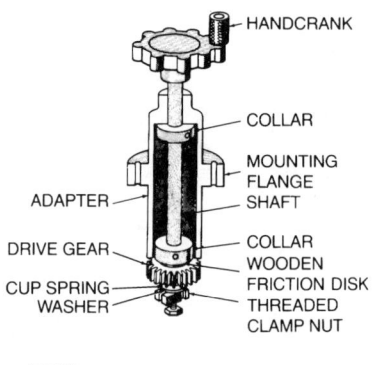

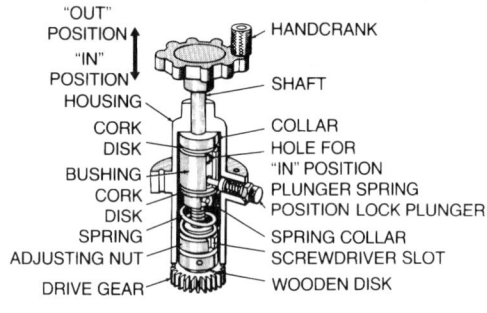

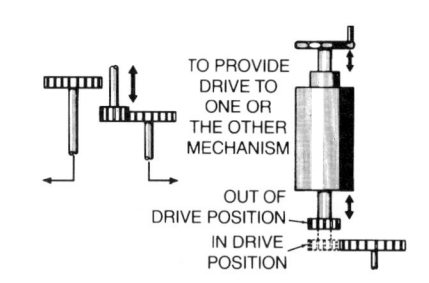

Figure 7.4 This excellent series of drawings integrates text with illustrations to enhance reader comprehension. [6]

Figure 7.5 This pictorial on a twelfth century B.C. Egyptian tomb shows the use of siphons to draw off Nile River water purified by sedimentation. It is one of the earliest descriptions of a technical process. [4]

180

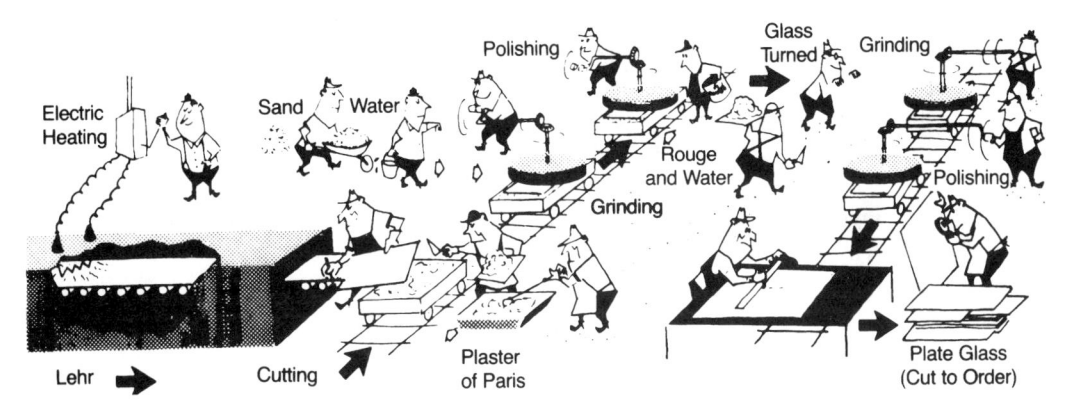

Figure 7.6 Appropriate cartoon drawings can be effective in technical presentations. They draw the reader's attention, hold interest, and provide relief from solid text material. Notice how the flow of flat glass manufacturing is enlivened by cartoon characters. [8]

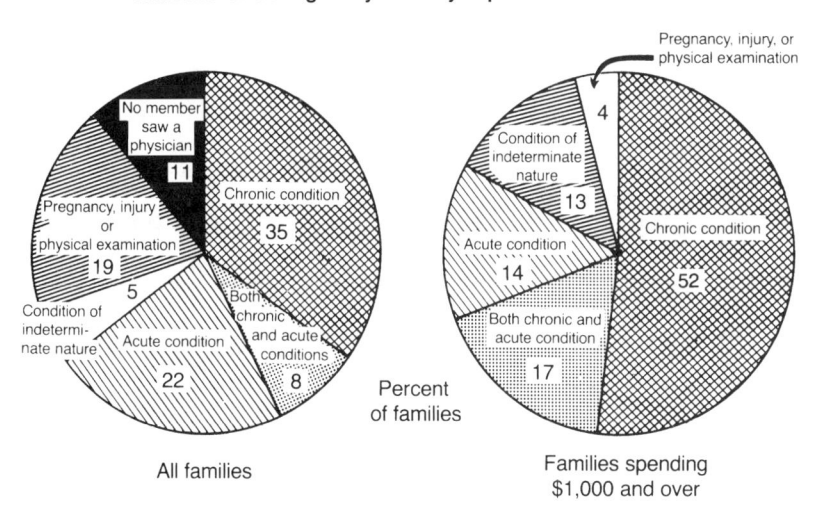

Figure 7.7 A circle graph or pie chart.

pare changes in value or interrelationships of variable quantities (Figure 7.7). Graphs, curves, and charts simplify statistical aspects of information and help in their interpretation (Figures 7.8 and 7.9).

Tables

Tables offer a convenient means for presenting characteristics of things, processes, and concepts. They offer the most precise way to present experimental data in a compact arrangement of facts, figures, and values in an orderly sequence such as lines and columns for convenient reference. Tables are boxed or framed on a page when the data are self-sufficient and self-explanatory; such tables are known as **independent** tables (Table 7.1). Where the significance and meaning of a table are dependent upon explanatory material preceding and succeeding the information in the columns, they become part of the text page and are called **dependent** tables, as in the following example:

The average surface wind velocities and direction at the Seattle Weather Station during the swimming season (for 20-year and 38-year averages) are as follows:

	June	July	August	September
Average wind velocity m.p.h.	4.2	3.9	3.7	3.9
Predominant direction	S	N	N	S

Thus, in summer, with light northerly or southerly winds, we could expect that the water in the swimming areas would be exchanged by surrounding lake water in from two to four hours.

Table 7.1 An Example of an Independent Table

Results of Colorado State University Laboratory Testing of Potential Sealants for the Coachella Canal

Sample No.	Material	Grit Content (%)	Colloidal Yield (%)	Wall Building Filter Loss (cc)	Wall Building Cake (in)	Viscosity (centipoises)
S1-1	Coyote Well	1.3	53.5*	40	3/32	3
S1-2	Ackins Claim	12.1	42.9*	189	8/32	2
S1-3	Thermo Claim	2.5	48.9*	88.5	1/8	2
S1-4	Burslem Claim	20.7	28.9	69	3/16	2
S1-5	Armaseal	4.2	65.2	41	1/16	<4
S1-6	Maas Clay	5.7	60.1	38	1/16	1
S1-7	Western Clay (Utah)	17.5	55.5	28.5	1/16	6
S1-8	Western Clay (Utah) reserves	5.0	41.3	33.3	1/8	3
S1-9	Bent. Corp. (Utah)	4.1	84.6	14.5	5/64	8
S1-10	Baroid (Wyo) crushed	4.8	89.4	16.5	1/8	22
S1-11	Baroid (Wyo) 200 mesh	2.9	88.2*	16	3/32	23

*Dispersant (sodium tripolyphosphate—0.75 gms) added where tendency for flocculation noted.

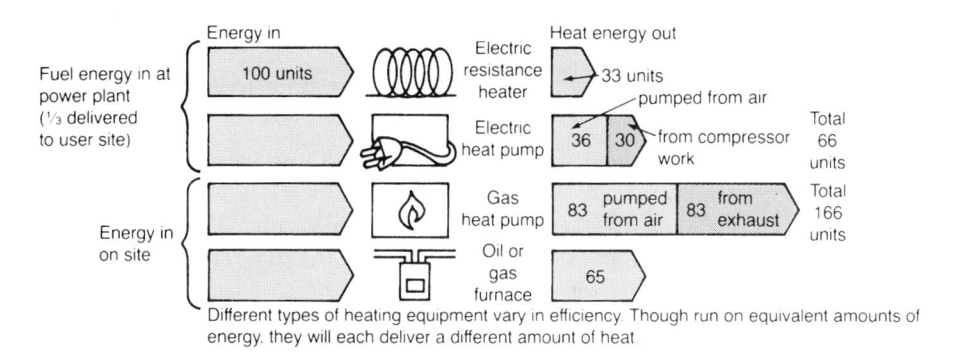

Figure 7.8 A pictorial chart [2].

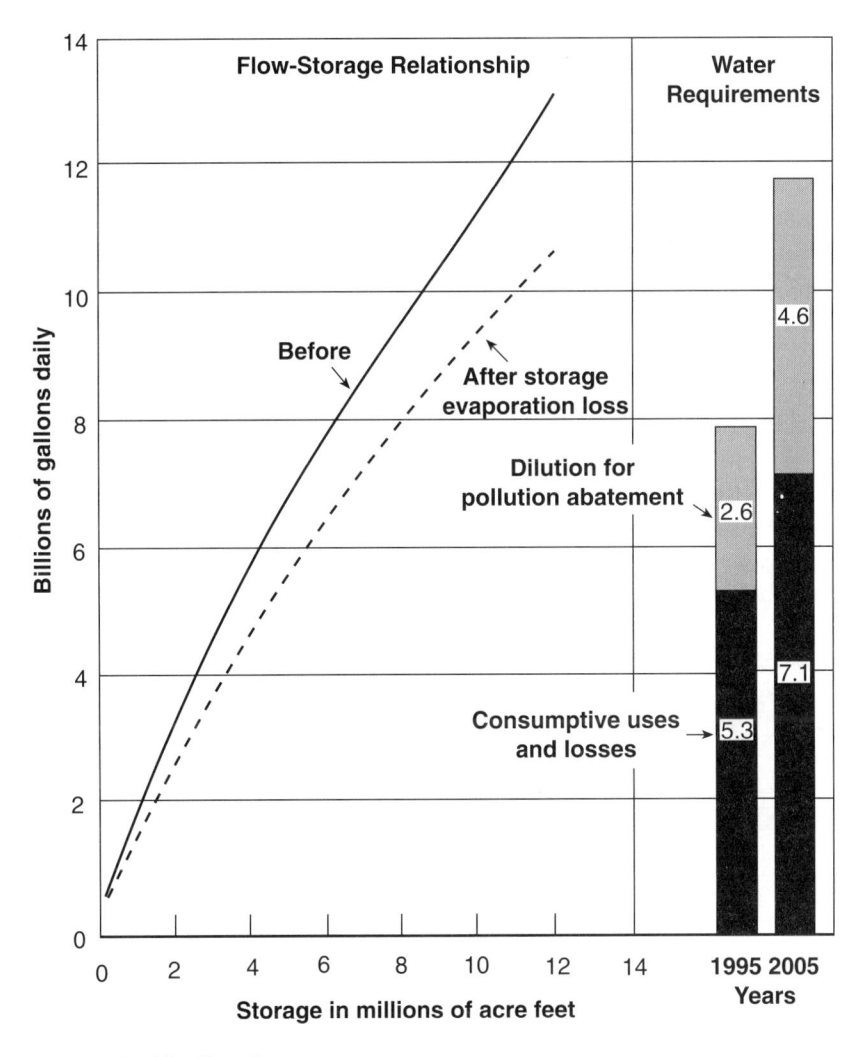

Figure 7.9 A bar/line chart.

Checklist for Constructing Tables

1. When four or more items of statistical information or data are to be presented, the material will be clearer in tabular form.
2. Quantitative, descriptive, and comparative data are more readily comprehensible in table form.
3. The data of a table should be crystallized into a logical unit. Extraneous data should be excluded; the table should be self-explanatory. Though self-contained, the table should be integrated with text matter for fuller explanation and interpretation.
4. The table should have both a number and title. Tables may be numbered in Roman numerals or in Arabic. The title should be concise yet clearly identify the contents. A subtitle may be used for providing precise details.
5. Each vertical column and, as necessary, each horizontal line should have an identifying head.
6. Standard terms, symbols, and abbreviations should be used for all unit descriptions. The same unit system of measurement should be used for comparable properties or dimensions; for example, in linear measurements, feet and meters should not be intermingled.
7. If all the numbers in the table are measurements in the same units, then the unit is stated in the title.
8. Data to be compared should be placed in a horizontal plane.
9. If headings are not self-explanatory, footnotes should be used. If an item is repeated several times in a table, it should be removed from the data in the table and placed in the title, in a footnote, or in a column or line head.
10. Footnotes should be numbered or identified in sequence, line by line, from left to right, across the table.
11. Figures in columns are aligned to similar digits—ordinarily the right digit. However, when the data set up in a column are composed of different units, they should be centered in the column or aligned on the left.

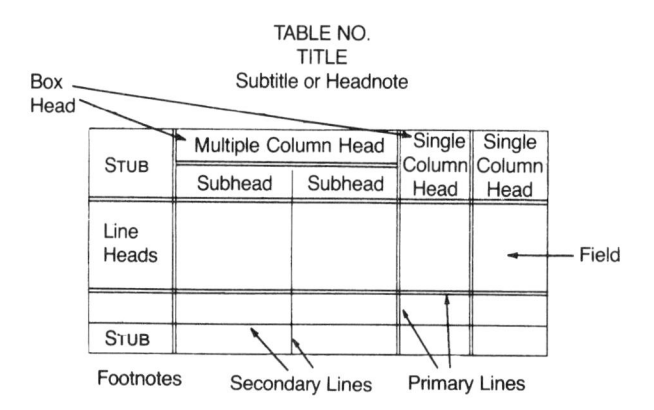

Figure 7.10 Elements of an independent table.

12. Fractions should be expressed in decimals. Decimal points are aligned in a column. When the first number of a column is wholly a decimal, a cipher is added to the left of the decimal point, as for example, 0.192.
13. Column or line headings should be used to group related data.
14. Whenever possible, a table should be designed and structured so it can be typed on one page. If the data cannot be made to fit on one page, a continuation page should be used. The word *continued* should be placed at the bottom of the first page, as well as at the top of the second page, to indicate that the table has not been completed. Column heads must also be shown on the second page.
15. Significant or summary tables are placed within the body of the report. Supporting tables of interest for the record are placed in the appendix.

How to Handle Equations

Mathematical equations are generally centered on a page. Lengthy equations should be typed completely on one line rather than broken into two lines:

. . . the cut-off frequency of a rectangular guide is

$$f_c = \frac{c}{\lambda c} = \frac{c\sqrt{\left(\frac{m}{a}\right)^2 + \left(\frac{u}{b}\right)^2}}{2}$$

Each new line of an equation should be positioned so that the equal signs are aligned with the equal signs of the preceding line:

$$\frac{\Delta Z_0}{Z_0} = \frac{1}{4\pi^2} \frac{w^2}{D^2 d^2}$$

$$K = \frac{\Delta Z_0}{2Z_0}$$

Many mathematical symbols must be penned by hand. The typist should leave the necessary space for hand lettering by the author. All complete equations are conventionally numbered consecutively within each chapter for easy reference purposes; the numbers appear within parentheses flush with the right margin of the text.

Example:

$$VSWR = \left(\frac{P_{s\,max}}{P_{s\,min}}\right)^{1/2} \tag{1}$$

$$P = c_1 s_{in}^2 \left(\frac{2\pi x}{g}\right) \tag{2}$$

A short formula within the text is set off by commas, as for example:

It can readily be seen that when $\lambda = 2a$, $\alpha = 90°$, or the waves are not propagated down the guide. . . .

Equations—no matter how short—containing fractions, square root signs, sub- or super-numerals, or letters require extra space above and below the text line and, therefore, should not be included in a text line but centered and placed on a line by themselves, as illustrated in preceding examples.
In summary:

1. Line up equal signs in a series of equations.
2. Keep all division lines (fraction bars) on the same level with equal signs.
3. Divide equations only after plus or minus signs but before equal signs in the second line.
4. In dividing equations, line up the second line with the equal sign or the first plus or minus sign in the first line.
5. Parentheses, braces, brackets, and integral signs should be the same heights as the expressions they enclose.

How to Handle Headings

Headings are mapping devices; they help make your report more readable. The features of the report are marked by sectional and subsectional titles or heads. Your headings correspond to the major divisions and subdivisions in your outline and in your table of contents. As mapping devices, headings serve to show relationships and subordinations; they should clearly indicate the logic of relationship and subordination throughout the report. A single system is recommended here, although in actual practice a number of conventions of showing this relationship and subordination are used (Figure 7.11).

First-Order Headings

First-order headings are written in all caps and centered 2 inches from the top of the page. Such a head constitutes a major text division and corresponds to the Roman and Arabic numerals of your outline. First-order headings begin on a new sheet of paper, and the text follows four typewriter spaces below.

Second-Order Headings

Second-order headings are placed flush with the left margin, two spaces below the last line of the preceding paragraph, and they are typed in all caps. They correspond to the capital letters in your outline and indicate major subdivisions of a section. The text follows two spaces below.

Documenting Your Report's References

> FIRST-ORDER HEADING
>
> SECOND-ORDER HEADING
>
> <u>Third-Order Heading</u>
>   <u>Fourth-Order Heading</u>. Text of paragraph follows on the same line as the fourth-order heading.

Figure 7.11 How to handle headings.

Third-Order Headings

Third-order headings are typed with initial caps of each word and are placed flush with the left margin and are underlined.

Fourth-Order Headings

These headings are indented five spaces and are also typed with initial caps. They are the same as the third-order headings except they are part of the paragraph of the text. The text follows on the same line.

Some reports follow through on the numbering system of the outline to conform with the various heads and their subheads of various rank. Certain organizations and many government agencies call for numbering of heads and subheads. The decimal system of numbering is frequently used.

Documenting Your Report's References

Why Documentation Is Necessary

Documentation is required in reports, professional papers, and other serious types of writing for three reasons:

1. To establish the validity of evidence. All important statements of fact not generally accepted as true, as well as other significant data, are supported by the presentation of evidence for validity if the exposition within the text itself does not offer the proof of the data or the facts. Direct reference to the source is provided so the writer's statements may be verified by the reader if he so chooses or if the reader wishes to extend his inquiry into the borrowed matter beyond the scope of this particular writing.
2. To acknowledge indebtedness. Each important statement of fact, data, or information and each conclusion or inference borrowed by the writer from someone

else should be acknowledged. A citation also is desirable when a conclusion or idea is paraphrased or its substance is borrowed and presented.
3. To provide the reader with information he might need or want about the subject matter a writer has borrowed or obtained from another source.

When any report, professional paper, book, or other type of serious writing contains information obtained from other publications, books, articles, and reports, such sources should be indicated under a list of references or a bibliography. Previously, I indicated that your report should have a bibliography if it uses information obtained from other sources. The bibliography follows the last page of the report and precedes the appendixes. The bibliography, as you will recall, is a list of the sources arranged alphabetically and numbered sequentially.

A Simple Documentation System

Scholarship has a long tradition of providing documentation for borrowed sources. The cited source material is documented in a footnote at the bottom of the page of the text upon which the borrowed material appears. However, this system of documentation is not as efficient as it might be. In this book, I have used what I consider an efficient and simple system of documentation. This system, instead of using a footnote at the bottom of the page, integrates the documentation reference within the text line following immediately the matter or source to be documented. The documentation reference begins with a bracket, then lists the sequential number of the bibliographic reference source being used, and is followed by a colon, the page numbers of that bibliographic reference, and a bracket; for example [7:113–19].

Let me illustrate more specifically how this system works. In Chapter 2, in my discussion of objectivity—a major characteristic of technical style—I used two quotations from the writings of T. H. Huxley. The first quote was from "The Lobster's Tail," a lecture Huxley gave before an uneducated but intelligent audience. I showed how he was able to reach and educate his audience by using the first person point of view and active voice. In the second quotation about a similar subject—"The Abdomen of the English Crayfish" (a small creature in the lobster family) taken from a college textbook—Huxley used the third person point of view and the passive voice. Please turn back to pages 18–19. You will note that the sources of the two quotations are documented as follows: [3:21] and [4:141]. Thus, in the documentation system I am recommending, instead of a superscript after the words, "modified in its details," and a footnote at the bottom of the page to document the reference, I use a bracket and the number 3 followed by :21. The 3 refers to the number in the sequential list of references at the end of Chapter 2. Similarly, [4:141] refers to item 4 in the list of references. Two things are accomplished by using this simple documentation system: 1) the concentration of the reader is not interrupted by shifting from the thought being read to a footnote at the bottom of the page detailing extraneous material, and 2) it saves you time and effort in providing the same documentation in both footnotes and the list of references.

Now let us suppose that instead of using a quotation, you used conclusions of an author derived from several different pages or different chapters of a book. This is handled simply. You would begin with a bracket, list the number with the sequence in the list of references, and supply the pages involved. Here is how it would work: [8:19; 23–30; 121–133; 140]. This documentation indicates that the paragraph you have written is a paraphrase of ideas expressed by source number 8 within the listed pages. What if you have paraphrased ideas from more than one source? In that case, your documentation would be similar; as for example: [7:237; 9:231–236; 13:88]. This indicates that you borrowed the expressed ideas from the sources and pages indicated.

This system is simple, efficient, and provides the reader with all the required information.

Using Footnotes

Although the above system has eliminated the need for footnotes to document borrowed reference material, footnotes may still be used and required in the following instances:

1. To amplify the discussion beyond the point permissible in the text
2. To provide cross-references to various parts of the report

For example, on page 8 of Chapter 1, I have a footnote of the first category. This footnote amplifies the information presented in the text. If this footnote of about 125 words were placed in the text, it would interrupt the continuity of the text matter for the reader. Although interesting, related, and amplifying, this information is not essential to the understanding of the text. Therefore, it is placed in the footnote.[2]

In the second type of footnote, where cross-references to various parts of the report are given, the writer is permitted to refer to material appearing in other parts of the report, such as the appendix or matters appearing in earlier or later portions of the report. This type of footnote aids the flow of the text, helps in clarity, and sends the reader, if he so chooses, to related information he may want to examine at that particular point.

I do want to make the point that documentation systems vary widely from college to college, discipline to discipline, journal to journal, and organization to organization. Journals and publishers within the same discipline may differ in the style they use to list references and where they place footnotes. Generally, in scientific fields, references are placed at the end of the paper or publication under headings such as "List of References" or "Literature Cited." The term *Bibliography* is usually reserved for a listing of literature pertinent to the topic reported but not necessarily mentioned in the paper. Thus, in this text I use the term *References* at the end of chapters to identify sources cited within those chapters. A bibliography

---

[2]Footnotes, as the term implies, are notes at the foot of the page, which the reader can read if he wants to or, after he reads the first line, he can see whether he wants to continue or not. The flow of the main text is not impeded by this device.

appears at the end of the book to identify sources providing supplementary information appropriate to technical report writing, the subject of this text.

In the fields of chemistry and physics, it is customary to omit the title of the article. Names of journals are given in abbreviated form, for example:

> M. Heaven, T. A. Miller, V. E. Bondybey, J. Chem. Phys. 80, 51 (1984)

Other journals, especially in the biological sciences, require not only inclusive pagination but also full titles of articles. The style manual of the Council of Biology Editors provides the following as a proper example of a citation for biological journals [1]:

> Steele, R. D. Role of 3-ethylthiopropionate in ethionine metabolism and toxicity in rats. J. Nutr. 112:118–125; 1982.

Note its stylistic characteristics:

1. Only the first word in the title is capitalized.
2. The volume and year but not the month are identified.
3. Full pagination is given.
4. *Journal of Nutrition* is abbreviated.
5. The title of the article does not have quotation marks around it nor is the title of the journal in italics.
6. A semicolon is used to separate the year of publication from the rest of the citation.

You can see that the number of documentation systems used in the various fields make the process more complicated and confusing than it ought to be. The system recommended in this text is used most often in the social sciences. Simple and efficient, it provides the reader all the information he needs. Nevertheless, you should become familiar with how the field of your discipline handles references and footnotes. An assignment at the end of this chapter will deal with that task.

Bibliography

The bibliography is a list of references used by the writer in his report. When the list of references is large, it is sometimes convenient to classify items according to types of references, listing in separate categories all books, periodical literature, publications of learned societies and organizations, government publications, encyclopedia articles, and manuscripts and unpublished materials. In most instances, the alphabetically and sequentially numbered bibliography is the most convenient.

Each bibliographic reference should list the complete elements that will help to identify the source. These bibliographical elements are author, surname first; title; place of publication; publisher; date; page numbers. In the case of a report or government publication that is classified, the security classification will be indicated. Listed below are examples of various bibliographic references and the conventional way of indicating them in a bibliography.

1. *Anglo-American Cataloging Rules,* prepared by the American Library Association, the Library of Congress, the Library Association, and the Canadian Library Association, 1967, 400pp.
2. Cain, Sandra E., and Jack M. Evans. *Sciencing, An Involvement Approach to Elementary Science Methods,* 3d ed. Columbus, Ohio: Merrill, 1990, pp. 84–91.
3. *Calloway Workshop, 1990.* Kansas City: Calloway Productions, 1995.
4. Clayman, Charles B., ed. *The American Medical Association Medical Encyclopedia,* vol. 1. Pleasantville, N.Y.: The Readers' Digest Association, Inc., published with permission of Random House, 1989, pp. 158–59.
5. Council of Biology Editors. *Style Manual,* 5th ed. Washington, D.C.: American Institute of Biological Sciences, 1983.
6. Directorate of Small and Disadvantaged Business Utilization, Office of the Secretary of Defense. *Guide to the Preparation of Offers for Selling to the Military.* Washington, D.C.: U.S. Government Printing Office, n.d.
7. Duran, Lise W., and E. S. Metcalf. "Analysis of the murine *Salmonella tythimurium*-specific B-cell repertoire." Posterboard presentation at the Annual Federation of American Societies for Experimental Biology, Chicago, April 11, 1983.
8. Duran, Lise W., and Larry R. Pease. "Tracing the Evolution of H-2D Region Genes Using Sequences Associated with a Repetitive Element." *The Journal of Immunology* (July 1, 1988): 295–301.
9. Flower, Linda, and John R. Hayes. "Plans that Guide the Composing Process." In *Writing: The Nature, Development, and Teaching of Written Communication,* edited by Carl H. Frederickson and Joseph F. Dominic. Hillsdale, N.J.: Lawrence Erlbaum, 1981, pp. 55–57.
10. Gilsdorf, J. W. "Writing to Persuade." *IEEE Transactions on Professional Communication,* PC-30.2 (June 1987):68–73.
11. Green, Bonnie L., "Overview and Research Recommendations." *Role Stressors and Supports for Emergency Workers, Proceedings from a 1984 Workshop by the Center for Mental Health Studies of Emergencies and the Federal Emergency Management Agency,* DHHS Publication No. (ADM)85-1408. Rockville, Md.: National Institute of Mental Health, 1985, pp. 1–20.
12. *Health Show.* Transcript, ABC Television Program, August 26, 1990.
13. Human Relations Commission. *Human Rights Laws.* Rockville, Md.: Montgomery Country Government, Maryland, n.d., 58pp.
14. Luhn, H. P. "Selective Dissemination of New Information With the Aid of Electronic Processing." In *H. P. Luhn Pioneer in Information Science, Selected Works.* edited by Clair K. Schultz. Yorktown Heights, N.Y.: Sparten Books, 1968, pp. 246–54. (Originally published by IBM Corporation, Advance Systems Development Division, Yorktown Height, NY, November 30, 1959.)
15. *The New York Times.* pp. 1, 26, December 21, 1996.

16. Norstrom, David M., Gerald A. Francis, and Rolland D. King. *Lifts and Wheelchairs, Securement for Buses and Paratransit Vehicles, A Companion Document to the Advisory Panel Accessible Transportation Guidelines Specifications.* (Prepared for the Architectural and Transportation Barriers Compliance Board.) Columbus, Ohio: Battelle Memorial Institute, n.d.

17. Oren, T. "The Architecture of Static Hypertexts." *Hypertext '87 Papers.* (Proceedings of a conference held at the University of North Carolina, Chapel Hill.) Chapel Hill, N.C.: University of North Carolina, 1988, pp. 291–306.

18. Stone, Richard. "An Artificial Eye May be Within Sight, Work Progresses on a Prosthesis for Reading." *The Washington Post,* August 20, 1990, p. A3.

19. *TDD (Telecommunication Devices for the Deaf).* Final report prepared for the U.S. Architectural and Transportation Barriers Compliance Board, Woodstock, Va.: Applied Concepts Corporation, August 3, 1984, 113 pp.

20. Tracey, J. R. *The Sequential Topical (STOP) Storyboarding Method of Organizing Reports and Proposals, A Group Book-building Technique.* Fullerton, Calif.: Hughes Aircraft Company, November, 1968.

21. Weisman, Alan. *La Frontera, The United States Border with Mexico.* (Photographs by Jay Dusard.) San Diego: Harcourt Brace Jovanovich, 1986, pp. 123–44.

22. Weisman, Harlan F. "Acute Infarct Expansion and Chronic Enlargement." Paper presented at the Post Graduate Seminar on Ventricular Remodeling after Myocardial Infarction, sponsored by the Council on Clinical Cardiology at the American Heart Association Annual Scientific Sessions, November 12–16, 1989.

23. Weisman, Harlan F., et al. "Soluble Human Complement Receptor Type 1: In Vivo Inhibitor of Complement Suppressing Post-Ischemic Myocardial Inflammation and Necroses." *Science* (July 13, 1990), 146–51.

24. Williams, Abbi J. Interview on Real Estate Pre-settlement Procedures, held at Beckett, Cromwell & Myers, Settlements Ltd., September 3, 1990.

25. Wolfe, W. M. (Moderator). "How Can Effectiveness of Analysis Centers Be Measured." Addendum to the *Proceedings of the Ad Hoc Forum for Information Analysis Center Managers, Directors, and Professional Analysts,* held at the Battelle Memorial Institute, Columbus, Ohio, November 9–11, 1965. (Unpublished manuscript, n.d., 53 pp.)

Proofreading

After you have finished typing your report, you must proofread the copy. You are making a quality control check of the typing. In this proofreading, you may find not only typographical errors but also other errors that you somehow missed earlier. Here is what you need to do in the proofing of the final draft:

1. Place the draft from which the final copy was typed next to the final copy. Use the index finger of each hand to make a word-for-word comparison between the two.

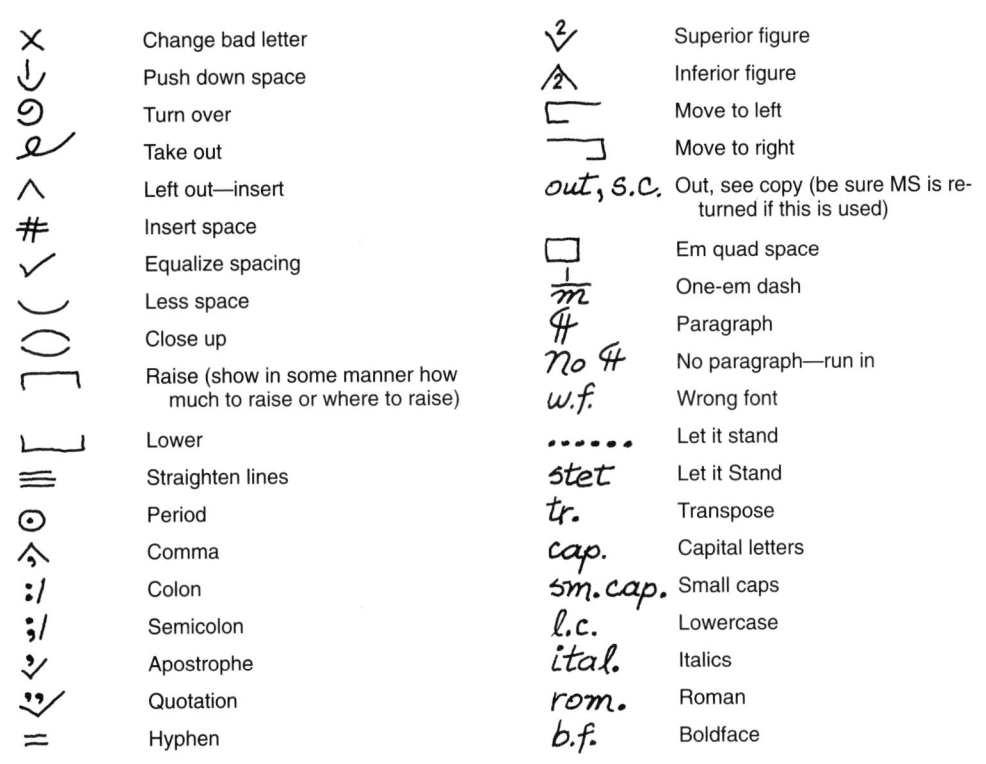

Mark	Meaning	Mark	Meaning
✗	Change bad letter	✌²	Superior figure
⌴	Push down space	⌃₂	Inferior figure
᧐	Turn over	⌐	Move to left
ℓ	Take out	⌐	Move to right
∧	Left out—insert	*out, s.c.*	Out, see copy (be sure MS is returned if this is used)
#	Insert space	⌑	Em quad space
✓	Equalize spacing	⊥/m	One-em dash
⌣	Less space	¶	Paragraph
◠	Close up	*no ¶*	No paragraph—run in
⌐	Raise (show in some manner how much to raise or where to raise)	*w.f.*	Wrong font
⌴ ⌴	Lower	⋯⋯	Let it stand
≡	Straighten lines	*stet*	Let it Stand
⊙	Period	*tr.*	Transpose
⌃	Comma	*cap.*	Capital letters
:/	Colon	*sm. cap.*	Small caps
;/	Semicolon	*l.c.*	Lowercase
᾽	Apostrophe	*ital.*	Italics
᾽᾽/	Quotation	*rom.*	Roman
=	Hyphen	*b.f.*	Boldface

Many of the proofreaders' marks may also be utilized in marking manuscripts.

Capitals	Comparative Data	COMPARATIVE DATA
Caps and small caps	COMPARATIVE DATA	COMPARATIVE DATA
Small caps	Comparative Data	COMPARATIVE DATA
Italic	Current Notes	*Current Notes*
Italic caps	Current Notes	*CURRENT NOTES*
Boldface	News and Notes	**News and Notes**
Boldface Italic	News and Notes	***News and Notes***
Boldface Italic Caps	News and Notes	***NEWS AND NOTES***
To change caps to caps and lowercase	CONCLUSIONS	
To change caps to caps and small caps	CONCLUSIONS	
Flush left	⌐	
Flush right	⌐	
Indented matter	⌐ ⌐	
Center	⟨COMMENT⟩	
Run in	COMPARATIVE TECHNICAL DATA	

◯   *Close up space.* Use when your typewriter skips a letter or when a letter is deleted in a word.

\#   *Open a space.* Insert a space between words run together.

Figure 7.12 Proofreaders' marks and how to use them.

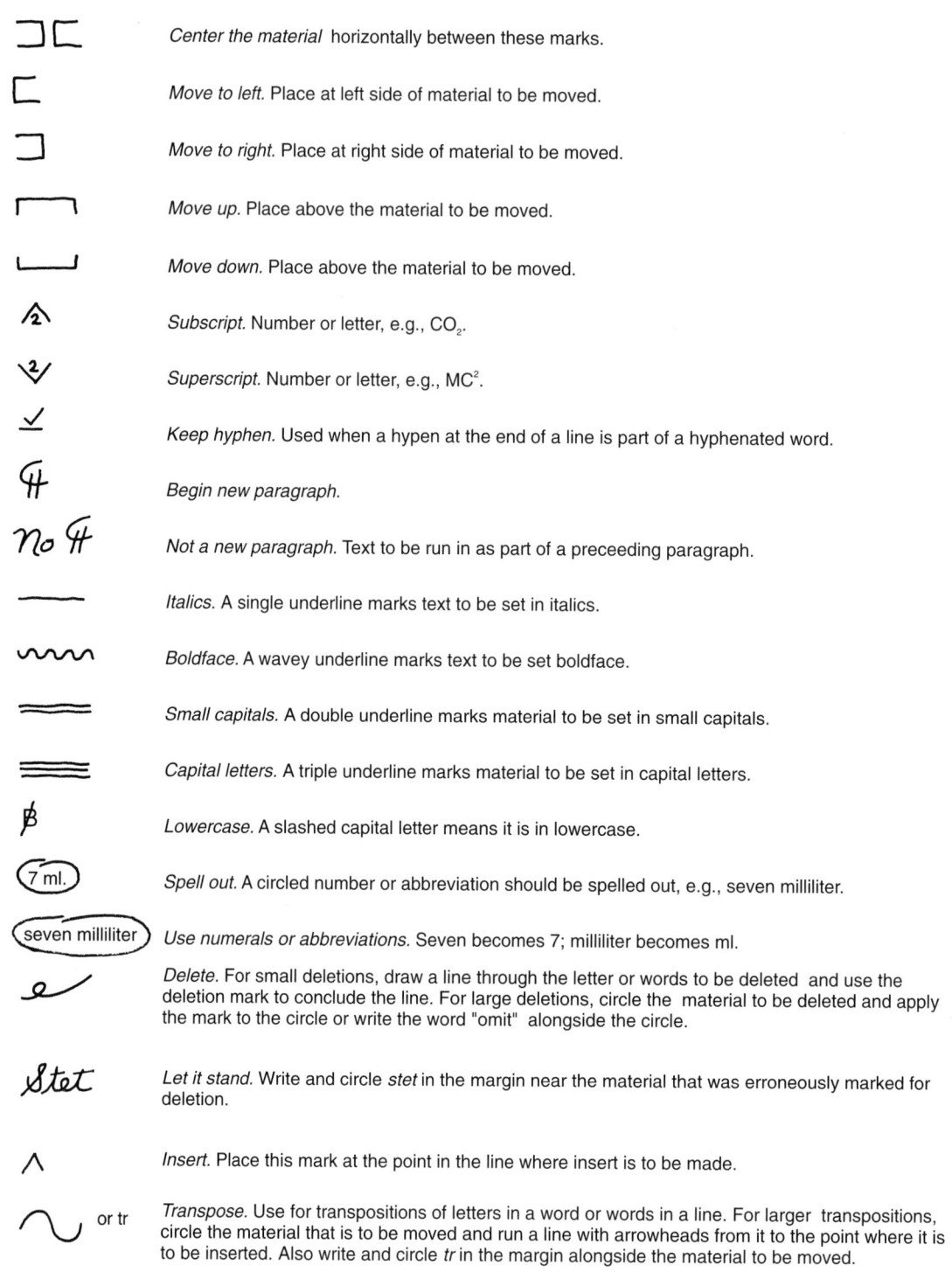

][	*Center the material* horizontally between these marks.
[	*Move to left.* Place at left side of material to be moved.
]	*Move to right.* Place at right side of material to be moved.
⌐¬	*Move up.* Place above the material to be moved.
⌊⌋	*Move down.* Place above the material to be moved.
/2\	*Subscript.* Number or letter, e.g., CO_2.
\2/	*Superscript.* Number or letter, e.g., MC^2.
‿	*Keep hyphen.* Used when a hypen at the end of a line is part of a hyphenated word.
¶	*Begin new paragraph.*
no ¶	*Not a new paragraph.* Text to be run in as part of a preceeding paragraph.
___	*Italics.* A single underline marks text to be set in italics.
∼∼∼	*Boldface.* A wavey underline marks text to be set boldface.
===	*Small capitals.* A double underline marks material to be set in small capitals.
≡≡≡	*Capital letters.* A triple underline marks material to be set in capital letters.
⌿B	*Lowercase.* A slashed capital letter means it is in lowercase.
(7 ml.)	*Spell out.* A circled number or abbreviation should be spelled out, e.g., seven milliliter.
(seven milliliter)	*Use numerals or abbreviations.* Seven becomes 7; milliliter becomes ml.
ℓ	*Delete.* For small deletions, draw a line through the letter or words to be deleted and use the deletion mark to conclude the line. For large deletions, circle the material to be deleted and apply the mark to the circle or write the word "omit" alongside the circle.
Stet	*Let it stand.* Write and circle *stet* in the margin near the material that was erroneously marked for deletion.
∧	*Insert.* Place this mark at the point in the line where insert is to be made.
∼ or tr	*Transpose.* Use for transpositions of letters in a word or words in a line. For larger transpositions, circle the material that is to be moved and run a line with arrowheads from it to the point where it is to be inserted. Also write and circle *tr* in the margin alongside the material to be moved.

Figure 7.12 (*continued*)

2. Examine each page to be sure that all corrections have been made and that the page is clean and neat in appearance.
3. Check that headings and text have consistent and proper spacing.
4. Read the text carefully to ensure that no words or lines have been omitted and that extraneous words or text lines or material have not been added.
5. Note any corrections lightly in pencil above the line. Use proofreading symbols if you are acquainted with them (Figure 7.12).
6. Check for proper pagination, numerical sequences (for section, figure, and footnote numbering), capitalization, consistency of style, and spelling.

Editors use printers' conventional proofreaders' marks to edit a manuscript. Figure 7.12 shows the range of proofreading marks. Editors use a selected number of these marks to indicate changes and instructions. All proofreaders' marks require a double marking—one in the body of the text at the point of correction and a corresponding mark in the margin, which calls attention to the fact that there is a correction to be made at this point. A correction marked only in the text and not in the margin may be missed by the printer.

Chapter in Brief

We examined the activities involved in the processes of writing, revising, editing, and printing the formal report. Included in our examination were matters of content, organization, language, and style. How computer technology helps in composition, revision, editing, use of graphics, and printing was also discussed. Format and mechanics considerations were then detailed.

Chapter Focal Points

- Writing process
- Revision and editing process
- Revising and editing with a word processor
- Software aids in revision and editing
- Format and mechanics
- Graphics and tables
- Documentation
- Proofreading
- Printing the report

Questions for Discussion

1. Recall your past written assignments both in this course and other courses. How did you revise and edit your written work? Can you describe step by step how you went about the revision and editing process to generate the final document you turned in? Share

your methods with the class, and discuss alternative editing procedures. Use the insights you gain from this class discussion to revise and edit your major report, following the assignments below.

Assignments

1. Write your instructor a memo addressing the following matters in the report you are writing in this course:
   a. On an average, how many words per sentence and how many syllables per hundred words do you have in your report?
   b. Are half the sentences in your report complex sentences? Simple sentences comprise what percentage of your paper? Compound? Other types of sentences?
   c. On your rough draft, underline the topic sentences in your report. Circle transition devices and structural paragraphs.
   d. Test each of your paragraphs by these criteria:

   What is the central idea (topic sentence)?

   What must the reader know to support it or explain it?

   Is there anything in it not related to the topic sentence?

   Are the sentences organized in a sequence that is sufficiently logical to support or explain the topic sentence clearly?

   e. Check your report for the common editing problems noted in this chapter.
   f. Check your report for the format considerations noted in this chapter.
   g. Does your report have sufficient variety in sentence length and structure to promote interest and avoid monotony? Does your report have transitional paragraphs, sentences, phrases?
   h. Do the subjects and verbs in your sentences agree grammatically?
   i. Does each "it," "who," "which," and "that" clause refer to a definite word?
   j. Does the punctuation help your reader reach the exact meaning you want him to reach?
   k. Are your words and phrases accurate and precise?
   l. Is all spelling accurate?
   m. Do your headings accurately and logically reflect the content matter they describe?
   n. Does your report have adequate graphics to describe and present its data efficiently?
   o. If you are using tables in your report, do they conform to the guidelines on pages 184–185?
2. Using the information in this memo and your instructor's comments, edit and rewrite the draft of the report text you prepared in Chapter 6.
3. Go to your library. Examine the documentation in a representative group of scientific/technical periodicals. What variations do you find among periodicals in the same field? In different fields? Are there variations in details of punctuation and capitalization or in content and arrangement? Report your findings to your class.
4. Write to a professional organization in your field or discipline to obtain a copy of the guidelines or manual for its documentation practices. As a separate assignment, prepare

the list of references/bibliography/footnotes required in your term assignment in accordance with those practiced in your declared professional field.
5. Prepare documentation, references, and bibliography for the report you are writing in accordance with the style and procedures recommended in this chapter. Turn these in to your instructor for comment.
6. Prepare a table of contents for your report.

References

1. *CBE Style Manual, Fifth Edition.* Bethesda, Md.: Council of Biology Editors, 1983.
2. *Energy Conservation, Gas Heat Pumps: More Heat from Natural Gas,* Washington, D.C.: Office of Public Affairs, Energy Research and Development Administration, 1977.
3. Ken Cook Company, Milwaukee, Wis., 1978.
4. *Nuclear Energy for Desalting.* Oak Ridge, Tenn.: U.S. Atomic Energy Commission, Division of Technical Information, September 1966.
5. U.S. Energy Research and Development Administration, Washington, D.C., n.d.
6. *Weapons Systems Fundamentals, Basic Weapons Systems Components,* NAVWEPS OP3000, vol. 1. Washington, D.C.: U.S. Government Printing Office, July 15, 1960.
7. Weisman, Harlan F., M.D., and Michelle K. Leppo. Division of Cardiology, Johns Hopkins Medical Institutions, 1990.
8. *Westinghouse Engineer.* Westinghouse Electric Research and Development Center, March 1960.

8
Technical Correspondence

Chapter Objective

Provide understanding of the principles and techniques of technical correspondence and provide proficiency in its various types with emphasis on job applications.

Chapter Focus

- Role of correspondence in science, technology, and industry
- Psychology of correspondence
- Prewriting
- Format considerations
- Employment letters
- Inquiries and responses
- Quotation letters
- Claim letters
- Letters of instruction
- Electronic technology in correspondence

Role of Correspondence in Industry and Technology

Correspondence is the basic communication instrument in business and industry. Much of the activity of science and technology is conducted through letters; many technical reports are written in letter form. It is not only technical administrators and their subordinates but also the people in the laboratory who daily must use correspondence to accomplish their work. Even the basic science researcher in the relative isolation of the laboratory is called upon to write letters. She sends out inquiries and requests, answers inquiries and requests, orders equipment, sends acknowledgments, writes letters of instruction, and on certain occasions writes sales letters and letters of adjustment. When she wants to change jobs, she will write an application letter.

Because the technical worker's successful activity depends very much on social interaction, we should examine the mechanics of correspondence, the form constituting a major portion of such interaction. Moreover, many of the principles of letter writing apply to report writing. Whereas letters are intended for a single reader and reports for a wide range of readers, letters, like reports or any piece of organized information, receive the classical structure of a beginning (which indicates the purpose), a middle (which elaborates on or develops the purpose), and an ending (which completes the purpose). Neither the report nor the business letter is written for the pleasure of the writer or reader. It is intended for some practical objective. The distinguishing dissimilarity between the report and the business letter is the definite intrusion of personal elements in the letter. Modern business letters are reader centered. Their style is based on the premise that a business letter communicates an attitude as well as a message. Reports, on the other hand, though directed toward a specific audience, are impersonal and objective. The letter tends to establish a personal relationship between the writer and the reader. The stress in the report is on fact; in the letter, it is on rapport.

The intention of this chapter is not to replace a text or handbook on business correspondence but to offer fundamentals, principles, and techniques of modern business correspondence that will be useful to the technical person. A list of some of the better texts on business correspondence will be found in the references at the end of the book.

Psychology of Correspondence

The modern business writer is much concerned with the reader. The "You Psychology" plays an important role in letter composition. "Put yourself in your reader's shoes" is the maxim. When you compose a letter, therefore, remember you are writing to a specific reader who is a human being. The reader of your letter is interested only in how your message will benefit *her*. She will not buy your product or service merely because you want her business. She will not hire you merely because you want to work for her. She will not accept delay in the delivery of your product only because you are having procurement problems. She will not buy for cash just because you ask her to. If your letter is to appeal to her, it must be constructed in terms of benefit to her. You must convince her that, by hiring you, she will get financial returns. You must show her that the material you want to use in the product she ordered is worth her waiting for. You must prove that her buying for cash is the best thing for her. Visualize your reader; tailor and personalize your letter specifically to her. Begin your letter with something that will be of interest to her. For example, do not say, "In order to help us simplify our problems in processing orders, we require customers to include our work order number in their correspondence to us." Would it not be better to say, "So that your order may be promptly serviced, please include our assigned work order number in your correspondence"?

Write simply, write naturally. Make your letter sound as if you were talking directly to your reader. Business English is not pompous English; it is a clear and friendly language. Stilted, formal letters build a fence between the writer and the reader. Compare "Please be assured, kind sir, of our continued esteem and constant desire to be of service in any capacity" with "We are always glad to help in any way we can."

Be sure that the general appearance of your letter creates a favorable impression. We like certain people because their appearance impressed us favorably the first time we met them. The same principle holds for letters. If you receive a letter that is neatly and evenly typed; well centered; correctly punctuated; and free from typing, spelling, and grammatical errors; your impression of the writer is likely to be a favorable one. Your letters can be one of the best public relations and advertising mediums because they reveal the quality of the service that can be expected from the writer.

Prewriting—Determining Your Purpose

No one can write a good letter without being exactly sure what she is after. Good letters are based on planning. Before starting to write, ask yourself: What do I want this letter to do? What action do I want the reader to take? What impression do I want to leave with the reader? If you have to answer a letter, read carefully the letter you have received; underline questions or statements to be answered; jot down comments in the margin. In composing a reply, it is often helpful to look through past correspondence. When you have gained all the background and facts, ask yourself: What is the most important fact to the reader? The most important fact should usually be dealt with first; let the rest follow in logical sequence.

Organizing Your Letter—Role of the Paragraph

Set a number of paragraphs—one for each main thought or fact—before you start. This will force you to order your thoughts and prevent confused ramblings. Make use of 1-2-3 or a-b-c lists wherever possible to streamline your message. This will help to clarify and emphasize.

Use the first paragraph to tell your reader what the letter is all about. Link it with any previous correspondence, but do not repeat the subject of the other person's letter as a preliminary to your reply. The result will be something trite and clumsy like, "In reply to your letter of April 25 requesting. . . ." Neither is the participial type of opening, like "Regarding your letter of April 25," any better. A simple "Thank you for your letter of April 25," or "Thank you for your quotation request of April 25" is effective. Business people do not read letters for pleasure. They want letters to be brief and to the point. Begin your letter directly. For example, "Production tells me we can now promise delivery of the 48 items of your order No. P-1465 on August 18, or a day or two sooner." Or "Here is some information about our multiplexers, which we are very glad to send you."

Try to see the closing paragraph before you begin; keep moving toward it when you set down your opening sentences. Use the last paragraph to make it easier for your reader to take the action you want taken, or use it to build a favorable attitude when no action is needed. When your message is completed, stop. For example, "Please send us the completed forms by May 15. We'll do the rest." Or "If you have a special measurements problem, our engineers might be able to help you. Just call us, and we'll be glad to send someone to see you."

Keep sentences and paragraphs short. Business letter experts recommend a sentence averaging twenty words; but vary sentence length. Opening and closing paragraphs should be brief. The longest paragraphs usually come in the middle of the letter. Paragraphs keep thoughts together that belong together. They enable the reader to get your meaning as easily and as certainly as possible.

Read your letter carefully before you sign it. Once it goes out, *you*, the signer, are responsible for any errors or confusion.

Format of the Letter

Although content is certainly more important than format or style, all of us recognize that style and format are to a letter what dress and appearance are to an individual. None of us would appear for a job or interview sloppily dressed or covered with mud. Similarly, when we send a letter, it speaks for us in a business situation. A single error may nullify an otherwise well-written letter. The receiver of the letter can evaluate the message only by the letter's total impression. If even a minor aspect suggests carelessness, slovenliness, or inaccuracy, the reader loses confidence in the more fundamental worth of the message. Therefore, an examination of format and style is important.

Most organizations and companies use one of three format styles in their letters—the **block,** the **semiblock,** and the **simplified** style. Examples are shown in Figures 8.1, 8.2, and 8.3.

Some organizations use all three styles or combinations of them. Many federal agencies have decreed the use of the simplified style to increase the productivity of their typists and word processor operators. Many companies have style manuals for letters and memoranda to achieve uniformity and excellence. If the organization or company for which you work has such a manual, follow its recommendations.

HILL AND KNOWLTON, INC.

Public Relations Counsel
150 East Forty-second Street
New York, N.Y. 10017

February 1, 19__

Professor Herman M. Weisman
1801 Richmond Road
Westport, MD 43214

Dear Professor Weisman:

I am sorry that it has taken so long to reply to your letter of November 27, requesting information about forms used in business correspondence.

Hill and Knowlton, Inc., has issued a <u>Secretarial Guide to Style</u> as a guide to the forms preferred when writing letters, memoranda, and reports. As can be noted from some of the samples given at the back of the Guide, indentation is preferred, but block form, which I am using, is also acceptable. Single space for letters and memoranda is also preferred, but length will sometimes dictate style.

I am sorry that we are not able to provide specimens of letters, memos, and reports, but feel that the material contained in the Guide will be helpful. As indicated in the introduction, the booklet is a supplement to the <u>Complete Secretary's Handbook</u> and the <u>Correspondence Handbook</u>, but does not conform in all instances to these aids.

I hope that we have been able to supply some of the answers you are seeking. We shall be happy to assist you if you wish additional information.

Sincerely yours,

Thelma T. Scrivens
Administrative Assistant
Education Department

TTS:lt
enclosure

Figure 8.1 *The block style.*

THE FORD MOTOR COMPANY

The American Road
Dearborn, Michigan
June 12, 19__

Dr. Herman Weisman
1801 Richmond Road
Westport, MD 43214

Dear Dr. Weisman:

Thank you for the opportunity to help you prepare your students for what the business world will require in the field of report and letter writing. The importance of this field cannot be emphasized too much, for the ability to write good reports and letters is a basic requirement for business success.

All of the Ford Motor Company training courses on writing stress three things:

1. Be brief—Businesspersons do not read letters and reports for pleasure, so make them short and to the point.

2. Be specific—Do not make the reader interpret your letter.

3. Be conversational—Stilted, formal letters build a barrier between the writer and the reader.

The type format preferred by our company is described in the enclosed copies of our standards on internal and external communications. Also enclosed are copies of letters and reports written by our employees.

If you need any additional information, please contact us.

Very truly yours,

FORD MOTOR COMPANY

W.J. Gough, Jr., Supervisor
Offices Services Section
Administrative Services Department
Finance Staff

WJG:rn
Enclosures

Figure 8.2 The semiblock style.

HANSON PRINTING MACHINERY

2222 22 Street S.E. Washington, D.C. 20020

10 July 19__

Dr. Herman M. Weisman
1801 Richmond Road
Westport, MD 43214

Enclosed is the Handy Type Index and Price List you recently requested from American Type Founders.

We are area distributors for American Type Founders and stock practically all of the currently popular faces in the Washington, D.C., area. You may be assured that prompt attention will be given to your order when it is received.

We will be pleased to furnish any further information concerning printing equipment or supplies that you may need. Please give us the opportunity of serving you.

W. Wayne Gilbert

WWG:mje
Enclosure

Figure 8.3 The simplified style.

205

The semiblock differs from the block format only in that the paragraphs in the body of the letter are indented. The block and simplified block formats are used in about 80 percent of all types of business letters. The simplified letter is very efficient in that it eliminates the need for indenting and tabulating by the typist, but some readers are disturbed by its unbalanced appearance and its omission of the salutation and complimentary close. Management consultant firms have a tendency to use this form because it gives the appearance of efficiency. Many advertising firms also use it because of the breezy appearance. The simplified letter form, on occasion, replaces the missing salutation with a subject line and frequently also omits the dictator's and typist's initials.

Mechanical Details

Stationery

Stationery should be of a good quality of unruled 8½-by-11-inch white bond paper. Company or organization preprinted letterhead should be used when appropriate. For continuation pages, bond of the same size, quality, and color as the letterhead should be used.

The first thing the recipient notices about your letter is its envelope. The envelope deserves as much care as the letter it contains. Assure its accuracy by checking it with the address printed on the letterhead of the company to which you are writing. The elements of neatness and attractiveness are just as important in typing the envelope as in typing the letter.

Addresses on envelopes should be typed in block style, double-spaced if the address is in three lines and single-spaced if the address contains more than three lines. Postal authorities require that the zip code be used. Foreign countries are typed in capitals. Use no abbreviations or punctuation for the end of the line. The person's name, title, and the name of the branch or department should precede the street address, city, and state. *Special delivery* or *registered* should be typed in capitals several spaces above the address. If an attention line is used in the letter, it should be typed on the envelope in the lower left-hand corner. If the notation *Personal* is desired on the envelope, it should appear in the same position as the attention line.

Ms. Jennifer Williams
Senior Vice President
Hill and Langer Company
93 Mill Pond Road
Dobbs Ferry, NY 10522

Personal

The Sawyer Corporation
62 Broadway
New York, NY 10004

Attention: Personnel Department

Framing a Letter on the Page

A typed letter should be placed on the page so the white margins serve as the frame around it. Practice and convention call for more white space at the bottom than at the top unless the length of the letter makes this impossible. The side margins should be approximately equal and usually should be no wider than the bottom margin. Side margins are usually from 1 to 2 inches, depending on the length of the letter. The bottom margin should never be less than 1 inch below the last typed word. The right-hand margin should be as even as possible. The body of the letter proper should be placed partly above and partly below the center of the page. A short letter makes a better appearance if it is more than half above the center of the page. The placement of the letter on the page, frequently referred to as centering, can be achieved by starting the first line of the inside address at a chosen depth to give the most pleasing appearance of white space above and below the letter. The shorter the message, the lower the inside address is placed.

The Heading

When a preprinted letterhead is not used, the writer includes a heading to help identify the source of the letter. The heading includes the address, but not the name, of the writer. The street address is on one line and the city, state, and zip code on another. The date follows the city and state line. The heading is placed at the right side of the page. Here are some examples of headings:

1303 Springfield Drive
Ft. Collins, CO 80521
November 8, 19__

87 Cherry Creek Lane
Minneapolis, MN 55421
March 29, 19__

605 West 112th Street
New York, NY 10026
December 21, 19__

The Date Line

The purpose of the date line is to record the date the letter is written and signed. When preprinted letterhead stationery is used, it is the first item typed on the page. If ordinary bond paper is used, in practice, the date line has become the last element of the heading. (Note the examples above.) With letterhead stationery, the date line can be centered or placed on the right or the left depending upon the style of layout. Sometimes the design of the letterhead will suggest one position or the other. When the date line is placed on the right, it should end flush with the right-hand margin of the letter. If the letter is very short, the date line should be dropped down to give a better balance to the page. The month should be spelled out in full and no period used after the year.

The Inside Address

The purpose of the inside address is to identify the receiver of the letter by giving the complete name and address of the person or organization to whom the letter is being sent. It is usually placed four to six lines below the date line. No punctuation is used at the end of any line in the address. Write out *street* or *avenue* as well as the name of the city.

For the state, use standard U.S. Postal Service two-letter abbreviations. Always include the zip code after the state abbreviation. Include the name and title of the addressee if one is appropriate. Otherwise, use a courtesy title such as Mr., Mrs., Miss, or Ms.:

> Mr. Thomas B. Morse
> 1620 Dakota Avenue
> Cincinnati, OH 45229

> Ms. Abbi J. Weisman
> 1303 Springfield Drive
> Fort Collins, CO 80521

When a title follows the name of an addressee, it is written on the same line, unless it is unusually long; then the title is placed on the next line:

> Mr. Jason Duran, President
> General Computers, Inc.
> 43 Madison Avenue
> Milwaukee, WI 53204

> Dr. Sylvia Tarkington
> Assistant Director, Engineering
> True Ohm Resistor Corporation
> 200 Market Street, Suite 2400
> Pennsylvania Building
> Philadelphia, PA 19102

The Attention Line and Subject Line

The attention line is intended to direct the letter to the person or department especially concerned. An attention line provides a less personal way of addressing an individual than placing his name at the head of the inside address. It is losing favor, however, since current practice is to address letters to individuals. If a subject line is to be used, it should be typed below or in place of the attention line.

> The J.B. McConnell Company
> 1812 Atlantic Avenue
> Brooklyn, NY 11233
>
> Attention: Mr. Joseph Rich, Comptroller
> Subject: <u>Payment for Crystal Diodes</u>
>
> Dear J.B. McConnell Company:

The attention line is placed two spaces below the last line of the inside address; it should not be in capitals, nor is it usually indented. Practice varies on how it appears. No end punctuation marks are used. Here is an example:

>General Motors Corporation
>General Motors Technical Center
>P.O. Box 117, North Penn Station
>Detroit, MI 41202
>
>Attention: Mr. Raymond O. Darling
>　　　　　Educational Relations Section

The purpose of the subject line is immediate communication of the topic of the letter, thus expediting its objective. The subject line is also an aid to filing. It should be placed conspicuously, though practice varies on exact placement. Some company correspondence manuals use the word *Subject* or *Reference* or the abbreviation for reference, *RE*. Others omit these. The prevailing use of the subject line in government correspondence has stimulated its wide use. The National Office Management Association also encourages its use. The subject line may be placed: on the same line with the salutation, two line spaces below the last line of the inside address, or so that it ends at the right-hand margin of the letter. Here are some examples:

>Avco Manufacturing Corporation
>420 Lexington Avenue
>New York, NY 10017
>
>Subject: <u>Our Purchase Order No. T1052</u>
>
>Avco Manufacturing Corporation
>420 Lexington Avenue
>New York, NY 10017
>
>Gentlemen: <u>Our Purchase Order No. T1052</u>
>
>Avco Manufacturing Corporation
>420 Lexington Avenue
>New York, NY 10017
>
>　　　　　　　　　　　　　　　　<u>Our Purchase Order No. T1052</u>
>
>Ladies/Gentlemen:

The first letters of important words in the subject line should be capitalized. Underscoring may or may not be used depending upon personal preference.

The Salutation

The salutation originated as a form of greeting. The simplified letter form omits it entirely as old-fashioned and superfluous. It is placed two line spaces below the inside address or six spaces if an attention or a subject line is used. Use a colon after the salutation. There is an increasing tendency to use the open pattern of punctuation. An open pattern omits commas and other punctuation marks unless meaning would be misinterpreted by the omission. A closed punctuation pattern makes liberal use of commas and other punctuation marks, placing one wherever tradition or grammatical structure allows. In the open punctuation pattern, the colon is omitted in the salutation and the comma omitted after the complimentary close. In business correspondence, if the writer and addressee have a friendly relationship, a comma often replaces the colon after the salutation. Conventionally, the word *Dear* precedes the person addressed unless a company or group is the recipient of the letter:

    Dear Mr. Smith: (Preferred) *or*
    Dear Sir: (closed)
    Dear Bill   (open)

    Dear Dr. Jones: (Preferred) *or*
    Dear Sir: (closed)
    Dear Dr. Jones   (open)

    Dear Mrs. Smith: (Preferred) *or*
    Dear Madam: (closed)
    Dear Mrs. Smith   (open)
    Dear Ms. Smith: (but never Dear Madam when Ms. is used)
    Dear J.B. McConnell Company: (closed)

Gentlemen: is the correct form in addressing a group of men, and *Ladies:* in addressing more than two women. When two persons are addressed, use both names:

    Dear Dr. Jones and Mr. Smith:
    Dear Mrs. Brewer and Ms. Handley:

Gentlemen has been the predominant way of addressing a company or organization. However, more women make up companies and organizations, more letters addressed to a group use the salutation, *Dear Ladies/Gentlemen:*.

    American Psychological Association
    1200 17th Street, N.W.
    Washington, D.C. 20036

    Dear Ladies/Gentlemen:

The Body of the Letter

Begin the body of the letter two line spaces below the salutation. Whether the body is indented, of course, depends upon the style used. Single-space letters that are of average length or longer. Short letters of five lines or less may be double-spaced. Always double-space between paragraphs in single-spaced letters. Quoted matter of three or more lines is indented at least five spaces from both margins. Very short letters that are double-spaced should use the semiblock form to make paragraphs stand out as separate units. Double-spaced material does not receive extra space between paragraphs.

The Complimentary Close

By convention, the purpose of the complimentary close is to express farewell at the end of the letter. In a simplified style, the complimentary close is frequently omitted, but conventionally the complimentary close should be typed two lines below the last line of the text. It should start slightly to the right of the center of the page, but it should never extend beyond the right margin of the letter. The comma is used at its end, unless the colon was omitted after the salutation. In that case, omit the comma after the complimentary close. Only the first word of the complimentary close is capitalized.

Yours truly, Very truly yours, Sincerely, and *Sincerely yours,* are the complimentary closes most frequently used. *Yours cordially* implies a special friendship; *Respectfully yours* implies that the person addressed is the writer's social or business superior.

The Signature

When the sender's name and title are printed in the letterhead, they are frequently omitted after the signature. Otherwise, the name and the title are typed three to five spaces directly below the complimentary close. First letters of each word are capitalized; no end punctuation is used. The letter is not official or complete until it is signed. Only after the dictator or writer has signed the letter does she become responsible for its contents. In routine letters, a secretary may, at times, sign the name of the official sender. In such a case, the secretary or stenographer signing the sender's name adds her initials. Sometimes her initials are preceded by the word *per*. The salutation and complimentary close must match in tone.

Yours truly, (closed)	Sincerely yours (open)
Stanley J. Duran	*Charlotte Billings*
Stanley J. Duran, C.P.A., J.D.	Charlotte Billings
Controller	President
Respectfully, (closed)	Cordially (open)
Tom Swift	*Marilyn Troupe*
Tom Swift	Marilyn Troupe, Ph.D.
Assistant Engineer	Chairman, Sociology

If a company, instead of the writer, is to be legally responsible for the letter, the company name should appear above the signature. The use of company letterhead does not absolve the writer. Therefore, if you want to protect yourself against legal involvement, type the company name in capitals one double-space below the complimentary close; then leave space for your signature before your typed name:

> Your truly, (closed)   Sincerely yours (open)
> STERLING PRODUCTS   AERO SPACE, INC.
> *James Joyce*   *Theodora Blum*
> James Joyce   Theodora Blum
> Design Engineer   Technical Editor

Enclosures

If there are enclosures, type *Encl.* in the lower left within the frame of the letter. If there is more than one enclosure, type *2 Encls.* or *3 Encls.*, as the case may be. If the enclosures are significant, spell out their identity:

> 2 Encls. (1 Contract No. N2021)
> (2 Proposals No. 42C)

Copy Notations

When a letter requires copies for someone other than the addressee, the designation *c:* for copy or *cc:* for courtesy copy should appear in the lower left-hand corner of the copies. Under certain conditions, the writer may wish to have the addressee informed of the distribution of copies, in which case, the notation should also appear on the original. In other instances, the sender may not wish the addressee to know that a copy was sent to a certain individual; then the letters *bc* (standing for "blind copy") are penned or typed under the *c* notation. The copy notation appears two lines below the enclosure data.

The Postscript

The postscript, years ago frowned upon, is now used more and more in business correspondence. It adds extra emphasis to some particular item or gives additional information. It is placed two line spaces below the referenced information, flush with the left-hand margin. The initials *P.S.* are sometimes used but frequently are omitted.

Second and Succeeding Pages

When a letter carries over to succeeding pages, use bond paper that matches the color and quality of the first page. Some firms have preprinted second-page stationery. Always start at least 1 inch from the top of the page. The name of the addressee should appear at the left margin. The page number, preceded and followed by a hyphen, should be centered, and the date should be at the right—forming the right-hand margin. Sometimes these elements are single-spaced, one below the other, at the left margin. The second page should carry at least three lines; five lines are preferable. Never divide a word at the end of a page.

  New Hampshire Electronics   -2-   July 6, 19__

  or

  New Hampshire Electronics
  Page 2
  July 6, 19__

The Memorandum

Purpose and Format

The **memorandum** or **memo** has been borrowed from the practice of military correspondence. It is the most common form of written communication in business and industry. Formerly, its use was restricted to interoffice, interdepartmental, or interorganizational communications. However, it is now being circulated with greater frequency out of the originating organization.

  The memorandum format is similar to that of the letter, but its tone is impersonal. Most organizations have printed memo forms for their internal communications. The format has been highly conventionalized, although details vary from one organization to another. There may be a preprinted heading identifying the company and department originating the memo. Instead of the inside address, the following three lines are used:

  TO:

  FROM:

  SUBJECT:

A date line is usually placed in the upper right-hand corner. A project or file number may also be included. In place of the complimentary close, there may be a signature of the writer, or the writer may sign or put her initials following her name in the "From" line. If the memorandum is a long communication, it may be organized into a number of sections and subsections with headings. A memorandum is frequently the most convenient mechanism to convey reporting information. (Figure 8.4).

  The purpose of a memo is to circulate information, to request others to take care of certain work, to report on what occurred in a meeting or on a trip, to keep members of an organization posted on new policies, to report on an activity or situation, and so forth.

  The basic purpose of the memo is to save time for both the reader and the writer. Amenities and courtesy are sacrificed for conciseness. Format and

```
                    INTERNATIONAL DYNAMICS CORPORATION
                    INTRA-CORPORATION COMMUNICATION

TO: Mr. F. R. Crane                                    New York
FROM: John Doe  J.D.                    Date: December 18, 19__
SUBJECT: Executive Orders Manual

Here is your copy of the General Dynamics Executive Orders
Manual containing the formal instruction, policy statements,
announcements, and other guidance from the President.

The Orders in the Executive Orders Manual have superseded
all previous Executive Orders and include all Orders
currently in effect. The Manual will be kept current by the
Office of the Vice President-Organization.

Your receiving a personal copy of the Executive Orders
Manual carries with it responsibility for complying with the
instructions and policies in the Manual and for ensuring
compliance by all personnel under your direction.

Enclosure
```

Figure 8.4 Sample memorandum.

language are directed to move the message along. Memos are frequently written under the pressure of time, and the writer is required to analyze a message situation quickly and to formulate it succinctly. The writer must reduce the subject—no matter how complex—to its substance in a terse, single statement in the "Subject" line. The reader is given direct, concise information and facts, with conclusions and recommendations (as appropriate) to provide clear but ample background to arrive at a proper decision and necessary action. Consider the following attempt at a memorandum as an illustration of a typical situation calling for this medium.

> TO: Mr. Stanley J. Duran, President
>
> FROM: Leslie S. Bruback, Administrative Assistant
>
> SUBJECT: Trip Report on the American Management Association (AMA) Conference on Employee Personnel Problems
>
> Due to very bad weather, my plane was delayed leaving the airport. It arrived more than two hours and thirty-three minutes late. Instead of landing as scheduled at Kennedy International Airport, it was rerouted to Newark, NJ. Fog

and other foul-ups delayed us at least another two hours and fifteen minutes.

I arrived at the Waldorf Astoria at 11 PM, five hours after the 6 PM deadline for my hotel reservation. As I feared, all the rooms were gone, and I had to settle for a hotel six blocks from the Waldorf where the conference was being held.

Despite the frustrations and inconveniences, the three days were worthwhile, due mostly to a session on the third day conducted by Dr. Dennis Nagel, a consultant in industrial psychology. I will detail all the sessions below.

The first session on Monday was on "Things to Watch for in Interviewing Salaried Staff," and so forth.

Ms. Bruback is reliving the trying three days of her trip to New York to attend a conference. Stanley J. Duran, though a kind and sympathetic boss, cares little about the inconveniences his assistant suffered while broadening her background at a conference and cares less to have them recorded formally. All Duran wants to know is: What did you learn that we might want to consider applying at our company? He wants information, short and sweet. Of course, he will not hesitate to let Leslie S. Bruback know this. A little red in the face, Bruback tries again. Mr. Duran shares her next effort with his division managers. That memo reads as follows:

TO: Division Managers

FROM: Leslie S. Bruback, Administrative Assistant to the President

SUBJECT: What Makes Good Employee Morale

I have just returned from an American Management Association Conference in New York. A session I found extremely valuable was on Improving Employee Morale, conducted by Dr. Dennis Nagel, a well-known industrial psychologist. Mr. Duran has suggested that I pass on to you a summary of Dr. Nagel's research and recommendations for improving employee morale.

Factors Important to Morale
1. Economic security
2. Interest in work
3. Opportunity for advancement
4. Appreciation
5. Company and management
6. Intrinsic aspects of job assignment
7. Wages
8. Supervision
9. Social aspects of job
10. Working conditions
11. Communication
12. Hours
13. Ease
14. Benefits

Please note that wages are halfway down the list. We should not jump to the conclusion that money is unimportant to an employee. Once her basic needs are satisfied through adequate pay, Dr. Nagel says, other nonmonetary factors of an employee's job take on an ever-increasing significance.

Recommendations for Improving Employee Morale

Dr. Nagel said that there are no simple ground rules. Every situation is unique—no two employees nor two companies are identical. However, psychological research on morale and employee attitudes has indicated the following recommendations:

1. Tell and *show* your employees that you are interested in their ideas on how conditions might be improved.
2. Treat your employees as individuals, never deal with them as impersonal ciphers.
3. Improve your general understanding of human behavior.
4. Accept the fact that others might not see things as you do.
5. Respect differences of opinion.
6. Insofar as possible, give explanations for management actions.
7. Provide information and guidance on matters affecting employee's security.
8. Make reasonable efforts to keep jobs interesting.
9. Encourage promotion from within.
10. Express appreciation publicly for jobs well done.
11. Offer criticism privately in the form of constructive suggestions for improvement.
12. Train supervisors to think about the people involved as much as is practical, rather than just the work.
13. Keep employees up-to-date on all business matters affecting them, and quell rumors with correct information.
14. Be fair.

Mr. Duran suggests that we be prepared to discuss the implementation of these recommendations at the next Management Circle Meeting on Monday, October 17.

Employment Letters—How to Apply for a Job

For a period of time, I was associated with an electronics company. One of my duties was personnel administration and recruitment of technical and professional personnel. During that period, I had the opportunity to read applications from several hundred people seeking positions with our company. I also interviewed a substantial number of applicants. I suppose within this group was a good cross-section of young people looking for their first job as well as those wishing to change from one position to another. The applications fell into four general categories.

The first included those so poorly written and/or so carelessly and sloppily done that I threw them into the wastebasket at once on the assumption that the person was so careless that he could not possibly be a first-rate, professional employee.

The second group contained resumes and cover letters that did not give sufficient information for me to form any judgment of the writer's prospects. Because our company was public relations conscious, these were acknowledged in polite terms but not filed.

The third included unsolicited applications written by people with fairly good backgrounds, training, and experience, but because no vacancy existed or seemed likely to occur for their particular backgrounds and capabilities, there was no reason at present for our further correspondence. However, these letters were acknowledged individually; the reply would indicate that we were impressed by the applicant's background and that we would keep the inquiry on file. If we had information about suitable vacancies at other companies, this was mentioned.

Finally, a few of the letters and resumes presented a clear picture of an individual who seemed capable, personable, well trained, and experienced for the opening, and seemed to have the personal qualifications most organizations want in their staff. Such persons were invited for a personal interview. When the interview confirmed first impressions, the individual was further interviewed by department heads in whose section or division her talents and experience would be appropriate. If the interviews further confirmed earlier impressions, a job offer ensued.

The situation I have just described is the typical one in the employment market. Many job applicants, no matter how capable or experienced, are so obsessed by their own personal situation that their approach in applying for the job is unfortunate. In business and industry, the resume plays a prominent role in helping to place individuals in appropriate openings. It might help to picture the setting into which an application arrives. For purposes of illustration, let us imagine that you are an employer. Let us say you have an opening for a responsible position that pays a competitive salary. You are anxious to find a qualified person to fill this vacancy. You place an ad in the Sunday edition of the city newspaper because you want it to receive a wide reading.

Response to the ad brings you more than 100 envelopes bearing resumes. Although you are delighted to get so many, you are also overwhelmed by the problem of how to select the right person for the position. As you look at the envelopes, you notice one that is lavender and scented. That is in such unbusinesslike form you file it promptly into the circular file (wastebasket). You notice another envelope that has misspelled both your name and street address. There is another with the remains of the applicant's breakfast on it. "Well," you tell yourself cheerfully, "I wouldn't want anyone so careless as these two filling this position," and you file both envelopes unopened in the circular file. As you continue to leaf through the pile, you find several more you can dispose of quickly, but about 100 still remain. You roll up your sleeves and start reading.

As you read the cover letters, each sounds like the previous one; the resumes also seem like clones: bunched text, their details running full up and down and across the page—words, words, dizzying words. You almost want to give up, but the need to fill the position urges you on.

After reading about ten letters, you find one that catches your interest; you read with eagerness. The first few sentences are not only appropriate but lead immediately into qualifications that have merit. Moreover, the writer is able to describe herself, her experience, and her background so that she appears to be an individual, apart from the others. "This person has character; she has ability; she has the background and the experience. I want to see this person!" you tell yourself, and you put her application carefully aside.

You return to read; for the most part you go no further than the first paragraph of the cover letter and give a perfunctory glance at the resume. You are looking for applications like the one that caught your interest previously; ones that make their writers come alive. After almost two hours, you have four piles of applications: those to be thrown away; those to be acknowledged politely; those to be acknowledged with more care and filed or entered into your computer for possible later openings; and those—about seven or eight—from candidates you want to interview.

From this hypothetical but typical situation, we can see that the reception your application will receive depends on these things:

1. Its initial impression and its appearance. If the cover letter and resume are neat and well-framed on the page, they color favorably the mood in which they will be read.
2. The first few sentences of the cover letter. If they are interesting (not bizarre) and lead the reader to the applicant's qualifications, the prospective employer will continue to read. The employer has a good idea of what she is looking for. The writer should emphasize at once her qualifications that she believes to be the most important to the opening. (An applicant's qualifications include, of course, experience, education, and personal matters.)
3. Establishing one's individuality. An employer becomes dizzy reading several scores of applications. One applicant, even though qualified, begins to sound like another. Hence, the writer needs to set herself apart from other applicants. She needs to make herself remembered. This, of course, is not easy, but we shall soon see how it can be done.

Job Strategy

So much for acquainting you with the job market environment. Let us now go to the beginning of the process. For the graduating student entering the job market, finding a job involves the following steps:

1. Self-appraisal (identifying salable qualifications and personal strengths)
2. Preparing a dossier
3. Researching job possibilities
4. Developing a resume
5. Writing a cover letter/executive briefing

6. Being interviewed for a position
7. Writing a post-interview letter
8. Writing a letter of acceptance or declination of the job offer

Self-Appraisal

You are the *product* you will want to sell to a prospective employer. Sales persons who are successful know their product. Therefore, before you prepare your sales instrument—the resume and its cover letter—you need to know yourself: You need to analyze and inventory your strengths, weaknesses, skills, experience, education, aptitudes, and goals. How do you do that? You ask yourself some questions and write down the answers honestly, after giving careful thought to each question. Consider such questions as the following:

What can I do well?
Can I speak well? Write? Draw? Socialize? Have I won any awards?
Do I speak or write any foreign languages?
Do I have military experience? Is any aspect of that experience appropriate to employment?
What skills have I acquired from my schooling? From jobs held? From hobbies?
What technical instruments or machine tools can I operate? How skillfully?
Do I have computer skills? How proficient am I?
How well do I get along with others? Am I a leader? A follower? Can I supervise others?
What important courses have I taken?
How good am I at working under stress?
What do I want out of life? What do I want from the job I am seeking? Security? Money? Power? Prestige? Excitement? Travel? Something else?
What is my goal? What is my career objective?

Your answers become an analytical inventory that will help you construct your job application material (resume and cover letter) and help you in a job interview.

Preparing a Dossier

Your college/university placement office is a valuable resource. It provides counseling, arranges on-campus job interviews, provides information on job openings, and helps you to establish a personal file, or **dossier,** and serves as its caretaker. The dossier contains information that substantiates your resume and cover letter, and contains other supporting documents such as transcripts of your college grades, listings of job experience, copies of awards and honors earned, unsolicited letters of praise, and other information that may benefit you or be of interest to a prospective employer. Copies of your dossier or some appropriate elements of it will be sent to a prospective employer at your specific request.

Researching Job Possibilities

Jobs do not come to you; you have to search for openings. Here are some suggested places to begin looking:

The Help Wanted section in newspapers, particularly the Sunday edition of a metropolitan paper

Your college placement office, which posts announcements of openings and arranges for job interviews with recruiters visiting your campus

The office of your department major, which also posts job opportunities (check with your faculty for placement suggestions.)

The professional journal(s) of your field, which carries national listings of openings

Regional and national professional and trade association meetings, which almost always include recruiting sessions for members

State and local employment offices

The Office of Personnel Management of the U.S. Federal Government, which you can write to for information on opportunities in your field

Your reference librarian, who can help you locate reference sources of information such as directories of corporations, government agencies, and professional organizations as well as guides to other business information

Job Analysis

Many persons, even the experienced and capable, approach an application for a position from the point of view of their own eagerness for it. They forget that a prospective employer has her own viewpoint and needs; therefore, the letters the applicants write express only their eagerness for this position, how much they would like the position, and how they feel the position would be right for them. Despite a great show of sincerity on the applicant's part, the employer cannot get interested. She is looking for a person who knows the employer's requirements and desires and who can show how the applicant's experience, training, and personal qualifications can be of benefit.

The first step—one that begins before the application is written—is to analyze the available position. This analysis must be based on the information describing the opening. This, of course, is found in ads or announcements revealing the availability of the opening. A good device is to itemize the position's qualifications listed in the announcement. Then, in a column alongside, list an inventory of your own qualifications, background, training, experience, and personal characteristics that would be appropriate for the opening. This type of inventory helps you understand, through comparative analysis, the type of qualifications and their importance to the employer.[1] It also allows you to look objectively at your

---

[1] Later, if appropriate, this comparative inventory can be converted into an executive briefing (see pages 242–243).

own qualifications in light of what the prospective employer is looking for. If you do not have what the employer wants, there is no point in applying. Save yourself the time, energy, and emotional investment. It is true, sometimes, that your qualifications may not be exactly what the employer is looking for, but you may have some of the qualifications plus additional ones that would be attractive to the prospective employer. There is no formula to gauge just how many qualifications you need to make it appropriate for you to apply. This depends on your analysis and knowledge of the requirements of the type of position being advertised.

If the ad reads:

> SOFTWARE ENGINEER WANTED
> with five years experience
> in defense industry in ADA/VAX software systems
> software configurations management, and
> IBM MVS/VM systems programming.

there is no point in applying if you have just graduated from engineering school and lack the necessary experience in the defense or intelligence communities.

Yet, it is also true that employers are looking for certain personal qualities, which no amount of schooling and actual work experience can provide. There have been many surveys to identify the reasons why employees lose their jobs. Incompetency is very low on the list. Very high on the list are personal factors—matters such as absenteeism, belligerency, hypochondria, alcoholism, drug addiction, inability to work with others, and so forth. Personnel managers, therefore, scrutinize applications very carefully for clues on prospective employees' instability, health and emotional problems, and personality difficulties. Employers are always on the lookout for prospective employees who will be responsible, who have stability, initiative, and characteristics of personal growth. Employers want not only individuals who have the personal knack of getting along well with others but also those who may have leadership and managerial abilities. Demonstration of such factors is eagerly searched for in resumes.

In your inventory, note carefully those qualities that would be attractive to employers. Granted, all of us have a sincere belief in our own abilities, popularity, and capabilities of working productively with others. However, that mere assertion is not enough. What is required is evidence in the form of proven accomplishments. If you have been elected to an office in your fraternity, sorority, or campus organization, you have demonstrated some leadership abilities. Recall any experience in extracurricular matters that offered challenges. Indicate instances of productive accomplishments.

Developing a Resume

In current practice, applications for positions have two parts. Part one is a cover letter or, in some instances, an executive briefing; part two is the resume, which is written before the cover letter and is the more important element.

The resume is a factual, succinct statement that highlights your qualifications. If this piece of technical writing is mechanically flawed or is too long, too detailed, too difficult to follow, or too sketchy, it will be discarded. A manager does not read resumes for fun or sport. The resume evolved as an employment instrument to save a manager's time. Most managers spend less than sixty seconds skimming an application. The resume must grab attention immediately and speak clearly, succinctly, and persuasively of your value as a potential employee.

Types of Resumes

Professional resume mavens say there are three approaches to presenting your credentials to a prospective employer:

Chronological
Functional
Chrono-functional (a combination of the above two)

The **chronological** resume lists and describes experience and education sequentially, beginning with the current or most recent and moving backward in time. For most students, education should be placed before employment experience, since education may be their most important qualification. Do not list your high school. Indicate your major field of study and the date or expected date of graduation. Do not list your courses unless some are significant to the position you are applying for. Honors, awards, professional affiliations, extracurricular activities, and offices held should also be indicated.

The **functional** resume focuses on experience and capabilities rather than on the time or context in which they were acquired. It is the approach to take when you have a specific career goal and you want to zero in on a specific job. This approach can help to convince the employer that you have the necessary experience, abilities, and aptitude for the opening.

The **chrono-functional** resume combines the previous two approaches. It is an apt resume tool for the person who is on a career track with a strong performance record. It contains a career summary either at the beginning or end of the resume, spotlighting professional skills, personal traits, and accomplishments, and aims toward future career growth. The chrono-functional resume starts with functional skills and experience relevant to job/career goals without reference to employers. This is followed by a chronological employment history, working backward, listing company names, dates, titles, duties, and responsibilities. A statement on education is then listed.

Preparing the Resume

Ideally, resumes, no matter which style is followed, should not be longer than two pages typed on one side. Note the attractive, framed appearance of the resumes in Figures 8.6, 8.8, and 8.10–8.12. Use paper of good quality, 20- to 25-pound bond of white or slightly off-white stock. Printing your resume on colored or pastel paper is poor form. The type should be black and clear. Avoid fancy or unusual type fonts, although you should take advantage of word processors to provide italics, bold, and capitalization for emphasis.

Basic Resume Ingredients

A resume is like a recipe. The ingredients of two entrées may be essentially the same, but what determines gourmet taste is the method of preparation and the special touches by which the ingredients are combined to produce a unique flavor. Some resume ingredients are universal, some may sometimes be included, and some are special touches that can be added to pique the interest for particular situations.

The basic ingredients of a resume are:

Contact information (your name, address, phone number)
Career/job objective statement
Experience
Education (include any special training or courses, and list any academic honors or awards)
Personal information (optional)
References (do not list but indicate availability)
Professional honors, awards, publications, patents, affiliations
Military service (if training and experience are appropriate to career/job)
Summary statement (used in chrono-functional resumes)

Let us examine these ingredients and see how they are combined to contribute to an effective resume.

Contact Information

Use your name as the heading, *not* the word *Resume*. Center and type it all in capitals at least 1 inch from the top. Give your complete address; do not abbreviate any part of it, except the state element. Include your zip code and your telephone number with the area code.

DANIEL M. WILLIAMS
12171 Carriage Square Court
Silver Spring, MD 20906
301-555-5980

Unless your current employer knows of your job search, do not include your business telephone in your resume. If appropriate, list the number in your cover letter with a caveat.

Career/Job Objective Statement

A career objective relates to your life work. A job objective relates to a specific occupational process; they are seldom interchangeable. Your career objective can change with the exigencies of time; a job objective relates to the opportunity of the moment as influenced by your qualifications. Young persons starting out on a professional career might delay indicating a career objective until they have attained enough work experience to be confident of the direction they want their careers to take.

A statement of a job objective provides a thematic conception to your resume. It helps the resume reader to focus on your qualifications as they relate to the opening to be filled, and it provides a retrievable index term under which to file your resume. Furthermore, a job objective statement indicates to a prospective employer your present level of competence and a willingness to work for advancement in the company. Job objectives are preliminary to career objectives.

An effective articulation of a career objective requires brainstorming, self-analysis, and self-evaluation. You have often faced the question, "What do you want to be when you grow up?" Now is the time to ask yourself, "What kind of job do I want? What am I qualified to do? What skills, talents, aptitudes do I have? What experience? What skills and experience do I need to have to obtain the kind of work that will lead me to the career I want? On the practical level, what kind of job am I qualified for that will send me on the road I want to go?" After careful thought and self-analysis, compose a job objective statement as precisely as you can that can lead to a career objective. Do not say:

> Objective: Chance for advancement in the computer industry. (This is too general and wishy-washy.)

Instead, say:

> Objective: To obtain a responsible and challenging position as a programmer where my initiative, education, and work experience with IDMS and COBOL would enable growth into advanced system design.

Experience and Education

In a chronological resume format the placement order of the next two categories, *Experience* and *Education,* varies. The applicant who has been out of college a number of years and whose experience has been extensive places the experience section before that of education. If you are an entry-level applicant, one just graduating, list your education before the experience entries. Use reverse chronology in listing experience and education.

Under *Experience,* your entries should tell not merely the title of the job but also specify the duties. Accomplishments should be listed. Recent graduates should include summer and part-time jobs. If you worked your way through college, fully or partially, you should so indicate. If you have computer literacy or proficiency, provide the information. Technical knowledge, especially expertise in computers, is critical in today's world.

Under *Education*, begin with the latest degree and work back, listing degrees, diplomas, and special training beyond high school. List college courses relevant to the opening. Note laboratory work, field work, and independent study. Indicate any accomplishments, honors, awards, and extracurricular activities.

Personal Information

In accordance with federal employment laws enacted to prevent discrimination, you are not required to give information about your gender, race, national origin, religion, or marital status. Nonetheless, plain sense should tell you what personal items to include that would add to your qualifications for the job. For example, if you are applying for a position requiring travel, by indicating that you are single, you inform the employer that you do not have family obligations that might prevent you from traveling. Therefore, include personal information that enhances your qualifications.

You should list affiliations with professional societies; that indicates a dedication to your profession. Omit references to religious, political, or potentially controversial affiliations. Your resume should reflect your professional, not personal, life. If you have publication credits, list them; these demonstrate creativity and extended effort.

References

There are differences among resume experts about the appropriateness of listing references in a resume. Some believe interviewers are not interested in checking references before they meet and develop an interest in an applicant. Also, according to the federal *Fair Credit and Reporting Act*, employers are forbidden to check references without your permission. Furthermore, listing references takes up valuable resume space. Most employers, these experts say, assume references are available for the asking. On the other hand, some resume experts feel that an employer may recognize a name on your list and thus pay special attention to your name and qualifications. I recommend using the simple statement: "References available on request."

Professional Affiliations, Honors, Awards, Publications, Patents

List, if any, your affiliations with professional associations and societies related to your field; such memberships show dedication to your career. Employers know that memberships can be helpful and important to networking. Include honors and awards received; they bespeak achievements and will impress a reader. Publications and patents manifest creative thought. They tell the prospective employer that you, the candidate, invest effort above the call of accepted professionalism. Publications carry much weight in professions and industries where literary visibility is important. Patents are a positive factor in technological and manufacturing fields. List publications and patents, if you have any, at the end of your resume as follows:

> PUBLICATIONS
>
> Jones, Mary, "A Program for Making DOS User-Friendly in the Russian Language," *Personal Computing* (October 1994).
>
> PATENTS
>
> Non-Carcinogenic Briquettes for Outdoor Grills. U.S. Patent 00,000,000, September 20, 1994.

Matters to Be Excluded From the Resume

Some information does not belong in the resume; its inclusion detracts and likely will fail to get you an interview. Among such matters are:

Written testimonials, which are in poor form (and no one believes them)

Salary expectations, which are best left to the interview

References to salary (past and present) because too high or too low will knock you out of the running

Photographs, unless you are seeking a job in the entertainment field

Exaggerated qualifications (or lies). Never, *never* lie about yourself or exaggerate your skills. Don't claim degrees or qualifications you don't have. Many employers have become skeptical of the data supplied in resumes and make it a point to verify a resume's claims. Stigmas of deceit can follow you for the rest of your life.

Preferences for work schedule, days off, overtime (The resume is not a negotiating instrument.)

Writing the Resume

Review what we have discussed about the resume. Now consider your background. Which organizational style is appropriate for you—chronological, functional, or chrono-functional? Examine the examples of each type in Figures 8.10, 8.11, and 8.12. The chronological approach seems a simpler form and can be effective. Try it first because it provides the basis for developing either of the other more difficult patterns. Now, examine the layout and page design of the resumes in Figures 8.6, 8.8, and 8.10–8.12 and use them as a model. You will have to tinker a little to fit your own situation.

Try a rough draft. Following the layout of the models, enter the contact information. Then compose your objective statement. Express it in as few words as possible, but in words that will bring a clear picture to the reader's mind. Keep the statement short, limiting it to one or two sentences.

If you have little work experience relevant to the position you are seeking, your next element will be Education. The sequence of data is degree, institution, its location (city and state), date graduated, course of study, thesis and supervisor if relevant, important courses if appropriate to job opening or job objective, and honors and awards, if any. Data in an entry are usually separated by commas. Periods are frequently used following dates. A period is used after a completed entry.

Under Experience, the sequence of data is date of employment, name of company, location (city and state), job title, and duties. Do not use complete sentences; use action verbs such as those in the following list:

> achieved, administered, advanced, analyzed, assembled, assisted, authored, built, chaired, coached, completed, computed, conducted, contributed, coordinated, created, decreased, demonstrated, designed, determined, developed, edited, engineered, established, evaluated, expedited, formulated, generated, guided, implemented, increased, initiated, invented, launched, led, marketed, monitored, operated, organized, performed, persuaded, planned, prepared, presented, processed, produced, programmed, provided, published, recommended, reduced, researched, restructured, retrieved, reviewed, scanned, screened, simulated, solved, specified, standardized, stimulated, streamlined, supervised, systematized, trained, trimmed, upgraded, wrote

In the Personal section, list activities that could support your candidacy, for example, the extent of your computer literacy or experience (if not previously covered), special skills, such as speaks, reads, and writes Spanish fluently; captain, University Golf Team; served on community's Big Brother organization, junior and senior years.

Under References, indicate they are available on request or available from the university placement office.

As you examine the resumes reproduced in this chapter you will note that sentences are truncated yet understandable. The pronoun *I* or the name of the applicant does not appear in the text lines; that saves space and allows you to "toot your own horn" without seeming boastful. There is an instance in which you can inject the personal *I*, which can give a human appeal to your resume. That instance is the inclusion of a *Personal Statement* at the end of your resume, as for example:

> I am competitive and frequently seek new approaches to solve problems, have excellent interpersonal skills, and am capable of working with and for people at all levels. I am able to plan, develop, organize, and implement ideas into viable projects.

A rule of thumb: The length of a resume is one page for every ten years of experience. For the entry-level candidate's resume, the length should be limited to one page. However, do not worry about length while writing your draft. Worry may hamper you. Usually two and one-half pages of double-spaced handwriting makes one page of typescript. If, after you have typed your resume, you find it is longer than a single page, review it to see what can be deleted. Ask yourself: Can I cut any superfluous words? Where have I repeated myself? If in doubt, cut. Leave nothing but facts and action verbs.

Appearance of the final resume is important—so important that a worthy candidate's document can be sent to the trash can unread if it contains typos, erasures, and misspellings, or if it does not conform to current practice in style and substance.

Type your own resume if you are a competent typist, or better yet, use a word processor if you have access to one. Preparing your resumes and cover letters with a word processor offers many conveniences and advantages. You can easily

- correct typos, misspellings, and punctuation errors,
- delete or insert words, phrases, and sentences without need for retyping the page,
- move items to more strategic locations on the page,
- change format of headings and their type style,
- update your resume as your situation changes,
- tailor your resume and cover letter to specific openings, and
- save different versions on diskette for quick retrieval.

Once your application material is stored, you have a permanent, easily recalled, attractive resume for use or revision as your situation requires.

After you are completely satisfied with the content and appearance of your resume, you need copies. Never send messy copies. If you have the use of a letter quality printer, you can run out any number of attractive, clean copies. If not, a photocopying machine is your best bet; or, for a modest cost, you can have your resume reproduced by a job shop that offers photocopy reproduction or offset printed copies. The neat, professional-looking copies are worth the cost.

I suggest you avoid resume preparing services. Whereas their final result appears attractive, their text material has a "canned" character. Employers often recognize the source by its style and might conclude that you are unable to communicate or organize data on your own.

Writing a Cover Letter

Now that you have completed your resume, your next challenge is its **cover letter.** The resume on its own may or may not lead you to the position you seek. The job market, especially for professional openings, is so crowded that employers receive numerous resumes as impressive as yours. How can you stand out? The cover letter or executive briefing can be the answer. (I will discuss the executive briefing later.) By writing an effective cover letter or executive briefing, you can persuade an employer to grant you an interview.

The cover letter of the resume is a sales letter, constructed to attract attention and to create interest on the part of the employer. It should speak with conviction about the applicant's "merchandise," and it should stimulate the recipient to the desired action.

To attract attention, the letter should have an interesting opening tailored to the specific position being applied for; the letter should describe the applicant's major qualifications in a way that will induce the reader to examine the resume. Descriptive language is not enough; the tone must be sincere, and the letter must convince the reader that the applicant has the desired qualifications.

Few people are hired on the basis of a letter and resume alone. The purpose of this application material is to create interest and stimulate the reader to invite the writer to appear for an interview.

How to Attract Favorable Attention

The first sentence or two of a cover letter are critical. Good opening sentences are unhackneyed, simple, and direct. There are a number of ways to begin a cover letter to interest the reader.

Original Openings

We have seen in our earlier hypothetical situation that a majority of the letters begin with the commonplace, "In reply to your Sunday's ad," or "Having read your ad in the morning *Post*," or "Regarding the ad you had in the recent issue of. . . ." Effective beginnings reflect the *you* attitude; they are simple, direct, distinctive but not odd or extravagant. Here are some examples of effective novel beginnings:

> The April 14 issue of *Science* had a feature story on IBM that convinced me that mathematicians employed by IBM have enviable opportunities for professional growth and personal advancement. As a graduating mathematical statistician, I believe I could do no better than to start my mathematical career under one of the training programs you are advertising. Won't you consider my qualifications?
>
> Your notice in a recent issue of *Computerworld* on developments in transaction processing caught my eye and your company name caught my attention. This letter is to introduce me and to explore any need you may have in VAX/VMS architecture.
>
> I am a young engineer eager to secure a position where I can earn my keep and, at the same time, learn how to be a better chemical engineer. I understand from Mr. Ben Holloway, of your Synthetics Department, that you are expecting to add a Junior Engineer to your staff. May I have a moment to acquaint you with my background and qualifications for this position?

In your effort to be original, be careful that you do not become bizarre. No one can deny that the following two openings are original and unhackneyed, but they defeat their intended purpose by their oddness:

> Stop! Go no further until you have read my letter and resume from beginning to end. I feel sure you will find me to be the best-qualified metallurgist for your position in the quality control department.
>
> Symbiosis is the biological term used to indicate cooperation between two or more parties toward a mutual goal. Your company has an outstanding

training program for young executives. I feel I am qualified to meet your expectations so let us get together.

Name Beginnings

If you have learned of the availability of a position through a person whom the prospective employer knows, or whose name or title will command respect, then beginning the letter with the name of that individual can be very effective. Here are some examples of name or reference beginnings:

>Professor J. K. Wagner, Department Head, Forest Recreation and Wildlife Conservation at Colorado State University, called me into her office this morning to see if I was interested in the permanent ranger position described in the notice you sent her.

>The Placement Office of our university has informed me that my qualifications might be of interest to you for the Management Trainee Position in your Overseas Service Department.

>Dr. James C. Donovan, Vice President of Engineering Research in your Denver office, suggested this afternoon that I write you concerning an opening in your Chicago office. He said, "Ted, because I know you have an unusual five-year educational combination of engineering and management, I think you have just the right background, and, of course, the ability to make yourself quite useful to the Industrial Engineering Department in our Chicago office. Would you be interested in dropping them a note at once?" I was happy to hear of this opportunity and am acquainting you with my interest and background.

Summary Beginnings

Another effective way to begin is to present immediately a summary of the most significant qualifications for the opening. Here are some examples:

>Since graduating from Wharton School of Business three years ago, I have served as Assistant Budget Officer in Keely and Company, with the principal duties of preparing budget requirements, undertaking statistical studies, making comparison of methods, costs, and results with those of other refining companies.

>My four years' work in the field servicing of electronic testing equipment, as well as a degree in Electrical Engineering, make me confident that I can qualify for the position you have open in your Quality Control Department.

Question Beginnings

Beginning a letter with a question can be effective, especially if you are applying for an unadvertised position. Here is an example:

>Do your plans for the future include graduating Electrical Engineers with practical experience in model shop and breadboard design? If so, please consider my qualifications.

Starting a cover letter with a question can be equally effective for an advertised opening.

> Wouldn't that Mechanical Engineer you advertised for in the Sunday *Post* be more valuable to your department if he had as much as three and a half years' experience as a maintenance technician in the U.S. Navy?

How to Describe Your Qualifications

The letter's beginning has the purpose of capturing the reader's attention. You must now create an interest in your qualifications. Entry-level applicants have four major qualifications: education, experience, personal qualities, and personal history. Just which of these four elements are emphasized in your letter will depend, of course, on your analysis of the requirements of the position. The principle is to write first and most about the qualification that your analysis deems most important to the position. If the ad reads: "Wanted—experienced design engineer," obviously the employer will want to know first and most about your experience as a design engineer. Although the employer will be interested to know that you graduated *magna cum laude*, that fact may not be as important as four years' experience designing certain kinds of instrumentation. If you have experience that is appropriate to the requirements of the opening, that is the most important qualification. Therefore, discuss it first and most fully.

If your strongest point has been your education, then that is what you need to start with. If your personal qualities are your strongest point, then show that you can develop or are capable of gaining the kind of experience necessary to do the job and that you are able to grow into more responsible positions within the company. After you have presented your strongest point, describe other qualifications you have that are important to the position. Details should be specific. Give the name of the firm where you acquired experience, the kind of position held, and the duties connected with the position. If you accomplished anything outstanding in the job, write about it.

> *General and ineffective:* "For three years, I served as a technician."
>
> *Specific:* "For three years, I served in the model shop of the research and development department of the Radio Corporation of America in Camden, NJ. My work consisted of making breadboards, fabricating prototype models from rough engineering sketches of development engineers. This required not only expert use of a soldering iron but also machine shop tools and equipment."

In discussing education, focus attention on those subjects directly or closely related to the position for which you are applying. For example, a student applying for a job with an agricultural machinery manufacturing company might indicate her educational qualifications as follows:

> My studies concentrated in the area of machine design, including such courses as kinematics of machines, dynamics of machinery, computer aided

design, machine analysis, agricultural power, and agricultural machinery. Some other pertinent courses include statics, dynamics, strength of materials, fluid mechanics, computer graphics, physics, chemistry, and robotics. In my Special Problems Course in Agricultural Machinery, I designed and built a corn conveyer feeding machine presently being used on our Agriculture Hog Farm.

By its substantiation of qualifications, the central portion of the cover letter creates an interest in and a desire to interview the applicant.

Securing Action

The final paragraph of the cover letter has the duty of persuading the reader to grant the applicant an interview. Mention should be made, either in the last portion of the letter or in the middle portion, that a resume with complete information on the applicant is attached. Give as much care to the ending of your letter as you did the beginning. Do not be hackneyed or weak and do not be impertinently brash or timorous:

> If you think I can qualify for your position, I'd be grateful if you gave me a chance [negative and timorous].
>
> I suppose it's only fair to tell you, you better call me before the end of this week, because I have several fine job offers I am considering and I would like to compare yours with the others before I reach my decision [brash and impertinent].
>
> Trusting you will grant me an interview at your convenience. I shall await your call [hackneyed].

To obtain the action you want—securing an interview—calls for a more effective close to your letter. Be direct yet circumspect. Here are some examples:

> I believe my qualifications are appropriate for the position you advertised. I would be happy to provide details beyond those outlined in my attached resume. May I have an interview at your convenience? Won't you write me at my home address or call me at 287-3873 between the hours of 5 and 9 PM?
>
> I will be in Chicago from December 22 to January 2. Would it be convenient for me to come in to tell you more about myself and to learn more about the position you have available?
>
> May I have an interview at your convenience? I have enclosed a self-addressed postal card for you to let me know when I might stop by to better acquaint you with my qualifications.
>
> Whether you have an opening at present or not, I would appreciate the opportunity to meet with you so that you may better judge my qualifications for possible employment with your organization. May I call you on the 15th to schedule a mutually convenient meeting?

Model cover letters and resumes appear in Figures 8.5–8.12.

698 South Grant
Fort Collins, CO 80521
January 6, 19__

Mr. John Koldchuk
Division Manager
Johnson Technology Corporation
Florence, CO 81226

Dear Mr. Koldchuk:

    Do your plans for this new year include graduating electronic engineers with a varied hands-on experience? If so, please consider my qualifications.

    My curiosity in the "magic" world of electronics prompted me to enlist in the navy where the opportunity to become an electronics technician was available. I was granted this opportunity and also the chance as an instructor to pass the knowledge I acquired on to others. I learned to operate and teach others about airborne equipment as well. I was able to make first-class petty officer during my four-year enlistment.

    The experience in the navy was but a mere acquaintance with electronics and an invitation to learn more. With an assist from the GI Bill, I enrolled in the College of Engineering at Colorado State University, where I took such courses as Circuit Analysis, Computer Systems, AC and DC Machinery, Robotics, and Human Engineering.

    To meet the financial requirements in acquiring my degree, it was necessary to supplement my military service benefits with part-time and summer employment. Besides financial assistance, these jobs offered acquaintance with, and some practical experience in, the agriculture and petroleum fields; these jobs also helped increase my sense of responsibility, gave me confidence, and taught me to appreciate my fellow workers.

    The knowledge, training, and experience I've acquired thus far have been mainly for my own satisfaction. I now want to put them to wider use. If my background and experience are of interest to Johnson Technology Corporation, I would appreciate an interview. You can contact me at the address and phone number listed on my attached resume. I look forward to hearing from you.

Sincerely yours,

Victor P. Norris

Figure 8.5 Sample cover letter.

VICTOR P. NORRIS
689 South Grant
Fort Collins, CO 80521
303-555-1367

EMPLOYMENT OBJECTIVE: To serve as an electronic test instrument design engineer with an opportunity to continue professional growth.

EDUCATION
B.S.E.E., Colorado State University, Fort Collins, June, 19__
    Important Courses: Electronic Circuits, Circuit Analysis, Computer Systems, Network Analysis, Robotics, Engineering Economics, Psychology, Technical Writing, Feedback Systems.

EXPERIENCE
September, 19__ to present. Part-time Handyman, Physical Plant, Colorado State University. Electrical repairs; designed automated feeders for large animals at Agriculture Station; carpentry.
Summers, 19__, 19__, 19__. Rustabout Pan American Petroleum Corporation., Midwest, Wyoming. Pulled rods and lines and helped maintain and repair oil well equipment and flow lines.

MILITARY EXPERIENCE
1985–1989. U.S. Navy, Great Lakes Naval Training Center, Aviation Electronics Technician. Norfolk Naval Air Station, AT1 rating; served as radar instructor.

PERSONAL
    Single; Excellent health; expert photographer

REFERENCES .
    Available on request.

Figure 8.6 Sample resume.

728 West Laurel Avenue
Fort Collins, Colorado
April 9, 19__

Mr. Thomas Welk
Supervisor
Mesa Verde National Park
Colorado 81330

Dear Mr. Welk:

Professor James Moss, department head of Forest Recreation and Wildlife Conservation at Colorado State University, called me into his office this morning to see if I was interested in the permanent ranger position described in the notice you sent to him.

The saying "opportunity knocks once" immediately flashed through my mind. To find this opportunity open at this point in my career was a pleasant surprise.

Why? I have two reasons: (1) I have long had a hobby and interest in Native American lore and archaeology, which would be of tremendous value in this type of position and (2) I have trained in a Forest Recreation major for National Park work, hoping to eventually secure a position where study and interpretation of Native American culture are carried on.

Professor Moss stressed the background needed for this position and the education necessary to qualify. My background has included various jobs where public relations were required. Helping manage a swimming pool one summer gave me invaluable practice in controlling groups of people and in gaining their confidence and interest. At Yellowstone National Park on busy weekends I helped guide tours to points of interest giving interpretive talks along the trail. From my hobby of Native American lore, I have gained a knowledge of various cultures that directly relate to Mesa Verde's Native American culture.

I will be in Mancos, Colorado, from May 22–29 doing research for the University on increased tourist visits to this community resulting from your location near the park. I will be happy to call at your convenience for a personal interview. If this is not convenient for you, I can be reached at my Fort Collins address after May 31.

Sincerely,

Rhonda D. Weeks

Figure 8.7 Sample cover letter.

RHONDA D. WEEKS
728 West Laurel Avenue
Fort Collins, CO 80521
Telephone: 303-555-3825

OBJECTIVE: A ranger position in a U.S. national park where study and interpretation of Native American culture are carried on.

SUMMARY OF QUALIFICATIONS
Varied experience with the National Park Service and the U.S. Forest Service; degree in Forest Recreation.

EDUCATION
B.S., Forest Recreation and Wildlife Conservation, Colorado State University, June, 199_.
Major courses: Principles of Wildland Recreation, National Park Management, Field Recreation Studies and Management, Ten-week Forestry Summer Camp, Principles of Wildland Management, Wildlife and Forestry Ecology.

EXPERIENCE
Summer, 199_, Grand Canyon National Park, AZ, Fire lookout and fire suppression.
Summer, 199_, Yellowstone National Park, WY, Tour guide.
Summer, 199_, Forest Field Summer Camp, Pingree Park.
Summer, 199_, Skyline Acres, Denver, Swimming pool manager and lifeguard.

PERSONAL
Single. Member, National Society of Park and Recreation; served as delegate, Western Clubs Convention, 199_ and 199_.

SPECIAL INTERESTS
Native American lore, mountain climbing, skiing.

Figure 8.8 Sample resume.

203 West Lake Street
Fort Collins, Colorado 80521
December 1, 19__

Mr. E. A. Ferris
Administrator of Training
Combustion Engineering, Inc.
Prospect Hill Road
Windsor, Connecticut 06095

Dear Mr. Ferris:

    Colorado State University has a steam heating system for its buildings on campus. One of the steam generators is a Combustion Engineering boiler erected in 1950. Since 1950 this boiler has performed satisfactorily with a minimum of maintenance. Modifications were recently completed for modernization of the heating plant and your boiler appears ready for another 45 years of service.

    The performance of this boiler and the reputation of your company have prompted me to write you. If your company has an opening for a graduating mechanical engineer with previous mechanical experience, please consider my qualifications.

    After attending college for one year, I joined the army to gain practical experience and maturity. While in the army, I attended school at Ft. Belvoir, Virginia, for the maintenance of engineering equipment. After equipment repair school, I was stationed in Germany where I had 2½ years of practical experience in the field repair of heavy equipment. My tour of duty convinced me that I had been right in choosing mechanical engineering for a career, so I returned to Colorado State University to finish my studies for a B.S.M.E. degree.

    To help pay college expenses, I supplemented my scholarship and savings by summer work and part-time work during the school year. Last summer I worked as a junior engineer at Boeing Company. My job involved an efficiency and cost analysis of both steam and hot water heating systems, evaluation of economy suggestions and inspection of building repairs, and maintenance.

    If my qualifications as outlined in the enclosed resume are of interest, I would appreciate an interview. I can be reached at the address and telephone number shown on my resume.

Sincerely,

John B. Dunne

Figure 8.9 Sample student employment letter.

JOHN B. DUNNE
203 West Lake Street
Fort Collins, CO 80521
303-555-1473

CAREER OBJECTIVE: A mechanical engineering position in which I can use my education, experience, and enthusiasm for challenges to advance to a supervisory position with an engineering equipment manufacturing company.

EXPERIENCE:
Summer 199_, Junior Engineer, Plant Services Section, Boeing Company, responsible for study to determine efficiency and cost analysis of steam heating system of factory, engineering, and administration buildings.
Summer 199_, Mechanic, Colorado State University, maintenance of motor pool trucks, tractors, bulldozers. Also repaired automatic machine tools.
1984–1989, U.S. Army Corps of Engineers. Specialist Second Class E-5, repair and maintenance of heavy equipment.
Summer 198_, Laborer, Gardner Construction Company, Colorado. Worked directly from blueprints. Duties included tying steel rods for concrete walls.

PROFESSIONAL AFFILIATIONS:
Member of A.S.M.E. student section. Honors: Sigma Tau, honorary engineering fraternity, and member of Phi Beta Phi.

SPECIAL INTERESTS:
Computers, mechanical repairs, skiing, reading, travel.

REFERENCES:
Available on request.

Figure 8.10 Sample chronological resume.

JOHN B. DUNNE
203 West Lake Street
Fort Collins, CO 80521
303-555-1473

CAREER OBJECTIVE: A mechanical engineering position in which I can use my education, experience, and enthusiasm for challenges to advance to a supervisory position with an engineering equipment manufacturing company.

SUMMARY: A B.S.M.E. degree with emphasis on computer-aided machine design, plus eight years of both hands-on and supervisory experience, maintaining and repairing engineering equipment from bulldozers to automatic screw machines.

MAINTENANCE and REPAIRS
    Crawler tractors, cranes, grader ditchers, bulldozers, bucket loaders, computer-controlled machine tools, and automatic screw machines.

RESEARCH
    Conducted efficiency and cost analysis study of heating systems of factory, engineering, and administration buildings at Boeing Company

MILITARY
    U.S. Army Corps of Engineers, 4-year enlistment, with 2-1/2 years in Germany, responsible for field repair of heavy equipment.

WORK EXPERIENCE
    Boeing Company, Junior Engineer, Summer, 199_
    Colorado State University, equipment mechanic, part-time and summers, 199_–199_.

EDUCATION
    B.S.M.E., Colorado State University, 199_.
    Certificate, Engineering Equipment, Corps of Engineering Service School, Fort Belvoir, VA., 198_.

REFERENCES
    Available on request.

Figure 8.11 Sample functional resume.

JOHN B. DUNNE
203 West Lake Street
Fort Collins, CO 80521
303-555-1473

OBJECTIVE

Employment with an engineering equipment manufacturing company in a position with supervisory potential.

SUMMARY

B.S.M.E. degree with emphasis on computerized machine design, plus eight years of both hands-on and supervisory experience, maintaining and repairing engineering equipment from bulldozers to automatic screw machines.

MAINTENANCE and REPAIRS

Crawler tractors, cranes, grader ditchers, bulldozers, bucket loaders, computer-controlled machine tools, and automatic screw machines.

RESEARCH

Conducted efficiency and cost analysis study of heating systems of factory, engineering, and administration buildings at Boeing Company.

MILITARY

Corps of Engineers, 4-year enlistment, 2-1/2 years in Germany, responsible for field repair of heavy equipment.

Figure 8.12 Sample chrono-functional resume.

Page 2 of 2   John B. Dunne   303-555-1473

EXPERIENCE
Summer, 199_, Junior Engineer, Plant Services Section, Boeing Company. Responsible for research study to determine efficiency and cost analysis of steam heating systems for factory, engineering, and administration buildings.
Summer, 199_, Mechanic, Colorado State University, maintenance of motor pool trucks, tractors, bulldozers. Operated and repaired heavy equipment and computerized machine tools.
199_–199_, U.S. Army Corps of Engineers, specialist second class E-5, field repair and maintenance of heavy equipment.
Summer, 199_, Laborer, Gardner Construction Company, Colorado. Worked directly from blueprints, duties included tying reinforcing steel rods for concrete walls.

PROFESSIONAL AFFILIATIONS
Member of A.S.M.E. student section; Sigma Tau Honorary Engineering Fraternity, and Phi Beta Phi.

REFERENCES
Available on request.

Figure 8.12 (continued)

Writing an Executive Briefing

The **executive briefing** has been developed by the employment recruiting field to replace the cover letter, particularly for a specific opening. It is based on the belief that the initial resume reviewer (a member of the personnel department) has only a vague understanding of the job opening. Cover letters, it was reasoned, have become stereotyped, so the executive briefing was developed as a streamlined, effective instrument to call attention to an applicant's qualifications for a specific opening. It is actually an abstract of an applicant's resume, high-lighting in "sound-bite" terms specific items of experience, competencies, and background as they relate to the opening. An aid to developing the executive briefing is to make use of the comparative inventory discussed on page 219.

The executive briefing is less appropriate for the person just beginning a career; it is, however, an effective device by which an experienced professional can call attention to the complete resume. Figure 8.13 is an example of an executive briefing.

Guidelines for Preparing Resumes

1. Do not use the word *Resume.* Begin with your name, centered, as the heading. (You want the contact information to stand out.) If you use a word processor, boldface the letters in your name. Center your address and telephone number below your name. Some resume writers place their address and telephone number on the same line to save space.

2. Your Career Objective statement follows below the contact information or heading. The words *Career Objective, Employment Objective,* or *Objective* may be centered with the statement across the page below it, or the objective statement may be placed in a prominent heading style at the left margin. Be consistent in your style when formatting headings. Refer to the sample resumes in this chapter.

3. If you decide to use a Summary statement (usually used in a functional or in a chrono-functional resume) place it after the Career or Employment Objective statement. (In some functional resumes, it replaces the Employment Objective statement.)

4. The chronological resume is most appropriate for the entry-level, less-experienced applicant. Use reverse chronology in your listings; that is, begin with your current or most recent experience and work backward in time.

5. For recent graduates, your education usually is your best qualification, so list it before the section on Experience. Again use reverse chronology in listing the items.

6. The usual sequence of data within each entry under Education is: degree, institution, location of institution (city and state), date graduated, course of study, grade-point average (optional), honors received, list of major courses significant to the opening or objective.

<u>EXECUTIVE BRIEFING</u>
for a senior programmer analyst
as advertised in <u>Computerworld</u>

Nathan M. Duran
118 Meadow Vista Way
Encinitas, CA 92024
619-555-4361

     To help you evaluate the attached resume and conserve your time, I have prepared this executive briefing. It lists your advertised needs on the left and my experience and skills on the right. My resume will give you further details.

<u>Job Title:</u>
Senior Programmer Analyst
Required Experience:
8 yrs. Programmer Analyst
of which at least 3 were
as a senior analyst

<u>My Current Title:</u>
Senior Program Analyst
Relevant Experience:
8 yrs. as a Program Analyst
of which 5 yrs. as a Senior Program
Analyst, in addition, 4 yrs. as a
Programmer with 2 yrs. as a Project
Leader

<u>Hardware:</u>
Prime 850, 750, 550
IBM360

<u>Hardware:</u>
DEC VAX, NETWARE, RISK, ES-9000,
DEC-Alpha, Network Protocol, TCP/IP,
Microcomputers

<u>Software:</u>
DOS, Primos, TAPR
Datatrieve

<u>Software:</u>
DOS, EXCEL, UNIX, DB2, ORACLES, CICS,
Harvard Graphics, FoxPro, DBase, Lotus, 4GL,
SAS, Windows

<u>Languages:</u>
COBOL, FORTRAN,
Info/Basic, PASCAL

<u>Languages:</u>
COBOL, C++, Visual Basic, SQL,
Power Builder

Figure 8.13 Sample executive briefing.

7. Sequence of data for each job experience is: job title, name of company, address (city and state), notation if part-time, dates worked, (sometimes dates are placed columnarly on the left), responsibilities and duties, and achievements if any. Be specific in describing duties; use action verbs, but do not clutter up your resume with too much data. Include only what reflects well on you. Avoid using personal pronouns. (Instead of saying, "I was responsible for maintaining UNISYS equipment," state, "maintained UNISYS equipment.")

8. Data in an entry are usually separated by commas. Some resumes use periods after dates. A colon follows after the item "duties." Items listed under duties are separated by commas. The completed entry is followed by a period. Be logical and consistent in the punctuation you use.

9. Do not include physical details (such as height, weight, health, gender). Use your date of birth, not your age. Marital status may be omitted. If you have computer literacy or proficiency, indicate it.

10. Do not list references, but indicate they are available on request.

11. Do not include so much data that your resume gives the appearance of clutter and runs three or four pages. The employer will not read it. A well-organized resume with carefully selected information need not run more than one page for an entry-level applicant.

12. An attractive, neat resume invites reading. Proofread it carefully. There must be *no* typographical errors, misspellings, or lapses in grammar. Do not bind the resume in a folder. Clip the cover letter to it; if your resume runs two pages, staple them together. The paper for both cover letter and resume should be a good quality white bond no less than 16 pounds, preferably 20-pound, 25 percent cotton/rag stock: A good quality business-size envelope should be used. Of course, the typing on the envelope should be neat, attractive, and accurate.

The Job Interview

The purpose of a job interview is to verify the impressions and credentials your application material provided to the prospective employer, and to judge whether you are the best of several candidates for the opening to be filled. The employer wants to see firsthand how you look, act, and react.

The prospect of an interview can be an anxiety-ridden experience, but it need not be a terrorizing one. It is normal for the prospect to give you butterflies in the stomach, but do not be frightened by it. Remember you have already passed a major hurdle—you have been invited for an interview! It is an opportunity for you to exhibit directly your qualifications.

The secret of success is preparation. Learn and research more information than you did before writing to the company/organization—details such as its products, services, history, achievements and successes, role/status in the industry/field, prospects, branch locations, and community activities. If time permits, request copies of company literature and annual reports. Research information in financial publications such as *Dun and Bradstreet* and *Standard and Poor's Corporation Records* as well as appropriate trade and professional periodicals. Your faculty is also an excellent source.

After you have all the useful information that is practical for you to obtain, give yourself time to analyze and relate it to your situation. With careful preparation, you will be competent and confident in your interview. To attain that type of security, consider the following factors:

You were not invited to be humiliated.

You are being given the opportunity to prove yourself: to perform one-on-one so you can be evaluated on how you behave and manage yourself in a stressful situation, how you think on your feet, how you speak, and how you interact.

With that in mind, here are some questions an employer may ask during your interview:

Tell me about yourself (in one or two minutes).

Why do you want to work here?

What sort of job are you looking for and why?

What do you know about our company/organization?

What qualifications do you have for the position?

What is your educational background/training? What did you learn? How does/did your course of study prepare you for this opening? What extracurricular activities did you have? What benefits did you derive from them?

What do you consider your strongest qualifications?

What do you see your greatest shortcomings to be?

What are you hoping to do in the future? (career objective)

Where would you like to be in ten years?

What is your secret ambition?

What makes you happy? What makes you unhappy?

You, in turn, should be prepared to ask some questions of your own:

What specifically does the position entail?

In what department/section is the work performed?

How does the department/section fit into the scheme of things in the company/organization's objectives/activities?

Whom will the selected candidate be working with and for?

What responsibilities/opportunities are there for the selected candidate and the department in which she works?

What is the stability of the position and of the company?

Consider carefully the answers to questions an employer may ask you. Consult with your faculty, knowledgeable friends, and family. They may have questions and topics not listed here. Write out the answers, but do not memorize them. Extemporize so that you are spontaneous in your responses during the interview. Practice the answers and rehearse the interview with a friend.

Bring a copy of your resume with you to the interview. The employer will have a copy of it, but it will help you to elaborate on any matter the interviewer may ask. If there are new additions to the resume's information, it is a good idea for you to present them at the interview. For example: "I received my degree two weeks ago," or "I have received notice that I am graduating *magna cum laude*."

If a silence occurs during the interview, do not feel obliged to talk unless you have something pertinent to say. It is the employer's ball game; let the interviewer make the next move. Perhaps the interviewer wants to gauge your reaction to the silence. Do not ramble on just to talk. Successful interviews last about an hour. When the interviewer wants the meeting to end, she will so indicate, usually by rising and saying something to the effect that the company/organization was pleased to meet you and that you will be informed about a decision after all interviews are completed. At the end of the interview, express tactfully but enthusiastically your interest in the position and thank the interviewer for the opportunity to present your qualifications. It is appropriate before leaving to ask when you can expect to hear the decision regarding your application.

Writing a Post-Interview Letter

The cover letter is a sales letter. Good salespeople know a sale frequently depends upon repeated efforts and follow-ups. Follow-up letters, after an interview, create a favorable impression upon a prospective employer. People admire determination and persistence. After you have been granted an interview, express your appreciation and reemphasize those particular qualifications that you determined, during the course of the interview, are important to the prospective employer. If you are able to present additional information or additional qualifications to enhance your application, do so in your follow-up letter. The follow-up letter should be neither too long nor too short and should be timed to reach your prospective employer as soon as possible, preferably the day following the interview (Figure 8.14).

Acceptance and Refusal Letters

When you receive an offer for a job, whether by telephone or letter, it is advisable and polite to write a letter accepting or declining the position. If you are informed by phone and are accepting the offer, it is appropriate to request a written confirmation and to respond with a formal letter of acceptance. The offer of employment can be considered a contract; the letter formalizes the terms of your employment. Your response should reiterate the terms you are accepting. Your letter, though formal and brief, should express your pleasure at the prospect of working for the company. Figure 8.15 is a sample acceptance letter.

Every now and then you may face the enviable problem of receiving more than one job offer and will have to turn an offer down. After due but prompt consideration, write a letter of refusal. Since an employer has invested time and effort

Dear Mr. Fisher:[2]

    I appreciate the time you spent with me yesterday discussing the sales engineering position you are seeking to fill. Your description of some of the problems the position entails offers a challenge I would like to tackle. My work as a Junior Applications Engineer for Moore Hydraulics Company during the summer of my senior year at Engineering College clinched my resolve that Sales Engineering would be my life's pursuit. It also gave me the kind of invaluable experience needed for engineering sales by working with customers on problems that needed modification of off-the-shelf Moore engineering products.

    The products of Digital Equipment Corporation, Mr. Fisher, were pointed out to me early in my laboratory courses by my professors as among the finest in the industry. Because a salesman must believe in the products he sells, I would be proud to be associated with your organization. The problems you mentioned in our conversation yesterday interested me. I would very much like to help you resolve them and look forward to doing so.

Sincerely yours,

Figure 8.14 Sample follow-up letter.

---

[2]In this and most subsequent sample letters, some headings, dates and signatures are omitted for purposes of saving space.

> Dear Mr. Beachem:
>
> I am happy to accept the position of Technical Writer at Interactive Software Company at a yearly salary of $28,600.
>
> I will telephone Ms. Stearns in your Personnel Office for instructions on the reporting date and employee orientation.
>
> I am looking forward to a fulfilling career with Interactive Software Company.
>
> Sincerely,

Figure 8.15 Sample acceptance letter.

considering your qualifications and interviewing you, you are obligated to explain your reason for not accepting the offer. Do not begin your letter with a blunt refusal. Lead into it with sincere, complimentary remarks about the interview and the position that was offered. Be candid but cordial, and always leave a door open for future possibilities. Sometimes, the job you accepted does not turn out the way you had hoped and you may wish to explore the job you turned down. Figure 8.16 is a sample of an effective refusal letter.

The policy of many firms with well-organized placement and personnel departments is to offer the courtesy of a letter explaining an unfavorable employment decision (see Figure 8.17). The graciousness expressed takes the sting out of the refusal. If you should receive a rejection letter like the example in Figure 8.17 and are still interested in working for the company, it would be good strategy to send a reply similar to the one in Figure 8.18.

How to Write Inquiries

Letters of inquiry are probably the most common type of correspondence in business and industry. This type of letter seeks information or advice on many matters, technical and otherwise, from another person who is able to furnish it. Sometimes the inquiry may offer potential or direct profit to the person or company addressed. Frequently, the person addressed has nothing to gain and much time and

Dear Mr. Ellis:

    I am gratified by your offer of employment as a junior mycologist in your clinical laboratory. I have discussed it with my major professor at State University, Dr. Edna Sapolsky. She tells me I should be flattered by it and I am. Dr. Sapolsky believes that I would find no better opportunity to pursue microbiology than in your laboratory. Unfortunately, while your offer has given me a great deal of happiness, it has also presented me with a conflict. You see, I had already decided to pursue studies in aquatic ecology before your letter arrived, and had been considering a similar offer from a laboratory in Cambridge, Massachusetts.

    After further discussion of my career aspirations with both Dr. Sapolsky and my parents, I have come to the decision that my interest in aquatic ecology can best be developed further by Ph.D. study. The offer from the other laboratory permits me to continue part-time graduate study at company expense. The Massachusetts Institute of Technology has accepted my application for this study. Under these circumstances, so advantageous to my aspirations, I have decided, not without mixed emotions, to accept the offer from the Cambridge laboratory.

    I do appreciate the wonderful opportunity you extended to me. I shall always recall the pleasant experience I had during my interview visit to your laboratories. I know it would have been a joy to have been part of your laboratory organization.

                                               Sincerely yours,

Figure 8.16 Sample refusal letter.

COLLINS RADIO COMPANY
CEDAR RAPIDS, IOWA 52403
May 14, 19__

Mr. James C. Mitchell
3520 East Jackson Boulevard
Lansing, MI 48906

Dear Mr. Mitchell:

Miss Williams has forwarded your completed application and your letter so that we may consider you for a possible association in our Controller's Division. We sincerely appreciate your interest in our company.

We would like to congratulate you on your efforts to acquire a specialized accounting education. You will find it an exceptionally fine background for any field of endeavor in which you engage.

The accounting system of Collins Radio Company is necessarily somewhat complex because we are engaged in both government and commercial enterprise. Your application indicated you have completed approximately nine semester hours of Accounting work with LaSalle Extension and Drake University. At the present time, we are using, almost exclusively, Accounting majors in our Controller's Division, which has the responsibility for the company's accounting program. Because of this fact, we think it unfair to you to consider your application at this time. Most of your competition in that division would have from two to three times as many hours of specialized accounting background as you have, in addition to considerable exposure in the area of economic theory. Most likely your progress here with that type of competition would be seriously limited.

May we suggest that you continue your Accounting studies and perhaps get in touch with us when you have completed that curriculum. Your application would seem to indicate you have the ambition and aggressiveness which we like to find in Collins' employees.

Thank you for your interest in Collins Radio Company. May we extend our best wishes for your continued success in your Accounting studies.

Very truly yours,

J. J. Field, Assistant Director
Treasurer's Division

JJF:DT

Figure 8.17 Sample company rejection letter.

> Dear Mr. Field:
>
> Thank you for writing me to explain why my application for employment with your company cannot be favorably considered at this time. Although I regret that there is nothing appropriate available for my background, I hope that with additional study and experience, which your letter has stimulated me to pursue, there will be an opportunity for which I may qualify in the future. I shall look forward to your examining my improved qualifications at that time.
>
> Sincerely yours,

Figure 8.18 Sample reply to a rejection letter.

energy to lose. Most organizations will answer all letters of inquiry as a matter of good public relations. Whether they send the inquirer the information requested frequently depends on the writer's ability to formulate her inquiry. A properly formulated inquiry will make the receiver want to answer it and makes the job of answering easier. A poorly written request may go unanswered or may receive an answer of little value.

A well-formulated letter of inquiry will have the following organizational pattern:

1. The opening paragraph should be a clear statement of the purpose of the letter. It should define for the reader the information desired or the problem involved: what is wanted, who wants it, why it is wanted.
2. The second paragraph should lead into the inquiry details. It should be specific and arranged in such a way as to make the answer as easy as possible. A good technique is to state specific questions in tabulated form. However, the request should be reasonable. The writer should not expect a busy person to take several hours to answer a long, involved questionnaire. Many companies will not answer inquiries from people who are not customers, unless they know why the writer wants the information. This is especially true if information requested is of a proprietary nature and would be of benefit to a competitor.
3. The final paragraph should contain an expression of appreciation with a tactful suggestion of action. The letter might conclude with a statement that the writer would return a similar favor or service.

The letter of inquiry falls into two categories: the solicited letter and the unsolicited letter. The solicited letter is written in response to an advertisement inviting the reader to write for further information about a certain product or service. The unsolicited letter is written when the writer takes the initiative for making the request or asking for information or advice. Figures 8.19 and 8.20 provide examples of solicited and unsolicited letters.

Answers to Inquiries

Replies should begin with a friendly statement indicating that the request has been granted or granted to the extent possible. Then there should follow the complete and exact information that was desired by the requester, including whatever explanatory data might be helpful. If part of the information wanted cannot be provided, this fact should be indicated next and accompanied with an expression of regret and an explanation of the reasons why the complete information cannot be given. Additional material that might be of value to the requester is also included. Finally, the reply could end with the courteous offer to provide any further information that might be wanted that is possible for the writer to provide. Figure 8.21 is an answer to an inquiry.

Sales Department
Bakelite Company
30 E. 42nd Street
Room 308
New York, N.Y. 10036

Ladies/Gentlemen:

I have noticed your advertisement in the September 10 issue of the <u>Wall Street Journal</u>. I would appreciate your sending me your booklet, "Products and Processes."

In addition, I am particularly interested in epoxies—and their application in the construction of dies and molds. I would like to know the physical characteristics of epoxies, such as bearing load limits, heat resistance, and wear resistance. Perhaps a representative of your company might call on us to discuss our possible uses of epoxies.

                                                            Yours truly,

---

Figure 8.19 *Sample solicited letter of inquiry.*

The Cumberland Company
80 Broad Street
Boston, MA 02401

Ladies/Gentlemen:

Will you give us the benefit of your experience? We, as a university, want to prepare our students going into business and industry to be able to write effective letters, memoranda, and reports. To make our course work as practical as possible, we would like to know what business and industry require in these areas. Will you give us your ideas?

Do you have a preference for, or a prejudice against, any of the forms presently used in business correspondence—block, semiblock, complete block, or the National Office Management's Simplified Letter Form? Why? Is any one form used universally throughout your company?

We have another favor to ask. Examples are often the best teacher. May we ask for copies of letters, memos, and reports that may be helpful in training our students along the line you suggest?

We hope you can help us to prepare our students to meet the communications problems they will find in business and industry.

Sincerely yours,

Figure 8.20 Sample unsolicited letter of inquiry.

THE CUMBERLAND COMPANY
PAPER MANUFACTURERS

Cable Address   Cumberland Mills
Cumberland Boston   Central Mill
                                                                                          Copsecook Mill

80 Broad Street, Boston, Massachusetts 02401

30 December, 19__

Professor Herman M. Weisman
1801 Richmond Road
Westport, Maryland 43214

SUBJECT: Correspondence and letter-writing practices

As you see, Professor Weisman—
we rate as an ardent supporter of the simplified form of letter-writing—so-called.

In fact, we're credited with being the originator of the practice. We've been using the simplified system of letter-writing, and successfully, for at least 50 years. Here's why:

There's no reason in the world for using the endearing term in the salutation part of a letter. In our opinion, the simplified form of correspondence automatically eliminates this practice, and the communication becomes "alive" immediately. That's what we call the fast start in letter-writing. Of course, there are many other reasons, too numerous to mention here in favor of the practice. But for the benefit of your students, perhaps the easiest way for us to demonstrate our technique is this: We'll arrange to send you, automatically, copies of typical correspondence covering a period of two weeks. Through this means, you can determine by actual experience, instead of theory, how we operate in progressing the practice of simplified letter-writing.

Incidentally, perhaps we should tip you off in advance that most of our correspondence is with people engaged in the advertising profession. And may we further add that the simplified form of letter-writing evidently appeals to them. We've never had even the semblance of a squawk from our customers to the effect that the technique is "flip" or undesirable.

Please believe, sir, we welcome this opportunity to be of some service to you. Here's wishing you much continued success in your worthy educational endeavors. With heartiest of season's greetings to you for the New Year; we are, as always,

Promotionally optimistic,

Randy Raymond

RR/emb
Advertising Department

Figure 8.21 Sample answer to an inquiry letter.

How to Write Claim Letters

As long as the human equation operates in business and industry, mistakes will be made, claims will be filed, and adjustments will have to be made. No matter what the cause, the claim or complaint needs to be expressed calmly, courteously, and objectively. Facts must be stated positively and truthfully. No matter how tempted the writer is and how justified she may be, any impatience, sarcasm, or discourtesy must be avoided. Vituperative or sarcastic language throws obstacles into the proceedings and makes adjustments more difficult and almost certainly will cause further delay in solving the problem.

The following suggestions are a practical guide in writing a letter of claim:

1. Explain what the problem is or what has gone wrong. Give necessary details for identifying the faulty product or service. Include dates of order and arrival or nonarrival. Specify breakage or the kind and extent of damage. Give model number, sizes, colors, and whatever information is necessary to enable the reader to check into the matter. It is proper to include a statement of inconvenience or loss that has resulted from the cause of complaint.
2. Motivate the reader for the desired action by appealing to her sense of fair play or pride.
3. Include a statement of what adjustment you would consider to be fair. Figures 8.21A and 8.21B are two examples of claim letters.

The Adjustment Letter

How adjustments are met is usually determined by company policy. Most companies grant adjustments whenever a claim seems justified. Claims are usually decided on their individual merits. However, every complaint or claim, no matter how trivial, is answered courteously and promptly. Where a claim is granted, the adjustment letter has the following structure:

1. The writer is thanked for calling attention to the difficulty or problem.
2. The problem may be reviewed and explained. Alibis are considered poor form; whenever possible and expedient, whatever caused the difficulty is dealt with frankly.
3. The writer grants the adjustment, emphasizing a sincere desire to maintain good relations with the customer and, finally, expresses appreciation for the customer's business.

When an adjustment is refused, the letter begins, similarly, on a positive note. The writer is thanked for calling attention to the difficulty. The situation is reviewed; particularly, the facts surrounding the claim are examined from the point of view of the decision.

The adjustment is refused with an explanation. The writer needs to show the reader that she understands the reader's problem. She must also, with friendly

Mr. A. H. Brown
Contracts Administrator
Homes Electronics
14 Lincoln Way
Lexington, Mass. 02173

Subject: Our Purchase Order No. BDLA83760

Dear Mr. Brown:

Our project engineer, Mr. T. H. Sherman, has informed me that despite an earlier agreement, your company has decided not to provide the feature of easy means and convenient interchangeability between crystal diode and bolometer in the instrumentation you are developing for us.

Please refer to our Purchase Order No. BDLA83760, which stipulates that the instrument under development will confirm to specifications.

I am sure this misunderstanding can be cleared up in time for delivery to be made in accordance with the required dates.

Sincerely yours,

R. H. Fanwell
Assistant Purchasing Agent

Figure 8.21A Sample claim letters.

> Knight Laboratories
> 2330 Eastern Avenue
> Los Angeles, California 90022
>
> Ladies/Gentlemen:
>
> Our last order included 1 × 100 Deserol Ampules. The order was delivered but the Deserol drug was not included within the packaged order, which arrived by United Parcel. Since your shipping document listed seven boxes of Deserol and this item was also included in your invoice attached with the shipment, we want to let you know of this discrepancy. What is more important, we are badly in need of this drug for filling our prescriptions.
>
> Sincerely yours,
>
> Barry Nelson

Figure 8.21B (continued)

candor, make sure that the reader will understand the writer's situation. Examine Figures 8.22 and 8.23 for some samples of adjustment letters.

The Letter of Instruction

Technical personnel, because of their specialized knowledge, are frequently called upon to instruct others who have a need for their specialized knowledge to perform a particular task. Letters of instruction are a convenient instrument toward this end. If the matter is a complex one, requiring diverse contributions by a number of people with a number of devices, tools, and equipment, the letter may be more conveniently structured as a report. Frequently, however, matters can be related most conveniently in the form of a letter or memo.

Instructions are mastered more readily, better remembered, and carried out more intelligently if the person being instructed knows the reasons for the procedures indicated. The letter of instruction, therefore, usually begins with a covering explanatory statement, which provides the background for the writing of the letter. The language of the letter is structured in accordance with the background, experience, and intelligence of the person for whom the instructions are intended.

The imperative mood is used for giving specific instructions. The imperative is the form of verb used in stating commands or strong requests. The subject of the verb is not expressed but understood. (The rest of this paragraph, for the sake of illustration, is structured in the imperative mood.) Be careful in using the

Mr. R. H. Fanwell
Assistant Purchasing Agent
King Electronics
1231 Jay Street
Brooklyn, N.Y. 11222

Subject: Your Purchase Order NO. BDLA31767

Dear Mr. Fanwell:

Your letter regarding the above purchase order has been reviewed with our Technical Personnel who have been working with your engineers on this instrumentation. Unknown to us, work requirements for this Purchase Order were left to informal understandings between some of our technical personnel and your engineers.

Our Contracts Department interpreted the work requirements in accordance with the written specifications of the purchase order and, accordingly, ruled that incorporation of a means for convenient and easy interchangeability between the crystal diode and bolometer was not called for. The interpretation was based on the note in purchase order BDLA31767, which reads: "Items 1a, 1b, and 1c to be in accordance with Proposal No. 1401 of May 24, 1990." Nowhere within Proposal No. 1401 is the requirement of interchangeability of crystal diode and bolometer mentioned.

Because of the informal understanding between our technical people and your project engineer, we will accomplish without any further cost the interchangeability requested. Delivery of the low-powered unit will be made within the next two-week period. We would appreciate notification of acceptability of that aspect of the work as soon as you have tested the delivered unit.

Sincerely yours,

Figure 8.22 Sample adjustment letter.

> Mr. Barry Nelson
> City Drugs
> 12 University Avenue
> Denver, Colorado 80206
>
> Dear Mr. Nelson:
>
> Thank you for calling our attention to the omission in your order of the Deserol drug. We did not intend to include it with your order. Listing it on the Bill of Lading and on the invoice was a mistake.
>
> Deserol is packaged one ampule per box, seven boxes to a shipping container. Since it is kept under refrigeration, we normally ship it by air parcel post, special delivery, rather than with regular orders. Because of this, and because we were uncertain of the amount you desired, we did not include it in your shipment. If you will send us your order indicating how many Deserol ampules you would prefer, we would be glad to make immediate air shipment.
>
> We appreciate your interest in our products. Please call on us if we can be of any further assistance.
>
> Very truly yours,

Figure 8.23 Sample adjustment letter.

imperative that you do not appear unduly brusque or imperious. This is especially advisable in dealings with clients or persons outside your organization. The imperative mood is used for the specific directions required, so be sure the instructions are in parallel grammatical construction; be sure, also, that your instructions are complete and that all words and statements are specific and clear. Whenever the reader is to use her own judgment, so indicate. Be sure there is logical order in the presentation of the steps of your directions. When instructions can be arranged in successive or chronological order, organize them in accordance with the demands of the situation so that they ensue as a planned sequence of activity. Write instructions concisely and precisely; avoid roundabout expressions, vague and unnecessary words, and generalities. Use such devices as numbering, underlining, and indention of headings because these help clarify the indicated procedures. Include the time or date by which the action must be accomplished. See Figures 8.24 and 8.25 for examples of letters of instruction.

Computer Technology in Correspondence

Computer technology has entered the technical writer's workplace. Three topics related to technical correspondence will be examined here.

Mr. James Mitchell
19 Cherry Creek Lane
Jericho, New York 11753

Dear Mr. Mitchell:

We are sorry that our salesman did not explain that all Hollywood beds are delivered unassembled. I am sure you understand that it would be most awkward and inconvenient to ship, in protected cartons, a bed completely assembled.

Such bulk would add to storage and transportation costs and would be reflected in the price we would have to charge you. Actually, assembling one of our Hollywood beds is a very simple process that can be done in four very easy steps. Won't you try them? We are sure you will find our instructions very easy to follow:

1. Place the two sections of the frame in a parallel position on the floor, so that both headboard plates are at the same end. Swing out the cross rails, until they are at right angles (90°) to the side rails.
2. Slip tension clamps on cross rails to your left, wing nuts facing out. <u>Do not tighten the clamps</u>. Overlap right and left cross rails so that left cross rail is on the <u>bottom</u> at the head end and on <u>top</u> at the foot end. Slide tension clamps to center of overlap of cross rails. <u>Do not tighten clamps</u>.
3. Measure the width of the boxspring across the bottom. Adjust the width of the bed frame to the same measurement. Tighten both clamps securely with the wing nut. Insert casters, glides, or rollers, whichever you have. Exert pressure downward on the frame until they click in.
4. Place boxspring and mattress on the frame, which should hold the boxspring securely. If not secure, loosen clamps, adjust frame for snug fit, and tighten clamps.

Thus you will have assembled the frame of your comfortable, but sturdy, Hollywood bed in not more than 15 minutes. I am attaching, also, for your information, drawings illustrating each step.

Sincerely yours,

Figure 8.24 Sample letter of instruction.

Mr. G. W. Schmidt
Field Engineer
Colorado Sugar Corp.
Berthoud, Colorado 80513

SUBJECT: Instructions for recording soil and drainage data

Dear Mr. Schmidt:

The data you collect on a soil and drainage investigation go to the Central Design office. The men who use your data have probably not seen the investigation site. In order that your data be complete and consistent, it is desirable that you follow a standardized procedure for recording such data.

Use Form D16, a copy of which is included. This form is available from the Engineering Office. Divide the recording data into three main parts:

A. Generalized site description
B. Specific soil and material description
C. Symbolic profile representation

A. Generalized site description

Use the spaces at the top of this form to record:

1. Area—the particular land development project.
2. Pit Number—the assigned number.
3. Photo Number—if the area is covered by an aerial photograph survey, note the photograph number and the scale of the survey. Example: 17–30, 1:8100 (Photos are filed by number under the survey scale).
4. Ground water: Record the depth of the ground water. If ground water was not present at the time of the survey, write "none."
5. Date: Date is important in conjunction with water table fluctuations.
6. Surveyor: Write your last name.
7. Site description: Note all conditions at the particular site. Land use, crop condition, if cultivated, natural vegetation, slope, salinity, and alkalinity.

B. Specific soil and material description

1. Indicate any changes in the soil profile by drawing a horizontal line across the form using the depth marks as guides.
2. Write out the soil texture for each horizon. Abbreviations can cause confusion.

Figure 8.25 Sample letter of instruction.

3. Indicate the structure of each horizon since structure is a guide to permeability.
4. Estimate the permeability of each horizon using standardized permeability classes.
5. Write out the moisture condition in each horizon.
6. Indicate any molting by standard nomenclature. Molting, when present, gives an indication of post ground water conditions. Example: Even when ground water was not encountered at the time of the survey, dark, rust-brown molting near the surface might indicate drainage problems sometime in the past.
7. If free water occurs in the pit, indicate by writing "Water Table" at the point of the Free Water Surface. Note the nature of the water table, true or perched.
8. Indicate any samplings of soil materials by blocking out the depth marks, "marks on the form corresponding to the depth of the sample."
9. Indicate water samples, by writing "Water Sample" in the supersaturated zone.

C. <u>Symbolic profile representation</u>

1. Use the space on the left side of the form, D16, to show the complete soil profile in symbolic form.
2. Use standard soil and material symbols.

If you follow this method of recording field data, you can be sure your data will be complete and clearly understood by those using it.

Sincerely yours,

Figure 8.25 (*continued*)

Electronic Mail

Electronic mail, sometimes referred to as **E-mail,** permits direct transmission of letters and memos electronically to a recipient's computer. It offers the speed and convenience of a telephone call plus the advantage of a permanent copy of the message. Though it costs more than a postage stamp, it is less costly than overnight air express mail. E-mail must be part of a dedicated system; it can be sent short distances between offices or very long distances across the world by satellite. The message can be read on the terminal, stored in the computer file, or printed at any time.

To use electronic mail, your computer must be linked to a system or service. You access the system or service by proper code identification. You key your message to your destination, which must have a linkage to your system or service. The message is received and placed in the recipient's file space (mailbox).

The two general types of E-mail are:

1. an inhouse network, which connects computers or terminals within an organization, and
2. an external network, connecting computers at different locations, even around the world.

Electronic Bulletin Boards

The **electronic bulletin board** is the equivalent of the conventional bulletin board with the exception that its system enables a linkage of enlarged readerships from great distances. Its purpose is to exchange information. Key to the electronic bulletin board is the system operator (or sysop), who oversees the activity. Connection to the bulletin board is made by a **modem,** a device that converts binary digital data to audio tones suitable for transmission over telephone lines and vice versa. Users can post messages for others to see; read messages posted by others; communicate with the system operator to ask questions, report problems, make suggestions, share programs, or obtain programs.

Electronic bulletin boards are often operated by individuals interested in computers, who wish to communicate with others with a similar interest to share information and software programs. Companies and organizations have also started electronic bulletin boards as a service to clients and members. Some businesses use them for customers to place orders, ask questions, and have problems solved. Electronic bulletin boards are a useful resource for technical writers in practicing their profession.

Facsimile (FAX)

In some ways similar to electronic mail, **facsimile (FAX)** is a technology using telephone links to provide a hard copy duplicate of an original document. The image of the document is scanned at the point of transmission, reconstructed at the receiving station by another FAX machine, and duplicated as hard copy.

Facsimile machines send an exact replica of a page—text, illustration, and even halftones—over telephone lines. The FAX uses a built-in scanner that passes over letters (including handwriting) or illustrations on a page, reading an "on" signal for a dark dot and an "off" signal for white space. At the receiving end, a high resolution printer translates the on/off signals to dot/no dot instructions and presents a picture of the page.

Advances in technology now permit personal computers to serve as FAX machines. A FAX modem, known as a fax board, allows both sending and receiving messages by way of a user's personal computer. Computer-generated outgoing FAXes are more readable and better appearing than messages sent by regular FAX machines because the image does not have to go through the degradation of the FAX machine scanner. Improved confidentiality is another advantage; messages enter the computer's disk instead of the FAX machine tray.

A recently available device combines a FAX, a copier, an image scanner, and a document printer and is designed to tie together these now-separate operations. Using this machine, a technical writer pushes a button on her computer to order up one or several hundred high-quality bound copies of a large report or send a FAX of the document to another computer user. In addition, the machine can electronically scan paper documents for storage into a computer, and that document later can be manipulated on the computer screen for other needs.

Chapter in Brief

In this chapter, we examined the role correspondence plays in science and industry. We looked into the psychology of correspondence, examined the conventions and formats of letters, and discussed how to organize and compose them. We concentrated on correspondence for the employment situation, particularly the resume and its cover letter. Other types of technical correspondence were examined—letters of inquiry and complaint, and responses to each, as well as letters of instruction. We ended the chapter by discussing aspects relating to correspondence utilizing computer technology—electronic mail, the electronic bulletin board, and facsimile.

Chapter Focal Points

- Psychology of correspondence
- Pre-writing—planning the message
- Format conventions
- Memorandums
- How to apply for a job
  Resumes
  Cover letters
  Executive briefings
- Claim and adjustment letters

- Letter of instruction
- Electronic mail
- Electronic bulletin board
- Facsimile

Questions for Discussion

1. Technical personnel often have secretaries type their letters. Do you think a "federal case" has been made in this chapter on correct format, layout, and typing considerations? Defend your answer.
2. Should a letter dealing with technical matters be concerned with the "you psychology"? Before you answer, recall that technical writing is objective and impersonal. Defend your answer.
3. One of the largest irrigation systems in Colorado has an opening for the position of assistant supervisor. The applicant must have a degree in irrigation, agricultural, or civil engineering, and must be between the ages of 25 and 35. Business ability is necessary. An applicant has written the following letter to the Fort Lyon Canal Company, La Junta, Colorado:

704 S. College Avenue
Fort Collins, CO 80521
October 5, 199__

Fort Lyon Canal Co.
Post Office Box 176
La Junta, CO 81050

Ladies/Gentlemen:

A coyote can live very well in a zoo, but he is not happy there. He longs to trade the security of his stuffy zoo quarters for his home on the prairie where he can battle the elements for himself and get away from dense population. I am like the coyote in many respects. I grew up in the Arkansas Valley and learned to love it. Cities, heavy traffic, and design rooms do not appeal to me. I am home in the Arkansas Valley working to try to increase its productivity. That is why I want to be assistant supervisor of your company.

I grew up on irrigated farms under the Fort Lyon and farmed there before entering the Air Force. As you know, my father farmed in the Arkansas Valley for 54 years, most of which was under the Fort Lyon. I am well acquainted with the problems of your company and of the farmers, a quality that would be useful not only in making decisions but also in gaining the confidence of the farmers.

I will receive a Bachelor of Science degree from Colorado State University next month in Agricultural Engineering, irrigation option. My technical electives were taken in irrigation, and most of my nontechnical electives were taken in the fields of business and economics.

I would like to have an interview on any Saturday this month. If this would be impossible, I can appear at your convenience.

Sincerely yours,

How do you think the prospective employer will react to the opening? If you suggest an unfavorable reaction, how would you rewrite the opening? Does the applicant meet the specifications called for in the ad? What specific information is lacking? Can this be supplied in the resume? Structure a resume supplementing the letter. What merits do you find in the letter? What elements would you improve upon?

4. What is your reaction to the following letter?

> Mr. J. R. Barnes, CLU
> General Manager
> New York Life Insurance Company
> 1740 Broadway, Suite B-304
> Denver, CO 80202
>
> Dear Mr. Barnes:
>
> I want to hitch my wagon to a star . . . not any star, but the New York Life star of the insurance galaxy.
>
> I can help put your district even higher into the insurance sales atmosphere than it is now . . . if I can only be given the opportunity.
>
> I will graduate from Colorado State University in June 19__, having completed my degree in the business administration field of study. I have no outstanding achievements that could be cited from my college records, but I have what I believe to be most essential to help you reach even higher sales records . . . the sincere desire to make a name for myself and your district by selling more insurance my first year than any previous salesman.
>
> I believe I am qualified to do this with your able training assistance in the insurance sales field. I have previously worked in the district sales category for Curtis Publishing Company, Wearever Aluminum, Norge, Frigidaire, Maytag, Zenith, and RCA on commission sales. Other sales work included advertising copy sales work for my hometown paper in high school and college paper at Kansas State College all in the period from age 16 until the present time.
>
> I like meeting people, making friends, doing things for these people, and most of all I like to make money. My motives are not entirely selfish because I don't have to say that to make this money in the insurance field one has to work hard . . . right? This I am ready to do.
>
> If you will glance up the left margin of this letter you can see that every paragraph starts with "I" . . . this is because I am thinking of what I can do for you and New York Life, if given the opportunity. May I have a personal interview with you at your convenience for furthering this discussion? My home telephone number is 555-5713, in case you are in town and wish to call.
>
> Sincerely yours,

What attitude is prevalent in the above letter? What kind of person do you think would write such a letter? Do you think it would impress a sales manager? How would you revise this letter?

5. What is your reaction to the following letter? Why? How would you revise it?

Room 115 Green Hall
Ft. Collins, CO 80521
May 13, 199__

Personnel Manager
King's Clothing
Lakeside Shopping Center
Westminster, CO 80030

Dear Sir or Madam:

Beautiful women! What do these words bring to your mind? Are the images tall, slender, immaculate, and graceful models? Do you see them sitting in a pseudo-swing, posing in a horse and buggy, or simply stepping from a fashion runway?

Without a doubt they will be lovely and a pleasure to look upon. I would like to be able to make these visions come alive for you and your customers. Fashion shows are the media through which I would work. My experience in this field was acquired by modeling for an American dress chain store and in fashion shows of Job's Daughters and high school. I love to organize and carry through brainstorms using lovely models and to select clothing such as you carry.

But even the best fashion show will not succeed without commentary that complements and emphasizes hidden features that make an outfit complete but are not obvious at a first glance. Journalistic training on the Denver Post, my high school newspaper, and *CSU Collegian* provide experience in composing proper comments and extensive college speech training make appearing before the public a pleasure.

Being 25, female, and in excellent health further qualify me to work with you to advance interest and sales through fashion shows. May I come in and talk with you about your position available as a fashion show director? I will call you at 2 PM Monday for an appointment.

Enclosed are three letters of recommendation you might be interested in referring to when considering me for employment. Also included is a recent photograph.

Thank you for your consideration.

Very truly yours,

4 Enclosures

Assignments

1. For training purposes, build up a collection of letters. Obtain them from friends and relatives in business, industry, and from various types of organizations. Study and analyze these letters in accordance with the various principles advocated in this chapter. In this analysis, write down the writer's purpose in each letter. If there are several

purposes, note if they are organized from an overall objective; if there is more than one purpose, do they create confusion? Rewrite such letters. Are there letters in which the writer does not seem to be successful in establishing her purpose? How would you revise those letters?

2. Study the want ads in the classified section of a major newspaper or the listing of positions available in a professional magazine of your field. Write a two-part cover letter for a permanent position on your graduation from college. Try at least three different types of opening paragraphs—original, summary, name beginning. What effect does each type of opening have on the rest of the letter?

3. Now compose a letter for an unsolicited opening—that is, write to a company for whom you wish to work although you do not know that it has a position available. How much of the previous letter (problem number 2) can you use? Should your resume or data sheet be slanted for each job you apply for, or does it remain constant? Why?

4. An influential friend of your family or a relative, who commands respect in the field in which you seek employment, has recommended you for a position. Apply for it by letter.

5. Write follow-up letters following interviews for positions in problem numbers 2, 3, and 4. Write job acceptance letters for problem numbers 3 and 4.

6. You have not been offered a job in the situation mentioned in problem number 4. Write a follow-up letter.

7. Write letters of acceptance for problem numbers 3 and 4.

8. Write two letters:
   a. A letter to a company, a government agency, or an educational institution in which you ask for information about a product, a piece of equipment, a bulletin, or a program of study
   b. A letter giving the information requested in problem number 8a

9. a. Write a letter to a manufacturer ordering six separate catalog items; for the sixth item, request certain changes from the catalog specifications. Ask for your order to be acknowledged and the acknowledgment to include a price list.
   b. Write the acknowledgment to the order in problem number 9a; indicate two alternatives to the special revision of the catalog item. Explain the advantages and disadvantages of each.

10. Write two letters:
    a. A letter giving instructions to a group of workmen under your supervision
    b. A letter report in response to the letter detailing the results after the instructions have been carried out.

11. Recall a product or service you have had that was unsatisfactory. Write a letter to the company concerned telling of your lack of satisfaction and asking for a refund or adjustment.

12. Write two replies:
    a. One granting the adjustment
    b. The other refusing the adjustment

13. Write a letter to a consulting engineer describing a technical problem; ask her whether she is interested in solving the problem for you and what her fee would be.

14. a. Write a letter to an eminent scientist inviting her to be the speaker at the annual banquet for your student scientific activity.
    b. Write a letter from the scientist accepting the engagement.
    c. Write a letter, after the banquet, thanking the scientist for helping to make your student affair a success.
15. Write a letter requesting information about price, efficiency, cost of operation, and maintenance of a piece of equipment for your college laboratory.
16. Reply to problem number 15 above.

9
Short Report Forms

Chapter Objective

Provide understanding of principles and techniques as well as proficiency in writing short reports.

Chapter Focus

- Letter report
- Memo report
- Recommendation reports
- Progress reports

So far, our emphasis in report writing has been on the formal report because principles and techniques applying to it also apply to reports covering simpler situations. Reports, as you will recall, are designed for the particular use a particular reader requires. Generally, its use forms the basis of a decision the reader must make. The report "form" is the package in which you wrap your facts and analysis. Choose or design a package that is suitable for your material, your purpose, and your reader. Let us now examine how to write some of the more common, shorter report forms.

The Letter Report

Frequently, in a reporting situation, the information to be transmitted is concerned with a relatively simple situation. The report's purpose is to provide the necessary information clearly, directly, and concisely. A letter of one to several pages best serves this purpose if the information is being sent outside one's organization. If the information is being sent within one's organization, the memo form is used.

The letter report's appearance is similar to the business letter, having many of its conventional format elements. The printed letterhead of the originating organization is used. Sometimes, a subject line and internal headings within the letter appear. The letter report does not exhibit a "you psychology" tone. The information conveyed is the most important factor, not the personal tone; the tone reflects objectivity. However, the writer is free to use personal pronouns such as "I," "we," and "you."

The letter report is composed of the following elements, usually in the order stated:

Purpose and scope
Findings
Conclusions
Recommendations, if appropriate

Letter reports of more than four pages may begin with a summary. Figure 9.1 is an example of a letter report.

The Memo Report

The memo report resembles the letter report, except that it is intended for members of the originating organization. There is a current tendency, however, to circulate reports in memorandum form to persons outside the originating organization. Like the letter report, it is used in situations that are informal, of immediate interest, and of lesser scope. Because its material is intended for one's own organization, its tone is less formal and less personal than that of the letter report. Its information is presented in the memo format with "From," "To," and "Subject" lines.

SMALL BUSINESS ADMINISTRATION
Washington, D.C. 20416
July 14, 19__

Mr. James Jacobi, President
Jacobi Paint Company
3200 East Monument Street
Baltimore, MD 21205
Subject: Market Aids Newsletter

Dear Mr. Jacobi:
Last February we wrote you as well as other subscribers of our Market Aids Newsletter about our publishing program. We asked whether you found our publication valuable enough to justify the costs of continuing to publish it. We also invited your comments on what uses you made of its information, what features you found useful, and what other subjects you wanted covered. Here are some of the findings:

Purpose and scope

  1. First of all, you told us that you do read the Market Aids Newsletters and that you analyze what they say in terms of your operations. Many people spoke of routing each new issue to key associates for similar study. A number mentioned keeping the back-numbers together in a notebook for handy reference. Still another large group said they use the Market Aids in customer- or employee-relations work, passing on certain issues of special interest. Some use them in discussions and training sessions. Quite a few re-read old Aids as "refreshers" when related problems come up.

Numbered paragraphs 1–4 are findings of the survey.

  2. You liked our short format with a summary at the start and frequent subheadings in boldface type. You asked us to continue listing a few references for further reading at the end of each Market Aids. Some of you hoped for "more elementary material"; others requested just the opposite. (We'll try to strike a balance and issue some of both.) You urged us to keep the language and examples down to everyday businessperson's levels. (We'll work extra hard to do so.)

  3. On suggested future subjects, you came up with scores of interesting ideas. The major areas of concern are human relations and communications, techniques of control, selling, money management, and computer programs for small businesses.

  4. More of you proposed potential authors than we had expected. This is good because many different fields of specialization are represented. You may be sure that all proposals will be carefully considered; you will see some in print later this year.

Figure 9.1 *Sample letter report.*

273

The last two paragraphs are the terminal section of this letter report, offering the conclusion of the survey. They also serve as a public relations device to express appreciation for the replies received and they recommend that there is still time for readers who have not responded to the survey to do so.

Based on your enthusiastic endorsement, we will continue to publish <u>Market Aids Newsletter</u>. We are grateful for the thoughtful help of all who wrote us. We wish we could have replied to each one of you individually, but the numbers were too great. Your interest, cooperation, and voiced support for the work we are trying to do on behalf of small businesses are very welcome.

To those subscribers who, for one reason or another, did not reply to our survey letter, let me say: It's never too late. We are always eager to get your reactions and ideas.

Sincerely yours,

Chief, Management Services Division

Figure 9.1 *(continued)*

WESTINGHOUSE

TO: J. W. Wagner
      Section Manager, Lighting Division
      Cleveland Works

FROM: W. J. Robertson
       Materials Engineering
       East Pittsburgh Works

DATE: February 15, 19__

SUBJECT: <u>Plaster Molding</u>

In your letter of February 5, you asked several questions regarding plaster molding as a method of producing one-of-a-kind castings to suit the needs of your Industrial Designer. Specifically you asked about the type of plaster, processing of molds, and types of alloys that could be handled. The castings to be made are required to have good surface finish and be as accurate as possible.

First of all, I want to point out that surface finish and accuracy (precise control of dimensions) are direct functions of pattern equipment regardless of the process used. Inherently, of course, different molding materials will have an effect but they cannot overcome defects in pattern equipment.

As far as molding processes are concerned, I believe there are several that can be considered for this application. Plaster molding is one, as you mentioned, but you might also consider the CO_2 molding technique, good dry sand molding such as applicable to critical core work, and investment type molds. Depending on the degree of surface smoothness and precision you need any one of these processes may be applicable.

There are two basic plaster molding processes—one using a permeable, foamed mixture, the other using a straight plaster mix, which is of low permeability. Plaster molding techniques do require considerable control in order to produce good molds and castings. Most commonly used are gypsum plasters, which work well on aluminum and copper base alloys except those copper alloys that are poured about 1100°C. In this temperature range, the plaster tends to break down giving very poor surface finish. Also, plaster molds are usually poured hot to assure that all moisture is driven off the mold. This is less critical with the foamed, permeable plasters but drying cycles are important and cannot be short-cut without trouble resulting. I am not familiar enough with plaster molding techniques to be able to spell out specific procedures for you to follow, but I suggest you contact one or more of the gypsum plaster manufacturers who can give you the details you want.

The first paragraph presents the background and purpose of the memo.

In the second paragraph, the writer gets immediately to the point and presents to the recipient the factors causing the problem.

In the middle paragraphs, three to six, the writer explains the methods, procedures, and factors involved in their successful use. Organizationally, these paragraphs represent findings based on experimental analysis.

Figure 9.2 Sample memo report.

Paragraphs seven to nine represent conclusions and recommendations. Because of the many variables involved in the successful use of plaster cast molding, the writer suggests several knowledgeable sources for more specific information on the several approaches he has suggested to solve the foundry operation problem.

In the final two paragraphs, the writer reaffirms the approaches he suggested and offers to be of further assistance.

You may also want to consider the investment type molds for this application but I suspect set-up and operation of this type of procedure for just occasional castings would not be justified. You would, however, get excellent finishes and dimensional control.

Sand molding procedures can also produce the type of quality you indicate if they are tailored to this need. Either the CO_2 process or dry sand procedures would be suitable. Surface finish would be directly related to sand composition in either case. The grain size and distribution of sizes of the sand would be important. I think Jim Drylie or one of his foundry sand experts could give you a good run-down on this possibility, although I don't know how familiar the foundry is with CO_2 molding. One big advantage to using a "precision" sand process lies in the greater size range that can be handled. If your interest in these special castings may range to large castings, i.e., larger than would fit in about a 12″ × 12″ × 12″ space, then plaster may have limitations. These larger items could be handled more readily in a sand process.

Sperry Gyroscope Company has used a carefully controlled sand process for producing a variety of "precision" microwave components. They claim very good dimensional control and surface finish. Unfortunately, I don't know the details of their sand mixes, but they use both dry and green sand practice.

I suggest you contact one or more of the following for detailed processing information:

Investment Molds "Curacast"	Kerr Manufacturing Company 6081 Twelfth Street Detroit, Michigan 48208
Plaster	U.S. Gypsum Company
Sand	Archer-Daniels-Midland Company Federal Foundry Supply Division 2191 West 110th Street Cleveland, Ohio 44102
	B.F. Goodrich Chemical Company 3135 Euclid Avenue Cleveland, Ohio 44115 ("Good-Rite CB-40" binder)

For the CO_2 process possibilities, I think DuPont or Linde Air Products or any good foundry supply house can give you detailed information. I know what I have written doesn't exactly answer your question concerning details of the plaster molding process, but I think the other processes are worth considering, especially since sand procedures would not be foreign to your present foundry operations.

If you want me to pursue this in more detail for you, please let me know.

Figure 9.2 (continued)

Memo reports are used mostly for communication between administrative levels and between members of different departments within an organization. The recipient is often familiar with much of the background of the reported situation. Therefore, more so than in the letter report, you should come directly to the point of your message.

Organizational Elements of a Memo Report

The opening paragraph states the purpose of the memorandum. The paragraph or paragraphs immediately following may present the conclusions reached, findings, or results obtained. The middle paragraphs provide whatever facts or explanations are needed to substantiate the conclusions or results. Tabular or graphic data may be used as needed toward that end. The final paragraph presents, as appropriate, recommendations for the recipient. Figure 9.2 illustrates a memo report.

Recommendation Reports

Recommendation reports are analytical reports based on the examination or investigation of a problematic situation. They are written for the purpose of decision making and action. For data, the investigator relies on:

1. Examination of the actual situation
2. Reading the literature about the problem
3. Interviews and consultations
4. Testing/experimentation
5. His own experience

Recommendations follow and are based on the analysis of the data. Because the client is interested in what to do about the problem, the major portion of the report is devoted to analytical considerations that lead to specific recommendations on actions to be taken. Very little space is devoted to the problem's background or the method of investigation. Most of the contents is devoted to an explanation of the data of the situation so as to lead the reader to the writer's conclusions and to acceptance of the writer's opinions and the recommended actions to solve the situation. Depending on the situation, recommendation reports can be in letter, memorandum, or formal report format.

The memorandum report in Figure 9.2 may also be considered a memorandum recommendation report. An example of a letter recommendation report is shown in Figure 9.3.

Mr. Darnell Winters
Production Superintendent
Palm Bay Boat Company
23719 Valley Road
San Diego, CA 92112

Dear Mr. Winters:

    In your letter of July 17 of this year, you commissioned me to recommend means and procedures to reduce premature corrosion at or near weld areas of ships you are building. After some thought and study, I believe I can suggest an effective and inexpensive way to eliminate this troublesome and expensive problem.
    When protective coatings break down in weld areas, it can usually be traced to the fact that harmful deposits formed during welding have not been fully removed before the coating process. Harmful deposits commonly found near weld seams are:

1. Alkaline slag from the weld flux, which reduces the adhesion and durability of the coating film;
2. Condensed flux fumes, which produce similar undesirable alkaline conditions;
3. Oxides produced by the heat of welding;
4. Weld metal spatter.

Beads of weld spatter may be as large as 6mm (¼ inches) in diameter, and their peaks are normally too high to allow adequate coverage by an average film thickness of coating. Spatter, therefore, presents vulnerable points for early rust formation.

    A simple three-step process will eliminate problems caused by all four types of deposits:

1. Treat the weld with 10% phosphoric or 10% hydrochloric acid to neutralize alkalinity. Scrub the acid into the weld area with a stiff brush. Commercial ready-made preparations (e.g., Rust-Oleum or Surfa-Etch) are also available for neutralizing the deposits, and they are easier to store and use. Be sure your workers wear protective rubber gloves, aprons, and goggles.
2. After the acid preheatment, rinse the entire area thoroughly with fresh warm water: While the surface is still wet, remove any rust spots or oxides near the weld by rubbing with fine steel wool. Then dry very carefully.
3. You can then remove the weld spatter by sand-blasting or grinding with power tools.

Figure 9.3 *Sample recommendation report.*

Surface preparation is, of course, only the first stage of weld protection; the primer coatings do the continuing rust prevention job. For optimum performance, use only those primer coatings specifically formulated to provide maximum anti-corrosive protection for steel surfaces, including welded areas. Examples include:

a. A lead-free red metal primer (X-60), which dries to the touch in 4-6 hours and may be exposed to the weather up to nine months before application of the finish coat.
b. A fast-drying (touch-dry in 30 minutes formulation C678).

Use an intermediate coat of 960 zinc chromate primer; it will help assure long term freedom from rust. Because of its light color, zinc chromate serves as an excellent undercoat when the finish coat is also light.

Durability of the coating system will depend on film thickness. Each coat, when dry, should be 25 (0.025mm; 0.001 in.) thick but not more than 50 (0.050mm; 0.002 in.). You must follow the instructions of the coating manufacturer for mixing, thinning, and application of the specific coating.

In case you do not have convenient referral to sources of primer and coating preparations, I am enclosing some catalog sheets on such preparations. If you have a need for any further information on steel weld corrosion problems, do please call on me again.

Sincerely yours,

Thomas F. Hood
Corrosion Consultant

Enclosures

Figure 9.3 (continued)

Progress Reports

All of us make progress reports; sometimes several times a day.

"What's new with your car, Fred?" a friend will greet you.

"Well, I got rid of that old clunker last week," you may reply. "It ate gas, burnt too much oil, and then the transmission went out. I bought a compact Saturday."

Or, your boss might say, "Cathy, how are you doing with the problem in the Newby Paper Company plant?"

"It's not the transformers, according to my inspection yesterday," you report. "Though the transformers need a good, new coat of protection paint. I'm looking at the synchronous motors that drive the drying rolls. They seem to be in good condition, but I need to give a closer look at the motors driving the rack and suction rolls at the wet end of the machines. They're covered with pulp and gook and don't operate well at all. I'm going to look at them today and let you know by tomorrow afternoon what's wrong and what should be done."

The main purpose of a progress report is to give an accounting. In a formal situation, progress reports are issued at specified intervals to show what has been done, what is being done, and what is expected to be done. Funding agencies, managers, and supervisors require such reports as a necessary communications link for control purposes and intelligent management decisions, often on whether a project should be maintained, expanded, reoriented, or abandoned. Progress reports also are helpful to the performer. They enable him to focus on and assess periodically the work done and the work remaining in relation to allocated resources, time, and effort.

Reporting periods are specified by the funding agency, client, or administrator. The form of the progress report varies. It may be a letter, memorandum (if in-house), or a bound document with formal trappings such as a title page, table of contents, abstract, separate text sections, and appendix material. What is covered in progress reports depends on the subject matter and what the reader wants and needs to know. The following elements are usually included:

Introduction
    Identification of grant, contract, or work order
    Purpose of grant, contract, or work order
    Project description
    Summary of earlier progress

Details of progress during report period (include dates)
    Procedures
    Problems
    Results
    Discussion (include conclusions and recommendations, if appropriate)

Work planned for next reporting period

Work planned for periods thereafter

Overall appraisal of progress to date

Most progress reports lend themselves to a chronological arrangement. In some cases, it may be more appropriate to arrange the progress by tasks or by subject matter such as equipment, materials, personnel, and costs in the case of production or construction work. Some progress reports are in letter format. A sample progress report is shown in Figure 9.4.

Chapter in Brief

In this chapter, we examined various types of short reports, their organization, formats, and techniques of composition.

Chapter Focal Points

- Letter report
- Memo report
- Recommendation reports
- Progress reports

Question for Discussion

Your institution, anticipating the future, is considering computer literacy as a requirement toward graduation. You are a member of the student council and a computer buff. You, personally, think the requirement is a good idea and long overdue, but as a student representative you want to check the pulse of your community. Each council member of the seven divisions of your institution—Humanities, Biological Sciences, Physical Sciences, Engineering, Home Economics, Social Sciences, and Computing Center—surveys the students in his division. When the results are tabulated, the majority, except in Humanities and Home Economics, favor the requirement. As a classroom discussion project, how would you go about preparing a memorandum report to the president? What would its contents be? What recommendations should the memorandum report have?

Assignments

1. The president of your university is making a fund drive to renovate a number of buildings in your institution. He has named you to a committee to make a preliminary survey to identify the most appropriate candidate buildings to be included in his appeal for renovation funds. Among the buildings surveyed were:

   Old Main—the Administration Building
   Library
   Gymnasium
   School of Home Economics
   Social Science/Humanities Building
   Computer Center
   Biology Building

Your committee will consider some of the following factors:

Need for air conditioning

Fire and other safety considerations

Classrooms and seating capacity

Comfort facilities

Heating system

Office space and student space

Parking

Laboratory and equipment resources

Write a memorandum recommendation report, identifying satisfactory and unsatisfactory building and space resources with recommendations to your university president.

2. After reading your report and discussing its recommendations with the university's board of trustees, your president decides it would be most practical to limit the fund drive to renovating just three buildings—Old Main, the Computer Center, and one more. He can't decide whether the third building should be the Gymnasium or the Library. He asks your committee to investigate and make a recommendation he can justify to both the alumni and the faculty. Write a report to meet your president's needs.

3. Your university president has appointed you to make a survey of traffic patterns in and around your campus with the object of determining whether student driving to or on campus should be banned. Write a memo report with recommendations for action the president should take. Your report might include tables and graphs to substantiate your conclusions and recommendations.

4. Write your instructor a progress report on your progress to date in writing the research report assigned for this course.

```
                    Fourth Quarterly
                   Progress Report on
            National Survey on Fires in Households
                   in the United States




















           Prepared for the U.S. Fire Administration
                       by XYZ Associates
                    1020 Connecticut Avenue NW
                      Washington, DC 20035













          Prepared under Contract No. 7915 for the period
                    October 1–December 31, 19__
```

Figure 9.4 Sample progress report.

Introduction

This is the fourth quarterly progress report on the work being done under Contract No. 7915 in the fulfillment of the performance requirements listed in paragraph 8e, covering the period of October 1 to December 31, 19__. The purpose of the contract is to conduct a national survey of a stratified, representative sample of U.S. households to help answer the following questions:

1. How many household fires occur per year in the U.S.?
2. Where do fires start?
3. When do fires start?
4. What starts the fire and what catches fire first?
5. Who gets hurt or killed?
6. What is the dollar fire loss?

Work Previously Completed

Following approval of the scientific design, 33,000 statistically selected households were surveyed. The survey was completed in the last reported period and computer tabulation and analysis of responses were begun.

Present Work

Tabulation was completed and analysis is continuing. There were 2,463 fire incidents reported during the calendar year of concern in the survey. Analyses of responses to the second and fourth questions being investigated provide the following indications:

Where do Fires Start?

Kitchen (cooking)	40%	} 65%
Kitchen (no cooking)	25%	
Living Room	12%	
Bedroom	8%	
Basement	4%	
Utility Room	2%	
Bathroom	1%	
Other	8%	
Total	100%	

What Starts Fires?

Appliances (involving grease or food)	34%	} 62%
Other Appliances	28%	
Wiring	8%	
Smoking	7%	
Matches and the like	4%	
Other, or do not know	19%	
Total	100%	

Figure 9.4 (continued)

What Catches Fire?

Grease, food	41%
Appliances	26%
Wall, Floor covering	6%
Furnishings	5%
Clothing	2%
Other, or do not know	<u>20%</u>
Total	100%

Problems

Despite a careful attempt to define for respondents what to classify as a fire incident—both the observation of flames and the start of smoke coming from wiring or appliances—there is an evident confusion in the responders on what constitutes a fire. The number of fire incidents may be more than what was reported.

Discussion

Preliminary analysis indicates that accidental fires are usually started by appliances. Nearly half the time, fire incidents are associated with cooking. Though analysis of dollar losses has not been completed, present evidence indicates the average "cooking" fire does comparatively little damage because someone is usually there to discover it. Fires that appear to do the most damage are those where either the wall or floor covering catches fire or where the start of the fire is unknown. These preliminary conclusions will be verified in the next reporting period.

Work Planned for the Next Reporting Period

1. Average dollar loss per fire will be determined (answer to Question 6) and extrapolated nationally.
2. Activities connected with the start of a fire will be determined. (Completion of answer to Question 4.)
3. The answer to Question 3 will be determined.
4. Annual casualties in deaths and injuries will be determined and extrapolated nationally (Question 5).

Completion of Project

Work in the performance of this contract is proceeding on schedule. We anticipate completing analysis of survey returns and delivery of the Final Report as required at the end of the quarterly period following the next.

Figure 9.4 (continued)

10
Oral Reports

Chapter Objective

To provide guidelines for oral presentations of reports.

Chapter Focus

- Informal, impromptu reports
- Semiformal, extemporaneous reports
- Formal oral presentations
- Preparation strategies
- Audience analysis
- Gathering information
- Organizing the information
- Practicing the delivery
- Techniques for delivering the oral report
- Audiovisual aids

Why should a text on technical writing be concerned with oral delivery of information? There are three principal reasons:

1. All of us daily are called upon to share and present information—to the class, to the boss, to colleagues, or, informally, to a friend or family member.
2. Speaking, like writing, is a medium of communication; principles of the process of communication, of language, of semantics, of exposition, of analysis, and of organization apply to both speaking and writing.
3. Principles of report preparation, organization, composition, and preparation of graphic aids are equally applicative.

As you advance professionally, your ability both to write and speak becomes more and more important. At conferences and meetings, you will be called upon to discuss your work, to propose solutions to problems, to analyze trends, and to justify budgets and activities. Many written reports often require an oral presentation.

The purpose of this chapter is to provide guidelines for making oral reports. It is not a substitute for a course or a text on speech. Like its counterpart, the oral report must be well prepared, factual, informative, clear, systematic, well organized, technically valid, and appropriate for its audience. There are significant differences, which translate into advantages and disadvantages, between the spoken and the written report.

Advantages

1. Immediate feedback enables you to adjust the content, style, and delivery of your information to make your report more relevant. (You can see immediately if your audience is with you.)
2. Your personality can help more directly to influence your audience's reception of your information.
3. Your information can be received simultaneously by many more people.
4. You have an opportunity to clarify obscure or complex points either in a question-and-answer period or during delivery.

Disadvantages

1. An oral report has limitations of time and complexity. Highly technical information must often be simplified and telescoped to fit a specific time frame and yet be valid. In a written report, readers can study complex data as long as they need to.
2. Nervousness on your part, poor delivery, or problems with projection of your visuals can pervert and becloud your carefully prepared information.
3. Your listener has only one opportunity to grasp your information and cannot go back to review and study it.
4. Your reader sets her own pace for comprehension of the written report, skimming some parts and pausing to study other elements. In an oral report, you es-

tablish the pace; if you misinterpret or ignore feedback, your listener may be lost.
5. Your audience cannot see headings between sections and subsections. (However, there is no reason why you cannot project these on a screen or note these on a blackboard or felt board.)

The differences between the two media not only identify the problems that exist in the speaker-listener relationship but also call attention to advantages of the oral communication situation: You can use your personality, voice, and gestures as well as eye contact, visuals, and feedback to engage your receiver's attention effectively and elicit direct response. On the other hand, your written report is easier to organize and refine, can be more complex, can be studied by your reader at her own pace, and can be more readily reviewed by decision makers. Keep these differences in mind when you plan any oral presentation.

Types of Oral Reporting Situations

Despite the previously identified distinctions, types of and forms for the oral report are similar to the written report. You should review Chapters 4, 5, and 6. Depending on the situation, your oral reports will vary in style, extent, complexity, and formality.

Informal, Impromptu Oral Reports

These are often casual, one-on-one presentations of information about a situation or problem. They can be as informal as telling a family member what you did at work today or bringing back to your boss information on why the gizmo you were assigned to design will not be finished today as you promised.

When you are unexpectedly called upon to comment on some matter, your response is impromptu, unprepared. How you respond can mark you as a professional or an amateur. Not all of us are walking, articulate encyclopedias; all of us, however, can avoid becoming embarrassed. With experience and practice we can learn to stay poised. You are not expected to give a formal speech in response to an impromptu question. Therefore, pause; take a deep breath; think while you're breathing about the subject you were asked about; take another breath; as items of recall start coming to mind, speak directly on what you know or what your opinion is on the matter. Say simply, "This is what I know" or "This is what my opinion is." Don't rattle on and on or fumble and fuss.

Listen to yourself as you speak; listen to others who express themselves well and clearly. Notice how they look and how they speak. Clear speaking is the result of clear thinking. Analyze what these articulate persons do and how they talk. Can you emulate them in the future? Try. Practice. Articulate expression comes with experience; experience comes with practice. Whereas you cannot practice responding to matters you know little about, you can practice responding clearly and with poise on what you know, and then offer to learn more for a future discussion.

Extemporaneous, Semiformal Reports

These types of oral presentations follow certain conventional formalities. One example of the semiformal report would be your presenting before your class a synopsis of your written report. In a work situation, you may be called upon to brief your colleagues or members of your work team on what you found out about the problem, task, or situation at hand. In staff meetings, including teleconferencing, we are often called to review progress, analyze work problems, predict trends, or present briefings on policies. A **briefing** is a short, factual summary of the details of a current or projected situation, or a concise rationale of a condition. For a briefing, you might make one- or two-word notes as reminders and to ensure the adequacy and accuracy of your information. These notes need be no more than a listing of topics in an order that provides focus, coherence, and unity.

Formal Reports

Like its written equivalent, the formal oral report follows the constructs of the reporting situation. In this category are talks at professional meetings, video presentations at teleconferences, reports at national conventions, and speeches to civic groups and to similar formal assemblies.

The Poster Board

The **poster board** is a flowchart that is part of a presentation for an oral report. The poster board, which is often used in conferences where many presentations must be made in a limited time period, enables a speaker to provide a pictorial summary of what happened in a project being reported. The speaker usually has about 15 minutes for her oral presentation and another 15 minutes for a question-and-answer period. With the aid of graphics on the poster board, the speaker's presentation is competently accomplished. It has the following structure:

Project description
Purpose and scope
Methods and materials (if appropriate)
Findings
Discussion and conclusions
Recommendations (if appropriate)

Figure 10.1 depicts a poster board for a presentation of the "Report on the Possible Origin of the Intrusive Bodies in Big Thompson Canyon," which appeared in Chapter 6, pages 156–167.

The effectiveness of your oral report depends on factors similar to the effectiveness of your written report. In an oral report, there are six major steps:

1. Prespeaking—preliminary analysis and planning
2. Gathering the information
3. Organizing the information

Origin of the Intrusive Bodies in Big Thompson Canyon

PROJECT: Determining the origin of intrusive granite material at base of Palisade Mountain, Big Thompson Canyon, Colorado.

PROJECT DESCRIPTION

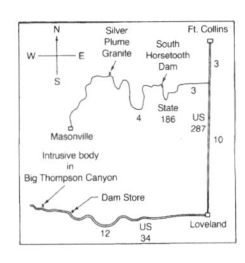

Figure 1

Figure 2

METHOD AND MATERIAL

Figure 3

Figure 4

FINDINGS

Figure 5

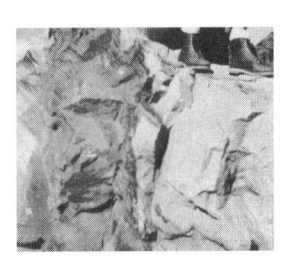

Figure 6

DISCUSSION AND CONCLUSIONS

Table 1

Mineral	Percentages	Color
Orthoclase Feldspar	60%	White
Quartz	20%	Clear, glassy
Biotite mica	15%	Black
Plagioclase Feldspar	5%	Gray-white

Table 2

Mineral	Percentages	Color
Orthoclase Feldspar	40%	Flesh-colored to white
Quartz	30%	Rose to clear, glassy
Biotite mica	25%	Black, vitreous
Plagioclase Feldspar	5%	White

RECOMMENDATION: Further Study

Figure 10.1 Sample poster board.

4. Composing the presentation
5. Practicing the delivery
6. Delivering the oral report

Prespeaking—Preliminary Analysis and Planning

Of course, the medium of communication for the oral report is different from that of the written. The principles, however, are the same. To develop the presentation, you go through similar analytical processes. You begin by establishing answers to a number of key questions:

1. Why am I speaking on this subject (problem)?
2. To whom am I speaking (layperson, executive, expert)?
3. What does the listener (audience) want or need to know?
4. Am I supposed to offer a solution to the problem?
5. Do I expect the listener to take any action? If so, what action?
6. Do I want questions, suggestions, or comments from the audience?
7. What is the purpose of my oral report? Is it to communicate information? To motivate my audience to accept my conclusions and recommendations? To stimulate them to take action?

Just as you did in the written report, formulate your purpose into a clear, concise statement. Once you have determined the purpose and identified the target audience, you can establish the scope of the information you need.

Gathering the Information

Procedures for gathering the information required to reach your purpose have been covered in Chapter 4.

Organizing the Information

The approaches to organization in Chapter 5 apply to the oral report as well as to the written. Factors governing organization are directed to (1) purpose, (2) needs of the audience, and (3) nature of the subject (problem).

Your organization should be geared to the following criteria:

1. Answers the question: Why am I making this presentation?
2. States the thesis of the presentation.
3. Presents substantiation for the thesis.
4. Accomplishes the desired audience response to the presentation.

Composing the Oral Presentation

Because of the factors of time available and the diverse mix of the usual audience, the oral report is, in effect, a summary of the written report. Plan on a fifteen- to twenty-minute delivery period. The approach taken in the composition of the Executive Summary to a formal report, discussed in Chapter 6, is appropriate. The oral report has three major divisions—the *Beginning* or *Introduction*, *Body (Middle)*, and *Conclusion (Close)* of the presentation.

The Beginning or Introduction

The *Beginning, Opening,* or *Introduction* serves to capture the attention of your audience, introduce the subject or purpose of your report, and establish your credibility for your conclusions and thesis. Your first few sentences must interest your listeners, or they will mentally drift away and never return. To catch your listeners' immediate attention, begin with a rhetorical device appropriate for your topic—a startling statement, an extraordinary statistic, a personal appeal, a striking figure of speech, or a humorous story relevant to your subject. Humor is universally appealing but it can be a two-edged sword if it is ill conceived or inappropriate to the thesis. Beginning with a visual aid or a sound effect can set the tone, establish the thesis, create audience identification with the subject, be dramatic, or result in an agglomeration of all these responses. Any one of the introductory approaches might be appropriate under one set of circumstances and inappropriate under a different set of circumstances. The job of the introduction is to get the attention of your audience, introduce your subject, and prepare your listeners for your thesis.

Body/Middle

Your subject, once introduced, needs to be explained in whatever details are necessary to accomplish the objective of your presentation. That is the purpose of the body of your speech. It develops the thesis by presenting the material to substantiate it. Remember your time is limited. To develop your thesis, you should consider what is the minimum information necessary to bring your ideas across and what the most effective logic for their sequence should be. Depending on the speech circumstance, you should also decide whether to handle questions from the audience during your presentation, at specific points, or at the end.

Methods for developing the body include these:

1. Examples illustrating points in spoken text or projections of visuals
2. Repetition of the major points leading to the thesis in order to drive the points home and to ensure audience comprehension
3. Statistics sparingly used and, more effectively, projected as visuals
4. Comparisons and contrasts to touch on the experience of the audience
5. Testimony of experts, participants, or witnesses to an event

Conclusion/Close

Good salespeople know they cannot "peter out" at the end of their sales pitch. Their final words must convince the potential customer and reinforce the points they have made. Similarly, in the speech situation, the last thing you say is as important as the first in which you gained your audience's attention. Your whole presentation must have a point—the thesis of your report. It is the "payload" you are delivering. To be sure your audience receives the payload, in your conclusion, review the purpose of your presentation, summarize and underscore the main points, and, if appropriate, appeal for the action you want your audience to take.

Your conclusion, or close, should not be lengthy, but it should be vivid and address the points you want your listeners to carry away with them. Sometimes an illustrative example of the effects of your thesis is a productive way to conclude your presentation.

To summarize the organization of your oral report: the Introduction states the idea of your presentation, the Body develops the idea, and the Conclusion restates and reinforces it.

In composing your oral report follow the encoding principles of communication[1] and the elements of the written report.[2] Mode of delivery also plays a role. In memorized delivery, you write out your report and then memorize it completely. Though it has the benefit of cohesive structure and careful use of language, unless you are experienced and can afford the time to practice, it often sounds mechanical. There is also the danger that you might forget a word, a phrase, a line, or even an important section. The result can be disastrous.

You may be tempted to read your report. You have the same benefit of careful structure, but you also face the hazard of boring and losing your listeners. Very few people can read a speech, maintain eye contact with the audience, and provide the necessary supplementary body language and tonal qualities that convey a live personality.

The **extemporaneous** delivery allows naturalness and spontaneity. Delivery is carefully planned, practiced, and based on notes, organized to keep you on track. The notes, either topical or in sentence outline form, enable you to stay in control of your report material.

Practicing the Delivery

Practice means rehearsal. The best way to rehearse your speech is to practice it as closely as possible to the actual speech situation. If you will stand when you speak, practice standing up; if you will not have a speaker's stand to hold your notes, practice holding your notes; if you will use a blackboard or felt board, have an actual model, or, if you are going to project slides or transparencies, practice with these visual aids. If you can practice in the actual room where you will make

---

[1] See Chapter 1.
[2] See Chapter 6.

your presentation, it will help to do so. If not, try to visualize the room's environment as you practice. Be sure to number your notes. Type or print them triple-spaced to make their reading easier.

Try to practice at least once before friends. If that is not possible, use a full-length mirror and a tape recorder. Revise any part of your presentation that your feedback indicates is unclear. Check not only your delivery but also your organization to ensure that your message is actually delivered.

Delivering the Oral Report

Many of us would like to think that what we have to say is more important than how we say it. Unfortunately, that is not the case, according to researchers in public speaking. They have found that effective, fluent delivery increases a speaker's credibility and improves audience comprehension and retention of a speaker's message.

"All right, so delivery is important!" you may say. "I have practiced my oral report, but delivering it in practice is not the same as giving it before an audience. I am scared stiff. What should I do?"

Your feelings of apprehension are not different from those of a quarterback before a big game or those of an actor on opening night. Your feelings are normal and actually healthy. You need an increase in adrenalin to perform what you have practiced. Winston Churchill, probably the greatest speaker in our century, was asked, "You are always so poised. Didn't you ever suffer from stage fright?" "When I was much younger, I did," said Sir Winston. "The day I had to make my first speech in Parliament I told a colleague how frightened I was. He was an experienced, wise, and kindly man, a brilliant orator. With a twinkle in his eye, he said, `You will do very well—as you rise, imagine that all of those distinguished old fogies before you are stark naked. That's what I do.' And I did just that. No audience stark naked is a frightening spectacle."

I am not suggesting necessarily that you imagine your audience as being stark naked. I am suggesting that even the most accomplished speakers have a certain amount of tension before a speech situation. Some tension is essential to effective speaking. Have you ever watched a racehorse at the starting gate? The horse is nervous and ready to go. The animal has been trained to perform at the sound of the gun and is straining to run. Its adrenalin is flowing. We behave similarly before a speech situation. Therefore, know that you will experience tension, but remember that the tension will help you deliver the report.

Communication, as you will recall from Chapter 1, is a two-way process. The advantage to the sender (you) is that you can obtain immediate feedback from the receiver (audience). Feedback, of course, can be negative as well as positive. Use the cues you receive to help you adjust and meet the requirements of the speech situation. If you have carefully taken the five previous steps before delivery, you will speak with confidence even though you are full of nervous tension. A confident speaker has poise; with confidence, you will find your audience reacting favorably. Be natural, be yourself. Your audience should not be a blur of faces. On the other hand, you cannot look directly into the eyes of every member unless your group numbers ten or less. Select some individuals with whom to establish firm eye contact so you can observe their facial reactions.

You will find the following guidelines helpful in your speech delivery.

Breathing

Breathing is the basis of speech. To make normal speech sounds, you must first inhale. Speech is manufactured when you exhale with pressure; the vibratory motion of your larynx (Adam's apple) sends sound waves out through your mouth and nose. Patterns of individual sound are formed by the tongue, hard and soft palates, the gum ridges, and teeth. You have been breathing and speaking all your life. Just continue doing what comes naturally. But before you speak, be sure you have a good supply of air in your lungs. Inhale. Pause and take several deep breaths. As your lungs fill, you can feel them push your diaphragm out. The pause, you will find, helps you to get your audience's attention. Look at your audience and inhale softly. Breathe frequently during your presentation. Break your speech material into small segments so that you do not run out of air before your next breath. Just be sure that your breath-group phrases are cohesive.

Pitch

Pitch is the level of sound or tone of your voice. It is based on the physics of the number of vibrations of your vocal chords. Variations in tone are called inflections. An interesting voice has varied inflections but uses a conversational tone. A pitch different from your natural speaking voice is distracting.

Voice Quality

Resonance, as you know from listening to stereo, adds richness to sound. In practicing your speech, experiment sending the sound waves through the resonating chambers of your speech mechanism—chest, mouth, head, and nasal cavities.

Intensity

Intensity is the force or loudness with which you project. Depending upon the size of your audience and the room arrangement, you should speak slightly louder than you would in normal conversation. Your volume should be loud enough for everyone to hear but not so loud that you overpower your listeners.

Rate

Rate or speed is the tempo of your speech. It is a factor in being understood. If you speak too fast or too slowly, you will irritate and lose your audience.

Pause

Related to rate, the pause can be effective in drawing attention to important points.

Pronunciation

Mispronunciations undermine an audience's confidence in the speaker. If you are unsure how a word is pronounced, look it up in the dictionary.

Enunciation

Enunciation is the way a speaker articulates words. It is the clear, precise formation of sounds of a word. Again, faulty enunciation is distracting and undermines an audience's confidence.

Body Language

Whether you use gestures or not, your body as well as your voice speaks for you. A poised speaker is one who appears self-confident, relaxed, and capable of doing what the speech situation calls for. Gestures do not come naturally to the inexperienced speaker, but they can be effective in emphasizing a point. Do what comes naturally. Gestures should call attention to an idea but not to the gesture. Your face is important. It reflects you in action. Your confidence, conviction, and sincerity will be communicated by your facial expression. Some people have distracting mannerisms—scratching their nose, tugging at an ear, twisting a lock of hair, or looking down or away from the audience. Check your delivery before a mirror or friends to catch any distracting mannerisms. Always try to be natural. Be comfortable with yourself and what you do, and your audience will be comfortable with you.

Audiovisual Aids in Oral Presentations

Visual aids serve three functions.[3]

1. They help keep the attention of your audience (keeping them interested).
2. They present information in clearer fashion by means of the visual channel.
3. They help your audience to retain the information.

The visuals most commonly used are models, graphs, maps, charts, photos, drawings, and short printed passages. They may be slides and transparencies projected on a screen; they may be drawn or lettered on a blackboard or displayed on a flannel board or poster board; or they may be held. They can be on sheets of paper, reproduced and distributed to the audience. Visuals have many advantages. You can often show an audience something more effectively than you can tell them about it. Showing *and* telling are often more successful than using either technique by itself.

---

[3] Review the sections on graphic aids in Chapter 7.

Using Audiovisual Aids

1. If you are using a microphone, be sure it is adjusted for volume and your height before you begin your presentation.
2. Check your audiovisual equipment: slides, transparencies, felt, chalk, and poster boards *before*, not after, your presentation begins. Be sure your slides, visuals, and transparencies are in proper order.
3. Be sure that your audience will be able to see illustrations and read the captions. The size of lettering and images should be determined by the size of audience and viewing room.
4. Firmly anchor illustrative materials on their felt boards so they do not fall off during your presentation.
5. Illustrate only one concept on a visual; two or more become confusing.
6. Do not block your audience's view by standing in front of the visuals you are explaining.
7. If you are using an overhead or slide projector, do not leave the visual on the screen after you are through using it; your audience will shift its attention from you to the projection. Also, turn off the projector when you finish. Its noise and lights are distracting.
8. If you have prepared handouts, be judicious about when to distribute them; your audience will read the material rather than tune in on you. Handouts are useful when you want your audience to follow specific or intricate details you wish to emphasize as you talk. If you want your audience to take the information with them, distribute the handout at the end of your presentation.

Guidelines for Oral Report Presentation

An oral report requires similar preparation to a written report. It is based on careful and thorough research and objective analysis. Like the written report, the oral one begins with an introduction, is followed by the body, which discusses findings, and ends with conclusions and recommendations. Because of time limitations and greater diversity of audience members, the oral report often follows the psychological organization scheme so that conclusions and recommendations are presented to follow the brief introduction.[4] The body, offering substantiating details, follows. The concluding section in this organizational scheme summarizes the entire report to reinforce the thesis of the presentation.

Steps in oral reporting are these:

1. Establish the purpose of your presentation.
2. Analyze your audience in terms of their knowledge and attitudes.
3. Research the problem or situation to be reported.

---

[4]See Chapter 5, pages 121–122.

4. Analyze the data in relation to the purpose.
5. Prepare an organizational scheme, concentrating on major points you want your audience to receive if your purpose is to be met.
6. Compose your presentation, formulating it for your intended audience and placing particular effort into a strong introduction and conclusion.
7. Practice your presentation—more than once in order to gain confidence and poise.
8. Deliver your presentation, using audience feedback to make adjustments if necessary.
9. Summarize and reinforce your ideas to make your thesis comprehensible and acceptable.
10. Conclude in time to allow questions from your audience.

After the presentation, evaluate your experience from audience feedback and reaction (from both classmates and instructor). The more you understand your successes or failures, the more likely you will be successful in your next oral presentation.

Though this chapter is not a substitute for a good course in speech, you will find, if you follow the guidelines, that your oral report was not a frightening experience and that you may even look forward to the next opportunity. The more experience you gain in speaking, the more confident, poised, and successful you will become. The attribute management looks for in professionals is facility in both written and oral communication.

Chapter in Brief

Similar to the written technical report, the oral report must be well prepared, factual, informative, clear, systematic, well organized, technically valid, and appropriate for its audience. Various types of oral reports were discussed in this chapter as well as how to prepare, organize, and deliver them. Techniques for oral delivery and guidelines for using audiovisual aids were presented.

Chapter Focal Points

- Informal, impromptu oral reports
- Semiformal extemporaneous oral reports
- Formal oral reports
- Prespeaking preparation
- Organizing the report
- Delivering the report
- Vocal techniques
- Audiovisual aids

Assignments

1. Observe a lecture or technical presentation at your college. Evaluate it according to the principles and guidelines in this chapter.
2. Each of us is an expert in some matter or idea or belief about which we feel strongly. Assume you have been asked to speak on that subject matter, belief, or idea. Prepare a four- to six-minute presentation to inform or persuade your audience.
3. Prepare a short presentation of four to five minutes describing a device/organism or one explaining a process. Include visuals.
4. Assume the instructor in one of the courses of your major field of study needs to be away from class and has asked you to take over the class for that class period. Prepare a ten-minute lecture on the subject to stimulate class questions and discussion. Your success in this assignment may be measured by the amount of discussion stimulated among your class members.
5. Prepare an oral report or a poster board presentation based on the formal report you have written for your technical writing class, following the suggestions in this chapter. Practice it. Present it to the class in ten to fifteen minutes (as your instructor may assign). A question-and-answer period will follow your presentation.
6. Write an evaluation of your presentation and turn it in to your instructor for comments.

Reference Index and Guide to Grammar, Punctuation, Style, and Usage

Some writers take refuge in the popular notion that grammar is not important. However, language is a code, and grammatical writing is easier to read and understand than ungrammatical writing. Unless people signal to each other in the same code, they cannot exchange intelligible messages. Their agreement to use the same code is the basis of correctness of grammar. Incorrect or ungrammatical means "not customary to the accepted code." You may not change the customary code without risking the possibility of your message being garbled.

This Reference Index is not meant to be a text on grammar and usage. Its purpose is to provide a ready and convenient guide to some of the more common problems the technical writer will meet in writing requirements. Fuller treatment of some of these problems will be found in the Selected Bibliography that follows.

a, an. *a* is used before words beginning with a consonant (except *h* when it is silent), before words beginning with *eu* and *u*, pronounced *yu*, and before *o*, pronounced as in *one*. *An* is used before all words beginning with a vowel sound and words beginning with a silent *h*.

a	*a*	*a*	*an*	*an*
beacon	hard disk	eugenicist	alloy	herb
drift	helix	one-hour rating	eel	H
shunt circuit	hydrate	unit	N	homage
tentacle	hysteresis	uropod	impulse	hour

abbreviations. Abbreviations are used frequently for convenience in technical writing. However, they are acceptable only if they convey meaning to the reader. You should explain nonstandard abbreviations fully when you introduce them in a report. Abbreviations are appropriate in compilations, tables, graphs, and illustrations where space is limited. Their use in the text should be limited except when preceded by numerals, as in giving dimensions or ratings. Unfortunately, the spelling of abbreviations is not universal. The American National

Standards Institute has a list that has been approved by many scientific and engineering societies. However, other professional societies, such as the Institute of Electric and Electronic Engineers, and government agencies have their own abbreviations. Dictionaries give frequently used abbreviations in their main listing of words; some also compile a list in a back section. You should consider including a glossary of abbreviations if you use a large number of them in a report. Always write the word out if you are unsure of the proper abbreviation. Use periods with abbreviations except for names of well-known organizations or government agencies, for instance: NOW, NSF, DOD, DOE, UNESCO, NATO, IEEE, PTSA, NAACP. To avoid confusion, use periods when the abbreviation spells out an actual word: W.H.O., C.A.B., A.I.D.; however, usage has ruled AIDS for acquired immunodeficiency syndrome and HIV for human immunodeficiency virus. In a company or corporation name, omit the period when the abbreviation has become the official name: the IBM Corporation. When letters within a single word are used as an abbreviation, they are capitalized but do not take periods: DDT, DNA, RNA, TB, TV. V.D. requires periods because it stands for two words. Stylistic convention within a field often determines whether an abbreviation is capitalized. We frequently see AI (artificial intelligence), PE (potential energy), and OD (outside diameter), but bp (boiling point), qid (four times a day), emf (electromotive force), and both nmr and NMR (nuclear magnetic resonance). This is true of ac and dc, frequently seen as AC and DC. It is true also of both ram and RAM (random-access memory) and rom and ROM (read-only memory). What should you do about the capitalization of abbreviations? Be consistent in their use. Incidentally, when ac and dc are used as nouns they are usually spelled out (alternating current and direct current), but as adjectives they are abbreviated. Through usage, abbreviations of many business terms are acceptable in formal writing: COD (cash/collect on delivery), EOM (end of the month), FOB (free on board), GDP (gross domestic product), LCL (less than carload lots), R&D (research and development).

above. Grammatically, this word occurs most frequently as an adverb (the equipment identified *above* [*above* modifies the verb *identified*]) or a preposition (*above* the lithosphere). *Above* is sometimes used as an adjective (the *above* diagram) or as a noun (the *above* is an equation of merit). Many competent writers avoid using *above* except as a preposition because the sentence has a stilted construction and the thought transmitted tends to be ambiguous since the reference of *above*, especially as a noun, is vague. *Above* as an adjective or adverb, in the context previously indicated, should be used with discretion and specificity. I would avoid its use as a noun entirely, unless you do not mind sounding stuffy.

accept, except. *Accept* (verb) means to take when offered, to receive with favor, to agree to. *Except* (verb) means to exclude or omit, *except* (preposition) means with the exclusion of, but. The customer *accepted* delivery of four of the equipments; of the five equipments built, only one was *excepted* from delivery. All *except* model 5 were delivered.

access, excess. *Access* means approach, admittance, admission (to gain *access* to the laboratory). *Excess* means that which exceeds what is usual, proper, or specified (there was an *excess* of 10 liters of liquid in the tank.)

acronym. An *acronym* is a pronounceable word formed with the first letter or letters of each of a series of words: *laser* from light amplification by stimulated emission of radiation; *radar* from radio detecting and ranging. WYSIWYG (pronounced "wizzy-wig") is an acronym for What you see is what you get. In the computer field, it refers to the image on the screen of the text or graphics as that image would look on the printed page. *ABM* is not an acronym but an abbreviation for antiballistic missile; NSF is the abbreviation for National Science Foundation.

activate, actuate. *Activate,* an old English word that was once considered obsolete, has been reintroduced as a special term in chemistry and physics to denote the process of making active or more active as: to make molecules reactive or more reactive; it is used especially in the sense of promoting the growth of bacteria in sewage and of making substances radioactive. The military has adopted *activate* to mean: to set up or formally institute a military unit with the necessary personnel and equipment. *Activate,* however, should not replace the word *actuate,* which means to set a machine in motion or to prompt a person to action.

adapt, adopt. These two words are often confused, even though their meanings are entirely different. *Adopt* means to take by choice into some sort of relationship (he *adopted* the older engineer's design). *Adapt* means to modify, to adjust, or to change for a special purpose (he *adapted* the cam to provide a slower movement).

adjective. An *adjective* is the part of speech that modifies or limits nouns and pronouns. Its purpose is to clarify for the reader the meaning of the word it modifies. The adjectives in the expression *electrostatic* reaction, *inverted-V* antenna, *igneous* magna, *alpha* particle, *standstill* torque, and *heat-resisting* steel provide more meaning to the reader than the nouns by themselves. Adjectives are classified as demonstrative, descriptive, limiting, and proper. A demonstrative adjective points out the word it modifies; *this* computer, *these* cells, *that* alloy, and *those* theories. A descriptive adjective denotes a quality or condition of the word it modifies: an *automatic* titration, a *progressive* disease, a *bent* pipe, a *dedicated* word processing system, and a *slower flow* rate. A limiting adjective designates the number or amount of the word it modifies: a *5 percent* potassium chloride solution; a *600,000 candela* intensity; 5 grams of ascorbic acid; and a *10 millimeter-per-second* flow. The articles *a, an,* and *the* are limiting adjectives. A proper adjective is one derived originally from a proper name: *Josephson* effect; *Schick* test; a *Hollerith* code; *Gibb's* function; *Californian* jade; and *Brownian* movement. Proper adjectives that have lost their sense of origin are written in lower case: *india* ink; *macadamized* road; and *angstrom* unit.

adverbs. An *adverb* is a word, phrase, or clause that modifies a verb (the experiment went *smoothly*); an adjective (the *very* slow titration took longer than I expected); another adverb (*almost* immediately the change occurred); or an entire sentence (*Fortunately,* the power had already been turned off). Most adverbs are adjectives plus the ending *ly: quickly,* completely, correctly, simply, finally. Some adverbs derived from Old English have no special adverbial sign: *now, quite, since, below, much,* and *soon.* Some adverbs have the same form as adjectives: *best, early, fast, slow, straight, well,* and *wrong.* Some of these adverbs also have an ly form: *slowly, wrongly.* When the adverb is used with a compound verb, it should *normally* be placed between the elements of the verb as this sentence and the following example illustrate: The cerebal cortical neuron of the cat will *usually* show a characteristic bursting firing pattern on injection of PTZ.

adverse, averse. *Adverse* means opposed to or being unfavorable to. *Averse* means unwilling to or reluctant to. The investigating committee was *averse* to making an *adverse* recommendation.

advice, advise. *Advice* is a noun meaning guidance, counsel, or a recommended opinion. The mechanic's *advice* was to install a new alternator. Statements without recommendations or opinions are not *advice*, as for example: The present *advice* is aspirin should not be used. In this instance, the use of *advice* is wrong. The sentence should read: Present knowledge indicates that aspirin should not be used in this situation. *Advise* is a verb meaning to give information, to recommend, to caution, to give counsel. The physician *advised* the patient to take two aspirins. The policeman *advised* the motorist to drive in first gear across the icy bridge.

adviser, advisor. Both spellings are acceptable. What adds to the confusion is that *adviser* is used more frequently, but the spelling of *advisory* is the correct one.

affect, effect. These words are frequently confused because many people pronounce them alike. *Affect* is almost always a verb, meaning to influence or to make a show of: The new economic measures *affected* the industry's recovery; he *affected* an English accent. *Affect* as a noun is used as a term in psychology, pertaining to feeling, emotion, and desire as factors in determining thought and conduct. *Effect* is used infrequently as a verb. As a noun, it means result or consequence. The *effect* of cooling on the system increased its efficiency; the *effect* of the design change was a saving in time and money. *Effect* as a verb means to bring about: The change in design *effected* a great saving.

agenda. *Agenda* is the plural of the Latin *agendum*. In today's usage, *agenda* is singular and *agendas* plural.

agree to, agree with, agree on, agree about. These are idiomatic expressions. You *agree to* things, *agree with* people, and people *agree on* something by mutual consent: He *agreed to* the contract; he *agreed with* the client; they *agreed on* the details of the contract; they *agreed about* the details.

all right. *Alright* is never *all right*. Do not use it.

allude, refer. To *allude* to something is to speak of it without direct mention; to *refer* to something is to mention it directly.

alphabetizing names. When dealing with *Mc* or *Mac*, alphabetize by the second letter: *Maberry, MacTavish; Mallard; McNeil*. In a listing, if family names are written before given names, the expression *Jr*. (or *Sr*. or *III*, and so forth) comes last: *Rockefeller, John D., Jr.,* not *Rockefeller, Jr., John D.*

alternate(ly), alternative(ly). As adjectives and adverbs, these two words are frequently confused. *Alternate* means by turn; *alternative* means offering a choice: The problem had two *alternative* solutions. The interstate highway is the shortest route to the city, but since it becomes crowded very early, there are several *alternative* routes to take. The weather *alternated* between rain and sunshine. The wall had *alternating* layers of brick and stone. *Alternate* as a noun means one that takes the place of or alternates with another: If you cannot attend, send an *alternate*.

although, though. Both words are often used interchangeably to connect an adverbial clause with the main clause of a sentence to provide a statement in opposition to the main statement, but one that does not contradict it. *Although* is preferable to introduce a clause that precedes the main clause; *though* for a clause that follows the main clause: *Although* we were short of test equipment, we managed to check out the system. We managed to check out the system, *though* we did not have all the test equipment.

A.M. and P.M., also a.m. and p.m. These are abbreviations for *ante meridiem* (before noon) and *post meridiem* (after noon). Some persons are confused about how to write "12 noon" and "12 midnight." Though *M* is the abbreviation for noon, writing 12 *noon* is used more commonly; midnight is written as 12 *P.M.* or 12 *p.m.*

among, between. *Among* denotes a mingling of more than two objects or persons; *between*, derived from an Old English word meaning "by two," denotes a mingling of two objects or persons: *Among* several designs, his was the most practical. The instrument's accuracy was *between* ±1 and ±2 percent. *Among*, however, expresses a collective relationship of things and *between* seems to be the only word available to express the relation of a thing to many and surrounding things, severally and individually: disagreement *among* bidders; to choose *between* courses; the space lying *between* three points.

amount, number. *Amount* refers to things or substances considered in bulk; *number* refers to countable items as individual units: the *amount* of gas in the container (but the *number* of containers of gas); the *amount* of corn in the silo (but the *number* of bushels of corn).

ampersand. *Ampersand* is the word for the symbol *&*. Its primary use is to save space. Its use as a substitute for the word *and* is frowned upon in formal writing. Many firms use the *ampersand* as a formal part of their official or incorporated name as in J.C. Mason & Co., Inc. In addressing firms, use the form indicated in their formal letterhead.

and/or. This expression, usually frowned upon in literary writing, is commonly used in agreements, contracts, business and legal writing, and technical writing to show that there are three possibilities to be considered: He offered his house *and/or* automobile as collateral.

apostrophe. The most common use of the *apostrophe* is to show possession and ownership: Dr. *Stanton's* equation; the *agency's* director; the *formula's* derivation; the *book's* index. The *apostrophe* is used to indicate omission of one or more letters in a contracted word or figure: '95 for 1995; *didn't* for did not; *they're* for they are. The *apostrophe* is used in the plural form of numbers, letters, and words: The *1990's*; *ABC's*; Programming is spelled with two *m's*; The second of the two *which's* is not necessary in the sentence. There is some tendency to omit the *apostrophe* in plurals of numbers and letters, such as 1920s, four Ws, or second of three thats. The *apostrophe* is not used with the possessive pronouns: his, hers, ours, theirs, yours, its. Sometimes a singular idea is expressed in words that are technically plural; in such a case, the plural form of the possessive is used: *United States'* scientists; *General Motors'* earnings. Almost all singular words ending in *s* require another *s* as well as the apostrophe to form the possessive: The *Times's* story, *Gibbs's* paper. However, the *s* after the apostrophe is dropped when two or more sibilant sounds precede the apostrophe: Kansas' wheat. When a name ends with a sibilant letter that is silent, the possessive is formed with *'s: Arkansas's* boundary; *Malraux's* writings. Plurals of names ending in *s*, such as Jameses', Charleses', Joneses' also have the apostrophe following the final *s*.

appendix. The plural most commonly used is *appendixes*. Purists prefer *appendices*.

appositives and their antecedents. An *appositive* is a term that modifies a noun or other expression by placing immediately after it an equivalent expression that repeats its meaning: the resistor, V101; videotext, an interactive electronic information system; our director, Dr. Roberts. *Appositives* should have clear antecedents. Vague appositive reference can be corrected by placing the appositive immediately after the word or phrase it modifies or by rewording the sentence.

Faulty: Maxwell formulated a new theory while experimenting with Faraday's concept, a major contribution to the study of electricity.

Revised: While experimenting with Faraday's concept, Maxwell formulated a new theory, a major contribution to the study of electricity.

or: Maxwell contributed greatly to the study of electricity when he formulated a new theory based on Faraday's concept.

appraise, apprise, apprize. *Appraise* means to evaluate; *apprise* means to inform; *apprize* is the British spelling.

Wrong: Employees were *appraised* of the new company policy.
Right: Employees were *apprised* of the new company policy.
Wrong: Employees were *apprised* only on their performance.
Right: Employees were *appraised* only on their performance.

Note the prepositions: *appraised on, apprised of*

articles. There are three articles in the English language: *a, an,* and *the. A* and *an* are indefinite articles: *a* dog; *an* apple; dog and apple refer to typical or unidentifiable things. *The* dog, *the* apple refer to a particular or identifiable dog and apple.

assay, essay. These two words are sometimes confused. *Assay* means to test; *essay* means to attempt. *Assay* also has the meaning of analyzing or appraising critically: We shall *assay* the sample to determine its properties. Having obtained a more precise instrument, the scientist again *essayed* the experiment.

as to whether. This phrase is used by persons who would rather use several words when one would serve, as in the sentence, *As to whether* the new software program would work was open to question. Are the words *as to* needed? Not really. *Whether the new software program would work was open to question* is all that is needed.

awhile, a while. *Awhile* is an adverb; *a while* is a noun phrase often used as the object of a preposition: the odor lasts *awhile*. For *a while*, the odor remained in the room.

back of, in back of. Though both are grammatically correct, *behind* is less wordy.

backward, not *backwards*.

because, for, since, as. *Because* is used to introduce a subordinate phrase or clause, providing the reason for the statement in the main clause: *Because* of its low boiling point, the substance could not be used in space applications. When a sentence begins with *The reason is* or *The reason why . . .* is, the clause containing the reason should not begin with *because* but with the word *that. Because* in this usage is an adverb; *that* is a pronoun. The linking verb *is* requires a noun rather than an adverbial clause. *For, since,* and *as* can be used in similar constructions, but these conjunctions are less formal and less emphatic.

before is better than the wordy and stilted *prior to.*

beside, besides. *Beside* means near, close by, by the side of. *Besides* means in addition to, moreover, also, aside from: The replacement assembly was placed *beside* the faulty instrument. *Besides* corrosion resistance, the new alloy had many other desirable properties.

biannual, biennial. *Biannual* means twice a year (as does *semiannual* and *semiyearly*); *biennial* means every two years.

biweekly, semiweekly. *Biweekly* means every two weeks; *semiweekly* means twice a week.

brackets [ ]. *Brackets* are used whenever it is necessary to insert parenthetical material within parenthetical material. *Brackets* are also used to make corrections or explanations within quoted material. In quoting material, use *sic* in brackets [sic] to indicate that an error was in the original quoted material: "He lives in New Haven, Conneticut [sic]."

building names. Capitalize the names of governmental buildings, churches, office buildings, hotels, specially designated rooms, and so forth: the Capitol (state or national), Department of Commerce Building, Washington Cathedral, Beth El, Kennedy Center, Oak Room.

but. *But* is the coordinating conjunction used to connect two contrasting statements of equal grammatical rank. It is less formal than the conjunction *however* or *yet* and is more emphatic than *although*: Not an atom *but* a molecule. The signal was short *but* distinct. The crew worked industriously under his supervision, *but* the minute he turned his back, they sloughed off.

can, may. *Can* expresses the power (physical or mental) to act; *may* expresses permission or sanction to act. In informal or colloquial usage, *can* is frequently substituted for *may* in the sense of permission, but this substitution is frowned upon in formal writing. *Could* and *might* are the original past tenses of *can* and *may*. They are now used to convey a shade of doubt or a smaller degree of possibility: We *can* meet your stringent specifications. Under the FDA regulations, products with 3 percent hexachlorophene solutions *may* be sold by prescription only. The absorbed hydrogen *might* be removed by pumping out the system. The use of *could* suggests doubt or a qualified possibility: The possibility is remote that under those conditions the contractor *could* meet his delivery schedule.

cannot, can not. Both forms are used. *Can not* is more formal, but *cannot* is used more often.

capital, Capitol. Use lowercase *capital* for the city that is the seat of national or state government. Washington, D.C., is the *capital* of the United States; Sacramento is the *capital* of California. The U.S. Senate meets in the *Capitol*.

capitalization. The rules for capitalization in technical writing are the same as in other formal writing. Use capitals for:

1. Titles, geographical places, and trade names: *Origin of Species*; Atlantic Ocean, Antarctica, Ohio; Freon, Polaroid, Teflon
2. Proper names and adjectives derived from proper names but not words used with them: Dundee sandstone, Pliocene period, Gaussian, Coulombic, Boyle's law, Huntington's chorea, Einstein's theory of relativity
Words derived from proper nouns and which, through long periods of usage, have

achieved an identity within themselves are no longer capitalized, for example: bunsen burner, galvanic cell, ohm, ohmic drop, petri dish

3. Scientific names of phyla, orders, classes, families, genera: *Decapoda, Megaloptera, Colymbiformes, Urochorda*
4. The first word of a sentence is capitalized.
5. In quotations, the first word of a quoted sentence or the first word of a part of a sentence is capitalized. When the quotation is interrupted, the second part is not capitalized unless it is a complete sentence:

> "Press the move key," the instructor told the word processing class, "the control F-4 key." He then added, "The status line at the bottom of the screen shows you have five choices."

6. Heads, subheads, and legends require capitalization.
7. Names of computer services and systems, software programs, and databases should be capitalized. Names of computer languages are regularly styled either with initial capitals or all capitals: DIALOG; NEXT; COBOL or Cobol; BASIC or Basic; WordPerfect; FORTRAN or Fortran; PL/1; Lotus; MS-DOS; Ventura Publisher; PRODIGY or Prodigy

catalog, catalogue. If you prefer the second spelling, you are a traditionalist fighting a losing battle.

cement, concrete. Cement and concrete are not interchangeable. *Cement* by definition is an adhesive. *Concrete* is produced by mixing Portland cement, water, sand, and gravel.

center about, center around, center on, center upon. In formal writing, the idiom is *center on* or *center upon;* in less formal writing, *center around* or *about* is the idiom found in use, but *revolve around* is better.

centigrade, Celsius. *Celsius* is the name of the Swede who invented the centrigrade system. The metric system has preferred to use his name for designating the centrigrade system: The boiling point of water at sea level is 100 degrees *Celsius.* In technical writing, use *Celsius.*

chairman, chairperson. *Chairperson* is preferable regardless of the presiding individual's gender.

chemical elements and formulas. Names of elements are not capitalized: *carbon, hydrogen, strontium 90.* In chemical formulas, the first letter of the abbreviation of the element is capitalized: H_2O; SO_2Na; Cl_2O; $KMnO_4$.

circumlocution. A long word meaning wordiness, excessive verbiage, dead wood. Perhaps because they have a subconscious belief that they are paid according to the number of words they write, technical writers often overwrite and pad. Excessive verbiage spreads ideas thin.

Wordy:	Caution must be observed. . . .
Revised:	Be careful, don't. . . .
Wordy:	We are about to enter an area of activity.

Revised:	We are ready to begin.
Wordy:	It is not desirable to leave filters in a system after resistance has increased to the point where there is a substantial decrease in the flow of air.
Revised:	Filters should not be left in a system after resistance has caused a substantial decrease in the flow of air.
Wordy:	On the basis of the foregoing discussion, it is apparent that. . . .
Revised:	This discussion shows. . . .
Wordy:	The pursuit and capture of winged, air-breathing arthropods is more easily effected when a sweet, as opposed to sour, substance is, for purposes of beguilement, made use of: For example, the viscid fluid derived from the saccharin secretion of a plant and produced by hymenopterous insects of the super family *Apoidea* has proved to be more successful in this endeavor than has dilute and impure acetic acid.
Revised:	More flies are caught with honey than with vinegar.

clause (subordinate). A *subordinate* or *dependent clause* is an element of complex and compound sentences (see pages 21–24); it usually has a subject and a verb and is grammatically equivalent to a noun, adjective, or adverb. The dependent clause is introduced by a subordinating conjunction, for example, *as, because, since, when;* or by a relative pronoun, for example, *that, who, which.*

> *That the waveguide overheated* was not a surprise to him (subject or noun clause).
> *Because the expert knows where to look for data on free-radical reactions in solution,* he seems to have little sympathy for the nonkineticist who needs such data (adjective clause).
> The administrator *who received the report* will not read it (adjective clause). The endogenous RNA was removed *when the preparation was subjected to alkaline hydrolosis* (adverbial clause).
> Few experiments have been carried out *because nematodes have little or no capacity for regeneration* (adverbial clause).

collective noun. A *collective noun* is one whose singular form carries the idea of more than one person, act, or object: army, class, crowd, dozen, flock, group, majority, personnel, public, remainder, and team. When the collective noun refers to the group as a whole, the verb and pronoun used with it should be singular. When the individuals of the group are intended, the noun takes a plural verb or pronoun: The committee *is* here; The committee *were* unanimous in disapproval; The corporation *has given* proof of its intention. The plural of a collective noun signifies different groups: *Herds* of deer graze in the upper valley.

colon (:). The colon is used as a mark of introduction to a word, phrase, tabulation, sentence, or passage to be quoted. It is also used in giving clock time. The first word after a colon is not capitalized if what follows is not a complete sentence. Use the colon:

1. After the salutation of a letter:
   Dear Dr. Reimann:
   Ladies/Gentlemen:

2. In memoranda following TO, FROM, and SUBJECT lines:
   TO:
   FROM:
   SUBJECT:
3. To introduce enumerations, usually *as follows, for example, the following,* and so forth. The components are *as follows:*
4. To introduce quotations:
   The statement read:
   We the undersigned members of the corporation believe:
5. To separate hours and minutes:
   The meeting will begin at 10:30 a.m.

comma. The modern tendency is to avoid *commas* except where they are needed for clarity. Use commas:

1. To set off nonrestrictive modifiers or clauses. A word, phrase, or clause that follows the word it modifies and that restricts the meaning of that word is called a restrictive modifier or restrictive clause. Restrictive clauses are *not* set off by commas. When such a modifier merely adds a descriptive detail, gives further information, it is called *nonrestrictive* and is set off by commas. If the modifier is omitted, will the sentence still tell the truth or offer the meaning you intend? If it does, then the clause or modifier is *nonrestrictive* and should be set off by commas. If it does not tell the truth and if it does not give the meaning intended, you must *not* use commas. Example: Our chief chemist, who got her Ph.D. degree from Stanford University, is now in Europe. *Who got her degree from Stanford University* is not necessary to the sense intended, so that clause is set off by commas. However: Our chief chemist who checked the computations of the experiment does not agree with the conclusions reached. The clause *who checked the computations of the experiment* is necessary to the sense of the sentence. It is restrictive and therefore should not be set off by commas.
2. With explanatory words and phrases or those used in apposition: To meet the deadline, Mr. Simon, our president, supervised the experiment.
3. With introductory and parenthetic words or phrases, such as *therefore, however, of course,* and *as we see it;* As you are aware, the legislation did not pass; this action, nevertheless, is necessary.
4. In inverted construction where a word, phrase, or clause is out of its natural order: That the result was unexpected, it was soon apparent.
5. To avoid confusion by separating two words or figures that might otherwise be misread: By 1990, 30,000 students are expected to enroll.
6. To avoid confusion by separating words in a series: The client manufactures furniture, pottery items, electric fixtures, and steel garden implements.
7. To make the meaning clear when a verb has been omitted: I covered the door, John covered the hallway, Bill covered the windows, and Tom, the remaining exit.
8. To separate two independent long clauses joined by a coordinating conjunction (*and, but, for, yet, neither, therefore,* or *so*): Analog recorders of .05 percent accuracy are available, but frequent maintenance is often required to hold this tolerance. (A comma is not used when the coordinate clauses are short and are closely related in meaning: A panel of experts might be chosen from particular areas of specialization and their report would be published).

9. To separate a dependent clause or a long phrase from its independent clause: For complex mixtures of acids such as those found in physiological fluids, a five-chamber concave gradient is generated. Although good recoveries of both methyl pyruvate and methyl lactate could be obtained at column temperatures below 100° Celsius, there was no indication that such recoveries could be achieved when either of the acids was in excess.
10. To separate the day of the month from the year:
December 21, 1916
When the day of the month is not given, the usual practice today is to omit the comma: December 1916. In construction in which the day precedes the month, no comma is used: 21 December 1916.
11. To separate town from state or country when they are written on the same line: Bethesda, Maryland; Washington, D.C.; Stockholm, Sweden; Fort Collins, Larimer County, Colorado.
12. In figures to separate thousands and millions: 528,121; 10,894,082.
13. To introduce a quotation: Professor Thomas said, "The new alloy will work."
14. To introduce a paraphrase similar in form to a quotation but lacking quotation marks: The question may be asked, Will this new approach work?

compare, contrast. There is some confusion in the application of these two words because *compare* is used in two senses: (1) to point out similarities (used with the preposition *to*); and (2) to examine two or more items or persons, to find likenesses or differences (used with the preposition *with*). *Contrast* always points out differences.

complement, compliment. These two words, though pronounced alike, are completely different in meaning. *Complement* means to fill up, to complete a whole: The *complement* of this 63 degree angle is the one of 27 degrees. *Compliment* means to praise: The professor *complimented* the student on her design.

compound predicate. A compound predicate consists of two or more verbs having the same subject. It is often used to avoid the awkward effect of repetition of the subject or the writing of another sentence: The Emperor Van de Graaff accelerator is precisely controllable. Another feature is that it is easily variable. It is also continuous. A more economical and smoother way of saying the previous sentences is to combine them with a compound predicate: The Emperor Van de Graaff accelerator is precisely *controllable, easily variable,* and *continuous.*

compound subject. Two or more elements that serve as the subject of one verb form: The *deposition time* and *amount of carbon available in the gases determine* (not determines) the resistance value in the film resistors.

computerese. (See also *jargon.*) Computerese is the special vocabulary or sublanguage evolved by people working with computers and information processing systems for communicating with one another. It is a user-unfriendly language, virtually incomprehensible to the uninitiated. Here is an example:

>1ON1 = 3 is a dBaseIII Plus work-alike. It is compatible with dBaseIII commands and functions in the dot prompt and programming mode; the assist mode, however, has been modified to make it easier to use. 1ON1 = 3 is

compatible with most dBaseIII Plus files and can read and report on information in dBaseII files. It requires 512K of RAM.

To the uninitiated, this unfriendly description of a program, to use a computerese term, is "GIGO" (garbage) and meaningless.

conjunction. Conjunctions introduce and tie clauses together and join series of words and phrases. Types of conjunctions include:

>coordinating: *and, but, for*
>correlative: *either . . . or, not only . . . but also*
>conjunctive adverbs: *however, therefore, consequently, accordingly, nonetheless*
>subordinating: *as, because, since, so that, when*

contractions. *Contractions* are words from which an unstressed syllable is dropped in speaking. Their use is acceptable in informal writing but not in formal writing.

>can't: use *cannot*
>didn't: use *did not*
>I'll: use *I will*

council, counsel, consul. These three words are sometimes confused. A *council* is an advisory group; *counsel* means advice and, in law, it means one who gives advice; a *consul* is an official representing the government of a foreign country.

dangling modifiers. The *dangling modifier,* the most prevalent fault in technical writing, is usually a verb form (often a participle) that is not supplied with a subject to modify, and which seems to claim a wrong word as its subject. It is said to dangle because it has no word to which it logically can be attached. Infinitive and prepositional phrases may also be dangling.

Wrong:	Calibrating the thermistor through the temperature range of 17° to 19° Celsius, a value of 4.0 ± 0.1°C.1 molar was obtained.
Revised:	Calibrating the thermistor through the range of 17° to 19° Celsius, we obtained a value of 4.0 ± 0.1°C.1 molar.
Wrong:	After adjusting the valves, the engine developed more power.
Revised:	The engine developed more power after the valves were adjusted.
or:	After adjusting the valves, the mechanic found the engine developed more power.
Wrong:	To write a program for our computer, it helps to know Fortran.
Revised:	To write a program for our computer, you would find it helpful to know Fortran.
Better:	A knowledge of Fortran is helpful in writing a program for our computer.
Wrong:	Near Kamchatka, Alaska, Figures 11 through 17 show the typical appearances in both the television pictures and the infrared data of several stages in the life cycle of the cloud vortices of a cyclonic storm.

Revised: Figures 11 and 17 show typical appearances in both television pictures and infrared data of several stages in the life cycle of the cloud vortices of a cyclonic storm near Kamchatka, Alaska.

dash (—). The *dash* is used to indicate a change of thought or a change in sentence structure. It is also used for emphasis and to set off repetition or explanation. The *dash* may be used in place of parentheses when greater prominence to the subordinate expression is desired. Dashes should not be used with numbers because they might be mistaken for minus signs.

> The rectifier—that was the guilty component.
>
> I am suspicious of prognosticators—but I would not be surprised if tangible evidence of extraterrestrial, intelligent life will be found before the end of the present century.
>
> A traveling wave tube has been made with a helix fifteen-thousandths of an inch in diameter—about three times the diameter of a human hair.
>
> These molecules—formic acid, acetic acid, succinic acid, and glycine—are the very ones from which living things are constructed.

data. The word *data* is the plural of the Latin word *datum*. The singular form *datum* is rarely used in English. The word *data* is often defined as raw facts or observations. In science and technology, *data* are characterized by their tendency toward quantification. Because the singular form is rarely used, the word *data* is becoming more acceptable in all but the most formal English as either singular or plural. In the computer field, *data* has come to mean a collection or mass of information; in that sense, it has lost its plural connotation: *Data is stored for retrieval.* Historically, Latin plurals sometimes become singular English words (for example, *agenda, stamina*). Some writers treat *data* as a collective noun and use the singular verb with the word. For instance: The experiment's *data* was made available to three laboratories. However, there is a loud and armed camp of data pluralists who will split an infinitive with alacrity but will scream with outrage and scorn at any usage of a singular English verb with the Latin plural form. My advice is that it is always safe to use the plural unless you can afford a battle—and can afford to lose it, because you may well do so.

dates. The more common form for writing dates is: August 11, 1994. The form, 11 August 1994, originating with the military services, is seeing more use because it makes a comma unnecessary. When only the month and year are used, August, 1994 is becoming obsolete; in more and more communications, the comma is being eliminated: August 1994. If saving space is important, months having more than four letters can be abbreviated: Jan., Feb., Mar., Apr., Aug., Sept., Oct., Nov., and Dec. In informal writing, figures are often used: 8-11-94 (for August 11, 1994). In England and other European countries, the day usually comes first: 11-8-94 (for August 11, 1994).

deadwood. See *circumlocution*.

decimals. Use figures for all numbers that contain decimals: 1.4 *liters of fluid;* 4.5 *inches of rain.* A zero is placed to the left of the decimal point when the fraction is less than a whole number: 0.3. Do not mix fractions with decimal fractions:

> *Not:* 2½ lb., 2.2 oz.
> *Instead* write: 2.5 lb., 2.2 oz.

defect. Use the preposition *in* for a defect in a thing: The defect *in* the engine caused the accident. Use *of* for a person's shortcomings. The astronaut's defect *of* perception caused the accident.

diagnosis, prognosis. *Diagnosis* is the process for determining by examination the nature of a circumstance for a disease. *Prognosis* follows diagnosis. It is the physician's educated guess as to the course and outcome of the disease. The words are not interchangeable.

different from, different than. *Different from* is the established usage. *From* is a preposition and *than* is a conjunction. Different things differ *from* each other. Many authorities recommend that *different than* be used (though *than* is a conjunction) if it avoids awkwardness or wasteful words. For example: *Computers use different programming languages now than they did ten years ago*, rather than *Computers use different programming languages today from those which they used ten years ago.*

dimensions, measurements, weights, and proportion. When any of these consist of two or more elements, or when a decimal is used, they should be rendered in numbers, even those below ten: *6 by 18; 12 feet 6 inches by 22 feet 9 inches; 7 years 5 months 15 days (age); 8 pounds 4 ounces; 5 parts gin, 1 part vermouth.* However, when a single dimension or measurement below 10 is given, it should be spelled out when it contains an ordinary fraction: *two-and-a-third* miles; *six*-feet tall; *seven*-pound baby. But when the fraction is given in decimal form, use figures: *21.6-inch* snowfall.

disc, disk. Dictionaries say each is a variant spelling of the other, but in the computer age, *disc* should be reserved for phonograph records and *disk* for the computer's magnetic information storage device.

discreet, discrete. *Discreet* means prudent. *Discrete* means separate or distinct. To use one for the other advertises ignorance.

disinterested, uninterested. *Disinterested* means fair, impartial, unbiased; *uninterested* means lacking interest or without curiosity. Although in recent years the two words have been used interchangeably in informal speech, your use of *disinterest* to mean lacking interest may raise some readers' eyebrows.

ditto marks ("). Ditto marks are a convenience in tabulation and lists that repeat words from one line to the next, but ditto marks should not be used in formal writing.

divided into, composed of. *Divided into* applies to a thing once whole that has been made into separate parts; *composed of* applies to a whole created from several or many parts.

division of words. Break words only between syllables. When in doubt about syllabication, look up the word in the dictionary. Avoid breaking up a compound word that requires a hyphen in its spelling. Do not divide words of two syllables if the division comes after a single vowel: *among, along, atom, enough.*

dollars and cents. Sums of dollars and cents are usually written in figures: *10 cents; 75 cents; $12; $24.95; $11,914.* However, *$1 million; $3.94 million; $4.6 billion* is acceptable. *$4 to $10 million* should be written as *$4 million to $10 million* to avoid confusion. With dollars and cents, the convention of spelling out numbers below 10 does not apply: *3 cents, $8.* Round amounts are written in words: one hundred dollars, three thousand dollars, a million dollars.

due to. Grammarians say that *due to* is properly used in the sense of *caused by* or *resulting from* when *due* is an adjective modifying a noun: The hissing sound was *due to* the malfunction of the number three pump. The modified noun is *sound*. However, *due to* should not be used when there is no noun modified. The malfunction occurred *due to* the leak in the number three pump is grammatically unacceptable. *Due to* in the present instance modifies the verb *occurred*. You will solve your problem and please grammarians by using an adverbial construction like *because of:* The malfunction occurred *because of* the leak in the number three pump.

ecology, environment. These words are not synonymous. *Ecology* is the science or study of the relationship between an organism and its environment. *Environment* is the totality of conditions surrounding an organism or organisms, including human beings.

editorial "we." The substitution of *we* when *I* obviously is intended is considered by many as affected and pompous. In those circumstances where there are several authors of a report, the use of *we* is certainly called for. However, a writer may want to take the reader with him over intellectual territory, as for example:

> We have seen the effect of X on variable Y in our experiment; we will therefore proceed now to add Z into the mixture to see whether thus and thus will then occur.

In correspondence, the use of *we* may be desirable when the writer is expressing his organization's policy or desires.

e.g. *e.g.*, an abbreviation of the Latin *exempli gratia*, meaning "for example," is used to introduce parenthetical examples.

either. *Either* means *one or the other of two*. It can be *either* an adjective or a pronoun: *Either* alternative is not sound. Nevertheless, I shall have to take *either* (one). To use *either* to refer to three or more objects is inaccurate:

Poor: *either* of three choices
Better: *any* of three choices

electric/electrical, electronic. The words are not interchangeable. Use *electric* to describe anything that produces, carries, or is activated by an electric current: *electric* appliance, *electric* charge, *electric* circuit. Use *electrical* to describe things that pertain to but do not contain or carry electricity: *electrical* analog, *electrical* engineer. Use *electronic* to describe devices that are activated by the flow of electrons: Computers, radio receivers, and television sets are *electronic* devices.

ellipsis (. . .). A punctuation mark of three dots indicates that something has been omitted within quoted material. Four dots are used to indicate that the omission occurs at the end of a sentence. The *ellipsis* also is used to indicate that a statement has an unfinished quality.

enormity, enormousness. *Enormity* means horror or great wickedness; *enormousness* refers to size: *the enormity of crime, the enormousness of the national debt.* (Some might call the national debt an *enormity*.)

ensure, insure, assure. *Ensure* and *insure* are often pronounced the same and in some contexts provide a similar meaning: to make certain. In common usage, *insure* means to protect against financial loss, as of life and property. *Assure* means to impart trust, an act of making a person so confident as to set his mind at ease. In England and Canada, life insurance companies use the word *assurance* in their name.

>We took the stereo to an authorized dealer to *ensure* it would be repaired properly.
>
>At any rate, we were glad we had *insured* the stereo.
>
>The technician *assured* us the Dolby Noise Reduction unit was fixed.

etc. *etc.*, an abbreviation for the Latin *et cetera*, which means "and so forth," is sometimes used at the end of a list of items. Unless there is some reason for saving space, avoid the use of *etc.* An effective way to avoid this use is to introduce the list with *such as* or *for example*. In textual material, such as this book or a long formal report, use *etc.* only in parenthetical or tabular material. In the body of the text, use *and so forth*. The use of *and* with etc. is redundant.

every, everybody, everyone. *Every* is an adjective; *everybody* and *everyone* are pronouns. *Every* and its compounds are grammatically singular:

>Every instrument in the bench setup was working.
>
>Everybody is here.
>
>Everyone who saw the phenomenon took back his own impressions.

Every one becomes two words when used in the sense of every or each one of a group name. *Every one of the six recommendations was adopted.* Though *every one* seems all-inclusive, it requires a singular verb.

exclamation mark (!). An *exclamation mark (or point)* is used after an emphatic interjection or forceful command. It may follow a complete sentence, phrase, or individual word. It should be used sparingly in technical writing.

farther, further. In informal speech, there is little distinction between the two words. In formal writing, *farther* applies to physical distances; *further* refers to degree or quantity.

>We drove on 60 miles *farther*.
>
>He questioned me *further*.
>
>The more he read about the matter, the *further* confused he became.

Federal. Capitalize the word when it is part of a name or when used as an adjective synonymous with the United States: *Federal Reserve Board, Federal courts, Federal government.*

fewer, less. Use *fewer* in referring to a number of individual persons or things. *Fewer than three transistors failed.* Use *less* in referring to quantity: *Less copper was used in this design.*

forego, forgo. To *forego* means to go before, to precede. To *forgo* means to give something up.

gender, the generic "he." Gender in language is a grammatical term that indicates the sex or sexlessness of the referent. Many languages have special endings for feminine, masculine, and neuter nouns and for adjectives modifying them. English abandoned this system several hundred years ago. Gender in English is determined by meaning. All nouns naming living creatures are feminine or masculine according to the sex of the individual, and all other nouns are neuter. In English, as in other languages, we attribute gender or personification to things, inanimate objects, and nouns generalizing persons:

> *The sun sent his warm rays down to earth.*
> *The moon cast her pale light. . . .*
> *The ship made her way through the channel.*
> *A good teacher will not lie to his pupils.*

The expression of gender in these examples is based not on grammar but on traditions of long usage. For most English words, gender is identifiable only by the choice of the meaningfully appropriate pronoun *(he, she, it)*:

> *The speaker chose his words carefully.* (a male speaker)
> *The playwright was brilliant in her characterization of the hero.* (a female playwright)
> *The storm made its impact felt.*

Today, most writers reject as sexist the use of the generic "he" for words or terms in which the sex of the referent is ambiguous. For example, the above sentence, *A good teacher will not lie to his pupils* becomes *A good teacher will not lie to his or her pupils*. This simple revision is more applicable to the thought expressed. In other cases, however, a similar revision might result in awkward phrasing. For example, *Every chairman must accept his responsibility to meet with each of his club members* would become *Every chairperson must accept his or her responsibility to meet with each of his or her club members*. Although the word *chairperson* has come into common usage, the repetition of *his or her* is clumsy. Such sentences can almost always be restructured to avoid these conflicts altogether. The above sentence could be written: *Every chairperson (or presiding officer) must accept responsibility for meeting with each club member*. A common way to avoid the use of awkward *his or her* is simply to make the referent plural whenever possible. For instance, *The client is usually the best judge of the worth of his therapy* becomes *Clients are usually the best judges of the therapy they receive*. Moreover, *A good teacher will not lie to his pupils* becomes *Good teachers will not lie to their pupils*.

In other examples, *humanity* or *people* could be substituted for *mankind*, and *workforce* or *personnel* for *manpower*.

genus, species. A *genus* is a taxonomic class of plants or animals that includes groups of closely related species. A *species* is a taxonomic category immediately below a genus. The name of the species is always preceded by the name of the genus, or larger category of which it is a subdivision. Only the genus is capitalized: *Homo sapiens; Myotis lucigigus*.

good, well. *Good* is an adjective; *well* is both an adverb and adjective. One can say:

>I feel good (adjective).
>I feel well (adjective).

However, the meanings are different. In the first sentence, *good* implies actual body sensations. In the second sentence, *well* refers to a condition of health—being "not ill." In nonstandard spoken English, *good* is sometimes substituted for *well*. For example:

>The centrifuge runs *good*.

Most educated persons would say:

>The centrifuge runs *well*.

Government, government. Capitalize when referring to a specific national government: the *U.S. Government*, the *Israeli Government*. Use lowercase for general state and local governments: the *city government* and so forth.

guarantee, guaranty. Used as nouns, each form is proper. Used as verbs, *guarantee* is more common.

hanged, hung. A person is *hanged*; a picture is *hung*.

heretofore. *Heretofore* is stilted; replace it with *until now*.

hertz, cycle. *Hertz* is a unit of frequency equal to one cycle per second; it has been adopted by the scientific community to replace *cycle*. Thus, it is kilohertz *not* kilocycle. The abbreviation is kHz. Kilohertz is used for both singular and plural.

historic, historical. *Historic* is preferred in the sense that something was or is momentous in human events. *Historical* means related to history: *historic* battle, *historic* invention, but *historical* accuracy.

however. As a conjunction, *however* is a useful connective between sentences to show the relation of a succeeding thought to a previous one in the sense of "on the other hand" or "in spite of." Inexperienced writers tend to overuse *however*. *But* is often more appropriate because it is a more direct connective. Compare the following uses of *however*:

1. In an attempt to make certain that only the fragments of the minus strand were synthesized, the recommended precautions were followed; *however,* when the reactions were carried out, the results indicated a vast excess of the plus strand.
2. In an attempt to make certain that only the fragments of the minus strand were synthesized, the recommended precautions were followed; *but* when the reactions were carried out, the results indicated a vast excess of the plus strand.
3. In an attempt to make certain that only the fragments of the minus strand were synthesized, the recommended precautions were followed. When the reactions were carried out, the results indicated a vast excess of the plus strand, *however*.

The more experienced writer will select use 2 or 3 over the usage in 1 above. *However* is also an adverb; it may modify an adjective or another adverb:

> *However* great the difficulty was, he still did his best.
> *However* hard he tried, he could not finish in time.

hyphen (-). *Hyphens* are a controversial point in style. Modern tendency is to eliminate their use. Consult a good dictionary or the style manual of your organization. A *hyphen* is a symbol conveying the meaning that the end of a line has separated a word at an appropriate syllable and that the syllables composed at the end of one line and the beginning of the next are one word. The *hyphen* is also used to convey the meaning that two or more words are made into one. The union may be ad hoc—for that single occasion—or permanent. Light-yellow flame has a different meaning than light, yellow flame. *Hyphens* are, therefore, used to form compound adjectival descriptive phrases preceding a noun: a beta-ray spectrum, cell-like globule, 21-cm radiation, less-developed countries. Conventionally, *hyphens* are used to join parts of fractional and whole numbers written as words: thirty-three, one-fourth.

Hyphens are used to set off prefixes and suffixes in differentiating between words spelled alike but having different meanings:

> Recover his composure, and re-cover his losses.
> Recount a story, re-count the proceeds.
> Fruitless endeavor, fruit-less meal.

Hyphens are used between a prefix and a proper name:

> pre-Sputnik, ex-professor
> Pro-relativistic quantum theory

Hyphens are used between a prefix ending in a vowel and a root word beginning with the same vowel:

> re-elected
> re-enter

Hyphenation has become more a publisher's worry than a writer's. Most organizations set a style policy in hyphenation. Some follow the style manual of the University of Chicago (the style used for this text) or the style manual of the U.S. Government Printing Office. Some professional societies have style manuals for the writing done in their fields (for example, the American Institute of Physics and the Conference of Biological Editors).

Word processing systems have a hyphenation feature to take care of hyphenation requirements. There are three types: a hard hyphen; a soft hyphen; and a nonbreaking hyphen. A hard hyphen is inserted by the user with a hyphen key. The *hard hyphen* stays with the word even if it is wordwrapped to the middle of a line after editing. If the word no longer requires hyphenation, the user must delete it. *Soft hyphens* are inserted by an automatic feature. If the position of the word changes during revision, rendering the hyphen unnecessary, the automatic hyphen feature removes the hyphen. A *nonbreaking hyphen* ensures that the word will not be broken at the end of a line; as for example, in the phrase: a

1-liter beaker, the character "1-" would not be separated at the end of the line from the word, "liter," which might otherwise appear at the beginning of the next line. The non-breaking hyphen feature keeps the phrase "1-liter" together.

i.e. The use of *i.e.,* the abbreviation of the Latin *id est* (meaning *that is*), often saves time and space, but the English *that is* is preferable.

if, whether. *If* is used to introduce a condition; *whether* is used in expressions of doubt.

>*If* the weather holds good, the space launch will be made.
>I wondered *whether* the space launch would be made.
>I asked *whether* the space launch would be made.

imply, infer. These two words are often confused. *Imply* means to suggest by word or manner. *Infer* means to draw a conclusion about the unknown on the basis of known facts.

in, into, in to. *In* shows location; *into* shows direction.

>He remained *in* the laboratory.
>He came *into* the laboratory.

The construction *in to* is that of an adverb followed by a preposition:

>He went *in to* eat.

in-, un-. The prefixes, *in-* and *un-* and their variants, *il-* and *im-*, usually give words a negative meaning: *in*adequate, *in*audible, *in*complete, *il*literate, *im*practical, *un*acceptable, *un*necessary, *un*responsive. Both *in-* and *un-* are used with some words: *in*decipherable, *un*decipherable; *in*distinguishable, *un*distinguishable; *in*supportable, *un*supportable. Problems arise because some related words use a different prefix: *in*digestible, *un*digested; *in*advisable, *un*advised. If you are not sure whether a word takes *in-*, *un-*, *im*, or *il-*, consult a dictionary. Not all words beginning with *in* are negative: *inflammable* means the same as flammable. Some other *in* words that do not have negative meaning are *incubate, indemnity,* and *invaluable*.

include. *Include* is used to introduce a number of items that do not constitute a complete listing: *The new generator included a mercury pump, a rotor, and a set of turbine wheels.*

incredible, incredulous. A statement, story, or situation is *incredible* (unbelievable); a person is *incredulous* (unbelieving).

indentation. *Indentation* in a manuscript or printed copy is beginning a line in from the left-hand margin. In typewritten or word processed copy, paragraphs are indented five spaces. In word processing, you indent by hitting the Tab key for a paragraph first line *indentation*. If you want the whole text material indented (for example, when you quote more than three lines) you hit the Indent key.

irregardless. The use of this word, having a negative prefix, *ir,* and a negative suffix, *less,* is considered nonstandard in formal writing. Use *regardless* or *irrespective* instead.

italics. A style of printing type patterned after a Renaissance script with letters slanted to the left. In handwritten or typewritten manuscripts, use of italics is shown by underlining. Use italics to indicate:

1. Titles of books, plays, musical compositions, motion pictures, periodicals, and newspapers. (Titles of articles, short stories, speeches, and poems are placed in quotation marks.) For example:

    Origin of Species
    War and Peace
    Hamlet
    Scientific American
    The New York Times
    Casablanca
    Beethoven's *Ninth Symphony*
    "The Snows of Kilimanjaro"
    "As We May Think"
    "Trees"
    Lincoln's "Gettysburg Address"

2. Foreign Words that have not become part of the English language:

    The footnote abbreviation for *loco citato*, "in the place cited," is *loc. cit.*
    Vitiglio or leukoderm is a condition in which pigment cells have stopped making pigment.

3. Latin scientific terms such as:

    Homo sapiens (modern human species)
    Cyanoeitta cristata (blue jay)
    Myotis lucifugus (little brown bat)

4. To emphasize words or statements:

    It was the *director of engineering* who was responsible for the calamity.

5. To call specific attention to words, letters, or numbers:

    The words *lay* and *lie* are often confused.
    The letter *g* in the word *length* is not pronounced.
    In the last paragraph, change the number *6* to number *9*.

Latin and foreign words that have become part of the English language are not italicized. For example:

| addendum (pl.-da) | barrage | camouflage |
| agenda | bona fide | carte blanche |

clientele	per capita	resume
data	per diem	status quo
delicatessen	pro rata	via
elite	queue	vice versa
entrepreneur	rapport	Weltanschauung
laissez-faire		

its, it's. *Its* is a possessive form and means belonging to it. *It's* is the contraction for *it is*.

-ize, -ise. English has many verbs ending in the sound of *iz*, some of which are spelled *-ise*, some *-ize*, and some both ways.

British spelling prefers *-ise*; American spelling, *ize*: anesthe*tise*, anesthe*tize*; standard*ise*, standard*ize*. In some words, *-ise* is the usual spelling in American English: *advise, devise, revise, surmise*. Both *-ize* and *-ise* are used in a number of words: *advertise, advertize; analyze, analyse*. If you are writing for an American audience, follow American usage.

jargon. *Jargon* or shoptalk is the term for the specialized words or phrases used in a particular profession, trade, science, field, or occupation, as for example: *input, output; throughput; infrastructure; metalanguage; heuristic; peer group; dichotomy; complex; party* (for *person* in law). Such words are the cliches of specialized fields and should be avoided or used with care to be sure the meaning is clear for the reader. (See *computerese, shoptalk*.)

kind, kinds; sort, sorts; type, types. As nouns, *kind, sort,* and *type* are singular nouns in form: This *kind* of illness. . . . This *sort* of equipment. . . . This *type* of system. . . . Informal usage, however, has added an *s* when the noun they stand before is plural: These *sorts* of problems. . . . These *kinds* of ideas. . . . These *types* of solutions. . . . In formal writing, the addition of an *s* should be avoided.

know-how. This term meaning technical skill has become acceptable in formal writing.

lay, lie. These verbs are often confused. *Lay* (principal parts: *lay, laid, have laid*) is a transitive verb meaning to put something down. *Lie* (principal parts: *lie, lay, have lain*) is an intransitive verb meaning to rest in reclining position.

> I *laid* the tool on the bench.
>
> The old man *lay* resting on the sofa.

lb., lbs. *lb.* is an abbreviation of the Latin *libra,* the plural of which is *librae*. Because there is no *s* in the Latin plural, some purists argue that *lb.* should be used for both singular and plural forms. Usage has brought acceptance of *lbs.* for the plural of the word *pound*.

leave, let. *Leave* means to go away or to part with; *let* means to allow or permit.

like, as. Despite common usage, *like* is not fully accepted as a conjunction. The preposition *like* is used correctly when it is followed by a noun or pronoun without a verb. In formal writing, avoid using *like* as a conjunction; *as* should be used instead.

> He writes *like* an ignoramus.
>
> He looks *like* me.
>
> Watch and do *as* I do.

literally. This word is often used when *figuratively* is meant: The strike has management *literally* walking a tightrope. The proper word in this sentence is *figuratively*.

madam, madame. *Madam* can be the keeper of a bordello.

material, materiel. *Material* is the term for the substance or substances of which a thing is made or composed. *Materiel* refers to apparatus, arms, and military equipment. The field of business has appropriated the term for the aggregate of things used or needed in an enterprise.

may be, maybe. These two forms are often confused. *May be* is a compound verb; *maybe* is an adverb meaning perhaps.

mean, median. In statistics, a *mean* is an average; a *median* is the figure that ranks midway in a list of numbers arranged in ascending or descending order. For example, in a discussion of the varying wages of 41 workers, the *mean* is the total of their pay divided by 41. The *median* is the wage that is higher than 20 of the wages and lower than the remaining 20.

Messrs. It is the abbreviation of the French word *messieurs*. It is used as the plural of *Mr.*: *Messrs.* Campbell and Hamilton. In the salutation of a letter when a firm name is addressed, as for example, Campbell and Hamilton & Company, the words *Ladies/Gentlemen:* should be used. *Messrs.* may be used in text material to avoid repetition of *Mr.* in a listing of three or more: *Messrs. Clark, Boehne, Markman, and Shaw attended the meeting.*

militate, mitigate. The meaning of these two words is sometimes confused. To *militate* (used with the preposition *against*) means to have weight or effect against; to *mitigate* means to ease or to soften a situation.

misplaced modifiers. Modifiers should be placed near the words they modify.

Wrong: Throw the horse over the fence some hay.
Revised: Throw some hay over the fence to the horse.

The accurate placing of the word *only* is critical to precise meaning in technical writing. Notice the change in meaning brought about by shifting the word *only* in the following sentences:

1. *Only* the physicist calculated the value of X in the equation.
2. The *only* physicist calculated the value of X in the equation.
3. The physicist *only* calculated the value of X in the equation.
4. The physicist calculated *only* the value of X in the equation.
5. The physicist calculated the *only* value of X in the equation.
6. The physicist calculated the value of *only* X in the equation.
7. The physicist calculated the value of X *only* in the equation.
8. The physicist calculated the value of X in the *only* equation.

Ms. This title may be used for either single or married women, analogous to Mr. for men; its plural is *Mss*.

namely. When you introduce a series of items, as in the following sentence: The apprentices were thoroughly grounded in the fundamental processes of the work, namely, planning, designing, and building, does the word *namely* add anything? Not really. Experienced writers would omit the word.

neither, neither . . . nor. *Neither* is a word used for two items or subjects and requires a singular verb: *Neither of the two alternatives was desirable.* After a *neither-nor* construction, if the subjects are singular, use a singular verb: *Neither the pump nor the exhaust was working.* If the subjects are both plural, use a plural verb: *Neither the personnel nor the systems were properly evaluated.* If one subject is singular and the other plural, use the number of the one after the *nor: Neither the director nor the scientists were surprised by the results.*

No. The abbreviation for number, *No.,* is written with an initial capital.

nobody, nothing, nowhere. All three are written as single words. *Nobody* and *nothing* are singular grammatically. *Nowheres* is nonstandard for *nowhere;* do not use it.

none, no one. *None* is commonly used to refer to things (but not always); *no one* is used to refer to people. *None* may take either a singular or plural verb, depending on whether a singular or plural meaning is intended. *None of the keypunchers are able to work Sundays. No one* always takes a singular verb.

number (the noun). *Number* is a collective noun, taking a singular or plural verb according to total or individual units meant: A number of pages in the manual *were* missing; the number of missing pages *was* exasperating.

number (of nouns and verbs). The singular and plural aspect of nouns and verbs is termed *number.*

1. A verb agrees in number with its subject; a pronoun or pronominal adjective (my, our, your, his, her, its, their) agrees in number with its antecedent. Examples:
   Right: Our greatest need *is* (not are) modernized plant designs.
   Right: The remaining two tubes of the circuit are V-101A and V-101B. *They* (not *it*) control the power input.
   Right: The closing sentence of both paragraphs and sections often *summarizes* (not *summarize*) the contents and *shows* (not *show*) their significance to the whole.
   Right: Determination of the choice and of the placement of punctuation marks *is* (not *are*) governed by the author's intention of meaning to be conveyed.
2. A compound subject coordinated by *and* requires a plural verb, regardless of the individual number of the member subjects.
   Right: A hammer and a saw *are* on the bench.
   Exception: When the compound subject refers to a unity, a singular verb is used.
   Right: A brace and bit *is* on the bench. (However, a brace and a bit *are* on the bench.)
   Right: Johnson and Sons *is* a reliable distributor.
3. Nouns or pronouns appearing between a subject and a verb have no effect upon the number of the verb. The number of the verb is determined solely by the number of its subject.

Right: The director of engineering, in addition to two senior engineers and an engineering aid, *was* in the laboratory.

Right: He, as well as I, *is* to be assigned to the project.

4. Collective nouns (for example, committee, crowd, majority, number) may be either singular or plural, depending on whether the whole or the individual membership is emphasized.

   Right: The committee *is* holding its first meeting.

   Right: The committee *are* in violent disagreement among themselves.

5. Expressions of aggregate quantity, even though plural in form, generally are construed as singular.

   Right: Two times two *is* four (some people say two and two are four).

   Right: Two-thirds of the corporation's income *has* been embezzled.

   Right: Forty kilowatt-hours *was* registered by the meter.

6. When the expressions of quantity not only specify an aggregate amount but also stress the units composing the aggregate, they are construed as plural.

   Right: Two hundred bags of Philippine Copra *were* piled on the dock.

   Right: More than a billion pounds of Copra *was* purchased in the Philippines.

7. A relative pronoun *(who, which, that)* should not be taken as singular when its antecedent is a plural object of the preposition *of* following the word *one.*

   Right: He was one of the ablest hydrographic engineers who *have* devoted *their* skill to the Coast and Geodetic Survey.

numerals. Practice varies in determining which numbers should be spelled out and which should be written as figures. Authorities frequently state rules that seem reasonable or preferable to them. A current trend is to use figures for all units of measure such as meter, gram, liter, volt, hectare, and kelvin. Aggregate numbers are those resulting from the addition or enumeration of items. The tendency to differentiate between the two is rapidly disappearing. Most authorities recommend the spelling out of numbers under ten. Round numbers above a million are frequently written as a combination of figures and words: a 56 million dollar appropriation, an employment force of 100 million.

Most authorities recommend writing out a number at the beginning of the sentence. When two numbers are adjacent to each other, the first is spelled out: six 120-watt lamps.

The practice is to spell out small fractions when they are not part of a mathematical expression or when they are not combined with the unit of measure: three-fourths of the area, one-third of the laboratory, one-half of the test population. However: use ½ mile, ¾ inch pipe, ¹⁄₅₀ horsepower, ¼ ton.

Decimals are always written as figures. When a number begins with a decimal point, precede the decimal point with a zero: an axis of 0.52.

Hours and minutes are written out except when A.M. or P.M. follow: 8:30 A.M. to 5:00 P.M.; six o'clock, nine-thirty, half past two; ten minutes for coffee breaks.

Street numbers always appear in numerals: 1600 Pennsylvania Avenue, N.W.

When several figures appear in a sentence or paragraph, they are written as numerals: In Experiment 2, there was a total of 258 plants. These yielded 8,023 seeds—6,022 yellow and 2,001 green.

Numbers indicating order—first, second, third, fourth, and so forth—are called *ordinal* numbers. (Numbers used in counting—one, two, three, and so forth—are *cardinal* numbers.) First, second, third, and so forth, can be both adjectives and adverbs. Therefore, the *ly* forms—firstly, secondly—are unnecessary and are now rarely used.

on, onto, on to. The distinction between these three words is similar to *in, into,* and *in to* (See entry). The first two words of each set are prepositions; the third term consists of an adverb and a preposition. *On* indicates position: the model on the bench. It also means "time when": *On September 13th;* or continued motion: the technicians worked *on through the night.* *Onto* suggests movement toward: He climbed *onto the roof* to adjust the antenna. When *on* is used as a separate adverb, the combination *on to* is written as two words: After visiting the library, she went *on to* the laboratory.

ongoing. This overworked adjective should be replaced by any of its many synonyms: *continuing, progressing, underway, growing.*

or. *Or* is a coordinating conjunction that connects words, phrases, or clauses of equal value.

oral, verbal. The literate individual does not use these terms interchangeably. *Oral* conveys the idea of spoken words. *Verbal* has the general meaning of words used in any manner spoken, written, or printed. In everyday usage, the distinction is often blurred so that we say a *verbal* agreement for a spoken agreement rather than an *oral* agreement.

page numbers. Unless beginning a sentence, use lowercase: page 1; pages 87–213. Abbreviations may be used: p. 5; 331 pp.; pp. 7, 18, 34, and 203; pp. 416–597.

parallel structure. Parallelism promotes balance, consistency, and understanding. Operationally, it means using similar grammatical structure in writing clauses, phrases, or words to express ideas or facts of equal value. Adjectives should be paralleled by adjectives, nouns by nouns; a specific verb form should be continued in a similar structure; active or passive voice should be kept consistently in a sentence. Shifting from one construction to another confuses the reader and destroys the sense of the meaning. A failure to maintain parallelism results in incomplete thoughts and illogical comparisons.

1. *Faulty:*	Assembly lines poorly planned and which are not scheduled properly are inefficient.
Revised:	Poorly planned and improperly scheduled assembly lines are inefficient.
Faulty:	This is a group with technical training and acquainted with procedures.
Revised:	This group has technical training and a knowledge of procedures.
Faulty:	Before operating the boiler, the fire fighter should both check the water level and be sure about the draft.
Revised:	Before operating the boiler, the fire fighter should check both the water level and the draft.
Faulty:	U.S. Highway 40 extends from the Coastal Plain, runs across the Piedmont, and into the mountains.
Revised:	U.S. Highway 40 extends from the Coastal Plain, across the Piedmont, and into the mountains.
2. *Illogical shifts:* *Shift in tense:*	These effects are usually concentrated in the blood system of the animal. The count of red and white blood cells is affected greatly. The percentage of hemoglobin was also reduced.

Revised:	These effects were usually concentrated in the blood of the animal. The count of red and white blood cells was affected. The percentage of hemoglobin was also reduced.
Shift in person:	First, a new filing system can be introduced. Second, you can train personnel to handle the present complicated system.
Revised:	First, a new filing system can be introduced. Second, personnel can be trained to handle the present complicated system.
Shift in voice:	The technicians began the tests on July 7, and the results were tabulated the following day.
Revised:	The technicians began the tests on July 7 and tabulated the results on the following day.
Shift in mood:	Class members should take meaningful notes on the lectures. Do not cram for quizzes that are to follow.
Revised:	Class members should take meaningful notes on the lectures. They should not cram for the quizzes that are to follow.
Confused sentence structure:	It was because of a natural interest that made me choose the profession of technical writing.
Revised:	A natural interest in writing led me to choose the profession of technical writing.

parentheses (). *Parentheses* are used to enclose additional, explanatory, or supplementary matter to help the reader understand the thought being conveyed. These additions are likely to be definitions, illustrations, or further information added for good measure. *Parentheses* are also used to enclose numbers or letters to mark items in a listing or for enumeration. When a clause in parentheses comes at the end of a sentence and is part of it, put the period outside the parentheses: *One of the many principles secreted into the blood stream by the anterior pituitary "master gland" is that which stimulates the secretion of the adrenal cortex (Adreno Cortico Tropic Hormone; ACTH).* If the parenthesized material is independent of the sentence, it requires a period. The period is placed inside the closing parenthesis mark: *When used for replacement or production of artificial hyperadrenatism, the corticosteroids are not curative. (They merely provide symptomatic relief.)* Do not place a comma before a parenthesis mark; if a comma is indicated after the parenthetical expression, the comma should be placed outside the closing parenthesis mark: *The laboratory (National Institute of Standards and Technology), he said, was not involved.*

people, persons. Use *people* for round numbers and groups (the larger the group, the more appropriate people sounds), and *persons* for precise or quite small numbers: *One million people were affected: The corporation notified 2,967 persons. Only two persons were infected.*

per. *Per* is a preposition borrowed from the Latin, meaning *by, by means of, through,* and is used with Latin phrases that have found their way and use in English: *per diem, per capita, percent* (or, archaically, *per cent*), *per annum. Per* has established itself by long range usage in business English.

percent, per cent, percentage, proportion. Generally written as one word, *percent* often replaces the word *percentage* or even the word *proportion: Only a small percent of the program was run.* With numerals, the *percent* symbol, %, is ordinarily used: 66.67%. *Percent* is used with definite figures. *Percentage* needs a qualifying adjective: A large *percentage* of the population favor the measure. The number of the verb used depends on the object of the preposition *of:* Ten *percent* of the boxes were empty. Ninety *percent* of the book is dull.

period. *Periods* are used to mark the end of complete declarative sentences and abbreviations. Periods are also used in a request, phrased as a question out of courtesy: *Won't you let me know if I can be of further service.*

phenomenon, phenomena. The plural form *phenomena* is frequently misused for the singular *phenomenon.*

plurals of abbreviations, letters, and figures. These plurals are formed by adding *'s* as in M.D.'s, C.P.A.'s, *q's*, and *size 7's*.

plurals of compound nouns. Plurals of compound nouns are formed by the addition of *s* to the most important word; The plural for assistant attorney general is assistant attorneys general, since they are *attorneys* not *generals*. But the plural for deputy associate director is deputy associate *directors*. Similarly, it is *sisters*-in-law, *editors*-in-chief and *points* of view.

possessive (for two names). When you are writing about one thing owned by two persons, it is permissible to use the possessive only once:

Correct: Jack and Jill's hill
Correct: Jack's and Jill's hill

When more than one item and separate ownership is involved, you should show two possessives:

> We shall use Jack's and Jill's computers.

possible, probable. Many things may be *possible* but not *probable*. If your meaning is that the matter is in the realm of likelihood, then the proper word is *probable*. If your meaning is that the matter can be achieved despite difficulties, the proper word is *possible*.

practicable, practical. Any thing that can be achieved or done is practicable, but whether it is *practical* depends on other factors: It could be practicable to develop pollution-free gasoline, but not *practical* because of cost and political factors.

prepositions. A *preposition* is a word of relation. It connects a noun, pronoun, or noun phrase to another element of the sentence. Certain prepositions are used idiomatically with certain words. For example:

knowledge of
interest in
hindrance to
agrees with (a person), agrees to (a suggestion)
agrees in (principle to a suggestion)
agrees to (a plan)
obedience to

responsibility for
fear of (high places), fear for (her safety)
means of (winning)
connected with
information on, information about

If a person uses an unidiomatic preposition, the reason is probably unfamiliarity with the word or confusion resulting from divided usage of that expression. We usually learn the use of the proper preposition by hearing or seeing it in its usual construction. Most prepositions, however, are governed by the logic of the relationship they bring to the noun, phrase, or clause from some other element of the sentence. Figure A illustrates the logic of the relationship provided by prepositions.

A number of years ago, it was fashionable for grammarians to put a stigma upon prepositions standing at the end of sentences. Actually, it is a characteristic of English idiom to postpone the preposition. Many technical writers still feel the pain inflicted in years gone by when some die-hard high school teacher slapped their wrists for ending a sentence with a preposition. Today, they still fall into very clumsy constructions to avoid it. Winston Churchill had the final word on final prepositions. Sir Winston, a famous stylist of his time, had little patience with rigid rules of grammar. When an assistant underlined a Churchillian sentence and noted solemnly in the margin, "Never end a sentence with a preposition," Sir Winston marginally noted back, "This is the sort of English up with which I will not put."

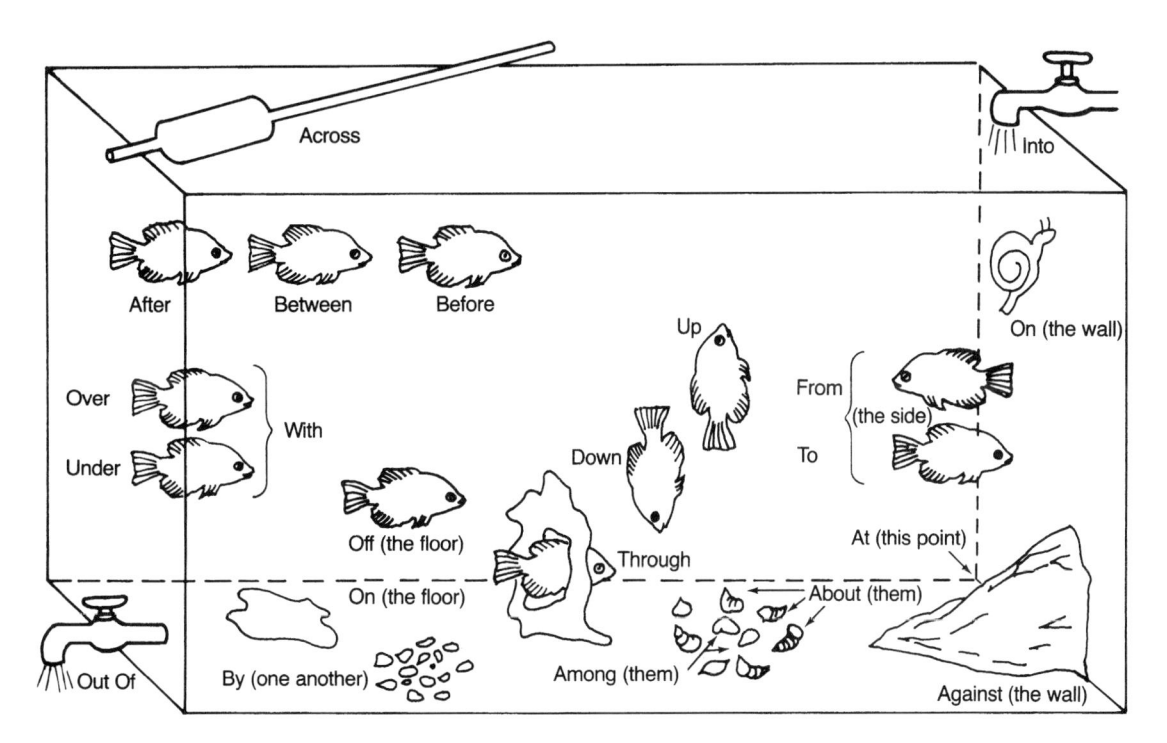

Figure A From I. A. Richards, *Design for Escape.* NY: Harcourt, Brace & World, 1968.

presume, assume. When you *assume* something, you suppose the matter to be a fact with or without a basis of belief. When you *presume* something, you regard the matter as true because there is a reason to do so and you have no evidence to the contrary.

principal, principle. *Principal* is used both as a noun and an adjective. As a noun, it has two meanings: (1) the chief person or leader; and (2) a sum of money drawing interest. As an adjective, *principal* means "of main importance" or "of highest rank or authority." *Principle* is always a noun and means fundamental truth or doctrine, or the basic ideas, motives, or morals inherent in a person, group, or philosophy.

prior to. This is a stilted expression. Replace it with *before*.

programed, programmed. Purists favor *programed* because they can cite the rule for doubling consonants: If a word is not accented on the last syllable, the consonant is not doubled. Scientists prefer the double consonant in *programmed*, and scientific publications use the double *M*. Your dictionary will tell you that both the single and double *M* are acceptable. Which form should you use? Use the form your community of readers feel most comfortable with, but be consistent in your usage.

pronoun. A *pronoun* refers to something without naming it. Its meaning in the reader's mind must be completed by a clear reference to some other word or group of words called its antecedent.

1. *Pronouns* must have definite, clearly understood antecedents.

    Antecedent implied but not expressed: The generator was overloaded and could not carry it.

    Revised: The generator could not carry the overload.

    or: The overload was so large that the generator could not carry it.

    Vague second-person reference: The generator is not satisfactory when shunt-excited. You must have separate excitation.

    Revised: The generator is not satisfactory when shunt-excited. It must have separate excitation.

2. A *pronoun* agrees with its antecedent in number.

    Plural: Multi-stage amplifiers are the heart of radio, television, and almost all electronic equipment. *Their* circuits have (not *its* circuit has) features of great practical importance.

    Singular: The *antibody* is a protein and is produced as a response to the presence in the blood of foreign antigens; *it* passes (not *they*) into the blood through the lymphatic vessels.

3. Place relative *pronouns (who, that, which)* as close as possible to their antecedents.

    Faulty: As transistors and amplifiers have become available that have higher powers and less noise, we have succeeded in developing instruments of improved ranges of operation.

    Revised: As transistors that have higher powers and as amplifiers that have less noise become available, we have succeeded in developing instruments of improved ranges of operation.

provided. Use *provided* not *providing* in the sense of *if*: the transducer will work, provided it is coupled to the amplifier.

punctuation. *Punctuation* is one means by which a writer can achieve clarity and exactness of meaning. Sloppy punctuation can distort meaning and confuse the reader. There are two principles governing the use of punctuation marks:

1. The choice and placement of punctuation marks are governed by the writer's intention of meaning.
2. A punctuation mark should be omitted if it does not clarify the thought.

There is a modern tendency to use open punctuation marks—that is, to omit all marks except those absolutely indispensable. A common mistake of the inexperienced writer is to overuse punctuation marks, especially the comma. A good working rule is to use only those marks for which there is a definite reason, either in making clear or in meeting some conventional demand of correspondence. To illustrate, notice the difference in meaning provided by the punctuation in the following two sets of sentences:

1. (a) The professor said the student is a fool.
   (b) "The professor," said the student, "is a fool!"
2. (a) All of your resistors, which were defective, have been returned.
   (b) All of your resistors which were defective have been returned.

The differences in meaning of sentences 1(a) and 1(b) because of the changes in punctuation are quite obvious. The use of commas in sentence 2(a) makes the sentence say that "all of your resistors were defective, and I have returned them all." Sentence 2(b) without the commas tells the reader that "only those resistors which were defective have been returned." The ultimate test for any punctuation mark is "Is the punctuation needed to make the meaning of my words clearer?"

question mark(?). This punctuation mark is used to denote the end of a question. The question mark is inside quotation marks only when the quoted matter itself is a question.

quotation marks ("). *Quotation marks* are used to enclose direct quotations, titles of articles and reports, and coined or special words or phrases. Quotations longer than three typewritten lines should be indented. No quotation marks are used, and in print, the size of type is usually reduced. In double-spaced typewritten papers, such quotations are single-spaced. The placement of punctuation marks that are not part of the quotation is controversial. Most American publishers place them inside the close-quote. The reason is that the quotes help fill the small spot of white that would be left if the punctuation marks came outside: *What is variously referred to as "inoculation," "homologous serum," "transfusion," or "syringe" jaundice is treatment-produced, resulting from injections of virus-contaminated substances or from injections given with virus-contaminated needles or syringes.* When quotation marks are to be used within a quotation, a single quotation mark is used around the inner quote. For example: *The Research Review Board concluded, "The evidence implicating oncogenes in the development of human cancers is still largely circumstantial. It is `guilt by association' at the moment, but the association is provocative."*

Re. *Re* is derived from the Latin *in re,* meaning "thing." *Re* is used to mean "in the matter of" or "in reference to." *Re* is used in business letters or memos preceding the text to indicate the subject of the communication; it can be used also in the body of the letter or memo. Its use is standard in legal papers, but is considered pretentious in nonbusiness or nonlegal writing.

re (as a prefix). As a prefix meaning "again," *re* is sometimes followed by a hyphen, sometimes not. When the word to which *re* is attached begins with an *e*, a hyphen is used; re-employed, re-enlist. If the hyphen is omitted between the prefix and the word and the result is a word with an unintended meaning, the hyphen is needed to avoid confusion: *recover* from an illness; *re-cover* a sofa.

rebut, refute. *Rebut* means to respond to a statement or speaker, to take issue; *refute* means to prove the statement or speaker wrong or false.

recourse, resource, resort. These three nouns are sometimes confused because they are similar in sound and there are some instances in which one might be substituted for another. A *resource* is a reserve asset that is readily available to a person as needed. A *recourse* is the act of turning to someone or something for help, or it is the person or something you *resort* to for aid, giving rise to the expression, "a last *resort*."

recurrence, reocurrence. *Reocurrence* means a second happening; *recurrence* gives the meaning of happening repeatedly or periodically.

redundancies. The same thing said twice is a *redundancy*, a waste of words, and is an annoyance to readers: His plan was increasingly *more* justified. The finance office is *up* above the third floor. Enclosed *herewith/attached* is the contract. It is customary *practice* to charge a higher interest for an unsecured loan. The words in italics are extra verbiage. The expressions are improved without the repetition.

reparable, repairable, irreparable. Both *reparable* and *repairable* have the meaning of capable of being mended, repaired, or remedied, but their usage differs. *Repairable* is used with things: a broken piece of furniture is *repairable*, but a bad situation might be *reparable*. If it cannot be *reparable*, then it is *irreparable*.

said. In legal documents, the use of *said* as a demonstrative pronoun (this, that, these, those) has a long tradition of use (for example, *said* Mr. Peterson, *said* dwelling). However, in business correspondence, it should be avoided as a cliché.

semicolon (;). The principal use of the *semicolon* is to separate independent clauses that are not joined by a conjunction or are joined by a conjunctive adverb or some other transitional term (for example, therefore, however, for example, in other words). A *semicolon* is also used to separate clauses and phrases in a series when they already contain commas:

> Among the articles offered for sale were a harpsichord, which was at least 200 years old; a desk, which had the earmarks of beautiful craftsmanship; and a table and four chairs, which were also antique.

shoptalk. *Shoptalk* is the specialized vocabulary used by specialists in their everyday work activity. It is a jargon usually known only to the initiated and is both obscure and obstructive to those not "in the know." It is not limited to the shop occupations. Physicians, lawyers, and college professors have their own "talk" that obfuscates. *Shoptalk* is appropriate in informal channels of communication within particular occupations, but it is out of place in formal writing aimed at persons or groups outside of that specialized activity. (See also *computerese, jargon*.)

should, would. *Should* and *would* are used in statements that suggest some doubt or uncertainty about the statement that is being made. Many years ago, *should* was restricted to the first person, but usage now is so divided in the choice of these words that personal preference rather than rule is the guide today. However, consistency in usage should be followed:

> I would greatly appreciate your granting me an interview.
> or:
> I should greatly appreciate your granting me an interview.

sic. *Sic* is Latin for *thus, so*. Placed in brackets, *sic* is used to mark an error in quoted matter. It shows the reader that the error was in the quoted material and was not made by the quoter:

> The Mississippi River starts at Lake Itaska, Minesota [sic].

since, because. Both words can be used interchangeably to indicate a reason for an action, serving to introduce a subordinate clause.

> *Since* he did not try, he failed.
> *Because* he did not try, he failed.

Since, however, functions as several parts of speech:

> As an adverb: She was searching ever *since*.
> As a preposition. The victim has been missing *since* last Tuesday.
> As a conjunction: She improved her SATC scores *since* she took them last year.

slow, slowly. *Slow* is both an adjective and an adverb; *slowly* is an adverb. As adverbs, the two forms are interchangeable, but *slow* is more forceful than *slowly*.

some, somebody, someone, somewhat, somewhere, and so forth. *Some* is used as a pronoun and an adjective.

> *Some* think otherwise (pronoun).
> He has *some* ideas on the problem (adjective).

Somebody (pronoun), *someone* (pronoun), *something* (pronoun), *someday* (adverb), *somehow* (adverb) are written as one word. As pronouns, they require singular verbs.

spacial, spatial. *Spatial* is the preferred adjectival form of *space*. *Spatial* is derived directly from the Latin word for space *spatium*. The word *space* came into English from the French word *espace*. The nonstandard word *spacial* creeps into news stories and articles frequently.

species, specie. The word *species* is both singular and plural. It refers to a logical division of a genus:

> This *species* of turtle is nearly extinct. (singular)
> Many *species* of turtles are amphibious. (plural)

The word *specie* means a coin, usually of gold or silver. Its plural is *species*. To use the term *specie* to represent a single organism of a certain class is erroneous.

spilled. Not split.

split infinitives. Usage has won out. To split an infinitive is no longer viewed as a grammatical misdemeanor. Frequently the interpolation of a word between the parts of an infinitive adds clarity and emphasis. For example:

>   To carefully examine the evidence
>   To forcefully impeach
>   To seriously doubt
>   To better equip

structure. This is an overworked transitive verb, which can often be replaced by *build, construct,* or *organize.* Similarly, *restructure* can often be replaced by *rebuild, recast, reconstruct, reorganize, revamp,* or *revise.*

target. *Target* as a verb is military or governmental jargon. *Targeted,* for example, should be changed to *set a target, aimed at,* or *concentrated on.*

tautology. Needless repetition or meanings differently expressed is an extreme form of wordiness. Here are examples:

>   true facts
>   when gases combine together
>   consensus of opinion
>   first and foremost
>   same identical
>   basic fundamentals
>   initial beginning

telephone numbers. Standard usage calls for placing parentheses around area code numbers: (301) 468-8119; (202) 634-7658. Current popular usage tends to forgo the parentheses and simply inserts a hyphen between the area code and the number: 301-468-8119. Either usage is acceptable.

than, then. *Then* is an adverb relating to time; *than* is a conjunction in clauses of comparison.

>   *Then* came the dawn.
>   Fortran is a more universal programming language *than* the other machine languages.

that, which. *That* is preferred in restrictive clauses: *The treatment that the physician selected was a diuretic to reduce intra-ocular pressure.* In nonrestrictive clauses, *which* is mandatory: *The diuretic, which was not expensive, helped reduce the intra-ocular pressure.*

there is, there are. These expressions delay the occurrence of the subject in a sentence. The verb in the expression must agree in number with the real subject.

> *There* is a difficult problem associated with the system.
> *There* are two solutions to the problem.

Often these expressions can be omitted with no loss to the sentence.

> A difficult problem is associated with the system. Two solutions are available for the problem.
>
> or:
>
> The problem has two solutions.

thousand, thousands, hundred, hundreds, million, millions, trillion, trillions. When the number of thousands, hundreds, millions, or trillions is given as in *ten thousand, ten hundred, ten million, a hundred trillion,* the form is singular. If the number is not given, the phrasing is *thousands of dollars . . . trillions of dollars.*

toward, towards. The two forms are interchangeable.

trademarks. Names of products and processes that are the exclusive property of an individual or company are capitalized: *Coca-Cola, Formica, Frigidaire, Kodak, Polaroid, Technicolor, Xerox,* and so forth.

underlining. In typewritten or handwritten copy, *underlining* is used in place of italics:

1. To indicate titles of books and periodicals
2. For emphasis: Words that would be heavily stressed when spoken are *underlined*.
3. To indicate foreign words

unique. The word means single in kind or excellence, unequalled; therefore, it cannot be compared. It is illogical to speak of (or to write): a more *unique* or most *unique* thing.

upward. Not upwards.

use, utilize. Technical writers often overuse *utilize* for the simpler verb *use*.

very. *Very*, an intensive word, has become so overused that its force is slight. If you are tempted to use *very* in a sentence or in the complimentary close of a letter, ask yourself what the word adds to the meaning you wish to convey. If the answer is negative, do not use it.

via. *Via* is the Latin word for *way, road,* or *path.* In English, *via* is used as a preposition to show a relationship to a place such as a highway or a route that passes through a geographical area: You can drive to Minneapolis *via* Chicago. They flew to Japan *via* Hawaii. Purists frown on extending the use of *via* to mean through the agency of or by the means of, since *via* in this context does not refer to a means of transportation. Purists prefer the preposition *by* over *via*: The information reached us *by* telex.

viz. *Viz.* is the abbreviation of the Latin *videlicet* meaning to wit or namely. Since the word *namely* hardly ever adds anything to the thought of a sentence, its Latin abbreviated equivalent certainly does not. Omit its use. Lawyers, alas, will not obey this injunction.

we. *We* is frequently used as an indefinite pronoun in expressions like *we find, we believe*. It is preferable to the passive and impersonal construction: *it is found; it is believed*. The use of *we* is especially recommended in conclusions and recommendations. The reader wants a living, warm-blooded human being giving him findings and beliefs based on judgments. Of course, if the writer represents a single individual the pronoun *I* is used rather than the "editorial" *we*.

when, where. Despite frequent informal usage, it is poor style to define a term by using the phrase *is when* or *is where*. *When* and *where* are adverbs and so cannot properly introduce noun clauses.

Wrong:	A simile is *when* two unlike things are compared.
Right:	A simile is a figure of speech in which two unlike things are compared.
Wrong:	An injunction *is where* the court orders you to do or not to do something.
Right:	An injunction *is a court writ* requiring the doing or refraining from doing a specified act.

Frequently *where* is wrongly used for *when*. *Where* should introduce an adverbial clause of place; *when*, of time: *Where* experts disagree, we should not rush to quick judgment. *When* should be used in the previous sentence.

which. *Which* is a pronominal word, used in both singular and plural constructions. It refers to things and to groups of people regarded impersonally (The crowd, which was large. . .).

who, whom. *Who* is the form used in the nominative case (as the subject) and *whom*, even in formal usage, is used only as the object of a preposition (objective case).

>He is the one *who* is responsible.
>For *whom* the bell tolls.
>He struck *whoever* was in his way.
>To *whomever* the rule applies.

who's, whose. *Who's* is a contraction of *who is; whose* is the possessive form of the pronoun *who*.

-wise. Use this suffix with care. It is acceptable in traditional forms like *clockwise, lengthwise, otherwise, pennywise, slantwise*. Many people frown on the faddish usage such as *energywise, healthwise,* or *wagewise*.

Xerox. Many people will frown if you use this trademark as a verb. Use *reproduce* or *photocopy*. There are many other reproduction technologies that do not use the Xerox process.

your, you're. *Your* is a possessive pronoun; *you're* is a contraction for *you are.*

> *Your* company is succeeding.
> *You're* to leave before noon.

Discussion Questions and Assignment Exercises in Grammar and Usage

1. Which indefinite article is used with the following words?

   a ___ an ___ aardwolf   a ___ an ___ herbaceous perennial
   a ___ an ___ helium diving bell   a ___ an ___ hour circle
   a ___ an ___ historical event   a ___ an ___ eutherian mammal
   a ___ an ___ M   a ___ an ___ urine specimen
   a ___ an ___ Henle's membrane   a ___ an ___ urea resin

2. What is the difference between an abbreviation and an acronym? List five acronyms.
3. Your instructor will not (accept ___ except ___) late reports unless a student has been (accepted ___ excepted ___) from the previous assignment.
4. Though the engineer (adapted ___ adopted ___) his supervisor's suggestion, the modified circuit would not (adapt ___ adopt ___) properly.
5. The subject's attitude (affected ___ effected ___) the outcome of the experiment.
6. a. Turn the gear (slow ___ slowly ___).
   b. The (slow ___ slowly ___) gear would not move.
7. The (Advisery ___ Advisory ___) Board reached its decision.
8. Professor Jones (alluded ___ referred ___) to the first chapter of *An Essay on the Principle of Population* by T.R. Malthus to substantiate his thesis.
9. The discussions (among ___ between ___) the three corporations ended in an agreement to divide the markets (among ___ between ___) them.
10. The (amount ___ number ___) of barrels with sediment in the experiment was greater than the (amount ___ number ___) of receptacles available, but the total (amount ___ number ___) of sediment was not as great as expected.
11. Place an apostrophe where it belongs in the following.

    Lises first experiment.

    The three electronic companies losses

    Everybodys mistakes

    Ours is not the reason why . . .

    The first of two thats

    United States crops during the 80s

    Sir James Jeans experiments

    O.K.d.

    Three cents worth

    Achilles heel
12. The apositive is misplaced in the following sentence. Revise the sentence to correct it.
    In acute intermittent porphyria, the liver produces an excessive amount of porphobilinogen, an inborn error of metabolism.

13. Explain why the following sentence is grammatically wrong and then correct it. The reason why the experiment failed is because the wrong specimen was used.
14. What is wrong with the following sentence?

    The foreman sent his report in biweekly, every Monday and Thursday.
15. Rewrite the following sentences to eliminate the excessive verbiage and to make the thoughts clearer.
    a. A class A fire is the type of fire that occurs in ordinary everyday materials such as wood, paper, animal and vegetable fibers which are the organic chemical compounds that contain carbon along with some hydrogen, oxygen, and nitrogen and which are normally almost always controlled and extinguished by cooling or the removal of fuel.
    b. Asbestos which has been known to be implicated as a contributing agent involving cancer of the chest and of abdominal membranes has obvious beneficial uses in the manufacture of any number of useful products in our modern complex society such as cement pipe, fireproof clothing, brake linings in automobiles, materials for roofs of houses and buildings, and for floor tiles, to name only a few of these.
    c. A decision tree branches out just like a tree's branches in the form of a network to illustrate basically two things, namely, decisions and results or sometimes these are called events to show the potential consequences of a series of decisions.
    d. In this study a unique field of research relative to fire casualty, i.e., the toxicity of metals in a fire atmosphere by means of concentrated analysis of soot given off during fires by means of atomic absorption spectography.
    e. In this paper I explore and describe the itinerary of personal concerns and experiences that led me to designing a grade school science curriculum which used food as a medium, and from there to another science syllabus, also for fifth graders in which food has become the message.
    f. After being ingested, zinc is absorbed from the digestive tract where it acts like an emetic, partly arresting the chance of systemic poisoning, but, nevertheless, its corrosive properties frequently cause severe gastrointestinal irritation, leading to marked nausea and diarrhea, as well as an inflammation of the stomach and duodenum and to gastric necrosis, resulting in congestion in abdominal viscera, the kidneys and the liver.
    g. Also known as tertiary recovery, a micellar solution of detergents, other chemicals, and water is pumped down injection wells, a multistage pumping operation dependent on chemical collection of rock-held oil.
    h. When the graphite soaks up light, taking in about 90 percent of the visible light that reaches it, heat is transferred to the flowing gas, drawing the heated gas ultimately from a large network of mirrors and pipes by means of a gas turbine coupled to an electric generator, such being a solar heat system.
    i. An every day example of convection heating is the blast of heat experienced when opening a hot oven door.
    j. Instead, a detector known as a heat flux transducer is used whose surface temperature increases in proportion to the intensity or heating rate of the radiation; which is important because it ultimately determines how long a firefighter can withstand the heat from a fire.
16. In the following sentences make the verb and or pronoun agree with (its ___ their ___) subject or antecedent.

a. Mr. Conway is one of those supervisors who (has ___ have ___) been very helpful with (his ___ their ___) suggestions.
b. This laboratory is one of several that (require ___ requires ___) a lot of expensive upkeep. We do not believe (it ___ they ___) (is ___ are ___) worth the money.
c. Many of our patients who (smokes ___ smoke ___) and (uses ___ use ___) saccharin (has ___ have ___) to be worried about the carcinogenic effects on (his ___ their ___) health.
d. Not one of the students in the chemistry class finished (his ___ her ___ their ___) test questions.
e. Perennial grasses offer year-round protection, even in a drought, if (it ___ they ___) are not overgrazed. However, grass provides no income for any of the region's farmers who (does ___ do ___) not have cattle.

17. If you think any of the following sentences are grammatically wrong, explain the error and correct the sentence.
    a. On reviewing the various compound gases, it was found there were examples of duplication of the volume of one of the constituents.
    b. To avoid, therefore, confusion and circumlocution, and for the sake of greater precision of expression than I can otherwise obtain, it will be necessary to garner succinct meaning into the framing of thoughts which reflect accurately and validly and not fallaciously the situation my fallible human frailty may allow.
    c. Visual observation was made that Ilford X-ray plates were used which were mounted in a plate-holder, the front of which was covered with opaque black paper.
    d. By the combustion of cyanic acid with copper oxide, it was obtained 2 volumes of carbon dioxide and 1 volume of nitrogen, but by the combustion of ammonium cyanate one must obtain equal volumes of these gases, which proportion also holds for urea.
    e. "d'Alembert's paradox" is when a uniformly translated body suffers no hydrodynamic drag by virtue of its motion through an infinitely extended inviscid fluid.
    f. In their efforts to summarize and systematize the great proliferation of nuclear particles that were being produced by accelerators on the high-energy frontiers of the 1950's, the quark was discovered.
    g. Silvicultural research in western larch forests prior to the mid-1960's were directed primarily at growing trees for commercial timber production, being a natural outgrowth of demands placed on the forest for timber at that time.
    h. The primary objective of most stand improvement work is to grow bigger and better trees, have a faster growth rate, as well as being economical.
    i. The tape inserted at system initialization is initialized by rewinding the tape and then you write a header record to the tape.
    j. Home fires in the U.S.A. resulted in an estimated 3×10^8\$ of damage in 1976, and the total cost of fire-related activities was 13×10^8\$.
    k. During operation of the system, it may be required to examine certain system parameters or initiating specific system functions.
    l. Two spectrographs are included among the space telescope instruments which split light up into its component colors or wavelengths, both measuring the intensity of radiation in each wavelength interval.

m. Within regularly coiled gastropods we can recognize two principal coiling types: isotrophic and anisostrophic, the former being bilaterally symmetrical and the latter which are not.

n. The electron is the most basic particle in chemistry and biology, being responsible for the initial light absorption that causes photochemistry and has been proved to initiate biological events such as photosynthesis as well as the visual transduction process.

o. Can techniques of in vitro fertilization and transplantation of the embryo damage the resulting fetus and lead to abnormal children was a question that is being considered.

18. The following sentences contain restrictive and nonrestrictive clauses or modifiers. Place the commas that are needed for clarity of meaning.

   a. This study will determine the conditions under which damaging moisture problems occur in the attic.

   b. This study which was to determine the conditions under which damaging moisture problems occur in attics was never funded.

   c. The National Institute of Standards and Technology recently completed its first validation test of a tiny electronic device that will be used to protect computer data in transmission and storage based on the Federal Data Encryption Standard.

   d. The National Institute of Standards and Technology recently completed its first validation test of a tiny electronic device that will be used to protect computer data in transmission and storage.

   e. On another front, scientists in the dental clinical research program are studying improvements in composite resins which will give restorations a smoother surface and make them bond better to the tooth.

   f. In the smog formation research project modeling consists of mathematical representation of an "airshed" which is the air over a certain region of the country.

19. The modern tendency is to avoid using commas except where they are needed for clarity of meaning. In the following sentences, place commas to ensure clarity. Some of these sentences will require full restructuring to achieve clarity:

   a. As children's requests change with increasing sophistication their mothers switch from establishing the sincerity of a request to identifying the object wanted.

   b. Characteristically less than 5 percent of the mother's responses to a child's requests before he is 17 months old have to do with agency or who is going to do or control something.

   c. The concept of addiction once thought to be clearly delineated in both its meanings and its causes has become cloudy and confused.

   d. Rather than deadening frustration and providing an excuse for aggressive and illegal acts the depression of inhibitory centers through alcohol lubricates cooperative social interactions at mealtimes and other structured social occasions.

   e. Plaques develop most often in people who suffer from high blood pressure, diabetes, or obesity and in those who smoke heavily include a great deal of fat in the diet or have a family history of severe cardiovascular disease.

   f. Were the top corporate tax rate cut to 42 percent and the top personal income tax rate to 50 percent pre-tax earnings need to net $300 of dividends to top-bracket stockholders would be reduced to $1034, equivalent to $3.45 for each $1 of the stockholder's after-tax dividends.

g. That all areas of temperature were properly monitored it soon became apparent was critical to the experiment.
h. Although checking the thermometer at the freezing level does not guarantee absolute accuracy at the working level say 100° it does assure with a little record keeping that it has not changed from the last "Ice Point" check.
i. The hot and cold water are fed separately into a mixing valve properly called a temperature control unit which in turn compensates for variations of temperature and pressure input thus providing output water of proper precision temperature to the processor.
j. When a pair of these lasers oriented at 90° was placed on a rotating table beat frequency excursions of about 275 kilohertz were observed associated entirely with laboratory-fixed environmental factors presumably the geomagnetic field.
k. In 1980 563 fossils from the Cambrian period 500–600 million years ago were discovered.
l. On the Coram Experimental Forest and elsewhere studies that have included site preparation as one of the variables have demonstrated that exposed mineral soil prepared either by prescribed burning Figure 21 or scarification Figure 22 provides the best environment for establishment of larch regeneration and also as shown in table 7 for other more shade-tolerant species.
m. You will find the data on page 12 Section III.
n. The project engineer wanted to continue the experiment the director of engineering decided to abort.
o. On the other hand that there are short-term fluctuations as measured by sun spots and solar-flare activity seems firmly established and there is mounting observational evidence that the so-called solar constant the amount of solar radiant energy striking a unit surface at the top of the atmosphere oriented perpendicular to the solar beam undergoes small but measurable and possibly regular changes.

20. Correct the dangling modifiers in the following sentences.
   a. Combining with tin dental amalgams have been experimented with gold alloys.
   b. This blight is known as urban or photo chemical smog interacting automobile emissions with the atmosphere and sunlight forming ozone.
   c. Measured and updated by laboratories around the world they require accurate data on chemical reactions rates.
   d. Charred, but still readable in the smoldering ruins of a burned out apartment the firefighters found a Smokey the Bear poster.
   e. Terrestrial agriculture being seen as inadequate to supply the world's food needs the oceans are a major source of food for humankind and have been looked to with increasing attention.
   f. To accept biorhythm it helps to know about circadian cycles.

21. Which of the following two sentences is correct? Explain why.
   a. Western larch is well adapted to direct seeding due to its seeds being small so they are not subject to rodent depredation.
   b. Failure of the spring seeding was due to moisture depletion.

22. Check the correct word to be used:
   a. The metallurgist was able to recover (fewer ___, less ___) than 1 milligram of the substance.

b. (Fewer ___, Less ___) than half of the committee members voted for the recommendation.
c. Most shoppers bought (fewer ___, less ___) coffee last year.
d. The (council ___, counsel ___) presented its recommendations.
e. The students exhibited their (disinterest ___, uninterest ___) in the professor's lecture by yawning.
f. The first arm of the radio telescope antenna extends 11.8 miles, the second, a little (farther ___, further ___).
g. He went (farther ___, further ___) in his reply than he intended.
h. Two Columbia University seismologists are worried (if ___, whether ___) the three nuclear power plants built on the Ramapo fault up the Hudson River from New York will be (affected ___, effected ___) by a quake.
i. (If ___, Whether ___) there is a 5 to 11 percent chance for a severe quake to occur, the Nuclear Regulatory Commission, they say, made a mistake in approving the plants.
j. His metabolism drove (literally ___, figuratively ___) with the speed of light.

23. Check the correct verb, pronoun, or pronominal adjective in the following sentences.
    a. "This pain from shingles (is ___, are ___) too much for me," the patient said.
    b. The therapist, using many strategies, (manipulate ___, manipulates ___) the expectations of his subjects.
    c. The patient population (has ___, have ___), in this setting, great faith in (its ___, their ___) therapists.
    d. One times many (is ___, are ___) a lot.
    e. The accelerated recovery and use of the most abundant fossil fuel on earth—coal (are ___, is ___) becoming increasingly complex.
    f. The use of electric vehicles (has ___, have ___) (its ___, their ___) pros and cons.
    g. Topics of the bilateral discussion (include ___, includes ___) the full spectrum of science.
    h. The Ames Laboratory with (its ___, their ___) team of scientists of many disciplines (have ___, has ___) prepared a feasibility study for detecting signals from extraterrestrial intelligence.
    i. Commercial reprocessing of these materials (is ___, are ___) among several answers to the dilemma facing this country.
    j. Taylor and Smith (is ___, are ___) an expert consulting firm.
    k. The president of the firm, as well as his two chief officers, (is ___, are ___) here to take charge.
    l. The committee (is ___, are ___) heterogeneous, divided into three groupings.
    m. Conscious attention to the comments and questions (provide ___, provides ___) awareness and (permit ___, permits ___) emphasis of elements of judgment that may otherwise be habitually overlooked.
    n. From this New Jersey study, it is apparent that the acknowledgment of risk and previous awareness of the cancer issue are additive; those who knew about the cancer rates show less interest in obtaining information than those who did not, and the same basic relationship between appraised risk and information seeking (is ___, are ___) observed for both groups.

24. Which of these numbers should be spelled out and which written as figures?
   a. (one ___ , 1 ___) gram
   b. (a million ___ , 1,000,000 ___) members
   c. (eighty-three ___ , 83 ___) liters
   d. six seventy-five-watt ___ , 6 75-watt ___ , six 75-watt) lamps
   e. (⅓ ___ , one-third ___) of the subjects in the test
   f. The Redskins scored in the (¼ ___ , fourth ___) quarter.
   g. There were (33 ___ , thirty-three ___) questions in the test.
   h. (Thirty-three ___ , 33 ___) white mice were used.
   i. There was (3 ___ , three ___) inches of snow on the ground.
   j. A (1/50 ___ , one-fiftieth ___) horsepower unit
25. Correct the following sentences for lack of parallelism and other faults:
   a. Microscopic examination of the centrifuged sediment was accomplished so you could see the contaminants and chemical determinations showed ketone, some yeasts and parasites revealed by the microscope as well as quantification of bacteria.
   b. Four barn owls were used in these experiments which injected a light anesthesia intramuscularly, so we could begin to explore the influence of sound source location on the response projectories of the owl's central auditory neurons for which a movable speaker was used to deliver sound stimuli under free-field conditions we placed in an anachoic chamber.
   c. Clean water is a basic human need, together with diminishing sources of energy, comprising ever increasing this country's current problems.
   d. Once the astigmatism has been corrected, other aberrations still remain, being called spherical aberration, coma, and curvature or field and they arise from the shape of the mirror surface cross section in the tangential plane.
   e. Scientists use the micron to express small distances and wavelengths of light, being denoted by µ and is equal to 10^{-3} mm. in length.
   f. He estimated that the world population of tigers was about 100,000 in 1900 and says the population is only about 7,000 today.
   g. The system has been used in hospitals around the country. You can get personal information in a matter of seconds. We don't have to tell you how important speed and efficiency are in a hospital.
   h. There are two kinds of coronary bypass operations. In the first and most common, you take a length from the saphenous vein in the leg and transplant it in the chest. The second, but less common, uses the internal mammary artery, a small artery that runs alongside the breastbone.
   i. Methadone is still being promoted as a treatment for addiction because it blocks the negative effects of heroin.
   j. There is more to communication than simply indicating and requesting. You use it for social change.
26. Check the correct idiomatic preposition.
   a. abstain (from ___ , to ___ , with ___)
   b. accede (on ___ , to ___)
   c. adhere (on ___ , to ___)

d. agree (on ___, to ___) a plan
e. agree (on ___, to ___) a proposal
f. agreeable (to ___, with ___)
g. concur (in ___, on ___) an opinion
h. concur (with ___, to ___) a person
i. consist (in ___, of ___) material
j. contend (against ___, for ___) an obstacle
k. contend (for ___, with ___) a principle
l. contend (against ___, with ___) a person
m. correspond (in ___, to ___, with ___) a thing
n. correspond (to ___, with ___) a person
o. differ (about ___, from ___, with ___) a question
p. differ (about ___, from ___, with ___) a quality
q. differ (about ___, from ___, with ___) a person
r. envious (about ___, of ___)
s. expert (about ___, at ___, in ___)
t. identical (to ___, with ___)
u. independent (of ___, on ___)
v. infer (from ___, about ___)
w. need (for ___, of ___, in ___)
x. part (from ___, with ___) a person
y. part (from ___, with ___) property
z. subscribe (in ___, to ___)

27. Relative pronouns are misplaced in the following sentences. If there are other faults, revise to make the corrections.
    a. A theory when lightning storms converted such molecules as water methane and ammonia into a "primordial soup" of prebiotic molecules such as amino acids and carbohydrates explains the life originated on earth.
    b. The oryx has traditionally scrabbled its living from sparse desert plants amid the sand and rock of the Arabian peninsula and which is a large beautifully marked antelope.
    c. When atomic nuclei combine with each other to form larger nuclei, some of the mass of the original nuclei is converted into energy according to Einstein's famous formula $E = mc^2$, which is a process we call fusion.

28. The following expressions have circumlocutions, or "deadwood," and redundancies (needless repetition). Revise.
    a. any and all
    b. advanced forward
    c. in this day and age
    d. give and convey
    e. vermilion in color
    f. rectangular in shape
    g. large in size

h. return back
   i. 33 in number
29. For restrictive clauses the pronominal, *that* is preferred. For nonrestrictive clauses, *which* is the pronominal of preference. Check the proper pronominal in the following sentences. Use commas as are needed.
   a. We believe the decrease (that ___, which ___) is associated with the trajectory of resonant energetic electrons is due to the drift they experience in the afternoon sector as they move away from the earth.
   b. Among nonflying mammals (that ___, which ___) regularly visit flowers for food are marsupials of Australia.
   c. The viscous boundary layer (that ___, which ___) is where the flow region is closest to the hull is greatly affected by the ambient pressure field generated by the body's motion through the fluid.
   d. For high-speed memories those (that ___, which ___) require less than about 1-nanosec access time the company uses three-junction interferometers.
   e. The structure (that ___, which ___) took four years to complete is laid out in the shape of a C.
30. Check the proper interrogative pronoun:
   a. Among the ten (who ___, whom ___) were chosen for the award were three women.
   b. The ten (who ___, whom ___) the Board recommended for an award included three women.
   c. The student (who ___, whom ___) the instructor described as the cheater, was not guilty.
   d. (Who ___, whom ___) do you think you are fooling?
   e. (Who ___, whom ___) do you think is responsible?

Glossary of Computer and Desktop Publishing Terms

A

Abort. The procedure for terminating a computer program when a mistake or a malfunction occurs.

Alphanumerics. Alphabetical letters A–Z, numerical digits 0–9, punctuation marks, and special characters such as: #, $, <, *, /, |, +, and so forth that are capable of being processed by a computer.

Application. The task to be performed by a computer program or system.

Application software. Software that enables the user to direct the computer to do certain tasks.

Architecture. The organization and interconnection of the components of a computer system.

Artificial intelligence (AI). The ability of computers to perform human-like thinking and intelligence.

Assembly language. Programming language that allows a computer user to write a program with mnemonics instead of numeric instructions (1s and 0s).

Automatic page numbering. A software feature the automatically places a consecutive page number on each page.

B

Back matter. The elements of a document that supplement its information such as a bibliography, appendix, glossary, and index.

Backup (BK). Copy of a file or data set kept for reference in memory in case the original is lost or destroyed.

Bar code. Code used on labels to be read by a scanner. Bar codes are used to identify retail sales items.

Basic input/output system (BIOS). A computer chip that determines how the computer reacts to software commands.

Batch. A group of records or programs that is considered as a single unit for processing on a computer.

Baud. A unit for measuring data transmission speed. One baud (B) is one bit per second.

Binary system. The base 2 numbering system that uses the digits 0 and 1. Computer data are represented by this system. 0 represents off and 1 represents on.

Bit. The smallest unit of information a computer stores. (It takes eight bits to make one character and those eight bits make one byte. A megabyte is a million characters. A double-spaced page of text is about 2,000 bytes or 2K. K is the symbol for 1,024 bytes. One megabyte is about 500 pages.)

Block move. Process in which a block of text is moved from one part of a document or file to another place in the document.

Boilerplate. Portions of text that get used over and over again, word-for-word in different documents. To boilerplate, as a verb, means inserting previously written text from another file into the document being worked on.

Bold. Type with heavier, darker appearance than regular type.

Boolean algebra. A branch of symbolic logic similar to algebra, which deals in logical relationships rather than numerical relationships.

Boot. To start or restart a computer. It involves loading part of the operating system into the computer's main memory. If the computer is already turned on, it is a "warm" boot; if not, it is a "cold" boot.

Bpi. The abbreviation for bits per inch. Bytes per inch is abbreviated BPI.

Break. The beginning or ending point of a line, column, or page.

Bug. A mistake in a computer's program or system, or a malfunction in a computer's hardware. To debug means to remove mistakes and correct malfunctions.

Bullet. A bold dot or a similar symbol used to emphasize or set off items in a list.

Bulletin board system (BBS). The electronic equivalent of a conventional bulletin board. A BBS is part of a communication network by which users can post messages, read those posted by other users, communicate with the system's operator, or upload or download programs.

Byte. A group of adjacent eight bits.

C

Callout. A label describing parts of a subject in an illustration, often with arrows pointing to the described object.

Camera-ready copy. Text and illustrations laid out for a page in proper size and position, ready to be photographed for a printing plate.

Caption. A title or explanation placed above, below, or to the side of an illustration.

Centering. A software feature that automatically places a word or a group of words in the center of a line or page.

Central processing unit (CPU). The component of a computer system that controls the function of interpreting and executing instructions to the computer.

Character. Any symbol, digit, letter, or punctuation mark, including a blank space, stored and processed by a computer.

Character enhancement. A software feature that allows the user to alter the typeface for purposes of emphasis, such as boldfacing or italicizing.

Character recognition. Technology of using electronic machines to identify human-readable symbols automatically and then to express their identities in machine-readable codes.

Chip. An electronic device, a type of complex on/off switch. The chip can be permanently rigged to perform a certain task, or it can be designed to store information. By adding more chips, the user enables the computer to perform more functions and tasks.

Clip art. Art items in public domain that can be used free of charge in publications.

Code. To write a program or routine for a computer. Used as a noun, it is a set of rules defining the way in which data are represented.

Coding. The writing of a set of instructions that will cause a computer to perform specified operations.

Cold boot. To turn on a computer and load an operating program in it.

Collate. To sort multiple reproduction pages into correctly ordered sets.

Commands. Action a user takes to enact a word processing function, usually by hitting a key or combination of keys.

Command-driven. A software program that requires the operator to enter or command the program to make a desired operation.

Compatibility. The ability of software and hardware of one computer system to work with that of another computer system.

Computer. An electronic machine that can accept data, perform certain functions on that data, and present the results of those operations. A machine that enables the use of a word processing program.

Computerese. The jargan or shoptalk of persons working with computers and information processing systems.

Computer ethics. A set of codes or rules governing the conduct of individuals and organizations in the use of computers. The accepted standard of behavior when dealing with computers and the information they contain.

Computer graphics. Images and pictures generated by computer software and the person using it. Also, a software program with the capability of converting digital information into illustrations on the display screen or hard-copy printer.

Computer literacy. A general knowledge of what computers are and how they are used.

Computer networks. Two or more computers linked by data communication channels.

Computer program. A series of instructions that direct the activities of a computer.

Computer science. The field of knowledge covering all aspects of the design and use of computers.

Copy-fitting. Editing text to fit a specific space.

Crop. To cut or trim an illustration or other graphic element.

Crop marks. Tiny marks on the corners or edges of drawings or photographs that tell the camera operator which portions of the illustration to include and which to eliminate (crop out).

Cursor. An on-screen position indicator such as a blinking line or square.

Cut-and-paste. A feature in some word processing and graphic programs that moves text or graphics from one location in a document to another.

D

Daisywheel printer. A type of printer that uses a print wheel resembling a daisy. At the end of each "petal" is a fully formed character.

Data. Representations of facts or concepts usually by means of letters, characters, or graphics suitable for communication, interpretation, or processing by persons or machines. Also, raw material or information.

Database. A collection of related files of information stored together in a logical manner.

Data processing. The process of transforming data into useful information by a computer. It is also referred to as information processing.

Debug. The activity of finding and correcting an error or malfunction in a program or computer system.

Dedicated word processing system. A computer system designed mainly for the function of word processing.

Default. A designed action that a program takes in the absence of another specified command.

Delete. A software feature that allows the user to remove existing text, data, records, or files.

Density. The amount of data that can be stored in a given area of a storage medium, such as a diskette. The higher the density, the more data can be stored.

Desktop publishing. A process for printing that combines the use of a computer with graphics-oriented page composition software and a high-quality laser printer to prepare the reproduction copy of a document. The quantity printing of that document can be done either by the laser printer, or the reproduction copy can serve as a master for offset printing.

Digitize. To convert an image into a series of dots stored by the computer so that the image can be manipulated and placed in publications.

Directory. A listing containing the names and location of all the files (documents) in a storage medium.

Disk. A magnetic device for storing information and programs in a computer. It can be either a rigid platter (hard disk) or a sheet of flexible plastic (floppy disk). Both types have tracks on which data are stored.

Disk drive. The device that reads data from a magnetic disk and copies it into the computer's memory so it can be used later.

Disk operating system (DOS). The set of programs that controls and supervises the computer; the system uses disks to assemble, edit, and apply programs.

Display. Physical presentation of data on the monitor's screen.

Distribution logic. A shared computer system that allows parts of memory and control circuits to be placed at individual work stations.

Document. Writing that has permanence and that can be read by people or machines.

Dot matrix printer. An impact printer that uses a print head containing from nine to twenty-four pins that produce characters by printing patterns of dots.

Downtime. Length of time a computer is inoperative because of a malfunction.

Drum printer. A line-at-a-time impact printer that uses a rotating drum of 80–132 print positions, with each print position containing a complete set of characters.

Dummy. A mock-up of a document. Sometimes it is a rough preliminary layout; other times it is made from blank pages or photocopies of galley pages.

E

Editing. Correction of typographical errors or incorrect data or information in an application program.

Electronic bulletin board. An information exchange technology that uses a computer and a modem for users to post and receive messages and information.

Electronic mail (E-mail). A communication service for computer users by which messages are sent to a central computer system ("electronic mailbox") and later retrieved by the addressee.

Electronic teleconferencing. A system for communicating via computers connected through a telephone system. Each user participates in the conference by keying in her conversation.

Ellipsis. Equally spaced periods—usually three—to indicate the omission of text.

End user. Anyone who uses a computer system or its output.

Error message. Messages that appear on the computer screen when the user makes an error. Some messages tell not only what the error is but also how to correct it.

Escape key. A control key on the computer keyboard used to take control of the computer away from a program or to stop a program.

Exchange mode. An editing software feature in which newly inserted characters take the place of (overwrite) existing material occupying the same place.

Exit key. The key to press when the user wants to leave the program in operation.

F

Facsimile (FAX). A form of electronic mail that copies and sends text and graphics via phone lines.

Fallback. Backup system brought into use in an emergency situation; the reserve database and programs that are switched on in the event of a detected fault in the system being operated.

Fanfold paper. One long, continuous sheet of paper perforated at regular intervals to mark page boundaries and folded fanstyle into a stack.

File. A collection of related records treated as a unit.

Floppy disk. A flexible magnetic disk (diskette) for storing a computer's data and programs.

Font. All letter characters, numbers, and symbols of one size and typeface.

Footer. Text of one or more lines of type programmed to appear automatically at the bottom of every page of a document.

Format. The overall appearance of a document based on its design elements such as page size, margins, column width, spacing, and page layout.

Formatting. Setting parameters such as margins or tabs to control the appearance of text; also preparing a disk or diskette for use.

Front matter. The pages that precede the main text of a document, including title page, copyright page, preface, acknowledgments, and table of contents.

Function keys. Keys on the keyboard that are preprogrammed so that when the user presses one, it performs a predetermined function.

G

Galley. A reproduction of a column of type, usually printed on a long sheet of paper.

Garbage in/garbage out (GIGO). A term used to describe bad data input into a computer, resulting in bad output.

Glossary. A word processing program that allows abbreviations to be typed instead of longer words or phrases. As the user types the abbreviations, the full word or phrase appears on the screen.

Gopher. A menu-based way to retrieve information from a data service.

Grammar and style checker. A software program that locates grammar, punctuation errors, and style inconsistencies in a document.

Graphics. Software that produces a computer-generated picture on screen, paper, or film. The graphics range from simple line or bar graphs to colored and detailed images.

Grayscale. The number of gradations of gray between white and black that can be generated by a scanner or by software.

Greeking. Simulating text as gray bars to show the position of that text on the page; used in layout design of a page.

Grid. A matrix of horizontal and vertical lines used by designers and pasteup artists to align and position the elements of a page.

Gutter. The space between two facing pages or the space between two columns.

H

Hacker. A term previously applied to a computer enthusiast who was experienced in using computers and enjoyed solving complex or unusual problems on a computer. Presently, it is being applied to persons who intentionally break into other computer systems, whether maliciously or not.

Halftone. The representation of a continuous tone photograph or illustration as a series of dots that look like gray tones when printed.

Hard copy. A form of permanent computer output such as paper or microform.

Hard disk. A hard metallic disk used for magnetically storing data. Its rigid construction allows higher storage densities, permitting more data storage and faster data access.

Hard hyphen. A hyphen required by the spelling of a term, for example: *two-level dwelling* or *re-enter*.

Hardware. The physical components of a computer system that enable it to do computer functions.

Header. Software programmed text that appears automatically at the top of a page, often a title, subtitle, author's name, or page number.

Help system. Messages on the screen to help users. Some software messages are always in view; others must be called up by command.

HyperCard. A hypertext system developed by Apple Computer. It is called HyperCard because the modules of information agglomerate like stacks of cards.

Hypertext. A generic term for computer systems that enable on-line identification, callup, and linkage of text modules on specific topics in a nonlinear way.

I

Impact printer. A printer that produces characters by using a hammer or pins to strike an inked ribbon on paper.

Information. Data that have been processed into an organized, usable form.

Information highway. An electronic community of people worldwide who use computers to exchange information and messages. (See *Internet*.)

Information service. An on-line computer service by which users can access large databases. Computer information services are usually offered for a fee and require a password to gain access.

Information system. A collection of information "messages" or documents, persons who produce and or use them, organizations that process them, and the conventions and rules by which these organizations and persons interrelate.

Initial caps. Text in which the first letter of each word is capitalized.

Inputting. Process of entering data into a computer.

Insert mode. An editing software feature in which all text to the right of an addition shifts to make room for new material.

Interactive. A system in which the user is in direct and continual communication with the computer.

Interface. Points of meeting between a computer and an external entity.

Internet. A vast international network of networks that enables a computer user to share information, share services, and communicate directly as if the user were part of one global computer system. Users of Internet become connected through membership in one of several on-line services such as Prodigy, Compu-Serve, or America OnLine.

Italic. A slanted typeface.

J

Joystick. An electromechanical lever to enable a user to move the cursor.

Justify. To place spaces between words and characters in a column or page so that both left and right margins are even.

K

Kerning. The reduction of excess white space between characters to make them fit more tightly on a line.

Keyboard. The input device—similar to a typewriter's—used to enter programs and data into the computer.

Keystroke. The action of pressing a single key or combination of keys on a keyboard.

Keyword. A significant and informative word in a title or document that describes the content of the document.

Kludge. A collection of mismatched components that have been assembled into a system.

L

Laptop computer. A portable computer, so-called because it is small enough to fit on one's lap and in a briefcase.

Laser printer. A nonimpact printer that produces images on paper by directing a laser beam onto a drum, leaving a negative charge in the form of a character to which positively charged toner powder will stick. The toner powder is transferred to paper as it rolls by the drum and is bonded to the paper by hot rollers, creating near-typeset quality text and graphics.

Layout. The arrangement and positioning of text, white space, and graphics on a page.

Letter quality print. Print of the highest quality, having fully formed characters, that is similar to a good typewriter print.

Light pen. A light-sensitive, penlike electronic device that allows the user to communicate with the computer by touching the pen to certain positions on the screen.

Line art. A drawing that contains no grays or middle tones; line art is made up exclusively of lines and white space.

Lowercase. Small letters, as opposed to capital letters.

M

Machine language. The basic language of computers. It is based on electronic states and operates on the binary system of 1s and 0s.

Macro. A software feature that makes use of previously recorded keystrokes or commands that can be executed with one or two keystrokes.

Magnetic disk. A mylar (floppy disk) or metallic hard disk on which electronic data can be stored.

Mainframe. A large-scale, general purpose computer, often having multiple users.

Makeup. The physical assembly of components of a page, usually on stiff cardboard. (Sometimes called pasteup.)

Mechanicals. Camera-ready pages on art boards, with text and art in position.

Memory. The computer's storage space.

Menu. A list of options in a software program that allows the user to choose which to operate.

Menu-driven. A software program that gives the user a menu (list) of choices—commands or directions on how to enter input.

Microfiche. A sheet of microfilm about 4 inches by 6 inches (10 cm $\times$ 15 cm) upon which images of a page or computer output can be recorded. Up to 270 pages of output can be recorded on one sheet.

Modem. A computerese abbreviation for modulator/demodulator. A device that enables computers to send information over telephone lines.

Monitor. A televisionlike device to display data.

Mouse. A small handheld device that allows the user to position the cursor on the screen of the monitor without using the keyboard.

Multimedia/hypermedia. Multiple forms of communication media, such as a book (text, photographs, and illustrations) and video (audio and moving visuals) that are controlled, coordinated, and integrated by a computer.

N

Natural language processing. The ability of a computer to understand and perform operations from commands issued in a natural language such as English.

Near letter quality print. Print made from dots rather than fully formed characters and which approach the appearance of letter quality print.

Network. A system of interconnected computer systems and terminals.

Node. Each computer or device in a computer network system.

Numeric pad. The set of numbered keys to the right of the typewriter keys on the keyboard. Most of these keys are preset to perform word processing functions.

O

Off-line. Equipment, devices, or persons not in direct communication with—not connected to—the central processing unit of the computer. Also, an operation or device in which data are not directly transferred to or from a computer.

Offset printing. A process by which a page is reproduced photographically on a metal plate attached to a revolving cylinder. Ink is transferred from the plate to a rubber blanket from which it is transferred to paper.

On-line. Equipment, devices, and persons in direct communication with—connected to—the central processing unit of the computer.

Operating system. Software that controls and supervises a computer system's hardware and provides computer services to users.

Optical character reader (OCR). An electronic device that accepts a printed document as input and processes it in the computer.

Orphan. The first line of a paragraph isolated at the bottom of a page.

Outliner. A software feature that helps the user to organize ideas by presenting them as headings or subheadings that can be arranged in a logical pattern.

Output. Information produced by the computer. In word processing, output is what the user keys into the computer and sees on the screen, or it is that which is printed.

P

Page break. A software feature that controls the number of lines to a page. After the set number of lines are reached, the additional text is automatically placed on the next page.

Pagination. The process of numbering pages. In desktop publishing, it is the process of laying out graphics and blocks of text for the purpose of designing all pages of a document.

Paintbrush. A graphics software program that provides the user with a variety of brush shapes on the display screen by means of a mouse or joystick. As the brush moves, it leaves behind a trail of shapes.

Pan. A graphics software feature that moves the entire graphic content on the screen from side to side, allowing the user to create and view images beyond the width of the screen.

Paper feed. Method by which paper is pulled through a printer.

Password. A special word, code, or symbol that must be presented to the computer system to gain access to its resources.

PC. Computerese for personal computer.

Peripheral equipment. Input/output devices and auxiliary storage units of a computer system attached by cables to the central processing unit. Sometimes called peripherals.

Pixel. Short for picture element, it is the smallest unit on a computer screen. The clarity of the screen depends on the number of pixels per inch on the monitor; the more pixels available, the clearer the image.

Preprogrammed keys (macros). Single keys or a limited number of keystroke combinations that are predefined and used to insert a word or a whole passage into a document.

Printer. Output device that produces hard copy.

Printout. Output printed on a page by a printer.

Processing. The steps a computer takes to convert data into information.

Program. A series of instructions that tells the computer what to do.

Prompt. A message the software provides to indicate it is ready to accept keyboard input. Usually, it is an on-screen question or instruction that tells the user what data to enter or what action to take.

Proof. A trial copy of a page or publication used to check the accuracy of its information. (Also, short for proofread—meaning to check for mistakes.)

Protocol. A set of rules and procedures for transmitting and receiving data so that different devices can communicate with one another.

Purge. To erase a file.

Q

Qwerty. The standard keyboard arrangement of characters. It is called Qwerty after the first six letters on the top alphabetic line of the keyboard.

R

Random access memory (RAM). The working but temporary memory of the computer. It is the memory into which the user enters information and instructions and from which the user can call up data. If power is shut off or lost before the user directs the computer to save it, the data are lost.

Read only memory (ROM). A solid state storage chip, programmed at the time of manufacture to have a set of frequently used instructions. ROM does not lose its programs when the computer is shut off, but the user cannot reprogram it.

Re-boot. To stop and boot the operating system again. It usually occurs by human intervention, resulting from a problem.

Record. A collection of related items of data treated as a unit.

Recto. A right-hand page.

Register. Precise alignment of printing plates or negatives.

Resolution. The density of dots or pixels on a page or display, usually measured in dots per inch (dpi). The higher the resolution, the finer the appearance of text or graphics. Fineness of resolution depends on the printer. In current desktop publishing technology, resolution ranges from 300 dpi in most laser printers to 2540 dpi in Linotronic imagesetters.

Retrieve. To call back from the computer's storage input that the user wants to review or edit.

Roman. A vertical style typeface as opposed to italics or oblique.

Roman-style typefaces. Typefaces having serifs in their characters.

Routine. A set of computer instructions for carrying out a specific processing operation; the term is sometimes used as a synonym for program.

Running head. A line at the top of the page that helps orient the reader, containing such information as title, author, chapter, date, or page number. (Synonym for header.)

S

Sans serif. A typeface without finishing strokes at the end of the character. *Sans* is the French word meaning "without." Sans serif typefaces are sometimes called block or gothic type.

Save. A word processing function that, when keyed, stores what is being written within the computer's random access memory. What is saved is stored permanently and can be retrieved for review, revision, and printing.

Scanner. A device that electronically converts text, photographs, or art renderings into a collection of dots that can be manipulated by a software program and placed into a page layout for reproduction.

Screen. The part of the terminal that displays what is being entered into the computer.

Scroll. A software feature that permits moving of the data into view on the screen—up, down, or across—so the viewer can review elements of the text that have been entered.

Search and replace. A software feature that allows the user to look for a word or phrase and replace the item with a corrected term wherever it occurs in the text.

Serif. A line or curve projecting from the end of a letter form.

Shared logic. Concurrent use of a single computer by multiple users.

Shareware. Free software that users can get from user groups and electronic bulletin boards.

Signature. A section of a book or document consisting of a large sheet of paper folded after printing into smaller page sizes within the final publication. Most printers use signatures of sixteen or thirty-two ultimate pages.

Soft copy. Data presented on the display screen of the terminal.

Soft hyphen. A hyphen printed only to break a word between syllables at the end of a line.

Software. The instructions that direct the operations of a computer.

Sort. To arrange data according to a logical system.

Spelling checker. Sometimes called dictionary, it is a software program that locates misspelled words or words not in the dictionary.

Split screen. Display screen that can be partitioned into two or more areas (windows) so that, within each screen area, formats, data, or help information can be shown at the same time.

Spreadsheet. A type of software that allows the user to spread out all related data on one sheet and show how it affects the other data.

Stand-alone system. A self-contained computer system that is not connected to another computer system.

Status line. One or more lines, located at the top or bottom of the display screen, that provide information about the document being worked on.

Storage. A device or medium that can accept data, hold them, and deliver them on demand; also called memory.

Store. To place what is keyed into the computer's memory.

Style sheet. Format and type specifications for a page design that can be stored and reused in desktop publishing programs.

Subhead. A heading, usually set in smaller type than a main heading, used to break up chapters or articles into smaller sections.

Syntax. The rules by which a programming language operates.

System. The combination of people, devices, and methods interrelated for the purpose of achieving a common goal. (These devices and methods often involve computers and software.)

System analyst. A person who works with a user to determine her data processing needs and then designs or recommends a program to meet those needs.

T

Tab setting. A software feature that sets indentations for a document and aligns columns and decimal numbers.

Telecommunication. The process or system by which communication facilities, such as the telephone or microwave relays, are used to send or receive data. (Also called teleprocessing.)

Template. A predesigned page used in desktop publishing with specified areas for text, heads, and illustrations.

Terminal. The computer hardware that contains the display screen, the keyboard, and the computer's operating system.

Text editing. The process of changing, adding, deleting, or revising text after it has been entered into the computer.

Text graphics. The method of creating a graphic image, such as a shape or line, by using alphanumerics and other special characters on the keyboard.

Thesaurus. A software program that provides synonyms for a given word in the document.

Thimble printer. A printer that uses a type wheel in the shape of a thimble. The thimble rotates, positioning the spokes so that the striking device can hit the spoke tip against the ribbon, thus printing the character on paper.

Time-sharing. A technology that allows more than one person access to the same computer at the same time.

Tone. In computer graphics, it is the degree of tint and shade in color.

Touch screen. A type of display screen on which the user can enter commands by pressing designated areas.

Typeface. A collection of letters, numbers, and symbols that share a distinctive appearance.

Type over. The ability of an impact printer to strike a character more than once to produce a boldface effect.

U

Undo. A software feature that allows the user to cancel the action of a previous instruction, putting the text back the way it was.

Uploading. Reading data from a user's disk and sending it to another computer.

Uppercase. Capital letters.

Usenet. A worldwide network of bulletin boards called newsgroups. Each bulletin board deals with a designated topic, ranging from the sacred to profane.

User. A person or group who uses the computer system.

User-friendly. A term for a particular computer or software that is easy to learn and use.

User group. A formal or informal group of users organized for the purpose of problem solving, sharing, and exchanging hardware and software information.

Utility program. A program that performs common or routine functions on the computer for the user, such as preparing a disk for use, copying, or saving a file.

V

Verso. The left-hand page.

Videotex. An electronic home information delivery system.

Videotext/viewdata. A home information delivery system that users can access and also transmit to the system.

Voice mail. A form of electronic mail that sends messages in the form of a computerized human voice.

W

Warm boot/warm start. Process of fooling the computer into thinking that its power has been turned off although the power is still on.

White space. The area of the page without text or graphics used as a deliberate element of design.

Widow. The last line of a paragraph isolated at the top of a page.

Window. A separate, defined area of the screen that is used to display data, menus, or another software. Windows also give the user the ability to look at two files (documents) at the same time.

Word. A logical group of bits, characters, or bytes considered an entity and capable of being stored in the computer.

Word processing (WP). The technique for electronically writing, editing, manipulating, storing, and printing text by using a computer and printer. The text is recorded on a magnetic medium, usually floppy disks. The final output is on paper.

Wordwrap. A word processing feature that automatically moves a word to the beginning of the next line if it will not fit at the end of the original line.

World-Wide Web (WWW). A type of global shopping mall with stores of data and information resources made available to the Internet. Essential components of the WWW system are:

> **Web browser.** A program that can retrieve documents from the World-Wide Web servers for display.
>
> **Web server.** A program that responds to requests from web browsers.
>
> Sources and types of information available through the WWW are publishers of magazines and books; some examples include: a *World Factbook,* produced by the CIA; the descriptive catalog of the Louvre Museum in Paris; and The Ahmanson Pediatric Center in Los Angeles, California.

Workstation. A combination of a monitor and keyboard used to enter input, view output, and edit within shared logic systems; it does not contain a central processing unit.

Wraparound. Text that wraps around a graphic; also called a runaround.

Writing. The process of entering data into a computer.

WYSIWYG (Pronounced wizzy-wig). The acronym for "What you see is what you get." It refers to the representation on a computer screen of text and graphic elements as they will look on the printed page.

X

Xerography. The process used by laser printers and photocopiers in which light conveys an image to an electrostatically charged surface. The image is picked up by toner and transferred to paper.

Z

Zoom. To view an enlarged (zoom in) portion or reduced (zoom out) portion of a page or screen.

Selected Bibliography

General References

Abbreviations for Use on Drawings and Text. New York: American Standards Institute, 1972.

American Heritage Dictionary of the English Language, Third Edition. Boston: Houghton Mifflin, 1992.

Barzun, Jacques, and Henry Graff. *The Modern Researcher.* 4th ed. New York: Harcourt Brace Jovanovich, 1985.

Berkman, Robert I. *Find It Fast: How to Uncover Expert Information on Any Subject.* New York: Harper and Row, 1987.

Bilner, John R. *Fundamentals of Communication.* 2d ed. Englewood Cliffs, N.J.: Prentice-Hall, 1988.

Bloom, Martin. *The Experience of Research.* New York: Macmillan, 1986.

Bordon, George H. *An Introduction to Human Communication Theory.* Dubuque, Iowa: Wm. C. Brown, 1971.

Brockman, John R., and Fern Rook, eds. *Technical Communication and Ethics.* Arlington, Va: Society for Technical Communication, 1989.

Caernarven-Smith, Patricia. *Audience Analysis and Response.* Pembroke, Mass.: Firman Technical Publications, 1983.

Chase, Stuart. *Power of Words.* New York: Harcourt Brace, 1954.

Chen, Ching-chih. *Scientific and Technical Information Sources.* 2d ed. Cambridge, Mass.: MIT Press, 1986.

Cohen, Morris R., and Ernest Nagel. *An Introduction to Logic and the Scientific Method.* New York: Harcourt Brace, 1934.

Condon, John C., Jr. *Semantics and Communication.* 3d ed. New York: Macmillan, 1985.

Council of Biology Editors. *Style Manual.* 5th ed. Washington, D.C.: American Institute of Biological Science, 1983.

DeGeorge, Richard T. *Business Ethics.* 3d ed. New York: Macmillan, 1990.

Dewey, John. *The Theory of Inquiry.* New York: Henry Holt, 1938.

Dobrin, David. *Writing and Technique.* Urbana, Ill. National Council of Teachers of English, 1989.

Dodd, Janet S., ed. *The ACS Style Guide: A Manual for Authors and Editors.* Washington, D.C.: American Chemical Society, 1986.

Dominowski, R. *Research Methods.* Englewood Cliffs, N.J.: Prentice-Hall, 1980.

Ebbit, Wilma R., and David R. Ebbitt. *Writer's Guide and Index to English.* Glenview, Ill.: Scott, Foresman and Company, 1983.

Emery, Donald W., John Kierzek, and Peter Lindholm. *English Fundamentals.* 9th ed. New York: Macmillan, 1990.

Fowler, H. W. *Modern English Usage.* (rev. ed. by Ernest Gowers.) New York: Oxford University Press, 1965.

Hayakawa, S. I. *Language in Thought and Action.* 4th ed. New York: Harcourt Brace Jovanovich, 1978.

Hibbison, Eric A. *Handbook for Student Writers and Researchers.* Englewood Cliffs, N.J.: Prentice-Hall, 1984.

Isaacs, Alan, et al. *The Oxford Dictionary for Scientific Writers and Editors.* New York: Oxford University Press, 1991.

Kirkman, John. *Good Style for Engineering and Scientific Writing.* London: E&FN SPON, 1992.

Klare, George R. *A Manual for Readable Writing.* Glen Burnie, Md.: REM, 1975.

Longyear, Marie M. *The McGraw-Hill Style Manual, A Concise Guide for Writers and Editors.* New York: McGraw-Hill, 1983.

Lutz, William O. *The Cambridge Thesaurus of American English.* New York: Cambridge University Press, 1994.

A Manual of Style. 13th ed. Chicago: Chicago University Press, 1982.

McDowell, Earl E. *Interviewing Practices for Technical Writers.* Amityville, N.Y.: Baywood Publishers, 1991.

McGraw-Hill Encyclopedia of Science and Technology. 6th ed. New York: McGraw-Hill, 1987.

Ogden, C. K., and I. A. Richards. *The Meaning of Meaning.* 8th ed. New York: Harcourt Brace, 1947.

Parker, Sybil P., ed. *McGraw-Hill Dictionary of Scientific and Technical Terms.* New York: McGraw-Hill, 1984.

Picket, Nell Ann, and Ann A. Lasker. *Technical English, Writing, Reading, and Speaking.* New York: Harper/Collins College Publishing, 1993.

Schramm, Wilbur. *The Story of Human Communication: Cave Painting to Microchip.* New York: Harper and Row, 1987.

Schramm, Wilbur, and Donald F. Roberts, eds. *The Process and Effects of Mass Communication.* rev. ed. Urbanna, Ill.: University of Illinois Press, 1971.

Scientific and Technical Reports—Organization, Preparation, and Production; ANSI Z39. New York: American National Standards Institute, 1987.

Sheehy, Eugene P., ed. *Guide to Reference Books.* Chicago: American Library Association, 1976.

Strunk, William, Jr. *The Elements of Style.* 3d ed. (rev. ed. by E. B. White.) New York: Macmillan, 1959.

Toulman, Steven, et al. *An Introduction to Reasoning.* New York: Macmillan Publishing Company, 1984.

Urban, Wilbur M. *Language and Reality.* New York: Macmillan, 1951.

U.S. Government Printing Office Style Manual. Washington, D.C.: U.S. Government Printing Office, 1984.

Webster's Encyclopedic Unabridged Dictionary of the English Language. New York: Crown Publishers, 1989.

Webster's Guide to Abbreviations. Springfield, Mass.: Merriam-Webster, 1985.

Weisman, Herman M. *Information Systems, Services, and Centers.* New York: Becker and Hayes; John Wiley and Sons, 1972.

Whorf, Benjamin Lee. *Language, Thought and Reality: Selected Writings of Benjamin Whorf.* Edited by John B. Carroll. New York: John Wiley and MIT Press, 1956.

Zimmerman, Donald E., and Michael Lynn Muraski. *Elements of Information Gathering, A Practical Guide.* Phoenix, Ariz.: Oryx Press, 1994.

Zinsser, William. *On Writing Well: An Informal Guide to Writing Nonfiction.* 4th ed. New York: Harper/Collins, 1990.

Technical Report Writing

Alley, Michael. *The Craft of Scientific Writing.* Englewood Cliffs, N.J.: Prentice-Hall, 1987.

Anderson, Paul V. *Technical Writing: A Reader-Centered Approach.* 2d ed. New York: Harcourt Brace Jovanovich, 1991.

Barnum, Carol M., and Saul Carliner, eds. *Techniques for Technical Communicators.* New York: Macmillan, 1993.

Blake, Gary, and Robert W. Bly. *The Elements of Technical Writing.* New York: Macmillan, 1993.

Burnett, Rebecca E. *Technical Communication.* 3rd ed. Belmont, Calif.: Wadsworth, 1994.

Cain, B. Edward. *The Basics of Technical Communication.* Washington, D.C.: American Chemical Society, 1988.

Chandler, Harry E. *Technical Writer's Handbook.* Metals Park, Ohio: American Society for Metals, 1983.

Damerst, William A., and Arthur H. Bell. *Clear Technical Communication.* San Diego: Harcourt Brace Jovanovich, 1989.

Fearing, Bertie E., and W. Keats Sparrow, eds. *Technical Writing: Theory and Practice.* New York: Modern Language Association of America, 1990.

Houp, Kenneth W., and Thomas E. Pearsall. *Reporting Technical Information.* 7th ed. New York: Macmillan, 1992.

Kapp, Reginald O. *Presentation of Technical Information.* New York: Macmillan, 1957.

Lannon, John M. *Technical Writing.* 4th ed. Glenview, Ill.: Scott, Foresman and Company, 1988.

Markel, Michael. *Technical Writing: Situations and Strategies.* 2d ed. New York: St. Martin's Press, 1992.

Mathes, J. C., and Dwight W. Stevenson. *Designing Technical Reports.* 2d ed. New York: Macmillan, 1991.

Michaelson, Herbert B. *How to Write and Publish Engineering Papers and Reports.* 3rd ed. Phoenix, Ariz.: Oryx Press, 1990.

Mills, Gordon H., and John A. Walter. *Technical Writing.* 5th ed. New York: Holt, Rinehart and Winston, 1986.

Moran, Michael G., and Debra Journet, eds. *Research in Technical Communication, A Bibliographic Sourcebook.* Westport, Conn.: Greenwood Press, 1985.

Pauley, Steven E., and Daniel G. Riordan. *Technical Report Writing Today.* 5th ed. Boston: Houghton Mifflin Company, 1993.

Pearsall, Thomas E., and Donald H. Cunningham. *How to Write for the World of Work.* 5th ed. Ft. Worth, Texas: Harcourt, Brace, Jovanovich, 1994.

Pfeiffer, William S. *Technical Writing: A Practical Approach.* 2d ed. New York: Macmillan, 1994.

Rook, Fern. *How to Prepare a Science Project Report, Write a Research Paper, Format a Report.* Phoenix, Ariz.: Fern Rook, 1982.

Rubens, Philip. *Science and Technical Writing: A Manual of Style.* New York: Henry Holt and Company, 1992.

Rude, Carolyn D. *Technical Editing.* Belmont, Calif.: Wadsworth, 1991.

Samson, Donald C., Jr. *Editing Technical Writing.* New York: Oxford University Press, 1993.

Sherman, Theodore A., and Simon A. Johnson. *Modern Technical Writing.* 4th ed. Englewood Cliffs, N.J.: Prentice-Hall, 1983.

Sides, Charles H. *Technical and Business Communication.* Phoenix, Ariz.: Oryx Press, 1991.

Stuart, Ann. *The Technical Writer.* New York: Holt, Rinehart and Winston, 1988.

Weisman, Herman M. *Basic Technical Writing.* 6th ed. New York: Merrill (an imprint of Macmillan), 1992.

Young, Matt. *The Technical Writer's Handbook.* Mill Valley, Calif.: University Science Books, 1989.

Zimmerman, Donald E., and David G. Clark. *The Random House Guide to Technical and Scientific Communication.* New York: Random House, 1987.

Graphics and Production

Bethune, James D. *Technical Illustration.* New York: John Wiley and Sons, 1983.

Burden, William J. *Graphics Reproduction: Photography.* New York: Hastings House, 1980.

Campbell, Alastair. *The Graphic Designer's Handbook.* Philadelphia: Running Press, 1987.

Cleveland, William S. *The Elements of Graphing Data.* Monterey, Calif.: Wadsworth Advanced Books and Software, 1985.

Demoney, Jerry, and Susan E. Meyer. *Pasteups and Mechanicals: A Step-by-Step Guide to Preparing Art for Reproduction.* New York: Watson-Guptill, 1982.

Haley, Allan. *The ABC's of Type.* New York: Watson-Guptill, 1992.

Hartley, James. *Designing Instructional Texts.* New York: Nichols, 1978.

Heller, Steven, and Seymour Chwast. *Graphic Style from Victorian to Post-Modern.* New York: Harry N. Abrams, 1988.

Jastrzebski, Zbigniew. *Scientific Illustration.* Englewood Cliffs, N.J.: Prentice-Hall, 1985.

Kelvin, George V. *Illustrating for Science.* New York: Watson-Guptill, 1992.

MacGregor, A. J. *Graphics Simplified: How to Plan and Prepare Effective Charts, Graphics, Illustrations, and Other Visual Aids.* Toronto: University of Toronto Press, 1979.

Matkowski, Betty S. *Steps to Effective Business Graphics.* San Diego: Hewlett Packard, 1983.

Nelms, Hemming. *Thinking With a Pencil.* New York: Barnes and Noble, 1964.

Parker, Roger C. *Looking Good in Print: A Guide to Basic Design for Desktop Publishing.* Chapel Hill, N.C.: Ventura Press, 1988.

Pratt, Dan, and Lev Ropes. *35mm Slides: A Manual for Technical Presentations.* Tulsa, Okla.: American Association of Petroleum Geologists, 1978.

Quick, John. *Artists' and Illustrators' Encyclopedia.* 2d ed. New York: McGraw-Hill, 1977.

Ressler, Sandy. *Perspectives on Electronic Publishing: Standards Solutions, and More.* Englewood Cliffs, N.J.: Prentice-Hall, 1993.

Robinson, Artur H., and Barbara Petchnik. *The Nature of Maps.* Chicago: University of Chicago Press, 1976.

Sanders, Norman. *Photographing for Publication.* New York: R.R. Bowker, 1983.

Schmid, Calvin F., and Stanton E. Schmid. *Handbook of Graphic Presentation.* 2d ed. New York: John Wiley and Sons, 1979.

Swann, Alan. *How to Understand and Use Design and Layout.* Cincinnati, Ohio: North Light Books, 1987.

White, Jan V. *Editing by Design: A Guide to Effective Word-and-Picture Communication for Editors and Designers.* New York: R. R. Bowker, 1982.

White, Jan V. *Graphic Design for the Electronic Age.* New York: Watson-Guptill, 1988.

White, Jan V. *Mastering Graphics, Design and Production Made Easy.* New York: R. R. Bowker, 1983.

Wileman, Ralph E. *Visual Communication.* Englewood Cliffs, N.J.: Prentice-Hall, 1993.

Business Communication

Anderson, Paul. *Business Communication.* New York: Harcourt Brace Jovanovich, 1989.

Andrews, Deborah C., and William D. Andrews. *Business Communication.* 2d ed. New York: Macmillan, 1993.

Backman, Lois J., Norman Sigband, and Theodore W. Hipple. *Successful Business English.* Glenview, Ill.: Scott, Foresman and Company, 1987.

Berryman, Gregg. *Designing Creative Resumes.* Los Altos, Calif.: William Kaufman, 1985.

Bowman, Joel P., and Bernadine P. Branchaw. *Business Report Writing.* Chicago: The Dryden Press, 1984.

Brusaw, Charles T., Gerald J. Alred, and Walter E. Oliu. *The Business Writer's Handbook.* 3d ed. New York: St. Martin's Press, 1987.

Croft, Barbara L. *Getting a Job, Resume Writing, Job Application Letters, and Interview Strategies.* Columbus, Ohio: Merrill, 1989.

Dumont, Raymond M., and John M. Lannon. *Business Communication.* Boston: Little, Brown and Company, 1987.

Frank, Darlene. *Silicon English: Business Writing Tools for the Computer Age.* San Raphael, Calif.: Royall Press, 1985.

Jacobi, Ernst, and G. Jay Christenson. *On the Job Communication for Business and Industry.* Englewood Cliffs, N.J.: Prentice-Hall, 1990.

Kogen, Myra, ed. *Writing in the Business Professions.* Urbana, Ill.: National Council of Teachers of English and the Association for Business Communication, 1989.

Leonard, Donald J., and Robert L. Shurter. *Effective Letters in Business.* 3d ed. New York: McGraw-Hill, 1984.

Munter, Mary. *Business Communication: Strategy and Skill.* Englewood Cliffs, N.J.: Prentice-Hall, 1987.

Murphy, Herta M., and E. W. Hildebrand. *Effective Business Communication.* 4th ed. New York: McGraw-Hill, 1984.

Olin, Walter E., et al. *Writing that Works: Effective Communication in Business.* New York: St. Martin's Press, 1992.

Sigband, Norman, and Arthur H. Bell. *Communication for Management and Business.* Glenview, Ill.: Scott, Foresman and Company, 1986.

Tebeaux, Elizabeth. *Design of Business Communications: The Process and the Product.* New York: Macmillan, 1990.

Weisman, Herman M. *Technical Correspondence: A Handbook and Reference Source for the Technical Professional.* New York: John Wiley and Sons, 1968.

Wilkinson, C. W., et al. *Writing and Speaking in Business.* 9th ed. Homewood, Ill.: Richard D. Irwin, 1986.

Yate, Martin John. *Resumes that Knock `Em Dead.* Holbrook, Mass.: Bob Adams, 1988.

Computers and New Information Technology

Barrett, Edward, ed. *Text, Context, and Hypertext: Writing With and For the Computer.* Cambridge, Mass.: MIT Press, 1988.

Bove, Tony, Cheryl Rhodes, and Wes Thomas. *The Art of Desktop Publishing: Using Personal Computers to Publish it Yourself.* 2d ed. New York: Bantam Books, 1988.

Burns, David, S. Venit, and Linda Mercer. *Using Ventura Publisher.* New York: Que Corporation/Macmillan, 1989.

Burns, Diane, S. Venit, and Rebecca Hausene. *The Electronic Publisher.* New York: Brady/Simon and Schuster, 1988.

Cavuoto, James, and Jesse Berst. *Inside Xerox Ventura Publisher,* 2d ed. Torrance, Calif.: Micro, 1989.

Chicago Guide to Preparing Electronic Manuscripts, for Authors and Publishers. Chicago: University of Chicago Press, 1987.

Constanzo, William. *The Electronic Text: Learning to Write, Read, and Reason with Computers.* Englewood Cliffs, N.J.: Educational Technology Publications, 1990.

Crown, James. *Effective Computer User Documentation.* New York: Van Nostrand Reinhold, 1992.

Dvorak, John C., and Nick Anis. *Dvorak's Guide to PC Telecommunications.* New York: Osborne McGraw-Hill, 1990.

Felici, Jim, and Ted Nace. *Desktop Publishing Skills: A Primer for Typesetting with Computers and Laser Printers.* Reading, Mass.: Addison-Wesley, 1987.

Foerster, Scott. *The Printer Bible.* Carmel, Ind.: Que Corporation, 1990.

Horton, William. *Designing & Writing Online Documentation.* 2d ed. New York: John Wiley and Sons, 1994.

Horton, William. *Illustrating Computer Documentation, The Art of Presenting Information Graphically on Paper and Online.* New York: John Wiley and Sons, 1991.

Kleper, Michael L. *The Illustrated Handbook of Desktop Publishing and Typesetting.* Blue Ridge Summit, Pa.: TAB Books, 1987.

Krull, Robert, ed. *Word Processing for Technical Writing.* Amityville, N.Y.: Baywood, 1988.

The Language of Computer Publishing. San Diego: Brenner Information Group, 1990.

Mitchell, Joan P. *The New Writer: Techniques for Writing with a Computer.* Redmond, Wash.: Microsoft Press, 1987.

Nelson, Ted. *Computer Lib/Dream Machines.* Redmond, Wash.: Microsoft Press, 1987.

Pfaffenberger, Brian. *Que's Computer User's Dictionary.* Carmel, Ind.: Que Corporation, 1990.

Ralston, Anthony, ed. *Encyclopedia of Computer Science and Engineering.* 2d ed. New York: Van Nostrand Reinhold, 1983.

Rardin, Kevin. *Desktop Publishing on the MAC: A Step-by-Step Guide to the New Technology.* New York: New American Library, 1986.

Ricson, Fritz, and John A. Vonk. *Easy Pagemaker, A Guide to Learning Pagemaker for the Macintosh Featuring Version 4.0.* New York: Macmillan, 1992.

Shushan, Ronnie, and Don Wright. *Desktop Publishing Design.* Redmond, Wash.: Microsoft Press, 1989.

Sitarz, Daniel. *The Desktop Publisher's Legal Handbook.* Carbondale, Ill.: Nova, 1989.

Szymanski, Robert A., et al. *Introduction to Computers and Information Systems.* 2d ed. Englewood Cliffs, N.J.: Merrill/Prentice-Hall, 1991.

Using Page Maker: Macintosh Version (developed by Que Corporation). New York: Que Corporation/Macmillan, 1989.

Venit, S., and Diane Burns. *Using Page Maker: IBM.* 2d ed. New York: Que Corporation/Macmillan, 1989.

Webster's New World Dictionary of Computer Terms. 3d ed. New York: Webster's New World, 1988.

Williams, Robin, and Steve Cummings. *Jargon, An Informal Dictionary of Computer Terms.* Berkeley, Calif.: Peachpit Press, 1993.

Woodcock JoAnn, et al. *Microsoft Press Computer Dictionary.* Redwood, Calif.: Microsoft Press, 1991.

Oral Communication

Adams, David. *Preparing and Delivering Technical Presentations.* Boston: Artech House, 1987.

Andrews, James. *Public Speaking: Principles and Practice.* Englewood Cliffs, N.J.: Prentice-Hall, 1987.

Beer, David F., ed. *Writing and Speaking in the Technology Professions, A Practical Guide.* New York: IEEE Press, 1992.

Bryant, Donald C., et al. *Oral Communication.* 5th ed. Englewood Cliffs, N.J.: Prentice-Hall, 1982.

D'Arcy, Jan. *Technically Speaking: Proven Ways To Make Your Next Presentation a Success.* New York: American Management Association, 1992.

Ehninger, Douglas, et al. *Principles and Types of Speech Communication.* 10th ed. Glenview, Ill.: Scott, Foresman and Company, 1986.

Selected Bibliography

Gronbeck, Bruce E., et al. *Principles of Speech Communication.* 10th ed. Glenview, Ill.: Scott, Foresman and Company, 1988.

Kenny, Peter. *A Handbook for Public Speaking for Scientists & Engineers.* Bristol, England: Adam Hilger, 1982.

Lucas, Stephen E. *The Art of Public Speaking.* 2d ed. New York: Random House, 1986.

Seiler, William J. *Introduction to Speech Communication.* Glenview, Ill.: Scott, Foresman and Company, 1988.

Smith, Terry C. *Making Successful Presentations, A Self-Teaching Guide.* New York: John Wiley and Sons, 1984.

Tacey, William S. *Business and Professional Speaking.* 4th ed. Dubuque, Iowa: Wm. C. Brown, 1983.

Turk, Christopher. *Effective Speaking, Communicating in Speech.* New York: Methuen, 1986.

Wiksell, Wesley. *Do They Understand You?* Englewood Cliffs, NJ: Prentice-Hall, 1960.

Index

abbreviations, use in technical writing, 301–302
abstract, in a report, 139
abstracting and indexing journals, use in literature searching, 90–91
acronyms, 302
adjectives, 303
adverbs, 303
analogy, definition by, 46
analysis, 62*ff*
  of data, 104
  definition by, 47
  definition of, 62
  in preparation of report writing, 84–86
  interpretation through, 66–67, 110
analysis, methods of, 62*ff*
  classification, 63*ff*
  definition of, 62
  partition, 64*ff*
  synthesis and interpretation, 66–67
analyzing components of a problem, 84–86
antonyms, definition by, 44
apostrophe, 305
appendix, in reports, 150–151
appositives, 305–306
audiovisual aids in oral presentations, 297–298

bibliography
  elements of, 88–89
  in reports, 150, 190–192
  selected references in technical writing, 363*ff*
  use in literature searching, 88–89
body language, in delivering oral presentations, 297
books, use of in literature searching, 90
brackets, 307
brainstorming, in report writing, 83
breathing, in delivery of oral presentations, 296
briefings, in oral reporting, 290

capitalization, 307
catalog, library, 87–88
checklist for constructing tables, 184–185
Chesterfield, Lord, 16
circumlocutions, 308–309
claim and adjustment letters, 255–257
classification, 63*ff*
  example of, 67–68
  as expository technique, 63
  guidelines for, 53–64
clauses, 21–24, 309
collective noun, 309
colon, 309
comma, 310–311
commercial computer data bases, 93–97
communication, 2*ff*
  definition of, 2–3
  factual communication, problems in, 9–10
  process of, 2–4

371

complex sentence, 22–24
compound sentence, 21–22
compound-complex sentence, 23
computer technology, in correspondence, 259, 263–264
computerized information services, 91*ff*
  advantages and disadvantages, 96
correspondence, 200*ff*. *See also* letters
  employment letters, 216*ff*
    developing resumes and cover letters, 224–244
  format and mechanics, 202*ff*
  how to apply for a job, 216–248
    job interviews, 244–246
    job strategies, 218
  letters, 201–203, 216*ff*
  memoranda, 213–216
  pre-correspondence writing strategies, 201
  psychology of, 200–201
  role of the paragraph, 201–202
  role of, in science, technology, industry, 200
  special types of, 248–262
cover/title page, in reports, 137, 139

dangling modifiers, 312–313
decimal outline, 128
definition, as expository technique, 41*ff*
  by amplification, 46*ff*
  by analogy, 46
  by analysis, 47
  by combination of methods, 47
  by comparison and contrast, 47
  by derivation, 46
  by distinction, 47
  by elimination, 47
  by example, 46
  by explication, 46
  formal, 42–43
  general principles of, 47–48
  by history, 47
  by illustration, 44
  informal, 43–44
  nature of, 46
  operational, 45
  by stipulation, 45
  by synonyms and antonyms, 44
delivering the oral report, 294–298
description, as expository technique, 48*ff*
  of mechanisms and organisms, 48*ff*
    examples of, 50*ff*
  of process, 53*ff*
    examples of, 56*ff*

Dewey, John, 66–67, 76
distribution list, in reports, 152
documentation, in reports, 187–189
drawings/diagrams, 178

electronic bulletin boards, 263
electronic mail, 263
employment letters, 216*ff*
encyclopedias, use in literature searching, 89
English, technical, 15*ff*
enunciation, in delivering oral reports, 197
equations, 185–186
ethics, in technical writing, 10–11
executive briefing, 242, 243
executive summary, in reports, 139, 143–144
experimentation, in research, 102*ff*
  planning for, 103
  rules of, 104–105
  use of controls, 104
exposition, 41*ff*
  by analysis, 62*ff*
  by classification, 63*ff*
  by definition, 41*ff*
  by description, 48*ff*
  process, explanation of, 53*ff*
  techniques for, 41*ff*

facsimile (Fax), 263–264
facts
  definition of, 8
  ingredients of reports, 80
footnotes. *See also* documentation
  use of, 189–190
front matter, in a report, 137–141

gender, the generic "he", 317
glossary
  for computer and desktop publishing, 347*ff*
  in reports, 150
graphics, use of, 177*ff*
  types of, 177*ff*
    drawings/diagrams, 178
    graphs, 178, 180
    tables, 180–184
      checklist for, 184
graphs, 178, 180

handbooks, in literature searching, 89
headings, 186–187
Huxley, T.H. 17–19

hypertext, 98
hyphen, 319–320
hypothesis, 78
   definition of, 78
   formulating the, 78
   role of, 78

illustration, definition by, 44–45
illustrations. *See* graphics
index, in reports, 152
inquiry letters, 248–256
instruction letter, 257–259, 260–262
intensity, in delivering oral presentations, 296
interviews and discussions
   how to, 106–107
   in research, 105–107
investigative procedures
   in report writing, 86*ff*
     experimentation, 105*ff*
     interviews and discussions, 105–107
     observation, 101–102
     questionnaires, 107–109
     searching the literature, 86*ff*
        computerized searching, 91*ff*
        manual searching, 87

jargon, 322
job interview, 244–246
Johnson, Samuel, 2

keywords, 92, 139

legal considerations, in technical writing, 10–11
letters, 200*ff*
   claim and adjustment, 255–257
   employment, 216*ff*
     executive briefing, 242, 243
     follow-up, 246–248
     resumes, 221*ff*
   format of, 202*ff*
   of instruction, 257–259
   mechanical details, 206–213
   planning, 201
   queries and responses, 248–256
   transmittal, 136, 137, 138
literature guides, 88
literature searching, 86*ff*
   suggestions for, 97–98
literature sources, 88*ff*
logical pattern, for organizing report material, 119–121

meaning, 4*ff*
   operation of, 4–6
   types of, 4
memoranda (memos), 213–216
memo reports, 272, 276–277
Molière, 8
modifiers, in grammar
   dangling, 312–313
   misplaced, 323

notes, taking, 99–100
number, in grammar, 324–325
numerals, 315

observation
   accurate method of, 9, 101–102
   how to conduct, 102
oral reports, 287*ff*
   advantages of, 388
   delivering, 295–297
     audiovisual aids, use of, 297–298
     guidelines for, 298–299
     stagefright, 295
   disadvantages of, 288–289
   types of, 289–292
     extemporaneous, 290
     formal, 290
     informal, 289
     posterboard, 290–292
   major steps in preparing, 290, 292
     the body, 293
     composing, 293–294
     the conclusion, 294
     preliminary analysis and planning, 292
     information gathering, 292
     the introduction, 293
     organizing the information, 292
   practicing delivery, 294
organizing report data, 115*ff*
   developing thesis sentence, 116–118
   guidelines for organizing data, 118
   patterns for, 118*ff*
     cause and effect, 121
     chronological, 119
     elimination of possible solutions, 120
     functional, 120
     general to particular, 120
     logical pattern, 119–121
     order of importance, 120
     particular to general, 120

organizing report data,
  patterns for, *continued*
    pro and con, 121
    simple to complex, 121
    spatial/geographical, 119–120
  psychological pattern, 121
outlines, 122–131
  format, 124*ff*
  types, 122*ff*
  computer outliners, 130
  organizing, 130
  requirements for, 130–131

paragraph, 24*ff*
  criteria for testing, 26
  function of, 24
  role of topic sentence, 24–26
  structural, 26–27
parallel structure in grammar, 326–327
parentheses, 327
partition, 64*ff*
  definition of, 64
  examples of, 68–69
  guidelines for, 65
pauses, in delivering oral presentation, 296
pitch, in delivering oral presentations, 296
plagiarism, 12, 100–101
prepositions, 328–329
pronouns, 330
post-interview letters (employment), 246–248
posterboard, 290–291
problem (concept)
  apprehending, 77
  hypothesis, role in solution, 78–79
  selecting for research, 83
  types of (in research), 76*ff*
process, describing a, 53*ff*
  examples of, 56–58, 59–61
  guidelines for, 54–56
  principles of, 58–62
progress reports, 277, 280, 283–285
  elements of, 280
pronunciation, in delivery of oral presentations, 297
proofreading, 192–195
psychological pattern, for organizing reports, 121
punctuation, 331

questionnaires, use in research, 107–109
quotation marks, 331

rate of speaking, in delivering oral presentations, 296
readability, 30*ff*
  advance organizers, 31
  factors to improve, 34
  graphic aids, 34
  inserted questions, 32
  overviews, 32–33
  prompting cues, 32
reader analysis, 27*ff*
recommendation reports, 277–279
reference index and guide to grammar, punctuation, style, and usage, 301*ff*
report, writing of, 75*ff*
  abstract, 139, 140, 142
  back matter, 150
  basic ingredients, 80
  body, writing the, 149–152
  conclusions and recommendations, writing the, 150
  decision making, role of in, 79
  definition of, 79–80
  executive summary, 139, 143–144
  final (completion) reports, requirements for 152–153
  first draft, writing the, 170
  formal reports, 146*ff*
  format mechanics, 176–177
  forms and classification of, 80–82
  graphics in, 177*ff*
  the introduction, elements of, 141, 146–149
  language and style in, 173–174
  letter, 272, 273–274
  memo, 272, 276–277
  oral report presentation, 287*ff*
    guidelines for, 298–299
  outlining, 122–131
  progress reports, 280–281, 283–285
  revising and editing with a word processor, 174–176
  revision process, 171–174
  structural elements of, 136*ff*
  student example of, 156–167
  terminal section of, 150
  types of, 81–82
  writing the, 169*ff*
research, relation to report writing, 79
resume, 221*ff*
revision, in report writing, 171–174
  using a word processor, 174–176

rules of experimental research, 104–105

Schramm, Wilbur, 3–4
science, 8
Seneca, 16
sense perception, 8
sentence outline, 123–128
sentence structure, capacity of sentence types, 21–24
shoptalk, 332
simple sentence, 21
split infinitives, 334
storyboard, as an outline technique, 128–129
style, technical, 15*ff*
   definition of, 16
   elements of, 21*ff*
   qualities of, 16*ff*
   in technical descriptions, 70
Swift, Jonathon, 16
synthesis
   of data, 109
   interpretation through, 109–110

systematizing data
   process in interpretation, 109

table of contents, 141, 145
tables, 181–185
technical writing, 6*ff*
   definition of, 8*ff*
   ethics in, 10–11
   legal considerations in, 11–12
topic sentence, 24–26
topical outlines, 122–123
transmittal letters, for reports, 136, 137, 138

voice, use in technical writing, 19–21
voice quality, in delivering oral presentations, 296

Whorf, Benjamin Lee, 79
word processing, use of in revising and editing, 174–176
WYSIWYG, 361

yearbooks, in literature searching, 91